33rd Conference on Computational Linguistics and Speech Processing (ROCLING 2021)

Taoyuan, Taiwan
15 – 16 October 2021

ISBN: 978-1-7138-3924-8

Printed from e-media with permission by:

Curran Associates, Inc.
57 Morehouse Lane
Red Hook, NY 12571

Some format issues inherent in the e-media version may also appear in this print version.

Association for Computational Linguistics
209 N. Eighth Street
Stroudsburg, Pennsylvania 18360

Phone: 1-570-476-8006
Fax: 1-570-476-0860

acl@aclweb.org

Additional copies of this publication are available from:

Curran Associates, Inc.
57 Morehouse Lane
Red Hook, NY 12571 USA
Phone: 845-758-0400
Fax: 845-758-2633
Email: curran@proceedings.com
Web: www.proceedings.com

ROCLING 2021: The 33rd Conference on Computational Linguistics and Speech Processing

第三十三屆自然語言與語音處理研討會

October 15-16, 2021

National Central University, Taoyuan, Taiwan, R.O.C.

主辦單位：

國立中央大學、國立臺灣科技大學、中華民國計算語言學學會

共同主辦單位：

科技部人工智慧技術暨全幅健康照護聯合研究中心、人工智慧普適研究中心、科技部人工智慧生技醫療創新研究中心

協辦單位：

科技部、教育部

贊助單位：

玉山金控、賽微科技股份有限公司、中華電信研究院

First Published in September 2021
By The Association for Computational Linguistics and Chinese Language Processing (ACLCLP)

Organizing Committee

Honorary Chair

Jing-Yang Jou, National Central University

Conference Chairs

Lung-Hao Lee, National Central University

Chia-Hui Chang, National Central University

Kuan-Yu Chen, National Taiwan University of Science and Technology

Program Chairs

Yung-Chun Chang, Taipei Medical University

Yi-Chin Huang, National Pingtung University

Tutorial Chair

Hung-Yi Lee, National Taiwan University

Publication Chair

Jheng-Long Wu, Soochow University

Special Session Chair

Chun-Hsien Hsu, National Central University

Shared Task Chair

Liang-Chih Yu, Yuan Ze University

Program Committee

Jenq-Haur Wang (王正豪), National Taipei University of Technology

Yu-Cheng Wang (王昱晟), Lunghwa University of Science and Technology

Jheng-Long Wu (吳政隆), Soochow University

Shih-Hung Wu (吳世弘), Chaoyang University of Technology

Jui-Feng Yeh (葉瑞峰), National Chiayi University

Liang-Chih Yu (禹良治), Yuan Ze University

Messages from Conference Chairs

As the Conference Chairs, we welcome you to the 33rd Conference on Computational Linguistics and Speech Processing (ROCLING 2021) in Taoyuan, Taiwan, during October 15-16, 2021. ROCLING 2021 is hosted by National Central University (NCU), National Taiwan University of Science and Technology (NTUST), and the Association for Computational Linguistics and Chinese Language Processing (ACLCLP) and co-organized by MOST Joint Research Center for AI Technology and All Vista Healthcare (AINTU), Pervasive Artificial Intelligence Research (PAIR) Labs, and MOST Artificial Intelligence Biomedical Research Center (AIBMRC).

We would like to thank the Program Chairs Prof. Yung-Chun Chang and Prof. Yi-Ching Huang, Tutorial Chair Prof. Hung-Yi Lee, Special Session Chair Prof. Chun-Hsien Hsu and Shared Task Chair Prof. Liang-Chih Yu for their hard work in coordinating the review process allowing for top quality papers and inspiring talks to be presented at the conference. We also thank Prof. Jheng-Long Wu for the publication of conference proceedings. The conference proceedings will be published from ACL Anthology.

Last but not least, we would like to thank all authors for submitting high-quality research papers, and all attendees for making the journey. Hope you all enjoy the conference program.

Lung-Hao Lee, National Central University
Chia-Hui Chang, National Central University
Kuan-Yu Chen, National Taiwan University of Science and Technology
ROCLING 2021 Conference Chairs

Messages from Program Chairs

The excellent program and activities of ROCLING 2021 are the result of collaborative efforts of more than 50 program committee members and conference organizers. Each paper has been reviewed by 2 to 3 PC members, and we thank all of them for their insightful reviews, from which we can build an outstanding technical program. We would also like to thank the Tutorial Chair, Prof. Hung-Yi Lee of National Taiwan University, for coordinating three excellent tutorials. We are very grateful to the Publication Chair, Prof. Jheng-Long Wu of the Soochow University, for editing the conference proceedings. We would also like to express our gratitude to the Special Session Chair, Prof. Chun-Hsien Hsu of National Central University, and Shared Task Chair, Prof. Liang-Chih Yu of Yuan Ze University, for organizing the special session and shared task that enable the outreach of conference events to many important communities. Last but not least, we appreciate the contributions of Conference Co-chairs, Prof. Lung-Hao Lee of National Central University, Prof. Chia-Hui Chang of National Central University, and Prof. Kuan-Yu Chen of National Taiwan University of Science and Technology, to the construction of the conference website and event coordination.

Yung-Chun Chang, Tapiei Medical University
Yi-Chin Huang, National Pingtung University
ROCLING 2021 Program Chairs

NLP Keynote by Prof. Vincent Ng

Event Coreference Resolution: Successes and Future Challenges

Speaker: Prof. Vincent Ng

Professor, The University of Texas at Dallas

Time: Friday, October 15, 2021, 09:10 - 10:10

Biography

Vincent Ng is a Professor in the Computer Science Department at the University of Texas at Dallas. He is also the director of the Machine Learning and Language Processing Laboratory in the Human Language Technology Research Institute at UT Dallas. He obtained his B.S. from Carnegie Mellon University and his Ph.D. from Cornell University. His research is in the area of Natural Language Processing, focusing on the development of computational methods for addressing key tasks in information extraction and discourse processing.

Abstract

Recent years have seen a gradual shift of focus from entity-based tasks to event-based tasks in information extraction research. This talk will focus on event coreference resolution, the event-based counterpart of the notoriously difficult entity coreference resolution task. Specifically, I will examine the major milestones made in event coreference research since its inception more than two decades ago, including the recent successes of neural event coreference models and their limitations, and discuss possible ways to bring these models to the next level of performance.

Speech Keynote by Dr. Jinyu Li

Advancing end-to-end automatic speech recognition

Speaker: Dr. Jinyu Li

Partner Applied Scientist and Technical Lead,
Microsoft Corporation, Redmond, USA

Time: Saturday, October 16, 2021, 09:00 - 10:00

Biography

Jinyu Li received the Ph.D. degree from Georgia Institute of Technology, Atlanta, in 2008. From 2000 to 2003, he was a Researcher in the Intel China Research Center and Research Manager in iFlytek, China. Currently, he is a Partner Applied Scientist and Technical Lead in Microsoft Corporation, Redmond, USA. He leads a team to design and improve speech modeling algorithms and technologies that ensure industry state-of-the-art speech recognition accuracy for Microsoft. His major research interests cover several topics in speech recognition, including end-to-end modeling, deep learning, noise robustness, etc. He is the leading author of the book "Robust Automatic Speech Recognition -- A Bridge to Practical Applications", Academic Press, Oct, 2015. He is the member of IEEE Speech and Language Processing Technical Committee since 2017. He also served as the associate editor of IEEE/ACM Transactions on Audio, Speech and Language Processing from 2015 to 2020.

Abstract

Recently, the speech community is seeing a significant trend of moving from deep neural network based hybrid modeling to end-to-end (E2E) modeling for automatic speech recognition (ASR). While E2E models achieve the state-of-the-art results in most benchmarks in terms of ASR accuracy, hybrid models still dominate the commercial ASR systems at current time. There are lots of practical factors that affect the production model deployment decision. Traditional hybrid models, being optimized for production for decades, are usually good at these factors. Without providing excellent solutions to all these factors, it is hard for E2E models to be widely commercialized. In this talk, I will overview the recent advances in E2E models with the focus on technologies addressing those challenges from the perspective of industry. Specifically, I will describe methods of 1) building high-accuracy low-latency E2E models, 2) building a single E2E model to serve all multilingual users, 3) customizing and adapting E2E models to a new domain 4) extending E2E models for multi-talker ASR etc. Finally, I will conclude the talk with some challenges we should address in the future.

Table of Contents

The 33rd Conference on Computational Linguistics and Speech Processing (ROCLING 2021)
Taoyuan, Taiwan, October 15-16, 2021. The Association for Computational Linguistics and Chinese Language Processing

Universal Recurrent Neural Network Grammar

Chinmay Choudhary
National University of Ireland
Newcastle, Galway
c.choudhary1@nuigalway.ie

Colm O'riordan
National University of Ireland
Newcastle, Galway
colm.oriordan@nuigalway.ie

Abstract

Modern approaches to Constituency Parsing are mono-lingual supervised approaches which require large amount of labelled data to be trained on, thus limiting their utility to only a handful of high-resource languages. To address this issue of data-sparsity for low-resource languages we propose **Universal Recurrent Neural Network Grammars (UniRNNG)** which is a multi-lingual variant of the popular Recurrent Neural Network Grammars (RNNG) model for constituency parsing. **UniRNNG** involves *Cross-lingual Transfer Learning* for Constituency Parsing task. The architecture of UniRNNG is inspired by *Principle and Parameter* theory proposed by Noam Chomsky. UniRNNG utilises the linguistic typology knowledge available as feature-values within WALS database, to generalize over multiple languages. Once trained on sufficiently diverse polyglot corpus **UniRNNG** can be applied to any natural language thus making it *Language-agnostic* constituency parser. Experiments reveal that our proposed **UniRNNG** outperform state-of-the-art baseline approaches for most of the target languages, for which these are tested.

Keywords: Constituency Parsing, Cross-lingual Transfer-learning

1 Introduction

Noam Chomsky proposed the hypothesis of **Universal Grammar (UG)** (Chomsky, 1986; Cook and Newson, 2014) which states that all human languages, while being superficially as diverse as they are, share some fundamental similarities. Thus he argues that deep down the specific grammars of various natural languages, there exists a *Universal Grammar*. Since then many linguists (Baker, 2008; Fodor and Sakas, 2004; Tomasello, 2005; Pinker, 1995; Fodor, 2001) attempted to outline the *principles and parameters* of this *Universal Grammar* manually, but with very limited success. If it is nearly impossible to identify and outline UG manually due to its anticipated large size and complexity (Roberts and Holmberg, 2005; Kayne, 2012; Cinque and Rizzi, 2010; Shlonsky, 2010), we can use a neural network to learn these automatically.

Recently Recurrent Neural Network based models for parsing (eg: *Recurrent Neural Network Grammars (RNNG)*(Dyer et al., 2016)) are proven to do excellent job in automatically learning and encoding (as model-parameters) the grammar of any language directly from its tree-bank corpus. This inspires us to make following assumption:

A Recurrent Neural Network based multi-lingual parser trained on a diverse polyglot treebank corpus would learn and encode the *Universal Grammar* as its model-parameters.

Based on this assumption, we propose **Universal Recurrent Neural Network Grammar (UniRNNG)** which is a multi-lingual variant of Dyer's RNNG model (Dyer et al., 2016). The architecture of **UniRNNG** is indeed inspired by the *Principle and Parameter* framework (Chomsky, 1993) advocated by linguists *Noam Chomsky* and *Howard Lasnik*. Hence unlike Dyer's RNNG, our proposed model comprises of two sets of model-parameters α and β. α would encode *Universal Principles* which are shared by all the languages and β would encode *Parameters* which are tuned to specific language of the sentence being parsed during run-time.

Our proposed model involves *Cross-lingual Transfer Learning (CLT)* from a polyglot corpus of high-resource source-languages to a low-resource target language. CLT has extensively been applied to numerous NLP-tasks including Dependency Parsing (Daniel et al., 2017a; Zeman et al., 2018a), Natural Language Inference (Conneau et al., 2018; Singh et al., 2019; Huang et al., 2019; Doval et al., 2019), Question Answering (Liu et al., 2019; Lee and Lee, 2019; Lewis et al., 2019), Text-classification (Bel et al., 2003; Shi et al., 2010; Mihalcea et al., 2007; Prettenhofer and Stein, 2010; Xu et al., 2016; Chen et al., 2018) etc. However, as far as we are aware, this is the first paper which evaluates the performance of CLT on *Constituency Parsing* task.

In order to generalize a mono-lingual constituency parsing model to multi-lingual settings, we utilize the knowledge of *Language typology* which is available as various typological feature-values in ***World Atlas of Language System (WALS)*** (Haspelmath, 2009) database.

It is observed that CLT based approaches do not perform well if the source and target languages are typologically very distinct (Ruder et al., 2019a). But since *UniRNNG* explicitly models over the typological features (as inputs) and is trained on a sufficiently diverse polyglot corpus, it is comparatively more robust to the typological differences between source and target languages. In other words, once being trained on sufficiently large and typologically diverse corpus it can be applied to any natural-language thus making it *Language-Agnostic*.

Section 2 provides a brief description of *Recurrant Neural Network Grammar (RNNG)* proposed by Dyer' et. al as background work. In section 3 we outline the architecture and intuition behind our proposed **UniRNNG**. Sections 4 and 5 describe the experiments performed and results obtained during the evaluation of proposed model.

2 Background

2.1 Cross-lingual Parsing

Cross-lingual *Model-transfer* approaches to Dependency Parsing such as (Daniel et al., 2017a; Zeman et al., 2018a; Duong et al., 2015; Guo et al., 2016; Vilares et al., 2015; Falenska and Çetinoğlu, 2017; Mulcaire et al., 2019; Vania et al., 2019; Shareghi et al., 2019) involve training a model on high-resource languages and subsequently adapting it to low-resource languages. Participants of CoNLL 2017 shared-task (Daniel et al., 2017b) and CoNLL 2018 shared task (Zeman et al., 2018b) also provide numerous approaches to dependency parsing of low-resource languages. Some approaches such as (Naseem et al., 2012; Täckström et al., 2013; Barzilay and Zhang, 2015; Wang and Eisner, 2016a; Rasooli and Collins, 2017; Ammar, 2016; Wang and Eisner, 2016b) used typological information to facilitate cross-lingual transfer. However all these approach utilise cross-lingual transfer learning for depndency-parsing task while our approach is for the cross-lingual Constituency-parsing/Phrase-parsing.

2.2 Recurrent Neural Network Grammar

RNNGs is a transition based approach to constituency parsing. Transition based parsing approaches reformulate the parsing problem as the task of prediction of best possible action-sequence.

A typical transition-based parser (Jurafsky and Martin, 2019) consists of a *Stack S* which stores the incomplete parse-tree, *Buffer B* which stores the sentence tokens and the set of all possible actions A. At every time-step t, the algorithm chooses the best action $a_t \in A$, given the current state of stack S_t, buffer B_t and history of actions $a_{<t}$. Depending upon the chosen action a_t, the Stack and Buffer are updated accordingly. The process is continued until the Buffer becomes empty and Stack consists of completed parse-tree.

(Dyer et al., 2016) proposed two variants of RNNGs namely *Discriminative* and *Generative* model. The *Discriminative* model computes most probable parse-tree y given the corresponding sentence x whereas the *Generative* RNNG is a language-model that generates sen-

Action	Description
NT(X)	Opens a non-terminal node 'X' and puts it on top of *Stack*. eg: NT(VP)==>(VP
SHIFT	Removes topmost token from the *Buffer* B and pushes onto Stack
REDUCE	Repeatedly pops completed sub-trees or terminal symbols from the stack until an open non-terminal is encountered, and then this open NT is popped and used as the label of a new constituent that has the popped sub-trees as its children. This new completed constituent is pushed onto the stack as a single composite item.

Table 1: Action Set for *Discriminative RNNG* (Dyer et al., 2016)

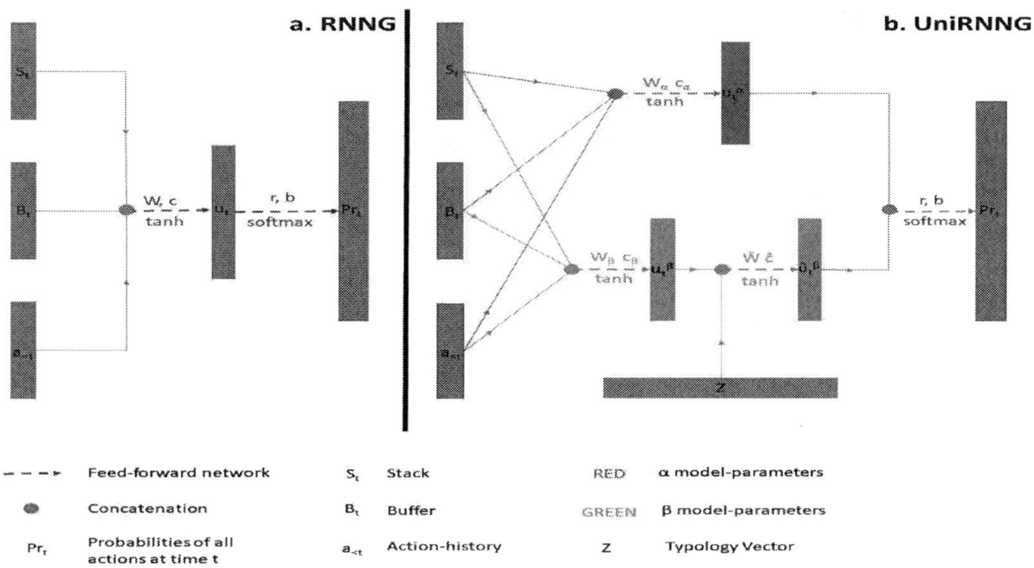

Figure 1: a. Recurrent Neural Network Grammar (RNNG) architecture. b.Universal Recurrent Neural Network Grammar (UniRNNG) architecture.

tence x and y simultaneously. Our proposed **UniRNNG** is a multi-lingual variant of the *Discrimantive* RNNG.

2.2.1 Discrimative RNNG

Table 1 describes the actions within action-set A for the *Discriminative RNNG (DiscRNNG)*. At any time-step t, RNNGs use a stack-LSTM (Dyer et al., 2015) to encode the current state of Stack S_t and use simple RNN to encode the current state of Buffer B_t and action-history $a_{<t}$. Given S_t, B_t and $a_{<t}$, the probability vector P_t comprising probabilities of all actions within A being the appropriate action to be taken at time-step t is computed by applying equation 1.

$$P_t = softmax(r^T u_t + b) \tag{1}$$

Vector u_t is vector representing the entire model-state at time t. u_t is computed by applying equation 2.

$$u_t = tanh(W[S_t; B_t; a_{<t}] + c) \tag{2}$$

Figure 1a depicts the neural-architecture for the entire action-prediction process at any time-step t by the RNNGs.
Given a sentence (token-sequence) x^i and its respective parse-tree y^i as a training example, the action-sequence that generated y^i from x^i can be extracted by depth-first, left-to-right traversal of y^i. The model-parameters are learnt by maximizing the likelihood of this extracted action-sequence for each training example.

3 UniRNNG Model

This section describes our proposed **Universal Recurrent Neural Network Grammar (UniRNNG)**. As being a multi-lingual variant of *DiscRNNG* (section 2.2.1), the

UniRNNG is also a transition based parser consisting of a *Stack* S, *Buffer* B and *action-set* A. At any time-step, the *Stack* stores incomplete parse-tree and *Buffer* stores token-sequence. At each time-step t, model predicts best action $a_t \in A$ given current state of Stack (S_t), Buffer (B_t) and Action-history ($a_{<t}$). Subsequently *Stack* and *Buffer* are updated as S_{t+1} and B_{t+1}, according to action a_t.

3.1 Architecture

Figure 1b depicts the architecture of the **UniRNNG**. At each time-step t the proposed model computes the Stack-encoding S_t, Buffer encoding B_t and action-sequence encoding $a_{<t}$ using stack-LSTM and RNN respectively, in similar way as *DiscRNNG.* (Section 2.2.1). However for **UniRNNG** *Cross-lingual Word-Embeddings* are used instead of Word-Identifier vectors during encoding of Stack and Buffer.

Once having computed S_t, B_t and $a_{<t}$ the model computes two distinct vector-representations of the entire model-state at time t namely *α-vector* (${u^\alpha}_t$) and *β-vector* (${u^\beta}_t$), unlike *DiscRNNG* which computes single representation u_t (equation 2). The ${u^\alpha}_t$ and ${u^\beta}_t$ are computed through equations 3 and 4.

$$ {u^\alpha}_t = tanh(W^\alpha[S_t; B_t; a_{<t}] + c^\alpha) \quad (3) $$

$$ {u^\beta}_t = tanh(W^\beta[S_t; B_t; a_{<t}] + c^\beta) \quad (4) $$

A *typology aware version of β-vector* $\hat{u}_t^\beta$ is computed by applying equation 5 (computation simply involves concatenation and dimension reduction through feed-forward network).

$$ \hat{u}_t^\beta = tanh(\hat{W}[{u^\beta}_t; Z] + \hat{c}) \quad (5) $$

Here $Z \in R^{|Z|}$ is a *Linguistic-typology* vector. Each value within Z represents a single typology-feature from *WALS* (Haspelmath, 2009) database having specific value as integer for the language being parsed. Both ${u^\beta}_t$ and $\hat{u}_t^\beta$ have same dimensions i.e. R^d. Final state-representation at time t is given as concatenation of *α-vector* (${u^\alpha}_t$) and *typology aware version of β-vector* ($\hat{u}_t^\beta$) as equation 6. Missing features for any language is assigned *zero* indicating no dominant value for it.

$$ u_t = [{u^\alpha}_t; \hat{u}_t^\beta] \quad (6) $$

To summarize *UniRNNG* is very similar to Dyer's *DiscRNNG* 2.2.1 with following modifications.

1. Cross-lingual Word-embeddings are used instead of unique word-identifiers
2. At each time-step t, two distinct model-state representations are computed namely *α-vector* ${u^\alpha}_t$ and *β-vector* ${u^\beta}_t$.
3. Final model-state representation u_t is computed as concatenation of *α-vector* and *typology aware version of β-vector.* This is unlike original *DiscRNNG* where u_t is computed directly from S_t, B_t and $a_{<t}$
4. Model is trained on a typologically diverse polyglot corpus.

The proposed architecture is inspired by the *Principle and Parameter framework* (Chomsky, 1993) framework proposed by linguists *Noam Chomsky* and *Howard Lasnik.* (Chomsky, 1993). The central idea behind the PP framework is that a person's syntactic knowledge can be modelled with two formal attributes namely a finite set of fundamental ***Principles*** that are shared by all languages (e.g.: A sentence must always have a subject) and a finite set of ***Parameters*** whose values characterize syntactic variability amongst various languages (eg: *Subject-Verb-Object* (S-V-O) order within a sentence).

Inspired by this PP theory, our proposed *UniRNNG* architecture comprises of distinct α (W^α,c^α) and β (W^β,c^β) parameters to encode the universal and language specific features.

4 Experiments

This section describes the experiments conducted to evaluate the performance of proposed **UniRNNG**. Each experiment comprises of a set of source languages L_s and a single target language l_t.

4.1 Experimental Settings

We evaluated the performance of **UniRNNG** under two experimental setups namely *Few-shot learning* and *Zero-shot learning* setups.

Few-shot Learning (Wang et al., 2019) is applied when only few training examples are

Language	Tree-bank	Family
English	Penn tree-bank (Marcus et al., 1993)	Germanic
Swedish (sd)	Talbanken05 (Nivre et al., 2006)	Germanic
French (fr)	FrenchTreebank (Abeillé et al., 2003)	Romance
Spanish (es)	Spanish UAM Treebank (Moreno et al., 1999)	Romance
Japanese (jp)	Tüba-J/S (Kawata and Bartels, 2000)	Altic
Arabic (ab)	Arabic PENN Treebank (Bies and Maamouri, 2003)	Afro-asiatic
Hungarian (hg)	Hungarian Szeged Treebank (Treebank)	Uralic

Table 2: List of source languages and their corpra used during experimentation. corpra are used to train both *Word-Embeddings* and *Parsers*

Language	Tree-bank	Family
German (de)	Negra Treebank (Skut et al., 1997)	Germanic
Danish (da)	Arboretum Treebank (Bick, 2003)	Germanic
Italian (it)	ISST Treebank (Montemagni et al., 2003)	Romance
Catalan (ct)	Catalan AnCora Treebank (Taulé et al., 2008)	Romance
Korean (kr)	Korean Penn Treebank (Han et al., 2002)	Altic
Heberew (hb)	(Sima' an et al., 2001)	Afro-asiatic
Estonian (est)	Estonian Arborest Treebank (Bick et al.)	Uralic
Hindi (hi)*	Hindi-Urdu Treebank (Bhat et al., 2017)	Indo-aryan
Vietnamese (vt)*	Vietnamese Treebank (Nguyen et al., 2009)	Austroasiatic

Table 3: List of target languages and their corpra used during experimentation. corpra are used to train both *Word-Embeddings* and *Parsers*. * these languages are used only in zero-shot settings

available in the *target language*. In this setup, the cross-lingual models (baseline and **UniRNNG**) are trained on a mixed corpus comprising of source-language sentences (covering over 80% corpus) and few available target language sentences. Hence for *Few-shot Learning* setup $l_t \in L_s$.

Zero-shot Learning (Socher et al., 2013) is applied when no labelled dataset is available in the *target language*. Hence $l_t \notin L_s$.

4.2 Baselines

This section describes the baselines used to compare the performance of our proposed *UniRNNG*.

4.2.1 Mono-lingual Models trained on Sparse Dataset

We used this baseline to compare the performance of our proposed *UniRNNG* only in the *Few-shot* learning settings. As our *UniRNNG* model is intended to be applied for low-resource languages, we compare the performance of it with that of the state-of-the-art mono-lingual models trained on sparse dataset. We experiment with three mono-lingual constituency parsers namely *DiscRNNG* 2.2.1, (Kuncoro et al., 2016) and Transformer (Vaswani et al., 2017).

These models provide over 95% F-Score when trained with sufficiently large dataset. But they would not show such high performance when trained on sparse dataset.

4.2.2 Unsupervised Recurrant Neural Network Grammar (URNNG)

Its a state of the art approach to *unsupervised constituency parsing*. We used this baseline to compare the performance of our proposed *UniRNNG* only in the *Zero-shot* learning settings.

4.2.3 Cross-lingual RNNG Parser trained on single source language (CL-RNNG-Mono)

Its the Dyer's RNNG model (Dyer et al., 2016) with only two modifications. Firstly the *Cross-lingual Word Embeddings* (Ruder et al., 2019b) are used rather than unique word-identifier vectors as used by Dyer et. al. Secondly the model is trained on a single source language *English* (UniRNNGs are trained on poly-

Hyper-parameter	Value
WE dims	768
S_t,B_t,$a_{<t}$ dims	450
$u^{\beta}{}_t$, $u^{\alpha}{}_t$ dims	450
Dropout prob.	0.01
Bach-size	32
Number of steps per epoch	Size of training corpus / 32
Epochs	150
BERT Model	bert_multi_cased_L-12_H-768_A-12

Table 4: Hyper-parameters

glot corpus) and tested on multiple target language. Within *Few-shot learning*, the training corpus also include small number of labelled target language sentences.

4.2.4 Cross-lingual RNNG Parser trained of multiple source languages (CL-RNNG-Poly)

It is the same model as described in 4.2.3, but trained on a mixed polyglot corpus of high-resource source languages.(*CL-RNNG-Mono* is trained on a single source language *English*). Similar to 4.2.3, a small number of labelled target-language l_t sentences are included as part of the training corpus within the *Few-shot* settings.

4.3 Dataset

Tables 2 and 3 list all the *Source* and *Target* languages as well as their tree-bank corpra used during experimentation. We evaluated our proposed *UniRNNG* model and all the baseline models on each of the target languages listed in Table 3 independently.
As already explained in section 4.1, the *CL-RNNG-Mono* parsers (4.2.3) are always trained on the single source-language *English*, whereas the *CL-RNNG-Poly* and the *UniRNNG* Parsers are always trained on a mixed polyglot corpus (in both *few-shot* and *zero-shot* setups). For each experiment, the source-language training corpus size is always fixed to 700,000 tokens to ensure controlled experiment-settings.
We created the source-language training-corpus for *CL-RNNG-Mono* parsers by randomly sampling sentences from the English-PTB corpus (one at a time), until the token-size becomes approximately equal to 700,000. On the other hand, to create the source-language training-corpus for *CL-RNNG-Poly* and *UniRNNG* models, we randomly sampled sentences from each of the seven source-language corpra listed in table 2 until the token-size becomes approximately equal 100,000, concatenated all these sampled datasets and randomly shuffled the order. Hence all the seven source-languages listed in table 2 are equally represented in the training-corpus for *CL-RNNG-Poly* and *UniRNNG* models.

4.3.1 Short tree-bank corpra

As explained in section 4.1, within *Few-shot learning* settings, only sparse target-language dataset should be used to train both *UniRNNG* and *Baselines*. Hence we extracted a small subset of entire large treebank corpus for each target language listed in table 3.
We extracted this subset by randomly sampling sentences from the target-language treebank corpus until the token-size becomes approximately equal to 3000. This is inspired by (Ammar et al., 2016) who used same yardstick to evaluate their *Multi-lingual Dependency Parser (MALOPA)*. This small target-language language corpus is added to the source-language training corpus for each experiment, within *Few-shot Learning* setup.

4.4 Universal Annotation

There are numerous tree-bank corpra for a diverse range of languages being developed during the years (some listed in Tables 2 and 3). But unlike *Dependency Parsing* tree-banks which are mostly annotated with the *UD Annotations* (McDonald et al., 2013) (for most languages), in case of *Constituency Parsing* various existing tree-bank corpra have their own independent tag annotations, thus making the application of multi-lingual approaches to it as impossible.
However, (Han et al., 2014) proposed a *Universal Phrase tag-set* with 9 common Phrase-tags. Furthermore, (Han et al., 2014) also provides a mapping table to map tags of popular constituency tree-banks (including all treebanks used by us in our experiments) to these *Unversal Phrase Tags*.

We used this mapping table to replace all tags within all tree-banks listed in Tables 2 and 3, with the universal tags. Subsequently we trained and evaluated all approaches (including baseline mono-lingual approaches) on these *Universally Tagged* tree-bank versions.

4.5 Cross-Lingual Word Embedding

As our model is a polyglot, we use *Cross-lingual Word-embeddings* during the encoding of Stack and Buffer state at any time-step t. We use a simple *Linear transformation based approach* (Ruder et al., 2019b) to compute such *Cross-lingual Word-embeddings.*
Given two languages l_1 and l_2, the simple *Linear Transformation* based approach first trains the mono-lingual WE for both l_1 and l_2 independently. Subsequently it uses a bi-lingual lexicon to learn a transformation matrix W^{l_1,l_2} to project embeddings of words of l_1 to the embedding-space of l_2 (considering l_2 as reference language).
To ensure that all WE are within same space, we use *English* as reference language. Mono-lingual WE of any other language l are thus transformed into the English space by learning the transformation matrix $W^{l,e}$ from word-pairs extracted from *English-l* bi-lingual lexicon.
We experiment with five common Word-embeddings namely *Skip-gram Word2vec* (Mikolov et al., 2013), *Fast-text* (Grave et al., 2018), Glove (Pennington et al., 2014), ELMo (Peters et al., 2018) and BERT (section 4.5.1). We use bi-lingual seed dictionaries provided by WOLD (Haspelmath and Uri Tadmor, 2009), ASJP (Wichmann and Brown, 2016) and IDS (Key and Comrie, 2015) which are elaborate multi-lingual lexical semantic databases.

4.5.1 BERT Word Embeddings

We computed language-independent BERT-Embeddings to be fed into UniRNNG using pre-trained Multilingual BERT (mBERT) (Wu and Dredze, 2019) model. mBERT is a multilingual variant of original BERT model (Devlin et al., 2018) trained on text from Wikipedia in 104 languages.
The Embeddings are calculated in same way as in (Kondratyuk and Straka, 2019). Given a sentence S, we tokenised the whole sentence using WordPiece tokeniser (Wu et al., 2016). Subsequently we fed this token-sequence into pre-trained mBERT provided by (Turc et al., 2019). Embedding of any word $w \in S$ i.e. e_w is computed by taking average of mBERT outputs of all Wordpiece tokens corresponding to word w.
Thus, mBERT based Word-embeddings do not require any Linear transformation.

4.6 Typology and Hyper-parameters

Table 4 outlines hyper-permeters used during experiments. These values are obtained by minimizing the training loss on *Development* dataset (Dev set) for *Penn Treebank Corpus* (Marcus et al., 1993).
Typology vector Z includes feature-values of all word-order and constituency features in WALS (Haspelmath, 2009) database excluding trivially redundant features as excluded by (Takamura et al., 2016).

5 Results and Inference

Tables 5 outlines results obtained from experiments conducted within the *Few-shot Learning* settings. Best results for *CL-RNNG-Mono*, *CL-RNNG-Poly* and proposed *UniRNNG* models are obtained with BERT Embedding. Table 6 outlines results obtained for experiments conducted under *Zero-shot* learning settings. As we obtained best results with BERT Embeddings within few-shot settings, we experimented with only BERT-embeddings 4.5.1 in *Zero-shot* settings indeed. As *CL-RNNG-Mono* is trained on the single source language English, it is expected to perform comparatively better on the target languages which are typologically closer to English and poorer on the target languages which are typologically apart from English. On the other hand, *CL-RNNG-Poly* and *UniRNNG* are expected to perform almost uniformly on all the target languages as these are trained on typologically diverse polyglot corpra. These expected trends are in-fact observed in both *Few-shot* and *Zero-shot* learning settings as evident in Tables 5 and 6. Hence for languages Danish (da) and German (de), *Cl-RNNG-Mono* outperformed both *CL-RNNG-Poly* and *UniRNNG* as these languages belong to the same language-family as English namely *Germanic* and are indeed

Model	de	da	it	ct	kr	hb	est
Transformers (Vaswani et al., 2017)	34.34	33.08	34.71	33.74	35.58	35.60	35.57
DiscRNNG 2.2.1	34.49	33.52	35.01	34.15	36.02	35.74	35.94
(Kuncoro et al., 2016)	34.98	33.68	35.53	34.46	36.3	36.42	36.23
CL-RNNG-Mono+Skip-Gram	65.63	70.85	54.59	58.05	22.95	30.44	53.43
CL-RNNG-Mono+Fast-text	67.13	72.55	56.39	60.35	24.75	31.94	55.83
CL-RNNG-Mono+Glove	68.73	74.15	57.29	61.15	25.45	33.84	55.93
CL-RNNG-Mono+ELMo	69.13	74.75	58.49	61.64	26.65	33.94	56.73
CL-RNNG-Mono+BERT	71.03	77.35	60.39	63.05	27.75	39.84	59.93
CL-RNNG-Poly+SkipGram	61.94	62.89	64.0	64.53	61.88	63.19	62.76
CL-RNNG-Poly+Fast-text	63.57	64.51	65.78	66.53	64.3	64.84	65.55
CL-RNNG-Poly+Glove	65.1	66.17	66.5	67.4	64.72	66.59	65.51
CL-RNNG-Poly+ELMo	65.48	66.86	67.61	68.16	65.89	66.64	66.01
CL-RNNG-Poly+BERT	67.48	69.41	69.55	70.46	69.18	69.88	69.19
UniRNNG+SkipGram	64.92	65.95	66.79	67.35	65.05	66.24	65.83
UniRNNG+Fast-text	66.42	67.65	68.59	69.64	67.05	67.74	68.23
UniRNNG+Glove	68.03	69.25	69.49	70.45	67.55	69.64	68.33
UniRNNG+ELMo	68.42	69.85	70.69	70.94	68.75	69.74	69.13
UniRNNG+BERT	70.33	72.44	72.59	73.35	71.85	72.64	72.33

Table 5: F1 Score in *Few-shot* learning settings. *Top:* Results for supervised approaches trained on sparse dataset. *Middle:* Results for baseline Cross-lingual Transfer Parser (CLT-P). *Bottom:* Results for proposed **UniRNNG**

Model	de	da	it	ct	kr	hb	est	hi	vt
URNNG (Kim et al., 2019)	11.84	11.58	10.53	12.43	9.97	10.46	8.52	9.36	3.12
CL-RNNG-Mono+BERT	68.13	70.94	61.99	56.85	20.91	27.82	52.61	48.66	37.61
CL-RNNG-Poly+BERT	64.43	64.13	64.5	66.37	63.32	64.99	63.5	56.2	57.21
UniRNNG+BERT	67.62	67.03	67.19	69.14	66.25	68.14	66.63	59.23	60.11

Table 6: F1 Score in *Few-shot* learning settings.

typologically very close to English. Whereas, on the other five target languages which are typologically and genealogically distinct from the source language English namely Italian (it), Catalan (ct), Estonian (est), Heberew (hb) and Korean (kr), it under-performed *CL-RNNG-Poly*.

Based on these observed trends we can infer that the polyglot training training increases the Cross-lingual transferring ability of the RNNG based Constituency Parser to a typologically distinct and unseen target language as it allows the model to better generalize over a diverse set of languages.

In both *Few-shot* and *Zero-shot* settings, *UniRNNGs* significant outperformed *CL-RNNG-Poly* on all the seven target languages namely Danish (da), German (de), Italian (it), Catalan (ct), Estonian (est), Heberew (hb) and Korean (kr) as evident in Tables 5 and 6. Hence it can be inferred inducing linguistic typology indeed leads to further improvement in Cross-lingual transferring ability of the RNNG based Constituency Parser to a typologically distinct and unseen target language.

Furthermore, in *zero-shot* learning settings, we evaluated our models on two additional target languages namely *Hindi* and *Vietnamese* (rightmost column in table 6). Languages *Hindi* and *Vietnamese* belong to linguistic families *Indo-aryan* and *Austro-asiatic* respectively. None of the source languages listed in Table 2 belong to these linguistic families. Thus languages *Hindi* and *Vietnamese* are typologically very distant form all the source languages in the polyglot training corpus of *UniRNNGs*. Hence scores obtained on these languages indicate true Language Agnostic nature of **UniRNNG** architecture.

Although the performance of **UniRNNG** for these two languages is comparatively lower than its performance on other target languages listed in table 3, yet this improved performance as compared to *CL-RNNG-Mono* and *CL-RNNG-Poly* provide even stronger evidence that **UniRNNG** architecture is more robust to typologically distinct unseen target languages than *CL-RNNG-Poly*. In other words, once trained on significantly diverse polyglot corpus, **UniRNNG** is *Language-Agnostic*.

6 Conclusion

In this work, we proposed and evaluated *Universal Recurrent Neural Network Grammar (UniRNNG)* which is a multilingual variant of Dyer's RNNG model. The architecture of *UniRNNG* is inspired by *Principles and Parameters* theory proposed by linguist Noam Chomsky. We evaluated the performance of *UniRNNG* in both *Few-shot* and *Zero-shot* learning settings. Results show that the *UniRNNGs* outperformed all baseline approaches for most of the target languages for which these are tested. As far as we are aware, this is the first paper which evaluated the performance of Cross-lingual Transfer Parsing for *Constituency Parsing* task.
Future work, would involve exploring the changes in performances of baseline and *UniRNNG* models with the varying degree of diversity in the training corpus.

References

Anne Abeillé, Lionel Clément, and François Toussenel. 2003. Building a treebank for french. In *Treebanks*, pages 165–187. Springer.

Waleed Ammar. 2016. *Towards a Universal Analyzer of Natural Languages*. Ph.D. thesis, Ph. D. thesis, Google Research.

Waleed Ammar, George Mulcaire, Miguel Ballesteros, Chris Dyer, and Noah A Smith. 2016. Many languages, one parser. *Transactions of the Association for Computational Linguistics*, 4:431–444.

Mark C Baker. 2008. *The atoms of language: The mind's hidden rules of grammar*. Basic books.

Regina Barzilay and Yuan Zhang. 2015. Hierarchical low-rank tensors for multilingual transfer parsing. Association for Computational Linguistics.

Nuria Bel, Cornelis HA Koster, and Marta Villegas. 2003. Cross-lingual text categorization. In *International Conference on Theory and Practice of Digital Libraries*, pages 126–139. Springer.

Riyaz Ahmad Bhat, Rajesh Bhatt, Annahita Farudi, Prescott Klassen, Bhuvana Narasimhan, Martha Palmer, Owen Rambow, Dipti Misra Sharma, Ashwini Vaidya, Sri Ramagurumurthy Vishnu, et al. 2017. The hindi/urdu treebank project. In *Handbook of Linguistic Annotation*, pages 659–697. Springer.

Eckhard Bick. 2003. Arboretum, a hybrid treebank for danish. In *Proceedings of TLT 2003 (2nd Workshop on Treebanks and Linguistic Theory, Växjö*, pages 9–20.

Eckhard Bick, Heli Uibo, and Kadri Muischnek. Preliminary experiments for a cg-based syntactic tree corpus of estonian.

Ann Bies and Mohamed Maamouri. 2003. Penn arabic treebank guidelines. *Draft: January*, 28:2003.

Xilun Chen, Yu Sun, Ben Athiwaratkun, Claire Cardie, and Kilian Weinberger. 2018. Adversarial deep averaging networks for cross-lingual sentiment classification. *Transactions of the Association for Computational Linguistics*, 6:557–570.

Noam Chomsky. 1986. *Knowledge of language: Its nature, origin, and use*. Greenwood Publishing Group.

Noam Chomsky. 1993. *Lectures on government and binding: The Pisa lectures*. 9. Walter de Gruyter.

Guglielmo Cinque and Luigi Rizzi. 2010. The cartography of syntactic structures. *Oxford Handbook of linguistic analysis*.

Alexis Conneau, Guillaume Lample, Ruty Rinott, Adina Williams, Samuel R Bowman, Holger Schwenk, and Veselin Stoyanov. 2018. Xnli: Evaluating cross-lingual sentence representations. *arXiv preprint arXiv:1809.05053*.

Vivian Cook and Mark Newson. 2014. *Chomsky's universal grammar*. John Wiley & Sons.

Zeman Daniel, Popel Martin, Straka Milan, Hajic Jan, Nivre Joakim, Ginter Filip, Luotolahti Juhani, Pyysalo Sampo, Petrov Slav, Potthast Martin, et al. 2017a. Conll 2017 shared task: Multilingual parsing from raw text to universal dependencies. In *CoNLL 2017 Shared Task: Multilingual Parsing from Raw Text to Universal Dependencies*, volume 1, pages 1–19. Association for Computational Linguistics.

Zeman Daniel, Popel Martin, Straka Milan, Hajic Jan, Nivre Joakim, Ginter Filip, Luotolahti Juhani, Pyysalo Sampo, Petrov Slav, Potthast Martin, et al. 2017b. Conll 2017 shared task: Multilingual parsing from raw text to universal dependencies. In *CoNLL 2017 Shared Task: Multilingual Parsing from Raw Text to Universal Dependencies*, volume 1, pages 1–19. Association for Computational Linguistics.

Jacob Devlin, Ming-Wei Chang, Kenton Lee, and Kristina Toutanova. 2018. Bert: Pre-training of deep bidirectional transformers for language understanding. *arXiv preprint arXiv:1810.04805*.

Yerai Doval, Jose Camacho-Collados, Luis Espinosa Anke, and Steven Schockaert. 2019. Meemi: A simple method for post-processing cross-lingual word embeddings. *arXiv preprint arXiv:1910.07221*.

Long Duong, Trevor Cohn, Steven Bird, and Paul Cook. 2015. Low resource dependency parsing: Cross-lingual parameter sharing in a neural network parser. In *Proceedings of the 53rd Annual Meeting of the Association for Computational Linguistics and the 7th International Joint Conference on Natural Language Processing (Volume 2: Short Papers)*, pages 845–850.

Chris Dyer, Miguel Ballesteros, Wang Ling, Austin Matthews, and Noah A Smith. 2015. Transition-based dependency parsing with stack long short-term memory. *arXiv preprint arXiv:1505.08075*.

Chris Dyer, Adhiguna Kuncoro, Miguel Ballesteros, and Noah A Smith. 2016. Recurrent neural network grammars. *arXiv preprint arXiv:1602.07776*.

Agnieszka Falenska and Özlem Çetinoğlu. 2017. Lexicalized vs. delexicalized parsing in low-resource scenarios. In *Proceedings of the 15th International Conference on Parsing Technologies*, pages 18–24.

Janet Dean Fodor. 2001. Setting syntactic parameters.

Janet Dean Fodor and William Gregory Sakas. 2004. Evaluating models of parameter setting. In *Proceedings of the 28th annual boston university conference on language development*, volume 1, pages 1–27. Cascadilla Press Somerville, MA.

Edouard Grave, Piotr Bojanowski, Prakhar Gupta, Armand Joulin, and Tomas Mikolov. 2018. Learning word vectors for 157 languages. In *Proceedings of the International Conference on Language Resources and Evaluation (LREC 2018)*.

Jiang Guo, Wanxiang Che, David Yarowsky, Haifeng Wang, and Ting Liu. 2016. A representation learning framework for multi-source transfer parsing. In *Thirtieth AAAI Conference on Artificial Intelligence*.

Aaron Li-Feng Han, Derek F Wong, Lidia S Chao, Yi Lu, Liangye He, and Liang Tian. 2014. A universal phrase tagset for multilingual treebanks. In *Chinese Computational Linguistics and Natural Language Processing Based on Naturally Annotated Big Data*, pages 247–258. Springer.

Chunghye Han, Narae Han, Eonsuk Ko, and Martha Palmer. 2002. Korean treebank: Development and evaluation. In *Proceedings of the 3rd International Conference on Language Resources and Evaluation*.

Martin Haspelmath. 2009. *The typological database of the World Atlas of Language Structures*. Berlin: Walter de Gruyter.

Martin Haspelmath and editors Uri Tadmor. 2009. WOLD.

Haoyang Huang, Yaobo Liang, Nan Duan, Ming Gong, Linjun Shou, Daxin Jiang, and Ming Zhou. 2019. Unicoder: A universal language encoder by pre-training with multiple cross-lingual tasks. *arXiv preprint arXiv:1909.00964*.

Daniel Jurafsky and James H. Martin. 2019. Transition-based dependency parsing (section 15.4). In *Speech and Language Processing (3rd Edition draft)*, chapter 15, pages 6–17.

Yasuhiro Kawata and Julia Bartels. 2000. Stylebook for the japanese treebank in verbmobil. In *Verbmobil-Report 240, Seminar für Sprachwissenschaft, Universität Tübingen*.

Richard Kayne. 2012. Some notes on comparative syntax, with special reference to english and french. In *The Oxford handbook of comparative syntax*. Oxford University Press.

Mary Ritchie Key and Bernard Comrie. 2015. IDS.

Yoon Kim, Alexander M Rush, Lei Yu, Adhiguna Kuncoro, Chris Dyer, and Gábor Melis. 2019. Unsupervised recurrent neural network grammars. *arXiv preprint arXiv:1904.03746*.

Dan Kondratyuk and Milan Straka. 2019. 75 languages, 1 model: Parsing universal dependencies universally. *arXiv preprint arXiv:1904.02099*.

Adhiguna Kuncoro, Miguel Ballesteros, Lingpeng Kong, Chris Dyer, Graham Neubig, and Noah A Smith. 2016. What do recurrent neural network grammars learn about syntax? *arXiv preprint arXiv:1611.05774*.

Chia-Hsuan Lee and Hung-Yi Lee. 2019. Cross-lingual transfer learning for question answering. *arXiv preprint arXiv:1907.06042*.

Patrick Lewis, Barlas Oğuz, Ruty Rinott, Sebastian Riedel, and Holger Schwenk. 2019. Mlqa: Evaluating cross-lingual extractive question answering. *arXiv preprint arXiv:1910.07475*.

Jiahua Liu, Yankai Lin, Zhiyuan Liu, and Maosong Sun. 2019. Xqa: A cross-lingual open-domain question answering dataset. In *Proceedings of the 57th Annual Meeting of the Association for Computational Linguistics*, pages 2358–2368.

Mitchell Marcus, Beatrice Santorini, and Mary Ann Marcinkiewicz. 1993. Building a large annotated corpus of english: The penn treebank.

Ryan McDonald, Joakim Nivre, Yvonne Quirmbach-Brundage, Yoav Goldberg, Dipanjan Das, Kuzman Ganchev, Keith Hall, Slav Petrov, Hao Zhang, Oscar Täckström, et al. 2013. Universal dependency annotation for multilingual parsing. In *Proceedings of the 51st Annual Meeting of the Association for Computational Linguistics (Volume 2: Short Papers)*, pages 92–97.

Rada Mihalcea, Carmen Banea, and Janyce Wiebe. 2007. Learning multilingual subjective language via cross-lingual projections. In *Proceedings of the 45th annual meeting of the association of computational linguistics*, pages 976–983.

Tomas Mikolov, Ilya Sutskever, Kai Chen, Greg S Corrado, and Jeff Dean. 2013. Distributed representations of words and phrases and their compositionality. In *Advances in neural information processing systems*, pages 3111–3119.

Simonetta Montemagni, Francesco Barsotti, Marco Battista, Nicoletta Calzolari, Ornella Corazzari, Antonio Zampolli, Francesca Fanciulli, Maria Massetani, Remo Raffaelli, Roberto Basili, et al. 2003. The italian syntactic-semantic treebank: Architecture, annotation, tools and evaluation.

Antonio Moreno, Susana López, and Manuel Alcántara. 1999. Spanish tree bank: Specifications, version 5. *Technical paper.*

Phoebe Mulcaire, Jungo Kasai, and Noah A Smith. 2019. Low-resource parsing with crosslingual contextualized representations. *arXiv preprint arXiv:1909.08744*.

Tahira Naseem, Regina Barzilay, and Amir Globerson. 2012. Selective sharing for multilingual dependency parsing. The Association for Computational Linguistics.

Phuong Thai Nguyen, Xuan Luong Vu, Thi Minh Huyen Nguyen, Hong Phuong Le, et al. 2009. Building a large syntactically-annotated corpus of vietnamese.

Joakim Nivre, Jens Nilsson, and Johan Hall. 2006. Talbanken05: A swedish treebank with phrase structure and dependency annotation. In *LREC*, pages 1392–1395.

Jeffrey Pennington, Richard Socher, and Christopher D Manning. 2014. Glove: Global vectors for word representation. In *Proceedings of the 2014 conference on empirical methods in natural language processing (EMNLP)*, pages 1532–1543.

Matthew E Peters, Mark Neumann, Mohit Iyyer, Matt Gardner, Christopher Clark, Kenton Lee, and Luke Zettlemoyer. 2018. Deep contextualized word representations. *arXiv preprint arXiv:1802.05365*.

Steven Pinker. 1995. *The language instinct: The new science of language and mind*, volume 7529. Penguin UK.

Peter Prettenhofer and Benno Stein. 2010. Cross-language text classification using structural correspondence learning. In *Proceedings of the 48th annual meeting of the association for computational linguistics*, pages 1118–1127.

Mohammad Sadegh Rasooli and Michael Collins. 2017. Cross-lingual syntactic transfer with limited resources. *Transactions of the Association for Computational Linguistics*, 5:279–293.

Ian Roberts and Anders Holmberg. 2005. On the role of parameters in universal grammar: A reply to newmeyer. *Organizing Grammar: Linguistic Studies in Honor of Henk van Riemsdijk. Berlin: Mouton de Gruyter*, pages 538–553.

Sebastian Ruder, Anders Søgaard, and Ivan Vulić. 2019a. Unsupervised cross-lingual representation learning. In *Proceedings of ACL 2019, Tutorial Abstracts*, pages 31–38.

Sebastian Ruder, Ivan Vulić, and Anders Søgaard. 2019b. A survey of cross-lingual word embedding models. *Journal of Artificial Intelligence Research*, 65:569–631.

Ehsan Shareghi, Yingzhen Li, Yi Zhu, Roi Reichart, and Anna Korhonen. 2019. Bayesian learning for neural dependency parsing. In *Proceedings of the 2019 Conference of the North American Chapter of the Association for Computational Linguistics: Human Language Technologies, Volume 1 (Long and Short Papers)*, pages 3509–3519.

Lei Shi, Rada Mihalcea, and Mingjun Tian. 2010. Cross language text classification by model translation and semi-supervised learning. In *Proceedings of the 2010 Conference on Empirical Methods in Natural Language Processing*, pages 1057–1067.

Ur Shlonsky. 2010. The cartographic enterprise in syntax. *Language and linguistics compass*, 4(6):417–429.

Khalil Sima' an, Alon Itai, Yoad Winter, Alon Altman, and Noa Nativ. 2001. Building a tree-bank of modern hebrew text. *Traitement Automatique des Langues*, 42(2):247–380.

Jasdeep Singh, Bryan McCann, Nitish Shirish Keskar, Caiming Xiong, and Richard Socher. 2019. Xlda: Cross-lingual data augmentation for natural language inference and question answering. *arXiv preprint arXiv:1905.11471*.

Wojciech Skut, Brigitte Krenn, Thorsten Brants, and Hans Uszkoreit. 1997. An annotation scheme for free word order languages. *arXiv preprint cmp-lg/9702004*.

Richard Socher, Milind Ganjoo, Christopher D Manning, and Andrew Ng. 2013. Zero-shot learning through cross-modal transfer. In *Advances in neural information processing systems*, pages 935–943.

Oscar Täckström, Ryan McDonald, and Joakim Nivre. 2013. Target language adaptation of discriminative transfer parsers.

Hiroya Takamura, Ryo Nagata, and Yoshifumi Kawasaki. 2016. Discriminative analysis of linguistic features for typological study. In *Proceedings of the Tenth International Conference on Language Resources and Evaluation (LREC'16)*, pages 69–76.

Mariona Taulé, Maria Antònia Martí, and Marta Recasens. 2008. Ancora: Multilevel annotated corpora for catalan and spanish. In *Lrec*.

Michael Tomasello. 2005. Beyond formalities: The case of language acquisition. *The Linguistic Review*, 22(2-4):183–197.

Hungarian Szeged Treebank. Szeged treebank 2.0: A hungarian natural language database with detailed syntactic analysis. *Hungarian linguistics at the University of Szeged*.

Iulia Turc, Ming-Wei Chang, Kenton Lee, and Kristina Toutanova. 2019. Well-read students learn better: On the importance of pre-training compact models. *arXiv preprint arXiv:1908.08962v2*.

Clara Vania, Yova Kementchedjhieva, Anders Søgaard, and Adam Lopez. 2019. A systematic comparison of methods for low-resource dependency parsing on genuinely low-resource languages. *arXiv preprint arXiv:1909.02857*.

Ashish Vaswani, Noam Shazeer, Niki Parmar, Jakob Uszkoreit, Llion Jones, Aidan N Gomez, Łukasz Kaiser, and Illia Polosukhin. 2017. Attention is all you need. In *Advances in neural information processing systems*, pages 5998–6008.

David Vilares, Carlos Gómez-Rodríguez, and Miguel A Alonso. 2015. One model, two languages: training bilingual parsers with harmonized treebanks. *arXiv preprint arXiv:1507.08449*.

Dingquan Wang and Jason Eisner. 2016a. The galactic dependencies treebanks: Getting more data by synthesizing new languages. *Transactions of the Association for Computational Linguistics*, 4:491–505.

Dingquan Wang and Jason Eisner. 2016b. The galactic dependencies treebanks: Getting more data by synthesizing new languages. *Transactions of the Association for Computational Linguistics*, 4:491–505.

Yaqing Wang, Quanming Yao, James T Kwok, and Lionel M Ni. 2019. Generalizing from a few examples: A survey on few-shot learning. *ACM Computing Surveys (CSUR)*.

Eric W. Holman Wichmann, Søren and Cecil H. Brown. 2016. The ASJP Database (version17).

Shijie Wu and Mark Dredze. 2019. Beto, bentz, becas: The surprising cross-lingual effectiveness of bert. *arXiv preprint arXiv:1904.09077*.

Yonghui Wu, Mike Schuster, Zhifeng Chen, Quoc V Le, Mohammad Norouzi, Wolfgang Macherey, Maxim Krikun, Yuan Cao, Qin Gao, Klaus Macherey, et al. 2016. Google's neural machine translation system: Bridging the gap between human and machine translation. *arXiv preprint arXiv:1609.08144*.

Ruochen Xu, Yiming Yang, Hanxiao Liu, and Andrew Hsi. 2016. Cross-lingual text classification via model translation with limited dictionaries. In *Proceedings of the 25th ACM International on Conference on Information and Knowledge Management*, pages 95–104.

Daniel Zeman, Jan Hajic, Martin Popel, Martin Potthast, Milan Straka, Filip Ginter, Joakim Nivre, and Slav Petrov. 2018a. Conll 2018 shared task: Multilingual parsing from raw text to universal dependencies. In *Proceedings of the CoNLL 2018 Shared Task: Multilingual parsing from raw text to universal dependencies*, pages 1–21.

Daniel Zeman, Jan Hajic, Martin Popel, Martin Potthast, Milan Straka, Filip Ginter, Joakim Nivre, and Slav Petrov. 2018b. Conll 2018 shared task: Multilingual parsing from raw text to universal dependencies. In *Proceedings of the CoNLL 2018 Shared Task: Multilingual parsing from raw text to universal dependencies*, pages 1–21.

The 33rd Conference on Computational Linguistics and Speech Processing (ROCLING 2021)
Taoyuan, Taiwan, October 15-16, 2021. The Association for Computational Linguistics and Chinese Language Processing

運用遷移式學習改善 BERT 於中文歌詞情緒分類模型之研發
A Study on Using Transfer Learning to Improve BERT Model for Emotional Classification of Chinese Lyrics

廖家誼 Jia-Yi Liao[1]
plusoneee@smail.nchu.edu.tw

林亞宣 Ya-Hsuan Lin [1]

林冠成 Kuan-Cheng Lin [1]

張家瑋 Jia-Wei Chang [2]
jiaweichang.gary@gmail.com

[1] 國立中興大學資訊管理學系
Department of Management Information Systems
National Chung Hsing University

[2] 國立臺中科技大學資訊工程系
Department of Computer Science and Information Engineering
National Taichung University of Science and Technology

摘要

音樂庫的爆炸增長讓音樂資訊檢索和推薦成爲重要議題，以音樂情緒辨識爲基礎的推薦系統逐漸受到研究者的重視。音樂情緒辨識主要以歌曲情緒爲主，部分研究關注英文歌詞，罕見對於中文歌詞情緒辨識的研究。因此，本研究提出利用 BERT 預訓練模型和遷移學習來改善中文歌詞的情緒分類任務。實驗結果顯示，在未針對歌詞情緒分類任務訓練下:(a) 使用 BERT 針對 CVAT 建立之分類模型，只能達到 50% 的歌詞情緒分類準確度。(b) 使用 BERT 針對 CVAW+CVAP 建立分類模型再對 CVAT 資料集遷移學習後，能提升到 71% 的歌詞情緒分類準確度。

Abstract

The explosive growth of music libraries has made music information retrieval and recommendation a critical issue. Recommendation systems based on music emotion recognition are gradually gaining attention. Most of the studies focus on audio data rather than lyrics to build models of music emotion classification. In addition, because of the richness of English language resources, most of the existing studies are focused on English lyrics but rarely on Chinese. For this reason, We propose an approach that uses the BERT pretraining model and Transfer learning to improve the emotion classification task of Chinese lyrics. The following approaches were used without any specific training for the Chinese lyrics emotional classification task: (a) Using BERT, only can reach 50% of the classification accuracy. (b) Using BERT with transfer learning of CVAW, CVAP, and CVAT datasets can achieve 71% classification accuracy.

關鍵字：音樂情緒辨識、自然語言處理、中文歌詞

Keywords: Music Emotion Recognition, Natural Language Processing, Chinese Lyrics

1 緒論

音樂搜尋通常以歌曲標題、詞曲作者、演唱者和演奏流派做檢索。然而，情緒可以作爲音樂的一個新且重要的搜尋屬性。隨著音樂串流平台使用者和歌曲庫的爆炸式增長，傳統的由專家進行情緒標註已不能滿足實際需求，推薦系統需要更快速的標註方法，自動情緒辨識因此成爲重要的議題。音樂情緒辨識 (Music Emotion Recognition) 用於觀察音樂與人類情感之相關性，對音樂抽取特徵並加以分析找出音樂特徵與人類對於音樂情緒感知的關聯。目前機器學習和深度學習方法已被廣泛用於辨識音樂的情緒。支持向量機 (Support Vector Machine，SVM) 和支持向量回歸 (Support Vector Regression，SVR) 等機器學習方法 (Han et al., 2009)。基於歌詞和音訊的歌曲情緒檢測方法，結合 ANEW 和 WordNet 來計算 Valence 和 Arousal 進行音樂情緒分類 (Jamdar et al., 2015)。用卷積神經網路預訓練模型對每 30 秒剪輯的印度古典音樂進行音樂情緒分類 (Sarkar et al., 2015)。

上述研究大多都集中利用聲學特徵進行音樂情緒辨識，並無討論歌詞對於情緒的影響。歌詞在引發人類的情緒以及預測音樂情緒扮演著重要的角色 (Hu and Downie, 2010b)。雖然旋律和歌詞會同時對聽眾產生影響，但聽眾對於歌詞内容的偏好能進一步反映聽眾的特徵和傾向 (Qiu et al., 2019)。Agrawal et al. (2021) 提出歌詞可視爲一連串彼此相關的句子，需捕捉上下文和長期依賴的關係，所以運用基於 Transformer 的模型進行歌詞情緒辨識，並在多個英文歌詞情緒資料集上取得良好的成果。上述的英文歌詞資料集皆基於 Russell 的 Valence-Arousal 環繞模型進行音樂情緒的標註。截至本研究發表之前，尚未有中文歌詞文本包含情緒標註的大型資料集，因此，本研究提出一新的中文情緒辨識方法，運用基於 Transformer 語言預訓練模型對中文文字與片語進行建模，將模型遷移至中文文本資料集，最後將模型直接用於無標註的歌詞文本進行情緒的自動標註。本研究其餘章節的組織如下：第二節説明情緒模型、基於 Transformer 之模型和遷移學習的相關工作，第三節介紹本研究使用的資料集、文本預處理並解釋本研究提出的架構，第四節爲本研究模型訓練和歌詞驗證的結果，第五節對實驗結果進行相關討論，第六節總結本研究的成果。

2 相關研究

2.1 情緒維度模型

現有的研究大多採用Russell (1980) 提出的環繞模型。Laurier et al. (2009) 的研究中表明，Russell 心理學情緒模型可以用於情緒分析或音樂情緒辨識任務。兩個維度的連續數值，分別爲 Valence 和 Arousal。Valence 代表所有情緒體驗所固有的積極或消極。Arousal 代表情緒的激動程度，歌曲的能量對應於 Arousal 值，代表歌曲強度 (Kim et al., 2011)。Çano and Morisio (2017a) 則基於 Russell 心理學情緒模型的四個象限將情緒分爲四類別，分別爲快樂、憤怒、悲傷和輕鬆 (Q1、Q2、Q3、Q4)，因此本研究在歌詞驗證也依此方法將歌詞情緒分爲四個象限類別。

2.2 基於 Transformer 之先進模型

歌詞被視爲是敘事而非彼此獨立的句子，需捕捉上下文的依賴關係，歌詞的音樂情緒分類任務若基於傳統詞典 (Barry 2017;Han et al. 2013) 進行效果有限 (Hu and Downie 2010a;Hu et al. 2009)。Abdillah et al. (2020) 運用捕捉時序關係的雙向長短期記憶 (Long Short-Term Memory，LSTM)，但遞歸架構難以具備平行運算的能力。Vaswani et al. (2017) 提出 Transformer 模型架構，該模型卓越的自注意力機制也使得目前自然語言處理領域中公認最先進的 BERT (Devlin et al., 2019) 亦以 Transformer 作爲模型設計的基礎。此外，Agrawal et al. (2021) 的研究使用基於 Transformer 作爲情緒分類的模型，在多個英文歌詞情緒資料集上達到傑出的成果，展現出 Transformer 的強大優勢。

2.3 遷移學習

在某些領域中標籤的標記昂貴，若原始資料中含有標籤的數量太少，容易過度擬合。遷移學習中有兩個常用的方法，特徵萃取和微調，特徵萃取技術是使用預先訓練好的模型作爲編碼器，爲目標任務提取有效的特徵。微調技術是將原有任務訓練所得到的模型結構和參數應用於目標任務的訓練，更新目標模型中的參數，達到提高訓練目標的學習能力。在自然語言處理領域，基於 Transformer 的預訓練模型 (Devlin et al., 2019) 已證明微調在大型無註釋語料庫上預訓練大規模語言模型的良好效能。Hung and Chang (2021) 則提到多層遷移學習在電腦視覺任務或自然語言處理任務的有效性，因此，本篇研究提出的模型架構便基於 Transformer 的語言預訓練模型對文本進行遷移學習。

3 方法論

3.1 資料集

- 中文情緒資料集 (Yu et al. 2016;Yu et al. 2017): 中文情緒字典 (CVAW)、中文情緒短語 (CVAP) 及中文情緒文本 (CVAT) 三個。CVAW 有 5,512 個中文情緒詞；CVAP 包含 2,998 個中文情緒片語；CVAT 從 720 篇來自 6 種不同類別的網路文章蒐集而來，共 2,009 個句子。每個詞或句子皆包含 Valence 和 Arousal 的數值，Valence 範圍從 1 到 9 分別代表極端負面和極端正面的情緒，Arousal 範圍從 1 到 9 分別代表平靜和激動，5 則代表沒有特定傾向的中性情緒。

- 歌詞資料集：本研究自行收集並標籤的資料集。標籤包含象限一 (Q1)、象限二 (Q2)、象限三 (Q3) 及象限四 (Q4)。Q1 共 43 首代表正向激昂，Q2 共 45 首代表負向激昂，Q3 共 43 首代表負向平靜，Q4 共 39 首代表正向平靜。V 和 A 分別代表 Valence 和 Arousal，V 標記 1 代表正向情緒、0 代表負向情緒，A 標記爲 1 代表激昂情緒、0 代表平靜情緒。

3.2 基於 BERT 的遷移式學習架構

本研究提出的模型架構如圖1，透過 BERT 預訓練模型建立 CVAT 中文維度情緒模型，將此模型直接用於歌詞情緒的標記，驗證在未學習過歌詞文本的情況下，模型對於歌詞情緒分類的成效。本章總共有三個小節，第一小節說明資料預處理，第二小節介紹模型實作的細節以及實驗的參數設定，第三小結討論將模型應用於歌詞文本情緒驗證的方法。

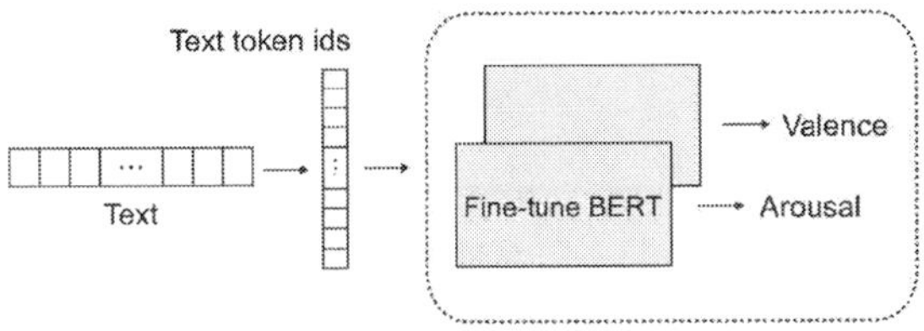

圖 1: 基於 BERT 的遷移式學習架構

3.2.1 資料預處理

CVAW、CVAP 和 CVAT 皆採用資料集內的文字、Valence 平均和 Arousal 平均，由於 CVAW、CVAP 的文字較短且類似，因此將兩個資料集合併成 CVAW+CVAP 資料集，以 8 比 2 拆分爲訓練集跟測試集。BERT 模型有別於傳統文本的方法，會將標點符號視爲一個特徵值進行訓練，因此 CVAT 文字不進行刪除標點符號的預處理。歌詞的資料集共 170 首，由三位標註者將每首歌曲的針對 Valence 和 Arousal 分別標註爲正或負，以中性情緒爲原點，依照 Valence 和 Arousal 的正跟負分標記到四個象限。BERT 能夠訓練的最大文本長度爲 512，考慮到 CVAP 和 CVAW 的文字都在 10 字以內，而 CVAT 的文本分佈大多集中在 100 字以內，爲避免產生過於稀疏向量，最大文本長度設定爲 256 而非 512。輸入 BERT 模型前必須在每個序列開頭加上特殊字元符號 [CLS]，此特殊字元代表整個輸入序列的向量表示，在序列尾巴則加上特殊字元符號 [SEP] 作爲文本的結束，每個中文字會對應到 BERT 中文字典的一個索引值稱爲 Token id，爲了讓每一則輸入序列的長度保持一致在文字序列後端填充特殊字元 [PAD]，最後，轉爲向量的序列和目標值轉爲 Tensor 至 BERT 模型進行訓練。

3.2.2 實施細節

本研究提出之模型架構如圖 1，模型輸出 Valence 和 Arousal 兩個數值，由於是數值的預測，因此損失函數選擇用均方誤差 (Mean square error，MSE)。實驗方法分別使用從 CVAW + CVAP 遷移至 CVAT 資料集的遷移學習方法比較從零直接訓練 CVAT 的未遷移的方法。基於微調方法進行實驗，微調方法的優點在於模型的許多參數不需要重新學習，即使只有少量訓練樣本也能達到良好的效果。在模型架構方面，在 BERT 欲訓練模型加上一層 Dropout 和一層線性分類層，優化器使用 Adam，學習速率在一開始嘗試多種學習速率，由於微調模型適合較小的學習速率避免預訓練的權重被修改破壞，最後選擇了 1e-05、1e-06 和 5e-05 三個超參數進行近一步實驗及比較，最大 Epoch 設定爲 100，並且加入 Early Stopping 的機制，將耐心 (Patience) 設至爲 10。

3.2.3 歌詞情緒之分類

此階段的目的在於驗證本研究提出的方法能在未學習過歌詞文本的情況下，對歌詞文本進行情緒的標註。將歌詞文本進行與第一小節同樣的預處理後送入模型進行數值預測，模型輸出 Valence 值和 Arousal 值。依照原資料集的敘述，Valence 和 Arousal 都以中性值 5 爲閾值 (Yu et al. 2016;Yu et al. 2017)，因此，當模型輸出的 Valence 大於 5，表示模型預測該歌詞爲正向情緒並它標記爲 1、Valence 小於 5 則表示模型預測該歌詞爲負向情緒並標記爲 0，若 Arousal 值大於 5 表示模型預測該歌詞爲激動情緒並標記爲 1、Arousal 值小於 5 表示模型預測該歌詞爲平靜情緒並標記爲 0。我們將 Valence 和 Arousal 標記之後的結果轉爲 Q1, Q2, Q3 和 Q4 的情緒分類之結果，最後驗證其分類效果。

4 實驗結果

本章節將實驗結果分爲兩個階段，第一階段是模型訓練的結果，第二階段是驗證模型預測歌詞情緒的成效。

4.1 建立中文情緒模型

訓練模型的資料集切分皆以 8 比 2 進行，CVAP+CVAW 資料集的訓練集和測試集分別爲 6808 筆和 1702 筆。模型架構的訓練結果，如表1，模型的 Valence 和 Arousal 的均方誤差分別爲 0.3788 和 0.77339，且最佳的學習速率皆爲 1e-05。表2爲從零訓練 CVAT 資料集和從 CVAP+CVAW 資料集模型遷移至 CVAT 資料集的結果。本實驗模型架構是分別預測 Valence 和 Arousal 兩個數值，因此分別討論 Valence 和 Arousal 的結果。首先比較 Valence 輸出的結果，未經遷移的均方誤差爲 0.50338，經遷移學習的均方誤差爲 0.46624，結果顯示經遷移學習的 CVAT 其結果優於未經遷移的結果。經遷移學習的最佳學習速率爲 1e-06，未經遷移的最佳學習速率爲 1e-5，就算同樣都在 1e-5 的學習速率下，經遷移學習的均方誤差 0.47898 還是優於未經遷移的均方誤差 0.50338。比較輸出爲 Arousal 的結果，經遷移的均方誤差爲 0.84259 優於未經遷移的 0.87107，從 Arousal 結果來看，經遷移學習的結果同樣優於未經遷移的結果。

Output	Learning Rate	Loss	Epoch
Valence	1e-5	**0.3788**	24
	1e-6	0.39498	35
	5e-5	0.51918	4
Arousal	1e-5	**0.77339**	12
	1e-6	0.92874	19
	5e-5	1.8867	12

表 1: 在 CVAW+CVAP 資料集的訓練結果

Method	Output	Lr	Loss	Epoch
From Scratch	Valence	1e-5	**0.50338**	12
		1e-6	0.51199	44
		5e-5	0.55236	6
	Arousal	1e-5	**0.87107**	5
		1e-6	0.93317	28
		5e-5	0.9303	10
Transfer Learning	Valence	1e-5	0.47898	4
		1e-6	**0.46624**	15
		5e-5	0.53422	5
	Arousal	1e-5	**0.84259**	1
		1e-6	0.88142	7
		5e-5	0.93479	11

表 2: 經遷移學習與未經遷移學習之結果

4.2 驗證中文歌詞分類之結果

歌詞情緒分類是將模型輸出的 Valence 和 Arousal 基於中性值 5 轉換爲坐標平面上的四個象限類別。經遷移學習 CVAT 與未經遷移學習模型的歌詞情緒分類結果，如表 3，經遷移學習的 CVAT 模型在歌詞情緒分類的準確度爲 0.71，標籤 Q1 和 Q4 的 F1-score 較低，分別爲 0.69 和 0.51，而 Q2 和 Q3 的 F1-score 較高，分別爲 0.83 和 0.72。未經遷移學習的 CVAT 模型在歌詞情緒分類的準確度爲 0.50，同樣是標籤 Q1 和 Q4 的 F1-score 較低，分別爲 0.41 和 0.29，而 Q2 和 Q3 的 F1-score 較高，分別爲 0.64 和 0.55。比較經遷移學習的模型與未經遷移學習的模型，經遷移學習的模型中每一個情緒標籤的分類結果

CVAT Transfer Learning			
Label	Precision	Recall	F1-score
Q1	0.96	0.53	**0.69**
Q2	0.72	0.98	**0.83**
Q3	0.63	0.84	**0.72**
Q4	0.61	0.44	**0.51**
Accuracy			**0.71**
CVAT Training from Scratch			
Label	Precision	Recall	F1-score
Q1	1.00	0.26	0.41
Q2	0.65	0.62	0.64
Q3	0.40	0.86	0.55
Q4	0.38	0.23	0.29
Accuracy			0.50

表 3: 經遷移學習與未經遷移學習的歌詞分類結果之分數

都優於未經遷移學習的模型。由上述可得知到在訓練階段 CVAT 模型學習效果較佳的模型，應用在歌詞的情緒分類能得到較佳的結果，證實經遷移學習的模型在 CVAW+CVAP 資料集中學習到的情緒特徵，有助於提升模型在歌詞文本的情緒辨識能力。

5 討論

從實驗結果可以看到 Arousal 的特徵較難學習其 loss 較高，在多個研究中都有提到中文或者英文的資料集上 Arousal 的維度難以區分，推測激動程度在文字上較難以顯示出來 (Malheiro et al. 2018; Yu et al. 2016;Çano and Morisio 2017b)。結果顯示經過遷移後的模型其結果都優於未經遷移的結果且提高了模型的收斂速度，證明在 CVAW 和 CVAP 兩個資料集所學習到的特徵，有助於模型對 CVAT 中文情緒文本的學習。在驗證模型能否應用於歌詞文本的實驗結果中觀察到，CVAT 訓練結果較佳的遷移模型，應用於歌詞文本分類使其結果也會較佳，優於未遷移的 CVAT 模型。實驗結果表明了經遷移學習學到的情緒特徵是有助歌詞文本的情緒辨識成果。最後，在未學習過歌詞文本的狀況下，歌詞情緒分類結果達到 71% 的準確率。

6 結論

本研究提出以基於 Transformer 的語言預訓練模型對中文情緒資料集進行學習，將中文情緒資料庫的模型直接用於歌詞的 Valence 和 Arousal 進行標註。實驗比較了有遷移學習與未經遷移學習的模型，結果證明在中文情緒字典與中文情緒片語學習到的特徵，有助於中文

情緒文本的學習。同時，將經遷移學習及未遷移的模型用於歌詞的情緒分類，發現經遷移學習的模型結果優於未經遷移的模型，證明在中文情緒資料集學習結果較佳的模型，用於歌詞情緒分類其結果也會較佳。

致謝

特別感謝科技部給予研究經費的支持，本論文爲科技部計畫「人工智慧音樂家-運用深度嵌入方法與生成對抗網路與和諧性爲導向的詞曲生成器之設計」(108-2218-E-025-002-MY3) 之研究成果。

References

Jiddy Abdillah, I. Asror, and Y. Wibowo. 2020. Emotion classification of song lyrics using bidirectional lstm method with glove word representation weighting.

Yudhik Agrawal, Ramaguru Guru Ravi Shanker, and Vinoo Alluri. 2021. Transformer-based approach towards music emotion recognition from lyrics. arXiv:2101.02051.

James Barry. 2017. Sentiment analysis of online reviews using bag-of-words and lstm approaches. In *AICS*.

J. Devlin, Ming-Wei Chang, Kenton Lee, and Kristina Toutanova. 2019. Bert: Pre-training of deep bidirectional transformers for language understanding. In *NAACL-HLT*.

Byeong-Jun Han, Seungmin Rho, Roger B. Dannenberg, and Eenjun Hwang. 2009. Smers: Music emotion recognition using support vector regression. In *Proceedings of the 2017 International Conference on Intelligent Systems*, pages 651–656. ISMIR.

Qi Han, J. Guo, and Hinrich Schütze. 2013. Codex: Combining an svm classifier and character n-gram language models for sentiment analysis on twitter text. In *SemEval@NAACL-HLT*.

Xiao Hu and J. S. Downie. 2010a. When lyrics outperform audio for music mood classification: A feature analysis. In *ISMIR*.

Xiao Hu and J. Stephen Downie. 2010b. When lyrics outperform audio for music mood classification: A feature analysis. In *Proceedings of the 2017 International Conference on Intelligent Systems*, pages 619–624. ISMIR.

Yajie Hu, Xiaoou Chen, and Deshun Yang. 2009. Lyric-based song emotion detection with affective lexicon and fuzzy clustering method. In *ISMIR*.

Jason C. Hung and Jia-Wei Chang. 2021. Multi-level transfer learning for improving the performance of deep neural networks: Theory and practice from the tasks of facial emotion recognition and named entity recognition. In *Applied Soft Computing*.

Adit Jamdar, Jessica Abraham, Karishma Khanna, and Rahul Dubey. 2015. Emotion analysis of songs based on lyrical and audio features. *Artificial Intelligence and Applications (IJAIA)*, arXiv:1506.05012.

Junghyun Kim, Seungjae Lee, Sungmin Kim, and Won young Yoo. 2011. Music mood classification model based on arousal-valence values. *13th International Conference on Advanced Communication Technology (ICACT2011)*, pages 292–295.

C. Laurier, M. Sordo, J. Serrà, and P. Herrera. 2009. Music mood representations from social tags. In *ISMIR*.

R. Malheiro, R. Panda, Paulo Gomes, and R. Paiva. 2018. Emotionally-relevant features for classification and regression of music lyrics. *IEEE Transactions on Affective Computing*, 9:240–254.

Lin Qiu, Jiayu Chen, Jonathan Ramsay, and Jiahui Lu. 2019. Personality predicts words in favorite songs. *Research in Personality*, 78:25–35.

J. Russell. 1980. A circumplex model of affect. *Journal of Personality and Social Psychology*, 39:1161–1178.

Uddalok Sarkar, Sayan Nag, Medha Basu, Archi Banerjee, Shankha Sanyal, Ranjan Sengupta, and Dipak Ghosh. 2015. Neural network architectures to classify emotions in indian classical musics. arXiv:2102.00616.

Ashish Vaswani, Noam M. Shazeer, Niki Parmar, Jakob Uszkoreit, Llion Jones, Aidan N. Gomez, Lukasz Kaiser, and Illia Polosukhin. 2017. Attention is all you need. *ArXiv*, abs/1706.03762.

L. Yu, Lung-Hao Lee, Shuai Hao, Jin Wang, Y. He, Jun Hu, K. Lai, and Xue-Jie Zhang. 2016. Building chinese affective resources in valence-arousal dimensions. In *HLT-NAACL*.

L. Yu, Lung-Hao Lee, Jin Wang, and Kam-Fai Wong. 2017. Ijcnlp-2017 task 2: Dimensional sentiment analysis for chinese phrases. In *IJCNLP*.

Erion Çano and M. Morisio. 2017a. Music mood dataset creation based on last.fm tags.

Erion Çano and Maurizio Morisio. 2017b. Moodylyrics: A sentiment annotated lyrics dataset. In *Proceedings of the 2017 International Conference on Intelligent Systems,*, pages 118–124, Hong Kong. Metaheuristics Swarm Intelligence.

The 33rd Conference on Computational Linguistics and Speech Processing (ROCLING 2021)
Taoyuan, Taiwan, October 15-16, 2021. The Association for Computational Linguistics and Chinese Language Processing

Nested Named Entity Recognition for Chinese Electronic Health Records with QA-based Sequence Labeling

Yu-Lun Chiang[1], Chih-Hao Lin[1], Cheng-Lung Sung[1], and Keh-Yih Su[2]
[1]Data Intelligence R&D Division, CTBC Bank, Co., Ltd, Taipei, Taiwan
[2]Institute of Information Science, Academia Sinica, Taiwan
{ylchiang914, mr.chihhaolin}@gmail.com
alan.sung@ctbcbank.com, kysu@iis.sinica.edu.tw

Abstract

This study presents a novel QA-based sequence labeling (QASL) approach to naturally tackle both flat and nested Named Entity Recognition (NER) tasks on a Chinese Electronic Health Records (CEHRs) dataset. This proposed QASL approach parallelly asks a corresponding natural language question for each specific named entity type. It then identifies those associated NEs of the same specified type with the BIO tagging scheme. The associated nested NEs are then formed by overlapping the results of various types. Compared with those pure sequence-labeling (SL) approaches, since the given question includes significant prior knowledge about the specified entity type and the capability of extracting NEs with different types, the nested NER task is thus improved, obtaining 90.70% of F1-score. Besides, compared to the pure QA-based approach, our proposed approach retains the SL features, which could extract multiple NEs with the same types without knowing the exact number of NEs in the same passage in advance. Eventually, experiments on our CEHR dataset demonstrate that QASL-based models greatly outperform the SL-based models by 6.12% to 7.14% of F1-score.

Keywords: Nested Named Entity Recognition, Chinese Electronic Health Records, QA-based Sequence Labeling

1 Introduction

Electronic health records (EHRs) contain rich medical information and treatment histories of patients (e.g., various event dates, diagnoses, and treatments). It is beneficial to understand the patients' conditions that all clinicians are

Figure 1: A common example of Chinese electronic health records (CEHRs).

involved in their care. In the past, this information was embedded in unstructured raw texts and extracted manually to databases. Therefore, Named Entity Recognition (NER) task, effectively identifying meaningful named entities (NEs) from unstructured raw texts, has emerged as a hot topic among researchers and practitioners these days.

In Chinese EHRs, a phenomenon often exists that NEs are overlapped or nested, especially in event date types. For example, as shown in Figure 1, The entity ("西元 2019 年 10 月 5 日", Oct. 5, 2019) in the passage has several roles such as the admission date and the emergency date. However, most models only focus on handling flat NER in which NEs do not overlap each other; only a few of them deal with nested NER in which overlapped NEs are allowed.

The NER task has been treated as a sequence labeling (SL) problem in previous works (Lafferty et al., 2001; Hammerton, 2003; Ratinov and Roth, 2009; Collobert et al., 2011; Huang et al., 2015; Ma and Hovy, 2016; Peters et al., 2018; Devlin et al., 2019). With this approach, flat (non-overlapping) NEs within a given passage could be simultaneously identified; however, they failed to detect nested NEs.

To address the issues, various approaches

have been proposed to solve both flat and nested NER with public datasets such as ACE2004 (Doddington et al., 2004), ACE2005 (Christopher Walker et al., 2006), GENIA (Kim et al., 2003), and NNE (Ringland et al., 2019). First, stack-based approaches utilize flat NER layers to sequentially extract entities from inner to outer or outer to inner (Alex et al., 2007; Ju et al., 2018; Wang et al., 2020a). Secondly, graph-based approaches apply constituency parse trees (Finkel and Manning, 2009), hypergraphs (Lu and Roth, 2015; Wang and Lu, 2018; Katiyar and Cardie, 2018), or bipartite graphs (Luo and Zhao, 2020) to identify nested NEs. Thirdly, region-based approaches decompose NER to two stages: detect all possible spans and classify them into pre-defined entity types (Xu et al., 2017; Fisher and Vlachos, 2019; Xia et al., 2019; Zheng et al., 2019; Wang et al., 2020b). Different from public datasets, our Chinese EHR dataset only contains flat NEs and nested NEs with different entity types, meaning that nested NEs with the same types are not in our consideration. Therefore, many above attempts are not the most suitable and intuitive methods for our CEHR dataset due to their complicated models or frameworks.

This study proposed a simple and effective framework of Question Answering Sequence Labeling (QASL). Inspired by Li et al., 2020 (Li et al., 2020), we also re-formalize the NER task to a Question Answering (QA) problem to naturally tackle both flat and nested NER. However, different from this work (Li et al., 2020), we modified the strategy of span selection from predicting start and end positions of entity spans to directly assigning BIO labels to tokens in the input passage. To be more specific, the QASL approach first adopts the corresponding string of the specified NE-type as the query. It then identifies NEs with the BIO tagging scheme by parallelly querying the corresponding NE-type-string (e.g. "入院日期," Admission Date) for each specific NE type. As shown in Figure 2, the QASL first assigns BIO labels (i.e., Begin (B), Inside (I), or Other (O)) (Ramshaw and Marcus, 1999) to the passage based on a given query/type ("入院日期," Admission Date). According to the assigned BIO labels, the NE-date (" 西元 2019 年 10 月 5 日", Oct. 5, 2019) is thus identified. Afterward, the QASL conducts the same procedure based on another query/type ("急診日期," Emergency Date), and thus identify the same entity with a different type. Last, by conducting the above procedure, all NEs in the passage could be extracted whether they are overlapped or not.

The modification of the span selection strategy has two advantages: (1) BIO labels implicitly tell models the start and end positions of entities and contain rich information among tokens (Wang et al., 2020b) for models. (2) BIO tagging scheme is simple and effective methods to select multiple spans for QA (Segal et al., 2020). It can do well no matter models know how many NEs exist in advance according to questions.

In summary, the contributions of this paper are:

- We propose a novel QA-based sequence labeling (QASL) approach to naturally deal with both flat and nested NER.
- We present the first work to handle the Chinese electronic health records (CEHRs) dataset for both flat and nested NER (To the best of our knowledge).
- We conduct the experiments on a CEHR dataset to show that the proposed QASL is effective.

2 QA-based Sequence Labeling

2.1 Task Formulation

Given a passage S = $\{s_1, s_2, ..., s_n\}$, where n is the length of the passage, find all the named entities in S with various entity types (according to a pre-specified type-set) $E = \{e_1, e_2, ..., e_m\}$, where m is the number of entity types. In the framework of QA-based Sequence Labeling (QASL), for each entity type $e \in E$, it is firstly mapped into a predefined query $q_e = \{q_1, q_2, ..., q_k\}$, where k is the length of query. Then, for each $q_e \in Q$, we find the corresponding named entities (with the same specified type) in S by simply labeling s_i as $l_i \in L = \{B, I, O\}$ according to the BIO scheme (Ramshaw and Marcus, 1999). The associated nested named entities are then formed by overlapping the NER result of each type.

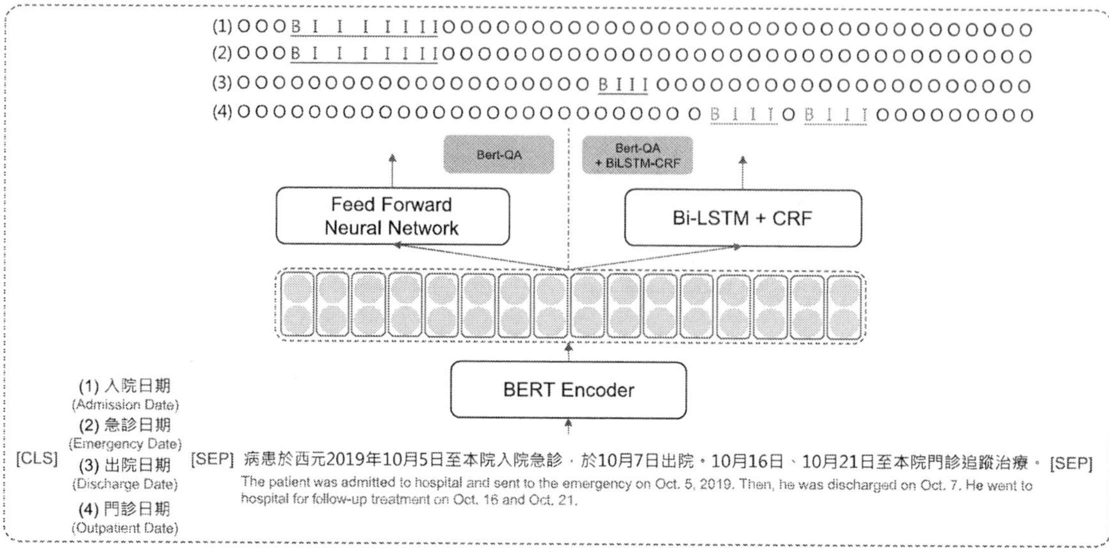

Figure 2: An overview of proposed Question Answering Sequence Labeling (QASL) framework.

2.2 Proposed QASL Model

2.2.1 Query Generation

Since the question could encode prior knowledge about entity types and significantly influence the final results, it is important to generate appropriate questions. To generate the benchmark questions, Li et al. (Li et al., 2020) adopted the Annotation Guideline Notes (e.g., Find locations in the text, including non-geographical locations, mountain ranges, and bodies of water.) to construct the required training data. They achieved the highest F1-score on English OntoNotes 5.0. However, it would not only require an expensive cost to generate the benchmark questions following the guidelines manually, but the questions generated by the guidelines also remain unknown to utilize for another dataset. To avoid those drawbacks mentioned above, we let the questions be keywords (i.e., Chinese NE-Types) in this study, as shown in Table 1. The questions can be easily transformed into the name of entity types, and they can be utilized by different datasets. Therefore, it does not require manual generation, which is expensive, and it is easily generalized by different datasets.

2.2.2 Input Layer

In this paper, we use BERT with whole word masking (BERT-wwm) as the backbone model (Cui et al., 2019). Follow the typical setup (Li et al., 2020), the question q_e and the passage S are concatenated with the special tokens $[CLS]$ and $[SEP]$, as shown in Figure 2. Then, word embeddings, segmentation embeddings, and positional embeddings for each token are summed together to generate final input representations.

2.2.3 BERT Encoder

The adopted BERT encoder consists of 12 Transformer blocks and 12 self-attention heads by taking the input representation from the input layer and then outputting a context representation. Different from the original BERT (Devlin et al., 2019), BERT-wwm focuses on Chinese language by pre-training with whole word masking (Cui et al., 2019). We only use the passage representations $C \in \mathbb{R}^{n \times d_1}$ from the last hidden layer of BERT-wwm, where d_1 is the dimension with a default value 768 and n is the length of the passage.

2.2.4 Output Layer

This study tests two different structures of output layers: a softmax classifier and a BiLSTM-CRF layer. First, the softmax classifier is that the model predicts the conditional probability distributions P overall categorical labels $L = \{B, I, O\}$, given the passage representations C from BERT encoder:

$$P(L|C;\theta) = softmax(C \cdot V) \in \mathbb{R}^{n \times 3} \quad (1)$$

Abb.	Entity Type	Abb.	Entity Type	Abb.	Entity Type
ADD	AdmissionDate	OPD	OutpatientDate	RTD	RadiotherapyDate
DCD	DischargeDate	OPDS	OutpatientDateStart	RTDS	RadiotherapyDateStart
ICD	InIntensiveCareDate	OPDE	OutpatientDateEnd	RTDE	RadiotherapyDateEnd
OCD	OutIntensiveCareDate	OPC	OutpatientCount	RTC	RadiotherapyCount
IBD	InBurnWaeDate	EMD	EmergencyDate	CTD	ChemotherapyDate
OBD	OutBurnWaeDate	EMDS	EmergencyDateStart	CTDS	ChemotherapyDateStart
IND	InNegativePressureDate	EMDE	EmergencyDateEnd	CTDE	ChemotherapyDateEnd
OND	OutNegativePressureDate	EMC	EmergencyCount	CTC	ChemotherapyCount
SGN	SurgeryName	SGD	SurgeryDate	SGDE	SurgeryDateEnd
DTN	Drug/TreatmentName	SGDS	SurgeryDateStart	SGC	SurgeryCount
DPN	DepartmentName				

Table 1: The names and abbreviation of entity types.

where θ is the set of all trainable parameters in the model. $V \in \mathbb{R}^{d_1 \times 3}$ is also the trainable parameter. On the other hand, the BiLSTM-CRF first outputs the concatenated hidden representations $H \in \mathbb{R}^{n \times d_2}$ given the passage representations C from BERT encoder, where d_2 is also the dimension with a value of 768. For each $h_i \in H$ and $c_i \in C$:

$$h_i = [\overrightarrow{h_i}; \overleftarrow{h_i}] \quad (2)$$

$$\overrightarrow{h_i} = LSTM(c_i, \overrightarrow{h}i-1; \overrightarrow{\theta}) \quad (3)$$

$$\overleftarrow{h_i} = LSTM(c_i, \overleftarrow{h}i-1; \overleftarrow{\theta}) \quad (4)$$

where $\overrightarrow{\theta}$, $\overleftarrow{\theta}$ are the trainable parameters in BiLSTM. Besides, the CRF layer (Lafferty et al., 2001) defines the probability of the predicted BIO label sequence Y given the input label sequence X transformed from a given passage S:

$$P(Y|X;\theta) = \frac{e^{score(X,Y)}}{\sum_{Y'} e^{score(X,Y')}} \quad (5)$$

The score (Lample et al., 2016) is defined as the sum of transitions and emissions from the BiLSTM:

$$score(X,Y) = \sum_{i=0}^{n-1} Tr_{y_i,y_{i+1}} + \sum_{i=1}^{n} Em_{y_i} \quad (6)$$

where Tr is a transition matrix in which $Tr_{y_i,yi+1}$ is the transition parameter from the label y_i to the y_{i+1}. Em is an emission matrix where Em_{y_i} represents the scores of the label y_i at the i-th position.

$$Em = H \cdot U \in \mathbb{R}^{n \times 3} \quad (7)$$

where $U \in \mathbb{R}^{d_2 \times 3}$ is the trainable parameters.

At test time in the structure of the softmax classifier, we take the labels with the largest probability as the predicted results.

$$Y^* = argmax(P(L|C;\theta)) \in \mathbb{R}^{n \times 1} \quad (8)$$

At test time in the structure of BiLSTM-CRF, we take the label sequence with the largest score as the predicted results by applying the Viterbi algorithm (Viterbi, 1967).

$$Y^* = argmax(score(X,Y')) \in \mathbb{R}^{n \times 1} \quad (9)$$

3 Experiments

3.1 Dataset

In this paper, all the experiments are conducted on our Chinese electronic health records (CEHR) dataset.[1] The CEHR dataset is annotated with SQuAD-like style by several well-trained annotators. It is a set of (Passage, Queries, Answers). There are 31 entity types in the CEHR dataset, as shown in Table 1. We extracted that dataset with only flat NEs from the original CEHR dataset as a flat NER dataset, and we took the original CEHR as a nested NER dataset. In the flat NER dataset, the number of passages is 4,328, and the average length of these passages is 70.43. The number of flat NE in these passages is 21,616. On the other hand, in the nested NER dataset, the number of passages is 7,907, and the average length of these passages is 76.08. The number of flat and nested NEs in these passages is 43,577 and 6,978, respectively. Eventually, the flat NER dataset and nested NER dataset are split for training, development, and test set with the ratio 8:1:1.

[1] The personal privacy information of all patients in CEHR has been de-identified during the labeling stage.

Model	P	R	F1
Bert	95.45	96.33	95.89
-BiLSTM-CRF	95.37	96.46	95.91
Bert-QA	94.24	95.23	94.73
-BiLSTM-CRF	95.06	95.98	95.52

Table 2: Model Performance on flat NER.

Model	P	R	F1
Bert	89.39	78.83	83.78
-BiLSTM-CRF	89.02	78.74	83.56
Bert-QA	87.67	**92.26**	89.90
-BiLSTM-CRF	**91.01**	90.40	**90.70**

Table 3: Model Performance on nested NER.

3.2 Baselines and Parameter Settings

In this study, we propose and test two different kinds of QASL-based models: BERT-QA and BERT-QA-BiLSTM-CRF. For comparison, we consider BERT and BERT-BiLSTM-CRF as two baselines, which treat NER as a traditional sequence labeling problem. For the parameter settings of all models, the max sequence length is 512. The batch size is 8. The learning rate is 5×10^{-5}. The number of layers, neurons, and dropout ratio in BiLSTM is 1, 384, and 0.5, respectively. The epoch is 40, and the model with the best F1-score in the development set will be the adopted system.

4 Results and Discussion

Table 2 and Table 3 show the experimental results on flat NER and nested NER, respectively. As shown in Table 2, for flat NER, QASL-based models are slightly inferior to the baseline models by -0.39% (in terms of F1-score) for BERT-QA (vs. BERT) and by -1.16% for BERT-QA-BiLSTM-CRF (vs. BERT-BiLSTM-CRF). The slight decrease in performance of QASL-based models results from two main reasons: (1) QASL-based models are primarily designed to solve nested NER. Thus, QASL-based models are much more complicated than SL-based models, so that they are overqualified for flat NER that is far simpler than nested NER. (2) searching spaces of QASL-based models are much larger than that of SL-based models. QASL-based models are designed to search for various possible NEs without knowing how many they are in given passages in advance. In contrast, SL-based models directly assume that each possible entity span only has one entity type. The above two reasons cause the slight decrease of F1-score of QASL-based models compared to SL-based models.

As shown in Table 3, for nested NER, we observed that QASL-based models significantly outperformed baseline models by +6.12% and +7.14% for BERT-QA (vs. BERT) BERTQA-BiLSTM-CRF (vs. BERT-BiLSTM-CRF), respectively. The substantial improvement of F1-scores is mainly from the boosted recall scores, attributed to the framework of QASL, which successfully detects nested NEs in the given queries and passages. Additionally, BERT-QA-BiLSTM-CRF achieves a 90.70% F1-score, which is +0.80% over that of BERT-QA. This is primarily because the BiLSTM-CRF structure makes QASL-based models assign more reasonable labels to tokens, reducing impossible outputs, thus leading to a higher F1-score.

5 Related Work

5.1 Named Entity Recognition

Most traditional feature-based approaches treated NER as a sequence labeling problem, thereby adopting Conditional Random Field (CRF) to resolve the NER task (Lafferty et al., 2001; Ratinov and Roth, 2009). Recently, deep learning techniques have achieved good results on NER tasks, such as LSTM (Hammerton, 2003), CNN-CRF (Collobert et al., 2011), BiLSTM-CRF (Huang et al., 2015), and BiLSTM-CNN-CRF (Ma and Hovy, 2016). Besides, transfer learning has been applied to language models to improve model performance, such as ELMo (Peters et al., 2018), and BERT (Devlin et al., 2019). However, nested named entities cannot be recognized by the above approaches.

5.2 Nested Named Entity Recognition

Stack-based approaches have been used to extract entities from inner to outer or outer to inner, can handle the nested NER task. Alex et al. (Alex et al., 2007) proposed two multi-layers CRF models to recognize nested named entities; however, this approach cannot handle nested entities of the same entity type. Ju et al. first (Ju et al., 2018) introduced a layered sequence labeling model to recognize innermost entities and then feed them into the next layer to extract outer entities. This method can deal with nested entities of the same type but suffers from error propagation among layers. Wang et al. (Wang et al., 2020a) proposed Pyramid, a novel layered model consisting of a stack of interconnected layers, to recognize entities without layer disorientation and error propagation.

Graph-based approaches have also been proposed to solve the nested NER task. Finkel and Manning (Finkel and Manning, 2009) used a CRF-based model to detect nested named entities with the assistance of constituency parse trees. Lu and Roth (Lu and Roth, 2015) introduced a hypergraph allowing edges to connect to multiple nodes to recognize overlapping entities. Wang and Lu (Wang and Lu, 2018) improved the spurious structures of the hypergraph by proposing neural segmental hypergraphs. Katiyar and Cardie (Katiyar and Cardie, 2018) used a LSTM model to learn a hypergraph representation for nested named entities. However, the hypergraph structure would become too complicated to be optimized if there are too many entities in the input sentences. Luo et al. (Luo and Zhao, 2020) proposed a novel bipartite flat graph network to recognize outermost entities and then use a graph module to extract inner ones.

Region-based approaches have utilized a pipeline framework with an end-to-end training paradigm to resolve the nested NER task. Specifically, these approaches first extract possible spans from the input sentence and then classify their entity types. Xu et al. (Xu et al., 2017) examined all possible spans (up to a certain length) of the input sentence and then fed their representation into a feed-forward neural network to classify entity types. Fisher and Vlachos 2019 (Fisher and Vlachos, 2019) first merged tokens into entities through real-valued predictions and then labeled them the corresponding entity types. Xia et al., 2019 (Xia et al., 2019) detected all possible spans through a detector and classified entities into pre-defined categories. Zheng et al., 2019 (Zheng et al., 2019) applied a single-layer sequence labeling model to identify the boundaries of potential entities using context information and then classify these boundary-aware regions into their entity type or non-entity. Wang et al., 2020 (Wang et al., 2020b) developed a head-tail detector and a token interaction tagger to identify nested named entities with appropriate model complexity.

Some researchers have attempted to transform NLP tasks into QA tasks, such as relation extraction (Levy et al., 2017; Li et al., 2019), summarization (McCann et al., 2018), named entity recognition (Li et al., 2020), and sentiment analysis (Yin et al., 2020). Li et al., 2020 (Li et al., 2020) treated NER as a QA problem. Each entity (y) and its entity type (x) can be parameterized as a question $(q(x))$ whose answer is (y). According to questions, models can parallelly identify nested named entities by using different questions. In addition, they can naturally solve flat NER as well.

6 Conclusion

This paper proposes a novel QA-based sequence labeling (QASL) approach to solve both flat and nested NER. The proposed framework comes with three key advantages: (1) It can recognize both flat and nested entities with a single model; (2) It combines QA and SL framework to solve NER and the problem of multiple spans selection; (3) The queries, encoding significant prior knowledge about entity types, are constructed without manual cost and are independent. The conducted experiments on Chinese electronic health records (CEHRs) have clearly shown the effectiveness of our proposed framework.

Acknowledgments

The research was supported by Data Intelligence R&D Division in CTBC Bank. We also thank Wen-Hsin Tseng for the assistance with data annotation.

References

Beatrice Alex, Barry Haddow, and Claire Grover. 2007. Recognising nested named entities in biomedical text. In *Biological, translational, and clinical language processing*, pages 65–72, Prague, Czech Republic. Association for Computational Linguistics.

Julie Medero Christopher Walker, Stephanie Strassel, and Kazuaki Maeda. 2006. Ace 2005 multilingual training corpus. Philadelphia 57. Linguistic Data Consortium.

Ronan Collobert, Jason Weston, Léon Bottou, Michael Karlen, Koray Kavukcuoglu, and Pavel Kuksa. 2011. Natural language processing (almost) from scratch. *Journal of machine learning research*, 12(ARTICLE):2493–2537.

Yiming Cui, Wanxiang Che, Ting Liu, Bing Qin, Ziqing Yang, Shijin Wang, and Guoping Hu. 2019. Pre-training with whole word masking for chinese bert. *arXiv preprint arXiv:1906.08101*.

Jacob Devlin, Ming-Wei Chang, Kenton Lee, and Kristina Toutanova. 2019. BERT: Pre-training of deep bidirectional transformers for language understanding. In *Proceedings of the 2019 Conference of the North American Chapter of the Association for Computational Linguistics: Human Language Technologies, Volume 1 (Long and Short Papers)*, pages 4171–4186, Minneapolis, Minnesota. Association for Computational Linguistics.

George Doddington, Alexis Mitchell, Mark Przybocki, Lance Ramshaw, Stephanie Strassel, and Ralph Weischedel. 2004. The automatic content extraction (ACE) program – tasks, data, and evaluation. In *Proceedings of the Fourth International Conference on Language Resources and Evaluation (LREC'04)*, Lisbon, Portugal. European Language Resources Association (ELRA).

Jenny Rose Finkel and Christopher D. Manning. 2009. Nested named entity recognition. In *Proceedings of the 2009 Conference on Empirical Methods in Natural Language Processing*, pages 141–150, Singapore. Association for Computational Linguistics.

Joseph Fisher and Andreas Vlachos. 2019. Merge and label: A novel neural network architecture for nested NER. In *Proceedings of the 57th Annual Meeting of the Association for Computational Linguistics*, pages 5840–5850, Florence, Italy. Association for Computational Linguistics.

James Hammerton. 2003. Named entity recognition with long short-term memory. In *Proceedings of the Seventh Conference on Natural Language Learning at HLT-NAACL 2003*, pages 172–175.

Zhiheng Huang, Wei Xu, and Kai Yu. 2015. Bidirectional lstm-crf models for sequence tagging. *arXiv preprint arXiv:1508.01991*.

Meizhi Ju, Makoto Miwa, and Sophia Ananiadou. 2018. A neural layered model for nested named entity recognition. In *Proceedings of the 2018 Conference of the North American Chapter of the Association for Computational Linguistics: Human Language Technologies, Volume 1 (Long Papers)*, pages 1446–1459, New Orleans, Louisiana. Association for Computational Linguistics.

Arzoo Katiyar and Claire Cardie. 2018. Nested named entity recognition revisited. In *Proceedings of the 2018 Conference of the North American Chapter of the Association for Computational Linguistics: Human Language Technologies, Volume 1 (Long Papers)*, pages 861–871, New Orleans, Louisiana. Association for Computational Linguistics.

J-D Kim, Tomoko Ohta, Yuka Tateisi, and Jun' ichi Tsujii. 2003. Genia corpus—a semantically annotated corpus for bio-textmining. *Bioinformatics*, 19(suppl_1):i180–i182.

John Lafferty, Andrew McCallum, and Fernando CN Pereira. 2001. Conditional random fields: Probabilistic models for segmenting and labeling sequence data.

Guillaume Lample, Miguel Ballesteros, Sandeep Subramanian, Kazuya Kawakami, and Chris Dyer. 2016. Neural architectures for named entity recognition. In *Proceedings of the 2016 Conference of the North American Chapter of the Association for Computational Linguistics: Human Language Technologies*, pages 260–270, San Diego, California. Association for Computational Linguistics.

Omer Levy, Minjoon Seo, Eunsol Choi, and Luke Zettlemoyer. 2017. Zero-shot relation extraction via reading comprehension. In *Proceedings of the 21st Conference on Computational Natural Language Learning (CoNLL 2017)*, pages 333–342, Vancouver, Canada. Association for Computational Linguistics.

Xiaoya Li, Jingrong Feng, Yuxian Meng, Qinghong Han, Fei Wu, and Jiwei Li. 2020. A unified MRC framework for named entity recognition. In *Proceedings of the 58th Annual Meeting of the Association for Computational Linguistics*, pages 5849–5859, Online. Association for Computational Linguistics.

Xiaoya Li, Fan Yin, Zijun Sun, Xiayu Li, Arianna Yuan, Duo Chai, Mingxin Zhou, and Jiwei Li. 2019. Entity-relation extraction as multi-turn question answering. In *Proceedings of the 57th Annual Meeting of the Association for Computational Linguistics*, pages 1340–1350, Florence, Italy. Association for Computational Linguistics.

Wei Lu and Dan Roth. 2015. Joint mention extraction and classification with mention hypergraphs. In *Proceedings of the 2015 Conference on Empirical Methods in Natural Language Processing*, pages 857–867, Lisbon, Portugal. Association for Computational Linguistics.

Ying Luo and Hai Zhao. 2020. Bipartite flat-graph network for nested named entity recognition. In *Proceedings of the 58th Annual Meeting of the Association for Computational Linguistics*, pages 6408–6418, Online. Association for Computational Linguistics.

Xuezhe Ma and Eduard Hovy. 2016. End-to-end sequence labeling via bi-directional LSTM-CNNs-CRF. In *Proceedings of the 54th Annual Meeting of the Association for Computational Linguistics (Volume 1: Long Papers)*, pages 1064–1074, Berlin, Germany. Association for Computational Linguistics.

Bryan McCann, Nitish Shirish Keskar, Caiming Xiong, and Richard Socher. 2018. The natural language decathlon: Multitask learning as question answering. *arXiv preprint arXiv:1806.08730*.

Matthew E. Peters, Mark Neumann, Mohit Iyyer, Matt Gardner, Christopher Clark, Kenton Lee, and Luke Zettlemoyer. 2018. Deep contextualized word representations. In *Proceedings of the 2018 Conference of the North American Chapter of the Association for Computational Linguistics: Human Language Technologies, Volume 1 (Long Papers)*, pages 2227–2237, New Orleans, Louisiana. Association for Computational Linguistics.

Lance A Ramshaw and Mitchell P Marcus. 1999. Text chunking using transformation-based learning. In *Natural language processing using very large corpora*, pages 157–176. Springer.

Lev Ratinov and Dan Roth. 2009. Design challenges and misconceptions in named entity recognition. In *Proceedings of the Thirteenth Conference on Computational Natural Language Learning (CoNLL-2009)*, pages 147–155, Boulder, Colorado. Association for Computational Linguistics.

Nicky Ringland, Xiang Dai, Ben Hachey, Sarvnaz Karimi, Cecile Paris, and James R. Curran. 2019. NNE: A dataset for nested named entity recognition in English newswire. In *Proceedings of the 57th Annual Meeting of the Association for Computational Linguistics*, pages 5176–5181, Florence, Italy. Association for Computational Linguistics.

Elad Segal, Avia Efrat, Mor Shoham, Amir Globerson, and Jonathan Berant. 2020. A simple and effective model for answering multi-span questions. In *Proceedings of the 2020 Conference on Empirical Methods in Natural Language Processing (EMNLP)*, pages 3074–3080, Online. Association for Computational Linguistics.

Andrew Viterbi. 1967. Error bounds for convolutional codes and an asymptotically optimum decoding algorithm. *IEEE transactions on Information Theory*, 13(2):260–269.

Bailin Wang and Wei Lu. 2018. Neural segmental hypergraphs for overlapping mention recognition. In *Proceedings of the 2018 Conference on Empirical Methods in Natural Language Processing*, pages 204–214, Brussels, Belgium. Association for Computational Linguistics.

Jue Wang, Lidan Shou, Ke Chen, and Gang Chen. 2020a. Pyramid: A layered model for nested named entity recognition. In *Proceedings of the 58th Annual Meeting of the Association for Computational Linguistics*, pages 5918–5928, Online. Association for Computational Linguistics.

Yu Wang, Yun Li, Hanghang Tong, and Ziye Zhu. 2020b. HIT: Nested named entity recognition via head-tail pair and token interaction. In *Proceedings of the 2020 Conference on Empirical Methods in Natural Language Processing (EMNLP)*, pages 6027–6036, Online. Association for Computational Linguistics.

Congying Xia, Chenwei Zhang, Tao Yang, Yaliang Li, Nan Du, Xian Wu, Wei Fan, Fenglong Ma, and Philip Yu. 2019. Multi-grained named entity recognition. In *Proceedings of the 57th Annual Meeting of the Association for Computational Linguistics*, pages 1430–1440, Florence, Italy. Association for Computational Linguistics.

Mingbin Xu, Hui Jiang, and Sedtawut Watcharawittayakul. 2017. A local detection approach for named entity recognition and mention detection. In *Proceedings of the 55th Annual Meeting of the Association for Computational Linguistics (Volume 1: Long Papers)*, pages 1237–1247, Vancouver, Canada. Association for Computational Linguistics.

Da Yin, Tao Meng, and Kai-Wei Chang. 2020. SentiBERT: A transferable transformer-based architecture for compositional sentiment semantics. In *Proceedings of the 58th Annual Meeting of the Association for Computational Linguistics*, pages 3695–3706, Online. Association for Computational Linguistics.

Changmeng Zheng, Yi Cai, Jingyun Xu, Ho-fung Leung, and Guandong Xu. 2019. A boundary-aware neural model for nested named entity recognition. In *Proceedings of the 2019 Conference on Empirical Methods in Natural Language Processing and the 9th International Joint Conference on Natural Language Processing (EMNLP-IJCNLP)*, pages 357–366, Hong Kong, China. Association for Computational Linguistics.

The 33rd Conference on Computational Linguistics and Speech Processing (ROCLING 2021)
Taoyuan, Taiwan, October 15-16, 2021. The Association for Computational Linguistics and Chinese Language Processing

AI Clerk Platform：資訊擷取 DIY 平台
AI Clerk Platform： Information Extraction DIY Platform

Ru-Yng Chang **Wen-Lun Chen** **Cheng-Ju Kao**
AI Clerk International Co., LTD.
13F., No. 502, Sec. 2, Ren'ai Rd., Linkou Dist., New Taipei City 244020 , Taiwan (R.O.C.)
changruyng889@gmail.com; lagame53@yahoo.com.tw; sports.exp@gmail.com

摘要

自然語言處理的一門核心技術資訊擷取（Information Extraction），將非結構化（Unstructured）或是半結構化（Semi-structured）的內容，擷取部分有意義的片語/子句對應到某一個特殊的主題。可說是許多語言技術和應用的核心技術，本論文提出 AI Clerk Platform，旨在加速和提升研發資訊擷取工具的整個流程和便利性，提供友善直覺視覺化的人工標記介面，設定符合欲擷取的語意類別，執行、分配與控管人工標記任務，讓使用者在不用寫程式的情況下，就可完成客製化資訊擷取模組，並提供三種方式瀏覽和使用自建模組與其 API，進而協助其它自然語言處理技術研發與應用服務的衍生。

Abstract

Information extraction is a core technology of natural language processing, which extracts some meaningful phrases/clauses from unstructured or semi-structured content to a particular topic. It can be said to be the core technology of many language technologies and applications. This paper introduces AI Clerk Platform, which aims to accelerate and improve the entire process and convenience of the development of information extraction tools. AI Clerk Platform provides a friendly and intuitive visualized manual labeling interface, sets suitable semantic label in need, and implements, distributes and controls manual labeling tasks, so that users can complete customized information extraction models without programming and view the automatically predict results of models by three method. AI Clerk Platform further assists in the development of other natural language processing technologies and the derivation of application services.

關鍵字：資訊擷取、資訊擷取平台、資訊擷取 API、自然語言處理、DIY、AI Clerk Platform

Keywords: Information Extraction, Information Extraction Platform, Information Extraction API, Natural Language Processing , DIY, AI Clerk Platform

1 背景動機

檔案中的內容常常是用連續性的字元所組成和表達，對電腦而言這樣的呈現和儲存是難以統計、分析、理解與應用的。自然語言處理的一門核心技術資訊擷取（Information Extraction），是將非結構化（Unstructured）或是半結構化（Semi-structured）的內容，擷取部分有意義的片語/子句對應到某一個特殊的主題（Appelt, 1999）。舉例，辨識實體--人、事、時、地、物，如圖 1。透過資訊擷取讓那些非結構化（Unstructured）或是半結構化（Semi-structured）的內容，自動轉化據語意的結構化資訊，所以可以知道圖 1 中“蔡桃貴”和“蔡阿嘎”是人名，“2018 年”是時間，台北市是地，“恐龍玩具”是物，在這串非結構化的內容中，出現兩次人名。也就是透過資訊擷取那些難以統計、分析、應用與理解的非結構（Unstructured）或是半結構化（Semi-structured）資料變成可以統計、分析的。

圖 1. 資訊擷取之釋例

資訊擷取也可說是很多自然語言處理應用服務或是語言技術研發的核心技術（Wilks,, 1997）。資訊擷取最直覺的應用就是幫助達到語意搜尋，可分別指定找出文件中意指水果的“蘋果”或是品牌名稱的“蘋果”。有學者將資訊擷取用於作為文本探勘的基礎找出文本之間的脈絡（Mooney & Bunescu, 2005)、也有學者用來輔助文本生成（Koncel-Kedziorski et al., 2019)（Venkatachalam, 2020）、甚至是輔助作文本摘要（Venkatachalam, 2020）、對話系統（Yoshino et al., 2011）、聊天機器人（Ali, 2020; Jiao, 2020）。為了達到不同應用服務，根據不同應用情境領域、應用技術研發和資料特性，其中資訊擷取和識別的語意類別各有不同，例如：譬如在 Yoshino 等人（2011）的對話系統，是資訊擷取技術獲得的術語論證結構（predicate argument structures）資訊來輔助對話系統技術研發，而 Ali（2020）研發的聊天機器人所應用的資訊擷取資訊是將聊天內容中所有的實體節取出，以“I want to know the taxi rate in Islamabad（我想要知道伊斯蘭堡計程車費率）”這句話為例，“Islamabad”和“taxi”就會被擷取出認為是一個實體值。同樣是聊天機器人技術研發，Jiao（2020）研發的與股票議題相關的聊天機器人所應用的資訊擷取資訊是股票、名稱、數量、上限符號、價格、名稱這類的語意。如果能加速資訊擷取的研發過程，而且是能夠符合不同應用情境和後續技術研發，資訊擷取工具能擷取並辨識不同語意，將大幅加速和衍生其它各式語言技術研發。

就如許多自然語言技術研發過程一樣，資訊擷取的技術研發過程，會需要先有人工標記的語料，接著是演算法建立模組，產生執行檔或 API 等型態供使用。傳統若需要針對不同領域、應用情境需要資訊擷取的核心技術，需要在技術研發環境裡開始自建人工標記語料，因為需要一定數量的標記語料所建立的模組，才比較容易達到一定效能，自建人工標記語料庫的過程變成是一非常耗時、又耗人力的過程，尤其資訊擷取是要在一堆文字內容中，找出要標記的字串，並且記錄下需要被標記的字串、被標記的字串位置和所對應的語意，因此，很耗眼力，往往人工標記的任務會是由多人一起分攤與執行。然而，「需標記的字串是哪些？需標記的邊際怎麼界定？」這是最常遇到的問題，往往也跟技術研發未來的應用有關，如果遇到比較需要標記比較專業的內容，譬如：前述的術語論證結構，更非一般人可應付。無論人工標記是哪種內容或挑戰難度，標記時的標準和品質都將影響後續自動化模組效能的表現。而且，多人一起分擔還衍生出標記的品質和進度控管的問題。

因此，若有一個友善直覺視覺化的人工標記介面，能讓標記人員清楚且便利的達成人工標記任務，也可將標記任務分配給不同人，讓眾人分攤並監管整個人工標記品質和進度，標記哪些語意也是根據不同需求而自行設定，讓使用者在整個資訊擷取工具的研發過程不用寫程式，透過簡單的設定和操作步驟便能完成一個資訊檢索的 API 供呼叫引用，也就是加速整個資訊擷取工具的研發流程，相信定可對許多自然語言處理技術的各式應用服務研發有很大的幫助，而其中最大的挑戰便在於怎樣讓各領域的人都可以透過這介面完成符合客製化需求的資訊擷取工具，必須將整個流程標準化而且操作介面易理解。本論文介紹的 AI Clerk Platform 就是基於這些緣由與目標。

2 相關工具

表 1.相關工具整理

競品名稱	用途與特色	效益
Apache cTAKES, MedLee (Friedman et al. 1994,Friedman et al., 1995),等	• toolkit 單機執行工具 • 特定（醫療）領域的資訊擷取工具 • 自動擷取固定的語意字串	• 降低研發人員技術研發過程中的寫程式的工作量，直接呼叫產生更多應用

US National Center SIFR annotator (Tchechmedjiev et al., 2018)	• API, Web Demo 介面 • 特定（醫療）領域的資訊擷取工具 • 自動擷取固定的語意字串	• 降低研發人員技術研發過程中的寫程式的工作量，直接遠端呼叫 API 產生更多應用
Google AuotML NLP	• 雲端 Platform • 匯入含可種自訂各種語意的人工標記語料 • 各領域的資訊擷取模組建置，產生自製客製化 API 供遠端呼叫	• 降低研發人員技術研發過程中的寫程式的工作量，直接呼叫遠端 API 產生更多應用
IBM Watson Knowledge Studio	• 雲端 Platform • 各領域標記語料建置 • 提供友善介面，建置人工標記資料 • 在平台上建立模組，減少建立模組時撰寫程式以進行語料格式轉換和特徵擷取，模組建完，讓其餘語料以自動化完成標記	• 降低研發人員技術研發過程中的資料建置時間
	• API • 特定一般領域的資訊擷取工具 • 自動擷取固定的語意字串（人事時地物等）	• 降低研發人員技術研發過程中的寫程式的工作量，直接呼叫 API 產生更多應用
AI Clerk Platform	• Platform、API • 免寫程式 • 提供友善介面，建置各領域標記資料 • 人工標記任務分配 • 可自訂欲自動擷取的語意 • 在平台上建立各領域模組，完成自動標記，減少建立模組時撰寫程式，產生 API 供遠端呼叫或在此平台直接引用。	• 讓無資訊背景的人都可使用。 • 降低技術研發過程中的資料建置時間 • 降低研發人員技術研發過程中的寫程式的工作量，直接遠端或在平台呼叫自製客製化 API 產生更多應用

相關工具的功能特色與效益，整理如表 1，可以發現相關工具多數著重在協助標記語料建置、協助模組建置或是提供既有資訊擷取工具的單一面向，提供既有資訊擷取工具提供固定擷取的語意，沒法滿足研發各種自然語言處理過程中針對不同應用情境可能會需要擷取不同語意的各種不同客製化資訊擷取，譬如：即便都是研發智能客服系統，但研發零售業智能客服系統和政府單位智能客服系統其中所需要的資訊擷取技術所要擷取的語意就不會相同。擷取人名、組織名等的資訊擷取結果，對零售業的智能客服的技術研發效益不大。

Google AuotML NLP 雖然可以協助各領域的資訊擷取模組建置，產生自製客製化 API 供遠端呼叫，但它是以對自然語言處理或是機器學習知識相當熟悉的技術人員所使用，必須書打很多指令，人工標記的過程則非 Google

AuotML NLP 想要便民處，連匯入的人工標記資料是經由工程師轉換的格式，如圖 2。

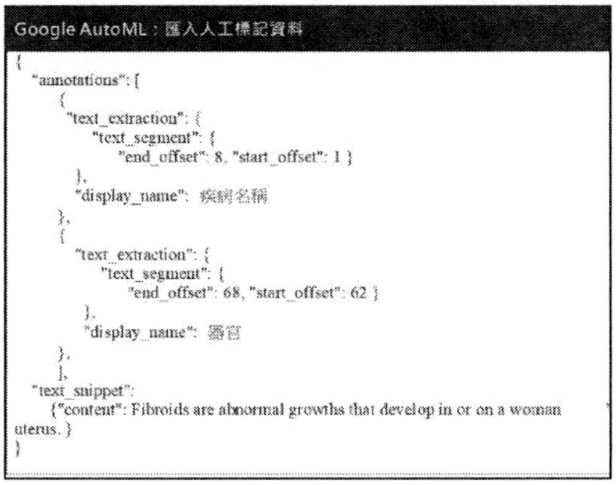

圖 2. Google AuotML NL 人工標記資料匯入

IBM 有提供協助人工標記和任務分配的功能，但建立好的模組僅限於在平台上自動標記其餘尚未標記的語料，所以目標著重在協助建立人工標記語料。

本論文提出的 AI Clerk Platform 則包含提供友善介面，將人工標記人物分配，協助人工標記語料建置，並且可自訂語意，在平台上建立各領域模組，完成自動標記，減少建立模組時撰寫程式，產生 API 供遠端呼叫或在此平台直接引用，所以整合並簡化了資料擷取技術研發過程中的各階段步驟，整個過程免寫程式，讓即便是非資訊人員的人，也可輕易的完成資訊擷取工具。

3 AI Clerk Platform 功能

- 協力建置領域標記語料

建立人工標記語料是自然語言處理領域最耗時的地方，改善人工標記是必要的，為了解決此情形，AI Clerk Platform 可以讓使用者根據自己的領域，自訂該領域的語意標籤，如圖 3，並且提供友善化人工標記介面，如圖 4，使用者只需要選取文字，再選擇語意標籤即可，介面會以顏色區隔標記文字，使用者可以更容易查看標記的文本以及輕鬆完成標記，不再需要建立 Excel 檔或自行撰寫標記介面。

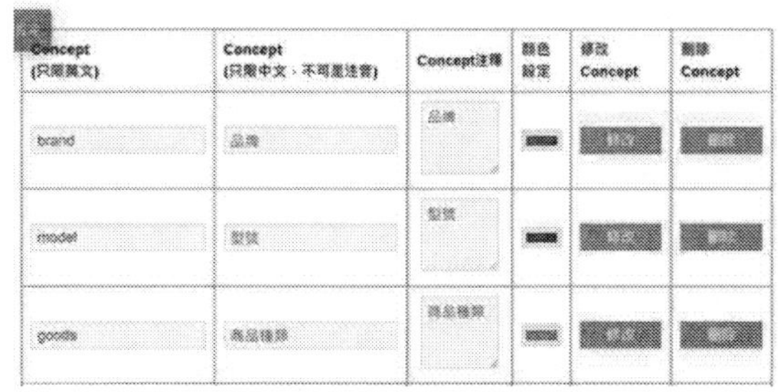

圖 3. 自訂欲自動擷取的語意標籤

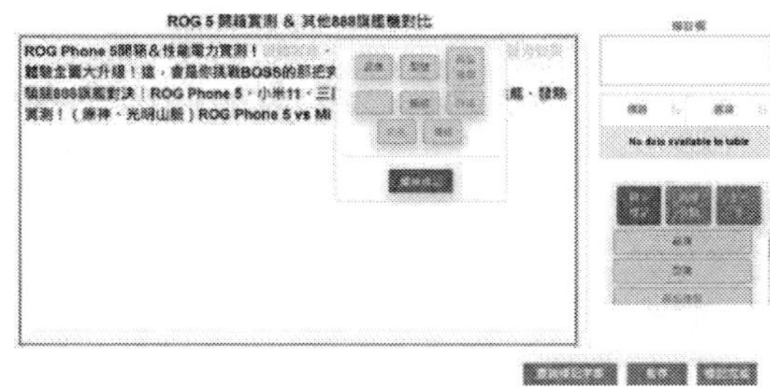

圖 4. 友善的人工標記介面

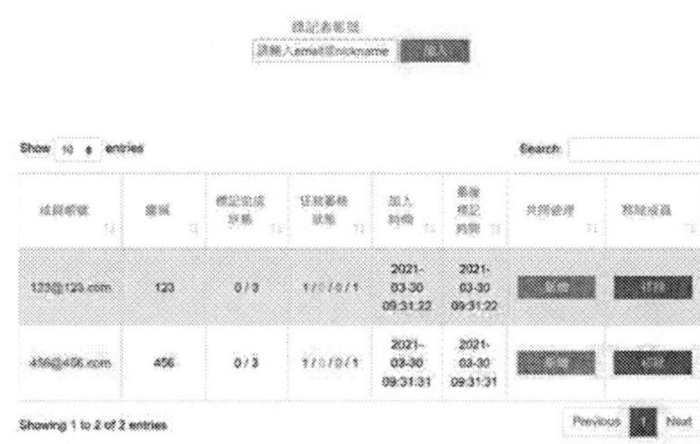

圖 5. 標記員任務管理

除此之外，AI Clerk Platform 提供任務管理機制，如圖 5，讓使用者將人工標記任務分割並分配給不同標記者，並且查看標記進度，與進行針對標記狀況進行審核，以利標記語料建置成果維持一定品質。

- 自建領域資訊擷取模組和 API

AI Clerk Platform 可以讓使用者建立資訊擷取模組和 API，如圖 6，使用者不需撰寫程式，只需點選按鈕即可進行模組訓練，平台提供包含常見的「訓練全部語料」、「80%訓練語料 20% 預測語料」、「5 Fold Cross Validation」三種訓練模式，滿足各種實驗設定，並降低了技術門檻和實踐過程，人人都可自建模組。

圖 6. 透過點擊與設定啟動模型之訓練

提供三種呼叫和瀏覽模組預測結果，如圖 7。第一種是線上預覽，使用者可以在平台上直接輸入文字，平台即時預測並顯示在介面上；第二種是遠端呼叫 API，系統會告知使用者呼叫方式，使用者就可以自行撰寫程式來進行大量呼叫使用；第三種是匯入 Excel 並執行自動預測，使用者將預測文本以 Excel 上傳至平台，同時預測多筆文本，並可下載包含預測結果的 Excel 檔案，如圖 8 為匯入 Excel 自動預測結果之釋例，Excel 是最普及且親民的文書處理軟體，使得人人都可以享受資訊擷取的強大效果。

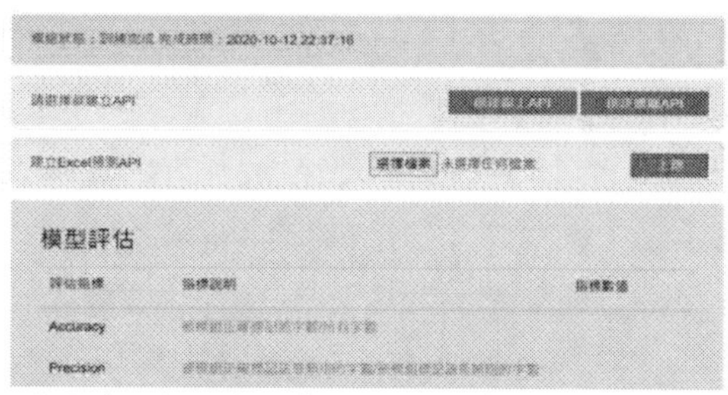

圖 7. 提供三種方式呼叫和瀏覽模組預測結果

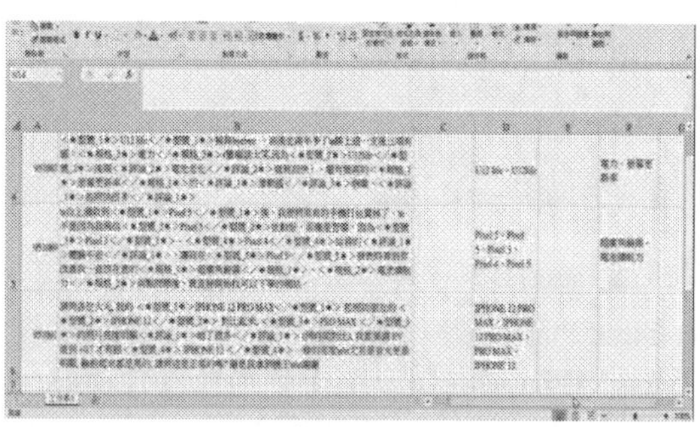

圖 8. 匯入 Excel 執行自動預測結果之釋例

● 提供資訊擷取特殊領域 API

建立特殊領域資訊擷取模組除了考驗人工標記人力，也考驗特殊領域的人力，標記人力也需要具備特殊領域的知識才可以標記，教育時間也更為曠日廢時。因此，AI Clerk Platform 提供一些訓練完成的資訊擷取特殊領域 API，讓使用者可以直接呼叫使用，目前已經有 3C 產品（如圖 9）以及保險商品領域可以使用，3C 產品 API 針對手機產品擷取效果最好，保險商品 API 可處理常見意外險、醫療險、壽險、罐頭保單的相關文本內容。

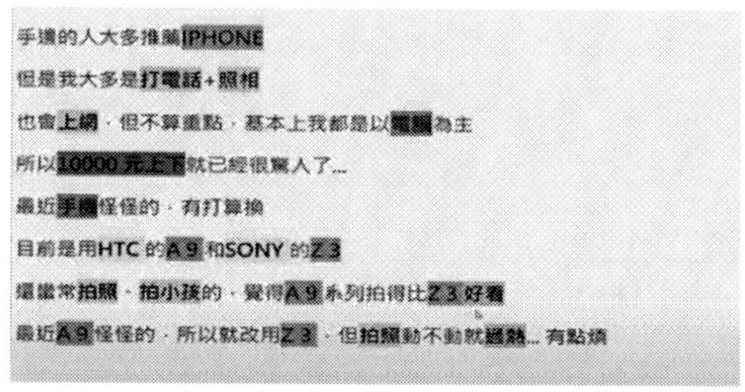

圖 9. 3C 產品資訊擷取 API 預測結果之釋例

4 AI Clerk Platform 平台效益

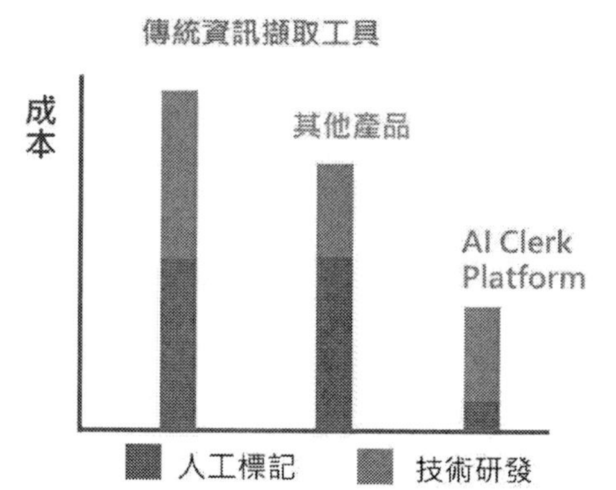

圖 10. 人力成本相對性比較示意圖

● 大幅縮減人工處理資料成本

AI Clerk Platform 藉由友善人工標記介面、任務管理並輔以後端演算法機制，大幅下降了人工標記人力，其餘競品都仍需要大量人力投入。如圖 10，AI Clerk Platform 與相關工具所提及的產品做比較，做了成本相對性比較示意圖，表達成本相對高低的概念，AI Clerk Platform 可以大量下降人力成本。根據本團隊針對建立 3C 產品領域模組為實驗，以手機類文章和其它相機、電腦類文章相比，手機類模組訓練全部此採用人工標記資料建置，而相機與電腦類文章僅有部分訓練語料是由人工標記，同樣是在論壇、業配文中找出商品種類、型號、規格、功能、描述、評論、價格的語意概念，透過後端演算法機制，當電腦類和相機類人工標記文章數量為手機類的20%時，就可達到和手機類文章同等級效益。因此，推估約可以節省80%的人工成本。因此可加速在更多特殊領域的技術研發和應用是可期待的。

● 不用寫程式，完成客製化資訊擷取 API

不用寫程式是 AI Clerk Platform 重要特色，使用者透過人工標記介面，可以用設定、選取的方式完成標記，模組與 API 建立只需點選按鈕進行，使用模組也可以透過匯入 Excel 執行和瀏覽自動預測結果，這些功能特色除了對研發更為便利，也更有助於連非資訊背景的人都可使用。

● 衍生各式資訊擷取或自然語言處理應用服務，減低技術門檻和成本

一般的競品需耗費大量的人力成本來建置資訊擷取模型，而且都需要仰賴工程師來建立模組，也意味著需耗費更多的時間成本來完成智慧應用服務。

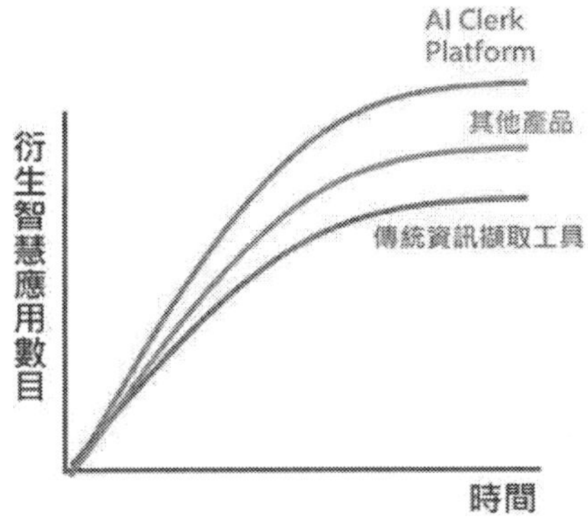

圖 11. 智慧應用相對性比較示意圖

AI Clerk Platform 搭配人工標記介面、任務管理和後端演算法機制降低人力成本與耗費時間，相對於其它競品來說 AI Clerk Platform 的功能可以大幅簡化了資料擷取技術研發過程，節省了人力成本等於也加快衍生各項以資訊擷取技術為基底的各類智慧應用服務之研發，如圖 11，與相關工具所提及的產品做比較，做了智慧應用數目相對性比較示意圖，以曲線相對高低來呈現數目相對多寡。

5 結論

本論文提出一個結合「協力建置領域人工標記語料」、「自建領域資訊擷取模組和 API」、「提供資訊擷取特殊領域 API」特色的 AI Clerk Platform。有別於現存的資訊擷取工具，AI Clerk Platform 可以讓使用者自訂語意標籤滿足客製化需求，透過任務管理機制和友善的人工標記介面，讓使用者可以輕鬆建置領域標記語料，並且可以在無需撰寫程式的前提下，自行建立領域資訊擷取模組和 API，並提供線上預覽、遠端呼叫以及匯入 Excel 執行和瀏覽自動預測結果，也提供特殊領域的資訊擷取 API，有 3C 產品以及保險商品。AI Clerk Platform 可以大幅縮減人工處理資料成本，並且快速衍生各種自然語言處理應用服務，相信 AI Clerk Platform 可以協助學界提升產能與效率。

參考文獻

Appelt, D. E. (1999). Introduction to information extraction. Ai Communications, 12(3), 161-172.

Wilks, Y. (1997, July). Information extraction as a core language technology. In International Summer School on Information Extraction (pp. 1-9). Springer, Berlin, Heidelberg.

Mooney, R. J., & Bunescu, R. (2005). Mining knowledge from text using information extraction. ACM SIGKDD explorations newsletter, 7(1), 3-10.

Koncel-Kedziorski, R., Bekal, D., Luan, Y., Lapata, M., & Hajishirzi, H. (2019). Text generation from knowledge graphs with graph transformers. arXiv preprint arXiv:1904.02342.

Venkatachalam, S., Subbiah, L. P., Rajendiran, R., & Venkatachalam, N. (2020). An ontology-based information extraction and summarization of multiple news articles. International Journal of Information Technology, 12(2), 547-557.

Yoshino, K., Mori, S., & Kawahara, T. (2011, June). Spoken dialogue system based on information extraction using similarity of predicate argument structures. In Proceedings of the SIGDIAL 2011 Conference (pp. 59-66).

Ali, N. (2020). Chatbot: A Conversational Agent employed with Named Entity Recognition Model using Artificial Neural Network. arXiv preprint arXiv:2007.04248.

Jiao, A. (2020, March). An intelligent chatbot system based on entity extraction using RASA NLU and neural network. In Journal of Physics: Conference Series (Vol. 1487, No. 1, p. 012014). IOP Publishing.

Apache cTAKES, https://ctakes.apache.org/

Friedman C, Alderson PO, Austin J, Cimino JJ, Johnson SB. A general natural language text processor for clinical radiology. J Am Med Inform Assoc. 1994; 1:161 – 74. [PMC free article] [PubMed] [Google Scholar]

Friedman C, Starren J, Johnson SB. Architectural requirements for a multipurpose natural language processor in the clinical environment. In: Gardner RM (ed). Proceedings of SCAMC 1995. Philadelphia: Hanley & Belfus, 1995:347 – 51.

Tchechmedjiev, A., Abdaoui, A., Emonet, V., Zevio, S., & Jonquet, C. (2018). SIFR annotator: ontology-based semantic annotation of French biomedical text and clinical notes. BMC bioinformatics, 19(1), 1-26.

Google AuotML NLP, https://cloud.google.com/natural-language/

IBM Watson Knowledge Studio, https://www.ibm.com/tw-zh/cloud/watson-knowledge-studio

The 33rd Conference on Computational Linguistics and Speech Processing (ROCLING 2021)
Taoyuan, Taiwan, October 15-16, 2021. The Association for Computational Linguistics and Chinese Language Processing

A Flexible and Extensible Framework for Multiple Answer Modes Question Answering

Cheng-Chung Fan
Shang-Bao Luo
Kuang-Yu Chang
Meng-Tse Wu
Tzu-Man Wu
Chao-Chun Liang
Kuan-Yu Chen◆
Keh-Yih Su
Institute of Information Science, Academia Sinica
▲ Research Center for Information Technology Innovation, Academia Sinica
{jjfan, newsboy3423, simonc, cwhsu, moju, doublebite, tzum.wu, alsm, ccliang, whm, kysu}@iis.sinica.edu.tw,

Chia-Chih Kuo◆
Pei-Jun Liao
Chiao-Wei Hsu
Shih-Hong Tsai
Aleksandra Smolka
Hsin-Min Wang
Yu Tsao▲
◆ Department of Computer Science and Information Engineering, National Taiwan University of Science and Technology
{jerrykuo7727, s2w81234}@gmail.com
kychen@mail.ntust.edu.tw
yu.tsao@citi.sinica.edu.tw

Abstract

This paper presents a framework to answer the questions that require various kinds of inference mechanisms (such as Extraction, Entailment-Judgement, and Summarization). Most of the previous approaches adopt a rigid framework which handles only one inference mechanism. Only a few of them adopt several answer generation modules for providing different mechanisms; however, they either lack an aggregation mechanism to merge the answers from various modules, or are too complicated to be implemented with neural networks. To alleviate the problems mentioned above, we propose a divide-and-conquer framework, which consists of a set of various answer generation modules, a dispatch module, and an aggregation module. The answer generation modules are designed to provide different inference mechanisms, the dispatch module is used to select a few appropriate answer generation modules to generate answer candidates, and the aggregation module is employed to select the final answer. We test our framework on the 2020 Formosa Grand Challenge Contest dataset. Experiments show that the proposed framework outperforms the state-of-the-art Roberta-large model by about 11.4%.

Keywords: QA, Framework, Divide-and-Conquer strategy, Answer Aggregation, Inference mechanism

1 Introduction

Natural Language Inference (NLI) is an important topic in the *Artificial Intelligence* (AI) field, and any NLI related issue can be checked by asking an appropriate corresponding question (Chen, 2018). Therefore, the *Question Answering* (QA) task has become a very suitable testbed for evaluating NLI models and checking the progress of current techniques. Accordingly, the Ministry of Science and Technology of Taiwan has organized the *Formosa Grand Challenge Open Contest* series[1] (FGC) in 2018, which mainly evaluates the reasoning/inference capability on natural texts, to promote the AI progress in Taiwan. Specifically, this open contest covers a variety of *answer modes*; that is, it needs different *inference mechanisms* (such as *Extraction*, *Entailment-Judgement*, *Aggregative-Operation*,

[1] https://fgc.stpi.narl.org.tw/activity/techai2018

etc.) to get the desired answer. As a result, the system/framework must be able to handle various answer modes at the same time.

The previous frameworks for the QA task could be classified into two main categories according to the number of answer modules adopted: (1) Single answer generation module (Trischler et al., 2017; Chen, 2018; Shoeybi et al., 2020; Zhang et al., 2020), which involves only one answer mode, and allows merely one type of replying format (such as identifying a span within the given passage, giving YES/NO answer, free text reply, etc.). (2) Multiple answer generation modules (Ferrucci, 2012; Andor et al., 2019; Hu et al., 2019), which adopts several answer generation modules, and each module conducts a specific inference mechanism (or, answer mode) with a specific replying format.

Since the first category only considers one answer mode, the types of questions that can be handled are quite limited. For example, it is not suitable for handling the FGC-2020 QA task[2], which covers various question types and needs different answer modes to get the desired answers. In contrast, the approaches under the second category adopt the *divide-and-conquer* strategy, which adopts a different answer generation module for each specific answer mode. Since each answer generation module only needs to consider a specific answer mode, it will be easier to design and add new inference mechanisms.

Among those second category approaches, the framework of Watson (Ferrucci, 2012) is not designed for end-to-end training; therefore, it is not suitable for modern neural-network multi-task learning due to the complicated flow/architecture under its statistics-based architecture. Also, the framework adopted in either (Andor et al., 2019) or (Hu et al., 2019) does not have an aggregation layer/module to merge the answers generated from different answer generation modules (i.e., the output is only picked from a specific module, and merging is not allowed). Therefore, their approaches not only have the error accumulation problem[3] (i.e., once a wrong module is selected, this error will propagate to the next answer-generation stage), but also lose the advantage of combining the strength of different inference mechanisms. Additionally, all modules will be activated in parallel under their frameworks (Andor et al., 2019), so computing resources on those modules that should not be activated for a given question would be wasted.

To overcome the problems mentioned above, a flexible and extensible framework is proposed in this paper. It adopts a divide-and-conquer strategy, and possesses the following main modules/functionalities: (1) A *supporting evidences locating module*, which extracts supporting evidences from the passage to narrow down the searching space. (2) A *dispatch module*, which would select and activate several appropriate answer generation modules; also, the answer type distribution will be provided to each answer generation module as a reference, based on the answer mode. (3) A set of *answer generation modules*, each of them generates a few local/module outputs (i.e., possible answers) if it is activated. (4) An *aggregation module*, which picks the best answer at the final stage by merging the answer candidates from those activated answer generation modules.

The strengths of the proposed framework are summarized as follows: (1) With the dispatch module, it is flexible for handling different question types with the same framework; as a result, it is extensible for adding more answer modes in the future. (2) With the aggregation module, it is able to merge the results from various modules; it thus possesses the capability of combining the strength of different inference mechanisms, and also reduces the error accumulation problem. (3) It is designed to fit the neural-network based end-to-end multi-task learning framework; therefore, it can be implemented with an appropriate neural network without much effort. (4) Since the dispatch module only activates the corresponding modules according to the given question, it will not waste computing resources on those modules that are irrelevant and should not be activated.

In comparison with IBM Watson framework, which adopts a complicated flow/architecture with probabilistic models, our proposed framework

[2] https://scidm.nchc.org.tw/dataset/grandchallenge2020

[3] The error accumulation problem of this kind of approaches is hard to avoid, as it is difficult to know which inference mechanism should be adopted before we actually see the related supporting statements (e.g., span-extraction mechanism is usually preferred if the desired answer is explicitly given in the supporting sentence; otherwise, a more complicated mechanism must be adopted).

adopts the neural-network based approach and can be optimized by the end-to-end training strategy. In comparison with the approaches from Andor et al. (2019) and Hu et al. (2019), which lack the mechanism to merge different answer candidates, our proposed framework only activates several possible/responsible modules and has the ability to aggregate the outputs from various modules.

The proposed framework is tested on the FGC-2020 QA dataset, which contains 1,322 questions. This dataset covers eight different answer modes (i.e., *Single-Span-Extraction*, *Multi-Span-Extraction*, *Yes/No*, *Aggregative-Operation*, *Arithmetic-Operations*, *Date-Duration*, *Kinship*, and *Summarization*) and ten different answer types (i.e., *Yes/No*, *Number-Measure*, *Kinship*, *Person*, *Date-Duration*, *Location*, *Organization*, *Object*, *Event*, and *Misc*). The experiment results show that our system outperforms the baseline RoBERTa-large (Liu et al., 2019) model by 11.4%.

In summary, this paper makes the following contributions: (1) We propose a novel *modular* framework/model that is more flexible for handling/adding various inference mechanisms. (2) We propose a novel aggregation model to merge various answer candidates. (3) We conduct experiments to show that the proposed framework outperforms the state-of-the-art RoBERTa-large model on the FGC-2020 QA dataset.

2 The Proposed Approach

In this section, the proposed divide-and-conquer QA model is first described in Section 2.1. The descriptions of the architecture of the proposed model is then presented in Section 2.2. Afterwards, Section 2.3 provides the concepts and principles of designing each answer generation module.

2.1 The Proposed Divide-and-Conquer QA Model

Given a Document D, Question Q, Wikipedia W_k and some external Knowledge Resources R (such as WordNet and ConceptNet), we would like to find out the most likely answer. To reduce the computation cost, we will first extract related Wikipages with an off-the-shelf IR tool (e.g., the Apache Lucene™ searching engine[4]). Let Wps denote the set of extracted Wikipages, the problem of finding the desired Answer $\hat{A}$ thus can be formulized as Equation (1). For conciseness, we will only use one notation (e.g., "D" (Document)) to denote both its content and its associated embedding vector when it can be interpreted without confusion.

$$\hat{A} = \mathrm{argmax}\, P(A|D,Q,W_k,R) \equiv argmax\, P(A|D,Q,W_{ps},R), \quad (1)$$

where A is a specific answer candidate, and $\hat{A}$ denotes the desired answer which can be: (1) A list of *string/NE/number/date* directly extracted from the document. This list might contain only one element, or even empty (The string "UNKNOWN" will be output in this case). (2) An aggregation result (such as *Summarization, Speaker's View, Arithmetic Result, Count/Min/Max/Avg, Entailment/Sentiment Judgment,* etc.) induced from the given document.

Since we will encounter various scenarios that request different answer modes (among which each adopts a different strategy to obtain the desired answer), a *Divide-and-Conquer* framework is thus proposed to convert a given complicated problem into a set of simple sub-problems:

$$P(A|D,Q,W_{ps},R) = \sum_{M,T,E_s,G_s} P(A,M,T,E_s,G_s|D,Q,W_{ps},R), \quad (2)$$

where M denotes a specific answer mode, T refers to a specific answer type that can be used for verification in each answer generation module, E_s stands for a specific set of supporting evidences, and G_s represents a specific set of paragraphs. By doing so, each answer generation module/model concentrates only on a specific answer mode. The probability $P(A,M,T,E_s,G_s|D,Q,W_{ps},R)$ can be further decomposed into five terms:

$$\begin{aligned} &P(A,M,T,E_s,G_s|D,Q,W_{ps},R) \\ &= P(A|M,T,E_s,G_s,D,Q,W_{ps},R) \\ &\times P(M|T,E_s,G_s,D,Q,W_{ps},R) \\ &\times P(T|E_s,G_s,D,Q,W_{ps},R) \times P(E_s|G_s,D,Q,W_{ps},R) \\ &\times P(G_s|D,Q,W_{ps},R) \\ &\approx P(A|M,T,E_s,Q,R) \times P(M|T,E_s,Q) \times \\ &P(T|E_s,Q) \times P(E_s|G_s,D,Q,W_{ps}) \times P(G_s|D,Q,W_{ps}), \end{aligned} \quad (3)$$

where $P(A|M,T,E_s,Q,R)$ will be generated by each specific answer generation module, both $P(M|T,E_s,Q)$ and $P(T|E_s,Q)$ will be generated by

[4] https://lucene.apache.org/

the Dispatch module, $P(E_s|G_s, D, Q, W_{ps})$ will be generated by the Supporting-Evidence-Locating module, and $P(G_s|D, Q, W_{ps})$ will be generated by another Paragraph-Locating module (Section 2.2).

Finally, $\sum_{M,T,E_s,G_s} P(A, M, T, E_s, G_s|D, Q, W_{ps}, R)$ will be taken care by the Aggregation module, which aggregates various answer-candidates generated by different answer generation modules to obtain the final answer. It predicts the best answer based on those obtained answer-module sextuplets (i.e., <answer mode *M*, the probability of the answer mode M_p, answer type *T*, the probability of the answer type T_p, answer-candidate *A*, its associated confidence-scores F_s>, to be specified later), where M, M_p, T, and T_p are from the Dispatch module, both *A* and F_s are from a specific activated answer generation module. Therefore, Equation (2) can be re-written as

$$P(A|D, Q, W_{ps}, R) = \sum_{M,T,E_s,G_s} P(A, M, T, E_s, G_s|D, Q, W_{ps}, R) \equiv \text{softmax}\,\sigma\left(H\left(\begin{matrix}(M; M_p; T; T_p; F_s)_{A,1}, \ldots, \\ (M; M_p; T; T_p; F_s)_{A,K}\end{matrix}\right)\right) \quad (4)$$

The above Eq (4) is implemented with a pre-processor, which first merges the same answer-candidate from various answer generation modules; afterwards, for each specific merged answer-candidate *A* (among a varying number of different merged candidates), it concatenates the corresponding information from each answer generation module[5] to form the input to a mapping function *H*. This mapping function *H* is mainly used to assign an overall-confidence-score to the given merged answer-candidate if it is supported/merged by/from several modules.

Specifically, for each merged answer-candidate *A*, we will have *K* different $(M; M_p; T; T_p; F_s)$ quintuplets, where *K* is a pre-specified/fixed number of available answer generation modules. Note that the relative position of each answer generation module within the concatenation is fixed (so that the corresponding NN weights can be learnt). The overall-confidence-score of *A* is input to a specific non-linear activation function σ, then a *softmax* function is used to normalize the obtained scores over various merged answer-candidates.

2.2 The Architecture and Operation Flow

Based on Equations (3) and (4), Figure 1 summarizes the proposed divide-and-conquer QA framework. Sequentially, the *Preprocessing-layer* first locates the related Wikipages and annotates the given question/passage (also those Wikipages) with their associated linguistic information via off-the-shelf language tools (e.g., the Stanford CoreNLP toolkit).

Afterwards, the *Embedding-layer* obtains contextual word embeddings through a pre-trained language model (e.g., BERT, RoBERTa (Liu et al., 2019) or XLNet (Yang et al., 2019)), and generates the associated hierarchical embeddings (including the document embedding, paragraph embeddings, and sentence embeddings). The hierarchical embeddings will be shared among subsequent layers.

The *Paragraph-Locating-layer* then narrows down the searching space to only refer to those closely related paragraphs/passages within documents/pages via the so-called "semantic retrieval" model (Nie et al., 2019).

The *Supporting-Evidence-Locating-layer* identifies the associated *Supporting Evidences* and also outputs an associated score of the specified configuration. Basically, only content similarity is considered here, and no reasoning is conducted (which will be done later in the Answer-Generation-layer). It can be implemented by a BERT-based model with output vectors connected to a binary classifier.

The *Dispatch-layer* generates the corresponding answer mode and answer type probability distributions for the given question-passage pair, and then activates the answer-generation-modules associated with the *top-D* answer modes; also, the answer type probability distribution will be sent to each answer generation module for reference. Please note that one answer mode can activate several corresponding answer generation modules simultaneously if the ensemble approach is adopted; also, all those activated answer generation modules will be operated in parallel. In the current implementation, the *Dispatcher-layer* is a BERT-based classification model.

[5] Please note that the corresponding information from all answer generation modules will be input to fix the input format (i.e., regardless of whether they are activated by the Dispatch module or not; however, for those inactivated modules, their associated fields will be set to null/zero).

The *Answer-Generation-layer* includes various answer generation modules and generates the local/module output (i.e., the answer-candidate) from each selected answer generation module. Furthermore, each module is expected to generate *top-N* answer-candidates with their associated confidence scores (Details are given in Section 2.3).

The *Aggregation-layer* generates the desired final answer via aggregating various local/module answer-candidates (Section 2.4). Please note that an answer mode may be handled by several different answer generation modules at the same time, if an ensemble approach is adopted. The influence of each answer generation module is implicitly decided by its associated NN weights of a feedforward neural network adopted in this layer.

The *External-Resources* and their accessing utilities/tools provide additional information (to supplement the training data-set and those on-line retrieved documents) to increase the knowledge coverage of the test data. Currently, they include WordNet, ConceptNet, Wikipedia, and other available resources/tools (e.g., Stanford CoreNLP).

Last, the *Online-Working-Memory* is a working-memory used to save the intermediate/linguistic-analysis results (e.g., Hierarchy Embeddings about the question/related-passages, POS/NE annotation, dependency-tree, etc.) that can be shared among various layers/modules later.

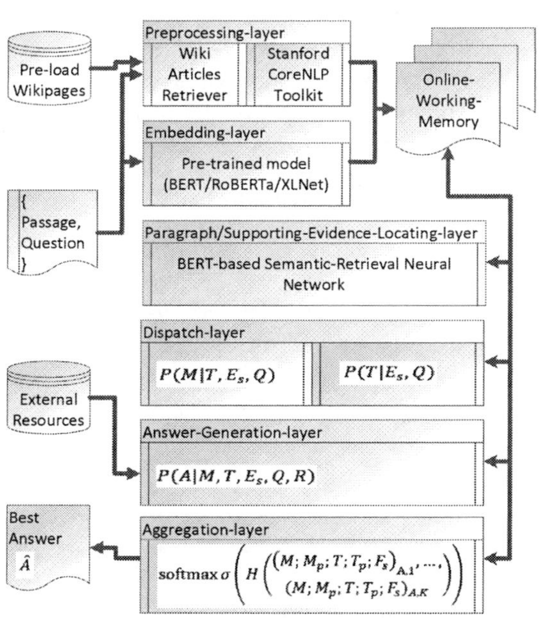

Figure 1. The proposed DNN system architecture

2.3 The Adopted Answer Generation Modules

Figure 2 shows the answer generation modules adopted in this work. Since this paper mainly addresses the framework design, we will only briefly sketch the adopted implementation of each module. The *Single-Span-Extraction* module adopts an ensemble approach. It is implemented by choosing 12 best RoBERTa-large models with AdaBoost algorithm (Yang et al., 2018). The implementation of the *Multi-Span-Extraction* module is based on the tag-based multi-span extraction model (Segal et al., 2020), which treats the task as a sequence tagging problem (i.e., for each token in the passage, decide whether it is part of the answer span). Since the implementations of the *Arithmetic-Operation* and *Date-Duration* modules are similar, we merge these two functionalities into one module in this task. In this merged module, a RoBERTa-base model is first used to extract top K candidates, and then a rule-based procedure is adopted for performing some arithmetic operations such as calculating the duration from the beginning and ending dates.

Furthermore, the *Entailment-Judgement* module is implemented by using a pre-trained BERT mode and fine-tuning it for the *Yes-No* task (Devlin et al., 2019). The *Common-Sense-Inference* is implemented with a template-based approach to answer *Kinship* questions. Firstly, the given question is tokenized by Stanford CoreNLP toolkit. The Chinese kinship associated terms (e.g., father, son, etc.) collected from related Wikipages are added to the dictionary of that toolkit to increase its accuracy rate. Afterwards, a rule-based procedure tries to fill in the slots of the question template with appropriate tokens. Last, the *Summarization* module is implemented by modifying an existing BERT-based extractive summarization algorithm (Liu, 2019)

Please note that some of the answer generation modules are not implemented here, which include the *Compare-Members* module and the *Speaker-View* modules, since they do not occur in the FGC-2020-pre dataset. Also, the *Aggregative-Operation* module is merged into *Multi-Span-Extraction* module, since there are only few questions in this dataset (and the Aggregative-Operation could be subsequently taken on the members that are extracted from the Multi-Span-Extraction module).

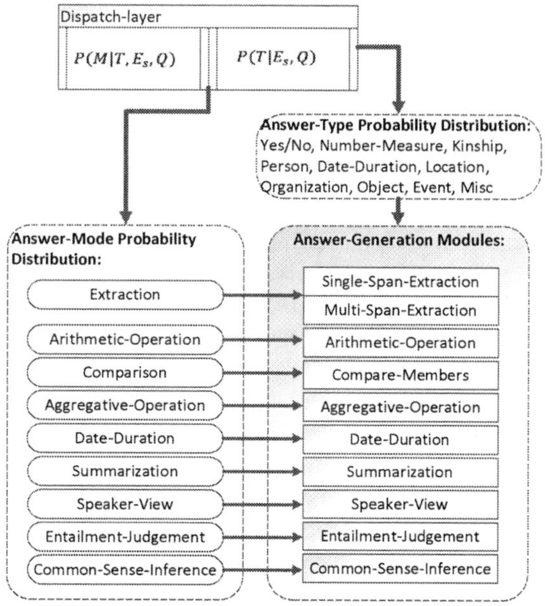

Figure 2. The adopted answer generation modules.

2.4 The Proposed Aggregation Module

As described in section 2.1, this module will adopt a pre-processor to first merge answer candidates from various answer generation modules. Figure 3 shows an example of the merging process. Suppose we have three answer generation modules (i.e., M_1, M_2, M_3) and pick top-3 answer candidates from each answer generation module, where C_{ij} denotes the *rank-j* answer candidate in answer generation *module-i*. After the merging process, there are four *merged answer-candidates* (i.e., MC_1, MC_2, MC_3, MC_4) left. For example, MC_1 groups two answer candidates C_{11} and C_{33} as they are identical.

$$\begin{array}{l} M_1:\ C_{11},\ C_{12},\ C_{13} \\ M_2:\ C_{21},\ C_{22},\ C_{23} \\ M_3:\ C_{31},\ C_{32},\ C_{33} \end{array} \xrightarrow[Merge]{} \begin{array}{l} MC_1:\ C_{11},\ C_{33}, \\ MC_2:\ C_{12},\ C_{21},\ C_{32} \\ MC_3:\ C_{13},\ C_{22},\ C_{31} \\ MC_4:\ C_{23} \end{array}$$

Figure 3. An example of merging answer candidates from different answer generation modules.

The mapping function H is implemented by a Feed-Forward network and its output is connected to a binary classifier (*T/F*) as showed in Figure 4. The *overall-confidence-score* of each merged answer candidate is given by the score of the output *T*. Take MC_1 as an example, we will have two quintuplets input from *module-1* and *module-3* while other modules are with zero vectors.

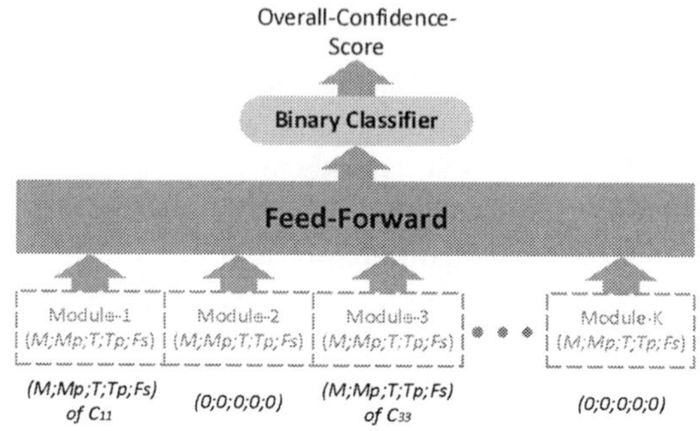

Figure 4. The NN-based aggregation module.

3 Evaluation

To verify the validity and effectiveness of the proposed framework, we have tested it on the FGC-2020 dataset. The details of the dataset and various experiments conducted are presented below.

3.1 Dataset

Officially, FGC-2020 organizer had released both FGC-2020-pre dataset, which is mainly used to let each team train their own model, and FGC-2020-final test set, which is mainly used to evaluate the final round performance. Since the FGC-2020-final test set is not open to various teams before the final contest, the following description is mainly for the FGC-2020-pre dataset. Each released question in the FGC-2020-pre dataset is associated with an official category tag among *Elementary*, *Advanced*, and *Argumentation*[6]. Table 1 shows the statistics of those question categories. Also, as those Argumentation questions do not have the golden answers provided by the FGC organizer, we exclude them from the FGC-2020-pre dataset.

Question Category	Count	Percentage
Elementary	929	70.27%
Advanced	378	28.59%
Argumentation	15	1.14%
Total	1,322	100.00%

Table 1. The statistics of the question categories in the FGC-2020-pre dataset.

To train the models and get a sense about our performance before the final competition, we further divide the remaining FGC-2020-pre data into our own training/development/test three subsets. To avoid distribution mismatch problem, we keep

[6] https://fgc.stpi.narl.org.tw/activity/2020_Talk2AI

the distributions of question categories in each subset as similar as possible while dividing them. The statistics of each subset are shown in Table 2.

Dataset	Count	Percentage
Training	875	66.94%
Development	242	18.52%
Test	190	14.54%
Total	1,307	100.00%

Table 2. The statistics of training/development/test subsets in the FGC-2020-pre dataset.

Figure 5 shows the distributions of answer mode and answer type in the training/development/test subsets, where the vertical axis displays various answer modes/types and the horizontal axis indicates their corresponding percentages. It is observed that the distributions of answer mode in training/development/test subsets are similar but that of answer type are significantly different (especially in the test subset); it is due to that we divide the dataset based on the given documents (and then adjust them according to answer modes), but each document is associated with a varying number of questions/types.

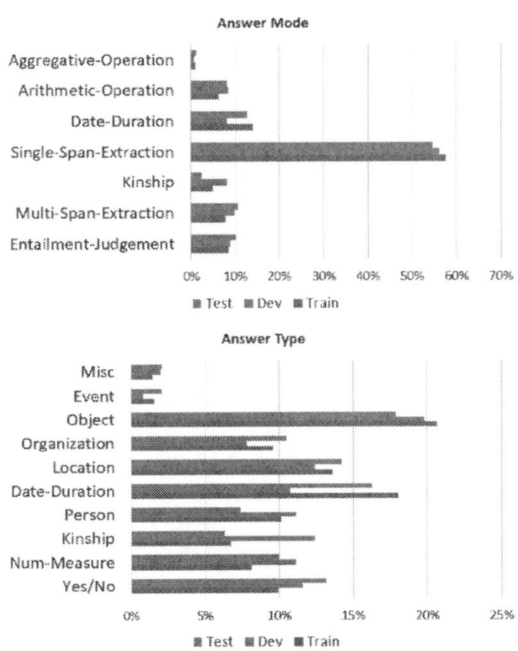

Figure5. The distributions of answer mode and answer type in the training/development/test subsets of the FGC-2020-pre dataset.

3.2 The Baseline Adopted

Since RoBERTa (Liu et al., 2019) is the state-of-the-art pre-trained model for single-span extraction (if ensemble approaches are excluded) on both SQuAD (Rajpurkar et al., 2016) and DRCD (Shao et al., 2018) datasets when we were preparing for the FGC preliminary round (2019/12/24), it was chosen as our baseline model.

3.3 Overall System Performance on Official Pre-released Dataset

Table 3 gives the performances of our proposed model and the above baseline (RoBERTa-large) on both the FGC-2020-pre test-set and the FGC-2020-final test-set. In comparison with the baseline, we have enjoyed 11.4% (= 70.5% - 59.1%) overall improvement on the FGC-2020-pre test-set. This shows when the dataset contains the questions with various answer modes, customizing the model architecture for each specific answer mode (which needs a different inference mechanism) is better than adopting a monolithic architecture (and then applying it to various answer modes). The advantage of adopting the proposed Divide-and-Conquer framework is thus shown.

Furthermore, the top-1 and top-2 accuracy rates of the answer mode are 98.9% and 100.0%, respectively; and those of the answer type are 93.7% and 95.3%, respectively. This shows that the Dispatch-layer is quite promising. The performance of answer type prediction is inferior to that of answer mode, as we have more answer types than answer modes.

Dataset	Baseline	Proposed
FGC-2020-pre test-set	59.1%	70.5%
FGC-2020-final test-set	36.9%	39.1%

Table 3. The EM (Exact Match) scores of the baseline and the proposed model on the FGC-2020-pre and the FGC-2020-final test-sets.

Last, an intuitive approach to implement the Aggregation-layer is to simply pick up the answer candidate with the highest score (which is calculated by multiplying its associated confidence score and the corresponding answer mode probability) among various candidates. It is surprised to find that this intuitive approach (with EM 70.5%) is 0.6% better than our proposed NN-based approach (with EM 69.9%) in this test-set. A possible reason could be that there is almost no overlapping among various top-3 candidate-sets (obtained from different answer generation modules) in this dataset; as the result, the advantage of merging the same answer-candidate generated from different inference mechanisms thus disappears.

3.4 The Performance on Official Final Test-set

Since we have got FGC-2020-final test-set after the contest, we also show its distributions of answer mode and answer type in Figure 6. It includes total 46 question-passage pairs (again, 4 Argumentation questions are excluded). It is observed that the distributions of both answer mode and answer type in the final run are very different from those in the FGC-2020-pre dataset. This indicates that we have a serious mismatch problem in both answer mode and answer type, which implies that shallow statistical information (which BERT mainly utilizes) would be less useful and deep understanding would be more demanding.

The obtained performance is given in Table 3. In comparison with the baseline, we only got 2.2% (= 39.1% - 36.9%) overall improvement. Comparing with the improvement obtained on the FGC-2020-pre test-set (11.4%), the gap shrinks considerably because the problems in the FGC-2020-final test-set is much more difficult (and thus beyond not only the capability of the baseline but also the capability of our proposed approach).

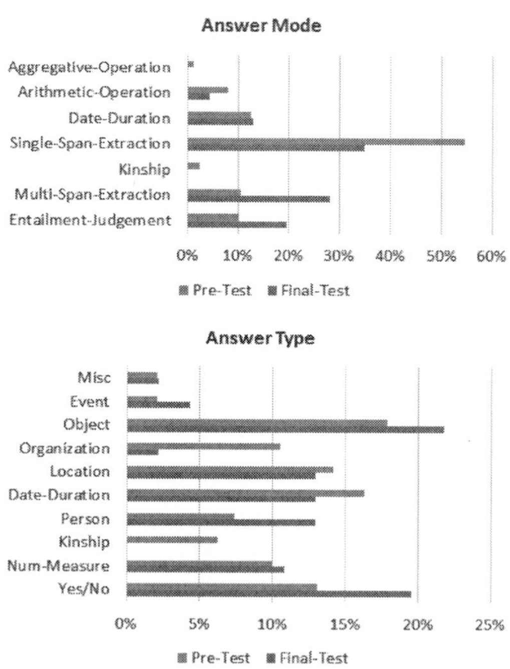

Figure 6. The distributions of answer mode and answer type in the FGC-2020-pre and FGC-2020-final test-sets.

Figure 7 further shows the overall system performance on the FGC-2020-pre and FGC-2020-final test-sets in each category. Surprising in coincidence, the accuracy rates on Elementary, Advanced, and Overall categories are 0.391, 0.391, and 0.391, respectively. In comparison with the overall performance of the FGC-2020-pre test-set, the accuracy rate drops 0.314 (from 0.705 to 0.391). Figure 8 additionally shows the accuracy rates associated with various answer-modes (Please note that there is no Kinship answer mode question in this test-set). We even have 0% and 15.4% accuracy rates for the Arithmetic-Operation and Multi-Span-Extraction answer modes, respectively. The obtained poor performances clearly indicate that these two answer-modes are more difficult to handle, which fits our intuition.

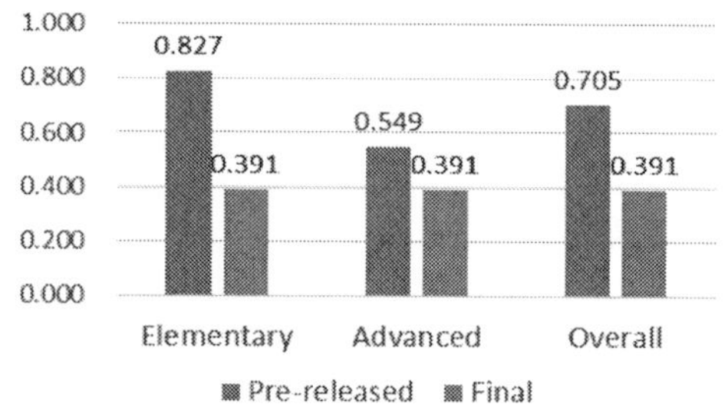

Figure 7. The overall system accuracy rate on the FGC-2020-pre and FGC-2020-final test-sets.

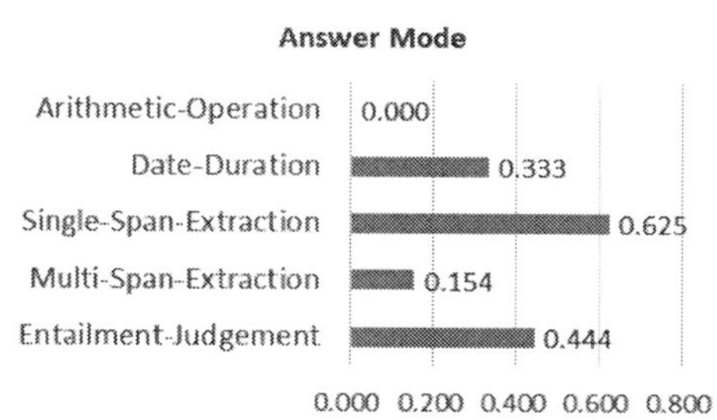

Figure 8. The accuracy rates associated with various answer modes on the FGC-2020-final test-set.

4 Error Analysis and Discussion for Official Final Test-set

As Figure 7 shows, the overall system performance degrades significantly (down 0.314, from 0.705 to 0.391) when we move from FGC-2020-pre test-set to FGC-2020-final test-set. It is mainly because the questions in the FGC-2020-final test-set is generally more difficult than that in the FGC-2020-pre test-set. And it is also because the involved topics (also their associated lexicons), the distributions of both answer mode and answer type drift significantly from FGC-2020-pre test-set to FGC-2020-final test-set (as shown in Figure 6).

Since almost all our current answer generation modules adopt BERT-based approaches, and it is well-known that BERT conducts the inference mainly based on surface-clues/hidden-distribution-bias (Naik et al., 2018; Poliak et al., 2018; Jiang and Marneffe, 2019; McCoy et al., 2019), the mismatch of those surface-clues/distributions thus causes serious degradation. On the other hand, it also implies that BERT-based approaches, although they have become state-of-the-art models, are still not capable to handle the FGC-2020 kind of tests (which require deep reasoning and cannot be falsely solved simply with surface-clues/distribution-bias).

Specifically, the performance of the Elementary questions drops more (down 0.436, from 0.827 to 0.391) in comparison with that of Advanced ones (down 0.158, from 0.549 to 0.391). The performance of the Advanced questions is less affected because those questions require deeper reasoning, and is thus less affected by the drift of topics and the distribution of answer mode/answer type mentioned above.

If we zoom into various answer modes, it is observed that the Multi-Span-Extraction causes most overall degradation in the FGC-2020-final test-set, which is mainly due to both its low accuracy rate (15.4% in Figure 8) and its high answer mode portion (28% in Figure 6)). It seems that the tag-based approach (Section 2.3) is not capable of handling the Multi-Span-Extraction questions involved in this dataset, as getting a multi-span answer needs to locate various list-members via matching the structures (Gentner and Markman, 1997) of the question and the passage, not just regarding it as a sequence-tagging task.

5 Conclusion

We proposed a divide-and-conquer model/framework for answering the questions in FGC-2020 QA dataset, which covers various answer modes. With the proposed Dispatch-layer, the proposed framework is flexible for handling various answer modes with different modules simultaneously, and is extensible for adding new answer modes and answer types in the future. Also, with the proposed Aggregation-layer, the proposed framework can take advantage of different inference mechanisms, and also reduce the error accumulation problem. Last, due to its design for fitting the end-to-end multi-task learning framework, the proposed framework could be implemented with an appropriate neural network and is thus more suitable for end-to-end optimization without much effort.

We have tested the proposed framework on 2020 Formosa Grand Challenge Contest QA dataset. The experiment results show that our system outperforms the baseline RoBERTa-large model about 11.4% on the FGC-2020-pre test-set. However, the overall system performance drops significantly (about 31.4%) from the FGC-2020-pre test-set to the FGC-2020-final test-set. On the other hand, together with our another dialog sub-system (tested on the FGC-2020-final *Dialog* test-set), we obtained 44.1 total score (out of 100; the human performance is 68.2), which outperforms that of the official top one system (announced in this contest) 7.4 points.

References

Daniel Andor, Luheng He, Kenton Lee, and Emily Pitler. 2019. *Giving BERT a Calculator: Finding Operations and Arguments with Reading Comprehension*. arXiv:1909.00109v2.

Dan-Qi Chen. 2018. *Neural Reading Comprehension and Beyond.* Ph.D. Dissertation. Stanford University.

Jacob Devlin, Ming-Wei Chang, Kenton Lee, and Kristina Toutanova. 2019. *BERT: Pre-training of Deep Bidirectional Transformers for Language Understanding*. arXiv:1810.04805v2.

David Ferrucci. 2012. *Introduction to 'This is Watson'*. IBM J. RES. & DEV. VOL. 56 NO. 3/4 PAPER 1.

Dedre Gentner and Arthur B. Markman. 1997. *Structure mapping in analogy and similarity.* American Psychologist, 52(1):45–56.

Ming-Hao Hu, Yu-Xing Peng, Zhen Huang, and Dong-sheng Li. 2019. *A Multi-Type Multi-Span Net-work for Reading Comprehension that Requires Discrete Reasoning*. arXiv:1908.05514v2.

Chu-Ren Huang, Shu-Kai Hsieh, Jia-Fei Hong, Yun-Zhu Chen, I-Li Su, Yong-Xiang Chen, and Sheng-Wei Huang. 2008. Chinese Wordnet: Design, Implementation, & Application of an Infrastructure for Cross-lingual Knowledge Processing. In *Chinese Lexical Semantic Workshop 2008.*

Nan-Jiang Jiang and Marie-Catherine de Marneffe (2019). Evaluating BERT for natural language inference: A case study on the Commitment Bank. In *Proceedings of the 2019 Conference on Empirical*

Methods in Natural Language Processing and the 9th International Joint Conference on Natural Language Processing. Association for Computational Linguistics, pages 6086–6091.

Cheng-Ru Li, Chi-Hsin Yu, and Hsin-Hsi Chen. 2011. Predicting the Semantic Orientation of Terms in E-HowNet. In *Proceedings of the 23rd Conference on Computational Linguistics and Speech Processing*, pages 151–165.

Yang Liu. 2019. *Fine-tune BERT for Extractive Summarization.* arXiv:1903.10318v2.

Yin-Han Liu, Myle Ott, Naman Goyal, Jing-Fei Du, Mandar Joshi, Dan-qi Chen, Omer Levy, Mike Lewis, Luke Zettlemoyer, and Veselin Stoyanov. 2019. *RoBERTa: A Robustly Optimized BERT Pretraining Approach.* arXiv:1907.11692v1.

Tom McCoy, Ellie Pavlick, and Tal Linzen. 2019. Right for the Wrong Reasons: Diagnosing Syntactic Heuristics in Natural Language Inference. In *Proceedings of the 57th Annual Meeting of the Association for Computational Linguistics. Association for Computational Linguistics*, pages 3428–3448.

Aakanksha Naik, Abhilasha Ravichander, Norman Sadeh, Carolyn Rose, and Graham Neubig. 2018. Stress Test Evaluation for Natural Language Inference. In *Proceedings of the 27th International Conference on Computational Linguistics. Association for Computational Linguistics*, pages 2340–2353.

Yi-Xin Nie, Song-He Wang, and Mohit Bansal. 2019. *Revealing the importance of semantic retrieval for machine reading at scale.* arXiv:1909.08041v1.

Adam Poliak, Jason Naradowsky, Aparajita Haldar, Rachel Rudinger, and Benjamin Van Durme. 2018. Hypothesis only baselines in natural language inference. In *Proceedings of the Seventh Joint Conference on Lexical and Computational Semantics. Association for Computational Linguistics*, pages 180–191.

Pranav Rajpurkar, Jian Zhang, Konstantin Lopyrev, and Percy Liang. 2016. *SQuAD: 100,000+ Questions for Machine Comprehension of Text.* arXiv: 1606.05250v3.

Sebastian Ruder. 2017. *An Overview of Multi-Task Learning in Deep Neural Networks.* arXiv:1706.05098v1.

Elad Segal, Avia Efrat, Mor Shoham, Amir Globerson, and Jonathan Berant. 2020. *A Simple and Effective Model for Answering Multi-span Questions.* arXiv:1909.13375v1.

Chih-Chieh Shao, Trois Liu, Yu-Ting Lai, Yi-Ying Tseng, and Sam Tsai. 2018. *DRCD: a Chinese Machine Reading Comprehension Dataset.* arXiv:1806.00920.

Mohammad Shoeybi, Mostofa Patwary, Raul Puri, Patrick LeGresley, Jared Casper, and Bryan Catanzaro. 2020. *Megatron-LM: Training Multi-Billion Parameter Language Models Using Model Parallelism.* arXiv:1909.08053v4.

Robyn Speer, Joshua Chin, and Catherine Havasi. 2018. *ConceptNet 5.5: An Open Multilingual Graph of General Knowledge.* arXiv:1612.03975v2.

Adam Trischler, Tong Wang, Xing-Di Yuan, Justin Harris, Alessandro Sordoni, Philip Bachman, and Kaheer Suleman. 2016. *NewsQA: A Machine Comprehension Dataset.* arXiv:1611.09830v3.

Dong-Dong Yang, Sen-Zhang Wang, and Zhou-Jun Li. 2018. Ensemble Neural Relation Extraction with Adaptive Boosting. In *Proceedings of the Twenty-Seventh International Joint Conference on Artificial Intelligence*, pages 4532–4538.

Zhi-Lin Yang, Zi-Hang Dai, Yi-Ming Yang, Jaime Carbonell, Ruslan Salakhutdinov, and Quoc V. Le. 2019. *XLNet: Generalized Autoregressive Pretraining for Language Understanding.* arXiv:1906.08237v2.

Yu Zhang and Qiang Yang. 2021. *A Survey on Multi-Task Learning.* arXiv:1707.08114v3.

Zhuo-Sheng Zhang, Jun-Jie Yang, and Hai Zhao. 2020. *Retrospective Reader for Machine Reading Comprehension.* arXiv: 2001.09694v3.

The 33rd Conference on Computational Linguistics and Speech Processing (ROCLING 2021)
Taoyuan, Taiwan, October 15-16, 2021. The Association for Computational Linguistics and Chinese Language Processing

基於 CNN+LSTM Model 之語音情緒識別
Speech Emotion Recognition Based on CNN+LSTM Model

Wei Mou[1], Pei-Hsuan Shen[1], Chu-Yun Chu[1], Yu-Cheng Chiu[1], Tsung-Hsien Yang[2] and Ming-Hsiang Su[1]
[1] Soochow University, Taiwan
[2] Telecommunication Laboratories Chunghwa Telecom Co. Ltd.
[1] weiswlight, claire1015069, tp973632, jean199925, huntfox.su@gmail.com
[2] yasamyang@cht.com.tw

摘要

由於智能對話助理服務的普及，語音情緒辨識已經變得越來越重要。在人與機器的溝通中，情緒辨識與情感分析能夠增強機器與人類的互動。本研究使用 CNN+LSTM 模型實作語音情緒辨識 (Speech Emotion Recognition, SER) 處理並進行預測。從實驗結果得知使用 CNN+LSTM 模型相對於使用傳統 NN 模型取得更好的效能。

Abstract

Due to the popularity of intelligent dialogue assistant services, speech emotion recognition has become more and more important. In the communication between humans and machines, emotion recognition and emotion analysis can enhance the interaction between machines and humans. This study uses the CNN+LSTM model to implement speech emotion recognition (SER) processing and prediction. From the experimental results, it is known that using the CNN+LSTM model achieves better performance than using the traditional NN model.

關鍵字：CNN、LSTM、情緒識別

Keywords: CNN, LSTM, Speech emotion recognition

1 Introduction

情緒定義為一種受到外在或內在刺激後引起的心理感受或反應 [1]。每種情緒都有其獨特的特徵：信號，生理和先前的事件。有別於「心情」的表現，「情緒」通常是起效快，持續時間短，發生率高的，因此也更能表現語者當下的反應。情緒的表現與分類，最早由 Tomkin 定義了八種情緒：驚訝、有趣、愉悅、憤怒、害怕、嫌惡、羞愧、痛苦 [2]。後續也有其他學者提出不同的分類方式，例如 Plutchik 以如同色輪一般的方式提出情緒輪的分類 [3]，如下圖一情緒輪所示，輪中接近的情緒是較為相似的，距離較遠之情緒則較無關聯性，而相對之情緒，如高興相對於悲傷則代表相反的情緒。不同的情緒如不同的顏色一般可互相混合而成。為了將情緒表現分類可視化，由 Posner、Russell和 Peterson 學者於 2005 年提出 [4] 將其投射在一個能表現情緒相互關係二維空間中，並以表現出的愉悅程度(valence)以及激發程度(arousal)劃分成四個象限，又稱為情緒空間(Valence-Arousal space)，如 Figure 1 所示。

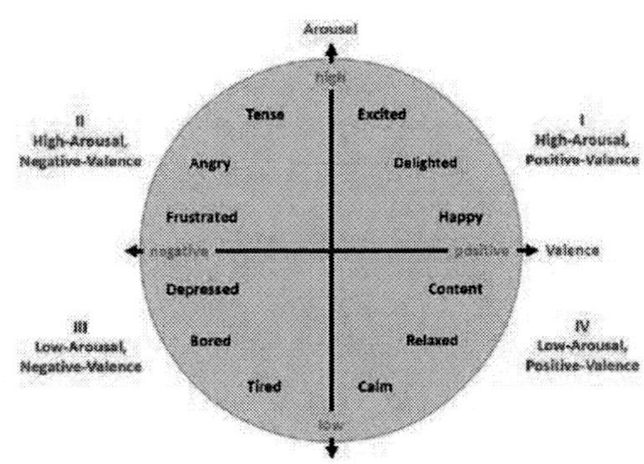

Figure 1: 情緒空間

如何自訊號中抽取利於辨識的情緒特徵，以及如何利用特徵正確辨識出情緒是重要的議題 [5-7]。常見語音訊號特徵如韻律特徵 (prosodic feature) 以及音訊頻譜特徵 (spectral features)。其中韻律特徵以音節及短語等口語斷點來計算該區段之音頻高低與聲音強度等 [5]，而音訊頻譜特徵以音框(frame) 作為音訊訊號之抽取單位，抽取各種低階語音特徵 (low-level descriptor, LLDs) 以及多個音框內低階語音特徵之統計資訊 [8]。這些特徵可能缺少對於情緒分析的客觀性 [9]，其忽略了訊號中隱含的情緒特徵，無法完整模擬人腦在做情緒辨識時所需的參考依據。近幾年，深度學習的研究日漸進步，其對於語音訊號之特徵抽取有重大的改進及貢獻，end-to-end 的特徵抽取方法，經由訓練網路層，找到輸入訊號與情緒目標之間的隱含關係，改善人為定義特徵不客觀的問題[10]，已有許多研究使用神經網路架構抽取音訊或頻譜 (spectrogram) 上之音訊特徵。Table 1 介紹使用神經網路架構的語音情緒辨識系統。

Table 1: 語音情緒辨識系統

Data	Feature Extraction	Corpus	Recognition
Spectrogram	1-layer 2D-CNN	Germany, English	LSTM [7]
Waveform	Auto-encoder	EMO-DB	SVM [11]
Waveform	2-layer 1D-CNN	eNTERFACE, MUSAN	BLSTM [12]
Spectrogram, waveform	Multi-layer 1D-CNN	Data from Cortana	CNN [13]
Waveform, Spectrogram	1-layer 1D-CNN, 1-layer 2D-CNN	NNIME	BLSTM [14]

由上述研究可以得知，現如今已有許多以神經網路進行情緒辨識之研究，他們多使用卷積神經網路 (convolution neural network, CNN) 進行特徵抽取，[7] 比較不同維度及層數的卷積層對辨識的影響，發現單層卷積層的效果較好，[7, 12, 14]皆使用長短期記憶模型(long short-term memory, LSTM)進行情緒特徵之分類，能有效處理訊號時序上的前後關係，以提升語音情緒之辨識效能。

2 Emotion Dataset

EMO-DB 資料集 [15] 是由柏林工業大學錄製的德語情感語音資料庫，由 10 位演員(5 男 5 女) 對 10 個語句 (5 長 5 短) 進行 7 種情感(中性/nertral、生氣/anger、害怕/fear、高興/joy、悲傷/sadness、厭惡/disgust、無聊/boredom，如 Figure 2 所示)的模擬得到，共包含 800 句語料，採樣頻率 48kHz (後壓縮到 16 kHz)，16 bit 量化。語料文本的選取遵從語意中性、無情感傾向的原則，且為日常口語化風格，無過多的書面語修飾。

Code of emotions:

letter	emotion (english)	letter	emotion (german)
A	anger	W	Ärger (Wut)
B	boredom	L	Langeweile
D	disgust	E	Ekel
F	anxiety/fear	A	Angst
H	happiness	F	Freude
S	sadness	T	Trauer
N = neutral version			

Figure 2: 英/德語情緒對照表

語音的錄製在專業錄音室中完成，要求演員在演譯某個特定情感前，必須通過回憶自身真實經歷或體驗進行情緒的醞釀，來增強情緒的真實感。經過 20 個參與者 (10 男 10 女) 的聽辨實驗，得到 84.3% 的聽辨識別率。這個資料集經過聽辨測試後，保留 535 句(男性情感語句 233 句、女性情感句 302 句)。其中語句內容具有較高情感自由度 (包含日常生活用語的 5 個短句和 5 個長句)，但不包含某一特定情感傾向。每個檔案的命名意義如下：Position1-2 對應該人的編號、Position3-5 對應語音內容編號、Position6 對應情感編號（表一紅框處，因檔名中以德語單詞首字母標記，表一為英/德語之情緒詞語對照表）、Position7 若有兩種版本以上，則以 a, b, c 依序命名。

3 Convolution Neural Network

卷積神經網路 (Convolutional Neural Network, CNN) 由一個或多個卷積層和池化層(pooling layer) 組成。CNN 最開始的概念是經由 Hubel 等學者在生物領域上的研究而啟發 [16]，而後在 1982 年由 Fukushima 等人將神經網路的架構提出 [17]。之後 1995 年的 B. Lo 等人 [18] 與 1998 年的 Y. Lecun 等人 [19] 在神經網路的架構中加入卷積層(convolution layer)、池化層(pooling layer)等逐漸完善成現在的卷積神經網路。基本的卷積神經網路包含卷積層以卷積的方式取得局部資訊並透過激化函數做為特徵、池化層將由卷積層而來的數值進行採樣做為代表值，而最後全連接(full connection)至目標輸出。本研究使用一維單層自適應卷積神經網路架構進行聲音特徵抽取，如 Figure 3 所示。

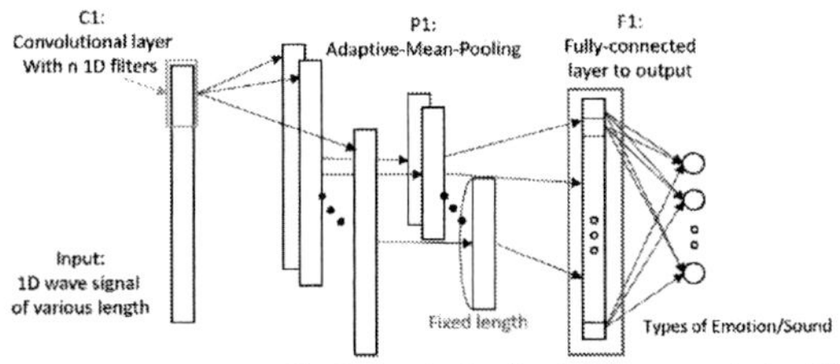

Figure 3: 一維單層自適應卷積神經網路架構

4 Long Short-Term Memory

長短期記憶神經網路 (long short-term memory, LSTM) 為一種遞歸神經網路 (recurrent neural network, RNN) 的變形。是為了解決傳統遞歸神經網路在損失函數從輸出層進行反向傳播時，可能造成梯度消失的問題，使得網路停在區域最佳解而難以學習節點間的連接關係。於是 Hochreiter 等人 [20] 提出長短期記憶單元構成的神經網路，可藉由記憶單元的特殊結構，學習到輸入間隔較長的資訊彼此的相互關係。

如 Figure 4 所示，長短期記憶單元的結構包含關鍵的細胞狀態 C_t 於圖片上方的水平線，而其中包含三個主要的閘(gate)，分別為遺忘閘、輸入閘、輸出閘，用以保護、控制細胞狀態，讓資訊選擇性的通過，而輸出皆會經過 sigmoid function(σ)使值介於 0 到 1 之間，用以描述通過的量。0 表示完全不通過、1 表示完全通過。

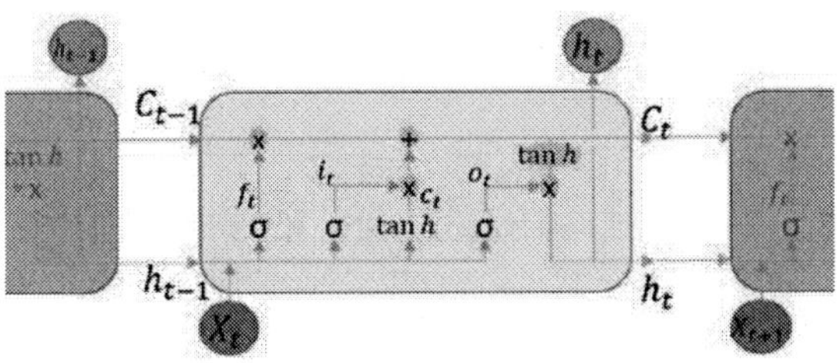

Figure 4: 長短期記憶網路

在 Figure 4 中，X_t 先經過遺忘閘，透過加權矩陣W_f和激活函數σ對上一時間的輸出與當下輸入的運算，來控制細胞狀態丟棄的資訊量。接著透過輸入閘來決定細胞狀態應該取得的新資訊，此部分有兩個步驟，第一步先由 sigmoid function 決定要更新的值。第二步通過 tanh function 決定細胞狀態的候選值c_t。得到遺忘閘與輸入閘的運算結果後，來對細胞狀態進行更新。其中前項以遺忘閘結果和舊的細胞狀態相乘決定要遺忘的資訊，後項由輸入閘結果與候選值相乘決定細胞狀態的新資訊，將兩者相加後即代表更新後的新細胞狀態。最後決定要輸出的值。由輸出閘決定要輸出多少資訊，再將細胞狀態透過 tanh function 與輸出閘結果相乘，計算出此細胞的輸出值。

$$f_t = \sigma(W_f \cdot [X_t, h_{t-1}] + b_f) \tag{1}$$
$$i_t = \sigma(W_i \cdot [X_t, h_{t-1}] + b_i) \tag{2}$$
$$c_t = tanh(W_c \cdot [X_t, h_{t-1}] + b_c) \tag{3}$$
$$C_t = f_t \times C_{t-1} + i_t \times c_t \tag{4}$$
$$o_t = \sigma(W_o \cdot [X_t, h_{t-1}] + b_o) \tag{5}$$
$$h_t = o_t \times tanh(C_t) \tag{6}$$

5 Experiment Settings and Results

本研究將數據利用 Root Mean Square normalization 進行數據歸一化，接著計算與分類各情緒中檔案個數。接著按照情緒分類，將 535 筆資料建立 20%為訓練集、64% 為測試集與 16% 的驗證集。，因為音檔轉換後的資料長度不一，最長 143652，最短為 19608，因此需要進行填補資料。於是我們將經歸一化的音頻數據進行切割，將一個音頻數據根據固定長度 (16000) 切割成數筆資料，最後不足的部分，進行補 0。最後可以每一個音頻可以形成 2 維資料以作為 CNN+LSTM 模型的輸入。

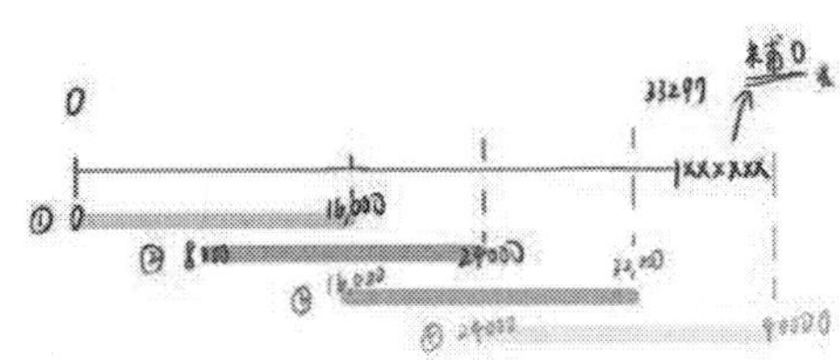

Figure 5: 音檔切割示意圖

本研究所提出的情緒識別模型是由四層 CNN、一層 LSTM 加上全連接層所建構而成。CNN 中含有 一維卷積層、批量標準化層、激活函數層、最大池化層。其中激活函數使用 Elu function(exponential linear unit)。對比 ReLu，Elu 可讓負的輸入值也有輸出值，相對較穩健。而 LSTM 中激活函數為 tanh function，編譯層中使用優化方式為SGD，其參數 momentum 用於 SGD 在相關方面上前進，抑制震盪，nesterov = True 表使用 Nesterov 動量。於訓練集使用 EarlyStopping 於出現過擬合或模型指標無明顯改進時提前中止訓練;利用 ModelCheckpoint 於每個訓練期後保存模型。實驗結果顯示以七種情緒進行識別，其情緒識別正確率為 57.83%，若改以四種情緒共 339 筆資料進行訓練及預測，則情緒識別正確率為 83%。

此外，本研究亦使用傳統類神經網路(neural network, NN) 進行情緒識別，輸入資料為 1 維資料 (原本 2 維資料藉由 flatten function 轉換為 1 維資料)。藉由不同的測試資料比例，可以看出傳統 NN 模型在測試資料集比例為 20% 時，得到最佳的辨識正確率，七種情緒辨識正確率為 53.30%，而四種情緒辨識正確率為 77.90%。

		全部（七種）情緒		四種情緒
test_size = 0.2	test	0.533	test	0.779
	random	0.477	random	0.765
test_size = 0.3	test	0.497	test	0.716
	random	0.491	random	0.676
test_size = 0.4	test	0.495	test	0.699
	random	0.519	random	0.706

Figure 6: 音檔切割示意圖

最後本研究僅使用 CNN 跟 LSTM 模型進行情緒識別，實驗結果顯示以七種情緒進行識別，其情緒識別正確率 CNN 模型為 45.80%，而 LSTM 模型情緒識別正確率為 50.50%。

6 Discussion

經過不同模型測試後，本研究發現在僅四種情緒的訓練及測試情況下，情緒辨識正確率明顯較高於七種情緒辨識正確率，我們認為可能原因為以下兩點：四種情緒間差異性較大及全部筆數較少無法有足夠的樣本進行訓練。若能再增加較多的樣本進行訓練及測試，應能提升情緒辨識正確率。

Table 2: 情緒識別正確率

Model	7 種情緒	4 種情緒
NN	53.30%	77.90%
CNN	45.80%	-
LSTM	50.50%	-
CNN+LSTM	**57.83%**	**83.00%**

7 Conclusion

本研究使用 CNN+LSTM 模型實作語音情緒辨識 (Speech Emotion Recognition, SER) 處理並進行預測。從實驗結果得知使用 CNN+LSTM 模型相對於使用傳統 NN 模型取得更好的效能。

未來可能嘗試的改進方法為將其他關於情緒辨識之開放資料與此 EMO-DB 資料共同進行訓練，可供訓練樣本增加可能會使準確度提升；另外，在資料前處理的部分對音訊嘗試進行更妥善的數據前處理方式以及不同的轉換方式測試，如傅立葉轉換等。

References

[1] Paul Ekman. 1992. An argument for basic emotions. *Cognition & emotion*, 6(3-4): 169-200, 1992.

[2] Paul Ekman, Wallace V. Friesen, and Ronald C. Simons. 1985. Is the startle reaction an emotion? *Journal of personality and social psychology*, 49(5): 1416.

[3] Robert Plutchik. 1980. *A general psychoevolutionary theory of emotion*, Chapter 1 in Theories of emotion: Elsevier, pages 3-33.

[4] Jonathan Posner, James A. Russell, and Bradley S. Peterson. 2005. The circumplex model of affect: An integrative approach to affective neuroscience, cognitive development, and psychopathology. *Development and psychopathology*, 17(3): 715-734.

[5] K. Sreenivasa Rao, Shashidhar G. Koolagudi, and Ramu Reddy Vempada. 2013. Emotion recognition from speech using global and local prosodic features. *International journal of speech technology*, 16(2): 143-160.

[6] Houwei Cao, Štefan Beňuš, Ruben C. Gur, Ragini Verma, and Ani Nenkova. 2014. Prosodic cues for emotion: analysis with discrete characterization of intonation. *Speech prosody*, 130-134.

[7] Namrata Anand and Prateek Verma. 2015. Convoluted feelings convolutional and recurrent nets for detecting emotion from audio data. In *Technical Report*: Stanford University.

[8] Tzinis, Efthymios, and Alexandras Potamianos. 2017. Segment-based speech emotion recognition using recurrent neural networks. In *Proceedings of the 2017 Seventh International Conference on Affective Computing and Intelligent Interaction (ACII)*. IEEE, pages 190-195. https://doi.org/10.1109/ACII.2017.8273599.

[9] Lianzhang Zhu, Leiming Chen, Dehai Zhao, Jiehan Zhou, and Weishan Zhang. 2017. Emotion recognition from Chinese speech for smart affective services using a combination of SVM and DBN. *Sensors*, 17(7): 1694.

[10] George Trigeorgis, Fabien Ringeval, Raymond Brueckner, Erik Marchi, Mihalis A. Nicolaou, Björn Schuller, and Stefanos Zafeiriou. 2016. Adieu features? end-to-end speech emotion recognition using a deep convolutional recurrent network. In *Proceedings of 2016 IEEE international conference on acoustics, speech and signal processing (ICASSP)*. IEEE, pages 5200-5204. https://doi.org/10.1109/ICASSP.2016.7472669.

[11] Jun Deng, Sascha Frühholz, Zixing Zhang, and Björn Schuller. 2017. Recognizing emotions from whispered speech based on acoustic feature transfer learning. *IEEE Access*, 5:5235-5246.

[12] Che-Wei Huang, and Shrikanth Shri Narayana. 2017. Deep convolutional recurrent neural network with attention mechanism for robust speech emotion recognition. In *Proceedings of 2017 IEEE International Conference on Multimedia and Expo (ICME)*. IEEE, pages 583-588. https://doi.org/10.1109/ICME.2017.8019296.

[13] Kim, Suyoun, and Michael L. Seltzer. 2018. Towards language-universal end-to-end speech recognition. In *Proceedings of 2018 IEEE International Conference on Acoustics, Speech and Signal Processing (ICASSP)*. IEEE, pages 4914-4918. https://doi.org/10.1109/ICASSP.2018.8462201.

[14] Kun-Yi Huang, Chung-Hsien Wu, Qian-Bei Hong, Ming-Hsiang Su, and Yi-Hsuan Chen. 2019. Speech emotion recognition using deep neural network considering verbal and nonverbal speech sounds. In *Proceedings of IEEE International Conference on Acoustics, Speech and Signal Processing (ICASSP)*. IEEE, pages 5866-5870. https://doi.org/10.1109/ICASSP.2019.8682283.

[15] Felix Burkhardt, Astrid Paeschke, M. Rolfes, Walter F. Sendlmeier, and Benjamin Weiss. 2005. A database of German emotional speech. In *Proceedings of Ninth European conference on speech communication and technology*.

[16] Hubel, David H., and Torsten N. Wiesel. 1962. Receptive fields, binocular interaction and functional architecture in the cat's visual cortex. *The Journal of Physiology*, 160(1): 106-154.

[17] Fukushima, Kunihiko, and Sei Miyake. 1982. Neocognitron: A Self-Organizing Neural Network Model for a Mechanism of Visual Pattern Recognition. In *Proceedings of Competition and Cooperation in Neural Nets*, Springer Berlin Heidelberg, pages 267-285. https://doi.org/10.1007/978-3-642-46466-9_18.

[18] Shih-Chung B. Lo, Heang-Ping Chan, Jyh-Shyan Lin, Huai Li, Matthew T. Freedman, and Seong K.Mun. 1995. Artificial convolution neural network for medical image pattern recognition. *Neural Networks*, 8(7): 1201-1214.

[19] LeCun, Yann, Léon Bottou, Yoshua Bengio, and Patrick Haffner. 1998. Gradient-based learning applied to document recognition. In *Proceedings of the IEEE*, 86(11): 2278-2324. https://doi.org/10.1109/5.726791.

[20] Hochreiter, Sepp, and Jürgen Schmidhuber. 1997. Long short-term memory. *Neural computation*, 9(8): 1735-1780.

The 33rd Conference on Computational Linguistics and Speech Processing (ROCLING 2021)
Taoyuan, Taiwan, October 15-16, 2021. The Association for Computational Linguistics and Chinese Language Processing

A Study on Contextualized Language Modeling for Machine Reading Comprehension (上下文語言模型化技術於閱讀理解之研究)

吳沁穎 Chin-Ying Wu
國立臺灣師範大學資訊工程學系
Department of Computer Science and Information Engineering
National Taiwan Normal University
elain1224@gmail.com

許永昌 Yung-Chang Hsu
易晨智能股份有限公司
mic@ez-ai.com.tw

陳柏琳 Berlin Chen
國立臺灣師範大學資訊工程學系
Department of Computer Science and Information Engineering
National Taiwan Normal University
berlin@ntnu.edu.tw

摘要

隨著深度學習的發展，機器閱讀理解的研究已有了長足的進步，並在許多實際應用情境上展露頭角。機器閱讀理解是一項用於評估機器對語言的理解能力的自然語言處理任務，其形式為：給定文章段落與相關問題，電腦自動根據文章段落與相關問題來進行回答。本研究嘗試使用兩種以 BERT 為基礎的預訓練語言模型：BERT-wwm 和 MacBERT，發展能夠達到更佳預測表現的機器閱讀理解方法。此外，考慮到閱讀理解中的文章類型可能對於回答模式有潛在影響，我們針對訓練資料集的文章段落進行分群，以此做作為額外資訊結合到語言模型的輸入。另一方面，我們也探索使用集成學習法來結合上述兩種預訓練語言模型，以進一步提升機器閱讀理解的表現。

Abstract

With the recent breakthrough of deep learning technologies, research on machine reading comprehension (MRC) has attracted much attention and found its versatile applications in many use cases. MRC is an important natural language processing (NLP) task aiming to assess the ability of a machine to understand natural language expressions, which is typically operationalized by first asking questions based on a given text paragraph and then receiving machine-generated answers in accordance with the given context paragraph and questions. In this paper, we leverage two novel pretrained language models built on top of Bidirectional Encoder Representations from Transformers (BERT), namely BERT-wwm and MacBERT, to develop effective MRC methods. In addition, we also seek to investigate whether additional incorporation of the categorical information about a context paragraph can benefit MRC or not, which is achieved based on performing context paragraph clustering on the training dataset. On the other hand, an ensemble learning approach is proposed to harness the synergistic power of the aforementioned two BERT-based models so as to further promote MRC performance.

關鍵字：深度學習、自然語言處理、機器閱讀理解、語言模型

Keywords: Deep Learning, Natural Language Processing, Machine Reading Comprehension, Language model

文章段落：
新北市的人口眾多，市區的交通流量十分龐大。每逢尖峰時段或假日，經常會有大量人潮、車潮流動於市區內或臺北、新北兩市之間，導致市區內各重要幹道常出現交通阻塞的情形。……
問題：
新北市的交通流量龐大的狀況與何有關？
可能回答：
人口眾多

圖 1、閱讀理解問題範例

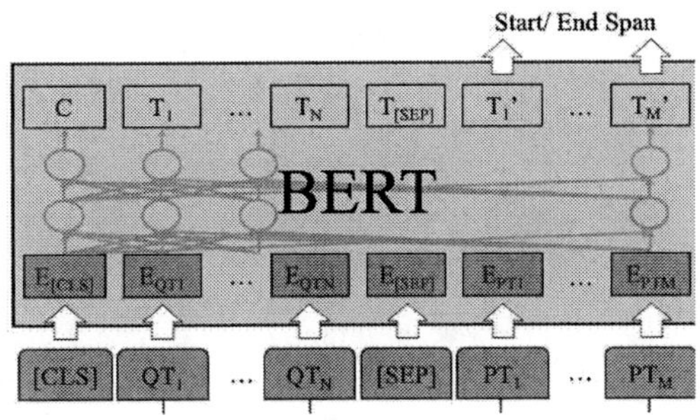

圖 2、BERT 在閱讀理解任務之應用示意圖

1 緒論

隨著各領域的文本數據大量產生，傳統的人工處理方式受限於速度、人力成本等因素使其逐漸成為產業發展的瓶頸；與此同時，能自動分析文本，並且從中抽取語意知識的機器閱讀理解 (Machine reading comprehension, MRC) 技術也漸漸開始受到關注。機器閱讀理解的主要應用的方向為：在既有的文本中查詢目標知識。例如：自動客服，可以從產品相關說明資料中找到與用戶描述相符的部分並給出詳細解答；在醫療領域，模型可以根據患者的症狀描述自動查詢大量病例與醫療論文，尋找相關的資訊與診療方式。舉凡需要分析大量文本的任務，都能夠以機器閱讀理解模型進行協助。

機器閱讀理解是一個典型的自然語言處理任務，用以評估機器對於語言的理解能力。任務的進行方法為：給定一段文章段落與一個相關的問題，機器需要根據文章進行回答。；此篇著重在段落擷取 (Span Extraction) 的類型，亦即，在任務中，模型在需要從給定的文章中擷取一個段落作為回答。範例如圖 1。

過去傳統的類神經網路架構是由多個不同功能的模組構成，研究的主軸在於如何運用注意力機制 (Attention-based) 讓模型取得更豐富的文章段落與問題之間的交互關係，例如：Attention Sum (Kadlec et al. 2016), Gated attention (Dhingra et al. 2017), Self-matching (Wang et al. 2017), Attention over Attention (Cui et al. 2017) Bi-attention (Seo et al. 2016) 。近年來，由於預訓練語言模型 (Pre-trained language model) 的出現，例如 ELMo (Peters et al. 2018) 、GPT (Radford et al. 2018) 、BERT (Devlin et al. 2019) ，使得機器閱讀理解中相當大一部分的模組功能都可以以此取代，並且因其具有更加豐富的語意資訊，使得後續模型皆以預訓練語言模型作為主幹進行研究。

本篇研究使用了兩個基於 Bidirectional Encoder Representations from Transformers (BERT) (Devlin et al., 2019) 架構的預訓練語言模型：BERT - Whole Word Masking (BERT-wwm) (Yiming Cui et al. 2019)、Masked As Correction BERT (Mac-BERT) (Yiming Cui et al. 2020)，兩者皆為針對中文語言特性提出的模型。使用的資料集為兩個機器閱讀理解資料集：簡體中文的 CMRC (Cui et al., 2019) 與繁體中文的 DRCD (Shao et al., 2018)。實驗有兩個主要的提升模型表現的方向。首先，考慮到資料集中的標題資訊可能帶有一些資訊，且可能對於回答模式有潛在影響，故利用此對所有文章進行分群 (Clustering) ，並以分群的結果作為額外資訊結合到語言模型的輸入，再以相同的方式重新訓練模型。最後一個部分，由於前述兩個語言模型都已經能達到一定的成果，故使用一個相對較簡單、快速的模型增進方法：集成學習法 (Ensemble Learning Method) ，將對於兩個模型的預測分數進行平均，以獲得更佳的結果。

2 相關研究

2.1 語言模型

由於語言模型有著可以提供更豐富的詞彙關聯性資訊、降低模型架構成本等優勢，在自

Strategies	Example
Original Sentence	使用語言模型來預測下一個詞的頻率。
+ BERT Tokenizer	使 用 語 言 模 型 來 預 測 下 一 個 詞 的 頻 率 。
+ CWS	使用 語言 模型 來 預測 下一個 詞 的 頻率 。
Original Masking	使用語言 [M] 型來[M] 測下一個詞的頻率。
+ WWM	使用語言 [M] [M] 來[M] [M] 下一個詞的頻率。
++ N-gram masking	使用[M] [M] [M] [M] 來 [M] [M] 下一個詞的頻率。
+++ Mac masking	使用語法建模來預見下一個詞的頻率。

表 1、不同切分策略與遮蓋策略示意圖。“+”代表沿用前述策略設定。

然語言處理的任務常選擇加入語言模型輔助以增進表現。近年來，預訓練的深層類神經網路語言模型，如 ELMo (Peters et al., 2018)、GPT (Radford et al., 2018)、BERT (Devlin et al., 2019) 等模型陸續被提出。這類的模型預先在其他相關的任務上以大量資料訓練，再將所學知識遷移到新的任務。如此一來，除了可以克服目標任務資料不足的問題，也能利用學到的知識提高目標模型的準確度。歸功於這些優點，預訓練的語言模型在各個自然語言處理領域都取得顯著的進展。其中，BERT 模型是最被廣泛運用在不同任務上的語言模型之一。BERT 運用 Transformer (Radford et al., 2018) 的自注意力機制 (Self-attention mechanism) 學習文本中單詞之間的上下文關係，並且由於其雙向進行的特性，使得上文與下文的資訊能更充分地被使用。BERT 在當時最知名的英文閱讀理解任務：SQuAD (Rajpurkar et al., 2016) 上展現了這方面的能力，不僅超越了當時所有的類神經網路模型，也改變了機器閱讀理解領域的研究模式，使得目前的模型大多是使用預訓練語言模型為主幹的方法。

2.2 機器閱讀理解

隨著資料集的發佈，機器閱讀理解開始受到越來越多研究者的關注。傳統類神經網路架構的機器閱讀理解模型可以分為四個核心模組，轉換文字為表徵的模組 (embedding)、特徵抽取模組 (feature extraction) 、文章段落與問題交互關係模組 (context-question interaction) 及預測答案模組 (answer prediction)。早期的研究趨勢在於文章段落與問題之間的交互關係，主要以基於注意力機制作為研究重點。研究包括 Attention Sum (Kadlec et al., 2016)、Gated attention (Dhingra et al. 2017)、Self-matching (Wang et al., 2017)、Attention over Attention (Cui et al., 2017)、Bi-attention (Seo et al., 2016) 等。近年來，預訓練語言模型陸續提出，由於其具備的豐富資訊，使得上述前三個模組的功能，都得以用一個預訓練語言模型就完全囊括。因此，預訓練的語言模型逐漸取代過去的注意力機制模型，開始作為機器閱讀理解模型的主要結構，並且在最近幾年取得了非常優秀的成果。這些預訓練語言模型包括 ELMo (Peters et al., 2018)、GPT (Radford et al., 2018)、BERT (Devlin et al., 2019)、XLNet (Yang et al., 2019)、RoBERTa (Liu et al., 2019)、ALBERT (Lan et al., 2020)、ELECTRA (Clark et al., 2020)。

3 研究方法

本研究主要探討 BERT 與兩種針對中文的語言模型：BERT-wwm (Yiming Cui et al. 2019)、MacBERT (Yiming Cui et al. 2020) 在閱讀理解任務上的表現，將分為三個部分進行。第一個部分，分別對三種語言模型進行最基本的微調。第二個部分，實驗目標是更有效利用文章的類別性質，故將資料集中的標題資訊作為分群基準，並將分群資訊加入模型的輸入端重新訓練模型。最後一個部分是集成模型，合併兩個模型的結果以提昇表現。

3.1 BERT

BERT 為由 Google 提出的預訓練語言模型，全名為 Bidirectional Encoder Representations from Transformers。主要架構為 Transformers 的編碼器 (Encoder)，使用 Masked Language model (MLM) 與 Next Sentence Prediction (NSP) 作為

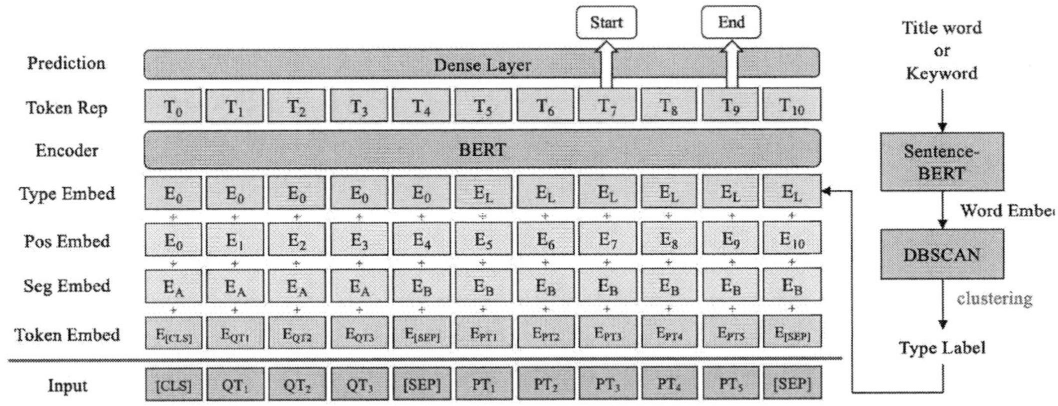

圖 3、文章標題分群與模型輸入整合之流程示意圖

訓練方式。句子在輸入模型後會切割句子，並以 tokenizer 轉換成以詞為單位的 token 序列；其中，MLM 是以特殊 token：[MASK] 隨機遮蔽 (Masking) 掉原始的 token 並進行遮蔽位置單詞的預測，目的是讓機器學習使用僅剩的上下文資訊推測目標 token 適合填入的單詞。此篇用的是同樣由 Google 提出的中文版的 BERT，使用的訓練語料為中文的維基百科文章，並且在所有文字間填入空格以利切分。切分前後狀態可參考表 1。

本實驗預計對模型進行微調，以建構成適合用於機器閱讀理解的模式。如圖 2 所示，首先將資料集中的一個問題與對應文章進行串接，前端會加入辨識輸出位置的特殊 token：[CLS]，兩段段文字之間則有 [SEP]，用以區別文章與問題。此串 token 序列作為模型的輸入，BERT 模型會根據每個 token 的資訊生成一個對應此 token 的表徵 (representation)，並依此算出文章中每個單詞適合作為起點和終點的機率。令 $\mathbf{T}_i$ 為 BERT 生成的第 i 個 token 的表徵，$\mathbf{S} \in \mathbb{R}^h$ 為起始點向量 (start vector)，其中 h 代表 token 表徵的大小。則起始機率可以表示為下列公式。

$$P_i = \frac{e^{S \cdot T_i}}{\sum_j e^{S \cdot T_j}} \quad (1)$$

終點機率算法概念相同。損失函數的計算為起點與終點的交叉熵損失 (cross-entropy loss) 平均值。模型最終會輸出根據起點與終點的一段文章段落。

3.2 BERT-wwm

BERT-wwm (Yiming Cui et al. 2019) 全名為 BERT - whole word masking，是考慮中文語言特性的 BERT 延伸模型。最早的 BERT 是使用英文作為訓練語料，以空格為基準所切分，切分出的英文單字是具有完整的意義的最基本單位，並以此作為遮蓋的單位；BERT 在運用到中文版本上時，會預先在所有字之間加入空格，再以字為單位進行切分，這也是訓練時的遮蓋的單位。然而，儘管字並非無意義，卻不一定會與中文使用者解讀句子的意思吻合。故以字作為單位訓練時，可能會產生一些誤差。考慮到中文的語言特性，BERT-wwm 在切分詞時使用 LTP (Che et al., 2010) 作為切分中文的工具 (Chinese Word Segmentation, CWS)，並以實際用於解讀意義的全詞作為 MLM 訓練時的遮蓋單位，用以接近中文在使用時的情境。實際使用情境與 BERT tokenizer 的比較可參考表 1 的範例。

3.3 MacBERT

MacBERT (Yiming Cuil et al. 2020) 全名為 Masked As Correction BERT，是另一個考慮中文語言特性的 BERT 延伸版本。在 MLM 的訓練任務上，除了沿用 BERT-wwm 的以全詞為單位訓練的概念之外，還修改了兩個部分的設定。首先，在選取欲被遮蓋的部分，以 N-gram masked 取代隨機遮蓋，先取得候選的 token，再從中選擇遮蓋目標。其次，更改遮

Dataset	Title	Paragraph
DRCD	函數	函數在數學中為兩集合間的一種對應關係：輸入值集合中的每項元素皆能對應唯一一項輸出值集合中的元素。氣溫的分布也能用函數表達，以時間和地點作為參量輸入…
CMRC	国际初中科学奥林匹克	国际初中科学奥林匹克（International Junior Science Olympiad）是一项给予 15 岁或以下的学生参与的国际科学比赛。此比赛最先在 2004 年举办，然后一年举办一次。…

表 2、資料集之文章段落與對應標題範例

蔽的內容，針對目標 token 先以 word2vec (Tomas Mikolov et al., 2013) 計算相似度以獲得相似的單詞，並且用此相似詞進行遮蓋，可以減少因為 [MASK] 只在預訓練使用而不會出現在微調階段所造成的差異，也可以藉此讓模型學到更多的相似詞與上下文之間的關係。遮蓋策略比較可參考表 1 的範例。

3.4 資料集分群與輸入整合

考慮到文章的類型可能會對於文章回答的形式有潛在的影響，故決定加入文章類型資訊。由於資料集中的文章沒有人工標記類別，此處根據資料集中既有的文章標題以及從文章取出的重要單詞等兩種來源作為依據進行分群，取得類似分類的資訊，將此資訊加入到模型中以提升表現。上述流程與模型架構如圖 3 所示。加入方式為新增一個 type token，於輸入 BERT 模型前將加入到所有 token 中。

其中，keyword 的取得方法為將全文進行分詞，取得每篇文章各自的詞庫後，再以 Term Frequency-Inverse Document Frequency (TF-IDF) 計算單詞重要性，最終取分數較高者作為此處輸入的內容。TF-IDF 包含兩個部分，詞頻 (Term Frequency, TF) 與逆向文件頻率 (Inverse Document Frequency, IDF)。其中 TF 表示單詞於單一文章中的出現頻率，IDF 表示單詞在整個資料集中出現過的文章數量，TF-IDF 則為兩者相乘。公式如下。

$$TF_{i,j} = \frac{n_{i,j}}{\sum_k n_{k,j}} \quad (2)$$

$$IDF_i = \log\frac{N}{n_i} \quad (3)$$

$$TFIDF_{i,j} = TF_{i,j} \times IDF_i \quad (4)$$

	Title#	Paragraph#	Question#
DRCD	2,108	10,014	30K
CMRC	3,251	3,251	20K

表 3、資料集之標題、文章、問題數量比較

上式中 TF 的 $n_{i,j}$ 為單詞 i 於文章 d_j 中的出現次數，分母為文章 d_j 中所有單詞的出現次數總和。 IDF 中的 N 為整個資料集的文章總數量，n_i 則為文章中包含文字 i 的文章數目。

前段得出分群根據的文字 (keyword) 與標題 (title word) 的後續方法相同。首先，利用 sentence-BERT (Nils Reimers and Iryna Gurevych, 2019) 取得標題或 keyword 的詞嵌入 (Word embedding)，再以基於密度的聚類演算法方法：DBSCAN (Density-based spatial clustering) (Martin Ester et.al., 1996) 分出數個相似度較高的群集。其中，只會將有一定數量的聚類識別為一個組別，在一定範圍內數量不足以構成組別的的離群值 (outlier) 將會被標記為雜訊 (noise)。

分組的結果會做為額外資訊提供給模型，並且作為 BERT 的輸入資訊之一整合在模型中。加入的方式如圖 3 所示，在 BERT 的輸入層中添加一層 Type Embed ，並在對應到的文章上進行組別標記，其中，被標記為離群值的部分會以 0 加入，等同於不加入任何額外資訊。

後續實驗步驟與一般閱讀理解任務相同，即 BERT 模型進行微調，預測出機率最高的起點與終點。可參考圖 2。

3.5 集成學習 (Ensemble Method)

集成學習指結合多個模型的結果來提升整體表現。段落擷取類型的閱讀理解模型最終會對文章中的每個詞進行兩種預測，分別為適

	Type	Title word	1 keyword	2 keywords
DRCD	Outlier	657	768	346
	Big group	1,097	5,105	8483
	Small group	10 ~ 193 (19)	10 ~ 436 (75)	10 ~ 40 (7)
CMRC	Outlier	810	678	591
	Big group	2,035	2,117	2453
	Small group	9 ~116 (14)	10 ~ 43 (26)	10 ~ 29 (12)

表 4、分群組別數量與樣本數量分佈結果，表格中數字代表樣本數，括弧為組數

合作為起點的機率以及適合作為終點的機率。每組機率值都會對應到文章內容並擷取起點與終點所對應的句子。使用單模型時取用機率最高的句子作為解答。使用兩個以上的模型結果時，將列出所有可能的預測句子，句子完全相同者對機率進行平均，不同者沿用單模型的機率作為新的句子候選。最終，再選出新的句子候選中機率最高者作為集成模型的輸出。

4 實驗結果與討論

4.1 實驗材料

本篇採用兩個公開的數據集：台達閱讀理解資料集 (Delta Reading Comprehension Dataset, DRCD) (Shao et al., 2018) 與訊飛杯中文機器閱讀理解評測 (The Third Evaluation Workshop on Chinese Machine Reading Comprehension, CMRC) (Cui et al., 2019)。兩者皆為段落擷取類型機器閱讀理解資料集，其訓練資料都來源於維基百科。其中，前者為繁體中文，包含 2,108 個主題 (Title) 的 10,014 個文章段落 (Paragraph)，以及三萬多個問題 (Query)；後者為簡體中文，包含 3251 個文章段落及兩萬多個問題。

在資料集分群的實驗，採用資料集中的文章主題名稱作為分群根據，主題與文章段落的關係可參考表 2。實驗用的兩個資料集在這部分有些差異：DRCD 的每個主題對應到多篇數量不等的文章段落；CMRC 則是一個主題只會對應到一篇文章。可參考表 3 的標題、文章以及問題的數量比較。另外，在以內容關鍵字作為分群依據的部分，則是用每篇文章的內容進行分詞與擷取，每篇文章都有對應的分群結果。

4.2 實驗設定

取得分群資訊的部分，使用 JIEBA 中文斷詞工具對目標文章進行分詞以取得 keyword，並且由於慣用語的不同，使用 JIEBA 的官方簡體中文字典與中央研究院資訊科學所繁體詞庫分別作為簡體中文與繁體中文的分詞依據；DBSCAN 分群中，title 與 keyword 的設定相同。兩點可作為鄰近點的最大距離閾值 (eps)為 3，每個群集中必須要有的最小鄰近點數量(min samples) 為 10。BERT 微調訓練的參數設定的部分，模型 learning rate 為 5e-5，訓練 batch size 為 32、training epoch 為 3；文字處理設定的部分，文章的最大長度為 384 個文字、問題的最大長度為 64 個文字、預測答案的最大長度為 30 個字。在文章與問題中，大於限制者會捨去超出字數的文字，小於限制者則會填空至此長度。

4.3 評估指標

採用 Exact match (EM) 與 F1-Score 兩種指標進行評估。EM 著重於預測回答與標準答案的完全匹配程度，有助於當正確答案為一個短句或單字時的回答精準度。例如，一個閱讀理解任務包括 N 個問題，每個問題對應的正確答案只有一個，此輪中回答正確的題數為 M 題。則完全匹配的回答數為 M 個，剩餘的 N-M 個為不完全匹配。不完全匹配包括與標準答案部分匹配的回答與完全無關的回答，其公式如下。

$$Exact\ Match = \frac{M}{N} \tag{5}$$

F1-Score 主要用來評估預測回答與標準答案的重合程度，相對於精準匹配值較具有彈性。

		DRCD		CMRC	
		EM (%)	F1	EM (%)	F1
Fine-tune	BERT	85.600	0.917	60.298	0.840
	BERT-wwm	85.686	0.921	61.479	0.844
	MacBERT	88.606	0.938	63.156	0.856
Add Clustering Info.	BERT-wwm				
	+ Title Label	85.377	0.919	61.819	0.844
	+ 1 Keyword Label	85.680	0.917	61.912	0.847
	+ 2 Keyword Labels	85.834	0.920	61.484	0.842
	MacBERT				
	+ Title Label	88.405	0.937	63.591	0.856
	+ 1 Keyword Label	88.262	0.936	63.778	0.855
	+ 2 Keyword Labels	88.892	0.940	63.156	0.858
Ensemble	MacBERT + BERT-wwm	88.663	0.938	64.461	0.864
	The two best model	**89.207**	**0.942**	**65.238**	**0.862**

表 5、使用 BERT-wwm、MacBERT、MacBERT 加入分群資訊及兩者集成的實驗結果。表中底線代表集成學習以外的方法中，表現較佳的兩個模型，亦為用於後續集成學習實驗；表中粗體代表表現最佳的分數

F1-Score 以準確率 (Accuracy) 和召回率 (Recall) 的調和平均數得出。公式如下。

$$precision = \frac{TP}{TP+FP} \quad (6)$$

$$recall = \frac{TP}{TP+FN} \quad (7)$$

$$F_1 = 2 \cdot \frac{precision \cdot recall}{precision + recall} \quad (8)$$

圖中的 TP、TN、FP、FN 分別代表四種可能的預測情況。True Positive (TP) 為將正確為預測為正確的情況；True Negative (TN) 為將錯誤預測為錯誤的情況；False Positive (FP) 為將錯誤預測為正確的情況；False Negative (FN) 為將正確預測為錯誤的情況。

4.4 分群結果

分群結果可參考表 4。根據分群後的狀態不同，將這些分群組別分成三種類型：離群值 (outlier)、一個大組別 (Big group) 與數個小組別 (Small group)。離群值指的是和其他文章相關性較低，或是存在相關性高的文章，但是其數量總和遠不足以構成一個新組別的文章樣本；大組別和小組別的區分主要是組內的樣本數量。根據實驗結果的觀察，資料集中都會有一個組別特別大，囊括了超過三分之一的文章類型，剩餘的文章分布則是數個具有一定樣本數的小組別。

標題分群的部分， DRCD 的離群值樣本數為 657 個，大組別的樣本數 1,097 個，小組別則是有 19 組，樣本數量分佈在 10 ~ 193 個。CMRC 的離群值樣本數為 810 ，大組別樣本數為 2,035，其餘共有 14 個小組別，樣本數分別分佈在 9 ~ 116。

在文章關鍵字分群的部分，分成只取一個和兩個關鍵字作為分群基準，以避免過多文字產生過多雜訊而造成分群效果不佳的情況。在取一個關鍵字分群的部分，DRCD 的離群值樣本數為 768 個，大組別的樣本數 5,105 個，小組別則是有 75 組，樣本數量分佈在 10 ~ 436 個。 CMRC 的離群值樣本數為 678 ，大組別樣本數為 2,117，其餘共有 26 個小組別，樣本數分別分佈在 10 ~ 43。取兩個關鍵字分群的部分，DRCD 的離群值樣本數為 346 個，大組別的樣本數 8,483 個，小組別則是有 7 組，樣本數量分佈在 10 ~ 40 個。CMRC 的離群值樣本數為 591 ，大組別樣本數為 2,453，其餘共有 12 個小組別，樣本數分別分佈在 10 ~ 29。

4.5 實驗結果

本篇實驗微調了 BERT 、 BERT-wwm 及 MacBERT 作為基線進行比較，如表 5 的前三

列，主要實驗為加入分群資訊與集成模型的兩個實驗。

加上分群資訊的部分，可參考表 5 中的 Add clustering info.的欄位。兩個 Bert-based 的模型加上標題資訊進行模型的重新訓練，並與原本的微調結果作比較。在微調表現較佳的 MacBERT 的實驗部分，差距主要在 EM 上，F1-Score 的變化不大。在加入標題資訊（+ Title Label）的方面， DRCD 資料集的 EM 微幅下降了 0.201 個百分點；在 CMRC 資料集的部分，EM 提高了 0.435 個百分點。在加入標題的實驗中，CMRC 的 EM 獲得提升，代表文章標題與內文關鍵字的資訊分類確實對模型有一定的幫助；在 DRCD 的表現卻差強人意，其原因可能是作為最初作為分群的標題資訊量不足所造成。DRCD 與 CMRC 在標題資訊上最大的差異是在於標題與文章的形式；DRCD 是多篇文章共用一個較大的標題；CMRC 則是一個文章對應一個標題不同，可能因此輸入了不足以代表文章內容的資訊，使得引入的雜訊影響原本的判斷，進而造成模型表現下降。

根據前述原因，使用了全文的斷詞並取出關鍵字（+ Keyword Label) 進行分群，此設定可以確保用於分群的資訊與文章內容是相關且具有一定重要程度的。實驗結果的部分，DRCD 在加入一個關鍵字的 EM 下降了 0.334 個百分點，但是加入兩個關鍵字時，提升了 0.286 個百分點；CMRC 加入一個關鍵字有 0.662 個百分點的提升，加入兩個則沒有變化。兩個資料集的實驗結果各有不同。DRCD 加入一個關鍵字的表現略差於兩個關鍵字的原因，可能是只使用一個關鍵字不足以代表整篇文章，分類資訊反而使表現下降。CMRC 則是在用一個關鍵字時有最佳的效果。BERT-wwm 的表現變化的趨勢與 MacBERT 相似。詳細數據可見表 5。另外，由於兩個資料集在不同數量 keyword 的分群數量表現變化差異較大，故此處不針對加入 keyword 數量造成的影響做探討。可參考表 4。

集成學習部分的結果，可參考表 5 的 ensemble 欄位。此處分成兩個實驗進行，結果將與兩個集成前的模型做比較，主要觀察是否比原先的模型有更佳的表現。首先是僅經過微調的預訓練模型集成學習，在 DRCD 資料集的實驗上，相較於原先就表現較佳的 MacBERT 微調結果，EM 提高了 0.063 個百分點，F1-Score 也有 0.011 個百分點的微幅進步。在 CMRC 實驗的部分，進步表現較為顯著，EM 提高了 1.305 個百分點，F1-Score 也有 0.843 個百分點的進步。另外，第二個部分是從前述的微調與加入分群資訊結果中，分別挑出最佳的兩個結果進行集成學習。DRCD 實驗結果中，選擇的是微調的 MacBERT 與加入兩個關鍵字的 MacBERT 模型，其 EM 結果相較於集成前的分數有 0.601 和 0.315 個百分點的進步，F1-Score 也有微幅提升；CMRC 的實驗中，選擇的是加入標題的 MacBERT 與加入一個關鍵字的 MacBERT 模型，其 EM 分別有 1.647 和 1.46 個百分點的進步，F1-Score 也有平均 0.0065 的提升。集成模型作為一個相對較簡單快速方法，也在此處讓模型預測進步方面達到了不錯的效果。

5 結論

本篇研究使用兩種基於 BERT 的語言模型：BERT-wwm 以及 MacBERT，分別在繁體中文語簡體中文的兩個機器閱讀理解任務上進行微調、加入分群資訊重新訓練與模型集成等實驗。加入分群資訊實驗的部分，兩個資料集的分群資訊皆讓模型學到與文章類型相關的潛在回答模式，使預測結果有所提升；在集成模型的部分，歸功於兩種預訓練語言模型的基礎能力，其合併預測結果的方式也得到了不錯的結果。

由於本篇實驗中的分群結果並不算理想，非常多文章被歸在同一個較大的聚類而無法顯示其差異性，可能因此浪費許多可以運用的資訊，也讓分群之間的結果較難做比較。未來，將會針對分群的部分做改進；另外，提升此篇單輪問答模型的表現也可以拓展到多輪問答上使用，故未來也將會針對加入歷史對話以運用在多輪的閱讀理解任務上進行進一步的研究。

參考文獻

Pranav Rajpurkar, Jian Zhang, Konstantin Lopyrev and Percy Liang. 2016. SQuAD: 100,000+ Questions for Machine Comprehension of Text. In *Proceedings of the 2016 Conference on Empirical*

Methods in Natural Language Processing, 2383–2392.

Chih Chieh Shao, Trois Liu, Yuting Lai, Yiying Tseng, and Sam Tsai. 2018. Drcd: a chinese machine reading comprehension dataset. arXiv preprint arXiv:1806.00920.

Yiming Cui, Ting Liu, Wanxiang Che, Li Xiao, Zhipeng Chen, Wentao Ma, Shijin Wang, and Guoping Hu. 2019b. A Span-Extraction Dataset for Chinese Machine Reading Comprehension. In *Proceedings of the 2019 Conference on Empirical Methods in Natural Language Processing and the 9th Inter- national Joint Conference on Natural Language Processing (EMNLP-IJCNLP)*, pages 5886–5891, Hong Kong, China. Association for Computational Linguistics.

Yiming Cui, Wanxiang Che, Ting Liu, Bing Qin, Ziqing Yang, Shijin Wang, and Guoping Hu. 2019a. Pre-training with whole word masking for chinese bert. arXiv preprint arXiv:1906.08101.

Yiming Cui, Ting Liu, Wanxiang Che, Li Xiao, Zhipeng Chen, Wentao Ma, Shijin Wang, and Guoping Hu. 2020. Revisiting Pre-Trained Models for Chinese Natural Language Processing. arXiv preprint arXiv:2004.13922.

Tomas Mikolov, Ilya Sutskever, Kai Chen, Greg S Corrado, and Jeff Dean. 2013. Distributed representations of words and phrases and their compositionality. In *C. J. C. Burges, L. Bottou, M. Welling, Z. Ghahramani, and K. Q. Weinberger, editors, Advances in Neural Information Processing Systems 26*, pages 3111–3119. Curran Associates, Inc.

Wanxiang Che, Zhenghua Li, and Ting Liu. 2010. Ltp: A chinese language technology platform. In *Proceedings of the 23rd International Conference on Computational Linguistics: Demonstrations*, pages 13–16. Association for Computational Linguistics.

Nils Reimers and Iryna Gurevych. 2019. Sentence-BERT: Sentence Embeddings using Siamese BERT-Networks. In *Conference on Empirical Methods in Natural Language Processing*.

Martin Ester, Hans-Peter Kriegel, Jörg Sander and Xiaowei Xu. 1996. A density-based algorithm for discovering clusters in large spatial databases with noise. In *Kdd*, volume 96, pages 226–231.

Shanshan Liu, Xin Zhang, Sheng Zhang, Hui Wang, Weiming Zhang. 2019. Neural Machine Reading Comprehension: Methods and Trends. *J. Applied Sciences*, 2019, 9(18): 3698

Rudolf Kadlec, Martin Schmid, Ondrej Bajgar and Jan Kleindienst. 2016. Text Understanding with the Attention Sum Reader Network. In *Proceedings of the 54th Annual Meeting of the Association for Computational Linguistics (Volume 1: Long Papers)*, 908–918.

Bhuwan Dhingra, Hanxiao Liu, Zhilin Yang, William W. Cohen and Ruslan Salakhutdinov. 2017. Gated-Attention Readers for Text Comprehension. In *Proceedings of the 55th Annual Meeting of the Association for Computational Linguistics (Volume 1: Long Papers)*, 1832–1846.

Wenhui Wang, Nan Yang, Furu Wei, Baobao Chang and Ming Zhou. 2017. Gated Self-Matching Networks for Reading Comprehension and Question Answering. In *Proceedings of the 55th Annual Meeting of the Association for Computational Linguistics (Volume 1: Long Papers)*, 189–198.

Yiming Cui, Zhipeng Chen, Si Wei, Shijin Wang, Ting Liu adn Guoping Hu. 2017. Attention-over-Attention Neural Networks for Reading Comprehension. In *Proceedings of the 55th Annual Meeting of the Association for Computational Linguistics (Volume 1: Long Papers)*, 593–602.

Minjoon Seo, Aniruddha Kembhavi, Ali Farhadi and Hannaneh Hajishirzi. 2016. Bidirectional Attention Flow for Machine Comprehension. In International Conference on Learning Representations. arXiv preprint arXiv: 1611.0160.

Ashish Vaswani, Noam Shazeer, Niki Parmar, Jakob Uszkoreit, Llion Jones, Aidan N Gomez, Lukasz Kaiser, and Illia Polosukhin. 2017. Attention is all you need. In *Advances in Neural Information Processing Systems*, pages 6000–6010.

Matthew E. Peters, Mark Neumann, Mohit Iyyer, Matt Gardner, Christopher Clark, Kenton Lee and Luke Zettlemoyer. 2018. Deep contextualized word representations. In *NAACL-HLT*, 2227–2237.

Alec Radford, Karthik Narasimhan, Tim Salimans and Ilya Sutskever, I. 2018. Improving language understanding by generative pre-training. *Technical report*.

Jacob Devlin, Ming-Wei Chang, Kenton Lee and Kristina Toutanova. 2019. BERT: Pre-training of Deep Bidirectional Transformers for Language Understanding. In *Proceedings of the 2019 Conference of the North American Chapter of the Association for Computational Linguistics: Human Language Technolo- gies, Volume 1 (Long and Short Papers)*, 4171–4186.

Zhilin Yang, Zihang Dai, Yiming Yang, Jaime Carbonell, Ruslan Salakhutdinov, Quoc V. Le. 2019. XLNET: Generalized autoregres- sive pretraining for language understanding. In *Advances in neural information processing systems*, 5753–5763.

Yinhan Liu, Myle Ott, Naman Goyal, Jingfei Du, Mandar Joshi, Danqi Chen, Omer Levy, Mike Lewis, Luke Zettlemoyer and Veselin Stoyanov. 2019. RoBERTa: A robustly optimized BERT pretraining approach. arXiv preprint arXiv:1907.11692.

Zhenzhong Lan, Mingda Chen, Sebastian Goodman, Kevin Gimpel, Piyush Sharma and Radu Soricut. 2020. ALBERT: A Lite BERT for Self- supervised Learning of Language Representations. In *International Conference on Learning Representations.*

Kevin Clark, Minh-Thang Luong, Quoc V. Le and Christopher D. Manning. 2020. ELECTRA: Pre-training Text Encoders as Discriminators Rather Than Generators. In *International Conference on Learning Representation.*

The 33rd Conference on Computational Linguistics and Speech Processing (ROCLING 2021)
Taoyuan, Taiwan, October 15-16, 2021. The Association for Computational Linguistics and Chinese Language Processing

長者日常對話與認知執行功能關係探討：使用詞向量與迴歸模型
Discussion on the relationship between elders' daily conversations and cognitive executive function: using word vectors and regression models

Ming-Hsiang Su, Yu-An Ko and Man-Ying Wang
Soochow University, Taiwan
huntfox.su,kelen850408, mywang.scu@gmail.com

摘要

隨著國人平均壽命攀升，老年人口的健康照護問題也更加多元，而且長期照護的需求也日漸增加，因此如何幫助高齡長者 擁有良好生活品質與尊嚴之維持，是我們需要思考的。本研究欲藉由深度模型進一步探討正常老化者自然語言的特性。首先以焦點團體的方式收集資料，使長者在過程中自然地與其他參與者互動。接著透過詞向量模型與迴歸模型建立基於對話資料的EF預測模型，幫助了解EF的退化軌跡與建立預警。

Abstract

As the average life expectancy of Chinese people rises, the health care problems of the elderly are becoming more diverse, and the demand for long-term care is also increasing. Therefore, how to help the elderly have a good quality of life and maintain their dignity is what we need to think about. This research intends to explore the characteristics of natural language of normal aging people through a deep model. First, we collect information through focus groups so that the elders can naturally interact with other participants in the process. Then, through the word vector model and regression model, an executive function prediction model based on dialogue data is established to help understand the degradation trajectory of executive function and establish an early warning.

關鍵字：詞向量、迴歸模型、認知執行功能

Keywords: word vector, regression model, cognitive executive function

1 Introduction

國家發展委員會指出台灣在 2018 年邁入高齡的社會，而在 2020 年時，超高齡人口已經占10.3%，進而推估在2025年台灣將邁入超高齡社會 (國家發展委員會, 2020)。隨著台灣人民的壽命延長， 對於銀髮族的健康照護問題也逐漸受到重視，對於銀髮族長期居家照護的需求也日漸增加。如何幫助銀髮族不僅在醫療層面受到照護，也能擁有優質生活品質與生命尊嚴，是一重要課題。

學者們的研究指出阿茲海默症 (Alzheimer's Disease, AD) 和輕度認知障礙 (Mild Cognitive Impairment, MCI) 患者在在疾病前驅期，它們的語言處理過程便出現缺陷 (Taler & Phillips, 2008)。如何識別早期跡象和症狀的能力對於干預措施的發展相當重要。藉由認知和思維障礙在說話方式和說話內容中的表現，我們可以藉由語言分析去洞悉神經功能，進而使用自動化或半自動化的語音和語言分析方法進行更深入的研究，以找出患者的語言與聲音特徵。

Calzà等人 (Calzà et al., 2021) 建立一個用於早期診斷和篩查的自動系統，旨在量化和描述由於認知能力下降導致的語言特徵變化。他們招募48名健康對照者和48名受損受試者。每個受試者接受了簡短的神經心理學篩查，並通過三個啟發任務收集了半自發語音產生的樣本。他們利用支持向量 (SVC) 和隨機森林分類器 (RFC) 來區分健康對照和 MCI 受試者。他們的實驗結果顯示他們所提出的方法是識別癡呆臨床前階段的一種很有前途的方法。Fraser 等人 (Fraser et al., 2019)考慮一種級聯方法來組合來自多種語言任務的數據。26名 MCI 參與者和 29 名健康對照組完成圖片描述、默讀和大聲朗讀三種語言任務。研究成果指出最好的分類結果是通過組合任務級別的數據來實現的（AUC＝0.88，準確度＝0.83）。這優於基於神經心理學測試分數（AUC = 0.75，準確度 = 0.65）以及多模態分類的“早期融合”方法（AUC = 0.79，準確度 = 0.70）訓練的分類器。Wang 等人 (Wang et al., 2019)的研究旨在檢驗情景圖片描述和自發自我介紹任務中的相關語音生成是否可用於區分具有 MCI 心理測量證據的個體和認知完整的個體。他們的研究揭示 MCI 參與者語義內容和句法複雜性的線性下降趨勢，以及明顯更大的不流暢跡象和語音生成減少。這些發現擴展了文獻中的報導，並對疑似 MCI 的篩查和診斷具有重要意義。

Fraser 等人 (Fraser et al., 2016) 展示從圖片描述任務引發的簡短敘述樣本中自動識別阿爾茨海默病的最先進的準確性，並通過統計因素分析揭示突出的語言因素。藉由 DementiaBank 語料庫訓練分類器，用以區分患有 AD 的參與者和健康對照組。為了檢查 AD 中語言障礙的異質性程度，他們對這些言語和語言的測量進行了探索性因素分析，並提供了對結果因素的解釋。在圖片描述任務中根據他們語言的短樣本，區分患有 AD 的個體和沒有 AD 的個體，獲得了超過 81% 的最先進的分類準確率。他們認為機器學習和語言分析在疑似 AD 的評估和聚類中非常有用。Asgari 等人 (Asgari et al., 2017) 認為輕度認知障礙 (MCI) 的指標可能存在於老年人口語內容中，並且有助於區分 MCI 患者和認知完好的患者。他們對參與臨床試驗的 MCI 參與者和具有完整認知的參與者的口語進行了語言分析，分類準確率為 84%，遠高於 60% 的機會。Polsinelli 等人(Polsinelli et al., 2020)調查了執行功能 (EF) 的可變性如何體現在日常用詞模式中。他們使用語言查詢和字數統計對捕獲的話語的逐字記錄進行了文本分析。 EF 使用經過驗證的測試電池組進行評估，測量 WM、移位和抑制控制。他們發現較高的整體 EF，尤其是工作記憶，與更多的冠詞和介詞、更長的單詞和更多的數字語言相關。

本研究期望探討台灣正常銀髮族的語言與認知執行功能之間的關係，藉由詞向量與迴歸模型建置，搭配彩色路徑描繪測驗 (CTT) 檢測銀髮族的執行功能，並且建立預測模型。

2 Dataset

本研究使用團體聊天方式來引導銀髮族語言使用的自然狀態。參與者為 53-74 歲的退休銀髮族 (36 位女性與 15 位男性)，參與者平均教育年數為 12.5 年。每場團體聊天人數為 2-5 人，他們會討論日常生活經常從事的活動，並且會針對有高共通性的議題進行深入討論，藉以了解其執行步驟、並接受彩色路徑描繪測驗，以測量執行功能與日常生活活動調查。

3 Word Embedding

本研究將參與者的語音資料轉成文字檔，並使用 CKIP API 進行斷詞處理，CKIP 為中研院中文語言小組開發，為中文自然語言處理提供相關的研究資料，包括中文詞知識庫、語料等。接著本研究使用 Word2vec 進行詞向量特徵抽取。Word2vec 是 Google 所提供的一個用來產生詞向量的模型，透過訓練可以將文本中的內容簡化成 n 維向量空間中的向量運算，此向量空間上的相似度可以用來表示文本語意上的相似度。訓練 Word2vec 方式可分為兩種：連續詞袋模型（continuous bag-of-words, CBOW）及 Skip-Gram 模型。在 CBOW 的方法裡，訓練目標是用一個詞的鄰近詞去預測該詞的機率；而 Skip-Gram 則是跟 CBOW 相反，訓練目標是用一個詞去預測該詞鄰近詞的機率。另外為了比較不同的詞向量對於系統效能的差異，本研究另外也使用 Doc2Vec 模型和 FASTText 模型進行詞向量模型訓練。

4 Regression Model

數據收集技術的進步大大增加了在科學與商業領域中預測變數的數量，此時就需要模型選擇的方法來找出重要的預測變數，傳統的模型選擇方法，如逐步 (stepwise) 和向前 (forward) 雖簡單，但被證實產生的模型準確性較低，特別是當預測變數的數量很大時 (Desboulets, 2018)。且變數大於觀測值個數時也可能造成過度適配 (overfitting) 的問題，因在樣本內的平方誤差和會越低，此時可使用正規化 (regularization)。

Lasso 是最小絕對收縮選擇和算子的簡稱，是一種採用了 L1 正則化（L1-regularization)的線性迴歸方法，採用了 L1 正則會使得部分學習到的特徵權值為 0，從而達到稀疏化和特徵選擇的目的。在考慮一般的線性迴歸問題，給定 n 個數據樣本點 $\{(x_1, y_1), (x_2, y_2), \ldots, (n, y_n)\}$，其中每個 $x_i \in R^d$ 是一個 d 維的向量，即每個觀測到的數據點是由d個變量的值組成的，每個 $y_i \in R$ 是一個實值。現在要做的是根據觀察到的數據點，尋找到一個映射$f: R^d \rightarrow R$，使得誤差平方和最小，優化目標為：

$$\beta^*, \beta_0^* = argmin_{\beta,\beta_0} \frac{1}{n}\sum_{i=0}^{n}(y_i - \beta^T x_i - \beta_0)^2 \quad (1)$$

$$\beta^* = argmin_{\beta} \frac{1}{n}\sum_{i=0}^{n}((y_i - \bar{y}) - \beta^T(x_i - \bar{x}))^2 \quad (2)$$

$$\beta^* = argmin_{\beta} \frac{1}{n}\|y - X\beta\|_2^2$$

由於有 d 個變量，所以稱之為 Multiple Linear Regression。一般來說，回歸問題是一個函數擬合的過程，那麼希望模型不要太複雜，否則很容易發生過擬合現象，所以要加入正則化項，而不同的正則化項就產生了不同的回歸方法，其中以 Ridge Regression 和 Lasso 最為經典，前者是加入了 L2 正則化項，後者加入的是 L1 正則化項。本研究將使用 Multiple Linear Regression、Ridge Regression 和 Lasso 進行實驗。

5 Experiment Settings and Results

本研究將斷詞後的資料集分別進行 Doc2Vec，FASTText 和 Word2Vec 詞向量模型訓練。在 Doc2Vec 詞向量模型中，文本向量維度為 300 維。而 Multiple Linear Regression 的實驗結果為訓練資料的 MSE: 1.20e-09；測試資料的 MSE: 1951.29；訓練資料的 R-squared: 1.00；測試資料的 R-squared: -1.94。另外我們進行 Multiple Linear Regression、Ridge Regression 和 Lasso 模型比較，如 Figure 1 所示，在 300 維詞向量中，我們可以發現 Ridge Regression 模型有較佳的結果。其中 Lasso 模型中，$\alpha = 1$時，僅使用了 28 個特徵（係數的非零值）；$\alpha = 0.01$時，僅使用了 37 個特徵；而$\alpha = 0.00001$時，則使用了 300 個特徵。

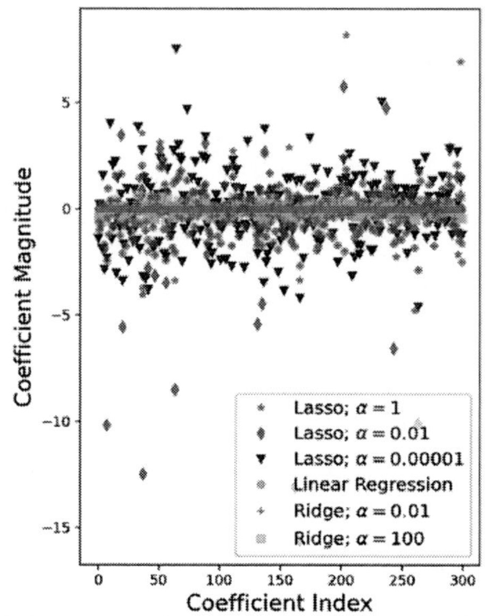

Figure 1: 不同 Regression 模型效能比較

在 FASTText 詞向量模型中，詞向量維度為 50 維。為了避免每個人的文本向量長度不同，所以我們採取每個人的文本只取 296 個詞，而整個文本向量維度為50×296維。而 Multiple Linear Regression 的實驗結果為訓練資料的 MSE: 2.82e-09；測試資料的 MSE: 702.15；訓練資料的 R-squared: 1.00；測試資料的 R-squared: -0.06。另外我們進行 Multiple Linear Regression、Ridge Regression 和 Lasso 模型比較，如 Figure 2 所示，在 300 維詞向量中，我們可以發現 Ridge Regression 模型有較佳的結果。其中 Lasso 模型中，$\alpha = 1$時，僅使用了 29 個特徵（係數的非零值）；$\alpha = 0.01$時，僅使用了 41 個特徵；而$\alpha = 0.00001$時，則使用了 346 個特徵。

在 Word2Vec 詞向量模型中，詞向量維度為 50 維。為了避免每個人的文本向量長度不同，所以我們採取每個人的文本只取 296 個詞，而整個文本向量維度為50×296維。而 Multiple Linear Regression 的實驗結果為訓練資料的 MSE: 2.62e-09；測試資料的 MSE: 809.47；訓練資料的 R-squared: 1.00；測試資料的 R-squared: -0.22。另外我們進行 Multiple Linear Regression、Ridge Regression 和 Lasso 模型比較，如 Figure 3 所示，在 300 維詞向量中，我們可以發現 Ridge Regression 模型有較佳的結果。其中 Lasso 模型中，$\alpha = 1$時，僅使用了 31 個特徵（係數的非零值）；$\alpha = 0.01$時，僅使用了 49 個特徵；而$\alpha = 0.00001$時，則使用了 532 個特徵。

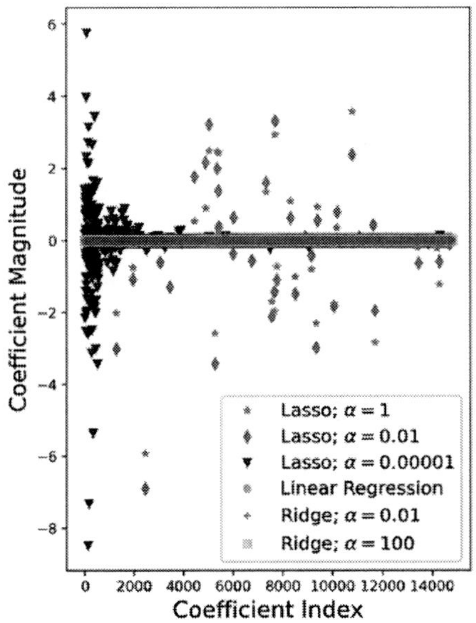

Figure 2: 不同 Regression 模型 FASTText 文本向量效能比較

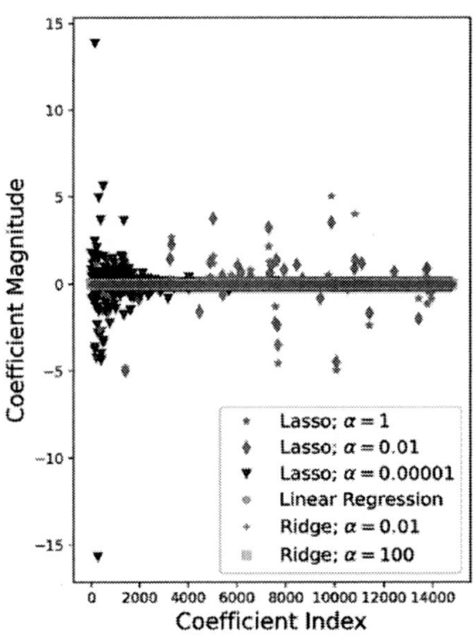

Figure 3: 不同 Regression 模型 Word2Vec 文本向量效能比較

6 Conclusion

本研究欲藉由深度模型進一步探討正常老化者自然語言的特性。首先以焦點團體的方式收集資料，使長者在過程中自然地與其他參與者互動。接著透過詞向量模型與迴歸模型建立基於對話資料的 EF 預測模型，幫助了解 EF 的退化軌跡與建立預警。實驗結果顯示，當詞向量使用 Word2Vec 模型而迴歸模型使用 Ridge 模型有較佳的預測效能。

在未來的研究中，本研究會持續增加資料集數量，另外也希望能加入 BERT 和 LSTM 等深度學習模型，以期能得到更好的結果。

References

[1] 國家發展委員會. 2020. 中華民國人口推估（2020 至 2070 年）報告. 取自 國家發展委員會，人口推估查詢系統網址 https://popproj.ndc.gov.tw/download.aspx?uid=70&pid=70

[2] Taler, Vanessa, and Natalie A. Phillips. 2008. Language performance in Alzheimer's disease and mild cognitive impairment: a comparative review. *Journal of clinical and experimental neuropsychology*, 30(5): 501-556. https://doi.org/10.1080/13803390701550128.

[3] Laura Calzà, Gloria Gagliardi, Rema Rossini Favretti, and Fabio Tamburini. 2021. Linguistic features and automatic classifiers for identifying mild cognitive impairment and dementia. *Computer Speech & Language*, 65: 101113. https://doi.org/10.1016/j.csl.2020.101113.

[4] Kathleen C. Fraser, Kristina Lundholm Fors, Marie Eckerström, Fredrik Öhman, and Dimitrios Kokkinakis. 2019. Predicting MCI Status From Multimodal Language Data Using Cascaded Classifiers. *Frontiers in aging neuroscience*, 11, 205. https://doi.org/10.3389/fnagi.2019.00205.

[5] Tianqi Wang, Chongyuan Lian, Jingshen Pan, Quanlei Yan, Feiqi Zhu, Manwa L. Ng, Lan Wang, Nan Yan. 2019. Towards the Speech Features of Mild Cognitive Impairment: Universal Evidence from Structured and Unstructured Connected Speech of Chinese. In *Proceedings of INTERSPEECH*. https://doi.org/10.21437/Interspeech.2019-2414.

[6] Fraser, Kathleen C., Jed A. Meltzer, and Frank Rudzicz. 2016. Linguistic features identify Alzheimer's disease in narrative speech. *Journal of Alzheimer's Disease*, 49(2): 407-422. https://doi.org/10.3233/JAD-150520.

[7] Asgari, Meysam, Jeffrey Kaye, and Hiroko Dodge. 2017. Predicting mild cognitive impairment from spontaneous spoken utterances. *Alzheimer's & Dementia: Translational Research & Clinical Interventions*, 3(2): 219-228. https://doi.org/10.1016/j.trci.2017.01.006.

[8] Angelina J. Polsinelli, Suzanne A. Moseley, Matthew D. Grilli, Elizabeth L. Glisky, and

Matthias R. Mehl. 2020. Natural, everyday language use provides a window into the integrity of older adults' executive functioning. *The Journals of Gerontology: Series B,* 75(9): e215-e220.

[9] Desboulets, Loann David Denis. 2018. A Review on Variable Selection in Regression Analysis. *Econometrics*, 6(4): 45. https://doi.org/10.3390/econometrics6040045.

The 33rd Conference on Computational Linguistics and Speech Processing (ROCLING 2021)
Taoyuan, Taiwan, October 15-16, 2021. The Association for Computational Linguistics and Chinese Language Processing

Chinese Medical Speech Recognition with Punctuated Hypothesis
(釋文內含標點符號之中文醫療語音辨識技術)

鍾聖倫 Sheng-Luen Chung; 范晉桓 Jin-Huan Fan
國立臺灣科技大學電機工程學系
Electrical Engineering Department
National Taiwan University of Science and Technology
Taipei, Taiwan
slchung@mail.ntust.edu.tw; m10807507@gapps.ntust.edu.tw

丁賢偉 Hsien-Wei Ting
衛生福利部臺北醫院神經外科
Department of Neurosurgery
Taipei Hospital, Ministry of Health and Welfare
Taipei, Taiwan
ting.ns@gmail.com

摘要

語音辨識可協助醫護專業人員節省其使用電子醫療系統的文書處理時間。中文醫療語音的內容爲中文爲主，之間摻入以英文的專業術語，所以本質上可視爲句中雙語 intra-sentential code switching speech corpus。先前在中文醫療語料庫 (Chinese Medicine Speech Corpus: sChiMeS) 上進行的語音辨識的譯文並沒有標點符號，不易人的閱讀，也不利後續機器翻譯等應用。據此，本論文提出一階段即可回復標點符號的語音辨識技術。爲此，在資料庫的準備上，將原本沒有標點符號標註的 ChiMeS 語料庫的標註加入標點符號成爲 psChiMeS，然後進行訓練。同時，爲取得更好的語音辨識效果，我們採用 ESPnet 框架中以 conformer 爲基礎並且彙整 CTC 辨識機制的 ASR 網路架構。在 psChiMeS-14 的語料庫上，本論文所提的方法得到 10.5% 的 CER 以及 13.10% 的 KER。對比之前在 Joint CTC/Attention 架構上最好的結果爲：15.70% 的 CER 以及 22.50% 的 KER。本技術可作爲發展線上醫療語音辨識系統的基石。

關鍵字：深度學習、語音辨識、醫療語料庫

Abstract

Automatic Speech Recognition (ASR) technology presents the possibility for medical professionals to document patient record, diagnosis, postoperative care, patrol records, and etc. that are now done manually. However, earlier research aimed on Chinese medical speech corpus (ChiMeS) has two shortcomings: first is the lack of punctuation, resulting in reduced readability of the output transcript, and second is the poor recognition error rate, affecting its application put to the fields. Accordingly, the contributions of this paper consist of: (1) A punctuated Chinese medical corpus psChiMeS-14 newly annotated from ChiMeS-14, which is the collection of 516 anonymized medical record readouts of 867 minutes long, recorded by 15 professional nursing staff from Taipei Hospital of the Ministry of Health and Welfare. psChiMeS-14 is manually punctuated with: colons, commas, and periods, ready for general end-to-end ASR models. (2) A self-attention based speech recognition solution by conformer networks. Trained by and tested on psChiMeS-14 corpus, the solutions deliver state-of-the-art recognition performance: CER (character error rate) 10.5%, and KER (Keyword error rate) of 13.10%, respectively, which is contrasted to the 15.70% CER and the 22.50% KER by an earlier reported Joint CTC/Attention architecture.

Keywords: deep learning, speech recognition, Chinese medical speech corpus

1 緒論

1.1 動機

醫療語音辨識有助於醫療專業人員進行病歷紀錄、巡房與診斷追蹤等。相較於一般大眾日常會話或是智慧家庭週邊商品所考量的情境語音，醫療語音的特殊性在於其中英文混雜的術語、筆記式的片斷句型、以及區域性醫護人員特殊的發音等特性。這些挑戰致使醫療情境中的語音無法直接使用一般語音辨識技術當作解決方案。

針對中文醫療語音辨識技術，先前的研究成果的貢獻有三項，分別是：(一) ChiMeS 語料庫，其爲時 14.4 小時，共 7,225 句語音。(二) 訓練好的 Joint CTC/Attention ASR 模型，其在 ChiMeS-14 的測試集上最好的字符錯誤率 (Character Error Rate：CER) 和關鍵字錯誤率 (Keyword Error Rate：KER) 分別爲 12.85% 和 17.62%。以及 (三) 評估其他 ASR 模型針對醫療語音辨識的基本績效測試平台。

大多數的語音辨識模型，在訓練時不包含標點符號。然而, 由 (Garg et al., 2018)、(Zhang and Zhang, 2020)、(Li et al., 2021) 所提出的文獻可以得知，標點符號不但能提高可讀性，同時也有助於翻譯的效能提升。另一方面，近兩年新的語音辨識技術的出現，也能對當前對 ChiMeS 的辨識績效更多提升的空間。上述內容統整出目前特別針對中文醫療語音辨識的兩項挑戰：(1) 先前的醫療語音辨識技術並沒有考量標點符號，導致辨識出的文本可讀性低；(2) 過去所採用的醫療語音辨識模型的 CER 仍有改善的空間。據此，本論文的貢獻如下：

(1) 含標點符號標註之中文醫療語料庫 (psChiMeS)：

參考教育部所頒定《重訂標點符號手冊》並依照醫療文本特性適時調整規則, 我們針對 ChiMeS 的文本重新進行標註，得到 psChiMeS，其可作爲後續針對中文醫療音辨識之端對端訓練的語料庫。

(2) 到目前爲止辨識績效最好的醫療語音辨識模型 Joint CTC-Conformer：

利用基於自我注意力機制 (Self-Attention) 和卷積網路 (Convolution) 機制的 Joint CTC-Conformer 語音辨識模型，在 psChiMeS 上的訓練與測試，實現了 10.5% 的 CER，以及 13.10% 的 KER，對比之前報導的 Joint CTC/Attention 經數據增強後所得的 15.7% 的 CER 和 22.50% 的 KER。

1.2 論文架構

本論文的第二節回顧自動化標註標點符號的技術和近年語音辨識模型的架構發展。第三節詳細介紹目前較先進的醫療語音辨識模型的相關技術與運作流程。第四節爲實驗結果與分析討論，包含語音辨識的效能比較；以及強調加註標點符號語音辨識的效能。最後，第五節爲本研究之結論與未來研究方向。

2 文獻審閱

2.1 自動化標註標點符號

針對語音辨識的釋文額外需要內含標點號的問題，文獻上主要作法爲兩階段，即先取得不含標點符號的文字串，然後再加上標點符號。以下先介紹對應這第二階段的自動化標註標點符號技術。之後再介紹一般端對端的 ASR 技術。

文獻上，自動化標點符號標註是將沒有標點符號的句子或 ASR 輸出的結果，進行額外塡入語意上需要停頓的標點符號還原 (punctuation restoration)，也就是將不含標點符號的文本輸入模型後，輸出爲含標點符號的文本。2017 年 (Salloum et al., 2017) 提出針對醫學報告的文本進行標點還原，其所採用的技術是使用 RNN 加上 Attention 的機制來進行標點符號恢復的任務。其作法是將相同字首或字尾的詞彙更換成統一表示方式來降低訓練詞彙量。此技術在逗號、句號、冒號的標點回復效果上都取得不錯的效能。2018 年由 (Garg et al., 2018) 所提出的自動標註標點符號模型，目標是爲了讓電子教學平台影片在做語言翻譯時，可以先進行標點符號的預測再送入翻譯模型，以提升翻譯品質，其提出的 CNN 加上雙向 LSTM 預測模型有最佳的效能。

2020 年 Amazon 針對醫療語音的辨識任務，進行標點符號的預測以及正確大小寫 (Sunkara et al., 2020) 的恢復。文中使用 BERT (Devlin et al., 2018) 預訓練模型對其任務進行微調，此架構用兩階段方式來訓練，最後在標點符號預測及恢復正確大小寫的任務上與 LSTM 架構相比，效能提升 3 ~ 4%。同樣在 2020 年，百度 (Zhang and Zhang, 2020) 爲了解決即時翻譯沒有輸出標點符號無法找出句子邊界的問題，使用 ERNIE (Zhang et al., 2019) 預訓練模型，以多分類的訓練方式來預測句子的邊界，最後 ASR 在搭配此模型運行下，BLEU 翻譯評測指標 (Papineni et al., 2002) 可以提升大約 2%。2020 年 Google 提出在翻譯實驗中 (Li et al., 2021)，透過句子邊界增量 (Sentence Boundary Augmentation)，在多個資料集上 BLEU 都有所提升，證明好的句子邊界不僅能提高可讀性，也能使翻譯品質有所提升。

2.2 端對端 ASR 模型

2.2.1 CTC

爲了解決語音辨識輸入與輸出序列長度不固定的問題，CTC (Graves et al., 2006) 對每一幀的輸入都會有相對應獨立的輸出結果，並學習語音與相對應標籤序列中如何自動對齊。2017 年由百度提出的 Deep Speech 2 (DS2)(Amodei et al., 2016)，編碼器是由 CNN 與雙向 LSTM 組成，用來提取每個語音時序上的前後文關係。摘要前後文資訊的的隱藏層狀態 (hidden state) 會被用來當作後續 CTC 輸出的依據。另一方面，解碼器爲單純一層全連接層 (fully connected layer)，不再需要額外使用詞典將音素映射至形素。端對端 ASR 的架構只需要一個架構進行訓練即可將語音轉換成文字。然而 CTC 的缺點是：針對每個輸入幀都被視爲獨立的對應輸出，所以常需搭配語言模型，來補足前後文關係較不足的問題。

2.2.2 Joint CTC-Attention

2017 年由 (Kim et al., 2017) 等學者提出同時具備 Attention 機制和 CTC 的 Joint CTC-attention 語音辨識模型。此模型主要分成三個部分：第一，Encoder 採用共用形式，主要由 CNN 和 LSTM 組成並在解碼階段將所有時序的隱藏層狀態輸出至 CTC Decoder 和 Attention Decoder。第二，CTC Decoder 在每一時間下的音頻輸入與對應字符爲條件獨立，因此在每一幀的音源輸入皆會有對應的文字輸出，最後以刪除重複的字和空白標籤 (Blank) 的縮減方式來對齊。第三，Attention Decoder 透過 attention 分數運算來獲取上下文關係。最後，透過合併使用這兩種 Decoder 的優點，並以 λ 來當作損失函數的調和參數，如式 1 所示，這樣所獲得得 Joint CTC-attention 模型能在當時達到更好的語音辨識效果。

$$L_{joint} = \lambda L_{CTC} + (1-\lambda) L_{Attention} \quad (1)$$

2.2.3 Self-Attention 機制用於 ASR 模型

在 2017 年，Google 提出 Transformer (Vaswani et al., 2017)，此模型是一個加入自我注意力機制 (Self-Attention) 的 Seq2Seq 模型。採用此機制的模型在訓練時可以對所有輸入的時序資料進行矩陣的平行運算，加速訓練。Transformer 在翻譯任務和 NLP 任務等時序資料處理的問通，都有很好的表現。之後，有學者將 Transformer 模型引入語音辨識。在 2018 年由 (Dong et al., 2018) 等學者首先提出 Speech-Transformer，其使用 Transformer 架構來取代 RNN 或 LSTM 等 Seq2Seq 模型，不僅在 Wall Street Journal (WSJ) 語料庫上可以取得到字錯誤率 (Word Error Rate：WER) 10.9% 的效能，所需的訓練時間也僅爲原本使用 RNN 或 LSTM 架構的 30%。

在 2020 年由 (Miao et al., 2020) 等學者所提出將 CTC 機制合併加入 Transformer 架構中，此架構可以保有 Transformer 在擷取大跨度的上下文特徵優異的特性，同時也結合 CTC 每一時間下預測的獨立性。最後在 HKUST 中文語料庫上，相較於 Joint CTC-Attention 模型的 CER 降低了 4%。

雖然 Transformer 對於大跨度的上下文特徵有不錯的表現，但對於局部特徵擷取較爲弱勢。因此 2020 年由 Google 另外在 Transformer Encoder 中加入 Convolution 機制，稱作 Conformer Encoder (Gulati et al., 2020)，其能有效的擷取全局與局部的音頻特徵。在搭配一層的 LSTM Decoder 架構下，可以在 LibriSpeech 語料庫取得 WER 2.1% 的效能；而搭配語言模型更取得 WER 1.9% 的效能。

3 研究方法

3.1 一階段直接標註標點符號的語音辨識技術

相較於一般文獻均是採用兩階段將語音轉譯成有附加標點符號的方法，本論文直接採用更爲簡潔與迅速的一階段訓練方式，如圖 1 所示。據此，我們首先針對原沒有加標點符號 ChiMeS 語料庫中，原音檔 w_i 所對應原沒有加標點符號的文本標註，重新進行人補註標點，加上包括：冒號、逗號與句號的文本，我們以 y_i^* 表示。接下來是建置同時合併使用 Self-Attention 機制的 conformer，以及 CTC 編碼器而成 Joint CTC/Conformer 架構的 ASR 網路。在此端對端的新架構上，直接使用有加標點符號的譯文 psChiMeS 作爲訓練的語料庫，而直接將額外標註的標點符號 (冒號、逗號與句號) 視同原本輸出字符字典中與中文字和英文單音節同樣的字符來處理，當作整個 ASR 網路的輸出字符處理。

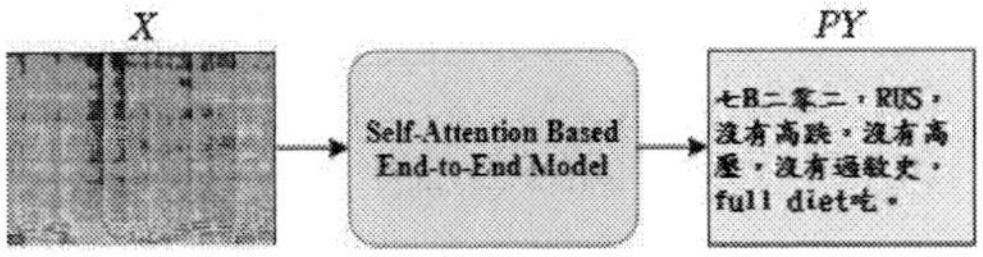

圖 1: 一階段訓練示意圖

3.2 重新標記之具標點符號語料庫

在本研究中，我們所採用的中文醫療語料庫 Chinese Medical Speech Corpus (ChiMeS)

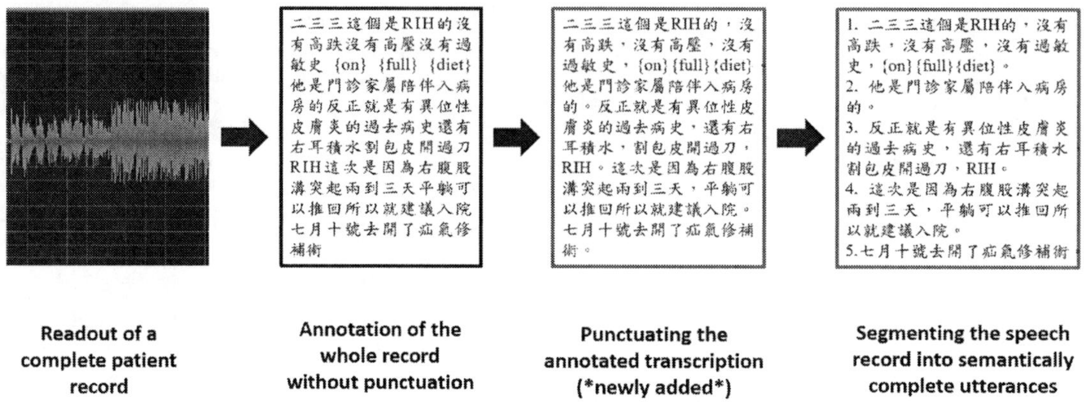

圖 2: psChiMeS 文本標註方式

共爲時約 14.4 小時，其由衛生服利部台北醫院的 15 位女性護理師，根據 516 份匿名化處理的住院病患病歷表，以交班時講話的方式進行語音的錄製，再按完整語義切割與中英文譯文的標註。如圖 2 所示，在標註時，我們是先將病歷表的朗讀檔先進行標註，得到沒有標點符號的譯文 (黑框處)。接著我們參考了教育部的標點符號手冊並且根據醫療文本的特性訂定了醫療文本標點符號規則，如表 1。將先前所標註的譯文加入標點符號，得到具標點符號的譯文 (藍框處)。

每一份病歷表的內容包括：病患匿名化之基本資料、入院狀態、目前病情，與每天狀況更新等四個部分。針對深度學習模型訓練與測試需要，我們透過前後文語意的完整性，將完整的病歷表譯文切割成多個句子 (紅框處)。最後，將 ChiMeS 語料庫切分爲訓練集與測試集，兩者的比例分配約爲 4：1，得到訓練集爲 5,682 句，而測試集爲 1,543 句。訓練集與測試集中沒有彼此重複的護理師。詳細的語料庫分布表如表 2, 其中 psChiMeS 爲含標點符號語料庫。

表 1: 標點符號標註規則

標點符號	規則
逗號（，）	前後意思銜接
	用來隔開檢查數值或是病名
冒號（：）	接下來要表示各個檢查數值
	接下來要敘述病人過去病史
句號（。）	語意上，敘述結束
	切分不同日期之間交班紀錄

表 2: sChiMeS 和 psChiMeS 資料分布表

語料庫	sChiMeS	psChiMeS
特性	語意完整	語意完整 有標點符號
句數 (訓練/測試)	7,225 (5,682/1,543)	7,225 (5,682/1,543)
平均時長 (秒/句)	7.2	7.2
平均字數	29.8	33.3
總時長 (分數)	867.86	867.86

3.3 Joint CTC-Conformer 模型

如圖 3 所示，Joint CTC-Conformer 是由 Conformer 編碼器，搭配 CTC 解碼器和 Transformer 解碼器所組成，其中編碼器的部分是由多個 Conformer Block 組成，每個 block 中依序包含前饋式網路 (Feed-Forward Netword)、多頭式注意力機制、卷積模組以及另一層前饋式網路。以下介紹 Joint CTC-Conformer 中的每個模組。

3.3.1 多頭式注意力機制 (Multi-Head Self-Attention，MHSA)

Self-Attention 的運算方式爲縮放點積注意力機制 (Scaled Dot-Product Attention)，其將每一時序特徵透過三個不同的線性層 (linear layer) 分別轉換爲 Q、K、V 後，送入縮放點積注意力機制。而縮放點積注意力機制運算如式 2，透過平行運算方式同時將所有時序的 Q 對各別時序的 K 兩兩做點積，接著將點積結果除以縮放因子 $\sqrt{d_k}$，然後再送入 softmax 得到相加爲 1 的注意力權重 (Attention Weight)，最後再使用此權重乘上 V 得到輸出

The 33rd Conference on Computational Linguistics and Speech Processing (ROCLING 2021)
Taoyuan, Taiwan, October 15-16, 2021. The Association for Computational Linguistics and Chinese Language Processing

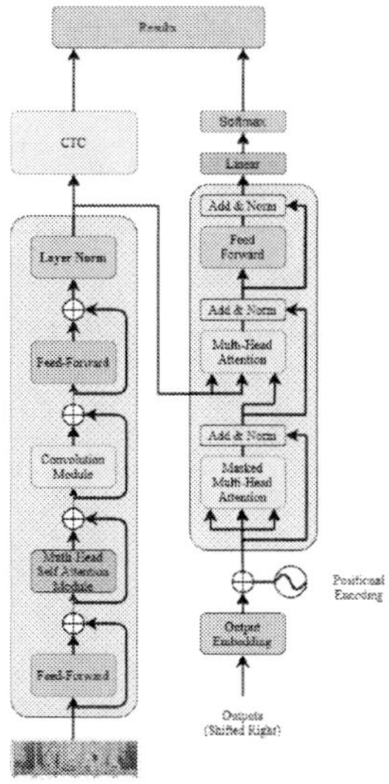

圖 3: Conformer ASR 架構圖

結果，再將每個時序的輸出結果合併就可得到注意力圖 (Attention Map)，其中使用縮放因子 $\sqrt{d_k}$ 的目的是在於讓 Q 和 K 點積後的數值不會因爲 Q 和 K 的維度太大，而造成數值過大，進而影響 softmax 的運算導致梯度變小，影響訓練的結果。

$$Attention(Q,K,V) = softmax(\frac{QK^T}{\sqrt{d_k}})V \quad (2)$$

多頭式注意力機制，如式 3 所示，是由多個縮放點積注意力機制所組成。同樣將每一時序特徵透過三個不同的線性層 (linear layer) 分別轉換爲 Q、K、V，接著再進一步將 Q、K、V 各別切分成 h 等分。多頭的概念是類似 CNN 卷積層中各通道對應的 convolution kernel 的效果，而每一顆頭 (head，h) 會各別關注不同來自不同時序的資訊，然後將每個時序切分後的 Q、K、V 序列送入縮放點積注意力機制進行平行運算最後得到注意力圖。其中 W^Q、W^K、W^V 爲參數矩陣，由訓練所得到。

$$MHSA(Q,K,V) = Concat(head_1, ..., head_H)W^o$$
$$where\, head_h = Attention(QW_h^Q, KW_h^K, VW_h^V) \quad (3)$$

3.3.2 卷積模組 (Convolution Module)

Conformer 中的 Convolution Module，有優異的局部特徵擷取能力，可以將相鄰語音的前後文特性塑模出來，像是能有效地重組醫療相關的關鍵詞，其架構主要先經由一層的點卷積層 (1-D pointwise convolution) 可以將通道 (channel) 加倍，然後依序是 GLU 激勵函數、一維深度卷積層 (1-D depthwise convolution)、Batch Normalize，接著使用 Swish 激勵函數，最後在接上點卷積層。

3.3.3 Self-attention 解碼器

此節我們說明 Self-Attention 解碼器的損失函數。來自編碼器的隱藏層狀態，經過解碼器多層的 Self-Attention 之後，會透過線性層與 softmax，輸出每個時序的聲學特徵序列與相對應字典中每個字符的預測機率。接著將 Ground Truth 轉換爲 one-hot 編碼形式，最後再與每個時序的預測機率進行交叉熵損失函數 (cross-entropy loss) 計算。公式如式 4 所示：

$$L_{self-attention} = -\sum_{u=1}^{U} y^* ln(y_u) \quad (4)$$

其中，y^* 表示爲正確標註 Ground Truth，y_u 爲與 y^* 相同字符的預測機率。最後將所有時序的計算結果相加。由於訓練時希望損失函數 (Loss Function) 最小化，因此取負對數 (Negative logarithm) 來計算損失函數。

3.3.4 CTC 解碼器

接著介紹 CTC 如何將隱藏層狀態 H 預測後的長度縮減成和 y^i 的長度相同。令 U 爲語料庫中所有預測的字典集合，包含中文字以及英文 Syllable 的所有類別，在 CTC 中會另外在字典中加入 Blank (-) 用來表示無發音、發音不清晰或模糊的類別。而語音辨識模型對於每一時序的輸入都會有相對應的輸出，以本研究爲例，即由 Self-Attention Based Encoder 所輸出每一時序的 hidden state 都會得到相對應的類別概率 $p_t(s_t|x)$，其中 s_t 是在 t 時刻從字典 U 中所預測的字符。透過網路輸出將各時序所預測的類別概率相乘可以得到各預測字串的機率，如下式 5 所示：

$$p(S|x) = \prod_{t=1}^{T} p_t(s_t|x) \quad (5)$$

其中 x、T 分別代表語音特徵序列和時序長度；$p_t(s_t|x)$ 表示爲在第 t 個時序所輸出爲某字符的機率，S 爲預測字串，而 $p(S|x)$ 則可理解成每一時序預測字符機率相乘後的預測字串的機率，也就是將每一時序所得到的 $p_t(s_t|x)$ 機率相乘所得到的預測字串機率。

由於 CTC 每一時序皆有相對應的輸出，其可能含有很多重複的預測字符與 blank，使得輸出字串的長度遠大於 y_i^* 的長度，因此在 CTC 中會透過特殊的刪減機制讓預測字串長度更接近 y_i^*。據此，CTC 的刪減規則會先將重複字符移除，接著將預測字串中的 blank 移除，最後得到刪減後的字串，例如：「醫醫-療–語語音音」經過 CTC 刪減後會得到「醫療語音」。

在解釋 CTC 的基本原理之後，我們如下說明如何定義 CTC 的損失函數，以計算輸入的特徵和 y_i^* 之間的損失，並藉此回調網路參數以提高辨識效果。爲了讓訓練和預測時，能讓預測結果更接近 y_i^*。損失函數定義如式 6 所示：

$$L_{CTC} = -log \sum_{s \in Align(x,y^*)} \prod_{t=1}^{T} p_t(s_t|x) \quad (6)$$

其中 x, y^* 分別代表輸入語音特徵序列和相對應的 Ground Truth；$Align(x, y^*)$ 爲所有預測組合經過 CTC 刪減後與 y_i^* 相同的組合，最後將所有屬於 $Align(x, y^*)$ 的組合機率相加。而由於訓練時希望損失函數 (Loss Function) 最小化，因此取負對數 (Negative logarithm) 來計算損失函數。

3.3.5 共同解碼機制 Joint Decoding

爲了讓語音辨識模型在解碼時能同時兼具 CTC 能專注語音局部的特性，以及 Self-Attention 能保持較大跨度前後文關係的優勢，本論文所提的網路架構在解碼階段採取共同解碼機制，也就是透過 λ 當作調和參數來調整 CTC loss 以及 self-attention 的 cross-entropy loss 的權重比例，如式 7 所示：

$$L_{total} = (1 - \lambda) L_{self-attention} - \lambda L_{CTC} \quad (7)$$

4 實驗與結果

我們對照 Joint CTC-Attention 模型與本研究所提出 Joint CTC-Conformer 模型，有使用與沒有使用資料增量時，在有標點符號 psChiMeS-14 進行訓練，對於輸出必需有標點符號標註的辨識效能。同時，我們也比較也進一步探討增加標點符號的標註對 ASR 效能的影響，也就是同樣採用 Joint CTC-Conformer 網路架構，但訓練與測試的語料庫爲 ChiMeS-14 與 psChiMeS-14 的差異時，CER 與 KER 的影響。

4.1 Attention 與 Conformer 的比較

關於實驗評測指標，除了使用語音辨識常見的字符錯誤率 (Character Error Rate：CER) 之外，考量醫療情境中，醫學術語的正確辨識極爲重要，我們也加入了關鍵字錯誤率指標 (Keyword Error Rate：KER)，其中，關鍵字是從訓練文本中另外經由人工擷取出六大類共 707 個醫療相關的關鍵字，其數量如表 3 所列。按此定義的 KER 計算公式如式 8 所示：

表 3: 醫療關鍵字類型

分類	病名	注射液	手術	傷口	藥物	檢查項目	總數
數量	354	60	99	19	60	115	707

$$KER = \frac{S_k + D_k + I_k}{N_k} \times 100\% \quad (8)$$

KER 的計算概念與 CER 類似，針對 Tabel 3 的關鍵字列表我們將 ground truth 的正確標註，以及預測結果中所出現的關鍵字，額外提取出來進行兩者的對齊比較。其中 N_k 爲所有正確的關鍵字數量，而 S_k、D_k 和 I_k 預測的關鍵詞與正確關鍵字比對後發現有替換 (翻錯)、刪除 (漏掉) 與插入 (多加) 動作等三種錯誤的個別次數。

此外，針對 Out Of Keyword (OOK) 也就是未曾出現在訓練集，卻出現在測試集的關鍵詞，我們也另外定義 OOK-KER 的評測指標，如式 9 所示：

$$OOK - KER = \frac{S_{ook} + D_{ook} + I_{ook}}{N_{ook}} \times 100\% \quad (9)$$

其算法基本上與 KER 的算法相同，僅是 OOK-KER 是針對從未出現於訓練集的關鍵字進行評比：N_{ook} 爲所有測試集中未出現在訓練中 ground truth 正確關鍵字的數量，而 S_{ook}、D_{ook} 和 I_{ook} 則爲比對測語音中，針對 OOK 的預測發生替換、刪除與插入這三種錯誤的次數。本研究將使用 CER、KER 和 OOK-KER 作爲評測標準來探討 ASR 績效，三種指標皆是數值越低，表示 ASR 效能越佳。

我們利用表 4 展示分別有使用波形增量的 Joint CTC-Attention 以及有使用速度增量之 Joint CTC-Conformer 訓練網路，在測試測試集中第 11 號錄音者所錄製的其中一份病歷表辨識結果。結果中翻錯、多翻和少翻分別使用 紅色、藍色刪除線 和綠色 <>表示。

如表 5 所示，兩模型在 baseline 不使用任何增量的條件下，Joint CTC-Conformer 的 CER 和 KER 分別優於 Joint CTC-Attention 大約 6.04% 和 9.51%，而 OOK-KER 也優於 Joint CTC-Attention 大約 14.3%。當各別使用數據增量後，Joint CTC-Attention 使用 wave 增量，也就是透過對原音檔上的音量 (volume)、音調 (pitch) 以及語速 (speed) 等進行隨機調整，並將因檔增加爲原來的 4 倍；而 Joint CTC-Conformer 則是使用語速

表 4: 比較 Joint CTC-attention 與 Joint CTC-Conformer 並模型的測試實例

實驗	文字	CER
Ground Truth	{co}{lon}{can}{cer}，沒有高跌，沒有高壓，沒有過敏史， DM{diet} 一天一千五百卡。有 DM，腹膜炎，{co}{lon}{can} {cer}。過去病史。然後此次是因爲發現 {co}{lon}{can}{cer}， 尚未開刀，在左鎖骨放 {port}A，預計行第二次化療入院。 左邊有一條 {port}A，到十月三號，{su}{gar} 測 QIDAC，沒事。	-
Joint CTC-Attention with wave augmentation	{co}{lon}{can}{cer}，沒有高跌，沒有高壓，沒有過敏史， DM{diet} 一千一千五百卡，有 DM<，>腹膜炎，{co}{lon} {can}{cer}。過去病史<，>：他此次< 是 >因爲排現 {co}{lon} {can}{cer}<，>上胃開刀，乀左鎖骨放 {port}A<，>預計先 第二次化療入院。左邊{an}一套口A<，>到十月三號<，> {su}{gar} 測 QIDAC，沒事。	16.81
Joint CTC-Conformer with speed augmentation	{co}{lon}{can}{cer}，沒有高跌，沒有高壓，沒有過敏 史，DM{diet} 一天一千五百卡，有 DM<，>腹膜炎， {co}{lon}{can}{cer}。過去病史<。>：他此次是因爲發 現 {co}{lon}{can}{cer}，上位開大，乀左鎖骨放 {port}AA 急性，DM次化療入院。左邊有一條 {port}A<，>打十月三 < 號 >，{su}{gar} 測 QIDAC<，>沒< 事 >。	15.25

增量 (speed perturbation)，也就是透過調整原音檔的語速 (0.9 和 1.1 倍語速)，將音檔增加爲原來的 3 倍。從數據上顯示，Joint CTC-Attention 在加入 wave 增量之後，相較於不使用的 baseline，其 CER 和 KER 分別下降 4.74% 和 7 %，而 OOK-KER 則持平。而 Joint CTC-Conformer 在加入語速增量後，相較於沒有使用的 baseline，其 CER、KER 和 OOK-KER 也分別下降了 3.9 %、6.89% 和 3.34 %。

由上述數據可知，在使用數據增量後，對於語音辨識效能提升是很有幫助。若進一步比較兩模型的效能，可發現 Joint CTC-Conformer 在 baseline 的條件下，三項指標都優於使用 wave 增量的 Joint CTC-Attention；在使用增量的情況下，Joint CTC-Conformer 的 OOK-KER 更是優於 Joint CTC-Attention 大約 17.69 %，再次驗證了 Conformer 加入 Convolution 的機制能有效補捉局部特徵，提升醫療關鍵字的辨識效能。

表 5: 不同架構在 psChiMeS-14 上的效能比較

ASR	Joint CTC-Attention		Joint CTC-Conformer	
Aug.	baseline	wave	baseline	speed
CER(%)	20.44	15.70	14.40	10.50
KER(%)	29.50	22.50	19.99	13.10
OOK-KER(%)	76.85	76.85	62.50	59.16

我們特別說明不曾出現在訓練集中 OOK 的辨識。相較於一般 ASR 不可能測試出不曾出現在訓練集的字符 (OOV)，對於醫療關鍵字，其本質上比較像是詞的概念，也就是由幾個獨立的字或是英文單音節所串接而成，只要一個由多個字是多個英文單音節所組成的關鍵詞 (keyword)，其各別組成的字或單音節曾出現在訓練集中，好的 ASR 就有機會將這從來沒有聽過的關鍵詞重組出來。在本研究所提出的 Joint CTC-conformer 架構中，不爲全錯的 OOK-KER 即代表：即使不曾在訓練集中出現的關鍵字，也有可能被正確辨識出來。也就是說，儘管沒有額外的 PM (pronunciation model) 以及 LM (language model) 的塑模，本研究所提出的 ASR 架構，仍可以從訓練集中出現過字符的前後文關係拼湊出先前不曾看過的關鍵字。表 6 與表 7 分別是一些被正確辨識出中文與英文 OOK 的例子。

4.2 增加標點符號的標註對 ASR 的影響

此外，我們也好奇，加入標點符號標註的文本對於端對端的語音辨識模型在辨識績效上的影響。我們固定使用 Joint CTC-Conformer 模型，比較當使用無標點符號的 ChiMeS 與有標點符號標註的 psChiMeS 這兩種語料庫，進行訓練與後續測試效果的比較。如表 8 所示，當 Joint CTC-Conformer 使用加上標點符號的 psChiMeS 訓練時，會比當使用沒有標點符號標註的 ChiMeS 訓練，CER 上升了 2.1 % 和 SER 上升大約 11%。我們解釋的原因是：標點符號占了 psChiMeS-14 整份文本中字數的大約 10%，而由整體標點符號正確辨識率的 F-Score 來看，約爲 83%，因此可以推知模型在 CER 上升 2% 的原因，主要應該是由標點符號所影響；而 SER (sentence error rate) 部分，由於 SER 計算方式較爲嚴格，也就是只要一句裡錯一個字即視爲全錯，再加上加入標點符號訓練所造成的標點符號錯誤，因此導致 SER 的上升。

表 6: 中文可辨識 OOK 範例

OOK	Conformer Results
膽管癌	七 B 五二二，男性其實歲診斷是膽管癌，UTI，然後他沒有高跌，是高壓的病人，沒有過敏史。
腸造口手術	他預計五月二二號進去開刀房做胰臟結腸切除跟吻合術，然後再加腸造口手術
心包膜積水	阿沒有心包膜積水齁，然後 IO 有都還好話，然後沒 S 二十九號辦出院。
輸尿管碎石	然後他的過去病史有：DM，尿路結石有開剖腹採，有輸尿管碎石，還有右側輸尿管狹窄開過刀。
肝囊腫	buscopan，buscopan 打過，有 follow A 加 P，A 腹部的 CTL 已沒有顯影的，就是肝囊腫，然後腸炎 X ray 沒有事，EKG sinus tachycardia。

表 7: 英文可辨識 OOK 範例

OOK	Conformer Results
kascoal	然後他有那個自備藥有一些藥 kascoal 齁，還有一些 primperan nexium 這些都把他停掉了。
bladder CA	男性八十二水診斷是 bladder CA，沒有高跌，沒有高壓，沒有過敏史，是 on full diet。
CAD	男性五素水診斷是 CAD ESRD，沒有高跌，沒有高壓。
on levophed pump	八月十七號因爲血壓低，給他 on levophed pump，之後血壓 OK 就 on 服。
右 lung tumor	男性六十五歲，他的診斷是右 lung tumor，沒有高跌，沒有高壓，沒有過敏史，目前是 on soft diet。

我們另外分析，標註文本加入標點符號後，對於原本中文字與英文單音節 (mon-syllable) 辨識的影響。爲此，我們將 psChiMeS-14 測試結果中的標點符號去除，重新計算前述三項效能指標，並與以文本中本身就沒有標點符號標註的 sChiMeS-14 訓練後模型的的測試結果進行比較。如同表 8中的第三列示，CER 並沒有太大的差異；SER 的部分些微下降了 0.45%，而 KER 下降了 1.14%。從數據上可以觀察出，模型使用加入標點符號的文本進行訓練，不僅不會造成中文字與英文單音節辨識效果下降，反而因爲加入標點符號後前後語意更爲完整，所以讓醫療關鍵字辨識率有些微的提升。

表 8: Joint CTC-Conformer 不同語料庫效能比較

Corpus	Joint CTC-Comformer		
	CER	SER	KER
sChiMeS-14	8.42	76.21	13.59
psChiMeS-14	10.5	87.60	13.10
psChiMeS-14 (remove punctuation)	8.40	75.76	12.45

5 Conclusion

爲了改良中文醫療語音辨識的結果也提供標點符號的需求，本研究透過重新標註原語料庫文本 ChiMeS-14 而得到有標點符號的訓練集 psChiMeS。然後，利用以 self-attention 機制爲基礎的 conformer 模型與 CTC 合併搭建的 Joint CTC-Attention ASR 的模型，在 psChiMeS-14 語料庫進行訓練與測試，我們獲得到目前爲止最好的語音辨識績效。一般說來，利用加上標點符號文本，在 Joint CTC-Conformer 的架構上進行端對端的訓練，基本上不會對 CER, SER 或是 KER 有明顯的影響。ASR 僅將這些額外標註的標點符號視同與中文字或是英文單音一樣的字符。

最後，由於目前病歷表的讀出較爲口語，未來將針對辨識結果中贅字虛字的校正與制式文書的轉譯謄寫，如：嗯、齁、痾等贅字可進行刪除。而醫療文本終有許多筆記型的陳述方式省略完整內容，不易一般人明瞭，因此未來也會使用後處理的機制進行轉譯，如高跌表示將轉譯爲高跌倒危險群等，方便大眾閱讀。此外，由 (Salloum et al., 2017) 等學者所提出的研究中，將語音辨識的結過再進一步透過

NLP 模型轉換成診斷報告。我們受到了啓發，未來將嘗試利用醫療文本中關鍵字建構智慧型的醫學診斷以及出院報告等，讓病歷報告可以自動化生成。

References

Dario Amodei, Sundaram Ananthanarayanan, Rishita Anubhai, Jingliang Bai, Eric Battenberg, Carl Case, Jared Casper, Bryan Catanzaro, Qiang Cheng, Guoliang Chen, et al. 2016. Deep speech 2: End-to-end speech recognition in english and mandarin. In *International conference on machine learning*, pages 173–182. PMLR.

Jacob Devlin, Ming-Wei Chang, Kenton Lee, and Kristina Toutanova. 2018. Bert: Pre-training of deep bidirectional transformers for language understanding. *arXiv preprint arXiv:1810.04805*.

Linhao Dong, Shuang Xu, and Bo Xu. 2018. Speech-transformer: a no-recurrence sequence-to-sequence model for speech recognition. In *2018 IEEE International Conference on Acoustics, Speech and Signal Processing (ICASSP)*, pages 5884–5888. IEEE.

Bhrigu Garg et al. 2018. Analysis of punctuation prediction models for automated transcript generation in mooc videos. In *2018 IEEE 6th International Conference on MOOCs, Innovation and Technology in Education (MITE)*, pages 19–26. IEEE.

Alex Graves, Santiago Fernández, Faustino Gomez, and Jürgen Schmidhuber. 2006. Connectionist temporal classification: labelling unsegmented sequence data with recurrent neural networks. In *Proceedings of the 23rd international conference on Machine learning*, pages 369–376.

Anmol Gulati, James Qin, Chung-Cheng Chiu, Niki Parmar, Yu Zhang, Jiahui Yu, Wei Han, Shibo Wang, Zhengdong Zhang, Yonghui Wu, et al. 2020. Conformer: Convolution-augmented transformer for speech recognition. *arXiv preprint arXiv:2005.08100*.

Suyoun Kim, Takaaki Hori, and Shinji Watanabe. 2017. Joint ctc-attention based end-to-end speech recognition using multi-task learning. In *2017 IEEE international conference on acoustics, speech and signal processing (ICASSP)*, pages 4835–4839. IEEE.

Daniel Li, I Te, Naveen Arivazhagan, Colin Cherry, and Dirk Padfield. 2021. Sentence boundary augmentation for neural machine translation robustness. In *ICASSP 2021-2021 IEEE International Conference on Acoustics, Speech and Signal Processing (ICASSP)*, pages 7553–7557. IEEE.

Haoran Miao, Gaofeng Cheng, Changfeng Gao, Pengyuan Zhang, and Yonghong Yan. 2020. Transformer-based online ctc/attention end-to-end speech recognition architecture. In *ICASSP 2020-2020 IEEE International Conference on Acoustics, Speech and Signal Processing (ICASSP)*, pages 6084–6088. IEEE.

Kishore Papineni, Salim Roukos, Todd Ward, and Wei-Jing Zhu. 2002. Bleu: a method for automatic evaluation of machine translation. In *Proceedings of the 40th annual meeting of the Association for Computational Linguistics*, pages 311–318.

Wael Salloum, Gregory Finley, Erik Edwards, Mark Miller, and David Suendermann-Oeft. 2017. Automated preamble detection in dictated medical reports. In *BioNLP 2017*, pages 287–295.

Monica Sunkara, Srikanth Ronanki, Kalpit Dixit, Sravan Bodapati, and Katrin Kirchhoff. 2020. Robust prediction of punctuation and truecasing for medical asr. *arXiv preprint arXiv:2007.02025*.

Ashish Vaswani, Noam Shazeer, Niki Parmar, Jakob Uszkoreit, Llion Jones, Aidan N Gomez, Łukasz Kaiser, and Illia Polosukhin. 2017. Attention is all you need. In *Advances in neural information processing systems*, pages 5998–6008.

Ruiqing Zhang and Chuanqiang Zhang. 2020. Dynamic sentence boundary detection for simultaneous translation. In *Proceedings of the First Workshop on Automatic Simultaneous Translation*, pages 1–9.

Zhengyan Zhang, Xu Han, Zhiyuan Liu, Xin Jiang, Maosong Sun, and Qun Liu. 2019. Ernie: Enhanced language representation with informative entities. *arXiv preprint arXiv:1905.07129*.

The 33rd Conference on Computational Linguistics and Speech Processing (ROCLING 2021)
Taoyuan, Taiwan, October 15-16, 2021. The Association for Computational Linguistics and Chinese Language Processing

Data centric approach to Chinese Medical Speech Recognition
以資料爲中心的中文醫療語音辨識技術開發

鍾聖倫 **Sheng-Luen Chung**; 李憶萱 **Yi-Shiuan Li**
國立臺灣科技大學電機工程學系
Electrical Engineering Department
National Taiwan University of Science and Technology
Taipei, Taiwan
slchung@mail.ntust.edu.tw; m10807310@gapps.ntust.edu.tw

丁賢偉 **Hsien-Wei Ting**
衛生福利部臺北醫院神經外科
Department of Neurosurgery
Taipei Hospital, Ministry of Health and Welfare
Taipei, Taiwan
ting.ns@gmail.com

摘要

針對中文醫療語音辨識技術，本研究以資料爲中心的觀點 (data centric)，按照機器學習中開發與佈署 (MLOps) 的流程進行研究。首先，本研究按語義完整性切割出 Chinese Medical Speech Corpus (ChiMeS)；其次是語音辨識模型的優化：在固定 Joint CTC/Attention 的自動語音辨識 (Automatic Speech Recognition，ASR) 網路架構後，針對語料庫極端受限的挑戰，利用波形之資料增量提升辨識效果。整體來看，爲了促進中文醫療語音辨識的發展，本研究的具體貢獻有三，分別是：(一) 收集並標註 ChiMeS 語料庫，其爲時 14.4 小時，共 7,225 句語音。(二) 針對中文醫療語音辨識應用，訓練好的 Joint CTC/Attention ASR 模型，其在 ChiMeS-14 的測試集上的字符錯誤率 (Character Error Rate，CER) 和關鍵字錯誤率 (Keyword Error Rate，KER) 分別爲 13.65% 和 20.82%。以及 (三) 提供用來評估其他 ASR 模型績效的測試平台。細節請參 ChiMeS 入口網站 (https://iclab.ee.ntust.edu.tw/home)。

關鍵字：深度學習、中文醫療語音庫、語音辨識

Abstract

Concerning the deleopment of Chinese medical speech recognition technology, this study re-addresses earlier encountered issues in accordance with the process of Machine Learning Engineering for Production (MLOps) from a data centric perspective. First is the new segmentation of speech utterances to meet sentences completeness for all utterances in the colllected Chinese Medical Speech Corpus (ChiMeS). Second is optimization of Joint CTC/Attention model through data augmentation in boosting recognition performance out of very limited speech corpus. Overall, to facilitate the development of Chinese medical speech recognition, this paper contributes: (1) The ChiMeS corpus, the first Chinese Medicine Speech corpus of its kind, which is 14.4 hours, with a total of 7,225 sentences. (2) A trained Joint CTC/Attention ASR model by ChiMeS-14, yielding a Character Error Rate (CER) of 13.65% and a Keyword Error Rate (KER) of 20.82%, respectively, when tested on the ChiMeS-14 testing set. And (3) an evaluation platform set up to compare performance of other ASR models. All the released resources can be found in the ChiMeS portal (https://iclab.ee.ntust.edu.tw/home).

Keywords: Deep learning, Chinese medical speech corpus, Speech recognition

1 緒論

機器學習與運作 Machine Learning and Operations (MLOps)(Spjuth et al., 2021) 的概念是：針對以深度學習爲架構的任務，通常仰賴大量的資料進行訓練與測試、需要不斷的驗證以進行錯誤分析、並要針對不夠理想的結果設法提升效能，以最終能夠發展成爲可上市產品的系統化技術開發流程。本研究所要探討的目的即爲：以深度學習技術爲基礎，發展中

文醫療語音辨識成文字的技術發展過程中，所涉及到 MLOps 流程中幾個關鍵點的考量。

傳統語音辨識技術 (Oh et al., 2008)，主要建構在以聲學模型 (acoustic model，AM)、拼音模型 (pronunciation model，PM) 以及語言模型 (language model，LM) 三個模型的基礎上。這些與語言學專業相關的模型需要個別訓練，過程繁瑣複雜。近年來，多虧 Deep Speech(Hannun et al., 2014) 等基於深度學習之端對端語音模型的出現，新的語音辨識技術可以讓深度學習網路直接學習到語音和字符之間的對應關係，而不再像傳統技術中需要獨立訓練再整合的處理，並可得到優異的辨識效果。

目前語音辨識技術大多針對一般日常應用情境的語句，如語音助理、會議紀錄的轉譯等。針對此類應用，文獻上有相當數量的語料庫，可支援相關語音模型的訓練。大部份商用的語音辨識技術，透過大規模語料庫的訓練，在常用對談的情境中，可得到相當好的辨識效果。相較而言，對於類似像醫護專業的應用情境來說，文獻上或是商用產品均較缺乏相關醫學語料庫以及語音辨識技術的報導。然而，醫護專業場景中，如有自動語音辨識的輔助，可帶來很大的便利性。以護理交班爲例，醫護人員在下班前要將其所負責病患的病歷內容交接給另外一位護理人員。護理師除了口述之外，還需要手動輸入至電子健康紀錄 (Electronic Health Record，EHR) 中，手工作業繁瑣且費時。本中文醫療語音辨識技術研究的目的之一，即在於協助護理人員在口述交班時，利用語音辨識技術，將口述的內容直接轉譯成文字，輔助輸入 EHR，以降低護理人員紙筆輸入、手動輸入病歷、以及操作電子設備的時間。

發展中文醫療語音辨識技術所面臨到最主要的挑戰是缺乏專業語料庫。首先，以深度學習爲主的語音辨識技術，需要大量的資料集進行訓練與測試。而在專業醫療領域上，語料庫的收集更是困難，以致於目前在華語地區尚未有以中文爲主的醫學語料庫的發佈。其次，一般中文醫護的語音雖然以中文爲主，但多輔以英文的專業術語，內含雙語 (sentential code-switching) 的語料庫對於語音辨識是一項挑戰。爲了解決上述兩個問題，本研究遵循著 MLOps 的流程：定義問題、蒐集資料庫、訓練模型，以及將模型部署於其他場域，並以資料爲中心進行研究。本研究之貢獻在於：(1) 收集並標註一個語意完整的中文醫學語料庫 (ChiMeS)；(2) 針對此醫學語料庫額外使用波形增量 (Ko et al., 2015) 的方法，得到 CER 和 KER 分別爲 13.65% 和 20.82% 的 ASR 模型；(3) 並提供 ChiMeS 入口網站，提供語料庫以及公平測試的平台。

本論文以下第二節的文獻審閱分爲語料庫與 ASR 的技術演進進行介紹。第三節的 ChiMeS-14 語料庫會詳述資料集的錄製來源、訓練與測試之資料統計數字，還有本研究所提供的入口網站。第四節介紹 Joint CTC/Attention 語音辨識架構，以及波形增量的應用。第五節爲實驗結果與分析效能之討論。第六節則是結論與未來研究之方向。

2 文獻審閱

2.1 語料庫

針對不同領域的語音辨識任務，需要不同的訓練資料。以下介紹從 2017 年至文獻上所發佈，與中文醫療語音稍有關連的語料庫，包括在臺灣、大陸與新馬地區的華語語料庫，以及英文版本的醫學語料庫。

當作全世界最重要的語言之一，中文有相當的地域性。臺灣與中國雖然語言都使用中文，但在字體的運用、發音，以及字義的表示上，兩個地區都有所不同。臺灣最具代表性的中文語料庫，如 FSW 語料庫 (Liao et al., 2020)，其爲透過臺灣國家教育廣播電台的錄製，提出總共約 610 小時。此語料庫中含有 98,089 句以及 14,631,829 個字符。若是忽略不計算 735 個廣播新聞，大約至少有 120 人參與共 800 場訪談的錄音。本語料庫並當作 2018 之 Formosa Grand Challenge 競賽之用。2019 年時，Common Voice(Ardila et al., 2019) 收集了 38 種不同的語言，其中臺灣口音的中文涵蓋約 43 小時，到了 2020 年更收集到 78 小時，錄製人員也從 949 增加至 1,444 位。

另一方面，2018 年在中國所發佈的 AIShell-2(Du et al., 2018) 含有接近 100 萬個句子，包含了 1,000 小時的語音資料，總共有 1,991 位人員參與錄音，爲目前最大量的中文語料庫。在 2020 年間，DiDiSpeech(Guo et al., 2021) 收集了 6,000 人的語音，相較其他語料庫含更多錄音者，有更多元的音色。爲了滿足不同語音辨識任務的需求，將此語料庫切割成兩個不同的子集：DiDiSpeech-1 和 DiDiSpeech-2。4500 位錄製者形成 DiDiSpeech-1 的 480,571 句子；而另外的 1,500 位錄製 171,361 句的 DiDiSpeech-2。

同樣在有許多華人的新加坡和馬來西亞，人們通常使用中英混雜的方式對談。2018 年釋出 SEAME(Lee et al., 2018)，爲 192 小時的語料庫，有 157 位錄音者，共有 162,290 句。

主要內容以採訪與對話爲主，在文本中以字 (word-level) 爲單位進行標註，並且含有語言標籤以及額外的六種分類標籤，分別爲目標語音、語助詞、其他語言、縮寫與專有名詞、口語化以及非語言訊號。

特別針對醫療語音辨識，2017 年時，Google (Chiu et al., 2017) 錄製超過 90,000 筆醫師與病患的醫療臨床對話，語料庫中最短的對話約爲 10 分鐘，而最長達到 2 個小時左右。此外，資料集中共有 100 名以上的醫師參與錄音，在訓練集與測試集的區分上，並不會有醫生的聲音重疊的情形，也就是出現在訓練集的醫生，就不會出現於測試集中。此英語內容的醫療語料庫極爲龐大，但並沒有釋出。

2.2 ASR 演進

傳統語音辨識技術中，kaldi(Povey et al., 2011) 的架構主要由：聲學模型、發音模型以及語言模型等三個模型所組成。其中，聲學模型主要是學習聲音上的特性；發音模型又稱爲詞典 (lexicon) 模型，其對應音素 (phoneme) 與形素 (grapheme) 的關係，協助聲學模型將發音映射到字形序列上；而語言模型則是學習文本中字與字之間的關係，提供傳統 ASR 語意上的幫助。由於這些模型需要個別訓練，因此需要仰賴語音的專業知識來對模型進行建模與優化。

近年來，以深度學習爲基礎的端對端語音辨識技術可直接學習如何語音特徵轉換成目標字符，免去了需要先針對傳統三個模塊個別建模與訓練的繁瑣流程，而有蓬勃發展。端對端語音辨識架構的本質是序列對序列的轉換，在將長度不固定的語音映射至可變長度輸出字符的技術上，主要分爲 Connectionist Temporal Classification(CTC) 和注意力 (attention) 方法。其中，爲了解決語音辨識輸入與輸出序列長度不固定的問題，CTC(Graves et al., 2006) 對每一幀的輸入都會有相對應獨立的輸出結果，透過 CTC 縮減的方式，將重複的字符先刪減，再移除空白標籤，最後得到短序列輸出的程序，來學習語音與相對應的標籤序列如何自動對齊。

另外一方面，基於注意力 (Attention) 機制的 ASR 也是透過編碼器和解碼器組成語音辨識架構：將輸入不固定長度的語音轉換成固定長度的語音特徵向量並得到隱藏狀態 (hidden state)，再利用基於 RNN 的解碼器，將語音的編碼器隱藏狀態解碼成序列表示的預測結果。和 CTC 機制不同的是，注意力機制的解碼器會同時參考編碼器中的所有隱藏狀態，可以捕捉時間跨度更長的前後文 (context) 的關係，如：拼音模型中的片語和語言模型的句型關係。注意力機制的代表架構如 Google 提出的 Listen, attend and spell (LAS)(Chan et al., 2016)，其中，稱爲 Listener 的金字塔型雙向 LSTM 將輸入序列轉變成高維特徵，而 Speller 在基於注意力的機制下，藉此學習前後文的關係，考慮過去輸入的情況下，輸出所有學過的字符機率分佈。

於 2017 年所發表的 Joint CTC/Attention (Kim et al., 2017) 語音識別模型結合 CTC 與注意力機制，提高架構的穩定性且使訓練能夠更快速收斂。藉由共用編碼器的方式，將聲學序列萃取後轉換成高維的特徵，在解碼器的部分則引用上述的 CTC 和注意力機制進行推斷以推測出最終結果。文獻上之後，也有許多針對基於結合這兩種方法的語音辨識架構，但主要是針對模型架構做調整與改善。舉例來說：(Zhu and Cheng, 2020) 的編碼器由雙向 LSTM (BLSTM) 組成的三角型架構組成，在沒有卷積層的情況下，來提升特徵萃取的能力。另外，(Li et al., 2019) 使用兩個獨立的編碼器先個別獲取聲音特徵以及各自的注意力分數，再將個別的注意力分數引入 Hierarchical Attention Network (HAN) 進行整合，得到更有效的訊息。

3 ChiMeS 語料庫與入口網站

語音資料庫採集不易，而專業領域情境下之語音更是如此。本研究針對 516 份住院病歷表朗讀語音檔，先按照語意完整性進行語句的切割與標註。之後，確認將此語料庫所切分出來的訓練集與測試集中錄音人員沒有重複。而對於評估語音辨識績效的指標，除了 CER 之外，由於專業語音中關鍵字相對重要，我們另外定義關鍵字錯誤率 Keyword Error Rate (KER)。相關語料庫、辨識評測標準以及工具一併公布至入口網站。

3.1 收集與標註

中文醫療語料庫 Chinese Medical Speech Corpus (ChiMeS) 共爲時約 14.4 小時，其由衛生福利部台北醫院的 15 位女性護理師，根據 516 份匿名化處理的住院病患病歷表，以交班時講話的方式進行語音的錄製，再經按完整語義切割與中英文譯文的標註而成。每份病歷表內容主要包括：匿名化病患之病史資料、入院狀態、目前病情，與每天狀況更新等四個部分。病歷來源包括：外科、泌尿科、耳鼻喉科、眼科、重症及安寧患者。此語料庫之音檔皆爲 wav 格式，採樣率 (sampling rate) 和取樣解析度 (bit resolution) 分別爲 16K Hz 及 16-bit，錄音文本則使用 UTF-8 編碼格式。

我們使用 ELAN(https://archive.mpi.nl/tla/elan) 標註工具，將專業護理師朗讀病歷表之語音，按照文本的語意完整性，以及大約時間長度爲 5 秒至 15 秒的條件下，將每份病歷表的朗讀切割成許多份語意完整的語音 (utterance) 檔案。由於病歷表中所記載之內容通常爲筆記型的摘要，不一定符合嚴謹的文法定義，我們儘量依據語意的完整性，先進行切分與文字標註。其中，語意的完整，指的是當語音內容描述完病患的一項狀態、一個診斷等完整的內容，即認定此爲完整的語意表達，進而做語音的分割，完成一句完整短語音，其流程如圖1所示。

語料庫中的字 (word) 或形素 (grapheme) 的標註，不僅決定 ASR 最終輸出字符的單位，也決定到最後 ASR 的績效評比，像是 CER 或是 WER 的計算。中文醫療語料庫標註的困難主要的原因在於其爲句中語系切換 (intra-sentential code switching)：雖然語音主體是中文句型，但文句中穿插有顯著比例的英文專業術語。針對句中語系切換語料庫的標註，不同語系的形素單位也有不同：在拼音系統中一般採用拼音字母，以英文而言，即爲 26 個英文字母，等同於 26 個形素。相對而言，中文字比較偏向表意符號 (ideogram)，每個中文字符本身即爲一個釋文代表。針對以字母標註的語料庫，ASR 除了要辨識各個字母，還要決定在連續字母之輸出後考慮是否爲一個單詞，並以空格做詞與詞間的區隔。而以表意文字標註的語料庫，不同的表意字符可能會發生同音字的情況，因此 ASR 架構需要仰賴前後文才能判定目前對應的字符輸出。爲了使 ASR 解碼一致，針對句中語系切換的 ChiMeS 語料庫，我們標註的原則是：中文以一個中文字符爲單位，而英文則以一個英文的單音節 (mono-syllable) 爲單位。本研究採用 How many syllables (https://www.howmanysyllables.com) 做爲將一個多音節的英詞 (word) 拆成由數個由英文單音節所串成標註的依據。舉例來說：'glucose' 分解成 'glu' 'cose'；而在英文縮寫上使用大寫表示，如 CRP。此外，由於病歷表中含有大量數值的內容，都使用中文標註，如：'10.3' 標註爲 '十點三'。

3.2 語料庫切分與評測依據

針對深度學習模型訓練與測試需要，ChiMeS 語料庫按約 4：1 的比例，切分爲錄音員不重覆的訓練集與測試。另外，音檔的命名方式以日期與第幾分病歷表爲標示，其次才爲此語句在整份病歷表中之編號，如：0522_01_1.wav。

配合跨科別測試，我們另外由 ChiMeS-14 的語料庫中，取出一個子集 ChiMeS-5，如表 1所示，其參與之錄製人員較少，病歷表涉及的科別涵蓋較小，只有外科、泌尿科、耳鼻喉科和眼科。而在人員錄製的病歷表份數上，訓練集中 01 和 02 號的份數不變，而編號 03、04 和 06 號護理人員，分別只含 86、33 和 9 份的病歷數；測試集的 05 號則是有 33 份的病歷表在子資料集 ChiMeS-5 中。在表 2爲 ChiMeS 的時長、句數、含中文字符與英文音節的總字數、平均時間長度等相關統計。值得一提的是，總字數的字符與音節分佈在 ChiMeS-14 中爲 167,409 和 48,110；而 ChiMeS-5 則爲 65,807 和 17,534。而不同字總數之字符和音節數在 ChiMeS-14 中爲 1,608 與 689；而 ChiMeS-5 則爲 1,268 和 553。

表 1: 語料庫分佈

語料庫	ChiMeS-14	ChiMeS-5
訓練護理師編號	{01~15}-{05,11,12}	{01~06}-05
測試護理師編號	{05,11,12}	05
訓練病歷表份數	394	166
測試病歷表份數	122	33

表 2: 語料庫細節

語料庫	ChiMeS-14	ChiMeS-5
時長	14.4hr (867mins)	5.5hr (335mins)
句數	7,225	2,987
總 tokens 數	215,519	83,341
不同 tokens 總數	2,297	1,821
平均時長 (secs)	7.2	6.7
平均 tokens 數	29.8	27.9
OOV 數	104	109

由於醫療語音辨識中，專業醫學術語的辨識上極爲重要，我們從 ChiMeS-14 中特別由人工萃取出 707 個與醫學相關的關鍵字，包括：病名、注射液、手術、傷口、藥物以及檢查項目，等六大類，如表 3 所示，各類醫學術語如：心臟病、limadol、扁桃腺切除、燙傷、vena 和核磁共振等中英文語詞。這些術語的正確辨識也將做爲專業語音辨識的績效依據。

表 3: 醫療關鍵字類型

分類	病名	注射液	手術	傷口	藥物	檢查項目	總數
數量	354	60	99	19	60	115	707

針對 ChiMeS 語料庫切分之測試集，我們

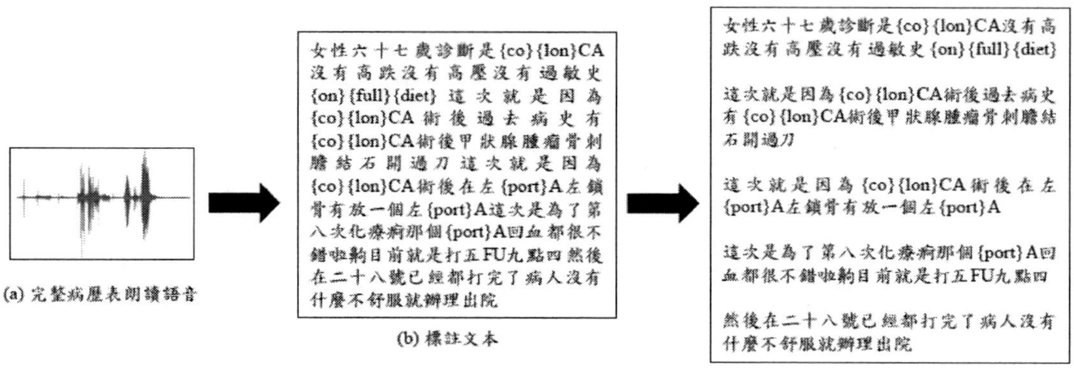

(a) 完整病歷表朗讀語音 (b) 標註文本 (c) 按語意切割語音

圖 1: 標註流程

使用兩種語音辨識的評判指標：CER、KER。其中，CER 的定義如式1 所示：

$$CER = \frac{S + D + I}{N} \times 100\% \tag{1}$$

在上式中，N 爲 ground truth 中正確標註的字符數目，而 S 、D 和 I 分別對應預測結果中，對應：替換 (錯判)、刪除 (漏掉) 和插入 (新加) 等三項錯誤結果的字符數。其中，中文的字符以一顆顆中文字爲單位，而英文則使用英文單音節爲單位進行計算。舉例而言，'glucose ' 分解成 'glu' 'cose'，在計算時視爲兩個字符，這剛好跟其中文意譯的 '血糖' 由兩個字符構成等權重。

除了 CER 的評測外，本研究也提供 KER 的計算，其公式如下式2：

$$KER = \frac{S_k + D_k + I_k}{N_k} \times 100\% \tag{2}$$

KER 的計算概念與 CER 類似，針對表 3的關鍵字列表，我們將 ground truth 中正確標註以及預測結果中所出現的關鍵字進行對齊以比較差異。其中，N_k 爲所有測試集中的 ground truth 中所出現正確關鍵字的數量，而 S_k 、D_k 和 I_k 分別爲預測結果中被替換、刪除與插入的錯誤之關鍵字的數目。

3.3 ChiMeS 入口網站

爲促進中文醫學語音辨識技的提供，我們建置了 ChiMeS 入口網站 (`https://iclab.ee.ntust.edu.tw/home`)，並於其中公佈相關的語料庫、利用 ChiMeS-14 所訓練的 ASR 語音辨識模型，以及提供比較 ASR 模型績效的測試平台。

ChiMeS 入口網站共含五個部分：首頁、資料集、語音模型、評測以及線上實例展示。首頁包含後續頁面的簡介；語料庫分頁中，提供授權後可下載之 ChiMeS 語料庫的訓練集和測試集的音檔和標註的文本。評測平台提供 ChiMeS-5 與 ChiMeS-14 測試集，以及評估工具，可提供其他 ASR 的解決方案的測試績效。此外，我們也提供使用 ChiMeS-14 訓練之 Joint CTC/Attention 進行即時語音辨識。透過直接上傳音檔或是使用麥克風進行即時錄音，即可得到 ASR 轉譯結果。最後線上實例展示分頁中，一樣透過錄音或者上傳音檔的方式，即時得到辨識結果，並可額外針對結果進行修改。

4 醫療語音辨識模型

本研究參考 (Hori et al., 2017) 之 Joint CTC/Attention 架構做爲中文醫療語料庫的基線解決方案。此外，還額外使用波形增量的方法，在有限的醫療病歷語料庫下，提升語音辨識的正確率。本節將分爲三個部分介紹。首先，概述本實驗之語音辨識基準方案在訓練與測試的流程。接下來說明 Joint CTC/Attention 架構訓練方法。最後，詳述有關資料增量方法的產生與應用。

在語音辨識的流程中，首先將波形資料進行預處理，形成長度爲 T 的聲學特徵序列 $X = (x_1, ..., x_T)$，再透過語音辨識模型輸出所有字符分佈機率，並在最後選出最大機率之句子作爲對應長度爲 U 的辨識結果 $Y = (y_1, ..., y_U)$。在訓練階段，本研究採用 Joint CTC/Attention 網路，根據 ground truth 正確標註來計算由 CTC 與注意力模型的損失函數，調整網路參數，並在解碼過程中，考量注意力模型與 CTC 之間的比重，來組合兩種解碼機制。另外一方面，在測試階段，在考量以上架構的輸出時，也會針對 CTC 和注意力機制，進行權重比例的分配。最後是採用光束搜

索 (Beam search) 的解碼方式，從所有的可能性中選擇出一個機率最大的句子作爲預測結果。

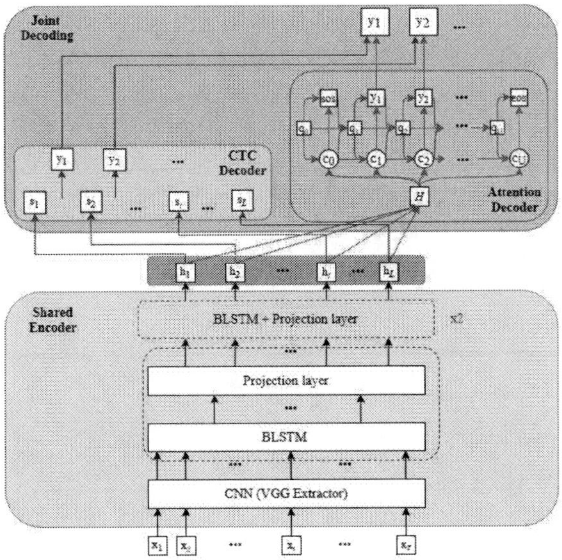

圖 2: Joint CTC/Attention

4.1 共同編碼器

我們將語料庫內的第 i 筆語音資料 w_i，其對應之逐字正確標註表示爲 y_i^*，這樣，語料庫中所有的資料可寫成 $W = \{(w_1, y_1^*), (w_2, y_2^*), .., (w_i, y_i^*)\}$。由於輸入 Joint CTC/Attention 網路架構的資料爲頻譜圖，因此將音檔透過快速傅立葉轉換 (Fast Fourier transform，FFT) 從時域轉換成頻域的形式，變成聲音特徵序列 $X = (x_1, ..., x_T)$。Joint CTC/Attention 網路架構共用一個編碼器，用來萃取語音特徵與學習時序關係，將長度 T 的序列 X 轉換成長度較短的高維表示，即編碼器的隱藏狀態爲 $H = (h_1, ..., h_L)$，如式3：

$$H = Encoder(X) \tag{3}$$

4.2 CTC 解碼器

CTC 機制能夠將長序列對應至短序列，並透過特殊的縮減方法來訓練語音模型。最主要的概念是針對每個語音幀都會有相對應的輸出字符，且不同字符的集合由字典 V 表示，其含中文字符與英文單音節，並有 blank 標籤 (<blank>) 代表發音模糊或是無發音的狀態。若要得知序列 Y 之機率，必須考慮刪減與移除前所有可能輸出 $S = (s_1, ..., s_L)$ 組合，公式如下式4：

$$p(Y|X) = \sum_{S \in Align(X,Y)} p(S|X) \tag{4}$$

在訓練階段，網路反向傳播誤差以用來更新權重參數。其中，CTC 的損失計算輸入序列與正確標註 Y^* 的差異，以在訓練時回傳與更新參數來學習對應關係。損失函數數值越小，代表此序列和正確標註越相似，模型學得越好。如式5所示：

$$L_{CTC} \triangleq -lnp(Y^*|X) \tag{5}$$

4.3 注意力解碼器

基於注意力機制之解碼器架構藉由式 6遞迴的方式，參考所有跨度的隱藏狀態 H，運算出在位置 u 的輸出字符分佈 y_u。如式 7所示，Attention 方法和 CTC 方法最大差別在於注意力除了將輸入聲音特徵序列 X 納入考量之外，也會參考過去輸出 $y_{1:u-1}$，以達到考慮前後文關係的完整序列 Y 預測。

$$y_u \sim AttentionDecoder(H, y_{1:u-1}) \tag{6}$$

$$p(S|X) = \prod_u p(y_u|X, y_{1:u-1}) \tag{7}$$

其損失函數計算如式 8，利用 cross-entropy 的準則學習編碼器的 $H = (h_1, ..., h_L)$ 和注意力解碼器的輸出 $Y = (y_1, ..., y_u)$ 兩種不同長度的序列。此外，爲了確保注意力編碼器能夠準確的學習到前後文的關係，使用強迫學習 (Teacher forcing) (Chang et al., 2019) 的方式，將過去的正確標籤序列 $y_{1:u-1}^*$ 作爲第 u 步的輸入資訊，進行網路的訓練。

$$L_{Attention} = -ln \sum_u p(y_u^*|X, y_{1:u-1}^*) \tag{8}$$

爲了計算出前後文向量 (Context Vector)，必須計算 location-based 的注意力權重 (Chorowski et al., 2015)，將編碼器的隱藏狀態 h_l 與基於注意力機制解碼器的隱藏狀態 q_{u-1} 融合，並透過所有跨度的隱藏狀態得出前後文向量。

最後，本研究所採用 Joint CTC/Attention 的 ASR 架構是將兩種不同的解碼方法使用 λ 參數調和，將 CTC 目標函式額外加入與注意力模型所組成的端對端架構一同進行訓練，藉此共享編碼器隱藏狀態。

$$L_{Joint} = \lambda L_{CTC} + (1 - \lambda) L_{Attention} \tag{9}$$

4.4 資料增量

針對基於深度學習之語音辨識模的訓練，收集大量的數據難度較高，而少量的訓練資料又會導致辨識效果無法達到最佳化。因此我們使用波形增量 (Ko et al., 2015)，針對原始訓練集音檔額外增加三倍音檔資料量，再將這些音檔轉換成頻譜的形式送進 ASR 進行訓練。

我們使用 Sound eXchange 語音編輯軟體 (http://sox.sourceforge.net/) 進行音頻的修改。爲了模擬不同人説話速度快慢、聲音高低和音量大小聲的差異，我們隨機在語速上調整 70% 至 120%；音高則是在-500 到 500 音分 (cent) 間；音量隨機放大 10dB 至減少 20dB 的範圍間；時移上則是移動 0 到 10ms 左右。除此之外，爲要強健模型面對吵雜語音的能力，參考文獻 (Amodei et al., 2016)，增加 10 到 15dB 噪音比的白噪音。透過隨機調整並組合以上五種聲音的特性，進而模擬不同人之聲紋與吵雜的背景音，增加訓練集資料的多樣性，以加強 ASR 的辨識能力。

5 實驗結果

爲了反映此模型的語音辨識能力，我們針對 ChiMeS 語料庫進行模型的訓練與測試，並比較使用波形增量前後之辨識結果。本研究實驗中有關 ASR 的參數設置，編碼器中的特徵萃取部分爲 VGG 萃取器之 4 層 CNN 外加兩層池化層的組合；而學習語言關係的部分則是由單層共有 640 個細胞 (cell) 的雙向 LSTM 共 3 層組合而成，且在每一層雙向 LSTM 後都會接續一層線性投影層 (linear projection layer)。而注意力解碼器則爲一層單向擁有 320 細胞的 LSTM 架構。Joint CTC/Attention 在訓練時，使用 0.0001 的學習率 (learning rate)、批量大小 (batch size) 爲 24，以及 Adam 優化器 (optimizer) 搭配梯度裁減的設置，CTC 和注意力之權重數值設爲 0.5。在測試時，光束寬度使用 6，來進行最佳結果的選擇。

爲了清楚説明不同組合條件下的實驗結果，我們引入以下的命名方式，以標註：(1) 所採用的 ASR 網路架構、(2) 針對哪一個語料庫進行訓練、(3) 訓練過程中是否有使用數據增量、以及 (4) 最後是否在相同語料庫的測試集上做測試。實驗的命名方式爲：ASR 模型 _ ChiMeS_ 資料增量/測試於不同語料庫的測試集上。舉例來說：使用 Joint CTC/Attention 模型，訓練 ChiMeS-14 並搭配波形增量，命名爲 JCA_14_w；若是在沒有使用增量的情況下訓練 ChiMeS-5 訓練集，並測試於 ChiMeS-14 測試集，則爲 JCA_5/14。

針對 Joint CTC/Attention 架構中兩種解碼機制，我們比較不同權重下所訓練模型的語音辨識效果，如表4。在只使用注意力方法的條件下，也就是 $\lambda = 0$ 時的效果極差，原因在於 ChiMeS 多以長句子爲主，若是前面出現辨識錯誤，易出現後續連續錯誤的情形。而在同時包含 CTC 和注意力解碼機制下，ASR 的預測相差不多，對於 λ 值並不敏感。最後，只包含 CTC 的方法，也就是 $\lambda = 1$ 時，因爲缺乏輸出間的語意關係，結果會略差於融合兩種解碼機制的結果。

表 4: 實驗結果

λ	JCA_14	JCA_14_w
0	92.01%	83.41%
0.2	21.57%	16.71%
0.5	19.82%	13.65%
0.8	21.51%	17.39%
1	33.49%	19.97%

受限語料庫大小有限的緣故，我們也比較有無使用波形增量的 ASR 辨識率，如表 5 所示，當使用波形增量訓練 Joint CTC/Attention 時，其 CER 可由不使用波形增量的 19.82%，大幅減少 6.17%；同時，在 KER 也可以展現出 10.82% 的改善。

表 5: 增量前後之實驗結果

評測標準	CER	KER
JCA_14	19.82%	30.90%
JCA_14_w	13.65%	20.82%

我們利用表 6 展示測試集中第 11 號錄音者所錄製的其中一份病歷表辨識結果，比較有無使用波形增量之效果。並將結果中翻錯、多翻和少翻分別使用 紅色、藍色刪除線 和綠色 <>表示。

6 結論

本研究提出一個由專業護理人員所錄製的中文醫療語料庫 ChiMeS，並提供一使用端對端的深度學習架構，在原始的訓練集下，利用波形增量的方法，加入額外音檔，有效提高語音辨識的效能。

未來的研究有三個方向：首先是針對醫學語料庫進行更全面的收集：不只要包含更多錄製人員，更要增加不同科別的病歷表內容，豐富語料庫的資料，以有助於在新佈署之場域辨識效果的穩定性。再來嘗試使用其他較新的端對端語音辨識架構，例如：Transformer(Dong et al., 2018)、Conformer(Gulati

表 6: 增量前後之實例

實驗	文字	CER
Ground Truth	{co}{lon}{can}{cer} 沒有高跌沒有高壓沒有過敏史 DM{diet} 一天一千五百卡有 DM 腹膜炎 {co}{lon}{can}{cer} 過去病史 然後此次是因爲發現 {co}{lon}{can}{cer} 尚未開刀 在左鎖骨放 {port}A 預計行第二次化療入院 左邊有一條 {port}A 到十月三號 {su}{gar} 測 QIDAC 沒事	-
JCA_14	<{co}>{com}{can}{cer} 沒< 有 >高跌沒有高壓沒有過敏史 D<M>{diet} 一天一千五帶卡有 DM 腹後炎<{co}><{lon}>看開過去病史 < 然 >< 後 >讓他是因爲< 發 >排線 {con}{can}{cer}上胃開大 內科說不放懷A 預計形 DN 吃排量入院 < 左 >這 B一條{po}A{gas}十A三{per}{su}{gar} 測 QIDAC名 {tive}	41.94%
JCA_14_w	{co}{lon}{can}{cer} 沒有高跌沒有高壓沒有過敏史 DM{diet} 一千一千五百卡有 DM 腹膜炎 {co}{lon}{can}{cer} 過去病史 < 然 >他此< 次 >日因爲發現 {co}{lon}{can}{cer}從維採大 乀左鎖骨放 {port}AA 底性第二次化療入院 左邊< 有 >一條痛A 到十月三號 {su}{gar}< 測 >QIDAC 沒事	15.97%

et al., 2020) 等提升辨識效果。最後，面臨醫療術語的多樣化，利用轉移學習 (Kunze et al., 2017) 的方式加快訓練速度，得到更佳的效果。

References

Dario Amodei, Sundaram Ananthanarayanan, Rishita Anubhai, Jingliang Bai, Eric Battenberg, Carl Case, Jared Casper, Bryan Catanzaro, Qiang Cheng, Guoliang Chen, et al. 2016. Deep speech 2: End-to-end speech recognition in english and mandarin. In *International conference on machine learning*, pages 173–182. PMLR.

Rosana Ardila, Megan Branson, Kelly Davis, Michael Henretty, Michael Kohler, Josh Meyer, Reuben Morais, Lindsay Saunders, Francis M Tyers, and Gregor Weber. 2019. Common voice: A massively-multilingual speech corpus. *arXiv preprint arXiv:1912.06670*.

William Chan, Navdeep Jaitly, Quoc Le, and Oriol Vinyals. 2016. Listen, attend and spell: A neural network for large vocabulary conversational speech recognition. In *2016 IEEE International Conference on Acoustics, Speech and Signal Processing (ICASSP)*, pages 4960–4964. IEEE.

Xuankai Chang, Yanmin Qian, Kai Yu, and Shinji Watanabe. 2019. End-to-end monaural multi-speaker asr system without pretraining. In *ICASSP 2019-2019 IEEE International Conference on Acoustics, Speech and Signal Processing (ICASSP)*, pages 6256–6260. IEEE.

Chung-Cheng Chiu, Anshuman Tripathi, Katherine Chou, Chris Co, Navdeep Jaitly, Diana Jaunzeikare, Anjuli Kannan, Patrick Nguyen, Hasim Sak, Ananth Sankar, et al. 2017. Speech recognition for medical conversations. *arXiv preprint arXiv:1711.07274*.

Jan Chorowski, Dzmitry Bahdanau, Dmitriy Serdyuk, Kyunghyun Cho, and Yoshua Bengio. 2015. Attention-based models for speech recognition. *arXiv preprint arXiv:1506.07503*.

Linhao Dong, Shuang Xu, and Bo Xu. 2018. Speech-transformer: a no-recurrence sequence-to-sequence model for speech recognition. In *2018 IEEE International Conference on Acoustics, Speech and Signal Processing (ICASSP)*, pages 5884–5888. IEEE.

Jiayu Du, Xingyu Na, Xuechen Liu, and Hui Bu. 2018. Aishell-2: Transforming mandarin asr research into industrial scale. *arXiv preprint arXiv:1808.10583*.

Alex Graves, Santiago Fernández, Faustino Gomez, and Jürgen Schmidhuber. 2006. Connectionist temporal classification: labelling unsegmented sequence data with recurrent neural networks. In *Proceedings of the 23rd international conference on Machine learning*, pages 369–376.

Anmol Gulati, James Qin, Chung-Cheng Chiu, Niki Parmar, Yu Zhang, Jiahui Yu, Wei Han, Shibo Wang, Zhengdong Zhang, Yonghui Wu, et al. 2020. Conformer: Convolution-augmented transformer for speech recognition. *arXiv preprint arXiv:2005.08100*.

Tingwei Guo, Cheng Wen, Dongwei Jiang, Ne Luo, Ruixiong Zhang, Shuaijiang Zhao, Wubo Li, Cheng Gong, Wei Zou, Kun Han, et al. 2021. Didispeech: A large scale mandarin speech corpus. In *ICASSP 2021-2021 IEEE International Conference on Acoustics, Speech and Signal Processing (ICASSP)*, pages 6968–6972. IEEE.

Awni Hannun, Carl Case, Jared Casper, Bryan Catanzaro, Greg Diamos, Erich Elsen, Ryan Prenger, Sanjeev Satheesh, Shubho Sengupta, Adam Coates, et al. 2014. Deep speech: Scaling up end-to-end speech recognition. *arXiv preprint arXiv:1412.5567*.

Takaaki Hori, Shinji Watanabe, Yu Zhang, and William Chan. 2017. Advances in joint ctc-attention based end-to-end speech recognition with a deep cnn encoder and rnn-lm. *arXiv preprint arXiv:1706.02737*.

Suyoun Kim, Takaaki Hori, and Shinji Watanabe. 2017. Joint ctc-attention based end-to-end speech recognition using multi-task learning. In *2017 IEEE international conference on acoustics, speech and signal processing (ICASSP)*, pages 4835–4839. IEEE.

T. Ko, V. Peddinti, D. Povey, and S. Khudanpur. 2015. Audio augmentation for speech recognition. volume 2015-January, pages 3586–3589.

Julius Kunze, Louis Kirsch, Ilia Kurenkov, Andreas Krug, Jens Johannsmeier, and Sebastian Stober. 2017. Transfer learning for speech recognition on a budget. *arXiv preprint arXiv:1706.00290*.

G. Lee, T.-N. Ho, E.-S. Chng, and H. Li. 2018. A review of the mandarin-english code-switching corpus: Seame. volume 2018-January, pages 210–213.

Ruizhi Li, Xiaofei Wang, Sri Harish Mallidi, Shinji Watanabe, Takaaki Hori, and Hynek Hermansky. 2019. Multi-stream end-to-end speech recognition. *IEEE/ACM Transactions on Audio, Speech, and Language Processing*, 28:646–655.

Yuan-Fu Liao, Yung-Hsiang Shawn Chang, Yu-Chen Lin, Wu-Hua Hsu, Matus Pleva, and Jozef Juhar. 2020. Formosa speech in the wild corpus for improving taiwanese mandarin speech-enabled human-computer interaction. *Journal of Signal Processing Systems*, 92(8):853–873.

Y.R. Oh, M. Kim, and H.K. Kim. 2008. Acoustic and pronunciation model adaptation for context-independent and context-dependent pronunciation variability of non-native speech. pages 4281–4284.

Daniel Povey, Arnab Ghoshal, Gilles Boulianne, Lukas Burget, Ondrej Glembek, Nagendra Goel, Mirko Hannemann, Petr Motlicek, Yanmin Qian, Petr Schwarz, et al. 2011. The kaldi speech recognition toolkit. In *IEEE 2011 workshop on automatic speech recognition and understanding*, CONF. IEEE Signal Processing Society.

O. Spjuth, J. Frid, and A. Hellander. 2021. The machine learning life cycle and the cloud: implications for drug discovery. *Expert Opinion on Drug Discovery*.

Tao Zhu and Chunling Cheng. 2020. Joint ctc-attention end-to-end speech recognition with a triangle recurrent neural network encoder. *Journal of Shanghai Jiaotong University (Science)*, 25(1):70–75.

The 33rd Conference on Computational Linguistics and Speech Processing (ROCLING 2021)
Taoyuan, Taiwan, October 15-16, 2021. The Association for Computational Linguistics and Chinese Language Processing

利用少量語碼轉換資料之中英語音辨識系統
Exploiting Low-Resource Code-Switching Data to Mandarin-English Speech Recognition Systems

林厚安 Hou-An Lin, 陳嘉平 Chia-Ping Chen
國立中山大學資訊工程學系
National Sun Yat-sen University
Department of Computer Science and Engineering
m093040066@nsysu.edu.tw, cpchen@cse.nsysu.edu.tw

摘要

本篇論文中，我們探討如何使用少量的語碼轉換 **(Code-Switching)** 資料來實現語碼轉換語音辨識系統。我們以 **Transformer** 端到端模型開發語碼轉換語音辨識系統，並使用中文資料集加上少量中英混合的課程語音資料集來訓練，作爲本篇論文的基準 **(Baseline)**，接著比較加入多任務學習 **(Multi-task learning)**、遷移學習 **(Transfer learning)** 對於系統效能的差異。實驗結果的部分，以字元錯誤率 **(Character Error Rate, CER)** 作爲評斷系統的標準，最後我們將三個系統分別結合了語言模型 **(Language model,LM)**，最終相比 **baseline** 的 **28.7%** 我們的最好的結果下降到了 **23.9%**。

Abstract

In this paper, we investigate how to use limited code-switching data to implement a code-switching speech recognition system. We utilize the Transformer end-to-end model to develop our code switching speech recognition system, which is trained with the Mandarin dataset and a small amount of Mandarin-English code switching dataset, as the baseline of this paper. Next, we compare the performance of systems after adding multi-task learning and transfer learning. Character Error Rate(CER) is adopted as the criterion for the system. Finally, we combined the three systems with the language model, respectively, our best result dropped to 23.9% compared with the baseline of 28.7%.

關鍵字：語碼轉換、語音辨識、語言識別、語言模型、遷移學習、少量資源

Keywords: code-switching, speech recognition, language model, language identification, transfer learning, low-resource

1 緒論

由於 2019 年新型冠狀病毒 (Covid-19) 在世界各地爆發，對各行各業造成衝擊，教育界也是其中之一。在這個大環境之下，各級學校開始採用了遠距離教學的策略，讓學生可以在家學習，而提供課程影片給學生觀看就是一種很受歡迎的遠距離教學的做法。

爲了增加學生觀看影片學習的效率，我們想爲課程影片加上字幕，所以先使用我們的中文語音辨識系統 (Automatic Speech Recognition, ASR) 來辨識影片中語音來生成課程内容的文本，但課程中時常會有少量的英文專有名詞，使得課程很容易出現語碼轉換 (Code-Switching) 的内容，因此本篇論文針對語碼轉換的情況下開發一個中英文語音辨識系統。

在本篇論文中，我們使用 Transformer 端到端 (End-to-End, E2E) 的架構 (Vaswani et al., 2017)(Karita et al., 2019a)，在訓練時使用論文 (Tsunoo et al., 2019) 提出的 contextual block processing 的 Transformer 編碼器，來開發我們的辨識系統。在 inference 時解碼器會使用 Blockwise Synchronous Beam Search 的方法 (Tsunoo et al., 2020)。

實驗的部份，我們以原先用於中文語音辨識系統的資料加入我們現有的少量語碼轉換資料訓練系統，同時以此作爲實驗的比較標準，並嘗試幾種方法來改善我們的系統。由於不同語言的發音方式有變異，因此我們參考論文 (Zeng et al., 2019)(Li et al., 2019)，在訓練階段加入 LID (Language identification) 分類器聯合訓練系統。同時我們擁有的語碼轉換資料有限，所以我們嘗試使用遷移學習來克服這個問題，遷移學習是一種在資料量不足時很有效的做法，我們將原先的中文語音辨識系統當作預訓練模型，再以現有的少量的語碼轉換資料訓練系統。

在剩餘的章節中，章節二會介紹我們所使用的系統架構以及訓練方法，在章節三中我們會介紹我們的實驗設置以及所使用的資料集，在

章節四會描述我們的實驗結果，最後一章會對於整個實驗做結論。

2 實驗方法

首先，我們使用中文資料集並加上課程內容的資料訓練一個語音辨識系統當作實驗的比較基準，同時也嘗試在訓練階段採用多任務學習的方法加入 LID 分類器作爲一個輔助的任務，並用相同的資料集訓練另一個語音辨識系統。

另外，我們以中文資料集先訓練出一個中文語音辨識系統，再應用遷移式學習的技術，加上包含語碼轉換內容的課程資料去微調一個辨識系統。最後對所有系統進行比較以及分析。

2.1 端到端模型

我們的端到端語音辨識模型 (E2E ASR model) 是使用論文 (Tsunoo et al., 2019) 提出使用 contextual embedding 的 Transformer 的架構如圖 1所示。同時以此 Transformer 架構並加入 LID 分類器，架構如圖 2所示，其中 LID 分類器的架構爲圖 2中左半邊的部分。

2.1.1 Transformer 編碼器

首先輸入的音檔會被表示爲一個 80 維的梅爾頻譜圖 (mel-spectrogram) 序列。接著我們會對特徵做降採樣 (Subsampling)，其中降採樣模塊 (Subsampling module) 是由兩層的卷積神網路 (Convolutional neural network, CNN) 組成，其中 kernel size 爲 3，stride 爲 2 還有 256 個 channel 以及 ReLU 的激活函數 (activation function)。我們使用加入 contextual embedding 的 Transformer 編碼器作爲我們的架構，自注意力機制 (self-attention) 能夠使輸入序列的每個位置都能關注到其他任意位置的資訊，以獲取輸入序列的全局信息，架構與原始 Transformer 一樣，架構在圖 1的左半部。

2.1.2 Transformer 解碼器

當 Transformer 的解碼器接收到編碼器的輸出 X_e 跟先前序列的 IDs $Y[1:u] = Y[1], ..., Y[u]$，最後解碼器會計算出輸出序列 $p_{\text{s2s}}(Y|X_e)$ 的後驗機率如下：

$$[p_{\text{s2s}}(Y[2]|Y[1], X_e), ..., p_{\text{s2s}}(Y[u+1]|Y[1:u], X_e)] = \text{softmax}(Z_d W_{\text{att}} + b_{\text{att}})$$

$$p_{\text{s2s}}(Y|X_e) = \prod_u p_{\text{s2s}}(Y[u+1]|Y[1:u], X_e)$$

其中 Z_d 是解碼器的輸出，$W_{\text{att}} \in \mathbb{R}^{d_{\text{att}} \times d_{\text{char}}}, b_{\text{att}} \in \mathbb{R}^{d_{\text{char}}}$ 是可學習的參數，d_{char} 爲字元的數量。Transformer 解碼器的架構爲圖 1的右半部。

2.1.3 語言辨識分類器

由於不同語言在發音方式會有差異，因此我們參考論文 (Zeng et al., 2019)(Li et al., 2019) 的方法，利用 LID 分類器當作一個輔助的任務，幫助我們提昇辨識系統的效能。分別分類輸入爲中文、英文還是語碼轉換的句子。而將此分類器接上原本的 Transformer 架構並使用多任務學習方法訓練系統，在 LID 分類器的損失函數 (Loss function) 是使用 cross entropy 損失函數，LID 分類器的架構如圖 2左半邊所示。

2.1.4 訓練方法

在訓練時我們使用論文 (Tsunoo et al., 2019) 提出的 contextual block processing 的方法來進行訓練，在解碼器的部分採取與原始 Transforemr 解碼器相同的批次 (batch) 訓練。

2.1.5 聯合訓練 CTC 與 Transformer

連續時序性分類 (Connectionist temporal classification, CTC)(Graves et al., 2006) 學習語音特徵與每個字元的對齊，CTC 聯合訓練也有效的加快了學習的速度，可以讓模型快速的收斂 (Kim et al., 2017; Karita et al., 2019b)。在訓練階段，我們採用多任務損失函數 (Multi-task loss)，損失函數結合了來自解碼器和 CTC 的負對數機率 (Kim et al., 2017; Karita et al., 2019b,a; Tsunoo et al., 2020)，損失函數如下所示：

$$L_{\text{mtl}} = -\alpha \log p_{\text{s2s}}(Y|X_e) - (1-\alpha) \log p_{\text{ctc}}(Y|X_e)$$

p_{ctc} 是 CTC 預測的後驗機率，α 是一個超參數，用於調整 CTC 和 S2S 模型之間的比例。

2.1.6 聯合訓練 CTC、LID 分類器與 Transformer

訓練中有新增 LID 分類器架構的系統，損失函數會加上 LID 的負對數機率，損失函數如下：

$$L_{\text{mtl}} = -\alpha \log p_{\text{s2s}}(Y|X_e) - (1-\alpha) \log p_{\text{ctc}}(Y|X_e) - \log p_{\text{lid}}(L|X_e)$$

其中 L 是該筆輸入的語言類別，p_{ctc} 是 CTC 預測的後驗機率，p_{lid} 是 LID 分類器的後驗機率，α 是一個超參數，用於調整 CTC 和 S2S 模型之間的比例。

2.1.7 聯合解碼 CTC、LM

在解碼 (Decoding) 階段，我們簡單的將 S2S 、CTC 以及語言模型的機率各取對數後合併起

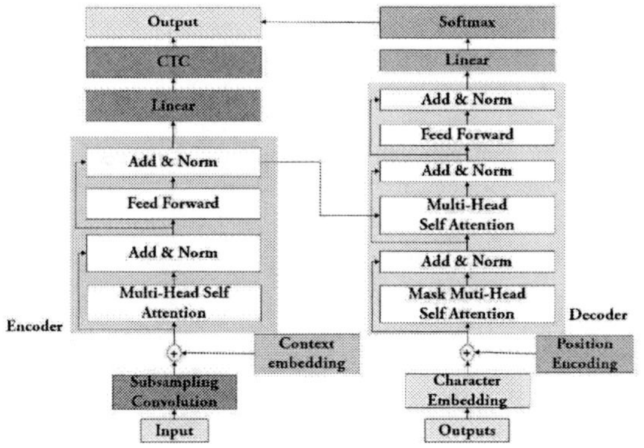

圖 1. 加入 contextual embedding 的 Transformer 架構圖

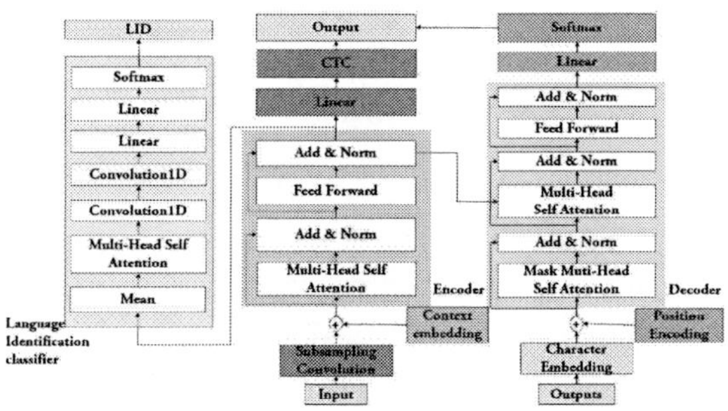

圖 2. 聯合訓練 LID 分類器且加入有 contextual embedding 的 Transformer 架構圖

來，並以 (Tsunoo et al., 2020) 提出的 Block Boundary Detection (BBD) 技術以及 block-wise synchronous beam search algorithm 取代原先的 beam search algorithm，其中 block-wise synchronous beam search algorithm 能夠在使用一定的的 block 數下，就能達到近似一般 beam search 的效果。由於 attention-based 的解碼器經常會出現過早預測出 <eos> 或者預測重複的 token，BBD 主要目的是判斷當前 block 新預測出來的假設是否爲可靠的 (reliable)，若判斷爲不可靠，就會讓解碼器使用編碼器下一個 block 的輸出以繼續解碼。其中 (Tsunoo et al., 2020) 提出的 Block Boundary Detection (BBD) 以及 blockwise synchronous beam search algorithm。我們自表 1的測試集中選取一筆音檔並觀察其搜尋過程，如圖3所示。圖中紅字的部份即爲預測出重複的 token，因此判斷此 block 在這一次新預測出的假設爲不可靠的，進而使解碼器使用編碼器下一個 block 的輸出繼續進行解碼。

資料集	音檔數	總時長 (小時)
Course-train	827	3.03
Course-val	90	0.31
Course-test	389	0.92

表 1. 課程資料集

$$\hat{Y} = \arg\max_{Y \in y^*} \{\lambda \log p_{\mathrm{s2s}}(Y|X_e)$$
$$+(1-\lambda)\log p_{\mathrm{ctc}}(Y|X_e) + \gamma \log p_{\mathrm{lm}}(Y)\}$$

其中 $p_{\mathrm{lm}}(Y)$ 是Y 的語言模型機率，λ 和 γ 爲超參數，用來調整他們各自所佔的比重，y^* 是一個輸出假設 (output hypotheses) 的集合。

2.1.8 遷移學習

遷移學習 (Transfer learning)(Wang and Zheng, 2015) 是一種被廣泛應用的技術，遷移學習可以將已經學習過的預訓練模型繼承到其他領域來訓練模型，可以省去重新從頭訓練所需要的工作，還可以解決我們在語碼轉換資料不足的問題。由於我們的語碼轉換資料較少，直接訓練可能會造成過度擬合 (Overfitting) 的現象。因此我們使用遷移學習，將先前訓練好的中文語音辨識系統當作預訓練模型，再加上表 1中少量的語碼轉換資料來微調 (fine-tune) 出中英語碼轉換語音辨識系統。

3 實驗設置與資料集

3.1 資料集

本篇論文中在語音辨識模型所使用的訓練集分爲三種，底下逐一說明，並以內容爲含有語碼轉換資料的課程資料集表 1中的 Course-test 資料集來作爲本篇論文的測試集。

3.1.1 課程資料集

此數據集是來自課程影片的資料 [1]，課程爲機率學的內容，其中包含語碼轉換的句子。全部共有 10 堂課程，我們將其中 2 堂課程內容作爲測試集而剩餘 8 堂課程以 90%、10% 的方式分爲訓練集以及驗證集。在表 1顯示了此數據集的資訊。

3.1.2 中文資料集

中文資料集由四個資料集組成，各別資料集的詳細資訊以表 2所示。

(1) NER-Trs-Vol：由國立教育廣播電台提供，其文本爲談話性節目以及新聞報導

[1] https://www.youtube.com/playlist?list=PL_Ks_ZHSKSQ5T2w4gEDCftEmbGNDBj48z

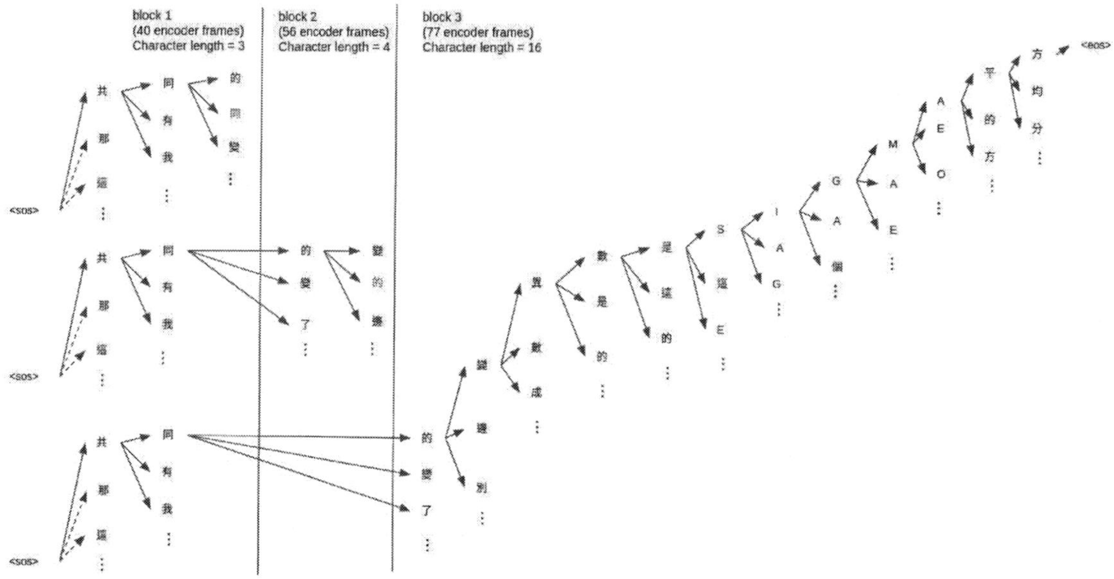

圖 3. blockwise synchronous beam search 演算法下搜尋”共同的變異數是 SIGMA 平方”其中 beam size 爲 10

資料集	音檔數	總時長 (小時)
NER-Trs-Vol1	21,089	126.65
AISHELL-1	20,000	24.82
AISHELL-2	20,000	19.87
科技大擂台	24102	50.50
total	85,191	221.84

表 2. 中文資料集

的朗讀式語音，其中總時長爲 126.8 小時，共 21,089 筆數據。

(2) AISHELL-1、AISHELL-2：由 AISHELL 公司提供 (Bu et al., 2017)，分別由 400、1991 位來自中國不同區域的人所錄製，其文本內容包含智能家居、無人駕駛等領域，我們同時將文本內容由簡體中文轉換爲繁體中文，並在兩個資料集中各隨機選取其中 20,000 筆資料加入訓練集。

(3) 科技大擂台 (Formosa Grand Challenge)：由國研院科技政策研究與資訊中心提供，內容爲華語文能力測驗，分爲文章、題目及選項。總時數約爲 400 小時，我們使用問題及選項中的部分資料，總時長約爲 50.5 小時，共 24,102 筆數據。

3.1.3 中文與課程資料集

此訓練集資料我們簡單的將課程資料集表 1中的 Course-train 資料集與中文資料集表 2合併，其資料集資訊如表 3所示。

資料集	音檔數	總時長 (小時)
NER-Trs-Vol1	21,089	126.65
AISHELL-1	20,000	24.82
AISHELL-2	20,000	19.87
科技大擂台	24,102	50.50
Course-train	827	3.03
total	86,018	224.87

表 3. 中文與課程資料集

3.1.4 語言模型資料集

在語言模型所使用的資料集爲內容含有中英文語碼轉換的課程資料集，其資料集資訊如表1所示。文本內容爲每一筆音檔所對應的文字，訓練集、驗證集以及測試集分別有 827、90 以及 389 筆文本，訓練集中 character token 總數爲 39796。

3.2 實驗設置

由於我們的資料量較少，因此使用了速度擾動 (speed perturbation) (Ko et al., 2015) 以及 SpecAugment(Park et al., 2019) 來對資料進行增強。其中，速度擾動會將訓練資料經過 0.9、1.0、1.1 三個參數來產生出三種不同聲音速度的訓練資料來增加訓練資料量，在 SpecAugment 的部分，會直接對頻譜圖進行三種變形，第一是時間扭曲 (Time Warping) 他會在時間方向上進行平移的動作，而其他兩個分別是在時間 (time) 跟頻率 (frequency) 方向上做遮罩 (mask)。礙於硬體資源限制，有

端到端模型	語言模型	CER(%)
Transformer	-	28.7
Transformer + LID	-	27.8
Transformer	√	27.3
Transformer + LID	√	26.5

表 4. 比較 baseline 與新增 LID 分類器架構系統的實驗結果

些許音檔經過速度擾動後使得音檔變長，在訓練階段造成顯示卡 (GPU) 記憶體不足的問題，我們將經過速度擾動後的資料中超過 47 秒的音檔刪除。其中在中文資料集表2以及中文與課程資料集表3在經過速度擾動後都分別刪除了 228 筆音檔，分別佔其資料集中的 0.089% 以及 0.088%。

我們的端到端架構爲 Transformer 的架構是由 12 層編碼器，6 層解碼器組成。在論文 (Tsunoo et al., 2019)(Tsunoo et al., 2020) 中有提出使所有輸入的 frame 有一半重疊的方法。同時會將每個 block 中所有的 frame 分爲三個部份，包括過去 (Past) 已經看過的 frame、當前 (Current) 使用的 frame 以及未來 (Future) 的 frame，其中過去和未來這兩部份的 frame 是提供給當前的 frame 上下文資訊，而這三個部份的 frame 數分別以 $\{N_l, N_c, N_r\}$ 表示，這部份我們的設置爲 $\{8, 16, 16\}$，而在論文 (Tsunoo et al., 2019) 提出的 contextual embedding，我們初始此 contextual embedding 的方式是將每個 block 中所有的 frame 取平均來作爲初始值，同時使用 position encoding 來幫助分辨 blocks 的序列。其中在多任務學習方法 (multitask learning) 的超參數 α 爲 0.3，decoding 階段的超參數 λ 和 γ 分別爲 0.5 以及 0.3，beam size 大小爲 10。

而 LID 分類器是由一層的 multi-head self attention 以及 2 層的 1D-convolution ，其中 kernel size 爲 3，stride 以及 padding 都是爲 1，最後再通過兩層 linear 所組成。

在語言模型的部份，我們使用 2 層 1024 個神經元的長短期記憶 (Long Short-Term Memory, LSTM) 來建立遞迴神經網路，並以表 1的訓練資料進行訓練。

我們的所有實驗都基於 ASR 工具 ESPnet2(Watanabe et al., 2018) 來開發。

4 實驗結果

由於課程內容多以中文爲主，英文專有名詞爲輔，因此我們以字元錯誤率作爲評估模型的標準。首先使用中文與課程資料集表 3當作訓練集，比較 Transformer 架構以及有加入 LID 分類器後兩者之間的結果，實驗結果如表 4所示。在未加入語言模型的情況下可以看到在加入 LID 分類器後字元錯誤率由 28.7% 下降到了 27.8%，在結果上可以看到加入 LID 分類器對於整體系統效能確實有幫助，再加入我們訓練的語言模型, 兩個實驗的結果皆有明顯的下降, 分別降至 27.3%、26.5%。

端到端模型	語言模型	CER(%)
Transformer	-	24.1
Transformer	√	23.9

表 5. 遷移訓練的實驗結果

接著我們以中文資料集表 2先訓練一個中文語音辨識系統當作預訓練模型，再使用遷移訓練的技術使用課程資料集表 1來進行微調，結果也下降至 24.1%，加入語言模型後, 結果也下降至 23.9%, 實驗結果如表 4所示。

5 結論

在這些實驗中，我們使用多任務學習方法加入了 LID 分類器來提昇系統效能，由於不同語言對於發音方式也不一樣，因此加入此分類器來判別當前語音爲哪種語言或是語碼轉換的聲音訊號，對於系統確實是有幫助的。同時我們使用了遷移學習的技術，基於原先用了較多訓練資料訓練出來的系統當成預訓練模型並只用了極少的語碼轉換資源微調語音辨識系統，實驗結果也有明顯的改善。

在未來，我們也將探討如何改善我們的系統，由於中英語碼轉換的語音資料不易取得。同時以實驗結果來看，語言模型對於系統的確是有幫助，因此我們會先針對語言模型系統進行改進，像是新增更多的語碼轉換的文本資料，且由於我們是以辨識課程爲目的，我們也會加入不同領域常用的英文專有名詞來對語言模型進行改善，以提升我們整體系統效能。

References

Hui Bu, Jiayu Du, Xingyu Na, Bengu Wu, and Hao Zheng. 2017. Aishell-1: An open-source mandarin speech corpus and a speech recognition baseline. In *Oriental COCOSDA 2017*, page Submitted.

Alex Graves, Santiago Fernández, Faustino Gomez, and Jürgen Schmidhuber. 2006. Connectionist temporal classification: labelling unsegmented sequence data with recurrent neural networks. In *Proceedings of the 23rd international conference on Machine learning*, pages 369–376.

Shigeki Karita, Nanxin Chen, Tomoki Hayashi, Takaaki Hori, Hirofumi Inaguma, Ziyan Jiang, Masao Someki, Nelson Enrique Yalta Soplin, Ryuichi Yamamoto, Xiaofei Wang, and et al. 2019a. A comparative study on transformer vs rnn in speech applications. *2019 IEEE Automatic Speech Recognition and Understanding Workshop (ASRU)*.

Shigeki Karita, Nelson Enrique Yalta Soplin, Shinji Watanabe, Marc Delcroix, Atsunori Ogawa, and Tomohiro Nakatani. 2019b. Improving Transformer-Based End-to-End Speech Recognition with Connectionist Temporal Classification and Language Model Integration. In *Proc. Interspeech 2019*, pages 1408–1412.

Suyoun Kim, Takaaki Hori, and Shinji Watanabe. 2017. Joint ctc-attention based end-to-end speech recognition using multi-task learning.

Tom Ko, Vijayaditya Peddinti, Daniel Povey, and S. Khudanpur. 2015. Audio augmentation for speech recognition. In *INTERSPEECH*.

Ke Li, Jinyu Li, Guoli Ye, and Yifan Gong. 2019. Towards code-switching asr for end-to-end ctc models. pages 6076–6080.

Daniel S. Park, William Chan, Yu Zhang, Chung-Cheng Chiu, Barret Zoph, Ekin D. Cubuk, and Quoc V. Le. 2019. Specaugment: A simple data augmentation method for automatic speech recognition. *Interspeech 2019*.

Emiru Tsunoo, Yosuke Kashiwagi, Toshiyuki Kumakura, and Shinji Watanabe. 2019. Transformer asr with contextual block processing.

Emiru Tsunoo, Yosuke Kashiwagi, and Shinji Watanabe. 2020. Streaming transformer asr with blockwise synchronous beam search.

Ashish Vaswani, Noam Shazeer, Niki Parmar, Jakob Uszkoreit, Llion Jones, Aidan N. Gomez, Lukasz Kaiser, and Illia Polosukhin. 2017. Attention is all you need.

Dong Wang and Thomas Fang Zheng. 2015. Transfer learning for speech and language processing.

Shinji Watanabe, Takaaki Hori, Shigeki Karita, Tomoki Hayashi, Jiro Nishitoba, Yuya Unno, Nelson Enrique Yalta Soplin, Jahn Heymann, Matthew Wiesner, Nanxin Chen, Adithya Renduchintala, and Tsubasa Ochiai. 2018. ESPnet: End-to-end speech processing toolkit. In *Proceedings of Interspeech*, pages 2207–2211.

Zhiping Zeng, Yerbolat Khassanov, Van Tung Pham, Haihua Xu, Eng Siong Chng, and Haizhou Li. 2019. On the end-to-end solution to mandarin-english code-switching speech recognition.

The 33rd Conference on Computational Linguistics and Speech Processing (ROCLING 2021)
Taoyuan, Taiwan, October 15-16, 2021. The Association for Computational Linguistics and Chinese Language Processing

探討領域泛化於跨裝置語者驗證系統
Discussion on domain generalization in the cross-device speaker verification system

林威廷 **Wei-Ting Lin**, 張育嘉 **Yu-Jia Zhang**, 陳嘉平 **Chia-Ping Chen**
國立中山大學資訊工程學系
National Sun Yat-sen University
Department of Computer Science and Engineering
m093040020@student.nsysu.edu.tw, m083040025@student.nsysu.edu.tw,
cpchen@mail.cse.nsysu.edu.tw
呂仲理 **Chung-Li Lu**, 詹博丞 **Bo-Cheng Chan**
中華電信研究院
Chunghwa Telecom Laboratories
chungli@cht.com.tw, cbc@cht.com.tw

摘要

本論文運用領域泛化改進跨裝置語者驗證系統的效能，我們基於一個可訓練的語者驗證系統，利用領域泛化演算法微調模型參數。首先我們使用 VoxCeleb2 資料集訓練 ECAPA-TDNN 作爲一個基準模型，接著利用 CHT-TDSV 資料集與以下領域泛化演算法來對其進行微調：DANN、CDANN、Deep CORAL。我們提出的系統在 NSYSU-TDSV 資料集中測試 10 種不同的模擬情境，包含單一裝置與多種裝置，最終於多個裝置的場景下，最佳等錯誤率從基礎模型的 18.39 下降至 8.84，成功在語者驗證系統達到跨裝置辨識的成效。

Abstract

In this paper, we use domain generalization to improve the performance of the cross-device speaker verification system. Based on a trainable speaker verification system, we use domain generalization algorithms to fine-tune the model parameters. First, we use the VoxCeleb2 dataset to train ECAPA-TDNN as a baseline model. Then, use the CHT-TDSV dataset and the following domain generalization algorithms to fine-tune it: DANN, CDNN, Deep CORAL. Our proposed system tests 10 different scenarios in the NSYSU-TDSV dataset, including a single device and multiple devices. Finally, in the scenario of multiple devices, the best equal error rate decreased from 18.39 in the baseline to 8.84. Successfully achieved cross-device identification on the speaker verification system.

關鍵字：語者驗證、領域泛化、深度神經網路

Keywords: Speaker Verification, Domain Generalization, Deep Neural Networks

1 緒論

在科技發達的現代社會當中，所見都不一定爲真，更何況是聲音，聲音也可以經過仿冒取得利益，像是透過模仿聲音來騙取語音客服提供客户的資料，因此確認這段聲音是否爲同一個人的語者驗證技術就相當的重要。然而在不同裝置下所聽到的聲音又會有所差異，這也增加語者驗證的辨識難度。因此本研究希望解決因不同裝置之間的差異性，導致語者驗證系統辨識不佳的問題。要在跨裝置語者驗證系統中加入領域泛化 (Domain Generalization) 技術必須先訓練語者驗證系統的模型，模型在訓練過程中透過損失函數分類來學習神經網路參數，進而在推論階段能夠擷取出語者嵌入向量 (Speaker Embedding)，透過比對 Speaker Embedding 可以得到語者之間的相似度，完成語者驗證的功能。而我們再將 Speaker Embedding 當作領域泛化演算法的特徵來微調 (Fine-Tuning) 我們的模型，經過微調後我們的模型具有強健性，同個語者在不同裝置的語音可以更好的被辨識出來。

Dataset	Voxceleb2
語者數量	5,994
男性語者比例	61%
影片數量	150,480
總時長 (hours)	2,442
句子總數	1,128,246
每人平均影片數	25
每人平均句子數	185

表 1. VoxCeleb2 的詳細資訊

2 研究方法

2.1 資料集

2.1.1 VoxCeleb2

VoxCeleb2(Nagrani et al., 2020)(Chung et al., 2018)(Nagrani et al., 2017) 屬於文本無關的資料集，內容是從 Youtube 上的影片擷取聲音的片段，有名人的演講、眞人節目上的訪談、大型體育館的演說等等，因此擷取下的聲音片段會包含背景雜音，甚至於人聲、笑聲等干擾。資料集的語者範圍廣泛，涵蓋了不同年齡、職業、口音、種族。語音的採樣率爲 16kHz，單聲道，WAV 格式，使用的語言爲英文。VoxCeleb2 其他的詳細資訊如表一所示。

2.1.2 CHT-TDSV

CHT-TDSV 是中華電信研究院開發的資料集。爲文本相關的資料集，語者數爲 32 人，每位語者約有 30 到 90 筆的語音，語言爲中文，語音的採樣率爲 8kHz，單聲道，WAV 格式，語音內容爲任意 9 碼數字所組成，平均長度約 2 秒。CHT-TDSV 適用於跨裝置語者驗證，共有三種不同的裝置，分別爲麥克風、手機和市話。

2.1.3 NSYSU-TDSV

NSYSU-TDSV 是我們實驗室自行錄製的資料集。語者數爲 12 人 (9 男 3 女)，資料數共有 1,080 筆音檔，語言爲中文，語音的採樣率爲 16kHz，單聲道，WAV 格式。NSYSU-TDSV 有三種不同的裝置，分別爲麥克風 (micro)、手機 (mobile) 和市話 (office)，由這三個裝置分別作爲註冊裝置及測試裝置可以分爲 9 種情況，測試配對可以分爲註冊及測試都是同一裝置 (micro、mobile、office)，以及底線前爲註冊裝置和底線後爲測試裝置 (micro_mobile、micro_office、mobile_micro、mobile_office、office_micro、office_mobile)，最後還有以上 9 種情況全部合在一起 (all)，共十種的測試情境。

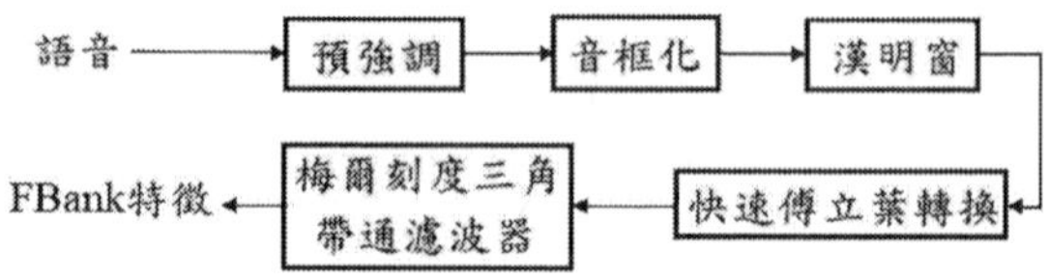

圖 1. FBank 聲學特徵處理流程

2.2 資料前處理

2.2.1 資料增強

在進行深度學習的訓練時，擁有大量的標記資料能使訓練的效果更好，也能確保訓練時不會發生過度擬合（Over-Fitting）的問題，因此我們利用資料增強的方法來增加我們訓練資料的數量及多樣性。我們採用兩種方法來進行資料增強，第一種是加入 MUSAN 語料庫 (Snyder et al., 2015) 的噪音，MUSAN 語料庫包含了演說 (Speech)、音樂 (Music) 與噪音 (Noise) 三個部分，演說部分的內容爲朗讀書本章節的內容或是美國政府部門的演講；音樂部分包含古典樂和現代流行樂；噪音部分包括技術性噪音 (撥號聲、傳眞機噪音等) 和環境噪音 (雷聲、雨聲、動物噪音等)，但不包括明顯可辨識說話內容的人聲。第二種爲利用房間脈衝響應 (Room Impulse Response) 加入迴響 (Reverberation)，房間脈衝響應是在房間內發出週期性的脈衝音 (Impulse Sound)，收集聲波經過房間內物體、牆面的反射所產生的迴響。

2.2.2 聲學特徵提取

在分析一段語音時，我們通常會將多個取樣點集合成一個單位，稱爲音框（frame），接著再從音框內提取聲學特徵作爲神經網路的輸入，這樣可以使我們的訓練更有效率。而我們採用濾波器組 (Filter bank, FBank) 作爲聲學特徵。FBank 的聲學特徵處理流程如圖一，首先語音訊號先經過預強調 (Pre-emphasis) 來對高頻的部分進行加重，使訊號的頻譜變得相對平坦，另外也是爲了補償語音訊號受到人類發音系統所限制的高頻部分。接下來將多個取樣點合成音框，再將音框代入漢明窗 (Hamming window) 函數來消除音框與音框之間可能造成的訊號不連續性。下一步是提取聲音訊號在時域上的特性，所以利用快速傅立葉轉換 (Fast Fourier Transfrom, FFT) 將其轉爲能量分布來觀察，不同的能量分布代表著不同的語音特性。再來將得到的頻譜乘上多組三角帶通濾波器來對頻譜平滑化，這樣可以使輸出的聲學特徵不受輸入語音的語調不同而有所影響。經過這些步驟後即完成 FBank 的聲學特徵提取。

2.3 ECAPA-TDNN

2.3.1 模型架構

ECAPA-TDNN(Desplanques et al., 2020)(Thienpondt et al., 2020) 是 VoxSRC-20 比賽第一名的模型，是基於時延神經網路 (TDNN)(Peddinti et al., 2015) 改進而成，我們所使用的 ECAPA-TDNN 模型 (Thienpondt et al., 2020) 架構如圖二。參數 T 代表輸入音框數、C 爲卷積通道數、k 爲卷積核大小、d 爲擴張率 (dilation rate)、S 爲語者數量，在我們的系統中，T 固定爲 200 個 frame，C 爲 2048，S 爲 5994。模型的輸入爲 80 維的特徵向量乘上 T。神經網路的第一層是 Conv1D+ReLU+BN。接下來會有 N 層的 1-D Squeeze-Excitation Res2Block(SE-Res2Block)，在 (Desplanques et al., 2020) 中只有三個 SE-Res2Block，而在 (Thienpondt et al., 2020) 中總共有四層的 SE-Res2Block，每層 SE-Res2Block 皆採用不同的擴張率，分別爲 2、3、4、5。下一層是 Conv1D+ReLU，這一層的作用爲多層特徵整合 (Multi-layer feature aggregation and summation)，將上一部分中不同擴張率的 SE-Res2Block 的輸出結合起來。接下來是 Attentive Statistical Pooling 層，計算加權平均值和加權標準差，將聚合之後的輸出進行池化。再來是一個全連接層加上 BatchNorm1d 層，用以將特徵做線性轉換得到 192 維的 embedding。最後一層是 AAM-Softmax(Deng et al., 2019)，將 192 維的 embedding 進行分類，輸出的個數等同於語者的數量 (5994)。

2.3.2 SE-Res2Block

ECAPA-TDNN 模型中最重要的部分就是 SE-Res2Block，SE-Res2Block 的架構如圖三，其實就是將 SE-Block(Hu et al., 2018) 加到 Res2Block 模組 (Gao et al., 2019) 的末端，並且將原先運用在 Res2Block 當中的 2 維卷積，改成適合語音特徵運算之具有擴張率的 1 維卷積。

SE 代表著壓縮 (Squeeze) 和激勵 (Excitation)。壓縮部分的計算方式爲公式 (1)，是針對長度 T 進行全域性平均池化 (global average pool)。h_t 代表一個 frame 的 feature map，維度爲 CxL，C 爲 channel 數，L 爲特徵幀數。經過壓縮，輸出 z 的維度成爲 Cx1。激勵部分先對每個通道的重要性進行學習，計算方式爲公式 (2)，W_1 爲 RxC 的向量，b_1 爲 Rx1 的向量，所以 W_1z + b_1 輸出一個 Rx1 的向量，其中 R 代表縮放的比例。接著 f 是一個

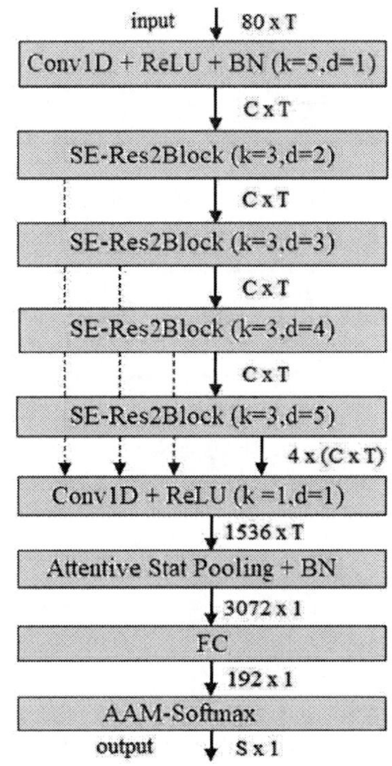

圖 2. ECAPA-TDNN 模型架構

非線性函數，在此我們使用 ReLU 函數。之後 W_2 是 CxR 的向量，b_2 爲 Cx1 的向量，所以 $W_2 f(W_1 z + b1) + b_2$ 輸出一個 Cx1 的向量。最後經過 σ 函數 (sigmoid 函數) 輸出 s，s 代表著經過全連接層、非線性層所學習到的 feature map 的權重，維度爲 Cx1。接著針對 h_t 中的每個 channel 乘上對應的權重，也就是對 h_t 做 channel-wise multiplication，如公式 (3) 所示，$s_c h_c$ 代表 s 中第 c 個 channel 和 feature map 中的第 c 個 channel 相乘，$\tilde{h_c}$ 爲第 c 個 channel 更新後的 feature map，在經過 SE 之後的 feature map 維度仍爲 CxL。

$$z = \frac{1}{T}\sum_{t}^{T} h_t \tag{1}$$

$$s = \sigma(W_2 f(W_1 z + b_1) + b_2) \tag{2}$$

$$\tilde{h_c} = s_c h_c \tag{3}$$

Res2Block 的架構如圖四，首先將特徵分爲 x1、x2、x3、x4 四組 (可以將特徵分爲任意組，這裡以四組爲例)，x1 不做任何動作即傳遞下去給 y1，而 x2 經過一組卷積大小爲 3 之卷積層提取特徵傳遞給 y2 和當作 x3 卷積層的輸入，x3 則將前一組 (x2) 的輸出和 x3 自己的輸入經過卷積層輸出給 y3 和當作 x4 卷

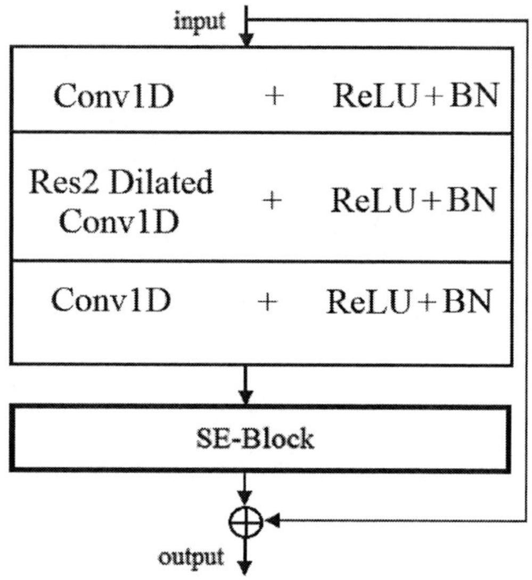

圖 3. SE-Res2Block 架構

積層的輸入，x4 則將前一組 (x3) 的輸出和 x4 的輸入經過卷積層輸出給 y4，經過這些步驟之後將每一組的輸出 y1、y2、y3、y4 連接起來放進 1x1 的卷積層來將收集到的特徵整合。

2.4 領域泛化

訓練好的 ECAPA-TDNN 模型可以去分辨兩段語音是否爲同一個語者所說，但語音在錄製時會受錄製的裝置不同而導致辨識效果有所影響。我們將 ECAPA-TDNN 作爲 pre-trained model 並用領域泛化方法以 CHT-TDSV 當作訓練集進行微調來強化跨裝置語者辨識的效果，我們使用了三種不同的領域泛化方法來進行實驗，分別爲 DANN、CDANN、Deep CORAL。

2.4.1 DANN

DANN(Ganin and Lempitsky, 2015) 的原理是運用生成對抗網路 (Generative Adversarial Networks) 中對抗的概念加上深度學習技術來達到領域泛化的效果，DANN 的架構如圖五所示，主要由特徵萃取器 (feature extractor)、標籤分類器 (label predictor)、域分類器 (domain classifier) 再加上 gradient reversal layer(GRL) 所組成。DANN 架構的流程如以下說明，首先在前向傳播時輸入 x 經過特徵萃取器萃取出特徵 f，接著特徵 f 作爲標籤分類器的輸入對特徵做分類，輸出 class label y，並計算一個 loss L_y；特徵 f 作爲域分類器的輸入對 domain 進行分類，輸出 domain label d，並計算一個 loss L_d。接下來進行反向傳播，其中 θ_f、θ_y、θ_d 分別代表特徵萃取器、標籤分類器和域分類器的參數，在 L_y 的

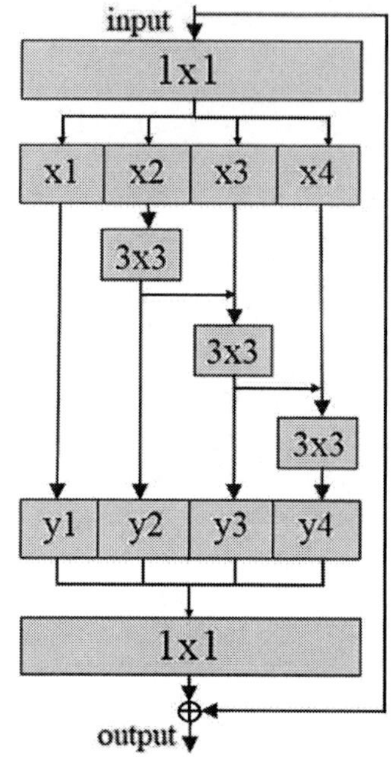

圖 4. Res2Block 架構

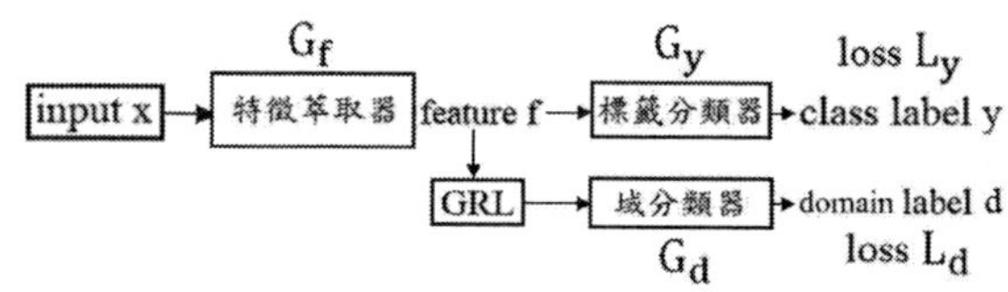

圖 5. DANN 架構

反向傳播中希望能最小化分類損失 L_y 來確保特徵 f 的判別性及分類的準確度，而在 L_d 的反向傳播過程中也希望能最小化損失 L_d，再透過 GRL 將參數乘以一個 $-\lambda$ 來反轉梯度，這樣做的目的是希望能讓域分類器不能區分源域 (source domain) 和目標域 (target domain)，從而達到領域泛化的效果。

綜合上述說明，DANN 要達到的目標是希望能最小化標籤分類器的損失 L_y，並尋找能使域分類器的損失 L_d 最大化的參數 θ_f 和能使域分類器損失 L_d 最小化的參數 θ_d，我們以公式 (4) 來表示，$\hat{\theta}_f$、$\hat{\theta}_y$、$\hat{\theta}_d$ 代表著我們要尋求的最佳解。E 函數的定義如公式 (5)，計算所有樣本在反向傳播時 loss 的總和，G_f、G_y、G_d 分別代表特徵萃取器、標籤分類器和域分類器，N 代表所有輸入的數目，x_i 表示第 i 筆輸入，y_i 表示第 i 筆輸入的 label，d_i 代表第 i 筆輸入的域標籤，0 則表示該域標籤爲源域。而 E 函數可以整理爲公式 (5) 中的第二行，L_y^i 和 L_d^i 爲在第 i 個輸入的 L_y 和

L_d。

$$\left(\hat{\theta}_f, \hat{\theta}_y\right) = arg \min_{\theta_f, \theta_y} E\left(\theta_f, \theta_y, \hat{\theta}_d\right)$$
$$\hat{\theta}_d = arg \max_{\theta_d} E\left(\hat{\theta}_f, \hat{\theta}_y, \theta_d\right) \quad (4)$$

$$\begin{aligned} E\left(\theta_f, \theta_y, \theta_d\right) &= \sum_{\substack{i=1..N \\ d_i=0}} L_y\left(G_y\left(G_f\left(x_i; \theta_f\right); \theta_y\right), y_i\right) - \\ &\lambda \sum_{i=1..N} L_d\left(G_d\left(G_f\left(x_i; \theta_f\right); \theta_d\right), y_i\right) \\ &= \sum_{\substack{i=1..N \\ d_i=0}} L_y^i\left(\theta_f, \theta_y\right) - \lambda \sum_{i=1..N} L_d^i\left(\theta_f, \theta_d\right) \end{aligned} \quad (5)$$

而公式 (4) 所追求的最佳解可透過公式 (6)-(8) 的梯度更新來尋求，參數 μ 爲學習率，公式 (6) 中的 $\frac{\partial L_d^i}{\partial \theta_f}$ 乘上 $-\lambda$ 就是參數在反向傳播時反轉梯度。

$$\theta_f \leftarrow \theta_f - \mu\left(\frac{\partial L_y^i}{\partial \theta_f} + (-\lambda)\frac{\partial L_d^i}{\partial \theta_f}\right) \quad (6)$$

$$\theta_y \leftarrow \theta_y - \mu\frac{\partial L_y^i}{\partial \theta_y} \quad (7)$$

$$\theta_d \leftarrow \theta_d - \mu\frac{\partial L_d^i}{\partial \theta_d} \quad (8)$$

我們可以將 ECAPA-TDNN 模型作爲 DANN 架構的特徵萃取器和標籤分類器，特徵萃取器萃取出來的特徵等同於 ECAPA-TDNN 模型中 FC 層所輸出的 192 維的 embedding，標籤分類器所輸出的 class label 等同於 AAM-Softmax 層的輸出，因此我們可以將 ECAPA-TDNN 模型改爲圖六的架構來將兩者結合。最終 loss L_{totalD} 的計算方式可由公式 (6) 的後半部份改寫成公式 (9)，$L_{speaker}$ 和 L_{domain} 分別爲 ECAPA-TDNN 模型和域分類器的輸出。

$$L_{totalD} = L_{speaker} + (-\lambda)\, L_{domain} \quad (9)$$

2.4.2 CDANN

CDANN(Li et al., 2018) 爲 DANN 的一種變化，CDANN 將原本 DANN 中的域分類器加上 Prior-Normalized 成爲類先驗歸一化域分類器 (class prior-normalized domain network)，另外再加入類條件域分類器 (class-conditional domain network)，CDANN 的架構如圖七，其中 L 爲類別數，L_y、L_{norm}、L_{con} 分別爲標籤分類器、類先驗歸一化域分類器、類條件域分類器的損失，θ_f、θ_c、θ_p、θ_d 則代表在特徵萃取器、標籤分類器、類先驗歸一化域分類器和類條件域分類器神經網路上的參數。加入 class prior-based normalization 的目的爲減少各個 domain 之間 label 的分佈不一致所帶來的負面影響，而類條件域分類器的作用爲針對每個類別的資料來區分 domain。

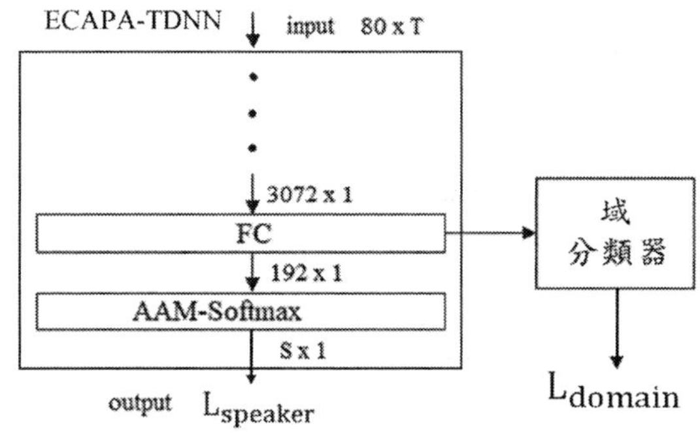

圖 6. ECAPA-TDNN + DANN 架構

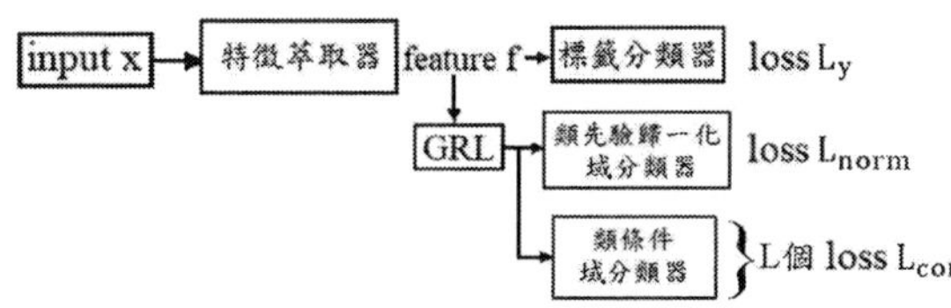

圖 7. CDANN 架構

CDANN 的訓練目標是希望能最小化標籤分類器的損失 L_y，並尋找能使類先驗歸一化域分類器和類條件域分類器的損失 L_{norm} 和 L_{con} 最大化的參數 θ_f，及尋找分別能使類先驗歸一化域分類器和類條件域分類器的損失 L_{norm} 和 L_{con} 最小化的參數 θ_p 和 θ_d，我們以公式 (10) 來表示，θ_f^*、$\left\{\theta_d^{*j}\right\}_{j=1}^{L}$、$\theta_p^*$、$\theta_c^*$ 爲我們所要尋求的最佳解，L 代表類別數，θ_d^j 代表在類別 j 中的 θ_d 參數，R 函數的定義如公式 (11)，是負責計算在反向傳播時 loss 的總和。

$$\left(\theta_f^*, \theta_c^*\right) = arg \min_{\theta_f, \theta_c} R\left(\theta_f, \left\{\theta_d^j\right\}_{j=1}^{L}, \theta_p, \theta_c\right)$$
$$\left(\left\{\theta_d^{*j}\right\}_{j=1}^{L}, \theta_p^*\right) = arg \max_{\left\{\theta_d^j\right\}_{j=1}^{L}, \theta_p} R\left(\theta_f, \left\{\theta_d^j\right\}_{j=1}^{L}, \theta_p, \theta_c\right) \quad (10)$$

$$R\left(\theta_f, \left\{\theta_d^j\right\}_{j=1}^{L}, \theta_p, \theta_c\right) = L_y\left(\theta_f, \theta_c\right) - \lambda\left(\sum_{j=1}^{L} L_{con}\left(\theta_f, \theta_d^j\right) + L_{norm}\left(\theta_f, \theta_p\right)\right) \tag{11}$$

公式 (11) 所要尋找的最佳解可由公式 (12)-(15) 的梯度更新來尋求，參數 i 為輸入的索引值，參數 μ 為學習率，公式 (12)、(14)、(15) 中的 $-\lambda$ 係數使參數在梯度更新時反轉梯度。

$$\theta_f^{i+1} = \theta_f^i - \mu\left[\frac{\partial L_y^i}{\partial \theta_f} - \lambda\left(\sum_{j=1}^{L} \frac{\partial L_{con}^i\left(\theta_f, \theta_d^j\right)}{\partial \theta_f} + \frac{\partial L_{norm}^i}{\partial \theta_f}\right)\right] \tag{12}$$

$$\theta_c^{i+1} = \theta_c^i - \mu\frac{\partial L_y^i}{\partial \theta_c} \tag{13}$$

$$\left(\theta_d^j\right)^{i+1} = \left(\theta_d^j\right)^i - \mu(-\lambda)\frac{\partial L_{con}^i\left(\theta_f, \theta_d^j\right)}{\partial \theta_d^j} \tag{14}$$

$$\theta_p^{i+1} = \theta_p^i - \mu(-\lambda)\frac{\partial L_{norm}^i}{\partial \theta_p} \tag{15}$$

我們可以將 ECAPA-TDNN 模型作為 CDANN 架構的特徵萃取器和標籤分類器，特徵萃取器萃取出來的特徵等同於 ECAPA-TDNN 模型中 FC 層所輸出的 192 維的 embedding，標籤分類器的輸出等同於 AAM-Softmax 層的輸出，因此我們可以將 ECAPA-TDNN 模型改為圖八的架構來將兩者結合，其中 L 為類別數。最終 loss L_{totalC} 的計算方式可由公式 (12) 的後半部份改寫成公式 (16)，$L_{speaker}$、L_{norm} 和 L_{con} 分別為 ECAPA-TDNN 模型、類先驗歸一化域分類器和類條件域分類器的輸出。

$$L_{totalC} = L_{speaker} + (-\lambda)\left(L_{norm} + \sum_{j=1}^{L} L_{con}\right) \tag{16}$$

2.4.3 Deep CORAL

Deep CORAL(Sun and Saenko, 2016) 的架構如圖九，我們所使用的 Network 就是 ECAPA-TDNN，所以 Deep CORAL 架構的上半部分為 ECAPA-TDNN 模型的實現，而下半部分所要達到的目標為最小化 CORAL loss，即是最小化裝置和裝置的特徵之間共變異數的差異。目的是希望能精確的將語者分類之外，又能使不同裝置的輸出分佈更為類似。

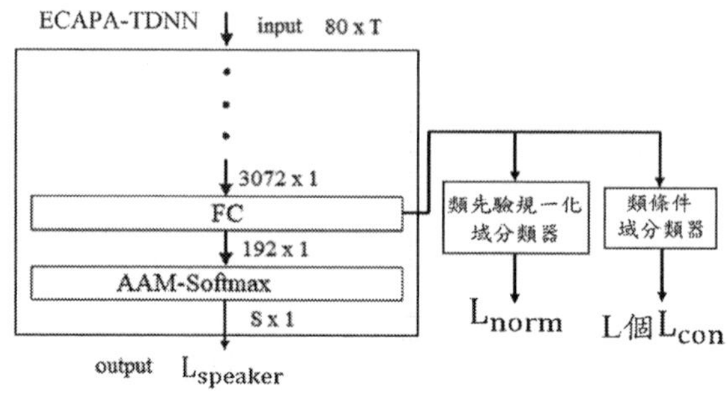

圖 8. ECAPA-TDNN + CDANN 架構

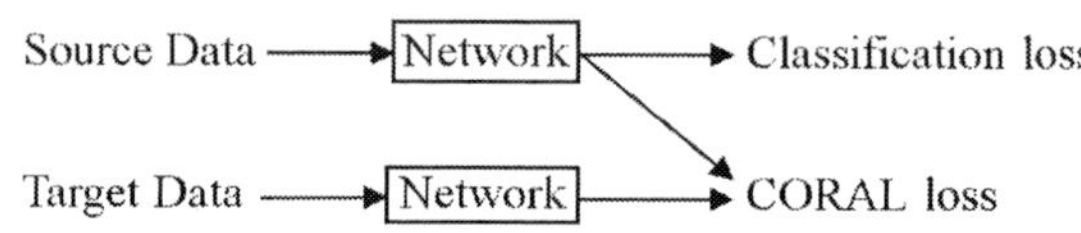

圖 9. Deep CORAL 架構

Deep CORAL 中的 CORAL loss 定義為源域和目標域特徵的共變異數之間的距離，計算方式如公式 (17)，d 可以理解為神經網路最後一層的輸出個數，$\|\cdot\|_F^2$ 表示 Frobenius 範數，C_S 和 C_T 分別為源域和目標域的共變異數矩陣，C_S 和 C_T 的定義如公式 (18) 所示，減號後面的項可以理解為平均值，D_S 為源域的資料，D_T 為目標域的資料，n_S 和 n_T 分別代表源域和目標域的資料個數，**1** 則是所有元素皆為 1 的一個列向量。

$$l_{CORAL} = \frac{1}{4d^2}\left\|C_S - C_T\right\|_F^2 \tag{17}$$

$$\begin{aligned} C_S &= \frac{1}{n_S - 1}\left(D_S^\top D_S - \frac{1}{n_S}\left(\mathbf{1}^\top D_S\right)^\top\left(\mathbf{1}^\top D_S\right)\right) \\ C_T &= \frac{1}{n_T - 1}\left(D_T^\top D_T - \frac{1}{n_T}\left(\mathbf{1}^\top D_T\right)^\top\left(\mathbf{1}^\top D_T\right)\right) \end{aligned} \tag{18}$$

最終 loss $L_{totalDC}$ 的計算方式為公式 (19)，$L_{speaker}$ 和 L_{CORAL} 分別為 Classification loss 和 CORAL loss，t 為超參數，代表 CORAL loss 神經網路的層數，γ 是用來平衡 classification loss 和 CORAL loss 的超參數。

$$L_{totalDC} = L_{speaker} + \sum_{i=1}^{t} \gamma_i L_{CORAL} \tag{19}$$

3 實驗設置

3.1 實驗流程

我們系統的實驗流程如圖十所示。首先先將所有資料集 (VoxCeleb2、CHT-TDSV、

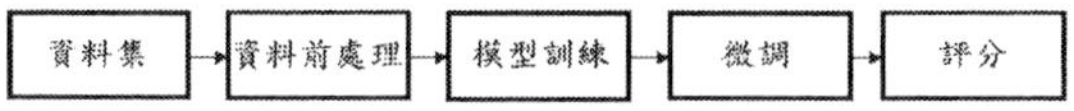

圖 10. 實驗流程圖

Test pair	Baseline	DANN	CDANN	Deep CORAL
all	18.39	8.84	13.19	9.44
micro	1.73	2.08	2.08	1.65
micro_mobile	13.25	6.07	9.17	5.30
micro_office	14.74	10.40	18.56	9.84
mobile	2.66	3.27	4.30	4.20
mobile_micro	12.87	6.62	10.60	6.21
mobile_office	11.74	8.81	15.21	8.38
office	1.56	2.60	4.16	2.60
office_micro	14.34	11.11	17.80	10.98
office_mobile	11.74	7.95	16.33	7.57

表 2. 實驗結果

NSYSU-TDSV) 經過資料前處理。之後以 VoxCeleb2 作爲訓練集訓練 ECAPA-TDNN 模型，訓練模型所使用的 batch size 爲 64，學習率爲 10^{-3}，學習率衰減爲 0.95。我們以訓練完成的 ECAPA-TDNN 模型當作 pre-trained model，使用領域泛化演算法並以 CHT-TDSV 作爲訓練集來進行微調，微調部分所使用的 batch size 爲 32，學習率爲 10^{-5}，學習率衰減爲 1。最後使用 NSYSU-TDSV 來進行測試，我們以 NSYSU-TDSV 三種不同裝置於註冊與測試之 10 種情況分別進行測試。

3.2 評分標準

我們以等錯誤率 (EER) 來當作實驗的評估標準。錯誤拒絕 (false rejection, FR) 率和錯誤接受 (false acceptance, FA) 率分別由公式 (20) 和公式 (21) 表示，其中參數 θ 代表接受或是拒絕的閥值，s 代表著第一筆語音 y_1 和第二筆語音 y_2 假設的相似性得分。如果 s 高於閥值表示兩段語音爲同一個語者，低於閥值則表示兩段語音爲不同的語者，透過調整閥值可以使錯誤拒絕率和錯誤接受率相等，此時的錯誤拒絕率或是錯誤接受率就是 EER。

$$P_{FR}(\theta) = P(s < \theta \mid y1 = y2) \quad (20)$$

$$P_{FA}(\theta) = P(s > \theta \mid y1 \neq y2) \quad (21)$$

4 實驗結果

實驗結果如表二所示，Baseline 爲不加任何領域泛化方法的 ECAPA-TDNN 模型，而 DANN、CDANN、Deep CORAL 爲各領域泛化方法之結果。

4.1 Baseline

Baseline 在三個裝置互相干擾之下有相比其他實驗方法還高的 EER，在只有兩個裝置組合的情況下也有同樣的結果，從這樣的結果可以看出跨裝置語者驗證因裝置差異導致效果變差的現象。而在相同裝置的情況下，反而是領域泛化演算法有較高的 EER，代表領域泛化演算法可能爲了要消除提取的特徵中不同裝置帶來的影響，而丟失了某些區分語者的特徵。

4.2 DANN

DANN 在三個裝置的測試得到所有演算法中最好的 EER，在其他的測試上也有良好的表現。DANN 簡單的透過反向傳播時的梯度反轉來將不同裝置的特徵分佈對齊，使裝置間的差異縮小，計算出來分數的分佈較爲接近，更能找到較好的閥值來區分語者。

4.3 CDANN

CDANN 的實驗結果爲三個領域泛化演算法中最差的。CDANN 新加入的類條件裝置分類器是想透過語者來區分不同的裝置，但語者的數量有 32 個，而且每個語者在不同裝置的特徵分佈的變換理論上是類似的，因此想透過語者來區分不同的裝置並沒有達到效果，甚至可能會讓模型的學習變得很雜亂。

4.4 Deep CORAL

在三個裝置的實驗下，Deep CORAL 的 EER 較 DANN 來的差，但在兩個裝置組合的實驗下，Deep CORAL 幾乎都表現得比 DANN 還要好。Deep CORAL 的方法爲最小化兩個域特徵的共變異數之間的距離，因此在裝置越多的情況下，不同域的特徵的共變異數會越難達到收斂，這可能是 Deep CORAL 在兩個裝置組合的實驗中較其他方法表現更好的原因。

5 結論

本論文實驗了在語者驗證系統上加入領域泛化演算法來達到跨裝置的成效，在多種領域泛化演算法的實驗下皆比原本的系統獲得大幅度的進步。不過當裝置越來越多變時，不同裝置所錄製的語音有可能差異更大，讓系統誤以爲是不同的語者，能否維持強健性是個問題，因此未來先朝實驗更多不同的裝置且達到一樣的成效爲目標。另外在領域泛化演算法上，近年來有很多應用於圖像上的領域泛化演算法，例如 Self-supervised Contrastive Regularization(Kim et al., 2021)、Smoothed-AND mask(Shahtalebi et al., 2021) 等，能否將這些演算法應用在語音領域中並套用在我們的系統上也是一個重要的改進方向。

References

Joon Son Chung, Arsha Nagrani, and Andrew Zisserman. 2018. Voxceleb2: Deep speaker recognition. *arXiv preprint arXiv:1806.05622*.

Jiankang Deng, Jia Guo, Niannan Xue, and Stefanos Zafeiriou. 2019. Arcface: Additive angular margin loss for deep face recognition. In *Proceedings of the IEEE/CVF Conference on Computer Vision and Pattern Recognition*, pages 4690–4699.

Brecht Desplanques, Jenthe Thienpondt, and Kris Demuynck. 2020. Ecapa-tdnn: Emphasized channel attention, propagation and aggregation in tdnn based speaker verification. *arXiv preprint arXiv:2005.07143*.

Yaroslav Ganin and Victor Lempitsky. 2015. Unsupervised domain adaptation by backpropagation. In *International conference on machine learning*, pages 1180–1189. PMLR.

Shanghua Gao, Ming-Ming Cheng, Kai Zhao, Xin-Yu Zhang, Ming-Hsuan Yang, and Philip HS Torr. 2019. Res2net: A new multi-scale backbone architecture. *IEEE transactions on pattern analysis and machine intelligence*.

Jie Hu, Li Shen, and Gang Sun. 2018. Squeeze-and-excitation networks. In *Proceedings of the IEEE conference on computer vision and pattern recognition*, pages 7132–7141.

Daehee Kim, Seunghyun Park, Jinkyu Kim, and Jaekoo Lee. 2021. Selfreg: Self-supervised contrastive regularization for domain generalization. *arXiv preprint arXiv:2104.09841*.

Ya Li, Xinmei Tian, Mingming Gong, Yajing Liu, Tongliang Liu, Kun Zhang, and Dacheng Tao. 2018. Deep domain generalization via conditional invariant adversarial networks. In *Proceedings of the European Conference on Computer Vision (ECCV)*, pages 624–639.

Arsha Nagrani, Joon Son Chung, Weidi Xie, and Andrew Zisserman. 2020. Voxceleb: Large-scale speaker verification in the wild. *Computer Speech & Language*, 60:101027.

Arsha Nagrani, Joon Son Chung, and Andrew Zisserman. 2017. Voxceleb: a large-scale speaker identification dataset. *arXiv preprint arXiv:1706.08612*.

Vijayaditya Peddinti, Daniel Povey, and Sanjeev Khudanpur. 2015. A time delay neural network architecture for efficient modeling of long temporal contexts. In *Sixteenth annual conference of the international speech communication association*.

Soroosh Shahtalebi, Jean-Christophe Gagnon-Audet, Touraj Laleh, Mojtaba Faramarzi, Kartik Ahuja, and Irina Rish. 2021. Sand-mask: An enhanced gradient masking strategy for the discovery of invariances in domain generalization. *arXiv preprint arXiv:2106.02266*.

David Snyder, Guoguo Chen, and Daniel Povey. 2015. Musan: A music, speech, and noise corpus. *arXiv preprint arXiv:1510.08484*.

Baochen Sun and Kate Saenko. 2016. Deep coral: Correlation alignment for deep domain adaptation. In *European conference on computer vision*, pages 443–450. Springer.

Jenthe Thienpondt, Brecht Desplanques, and Kris Demuynck. 2020. The idlab voxceleb speaker recognition challenge 2020 system description. *arXiv preprint arXiv:2010.12468*.

The 33rd Conference on Computational Linguistics and Speech Processing (ROCLING 2021)
Taoyuan, Taiwan, October 15-16, 2021. The Association for Computational Linguistics and Chinese Language Processing

Integrated Semantic and Phonetic Post-correction for Chinese Speech Recognition

Yi-Chang Chen
E.SUN
Financial Holding Co., Ltd.
ycc.tw.email@gmail.com

Chun-Yen Cheng
E.SUN
Financial Holding Co., Ltd.
quadratic999@gmail.com

Chien-An Chen
E.SUN
Financial Holding Co., Ltd.
lukechen419@gmail.com

Ming-Chieh Sung
E.SUN
Financial Holding Co., Ltd.
mingchieh-17908@email.esunbank.com.tw

Yi-Ren Yeh
Department of Mathematics
National Kaohsiung Normal University
yryeh@nknu.edu.tw

Abstract

Due to the recent advances of natural language processing, several works have applied the pre-trained masked language model (MLM) of BERT to the post-correction of speech recognition. However, existing pre-trained models only consider the semantic correction while the phonetic features of words is neglected. The semantic-only post-correction will consequently decrease the performance since homophonic errors are fairly common in Chinese ASR. In this paper, we proposed a novel approach to collectively exploit the contextualized representation and the phonetic information between the error and its replacing candidates to alleviate the error rate of Chinese ASR. Our experiment results on real world speech recognition datasets showed that our proposed method has evidently lower CER than the baseline model, which utilized a pre-trained BERT MLM as the corrector.

Keywords: language error correction, masked language modeling, phonetic distance

1 Introduction

A variety of real-world applications have been benefited from the recent advances of Automatic speech recognition (ASR), such as voice-activated banking, meeting minutes transcription, and voice content inspection. In ASR, hidden Markov model (HMM) based models (Rabiner and Juang, 1986; Rabiner, 1989; Povey et al., 2011) and end-to-end models (Chan et al., 2016; Bahdanau et al., 2016; Graves, 2012; Jaitly et al., 2016) are two popular types of modeling methods. For end-to-end models, it typically requires a huge amount of data for the model training due to the complicated architectures of neural networks. However, it is not easy to collect sufficient voice data in many real-world scenarios.

In contrast to end-to-end models, conventional HMM-based models, such as Kaldi (Povey et al., 2011), require less data and are quite popular in practice. HMM-based models are comprised of the acoustic model and language model. The acoustic model is used to produce phonetic units from the speech signals. Language models are responsible for obtaining the probabilities of next words by given past words. Typically the N-gram model is used as the language model in HMM-based models. One drawback of the N-gram model is the lack of long-term contextual clues by comparing with RNN-based or transformer-based language models.

For Chinese speech recognition, we found that many homo-phonic errors are produced in HMM-based models with the N-gram model. It shows that the näive N-gram model might sacrifice the performance of HMM-based models even a well-trained acoustic model is given. However, it is not easy to replace the N-gram model due to the structure of interaction between the acoustic model and language model within HMM-based models. To overcome this problem, many methods have been proposed for the post-correction of speech recognition (Kumar et al., 2017; Xie et al., 2016; Guo et al.,

2019; Liu et al., 2013; Zhang et al., 2020).

Recently, many successful methods have been proposed in natural language processing, such as BERT (Devlin et al., 2019). For those pretraining tasks in BERT, masked language modeling (MLM) is a task of interest for our post-correction. The goal of MLM is to predict those masked tokens within a sentence in which certain input tokens are randomly masked. The prediction of masked tokens can be regarded as a kind of error correction. As shown in (Devlin et al., 2019), MLM also could be applied as a post-correction for speech recognition. To be more precise, we apply the fine-tuned BERT to detect the errors within a recognized sentence from ASR. Followed by the detection, MLM is applied to correct these words.

The post-correction by MLM could reduce the deficiency of long-term contextual information in the N-gram model. However, the conventional MLM did not take the phoneme into account. To address this issue, we aim to propose a phonetic MLM as the post-correction for speech recognition by leveraging the phoneme information from the predicted words.

2 Related Work

Many methods have been proposed for correcting the outputs of ASR systems (Errattahi et al., 2018). These existing approaches of language correction typically can be divided into three categories. The first group of them uses external language models to rescore k-best candidates in ASR system. For example, (Kumar et al., 2017) picks k-best candidates of each word from the original ASR system. Once these k-best candidates are determined, RNN-LM is applied to re-score the k-best candidates of each word. From (Kumar et al., 2017), it also shows that the improved performance can be achieved since RNN-LM is a more effective model for the representation of natural languages.

The second category of language correction methods adopts the sequence to sequence learning framework (Sutskever et al., 2014). Based on this architecture, (Xie et al., 2016) adopts a character-based attention mechanism to generate a corrected sentence. On the other hand, (Guo et al., 2019) also proposes a RNN with attention to correct the output from Listen, Attend, and Spell (LAS) model.

The third group of language correction methods adopts a two-step correction. For example, (Liu et al., 2013) uses the language model and statistical machine translation model to detect error words in a sentence. After the error detection, SVM is used to replace the predicted error words with the most likely word. In (Zhang et al., 2020), the authors proposed a bi-GRU model as the error detection network. Given a sequence of embeddings from BERT, the detection networks generate the probability of being an incorrect word. Followed by the detection network, the input of the correction model is the convex combination of mask token embedding and token embedding with the probability of incorrectness. Once the integrated embedding is calculated, a sequential multi-class labeling model based on BERT is applied to generate the corrected sentence.

3 Methodology

In our proposed method, we integrate semantic and phonetic information for the post-correction of ASR. More specifically, the mask language model (MLM) based on BERT is used for semantic error correction. Besides, we also apply a phonetic distance to re-rank the candidates of being corrected from MLM. The details will be addressed in Section 3.1 and Section 3.2 respectively.

3.1 Semantic Post-correction by MLM

In our work, we first apply a token classifier to detect the errors within a recognized sentence from ASR. To learn the binary classifier, we regard the incorrect words within a sentence as the positive examples and fine-tune the model with Chinese pre-trained BERT. Followed by the detection, MLM is applied to correct these words. MLM is one of the pre-training tasks of BERT and originally aims to predict those masked tokens within a sentence in which certain input tokens are randomly masked. In the original design for the pre-training BERT, MLM predicts all masked tokens (i.e., the error words in our task) in a sentence simultaneously as shown in Figure 1(a). That is, the

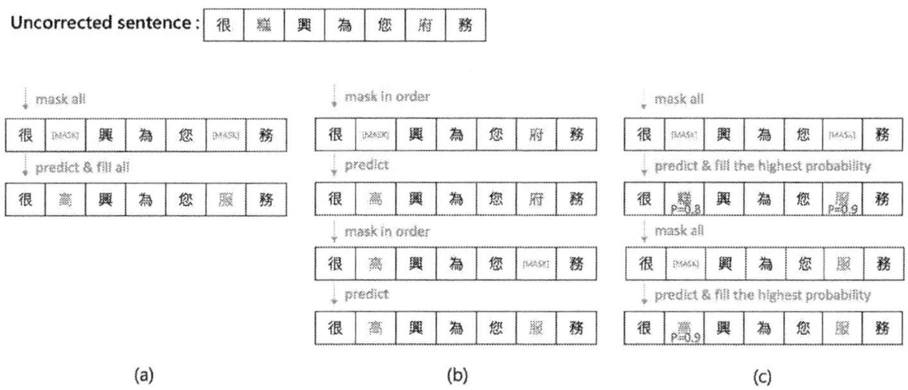

Figure 1: Different masking and replacement strategies of MLM for post-correction: (a) mask-all-and-replace-all, (b) mask-one-and-replace-one, and (c) mask-all-and-replace-one.

mask-all-and-replace-all strategy applied the error token classifier to detect all candidates of incorrect words. Once the detected error words are determined by the token classifier, we replace all of them by the "[MASK]" token and predict the correct words by MLM at the same time.

In addition to the mask-all-and-replace-all strategy, we also propose two other strategies to investigate the influence of the sequential masking and replacement of the detected error words. Different to mask-all-and-replace-all, our first strategy, mask-one-and-replace-one as shown in Figure 1(b), applies MLM to predict the correct words for each error token sequentially from left to right after the positions of error tokens are determined.

Similar to mask-all-and-replace-all, our second strategy, mask-all-and-replace-one, also masks all the candidates at the beginning. Rather than replace all the candidates at once, only one candidate associated with the highest probability will be replaced at one time as shown in Figure 1(c).

Based on the strategies mentioned above, the edited sentence will go through the same process all over again until all detected error words has been corrected. In our experiments, we also evaluate the performance of using these different strategies. The detailed results will be discussed in Section 4.1.

3.2 Phonetic MLM for Post-correction

Using conventional MLM as post-correction of speech recognition only takes the semantic context into account. As the example recognized sentences shown in Figure 2, we found that many homo-phonic errors of correction are made in HMM-based models with the N-gram language model. To overcome this problem, we proposed a phonetic MLM by leveraging the phonetic distance to integrate semantic and phonetic information for the post-correction.

In our proposed framework as shown in Figure 2, we first apply the fine-tuned BERT of token classification to detect the positions of errors. Once the errors are determined, we simply mask them and apply MLM to get the probabilities of candidates denoted by $P_{candidate}$. As the example in Figure 2, we first detect the error "糕" in the recognized sentence, and then "糕" is replaced by "[MASK]". After masking "糕", our MLM will predict candidates of replacement, such as "有", "高", and "羔", with the corresponding probabilities 0.4, 0.2, and 0.1 respectively.

In addition to the semantic correction by the conventional MLM, we also take the phonetic information into account. To obtain the phonetic information, we apply DIMSIM (Li et al., 2018) to obtain the Chinese phonetic distance. In DIMSIM, each pronunciation of Chinese characters is encoded in a high dimensional space. The phonetic distance S between Chinese characters c and c' is defined as follows:

$$\begin{aligned} S(c, c') = \\ S_p(p_c^I, p_{c'}^I) + S_p(p_c^F, p_{c'}^F) + S_T(p_c^T, p_{c'}^T), \end{aligned} \quad (1)$$

where p_c^I, p_c^F and p_c^T represent the initial, final, and tone components of c in Pinyin, re-

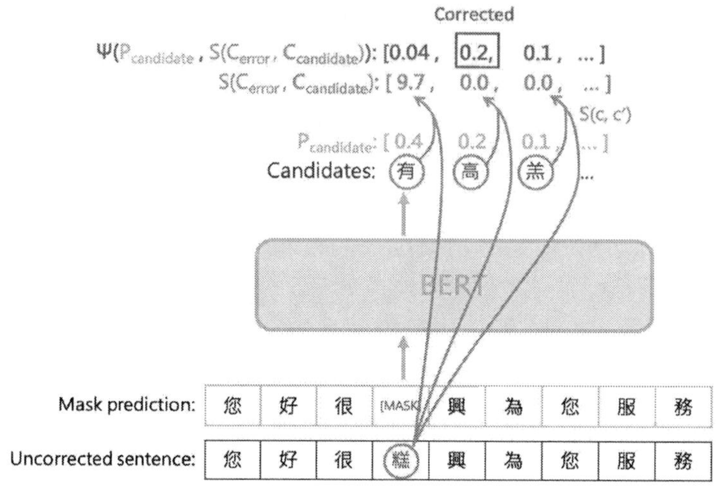

Figure 2: An example of our proposed semantic and phonetic post-correction. $P_{candidate}$ is the probabilities of candidates from MLM. $S(c_{error}, c_{candidate})$ is the the phonetic distances between the detected error character of interest (c_{error}) and the candidates ($c_{candidate}$) based on (1). $\Psi(\cdot,\cdot)$ controls the trade-off between semantic and phonetic metrics as defined in (2).

spectively. S_p and S_T are denoted as the Euclidean distance and phonetic tone distance between c and c', respectively. We note that the phonetic distance S between two homophonic characters is 0, and the phonetic distance $S(c, c') \geq 0$. In (1), by given two Chinese characters, the phonetic distance will be larger while the phonic difference is more significant.

Based on (1), we could calculate the phonetic distances between the detected error character of interest (c_{error}) and the candidates ($c_{candidate}$) of replacing c_{error} by $S(c_{error}, c_{candidate})$. For example, we will calculate S(“糕”,“有”), S(“糕”,“高”), and S(“糕”,“羔”) as their phonetic distances in Figure 2. To consider the semantic correction and phonetic distance for the selection of candidates simultaneously, we first estimate $P_{candidate}$ of all candidates by MLM. Once $P_{candidate}$ and $S(c_{error}, c_{candidate})$ are obtained, we balance these two metrics by the function Ψ as follows:

$$\Psi(P_{candidate}, S(c_{error}, c_{candidate})) \\ = P_{candidate} \times exp(-\alpha \times S(c_{error}, c_{candidate})), \quad (2)$$

where α is a positive number that controls the trade-off between semantic and phonetic information. In our experiments, this hyperparameter is determined by grid search with a validation set. As the example in Figure 2, given the error of interest (i,e., “糕”), S(“糕”,“有”), S(“糕”,“高”), and S(“糕”,“羔”) are calculated as 9.7, 0.0, and 0.0 by (1), respectively. For the correction, we use (2) to obtain the final scores 0.04, 0.2, and 0.1 for “有”, “高”, and “羔”, respectively. Based on the scores from (2), we chose the character with the highest score as the replacement (i.e., “高” in Figure 2).

4 Experiments

Different to the conventional typo correction, we aim to correct the error after ASR in this work. To obtain the results of ASR, we use Kaldi (Povey et al., 2011) as the speech recognizer in our experiments. Once the ASR results are generated, the correction methods are applied to refine the sentences. To evaluate our proposed methods, we conduct two experiments in this section. For the first one, we evaluate the performance of the semantic-only post-correction with MLM in Section 3.1. In the second experiment, our proposed semantic and phonetic post-correction in Section 3.2 is also evaluated. The details will be addressed in the following sections.

	Datasets	
	AISHELL-3	Wiki
mask-all-and-replace-all	11.69 %	75.14 %
mask-one-and-replace-one	9.89 %	73.84 %
mask-all-and-replace-one	11.75 %	75.62 %

Table 1: The correction accuracies for different masking and replacement strategies.

	Correction			
	Pre.	Rec.	F_1	CER
MLM	0.099	0.061	0.075	10%
Ours ($\alpha = 500$)	**0.404**	**0.179**	**0.248**	**8.3%**

Table 2: The evaluation results of our proposed method and the baseline model on AISHELL-3 dataset. Pre., Rec., F_1 represent the correction precision, recall and F_1-score denoted in (Tseng et al., 2015), respectively.

4.1 Evaluation on Semantic-only Post-correction

In this experiment, we aim to evaluate the effectiveness on the semantic-only post-correction with MLM by considering different masking and replacement strategies as described in Section 3.1. For the error detection, we assume that our detection network could detect all the incorrect words perfectly. Based on the setting, we calculate the accuracy of correction by given the detected incorrect characters. In our evaluation, we use two benchmark datasets in this experiment. The first one is a Chinese open speech dataset: AISHELL-3 (Shi et al., 2020). AISHELL-3 contains 63,262 and 24,773 sentences as the training set and test set respectively. It is worth noting that we directly use the pre-trained MLM of BERT with different masking strategies. Thus, we did not use the training set and only sampling 20,000 sentences from the testing set for the evaluation. The second one is Wiki dataset. The dataset contains 286,975 sentences, and all of them are used for the evaluation.

From the evaluation on Wiki dataset, as the results are shown in Table 1, the mask-one-and-replace-one strategy produces the lowest accuracy. This indicates that if we only mask one incorrect character, the other unmasked incorrect characters will sacrifice the performance of MLM. On the other hand, if the incorrect characters are all masked, such as mask-all-and-replace-all and mask-all-and-replace-one strategies, the incorrect semantic information will not propagate to the task of token replacement. For AISHELL-3 dataset, we also can obtain similar results from the evaluation even if there are a lot of proper nouns in the sentences. Besides, the results from Table 1 also show that mask-all-and-replace-all and mask-all-and-replace-one strategies produce similar results for the token correction. For the sake of simplicity, we applied the mask-all-and-replace-all strategy in our experiment as the origin MLM of BERT did.

4.2 Evaluation on Our Semantic and Phonetic Post-correction

In the second experiment, we evaluate our proposed phonetic MLM post-correction mentioned in Section 3.2 with only AISHELL-3 dataset since the phonetic information is not available in Wiki dataset. Different to the setting in Section 4.1, we randomly split 6,000 sentences from the training set as the validation set to find the proper hyper-parameters in our proposed method, and all the testing data are used for the evaluation. To evaluate the performance of the post-correction for ASR, we adopt correction F_1-score and CER (character error rate) as the metrics. Correction F_1-score is calculated by examining whether each error is corrected or not. Most Chinese error correction tasks adopt this metric as the evaluation (Tseng et al., 2015). On the other hand, CER is calculated by the average error rate in every sentence. It is often used to evaluate the results of speech recognition. To evaluate the

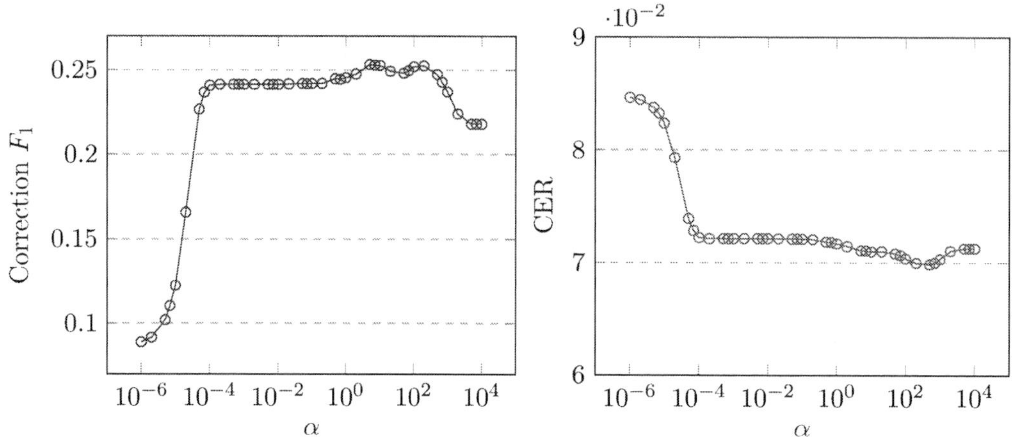

Figure 3: Comparisons of correction F_1 and CER using different α in (2) for ALSHELL-3 dataset.

performance in practices, we also report CER of the correction results in our experiments.

Followed by experimental results in Section 4.1, we use the pre-trained MLM model from the official bert-base-chinese package[1] for the semantic correction. This semantic-only approach is also the baseline in this experiment. As shown in Table 2, our proposed method could achieve 0.248 correction F_1-score while the baseline model only has 0.075 correction F_1-score. It shows that our proposed improve the performance of post-correction by leveraging the phonetic distance defined in (2).

In addition to the correction F_1-score, we also evaluate the performance of these two models with CER due to the practical usage. Similar to the results with correction F_1-score, our proposed method also achieves better CER by comparing with the baseline model. Based on the results from Table 2, we confirmed that the usage of phonetic information of characters is beneficial to post-correction of ASR.

4.3 Sensitivity of Phonetic Distance

As discussed in Section 3.2, we need to determine the hyper-parameter α in (2). This hyper-parameter controls the trade-off between semantic and phonetic information. In our experiments, we use the validation set to determine the value of α by the grid search. According to the range of phonetic distances from DIMSIM, we set 10^{-6} to 10^{4} as the search range, and calculate correction F_1-score and CER with the validation data. Typically the

[1]https://github.com/huggingface/transformers

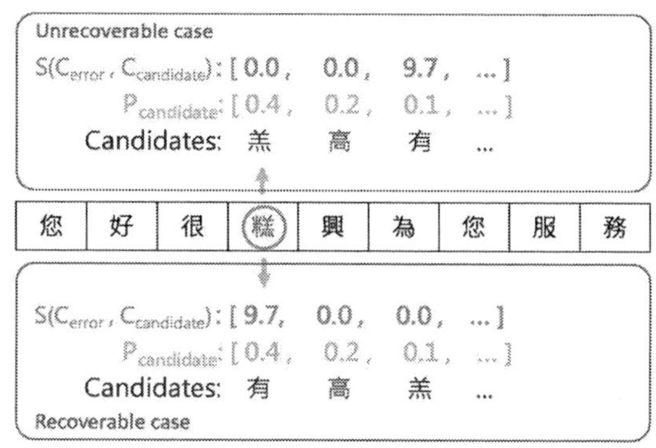

Figure 4: Examples of recoverable and unrecoverable cases in our scenario.

larger α value we have, the more influence of the phonetic distance it will increase. As shown in Figure 3, we plot the correction F_1-score and CER according to different values of α. It can be observed that slightly increasing the value of α will improve the performance dramatically. This also indicates that many homo-phonic errors can be corrected by our proposed method. On the other hand, a too large value of α will also cause the opposite effect due to the over-emphasizing of phonetic information. Besides, it also shows that the results are quite robust within a wide range of α. Thus, the proper value of α in (2) could be easily searched.

4.4 Recoverable Ability of Phonetic Distance

In our proposed method, it is obvious that not all the incorrect characters can be corrected by adding the phonetic information. To be more precise, an error word of interest is unrecoverable if there exists a candidate that satisfies the following two conditions:

$$P_{error\ candidate} \geq P_{correct\ candidate} \quad (3)$$

and

$$\begin{aligned} &S(C_{error}, C_{error\ candidate}) \\ \leq &S(C_{error}, C_{correct\ candidate}), \end{aligned} \quad (4)$$

where C_{error} is the error word of interest, $C_{correct\ candidate}$ is the ground truth, and $C_{error\ candidate}$ is the incorrect word of the candidates. For example, as the unrecoverable case shown in Figure 4, it is not possible to recover the correct character "高" since "羔" satisfies (3) and (4). On the other hand, one can recover the correct character "高" as shown in the recoverable case of Figure 4 since no candidate satisfies (3) and (4).

In our experiments, we have 21,865 Chinese characters that are not able to be corrected properly by the baseline model. Among these error corrections, we have 6,483 recoverable characters (~29.7%). By given these recoverable characters, our proposed method can refine 4,671 characters (~72.1%) correctly by using the phonetic distance. This indicates that our proposed phonetic feature could fix most recoverable characters.

5 Conclusion

In this paper, we proposed a novel approach for the post-correction of speech recognition. By exploring the phonetic distance derived from DIMSIM, we integrated semantic and phonetic information based on the pre-trained MLM of BERT. By taking the phonetic distance into account, many homophonic errors can be corrected by our proposed method. Experimental results on a real-world speech recognition dataset confirmed the use of our proposed method for improved post-correction of ASR.

Acknowledgments

This work was supported in part by the Ministry of Science and Technology of Taiwan under Grants MOST 108-2221-E-017-008-MY3.

References

Dzmitry Bahdanau, Jan Chorowski, Dmitriy Serdyuk, Philémon Brakel, and Yoshua Bengio. 2016. End-to-end attention-based large vocabulary speech recognition. In *IEEE International Conference on Acoustics, Speech and Signal Processing (ICASSP)*.

William Chan, Navdeep Jaitly, Quoc Le, and Oriol Vinyals. 2016. Listen, attend and spell: A neural network for large vocabulary conversational speech recognition. In *IEEE International Conference on Acoustics, Speech and Signal Processing (ICASSP)*.

Jacob Devlin, Ming-Wei Chang, Kenton Lee, and Kristina Toutanova. 2019. Bert: Pre-training of deep bidirectional transformers for language understanding. In *Proceedings of the 2019 Conference of the North American Chapter of the Association for Computational Linguistics: Human Language Technologies, Volume 1 (Long and Short Papers)*.

Rahhal Errattahi, Asmaa El Hannani, and Hassan Ouahmane. 2018. Automatic speech recognition errors detection and correction: A review. In *Procedia Computer Science, 2018*.

Alex Graves. 2012. Sequence transduction with recurrent neural networks. In *International Conference of Machine Learning (ICML) 2012 Workshop on Representation Learning*.

Jinxi Guo, Tara N. Sainath, and Ron J. Weiss. 2019. A spelling correction model for end-to-end speech recognition. In *2019 IEEE International Conference on Acoustics, Speech and Signal Processing (ICASSP)*.

Navdeep Jaitly, David Sussillo, Quoc V. Le, Oriol Vinyals, Ilya Sutskever, and Samy Bengio. 2016. An online sequence-to-sequence model using partial conditioning. In *NIPS*.

Shankar Kumar, Michael Nirschl, Daniel Holtmann-Rice, Hank Liao, Ananda Theertha Suresh, and Felix Yu. 2017. Lattice rescoring strategies for long short term memory language models in speech recognition. In *Proceedings of ASRU*.

Min Li, Marina Danilevsky, Sara Noeman, and Yunyao Li. 2018. Dimsim: An accurate chinese phonetic similarity algorithm based on learned high dimensional encoding. In *Proceedings of the 22nd Conference on Computational Natural Language Learning*.

Xiaodong Liu, Fei Cheng, Yanyan Luo, Kevin Duh, and Yuji Matsumoto. 2013. A hybrid chinese spelling correction using language model and statistical machine translation with reranking. In *Proceedings of the 7th SIGHAN Workshop on Chinese Language Processing (SIGHAN-13)*.

Daniel Povey, Arnab Ghoshal, Gilles Boulianne, Lukas Burget, Ondrej Glembek, Nagendra Goel, Mirko Hannemann, Petr Motlicek, Yanmin Qian, Petr Schwarz, Jan Silovsky, Georg Stemmer, and Karel Vesely. 2011. The kaldi speech recognition toolkit. In *IEEE 2011 Workshop on Automatic Speech Recognition and Understanding*.

L. R. Rabiner. 1989. A tutorial on hmm and selected applications in speech recognition. *IEEE Proceedings*, pages 257–286.

L. R. Rabiner and B. H. Juang. 1986. An introduction to hidden markov models. *IEEEASSP Mag. (June)*, pages 4–16.

Yao Shi, Hui Bu, Xin Xu, Shaoji Zhang, and Ming Li. 2020. Aishell-3: A multi-speaker mandarin tts corpus and the baselines. *arXiv preprint arXiv:2010.11567*.

Ilya Sutskever, Oriol Vinyals, and Quoc V. Le. 2014. Sequence to sequence learning with neural networks. *NIPS, 2014*, pages 3104–3112.

Yuen-Hsien Tseng, Lung-Hao Lee, Li-Ping Chang, and Hsin-Hsi Chen. 2015. Introduction to sighan 2015 bake-off for chinese spelling check. In *Proceedings of the Eighth SIGHAN Workshop on Chinese Language Processing*, pages 32–37.

Ziang Xie, Anand Avati, Naveen Arivazhagan, Dan Jurafsky, and Andrew Y. Ng. 2016. Neural language correction with character-based attention. *arXiv:1603.09727*.

Shaohua Zhang, Haoran Huang, Jicong Liu, and Hang Li. 2020. Spelling error correction with soft-masked bert. In *Association for Computational Linguistics*, pages 882–890.

The 33rd Conference on Computational Linguistics and Speech Processing (ROCLING 2021)
Taoyuan, Taiwan, October 15-16, 2021. The Association for Computational Linguistics and Chinese Language Processing

環境音分類使用大規模預訓練模型以及半監督式訓練之初步研究

A Preliminary Study on Environmental Sound Classification Leveraging Large-Scale Pretrained Model and Semi-Supervised Learning

You-Sheng Tsao, Tien-Hong Lo, Jiun-Ting Li, Shi-Yan Weng, Berlin Chen
Department of Computer Science and Information Engineering, National Taiwan Normal University
{60947058s, teinhonglo, 60947036s, 60947007s, berlin}@ntnu.edu.tw

摘要

隨著智慧裝置的應用日漸普及，環境音分類技術的研究也越加受到重視。本論文探究環境音分類使用大規模聲音預訓練模型以及半監督式模型訓練模式。為此，我們首先使用大規模聲音預訓練模型來發展環境音分類方法；並且在假設標記資料匱乏的情境下，基於遷移學習(Transfer Learning)的概念下，使用近期被提出的 FixMatch 訓練演算法以及 SpecAugment 資料擴增技術來達到半監督訓練的目的。在環境音分類標竿資料集 UrbanSound8K 的實驗顯示，我們所提出的方法能較現有的基礎方法有 2.4%準確率提升。

Abstract

With the widespread commercialization of smart devices, research on environmental sound classification has gained more and more attention in recent years. In this paper, we set out to make effective use of large-scale audio pretrained model and semi-supervised model training paradigm for environmental sound classification. To this end, an environmental sound classification method is first put forward, whose component model is built on top a large-scale audio pretrained model. Further, to simulate a low-resource sound classification setting where only limited supervised examples are made available, we instantiate the notion of transfer learning with a recently proposed training algorithm (namely, FixMatch) and a data augmentation method (namely, SpecAugment) to achieve the goal of semi-supervised model training. Experiments conducted on benchmark dataset UrbanSound8K reveal that our classification method can lead to an accuracy improvement of 2.4% in relation to a current baseline method.

關鍵字：環境音分類、遷移學習、半監督學習
Keywords: Environmental Sound Classification, Transfer learning, Semi-supervised learning

1 緒論

隨著人工智慧與硬體技術的普及，在智慧裝置上應用語音辨識來下達指令已然成為司空見慣的事情，但是除了語音以外，若能夠辨識音訊種類也能夠為智慧裝置帶來更多的可能性，像是使用智慧音箱來對居家環境進行感知，以避免意外發生，又或者在智慧型手機上透過辨識周圍的環境音來套用相應的收音設定等。

本文從音訊標記 (Audio Tagging) 中的環境音分類 (Environmental Sound Classification) 任務著手，透過對輸入的聲音片段進行分類任務來辨別該聲音的種類。我們注意到，在發展環境音辨識時，尤其是針對特定環境的音訊標記任務，容易面臨到資料稀缺的問題，儘管相較於語音辨識，對音訊標記的資料集標註或許不需耗費龐大的人力資源，但對於監督式學習來說，如果想要讓模型能夠有更好的表現，勢必得提供大量的標記資料給模型進行訓練，若能使用少許的標註資料就能夠讓模型有相當的表現，又或者能夠利用未標註資料讓模型有辦法適應資料的分布，便可以在有限的資源下提升模型的能力。

為了突破訓練在目標領域 (Target Domain) 時標記資料稀缺的情況，我們提出一個結合兩

種做法的架構：首先使用預訓練模型來解決資料不足以讓模型學習特徵的問題，有了這樣的作法便能夠快速且強力的將訓練結果提升到一定的水準；接著，我們進一步以半監督式的遷移學習配合預訓練模型進行訓練，這樣的方式除了能夠在標註資料的音訊分類上保持該有表現外，也能夠善用未標註的資料，在目標領域的資料上有更好的擬合。細節上，我們使用音訊大規模預訓練模型專案 PANN (Pretrained Audio Neural Networks) (Kong et al., 2020) 作為基底，進行監督式的遷移學習，而在半監督學習的作法上，我們使用架構簡單但效果卓越的 FixMatch (Sohn et al., 2020) 對未標註的測試資料擬合，並為了實現 FixMatch 的技術需求，我們在音訊標記的任務上引入近期在語音辨識熱門的的資料增補技術 SpecAugment (Park et al., 2019)，對這個系統則使用環境音資料集 UrbanSound8K (Salamon et al., 2014) 進行評估，並分別對 FixMatch 的參數與方法上進行效果的比較，據我們所知，儘管在此類任務上有眾多個別使用預訓練或半監督學習的研究，但將預訓練模型與 FixMatch 結合仍尚未被討論過。

接下來會依序介紹相關研究，描述使用的模型與半監督訓練方法，在實驗設定章節會簡介資料集的結構與處理，並詳述訓練的參數，在實驗結果的部份，首先會對提出的架構與其他方法進行比較，再分析各項參數的調整，最後一節則是結論。

2 相關研究

這個章節主要會介紹音訊標記的相關做法、音訊標記之預訓練模型概述，以及本論文所聚焦的半監督訓練方法考察。

2.1 音訊標記

早期的做法中，音訊標記的流程與自動語音辨識的做法類似，同樣將音訊透過人為定義的函數提取特徵，再將這些特徵輸入如高斯混合模型 (Gaussian Mixture Model, GMM) 或是隱含馬可夫模型 (Hidden Markov Model, HMM) (Vuegen et al., 2013; Mesaros et al., 2010) 以得到機率的分佈後，使用這些模型做為辨識器來使用。近年來深度學習的發展如日中天，使用卷積網路架構 (Convolutional Neural Network, CNN) 來進行特徵辨識的做法逐漸變成主流，在電腦視覺的領域中，CNN 成功證明了它的有效性 (Krizhevsky et al., 2017)，而在音訊辨識方面，無論是對特定資料集的表現或者是知名的音訊辨識比賽 DCASE[1] 中，表現優異的做法也大多使用 CNN 作為基礎模型，再加上額外的特徵或是使用新穎的訓練手法 (Su et al., 2019; Sharma et al., 2020) 來增加模型的表現。

在 Google 發表了 Audioset 資料集後，音訊標記的發展便有了大幅的進步，該資料集包含5000多個小時從 Youtube 影片分離的音訊，並分成 527 種分類，而如同電腦視覺領域的 ImageNet (Deng et al., 2009) 一樣，在如此規模的資料幫助下，訓練出來的模型一般都有很不錯的泛化能力，方便進行後續的延伸應用，這也就引起大家對於預訓練模型的興趣。除了本篇論文引用的 PANN 以外，進一步的做法如 PSLA (Gong et al., 2021) 則是使用更多額外的訓練手法來增加對模型對 Audioset 的適應，而除了使用音訊資料集預訓練外，近來也有透過加入與分類相應的不同形式資料，如文字、圖像等讓模型能夠對於各個分類學到更強健的關聯性 (Jaegle et al., 2021; Guzhov et al., 2021) 或是一並使用圖像資料集預訓練的研究，如 Palanisamy et al. (2020) 就提出，將頻譜當成圖像在 ImageNet 預訓練模型上進行遷移學習，可以在更短的訓練次數內達到相當的辨識率，這樣的作法也在前述提到的 PSLA 中被應用。但綜合考量這些做法的易取用性以及結果上的表現後，我們挑選了易於修改的 PANN 做為實驗的框架。

2.2 半監督學習

在語音辨識的領域中，為了善用沒有譯文的資料，半監督學習也是一個熱門的研究領域，畢竟語音的資料集相較於普遍的分類任務，會需要花費更多資源進行標註，在這樣的背景下，將半監督學習套用在音訊標記的做法便迅速獲得我們的注意。

為數不少的半監督訓練方法是使用偽標籤 (Pseudo-Label) 來處理未標註資料集，具體做法為預先使用訓練過的模型來辨識這些未標

[1] http://dcase.community/challenge2020/index

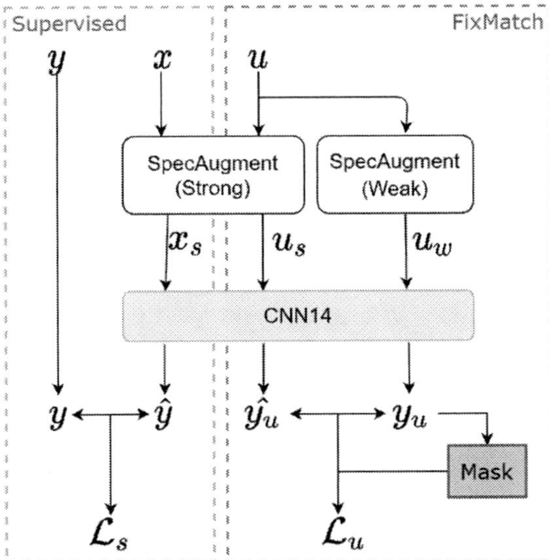

圖 1. 預訓練模型結合半監督方式訓練流程，藍色區塊為監督式學習，紅色為半監督學習，在一次的迭代中結合兩者的損失來進行訓練。

註資料，再根據如銳化函數 (Sharpening)、信心度等設定的條件來過濾及調整偽標籤的分布，最後便能將這些加上偽標籤的資料當成標註資料放進標註資料集進行訓練。

在近期常見的做法中，分別有對模型進行迭代，每次的新迭代都以新的模型加上前次計算的偽標籤進行訓練的 Teacher-Student 模式 (Xie et al., 2020)，以及整個訓練流程均使用同一個模型，並使用一致性正則化 (Consistency Regularization) (Sajjadi et al., 2016) 為核心概念的 MixMatch (Berthelot et al., 2019) 系列研究，前者需要多次迭代模型使得實作上稍微複雜，因此在這篇論文中我們使用了 MixMatch 的延伸研究，將流程去蕪存菁的 FixMatch 來進行實作，詳細作法會於下個章節詳述。

3 研究方法

為了弭平標註資料稀缺的問題，我們使用預訓練模型 PANN 讓模型有一定的能力對音訊特徵辨認，除了能夠短時間讓模型收斂，在收斂時也能夠達到比從頭開始訓練更好的效果，而為了應對未來模型在推論時會遇到的資料分布，我們進一步的使用了 FixMatch 對目標域進行偽標籤一致性的訓練，以更好的對未標註資料集做擬合。我們將提出的架構展示如圖 1，並對各部件做詳細的介紹。

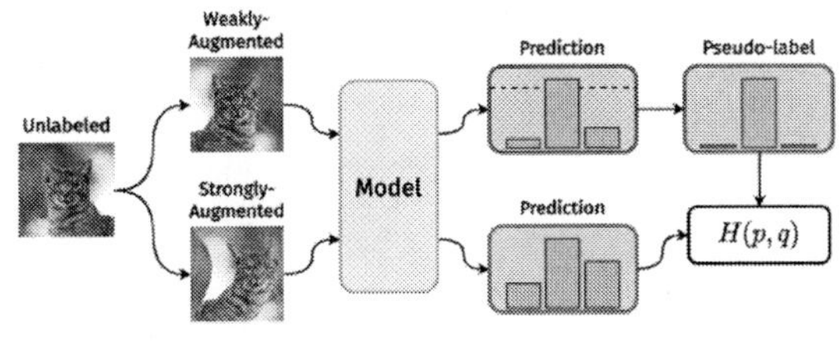

圖 2. FixMatch 訓練流程圖解

3.1 PANN

PANN 的主要目標是提供一系列不同架構的預訓練模型，訓練資料基於 Google 所發表的 AudioSet 資料集，期望能像 ImageNet 一般，以如此規模的資料集作為特徵抽取或是遷移學習的基礎模型。

在該論文中他們針對了不同的超參數與訓練方式做了多種實驗，發現使用 14 層的 CNN 模型能在嘗試過的架構中取得最佳的結果，並提出了一個對時間維度擷取的 1D-CNN 作為額外的特徵，稱做 Wavegram，將此特徵與 CNN-14 結合，成為他們的論文中成效最好的模型，但由於在初步實驗中對於 Wavegram 套用資料增補的成效不彰，最後我們只使用了 CNN-14 的結構。

PANN 在訓練的策略上，根據 AudioSet 中每個類別所包含的樣本數不一致問題做均勻取樣，實際做法為先從所有類別中抽樣，再從挑中的類別中隨機挑選樣本，以這樣的方式來避免訓練過程中因為特定類別的樣本太多而造成模型過於偏袒。

PANN 也使用了 Mixup (Zhang et al., 2018; Cances et al., 2021) 與 SpecAugment 等資料增補技術來增強模型的表現，在後續的遷移學習實驗中我們也沿用了這些資料增補技術。以這些方式訓練 AudioSet 能夠在 Wavegram-Logmel-CNN 與 CNN-14 的模型上，以平均正確率均值 (mean Average Precision, mAP)，即對所有分類的平均正確率作為評量標準，分別得到 0.439 與 0.431 的成績。

除此之外，考慮到訓練這樣的模型是為了便於在下游任務上使用，該論文中近一步的比較將 PANN 做為特徵抽取器，或是以微調 (Fine-tune) 方式進行遷移學習的方法優劣，前者會固定輸入側的訓練層參數，後者則是在輸出層換上新的全連接層進行訓練，在最後的實驗結果中則顯示，以微調方式進行訓練能夠在多數的下游任務中取得較佳的結果。

3.2 FixMatch

FixMatch 的訓練流程如圖 2 所示，主要的概念為一致性正則化 (Consistency Regularization) 的使用，翻成白話即是，即使對一個訓練樣本做了資料增補 (Data Augmentation) 之後，因為來源的樣本一致，結果的分布應該會是在同樣的領域內，所以模型需對這兩個樣本給出相近的標籤，在使用這樣的訓練限制下，透過訓練將兩個樣本的損失最小化，就可以運用這些未標記資料來增加模型的泛化性。

在取得偽標籤的做法中，對於同個未標註資料樣本 u 將會分別套用弱增補 u_{weak} 以及強增補 u_{strong}，弱樣本經過模型得到預測後會使用閾值 τ 將可能性低於 τ 的預測遮住得到 mask，並將結果作為該樣本的偽標籤：

$$y_u = P_m(u_{weak}) \quad (1)$$

$$mask = 1(\max(y_u) \geq \tau) \quad (2)$$

有了偽標籤便能與同個樣本的強增補計算損失函數，將預測的損失能最小化：

$$\mathcal{L}_u = mask \cdot CE\left(P_m(u_{strong}), \text{argmax}(y_u)\right) \quad (3)$$

之後使用交叉熵 (Cross-Entropy) 作為損失函數，將監督學習的損失與未標註資料損失相加，成為最終的損失函數：

$$\mathcal{L}_s = CE(P_m(x), y) \quad (4)$$

$$\mathcal{L} = \mathcal{L}_s + \lambda_u \mathcal{L}_u \quad (5)$$

在此處的 λ_u 為在兩者的損失做取捨的權重，我們參考的兩篇論文均將參數固定為 0.5。

也因為未標註資料會被過濾，故每次訓練的樣本數會是標註樣本的 μ 倍，這裡我們也參考原始論文的設定，使用 μ =7。

4 實驗設定

4.1 資料集

我們使用 UrbanSound8K 來進行效果的比較，這個資料集提供都市中多種類的環境音，包含了 10 種類別共 8,732 個標記音檔，每個音檔長度均少於 4 秒，並由官方提供 10 等分的交叉驗證 (10-fold cross validation)，每個等分大略包含了 870 個音檔，半監督訓練時的資料佔比則採訓練：驗證：未標註 = 1:1:8 的方式來驗證半監督訓練的有效性。

SpecAugment	Frequency		Time	
	max drop	drop nums	max drop	drop nums
Weak	8	1	32	1
Strong	35	2	64	2

表 1. SpecAugment 參數設定

輸入音檔的處理上，參考 PANN 提供之遷移學習專案的參數，將音檔重新取樣至 16kHz 以符合模型設定，並用 64 mel-bins 轉換至 log-mel spectrograms，並且為了實驗的簡單化，我們沿用專案的設定，所有音檔在讀取後填充至 5 秒長度。。其餘固定的訓練參數為學習率 = 5e-4，批數量 (batch_size) = 32。

4.2 資料增補

資料增補的部分，我們使用不同參數的 SpecAugment 作為半監督訓練的強增補與弱增補，監督式訓練則套用強增補參數，參考了 Weninger et al. (Weninger et al., 2020) 的設定以及 PANN 預設的參數，列於表 1。

在 Mixup 的部分我們比較了在遷移學習上使用與否對結果的影響。而在初步實驗中，我們也試著使用 Label-smoothing (Müller et al., 2020) 來增加模型的在偽標籤訓練過程的穩健性，或嘗試對標記資料加入 Pitch Shift 以及 Background Noise 進行實驗，但效果並沒有進一步的提升，故在最終實驗中沒有使用這三種方法。

4.3 訓練方式

PANN 的架構基於原論文的遷移學習專案[2]，並使用微調方式訓練整個模型及分類器層，預訓練模型則採用 CNN-14-16k 作為基準，原因除了對於 Audioset 的表現較好外，其架構相較 Wavegram-Logmel-CNN 更為簡潔，考慮到多了一種特徵增加訓練時間，進步卻有限的取捨中，我們便捨棄了 Wavegram 這個特徵；另外，在套用 FixMatch 的實驗裏，儘管我們嘗試將 SpecAugment 套用至 Wavegram，但訓練的效果上不但不會進步，甚至會傷害模型的表現，這樣的結果導致依賴資料增補技術的 FixMatch 實作變的困難，我們推測若沒有對 Wavegram 一併進行資料增補，FixMatch 在

[2] https://github.com/qiuqiangkong/audioset_tagging_cnn

	Accuracy	$AUC_{weighted}$
CNN14	39.55	84.00
PANN	74.55	**95.54**
+ FixMatch	**75.23**	93.28
-- w/o mixup	73.91	92.60

表 2. 僅使用單個等分資料與相同迭代次數的情形下，比較加入預訓練模型、FixMatch 以及去除 Mixup 時的表現，這裡的 FixMatch 閥值 $\tau = 0.95$

訓練的過程中很有可能會過於依賴 Wavegram 這個相對容易的特徵，且預訓練模型也沒有訓練到 Wavegram 進行資料增補的部分，這些因素都增加了模型收斂的困難度。

我們將進行 FixMatch 訓練時的批數量減半至 16，為了應對 FixMatch 與 Mixup 合併使用的批數量需求，合併使用時未標註樣本的批數量會變成 $2 * \mu *$ batch_size，因此我們額外對梯度累加 (Gradient Accumulation) 技術進行實驗，以便於和監督式學習於同樣的參數上比較，並參照原始論文的做法，使用餘弦退火學習率排程器 (Cosine Annealing Learing Rate Schedular)，將其設定在每 35 輪 (epoch) 調整學習率，在原始論文及我們多次的實驗中發現，這樣的設定能夠有效的避免模型在訓練過程中被未標記資料過度影響而導致成效的衰退，或是訓練無法收斂。

5 實驗結果

在此章節中，我們先以一個等分的資料模擬資料稀缺的情境，呈現使用預訓練模型與 FixMatch 的差異，接著再比較 FixMatch 訓練時，使用 Mixup、調整閥值、梯度累加技術，及優化器 (Optimizer) 的差異，最後再以最佳參數進行 10-fold 交叉驗證的訓練，與其他模型進行比較。除了進行交叉驗證的訓練以外，其他均僅使用第一個等分訓練，第二個等分驗證，其餘等分做為未標記或不使用。

我們使用準確率 (Accuracy) 與 Area Under the ROC Curve (AUC ROC) 分數進行效能的評估，其中 AUC ROC 所測量的是模型能夠正確判斷出正負樣本的能力，該評量計算接收者操作特徵 (Receiver Operating Characteristic, ROC) 的曲線下面積 (Area Under Curve, AUC)，ROC 曲線若越往上凸則代表模型整體表現較佳，透過計算曲線下面積便可得到一個分數來衡量模型的表現。

FixMatch	Accuracy	$AUC_{weighted}$
$\tau = 0.95$	75.23	93.28
$\tau = 0.85$	75.44	91.79
$\tau = 0.75$	**79.66**	**94.94**
+ Gradient Accum.	78.41	93.77

表 3. 使用不同閥值訓練之結果，並針對表現最好的閥值進行梯度累加實驗

5.1 使用 FixMatch 進行訓練

我們在一開始的實驗中先參考 Cances et al. (2021) 一文，套用他們對 US8K 訓練的 $\tau =$ 0.95，在表 2 的部分呈現相同迭代次數下，使用隨機權重從頭訓練，以及逐步套用本論文提出的架構訓練的效果比較，可以看到在相同迭代次數時，PANN 可以很輕易的大幅度超越沒有經過預訓練的模型，這也是使用預訓練模型的優勢所在，並且再進一步使用 FixMatch 訓練的時候，因為有了未標註資料的幫助，所以能夠再推進 1% 的相對準確度。

接著我們實驗了使用 Mixup 與否的差異，這個技術的限制在於，訓練時會先取得批數量兩倍的樣本，再將樣本兩兩融合，這樣的資源需求在一般訓練上可能差異不大，但若配合上 FixMatch 必須先取得批數量 7 倍的未標註樣本進行過濾的限制後，一次迭代所需的樣本數就會來到原本的 16 倍之多，但在我們實驗的數據中顯示，不使用 Mixup 會讓模型表現的比僅用監督學習還差的情況，在這裡我們推測因為 PANN 是經過 Mixup 訓練過的模型，若在半監督遷移學習時不使用的話，這一階段的學習難度會就大幅下降，並且在難度低的情況下多次對目標域擬合，就會造成整體預測結果的衰退。

接下來會比較不同閥值的結果，以及前文提到之大量資料需求下，使用梯度累加的差異。儘管相關論文 (Sohn et al., 2020; Cances et al., 2021) 對於閥值的設定均有至少高於 0.75 的共識，但在預訓練模型的影響下，是否需要額外調整閥值仍值得探討。直覺上，我們會認為模型需要對預測結果非常肯定，這樣的預測才會對模型有幫助，我們在前一個實驗中選擇了 0.95 來實驗，但在圖像分類的原論文中，卻是以 0.75 得到最佳表現，於是我們依序的從 0.95 至 0.75 實驗了三個權重，得到結果如表 3。可以發現隨著閥值的下降表現也逐漸的進步，我們的解釋是，歸功於預訓練

FixMatch $\tau = 0.75$	Accuracy	$AUC_{weighted}$
SGD	71.29	94.86
ADAM	**79.66**	**94.94**
Ranger	75.17	94.54

表 4. 在 $\tau = 0.75$ 使用不同優化器訓練之結果

的優勢，使得在訓練上我們可以給比較低的閾值，讓半監督的結果不會被遷移學習的初期被某些少數超過閾值，但仍有可能分類錯誤的樣本給誤導，我們在分析資料集的過程中發現到，儘管使用了所有資料集進行監督學習，還是有模稜兩可的樣本容易混淆。

在得到最佳閾值為 0.75 後，我們使用梯度累加方式，試圖模擬批數量 32 的訓練結果，結果卻得到 1%的分數下降，推測是儘管在同樣的迭代次數下，多次更新的結果還是對半監督訓練比較有優勢的。

最後則比較了不同優化器在此次架構中的影響，我們比較了三種優化器，分別為 FixMatch 原始論文中表現最好的 SGD，PANN 預設的 AdamW，以及在機器學習比賽中號稱可以推進成績的 Ranger (Wright, 2019)，結果如表 4。出乎意料的，儘管訓練中我們使用了與原論文中一致的排程器，但在同樣的訓練次數中 SGD 卻是落後一大截，反而是 AdamW 能夠穩定的成長並得到最佳的表現，而 Ranger 雖然表現得不錯，但訓練過程中的驗證集卻會得到不穩定的辨識率，導致難以預測整體的結果。

5.2 與其他方法的比較

在監督式學習的部分，我們以兩種資料量來進行比較，表 5 中標有 100% 為使用所有可用標記資料來進行訓練，也就是資料充足的情況，而 10% 則是使用單個等分進行訓練，並且列出幾個使用所有標記資料進行訓練的方法做為此資料集目前準確率上限的參考。而在半監督學習的部分，我們主要與 Cances et al. (2021) 的實驗結果進行比較，該結果使用不含預訓練權重的 ResNet 模型進行 FixMatch 訓練，此表格內的分數均採用交叉驗證所得到的平均分數來呈現。

從監督訓練的結果發現，在預訓練模型的幫助下，使用所有資料訓練 PANN 最佳可以達到 95.5% 的準確度，相較於 ResNet 多出 13.45%，就算僅用單個等分，在同個結構上

	UrbanSound8K **Supervised**	Accuracy (%)	$AUC_{weighted}$ (%)
Others	ResNet – 10%	76.25	--
	– 100% (Cances et al., 2021)	82.04	--
	AudioCLIP (Guzhov et al., 2021)	90.07	--
	TSCNN-DS (Su et al., 2019)	97.20	--
	ADCNN-5 (Sharma et al., 2020)	97.52	--
Ours	CNN14 – 10%	69.83	94.40
	PANN – 10%	81.68	97.97
	– 100%	95.49	99.83
	Semi-Supervised		
	ResNet + FixMatch (Cances et al., 2021)	81.73	--
	CNN14 + FixMatch	79.42	97.60
	PANN + FixMatch	**84.07**	**98.35**

表 5. 實驗結果，表格呈現交叉驗證的分數，比較相關研究及使用預訓練與半監督學習的效果，標註 CNN14 為乾淨的模型，PANN 則為預訓練模型

也比乾淨模型高出 11.85% 的準確度，使用極少比例的資料就足以與使用所有資料訓練的 ResNet 匹敵，而接下來為了能充分利用未標註資料，我們便進一步比較使用半監督訓練的效果。

我們將前個小節中得到的最佳參數對 FixMatch 進行訓練並呈現於同個表格，使用 $\tau = 0.75$、AdamW 優化器且不使用梯度累加的情況下，可以提高準確度 2.39%。儘管在這樣的實驗結果上進步的幅度不大，但仍顯示了加入未標記資料可以讓模型學得更多，並贏過其他兩者，對於這樣小幅度的成長，我們推測可能是因為 PANN 已經充分地對音訊特徵擬合，使得 FixMatch 的長處，也就是適應目標領域特徵的能力，無法明顯的表現，不過以資源的消耗來說，使用預訓練模型的優勢就是能快速的立於良好的起跑點，對比的 ResNet 模型必須以每批次 256 個樣本訓練 300 輪 (epoch) 才能得到 81.73% 的成績，PANN 只需以 16 個樣本訓練 70 輪就能得到相近、甚至更佳的準確度，而這樣的訓練方式讓不管是標記資料或未標記資料都能對模型有所助益。

6 結論

此篇論文中，我們呈現了利用語音辨識技術的 SpecAugment 套用 FixMatch 半監督訓練於大規模預訓練模型的結果，並與未使用預訓練模型的作法相比，得到了微幅的成長，為我們所知在音訊標記領域中，首次以 FixMatch 搭配預訓練模型的做法，儘管這大部分歸功於預訓練模型對音訊特徵的適應，但相較於未使用預訓練的情況，可以大幅縮短訓練的時間，同時達到準確度的增加。在未來的半監督學習研究上，我們計畫能夠在訓練能時應對未標記的例外樣本進行排除，如 FixMatch 的延伸研究 OpenMatch (Saito et al., 2021)，使得模型在訓練時能夠更好的利用未標記資料。

參考文獻

David Berthelot, Nicholas Carlini, Ian Goodfellow, Nicolas Papernot, Avital Oliver, and Colin Raffel. 2019. MixMatch: A Holistic Approach to Semi-Supervised Learning. *arXiv:1905.02249 [cs, stat]*, October. arXiv: 1905.02249.

Léo Cances, Etienne Labbé, and Thomas Pellegrini. 2021. Improving Deep-learning-based Semi-supervised Audio Tagging with Mixup. *arXiv:2102.08183 [cs, eess]*, February. arXiv: 2102.08183.

Jia Deng, Wei Dong, R. Socher, Li-Jia Li, K. Li, and Li Fei-Fei. 2009. ImageNet: A large-scale hierarchical image database. In *CVPR*.

Yuan Gong, Yu-An Chung, and James Glass. 2021. PSLA: Improving Audio Tagging with Pretraining, Sampling, Labeling, and Aggregation. *arXiv:2102.01243 [cs, eess]*, May. arXiv: 2102.01243.

Andrey Guzhov, Federico Raue, Jörn Hees, and Andreas Dengel. 2021. AudioCLIP: Extending CLIP to Image, Text and Audio. *arXiv:2106.13043 [cs, eess]*, June. arXiv: 2106.13043.

Andrew Jaegle, Felix Gimeno, Andrew Brock, Andrew Zisserman, Oriol Vinyals, and Joao Carreira. 2021. Perceiver: General Perception with Iterative Attention. *arXiv:2103.03206 [cs, eess]*, March. arXiv: 2103.03206.

Alex Krizhevsky, Ilya Sutskever, and Geoffrey E. Hinton. 2017. ImageNet classification with deep convolutional neural networks. *Communications of the ACM*, 60(6):84–90, May.

Qiuqiang Kong, Yin Cao, Turab Iqbal, Yuxuan Wang, Wenwu Wang, and Mark D. Plumbley. 2020. PANNs: Large-Scale Pretrained Audio Neural Networks for Audio Pattern Recognition. *arXiv:1912.10211 [cs, eess]*, August. arXiv: 1912.10211.

Annamaria Mesaros, Toni Heittola, Antti Eronen, and Tuomas Virtanen. 2010. Acoustic event detection in real life recordings. In *2010 18th European Signal Processing Conference*, pages 1267–1271. August.

Rafael Müller, Simon Kornblith, and Geoffrey Hinton. 2020. When Does Label Smoothing Help? *arXiv:1906.02629 [cs, stat]*, June. arXiv: 1906.02629.

Kamalesh Palanisamy, Dipika Singhania, and Angela Yao. 2020. Rethinking CNN Models for Audio Classification. *arXiv:2007.11154 [cs, eess]*, November. arXiv: 2007.11154.

Daniel S. Park, William Chan, Yu Zhang, Chung-Cheng Chiu, Barret Zoph, Ekin D. Cubuk, and Quoc V. Le. 2019. SpecAugment: A Simple Data Augmentation Method for Automatic Speech Recognition. *Interspeech 2019*:2613–2617, September. arXiv: 1904.08779.

Kuniaki Saito, Donghyun Kim, and Kate Saenko. 2021. OpenMatch: Open-set Consistency Regularization for Semi-supervised Learning with Outliers. *arXiv:2105.14148 [cs]*, May. arXiv: 2105.14148.

Mehdi Sajjadi, Mehran Javanmardi, and Tolga Tasdizen. 2016. Regularization With Stochastic Transformations and Perturbations for Deep Semi-Supervised Learning. *arXiv:1606.04586 [cs]*, June. arXiv: 1606.04586.

Justin Salamon, Christopher Jacoby, and Juan Pablo Bello. 2014. A Dataset and Taxonomy for Urban Sound Research. In *Proceedings of the 22nd ACM international conference on Multimedia*, pages 1041–1044, Orlando Florida USA, November. ACM.

Jivitesh Sharma, Ole-Christoffer Granmo, and Morten Goodwin. 2020. Environment Sound Classification Using Multiple Feature Channels and Attention Based Deep Convolutional Neural Network. In *Interspeech 2020*, pages 1186–1190. ISCA, October.

Kihyuk Sohn, David Berthelot, Chun-Liang Li, Zizhao Zhang, Nicholas Carlini, Ekin D. Cubuk, Alex Kurakin, Han Zhang, and Colin Raffel. 2020. FixMatch: Simplifying Semi-Supervised Learning with Consistency and Confidence. *arXiv:2001.07685 [cs, stat]*, November. arXiv: 2001.07685.

Yu Su, Ke Zhang, Jingyu Wang, and Kurosh Madani. 2019. Environment Sound Classification Using a Two-Stream CNN Based on Decision-Level Fusion. *Sensors*, 19(7):1733, January.

Lode Vuegen, Bert Van Den Broeck, Peter Karsmakers, Jort Florent Gemmeke, and Hugo Van hamme. 2013. An MFCC GMM approach for event detection and classification. October.

Felix Weninger, Franco Mana, Roberto Gemello, Jesús Andrés-Ferrer, and Puming Zhan. 2020. Semi-Supervised Learning with Data Augmentation for End-to-End ASR. *arXiv:2007.13876 [cs, eess]*, July. arXiv: 2007.13876.

Less Wright. 2019. New Deep Learning Optimizer, Ranger: Synergistic combination of RAdam + LookAhead for the best of both. September.

Qizhe Xie, Minh-Thang Luong, Eduard Hovy, and Quoc V. Le. 2020. Self-training with Noisy Student improves ImageNet classification. *arXiv:1911.04252 [cs, stat]*, June. arXiv: 1911.04252.

Hongyi Zhang, Moustapha Cisse, Yann N. Dauphin, and David Lopez-Paz. 2018. mixup: Beyond Empirical Risk Minimization. *arXiv:1710.09412 [cs, stat]*, April. arXiv: 1710.09412.

The 33rd Conference on Computational Linguistics and Speech Processing (ROCLING 2021)
Taoyuan, Taiwan, October 15-16, 2021. The Association for Computational Linguistics and Chinese Language Processing

Mining Commonsense and Domain Knowledge from Math Word Problems

Shih-Hung Tsai, Chao-Chun Liang, Hsin-Min Wang, Keh-Yih Su
Institute of Information Science, Academia Sinica, Taiwan
{doublebite,ccliang,whm,kysu}@iis.sinica.edu.tw

Abstract

Current neural math solvers learn to incorporate commonsense or domain knowledge by utilizing pre-specified constants or formulas. However, as these constants and formulas are mainly human-specified, the generalizability of the solvers is limited. In this paper, we propose to explicitly retrieve the required knowledge from math problem datasets. In this way, we can determinedly characterize the required knowledge and improve the explainability of solvers. Our two algorithms take the problem text and the solution equations as input. Then, they try to deduce the required commonsense and domain knowledge by integrating information from both the problem text and equation. To show the effectiveness of our algorithms, we construct two math datasets and prove by experiments that our algorithms can retrieve the required knowledge for problem-solving.

Keywords: Math word problem solving, knowledge retrieval

1 Introduction

Math word problem (MWP) solving is a special subtask of question answering in which machine solvers need natural language understanding and numerical reasoning capability to solve a given problem. Traditionally, feature-based solvers (Kushman et al., 2014; Hosseini et al., 2014) learn to apply the corresponding operations with the help of salient features or indicators (e.g., "*buy A, B and C in total*" may indicates a series of addition).

Benefiting from the availability of large scale datasets, neural solvers have emerged. They utilize encoder-decoder architectures to encode the problem text into hidden representations and learn to decode them into equation strings or operation trees (Wang et al., 2017; Amini et al., 2019; Xie and Sun, 2019; Zhang et al., 2020). During the decoding stage, pre-specified constants and formulas are either added to the vocabulary or introduced by some special mechanisms so that the solver can generate equations that carry mathematical knowledge. In most cases, the constants or formulas are limited and human-specified, impeding the generalizability of the solvers to different types of problems (e.g., commonsense problems, geometry problems, etc).

In this paper, we propose to alleviate this issue by automatically retrieving the required knowledge from MWP datasets. To do so, our algorithms try to identify **numbers** and their **associated concepts** or **units** in the text (e.g., in "*the length is 5 m*", *length* is the concept and *m* is the unit) and then deduce the required knowledge by aggregating information from solution equations. For example, if there are two different units in the problem (e.g., "*the length is 5 m and width is 50 cm*"), then our algorithms will try to find the ratio that possibly **bridges** these two units. In this way, our algorithms may be able to retrieve the unit conversion knowledge that there is a conversion ratio *100* between "cm" and "m". Technically, this task differs from standard problem solving tasks in which we aim to characterize all the required knowledge in a dataset rather than predicting the required knowledge for a single problem.

To verify our algorithms, we construct two middle-sized MWP datasets and annotate each problem with the associated knowledge. Experimental results show the effectiveness of our algorithms that they can retrieve 69.8% and 62.5% of the required knowledge for these two datasets, respectively.

Type	Example	Example Problem
Object property (commonsense)	A chicken has two feet and a rabbit has four.	There are 15 chickens and 10 rabbits in the cage. How many animal feet are in there? ($animal\_feet = 15 \times 2 + 10 \times 4$)
Hyper/hyponym (commonsense)	A daisy or rose is a kind of flower; a flower pot is not a flower.	Mary bought 3 daisies, 2 roses, and 5 flower pots from a flower store. How many flowers does she have?
Unit conversion (commonsense)	One kilometer equals 1000 meters.	Sam just ran a race of 3400 meters long. How many kilometers was the race?
Geometry (domain)	Formulas like "area = length×breadth".	The length of a rectangular plot is thrice its breadth. If the area is 972 sq. m, then what is the perimeter of the plot?

Table 1: Commonly used commonsense and domain knowledge in MWP solving

2 External Knowledge in MWP Solving

As with other QA tasks, solving MWPs usually requires external knowledge that is beyond the given information in the problem. Table 1 lists the common types of commonsense and domain knowledge used in MWP solving with prototypical examples.

Commonsense Knowledge is the set of prior knowledge that solvers are presumed to hold when dealing with problems concerning some real world scenarios. For example, as shown in Table 1, object-property or hyper/hyponym knowledge is critically needed to perform arithmetic operations between different objects. To calculate the number of flowers, a solver needs to know "daisy and rose are hyponyms of flower". As another example, the knowledge "a chicken has two feet; a rabbit has four" is required to calculate the number of animal feet.

Domain Knowledge On the other hand, domain knowledge also plays an essential role in MWP solving. Ranging from geometry and probability to combinations and permutations, a solver needs to apply some particular domain knowledge to solve the MWPs. In most cases, the domain knowledge is in the form of formulas. For example, a solver applies "the area formula for rectangle" to solve the geometry problem in Table 1. As another example, a solver may apply the conditional probability formula to solve a probability problem. Therefore, in this work we target on the domain knowledge that can be represented as formulas.

3 Retrieving Commonsense Knowledge

Our first step is to retrieve from MWP datasets the commonsense knowledge for problem solving.

3.1 Commonsense Knowledge as Mapping Ratios

Typically, commonsense knowledge concerns the introduction of extra numerical information, most of which can be regarded as *specific ratios* between concepts. For example, in the first MWP in Table 1, a solver introduces the object-property knowledge to calculate the total number of animal feet, where "a chicken has two feet" and "a rabbit has four feet". In fact, "2" and "4" serve as the associated mapping ratios that convert the concepts of "chicken" and "rabbit" to "animal feet".

Likewise, the knowledge of hypernym and hyponym can be considered as a 1-to-1 ratio that maps a hyponym to its hypernym or vice versa. On the other hand, the unit-conversion knowledge, obviously, can be represented as a mapping ratio between two units.

3.2 Identifying Mapping Ratios in Equations

To identify the ratios, our algorithm first extracts numbers in the text, and then creates mappings that map numbers to their corresponding concepts or units, as shown in the first step in Figure 1. For example, the noun "pennies" is captured as the unit for the number "9". Specifically, we use StanfordNLP toolkit (Manning et al., 2014) for dependency parsing in order to locate the numbers and their head nouns (concepts/units).

On the other hand, for variables, our algorithm uses five simple semantic patterns to capture the problem target as the corresponding concept or unit, as shown in Table 2. For example, we capture "cent" from "how many cents ..." as the unit for variable "x". In our pilot study, this heuristic handles about 90% of the cases.

Pattern	Rule
how many A (and B) ...	The goal object is A (and B)
(what is / find) the (length / distance) ...	We take the first length unit in the problem as the goal unit.
(what is the / find the / how much) time ...	We take the first time unit as the goal unit.
how much weight ...	We take the first mass unit as the goal unit.
how much ...	The default unit is dollar.

Table 2: Patterns for capturing the goal concept/unit of the variables

Next, the algorithm deduces the mapping ratios using these number-to-concept mappings. Here we use basic arithmetic principles for ratio deduction. For an equation to make sense, every term must correspond to the same concept/unit. As in the equation "$9 + 4 \times 5 + 10 \times 10 = x$" in Figure 1, "9", "4×5", "10×10", and "x" should share the same concept. Based on the fact that "9" and "4" corresponds to "penny" and "nickel", respectively, we can thus infer that "5" serves as the mapping ratio that maps "nickel" to "penny". Figure 1 illustrates the overall deduction flow for a single MWP.

Finally, the algorithm collects the ratio candidates for the whole dataset. It calculates the

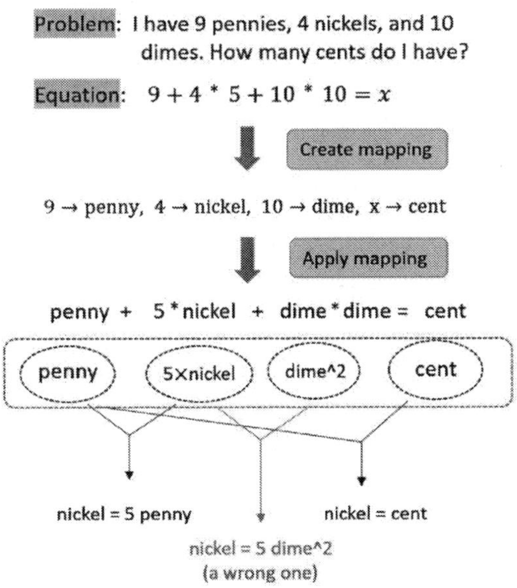

Figure 1: Flow of commonsense knowledge retrieval

occurrence frequency for each candidate and then removes the ones whose counts are less than a pre-specified threshold λ, as a way to filter wrongly generated ratios (like the one in red in Figure 1).

4 Retrieving Domain Knowledge

Our next target is to retrieve the domain knowledge involved in MWP solving. We consider the types of domain knowledge used in the form of formulas, and assume they (at least the common ones) appear in more than one problem in a dataset so that our algorithm can discover them by finding common patterns.

4.1 Formulas and Concept Mappings

Generally, a solver uses a formula by substituting values (numbers) into it and then generating corresponding equations. As a result, the generated equations more or less keep the skeleton of the source formula, as shown in Figure 2. Thus, our goal is to retrieve the underlying formula from equations by considering the mapping between numbers and domain concepts.

To find the mapping, our algorithm performs entity recognition and relation prediction to identify domain concepts, numbers, and their mapping relationships, respectively.

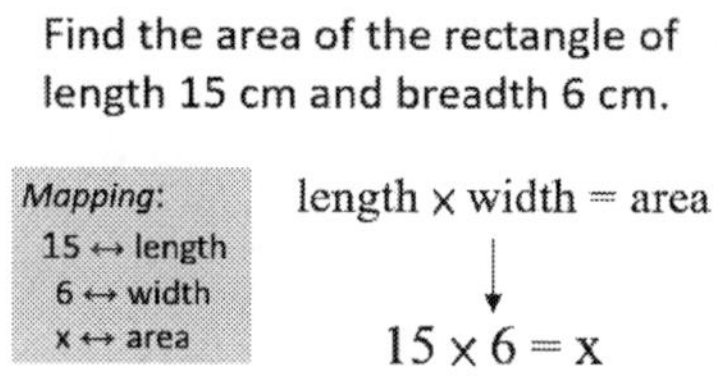

Figure 2: Simple example showing the idea that we have a mapping in mind when using formulas

As different domains may come with different domain language in their problem description, here we use neural models (which are more generalizable than semantic rules) for this task. Our pilot study showed that little labeled data is enough to train the models. Specifically, we employ two intuitive Bert-based models for entity recognition (Devlin et al., 2018) and relation prediction (Shi and Lin, 2019), and label a small amount of data to finetune both models.

Here we describe the entity and relation types as well as the model architectures we use in details. In this work, we consider geometry as the sample domain knowledge, and we identify four important entity types that are related to geometry domain: *object*, *attribute*, *value*, and *target*. Table 3 gives a detailed description for each entity. We use the architecture in Figure 3 to discern these entities in the problem text. Specifically, the model is based on Bert (Devlin et al., 2018) and fine-tuned on our MWP entity data using IO tagging.

Next, we seek to predict relationships between these entities. The relation types that we use are: *attribute-of*, *value-of*, and *none*, as described in Table 4. We adopt the framework of (Shi and Lin, 2019) for our model, as shown in Figure 4. In this framework, a special format is used for the input, in which entity mentions are replaced with entity-type masks in their original position and then moved to the end of the input. Such arrangement helps inform the model the two entities to focus on. Specifically, the model takes the problem text and two entities as input and is fine-tuned to predict their corresponding relation. Finally, we construct a concept mapping between an attribute and a number if there is a "value-of" relationship between them.

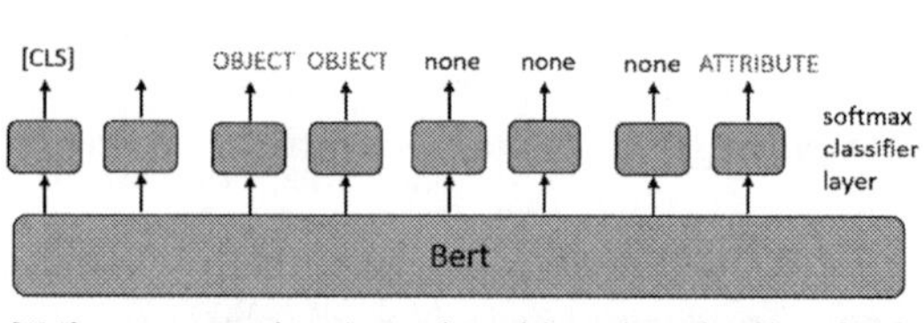

Figure 3: Architecture of entity recognition model

Entity types	Description
object	A geometric shape or real-world object, such as "circle" or "cylindrical container".
attribute	Attribute of the objects, such as "length", "width".
value	Number or value of a quantity, such as "two" triangles and "5" cm.
target	The goal of the problem, such as "volume" in "*what is the volume of X*".

Table 3: Entity types and their descriptions

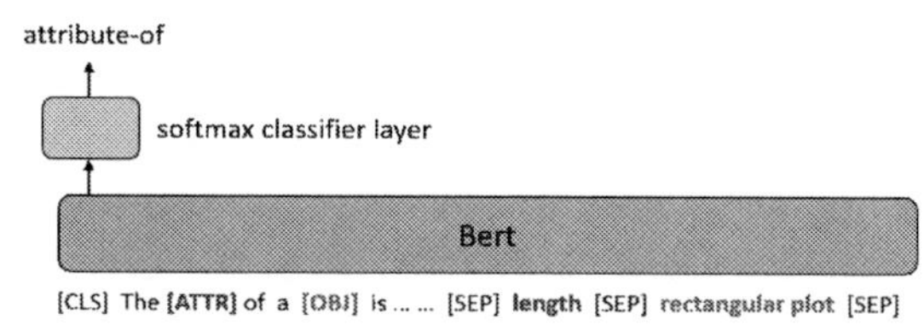

Figure 4: Architecture of relation extraction model. The original sentence "The length of a rectangular plot ..." becomes "The [ATTR] of a [OBJ] ... " and both entities are moved to the end of the input.

Types	Description
attribute-of	Relation between *object* and *attribute*, such as "circle" and "radius" in the description "the radius of the circle".
value-of	Relation between *value* and *attribute*, such as "radius" and "4" in "the radius is 4 cm".
none	None of the relations above.

Table 4: Relation types and their descriptions

4.2 Formula Candidate Generation

As shown in Section 3, our algorithm uses the mappings generated by entity recognition and

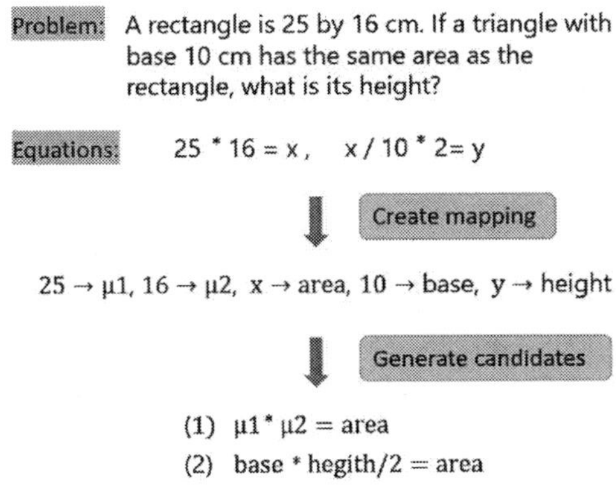

Figure 5: Flow of domain knowledge retrieval. We use μ_n to indicate that the concept of the number is unknown.

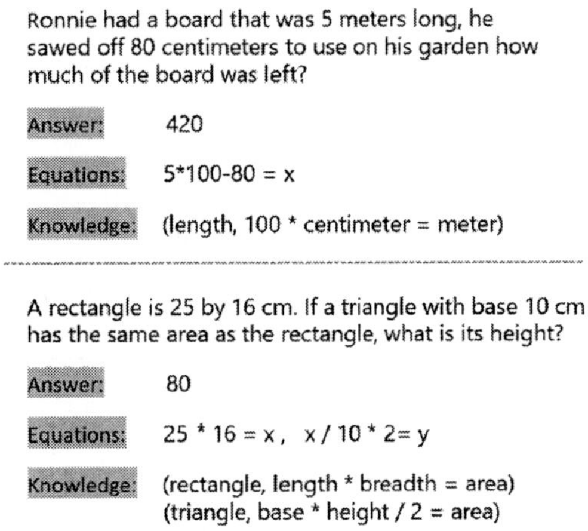

Figure 6: Sample MWPs from UnitQA (above) and GeometryQA (below). The annotation is in the form of "(*type*, *knowledge*)".

relation extraction models to generate formula candidates from the equations. Then, it splits long candidates into shorter ones by addition and subtraction operators, and normalize the resulted candidates in order to reduce the degree of freedom. After that, the algorithm gathers all formula candidates for each MWP in the dataset and calculates the occurrence frequency of these candidates. Finally, it removes the candidates whose counts are less than a pre-specified threshold λ.

5 UnitQA & GeometryQA

To check the effectiveness of our methodology, we construct two middle-sized MWP datasets: *UnitQA* and *GeometryQA*. The first dataset contains 1128 MWPs that require the commonsense unit-conversion knowledge, while the second dataset contains 675 MWPs that require geometric domain knowledge.

Problems of both datasets are collected from two large-scale datasets: *Dolphin18K* (Huang et al., 2016) and *MathQA* (Amini et al., 2019). We collect these MWPs using some domain-relevant keywords. Then, we manually annotate the required external knowledge (if any) for each problem, as shown in Figure 6. We select only a subset of problems from the large datasets because we would like to focus on basic problems first. The more advanced ones are left for future work.

Table 5 shows the statistics of UnitQA. It contains a total of 1128 MWPs, 305 out of which require unit-conversion knowledge across 43 different types, including the conversion knowledge between units of money, time, length and so on. To test the capability for retrieving other types of commonsense knowledge, we also heuristically select 25 problems that require **object-property** or **hypernym/hyponym** knowledge. Due to data sparsity, these problems are not large enough to form a dataset, yet they should help demonstrate the effectiveness of our algorithm (details described in Section 6.2).

Table 6 shows the statistics of GeometryQA. It contains 675 MWPs, 570 out of which require 40 different formulas for 18 different geometric objects, including circle, rectangle, and so on. In addition, we annotate an extra 193/46 geometric MWPs with corresponding entities/relationships to train the two different BERT models. We found that a small amount of annotated MWPs are enough to make accurate entity and relation predictions.

UnitQA	
Total problems	1128
Knowledge required	305
Total knowledge types	43
Types of unit conversion: money(34.9%), length(32.6%), time(14%), mass(11.6%), volume(4.7%), and area(2.3%).	

Table 5: Dataset statistics of UnitQA

GeometryQA	
Total problems	675
Knowledge required	570 (84% of 675)
Total formula types	40
There are 40 types of geometric formulas for 18 objects, including the area, perimeter, and volume formulas for square, circle, cubic, sphere, and so on.	

Table 6: Dataset statistics of GeometryQA

6 Experimental Results

6.1 Experimental Settings

We use exact the same setting for both models and implement them based on HuggingFace[1]. The dropout rate is set to 0.1. The parameters are optimized by Adam (Kingma and Ba, 2014), with learning rate 1e-4, batch size 50, and a max sequence length for the input 68.

6.2 Retrieving Commonsense Knowledge

We first conduct experiment on *UnitQA* to retrieve the commonsense unit-conversion knowledge. We test with threshold $\lambda = 0, 2, 5$ (for larger dataset, the λ should be adjusted accordingly.) Table 7 shows the overall performance of the experiment. When $\lambda = 0$, where no candidate is eliminated for insufficient frequency, it shows an upper bound of the recall (79%). As expected, when the threshold increases, it causes a decrease in recall and an increase in precision. We found that for $\lambda = 2$, about 67% of the unretrieved cases are due to concept identification errors, where the concept for numbers are wrongly identified. This suggests the limit of our rule-based deduction strategy.

Due to data sparsity, we have not collected enough problems that require object-property or hyper/hyponym knowledge. Yet, in our small-scale experiment (about 25 problems), our algorithm can identify about 68% of the required knowledge and retrieve something like "chicken $\leftrightarrow$ 2 feet" , "rabbit $\leftrightarrow$ 4 feet" , and " bicycle $\leftrightarrow$ 2 wheels" for the first and second types of knowledge in Table 1.

[1] https://github.com/huggingface/transformers

	Precision	Recall
$\lambda = 0$	47.8% (33/69)	79.1% (34/43)
$\lambda = 2$	**90.9%** (30/33)	**69.8%** (30/43)
$\lambda = 5$	100% (9/9)	20.9% (9/43)

Table 7: Precision and recall for retrieving the unit-conversion knowledge in UnitQA with $\lambda = 0, 2, 5$

6.3 Retrieving Domain Knowledge

In this experiment, we test the effectiveness of our algorithm for retrieving domain knowledge on *GeaometryQA*. We test with $\lambda = 0, 2, 5$. Table 8 presents the overall knowledge retrieval result. When $\lambda = 0$, where no candidate is eliminated for insufficient frequency, it shows an upper bound of recall (70%). As expected, when the threshold increases, it causes a decrease in recall and an increase in precision. We conduct error analysis on $\lambda = 2$ and find that about 75% unretrieved formulas are also caused by concept identification errors. That is, if an equation contains several variables, our algorithm cannot always find the corresponding concept for each variable and thus unable to retrieve the correct formula.

	Precision	Recall
$\lambda = 0$	71.8% (28/39)	70% (28/40)
$\lambda = 2$	**92.6%** (25/27)	**62.5%** (25/40)
$\lambda = 5$	80% (8/10)	20% (8/40)

Table 8: Precision and recall for knowledge retrieval on GeometryQA with $\lambda = 0, 2, 5$

7 Conclusion

In this paper, we introduced a task of retrieving the required knowledge for math word problem datasets. By explicitly identifying the required knowledge, we can characterize the datasets and assist current neural solvers. We then proposed two algorithms which retrieves the commonsense and domain knowledge, respectively, and constructed two datasets with each MWP annotated with the required knowledge. Experimental results demonstrated the effectiveness of our algorithms.

References

Aida Amini, Saadia Gabriel, Peter Lin, Rik Koncel-Kedziorski, Yejin Choi, and Hannaneh Hajishirzi. 2019. Mathqa: Towards interpretable math word problem solving with operation-based formalisms. *arXiv preprint arXiv:1905.13319.*

Jacob Devlin, Ming-Wei Chang, Kenton Lee, and Kristina Toutanova. 2018. Bert: Pre-training of deep bidirectional transformers for language understanding. *arXiv preprint arXiv:1810.04805.*

Mohammad Javad Hosseini, Hannaneh Hajishirzi, Oren Etzioni, and Nate Kushman. 2014. Learning to solve arithmetic word problems with verb categorization. In *Proceedings of the 2014 Conference on Empirical Methods in Natural Language Processing (EMNLP)*, pages 523–533.

Danqing Huang, Shuming Shi, Chin-Yew Lin, Jian Yin, and Wei-Ying Ma. 2016. How well do computers solve math word problems? large-scale dataset construction and evaluation. In *Proceedings of the 54th Annual Meeting of the Association for Computational Linguistics (Volume 1: Long Papers)*, pages 887–896.

Diederik P Kingma and Jimmy Ba. 2014. Adam: A method for stochastic optimization. *arXiv preprint arXiv:1412.6980.*

Nate Kushman, Yoav Artzi, Luke Zettlemoyer, and Regina Barzilay. 2014. Learning to automatically solve algebra word problems. In *Proceedings of the 52nd Annual Meeting of the Association for Computational Linguistics (Volume 1: Long Papers)*, pages 271–281.

Christopher D Manning, Mihai Surdeanu, John Bauer, Jenny Rose Finkel, Steven Bethard, and David McClosky. 2014. The stanford corenlp natural language processing toolkit. In *Proceedings of 52nd annual meeting of the association for computational linguistics: system demonstrations*, pages 55–60.

Peng Shi and Jimmy Lin. 2019. Simple bert models for relation extraction and semantic role labeling. *arXiv preprint arXiv:1904.05255.*

Yan Wang, Xiaojiang Liu, and Shuming Shi. 2017. Deep neural solver for math word problems. In *Proceedings of the 2017 Conference on Empirical Methods in Natural Language Processing*, pages 845–854.

Zhipeng Xie and Shichao Sun. 2019. A goal-driven tree-structured neural model for math word problems. In *IJCAI*, pages 5299–5305.

Jipeng Zhang, Lei Wang, Roy Ka-Wei Lee, Yi Bin, Yan Wang, Jie Shao, and Ee-Peng Lim. 2020. Graph-to-tree learning for solving math word problems. In *Proceedings of the 58th Annual Meeting of the Association for Computational Linguistics*, pages 3928–3937.

The 33rd Conference on Computational Linguistics and Speech Processing (ROCLING 2021)
Taoyuan, Taiwan, October 15-16, 2021. The Association for Computational Linguistics and Chinese Language Processing

RCRNN-based Sound Event Detection System with Specific Speech Resolution
具有特定語音分辨率的 RCRNN 聲音事件偵測系統

黃頌仁 Sung-Jen Huang, 王奕雯 Yih-Wen Wang, 陳嘉平 Chia-Ping Chen
國立中山大學資訊工程學系
National Sun Yat-sen University
Department of Computer Science and Engineering
m093040011@student.nsysu.edu.tw, m083040011@student.nsysu.edu.tw, cpchen@cse.nsysu.edu.tw
呂仲理 Chung-Li Lu, 詹博丞 Bo-Cheng Chan
中華電信研究院
Chunghwa Telecom Laboratories
chungli@cht.com.tw, cbc@cht.com.tw

摘要

聲音事件偵測的目標是標記出音訊中的聲音事件及其時間界線。我們基於半監督式學習的均值教師框架，提出一個帶有殘差連接與注意力機制的 RCRNN 網路架構，其可用大量弱標註/未標註資料來訓練。而在許多聲音事件中，語音具有更豐富的訊息量，因此我們使用特定的時間頻率參數來擷取該類別的聲學特徵，並且利用資料增強與後處理來進一步提升效能。我們提出的系統於 DCASE 2021 Task 4 的驗證集上，PSDS (Polyphonic Sound Detection Score)-scenario 1、2 和 Event-based F1-Score 分別達到 38.2%, 58.2% 和 44.3%，優於 baseline 的 33.8%, 52.9% 和 40.7%。

Abstract

Sound event detection (SED) system outputs sound events and their time boundaries in audio signals. We proposed an RCRNN-based SED system with residual connection and convolution block attention mechanism based on the mean-teacher framework of semi-supervised learning. The neural network can be trained with an amount of weakly labeled data and unlabeled data. In addition, we consider that the speech event has more information than other sound events. Thus, we use the specific time-frequency resolution to extract the acoustic feature of the speech event. Furthermore, we apply data augmentation and post-processing to improve the performance. On the DCASE 2021 Task 4 validation set, the proposed system achieves the PSDS (Poly-phonic Sound Event Detection Score)-scenario 1,2 of 38.2%, 58.2% and event-based F1-score of 44.3%, outperforming the baseline score of 33.8%, 52.9% and 40.7%.

關鍵字：聲音事件偵測、均值教師模型、卷積注意力機制、語音

Keywords: Sound event detection, Mean teacher model, CBAM, Speech

1 緒論

聲音在人類的日常生活中無處不在，人們對聲音的接收，是許多行動和反應的判斷基礎，而這通常是基於聲音的事件類別，例如：假若有人呼喊你的名字，你會回頭查看，而若是突然有短促的警報聲，人們則會迅速進入警戒狀態，因此輔助或是代替人們做出決定的決策型機器亦是需要這種判斷聲音事件的能力，由於機器需要能準確的判斷發生的事件類別以及其發生的開始和結束時間，即帶出了聲音事件偵測這個主題，而聲音事件偵測可以簡單的分爲兩類，一類是訓練和測試資料中事件的發生會存在部份重疊，另一類則不會如此，前者在預測上較爲困難，後者則相對容易，DCASE(Detection and Classification of Acoustic Scenes and Events) Challenge Task 4: Sound Event Detection and Separation in Domestic Environments 即是屬於前者，目標

是希望在多個聲音事件彼此重疊的情況下，仍可預測出音訊中所發生的聲音事件及其時間界線。此外，蒐集大量具有時間及事件標註的資料是相當高成本的，因此該任務期望系統可同時利用標註不完全的資料進行訓練。

DCASE 2021 Task 4 的 baseline (Turpault et al., 2019) 是一個基於 CRNN 模型架構的聲音事件偵測系統，且利用均值教師模型 (Tarvainen and Valpola, 2017 ; Lionel and Cyril, 2019) 對弱標註/未標註資料進行半監督式學習。爲了更好的分出十種類別的事件，我們參考 Kim and Kim (2021) 提出的 RCRNN 模型並加以改動，利用由兩層卷積層 (convolution layer) 組合而成的殘差卷積模塊 (residual convolution block) ，目的是希望透過加深層數來增強學習的效果，而其中跳層連接部份的設計則避免了層數過深導致的梯度消失，此外，在十種類別中，我們更加注重語音類別的預測準確度，因此使用了不同解析度的聲學特徵 (Park et al., 2010 ; Zhang et al., 2007)，其中解析度代表的即是透過設定特定的短時傅立葉轉換和梅爾頻率參數來取得與原先不同大小 (對特徵的表現也不相同) 的梅爾頻譜圖。

論文其餘章節的編排方式將如下安排，章節二：研究方法描述 baseline 系統以及所提出的改進；章節三：實驗設置描述資料集、訊號處理，以及網路參數設定；章節四：實驗結果比較 baseline 系統與改進後系統的效能差異；章節五：結論總結我們系統的優點和未來的研究方向。

2 研究方法

本章節將詳細描述我們提出的聲音事件偵測系統，包含模型架構和半監督式學習的運用，也將說明資料增強的方法以及後處理之具體流程。

2.1 模型架構

2.1.1 CRNN

DCASE Task4 官方提出的 baseline 系統是基於 CRNN 的架構，顧名思義，該架構是由卷積網路 (Convolution Neural Network,CNN) 和遞歸網路 (Recurrent Neural Network,RNN) 組成，其中卷積層可以更好的學習到局部特徵，與之相對的遞歸層則在學習全域特徵上有更佳的表現，而將兩種架構結合後，可同時擁有擷取不同特徵的能力。我們實作了 DCASE Task4 官方提出的 CRNN 系統 (參照圖 1)，此架構使用的是七層卷積層，卷積核大小 (kernel size) 皆是 3×3、激勵函數全部使用門控線性單元 (Gated Linear Unit,GLU)，濾波器 (filter) 數則分別是 16, 32, 64, 128, 128, 128 和 128 個，每層亦使用了批標準化 (batch normalization) 和平均池化 (average pooling)，平均池化的卷積核大小個別是 2×2, 2×2, 1×2, 1×2, 1×2, 1×2 和 1×2，接著連接兩層 128 個單元的雙向門控循環單元 (Bidirectional Gated Recurrent Unit,Bi-GRU) 之遞歸網路架構，最後連接一層乙狀函數 (sigmoid) 的全連接層作爲分類器輸出十個類別的幀級預測 (frame-level prediction or strong prediction)，該預測結果包含事件類別及其時間界線的資訊，接著進一步透過注意力池化層 (Attention pooling) 對幀級預測的時間軸取平均，以得到剪輯級預測 (clip-level prediction or weak prediction)，該預測結果則僅包含事件類別。

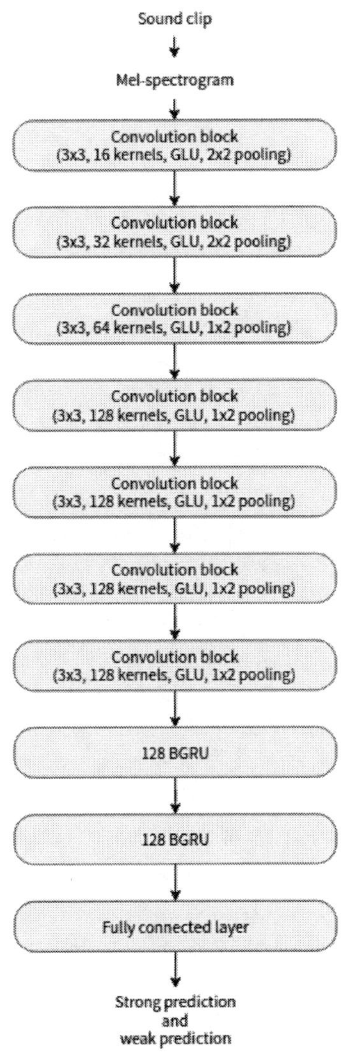

圖 1. Baseline：卷積層中的描述依序代表卷積核大小及濾波器數量、激勵函數和池化層卷積核大小，雙向門控循環單元層的數字則表示單元數。

2.1.2 RCRNN

啓發於 (Kim and Kim, 2021)，我們改良 baseline 模型並實作一個類似的 RCRNN 架構系統，參照圖 2，與其提出的模型相比，我們將殘差連接的部分做了些微改動，此架構將原本 baseline 模型的前兩層卷積核大小改爲 7×7，後五層則將每層改成由兩層卷積模塊和卷積塊的注意力機制 (CBAM,Convolution Block Attention Module) 以及殘差連接組成的殘差模塊（參見圖 2 右半部分），每層卷積模塊使用了與原先大小和數量相同的濾波器（每個殘差模塊視爲一層），同樣使用了批標準化和平均池化，主要不同的是把激勵函數改爲線性整流函數 (Rectified Linear Unit,ReLU)，卷積塊的注意力機制 (Woo et al., 2018) 的運作是如下面公式所示

$$F' = M_c(F) \otimes F \tag{1}$$

$$F'' = M_s(F') \otimes F' \tag{2}$$

$$\begin{aligned} M_c(F) = \sigma(&MLP(Avgpool(F)) \\ &+MLP(Maxpool(F))) \end{aligned} \tag{3}$$

$$M_s(F) = \sigma(f^{(7\times7)}(Avgpool(F); Maxpool(F)) \tag{4}$$

，與常見的注意力模型不同，卷積塊的注意力機制使用乙狀 (sigmoid) 函數（以 σ 表示），而不是歸一化指數函數（softmax），其中 F 爲前一層的輸出，M_c/M_s 是通道/空間注意力機制，$Avgpool/Maxpool$ 是對特徵做平均/最大池化 (即先做通道注意力機制再做空間注意力機制，而通道/空間注意力是使用在空間/通道維度上)，MLP 和 $f^{(7\times7)}$ 分別是僅有一層隱藏層的多層感知器和 7×7 的卷積操作。

由兩層卷積模塊組成是透過加深層數更好的學習十種類別，而加入卷積塊注意力機制的目的則是希望專注於更重要的特徵，最後殘差的設計是避免層數加深導致的梯度消失問題。

2.1.3 半監督式學習

我們參照 baseline 所使用的均值教師框架 (Mean-Teacher framework)，來作爲半監督式學習的方法，一個均值教師模型是由兩個結構完全相同的學生和教師模型組成，只有學生會隨著訓練資料調整其模型的網路參數，教師模型的網路參數則是透過對學生模型的參數進行指數移動平均 (exponential moving average) 後得到，如下式

$$\theta'_t = \alpha\theta'_{t-1} + (1-\alpha)\theta_t \tag{5}$$

，θ 和 θ' 分別表示學生模型和教師模型的參數，t 則代表當前時刻，α 是數值介於 0 和 1 之間的超參數，該框架包含兩種損失函數，分別爲監督式損失 (Supervised loss) 與一致性損失 (Consistency loss)，前者使用二元交叉熵 (Binary Cross-Entropy,BCE)，後者使用平均方差 (Mean Square Error,MSE)。監督式損失用二元交叉熵來計算學生模型對於有標註資料的預測結果與眞實答案的差值，一致性損失則使用平均方差來計算學生模型與教師模型彼此對所有資料預測結果的一致性。此外，一致性損失具有額外的權重，於訓練初期時，將其設定爲零，以便模型優先學習有標註的資料，隨著訓練步數增加，權重亦提高進而開始學習無標註的資料，整體流程如圖 3。

2.2 資料增強

爲了進一步提升效能，我們參照 baseline 所使用的資料混和 (Mixup) 來作爲資料增強的方法 (Zhang et al., 2018)，將兩個資料樣本進行線性組合，以得到新的樣本資料，過程如下

$$\hat{x} = \lambda x_i + (1-\lambda)x_j \tag{6}$$

$$\hat{y} = \lambda y_i + (1-\lambda)y_j \tag{7}$$

，其中 x_i 和 x_j 是隨機選取的兩個樣本的特徵向量，y_i 和 y_j 代表這兩個樣本的標註，$\lambda \in [0,1]$，而其特徵 $\hat{x}$（標註 $\hat{y}$）爲其線性組合產生的新樣本及對應的標註。

2.3 後處理流程

神經網路的幀級預測 (frame-level prediction) 需進一步執行後處理方可得到最終輸出。首先，透過閾值 (Threshold) 將各機率值轉換成二元輸出，接著，再透過中值濾波器 (Median filter) 進一步平滑結果，以避免虛假的預測。我們參照 baseline 所使用的設定，所有事件類別的閾值皆爲 0.5，中值濾波器大小皆爲 7 (即爲 0.45 秒)。

3 實驗設置

3.1 資料集

資料集使用的是由 DCASE 2021 Challenge Task 4 釋出的 DESED(Domestic Environment Sound Event Detection)，當中含有具備兩種資料屬性的三類資料，分別是生成資料：透過 Scaper 工具生成的強標記資料 (標註了音檔中所有發生事件的類別和時間界線) 以及眞實資料：擷取於 Audioset 的弱標記資料 (僅標記發生的事件類別) 和未標記資料，三類資

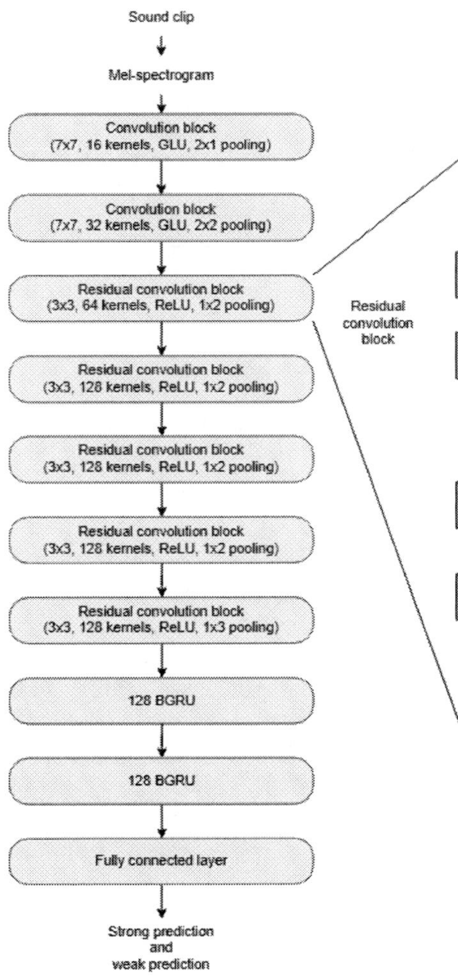

圖 2. 提出的模型：左半部分與圖 1 相似，卷積層和殘差卷積模塊的描述依序爲卷積核大小及濾波器數量、激勵函數和池化層卷積核大小，右半部分則是 residual convolution block 的內部架構

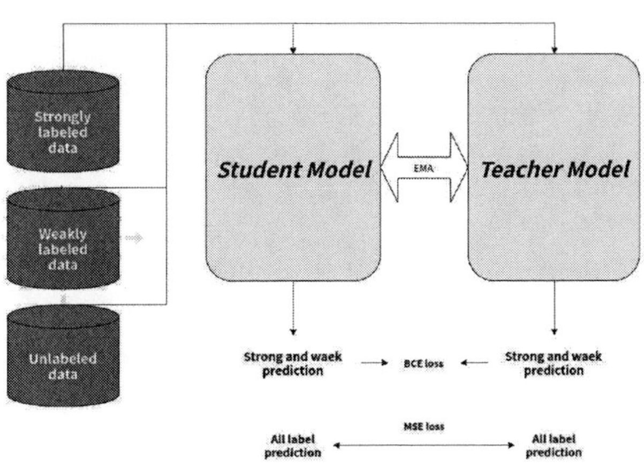

圖 3. 均值教師框架 (Mean-Teacher framework)：將網路架構視爲兩種身分，分別爲學生模型與教師模型。所有資料皆會作爲兩模型的輸入，其中學生模型的參數使用一般梯度更新方式，而教師模型則將學生模型參數進行指數移動平均，以得到當前時刻的參數。此流程包含兩種損失函數，分別爲監督式損失與一致性損失。

	Baseline	RCRNN(A)	RCRNN(B)
Alarm/bell/ringing	42.5%	44.7%	**46.0%**
Blender	46.8%	37.9%	**48.7%**
Cat	42.4%	46.6%	**48.2%**
Dishes	22.7%	32.2%	**33.4%**
Dog	25.8%	**27.1%**	**27.1%**
Electric shaver/toothbrush	45.4%	**59.0%**	51.0%
Frying	34.3%	**42.6%**	37.2%
Running water	37.8%	39.4%	**43.8%**
Speech	53.0%	53.6%	**61.4%**
Vacuum cleaner	**56.1%**	47.7%	46.3%

表 1. 各類別比較：在不同解析度與不同網路架構下，各類別的 Event-based F1 (event-f1) Score

料個別有 10000、1578 和 14412 筆，驗證資料和測試資料分別是 2500 和 1168 筆強預測資料，詳細資訊如表 2 所示。

	訓練資料			驗證資料	測試資料
	強標記	弱標記	未標記	強標記	強標記
數量	10000	1578	14412	2500	1168
種類	生成	真實	真實	生成	生成
長度	至多 10 秒				
通道數	1	2	2	1	1
採樣率 (kHz)	16	44.1	44.1	16	16

表 2. DESED 資料集

3.2 訊號處理

在 DESED 資料中，所有音檔的採樣率與聲道數並非一致，因此我們先利用 FFmpeg 工具將所有資料屬性統一爲 16000 Hz 和單聲道，接著透過 Librosa 工具從音檔中擷取聲學特徵來做爲神經網路的輸入，而這裡擷取的聲學特徵是梅爾頻譜圖。

3.3 訓練設定

我們提出的系統使用的皆是 RCRNN 架構，下面會分爲是否改動解析度的兩類描述，如此改動是爲了提升語音類別的準確度，主要差異爲梅爾頻譜圖參數設置及池化層稍有改動，而 baseline 的設置則參照章節 2.1.1 描述（解析度與未改動的 RCRNN 模型相同）。

3.3.1 未改動解析度的 RCRNN 模型

參數設置如圖 2 左半部分所示，生成梅爾頻譜圖的參數 (版本 A) 爲 n_mels: 128 (128 個 mel-filter bank)、n_filters: 2048 (離散傅立葉轉換的樣本數)、hop_length: 256 (短時傅立葉轉換的 window 間隔)、n_window: 2048 (短時傅立葉轉換的 window 大小)。

3.3.2 改變解析度的 RCRNN

爲了能在語音類別上有更佳的準確度，將聲學特徵擷取參數改變以擷取到更爲清晰的語音類別特徵，因此在採樣頻率保持 16000 Hz 下將生成梅爾頻譜圖的參數 (版本 B) 改爲 n_mels: 96、n_filters: 2048 、hop_length: 192 、n_window: 1536（參考表 3），以上的單位除了 mel-filter bank 外皆是樣本數，另外爲了維持最終輸出大小與擷取出的標註大小相同，將第一層和最後一層池化層大小改爲 2×1 和 1×3，如此的設計是由於在 (Benito-Gorrón et al., 2021) 的實驗中 PSDS 近似的情況下，語音類別的準確度有相當的提昇，其中的研究也指出不同類別事件在不同聲學特徵下有不同表現（例如電動刮鬍刀的聲音類別在頻率擷取更密集的聲學特徵下有更清晰的表現，警示聲則在時間擷取更密集的特徵下更明顯）。

	A	B
n_mels	128	96
n_filters	2048	2048
hop_length	256	192
n_window	2048	1536

表 3. 聲學特徵參數設定：爲了提升語音類別準確度，將聲學參數由版本 A 改爲版本 B

	PSDS-1	PSDS-2	event-f1
Baseline	0.338	0.529	40.7%
RCRNN	**0.374**	**0.563**	**43.1%**

表 4. 架構改動結果：在相同解析度下，不同網路架構的實驗結果

	解析度	PSDS-1	PSDS-2	event-f1
Baseline	A	0.338	0.529	40.7%
RCRNN	A	0.374	0.563	43.1%
	B	**0.382**	**0.582**	**44.3%**

表 5. 解析度改動結果：在不同解析度與不同網路架構下的實驗結果

4 實驗結果

4.1 模型架構改動結果

表 4 呈現 baseline 系統與我們所提出的系統之效能比較。在各評估標準下，RCRNN 模型皆明顯優於 CRNN 模型，於 PSDS scenario 1 由 0.338 提升至 0.374，PSDS scenario 2 亦由 0.529 提升至 0.563，event-f1 則由 40.7% 提升至 43.1%，顯示層數加深並且使用卷積注意力機制對於效果有顯著提昇。

4.2 解析度改動結果

表 5 列出在不同解析度設定的情況下，不同網路架構的實驗結果，而在表 1. 各類別比較中顯示了在 CRNN 模型和兩種解析度的 RCRNN 模型中各個類別事件預測的 f1-score，從表 1、4 和 5 的結果可以看出 RCRNN 模型在提升所有分數的同時，語音類別也能有更高的正確性，而改動解析度的模型除了所有分數再次提昇外，語音類別的分數亦大幅提昇，令語音類別 f1-score 達到 61.4%，可見在稍微增加時間解析度且少量減少頻率解析度下對於識別語音類別是有明顯幫助的。

5 結論

我們提出了一個運用不同聲學參數梅爾頻譜圖的 RCRNN 架構系統，透過模型架構的改動提升了整體的分數，而改變解析度極大的提升語音類別的準確度，同時，整體分數（PSDS、event f1-score）也有小幅提昇，觀察 baseline 系統和 RCRNN 系統的比較表可見，RCRNN 是明顯優於 baseline 系統的，使用不同的解析度後，語音類別的預測有明顯的提昇，而未來研究的方向大致有兩個面向，其一是研究 RCRNN 模型架構下適合何種參數設置（例如 CNN 的卷積核大小和濾波器數量），二則是研究何種解析度對於語音類別是最佳的，以及探討此種解析度會更好的原因。

References

Diego De Benito-Gorrón, Daniel Ramos, and Doroteo T. Toledano. 2021. A multi-resolution crnn-based approach for semi-supervised sound event detection in dcase 2020 challenge. *IEEE Access*, 9:89029–89042.

Nam Kyun Kim and Hong Kook Kim. 2021. Polyphonic sound event detection based on residual convolutional recurrent neural network with semi-supervised loss function. *IEEE Access*, 9:7564–7575.

Delphin-Poulat Lionel and Plapous Cyril. 2019. Mean teacher with data augmentation for dcase 2019 task 4. In *Detection and Classification of Acoustic Scenes and Events 2019*.

Dennis Park, Deva Ramanan, and Charless Fowlkes. 2010. Multiresolution models for object detection. In *European Conference on Computer Vision(ECCV) 2010*, pages 241–254.

Antti Tarvainen and Harri Valpola. 2017. Mean teachers are better role models: Weight-averaged consistency targets improve semi-supervised deep learning results. In *Advances in Neural Information Processing Systems 30 (NIPS 2017)*.

Nicolas Turpault, Romain Serizel, Ankit Parag Shah, and Justin Salamon. 2019. Sound event detection in domestic environments with weakly labeled data and soundscape synthesis. In *Detection and Classification of Acoustic Scenes and Events*.

Sanghyun Woo, Jongchan Park, Joon-Young Lee, and In So Kweon. 2018. Cbam: Convolutional block attention module. In *Proceedings of the European Conference on Computer Vision (ECCV), 2018*, pages 3–19.

Hongyi Zhang, Moustapha Cisse, Yann N. Dauphin, and David Lopez-Paz. 2018. mixup: Beyond empirical risk minimization. In *6th International Conference on Learning Representations(ICLR 2018)*.

Wei Zhang, Gregory Zelinsky, and Dimitris Samaras. 2007. Real-time accurate object detection using multiple resolutions. In *2007 IEEE 11th International Conference on Computer Vision*.

The 33rd Conference on Computational Linguistics and Speech Processing (ROCLING 2021)
Taoyuan, Taiwan, October 15-16, 2021. The Association for Computational Linguistics and Chinese Language Processing

結合端對端語音辨識與發音模型於英文錯誤發音偵測之研究

Exploring the Integration of E2E ASR and Pronunciation Modeling for English Mispronunciation Detection

Hsin-Wei Wang[1], Bi-Cheng Yan[1], Yung-Chang Hsu[2], Berlin Chen[1]

[1] Department of Computer Science and Information Engineering National Taiwan Normal University

[2] EZ-AI Inc.

Taipei, Taiwan

{ hsinweiwang, bicheng, berlin }@ntnu.edu.tw

mic@ez-ai.com.tw

摘要

電腦輔助發音訓練需求日益漸增，它能讓第二外語學習者根據電腦所產生的回饋來改進發音並重複練習。然而現階段基於語音辨識的發音檢測系統在該任務的效能上仍未臻完美，在缺少非母語學習者的語料下，電腦輔助發音訓練系統的表現常受到自動語音辨識性能不佳而影響。有鑑於此，本論文發展一個兩階段的英文錯誤發音偵測方法：第一階段針對學習者的語音輸入進行端對端自動語音辨識，而第二階段將自動語音辨識產生的前 N 個最佳音素序列假設輸入到發音模型以預測出最接近學習者實際所發出音素序列的假設來與提示文字的音素序列進行比對，藉此提升錯誤發音偵測的效能。本論文經由在一套英語標竿資料集所進行的一系列實驗確認了我們所提出方法的可行性。

Abstract

There has been increasing demand to develop effective computer-assisted language training (CAPT) systems, which can provide feedback on mispronunciations and facilitate second-language (L2) learners to improve their speaking proficiency through repeated practice. Due to the shortage of non-native speech for training the automatic speech recognition (ASR) module of a CAPT system, the corresponding mispronunciation detection performance is often affected by imperfect ASR. Recognizing this importance, we in this paper put forward a two-stage mispronunciation detection method. In the first stage, the speech uttered by an L2 learner is processed by an end-to-end ASR module to produce N-best phone sequence hypotheses. In the second stage, these hypotheses are fed into a pronunciation model which seeks to faithfully predict the phone sequence hypothesis that is most likely pronounced by the learner, so as to improve the performance of mispronunciation detection. Empirical experiments conducted a English benchmark dataset seem to confirm the utility of our method.

關鍵字：端對端語音辨識、發音檢測與診斷、N-best 重新排序

Keywords : End-to-End Speech Recognition , Mispronunciation Detection and Diagnosis , N-best Rescoring

1 緒論 (Introduction)

在全球化趨勢下，外語變成現今國際化人才最需具備的能力之一。近年教育方式也順應科技日新月異不斷改變，許多研究早已開始探討如何利用資訊科技及網際網路的優勢來加速語言的學習 (Mark Warschauer, 1995; Mark Warschauer et al., 2000)。語言學習的熱潮讓電腦輔助發音訓練 (Computer Assisted Pronunciation Training, CAPT)的研究逐漸受到重視，讓電腦具備與英語教師相當的專業能力。

學習者會根據 CAPT 系統提供的文本提示(prompt)進行朗讀，系統即時針對錄音結果進行偵測並診斷發音，最後提供回饋以便學習者可以改進並重複練習。

開發電腦輔助發音訓練系統與語音辨識技術息息相關，常見的實踐方法是透過識別學生的發音音素序列，將其與作為規範音素(canonical phone)的母語人士發音音素序列進行比對。最近端對端混合模型架構已逐漸取代深度類神經網路結合隱藏式馬可夫模型(Deep Neural Network-Hidden Markov Model, DNN-HMM)(Geoffrey Hinton et al., 2012)作為主流語音辨識模型架構；使用單一的深度網絡架構取代複雜的模組組合，大大簡化了傳統語音識別系統的建立過程。常見 CAPT 系統基於語音辨識能以高準確度自動識別音素的假設下，直接從語音辨識結果診斷錯誤發音。然而在非英語母語者(non-native speaker)發音標記資料相對少量的訓練情況下，系統診斷準確率常受語音辨識性能下降影響。因此本論文設計發音模型(pronunciation model)結合端對端語音辨識，用來提升英文錯誤發音偵測性能與錯誤發音診斷準確率。論文還分別採用兩種不同的編碼/解碼器的端對端語音辨識模型進行實驗與效能評估。

2 端對端自動語音辨識技術 (E2E ASR)

2.1 CTC (Connectionist Temporal Classification)

連結時序分類最早於 2006 年提出(Alex Graves et al., 2006)，概念為給定一段長度為 T 的聲學特徵序列 X， $X = \{x_t \in \mathbb{R}^D \mid t = 1, \dots, T\}$ (x_t表示為第 t 音框的 D 維語音特徵向量) 及一段長度 L 的標籤序列 C，$C = \{c_l \in U \mid l = 1, \dots, L\}$ (U 為存在的標籤集合)，目標估計聲學特徵對應字符的後驗概率 $P(C|X)$。CTC 在訓練時引入了額外的空白標籤(blank symbol)，作為標籤間的分界，每個音框的標籤序列可表示為 $Z = \{z_t \in U \cup \{<b>\} \mid t = 1, \dots, T\}$ 。CTC 的目標函數表示如下：

$$P_{ctc}(C|X) \approx \sum_Z \prod_{t=1}^{T} P(z_t|z_{t-1}, C) P(z_t|X) \quad (1)$$

其中$P(z_t|z_{t-1}, C)$表示為狀態轉移機率。$P(z_t|X)$ 為 CTC 聲學模型，可由透過鏈式法則展開後利用條件獨立的假設求得。

2.2 注意力機制 (Attention Mechanism)

與 CTC 方法不同，基於注意力機制的方法(Jan Chorowski et al., 2015)不做任何條件獨立假設，而是直接估計後驗機率 $P(C|X)$。注意力模型的目標函數表示如下：

$$P_{att}(C|X) \approx \prod_{l=1}^{L} P(c_l|c_1, \dots, c_{l-1}, X) \quad (2)$$

上式中的 $P(c_l|c_1, \dots, c_{l-1}, X)$ 可由下列式子求得：

$$h_t = Encoder(X) \quad (3)$$

$$a_{lt} \begin{cases} ContentAttention(q_{l-1}, h_t) \\ LocationAttention(\{a_{l-1}\}_{t=1}^{T}, q_{l-1}, h_t) \end{cases} \quad (4)$$

$$r_l = \sum_{t=1}^{T} a_{lt} h_t \quad (5)$$

$$P(c_l|c_1, \dots, c_{l-1}, X) = Decoder(r_l, q_{l-1}, c_{l-1}) \quad (6)$$

第(3)與(6)式分別為編碼器(encoder)網路與解碼器(decoder)網路。上述 4 式的符號定義分別如下：h_t為 encoder 的隱藏向量、 a_{lt}為注意力權重、 q 表示為前一個解碼隱藏向量。r_l表示字母級別的隱藏向量。注意力機制與 CTC 的差異在於注意力機制計算時會考慮過去輸出的字元。

2.3 CTC-Attention 混和模型 (Hybrid CTC-Attention Model)

由 Shinji Watanabe (2017)等人於提出的 CTC-Attention 混和模型架構如圖 1 所示，以 CTC 目標函數作為輔助任務，運用多任務學習框架訓練注意力模型的編碼器。CTC-Attention 混和模

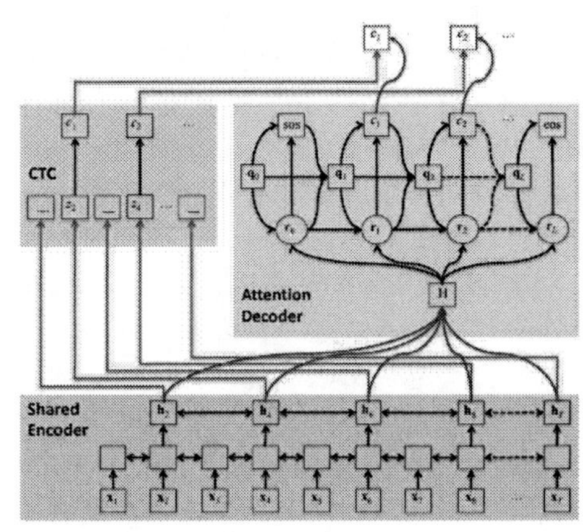

圖 1. CTC-Attention 混和模型端對端架構 [1].

[1] 圖片取自論文 Hybrid CTC/Attention Architecture for End-to-End Speech Recognition.

型共享編碼器的網路，藉由注意力模型的前後資訊改善了CTC對每個音框的對應字符輸出的獨立假設所面臨與真實情況偏離的問題，並透過 CTC 的嚴格單調特性減少對齊計算範圍加快注意力模型對齊過程。CTC-Attention 混合模型訓練的損失函數為兩種模型目標函數的線性組合，表示如下：

$$\mathcal{L}_{MOL} = \lambda logP_{ctc}(C|X) + (1-\lambda)logP^{*}_{att}(C|X) \quad (7)$$

本論文提出的英文錯誤發音偵測實驗中第一階段採用 CTC-Attention 架構進行訓練的語音辨識模型，並實驗兩種編碼與解碼器的模型(VGG-BiLSTM & Transformer)在兩階段錯誤發音偵測上的性能。

3 發音模型 (Pronunciation Model)

語言學家將第二外語學習者常見的發音錯誤情形分為以下三類(以 North, */n ao r th/*為例)：①語言轉移(Language transfer)：學習者使用母語發音去近似目標發音。例如：以中文發音諾斯進行朗誦 */ no⁴ ssu/*。②不正確字母的聲音轉換：某些不常見的word，學習者使用拼音知識去猜測。例如：*/n ow r th/*。雖然發音聽起來可能很相似，但以音素級別角度進行診斷時，其音素序列(phone sequence)還是與標準發音的音素序列不同。③誤讀文本提示：學習者朗讀與文本內容不相關的語句。

基於端對端語音辨識模型的錯誤發音偵測與診斷方法是透過計算編集距離將辨識結果與文本提示進行對齊，並直接給予回饋。開放的語料庫中英語母語者的標記訓練語料資源相對豐富，針對英語非母語學習者的標記語料反而很少或是不易取得。由於訓練受缺少非母語者發音標記的語料限制，導致自動語音辨識系統(ASR)針對錯誤發音的辨識率下降，進而影響僅一階段的電腦輔助發音訓練系統整體性能。其實錯誤發音診斷與自動語音辨識目標任務本質不同，如圖 2 所示，比起紅色為學習者可能的候選錯誤發音路徑，語音辨識系統更有可能優先輸出藍色的正確發音路徑。因此本論文提出兩階段的電腦輔助發音訓練系統，於第二階段加入發音模型(pronunciation model)輔助提升錯誤發音偵測的性能與錯誤發音診斷任務的準確率。

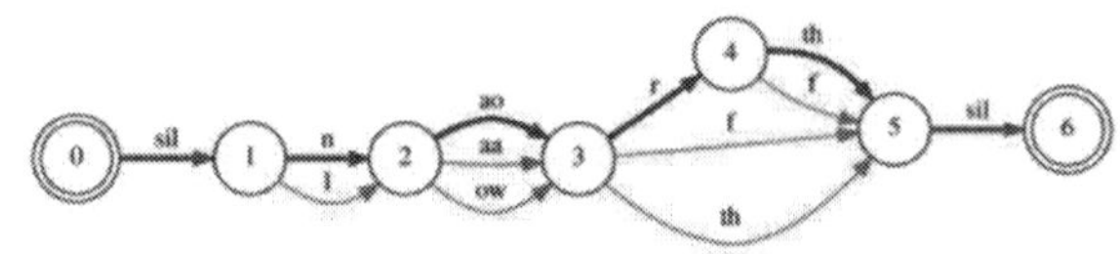

圖 2. 單字 North 的可能發音路徑.

具體來說給定一組候選 N-best 語音辨識結果，利用共享Bi-LSTM參數萃取出對各個候選發音路徑有用的資訊，讓發音模型學習重新選擇辨識結果。模型架構如圖 3 所示。首先將候選 N-best 結果逐一透過嵌入層(embedding layer)轉成指定大小的音素嵌入(phone embedding)；接者輸入進Bi-LSTM，Bi-LSTM會自動編碼成序列表示法 ***h**** (如圖3深綠色長方形所示)；最後由於這是一個分類問題，因此需要再將最後一個時間點的輸出 ***h**** 經過一層線性層(linear layer)轉換，方可進行多類別預測任務。發音模型的訓練首先計算第一階段語音辨識產生的候選N-best 序列在錯誤發音偵測任務的 F1 分數，將分數高低排名作為優異與否的分類依據，成為第二階段發音模型多類別分類(Multi-class Classification)的預測目標。交叉熵被廣泛應用於許多多類別分類任務中，本篇論文訓練也採用交叉熵(Cross Entropy)作為損失函數。測試時取分類類別為最優的發音序列作為發音模型的輸出，以進行後續發音偵測任務與診斷任務。

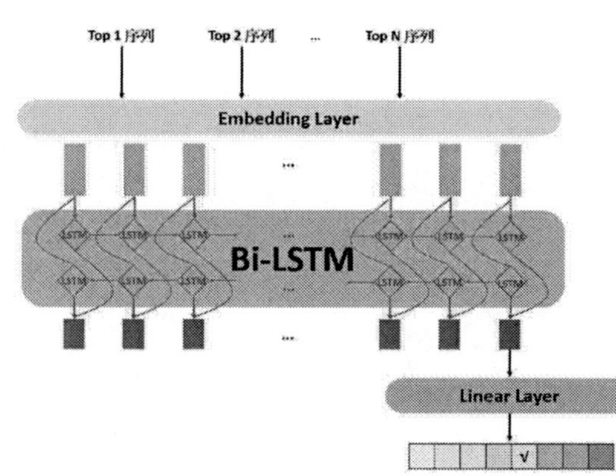

圖 3. N-best 辨識結果與聲學分數分類模型架構.

4 實驗 (Experiments)

4.1 資料集

實驗使用兩個資料集，分別為美式英語母語者(L1 speaker) 的 ***TIMIT*** (J. S. Garofolo et al., 1993) 以及英語非母語者(L2 speaker)的 ***L2-ARCTIC*** (Guanlong Zhao et al., 2018)。

TIMIT 由來自美國八個主要方言地區的 630 位美式英語母語人士錄製指定的 10 句文本提示 (prompt)，共計 5.4 小時，所有的錄音都提供經時間對齊的音素級別轉錄。該資料集語句分為 3 種類型，詳細資料如表 1 所示，SA 為方言語句，SX 與 SI 則為一般類型語句。將該資料集切割為訓練集 3.15 小時與驗證集 0.34 小時作為實驗使用，統計如表 2 所示。

L2-ARCTIC 包括二十四位英語非母語人士的錄音，每位語者錄製大約一小時取自 CMU ARCTIC 的文本提示。錄音者的母語分別為印度語、韓語、華語、西班牙語、阿拉伯語和越南語，共計 6 種不同語言，詳細資料如表 3 所示。該資料集除提供經強制對齊的音素級別轉錄外，也提供每位語者 150 句的專家標記(annotation)語句，其中 150 句分別選自相同的 100 句文本提示，以及 50 句針對各母語特性挑選的易犯發音錯誤的文本提示，增加發音錯誤情形。將該資料集切割為訓練集 2.66 小時，驗證集 0.12 小時及測試集 0.88 小時作為實驗使用，統計如表 4 所示。

表 1. TIMIT 資料集.

類型	SA	SX	SI	統計
總文本數	2	450	1890	2342
各文本所含語者數	630	7	1	-
各語者所唸文本數	2	5	3	10
總句數	1260	3150	1890	6300

表 2. 實驗中 TIMIT 資料統計.

	訓練	驗證
總語者數	462	50
各語者所唸句數	8	8
總句數	3696	400
總音素個數	139,940	15,342
時長統計(hrs)	3.15	0.34

表 3. L2-ARCTIC 資料集.

語者	母語
ABA / SKA / ZHAA / YBAA	阿拉伯語
BWC / LXC / NCC / TXHC	華語
ASI / RRBI / SVBI / TNI	印度語
HJK / HKK / YDCK / YKWK	韓語
EBVS / ERMS / MBMPS / NJS	西班牙語
HQTV / PNV / THV / TLV	越南語

表 4. 實驗中 L2-ARCTIC 資料統計.

	訓練	驗證	測試
語者數	2549	150	900
正確發音音素個數	71,935	4,054	25,690
錯誤發音音個數	13,236	903	4,314
時長統計(hrs)	2.66	0.12	0.88

4.2 發音偵測與診斷任務評估指標

在發音偵測任務我們會分別關注正確發音以及錯誤發音的判定成效，兩者的評估指標 Recall(RE)、Precision(PR)與 F 度量(F1)計算方式如下：

- 正確發音：

$$\mathrm{RE}_{cor} = \frac{\text{正確接受數量}}{\text{實際正確發音數量}} = \frac{TA}{TA+FR} * 100\% \quad (8)$$

$$\mathrm{PR}_{cor} = \frac{\text{正確接受數量}}{\text{系統判定正確發音數量}} = \frac{TA}{TA+FA} * 100\% \quad (9)$$

$$\mathrm{F1}_{cor} = \frac{2\times\mathrm{RE}_{cor}\times\mathrm{PR}_{cor}}{\mathrm{RE}_{cor}+\mathrm{PR}_{cor}} * 100\% \quad (10)$$

- 錯誤發音：

$$\mathrm{RE}_{mis} = \frac{\text{正確拒絕數量}}{\text{實際錯誤發音數量}} = \frac{TR}{TR+FA} * 100\% \quad (11)$$

$$\mathrm{PR}_{mis} = \frac{\text{正確拒絕數量}}{\text{系統判定錯誤發音數量}} = \frac{TR}{TR+FR} * 100\% \quad (12)$$

$$\text{F1}_{mis} = \frac{2\times\text{RE}_{mis}\times\text{PR}_{mis}}{\text{RE}_{mis}+\text{PR}_{mis}} * 100\% \quad (13)$$

錯誤發音偵測評估指標中的正確拒絕 TR，其實又可以分成診斷正確 CD (不僅檢測出學習者唸錯，又正確診斷唸錯成哪個音素)與診斷錯誤 DE (雖然判定學習者唸錯，但無法正確診斷唸錯成哪個音素)。因此錯誤發音診斷正確率(DAR_{mis})的計算方式如下：

$$\text{DAR}_{mis} = \frac{\text{正確診斷數}}{\text{正確診斷數}+\text{診斷錯誤數}} = \frac{\text{CD}}{\text{CD+}} * 100\% \quad (14)$$

4.3 實驗設定

本論文的第一階段實驗使用了開源端對端語音辨識工具 **Espnet** (Shinji Watanabe et al., 2018) 完成，端對端語音辨識模型使用 CTC-Attention 混合模型架構，並進行兩個不同的實驗設定。分別採用 VGG-BiLSTM 與 Transformer 的編碼器與解碼器進行實驗，具體設定如表 5 所示。

表 5. 端對端語音辨識實驗設定.

VGG-BiLSTM			
feature		80-dim fbank + 3-dim pitch	
encoder / decoder		BiLSTM	
encoder		decoder	
layers	2	layers	3
hidden size	1024	hidden size	1024
CTC/Attention 混和比		0.6/0.4	
Transformer			
feature		80-dim fbank + 3-dim pitch	
encoder / decoder		Transformer	
encoder		decoder	
attention heads	8	attention heads	8
linear units	2048	linear units	2048
blocks	12	blocks	6
dropout rate	0.1	dropout rate	0.1
CTC/Attention 混和比		0.3/0.7	

4.4 實驗結果與討論

實驗分別使用兩個語音辨識模型進行解碼，將產生的 5-best 候選結果用於第二階段發音模型的訓練。訓練完成後，將發音模型分別測試在測試集解碼的 5-best 候選結果。

在第一階段的語音辨識結果與專家標記(annotation)進行比對的音素錯誤率(phone error rate)表現如表 6 所示。可以看到 VGG-BiLSTM 的語音辨識結果表現均較 Transformer 表現差，這將會影響採用 VGG-BiLSTM 的電腦輔助發音訓練系統在後續錯誤發音診斷任務上的準確率不如採用 Transformer 的發音訓練系統表現。

表 6. L2-ARCTIC 測試集中各語者音素錯誤率.

語者	VGG-BiLSTM	Transformer
NJS	23.3	15.7
TLV	25	18.2
TNI	32.3	19.7
TXHC	28	18.3
YKWK	24.9	15.7
ZHAA	26.1	15.3
平均	26.6	17.1

測試集經過發音模型後最後輸出的發音序列與文本提示(prompt)進行比對的發音檢測與診斷表現如表 7 與表 8 所示。Baseline 為一階段基於語音辨識的發音訓練系統結果，N=5 為本論文提出的兩階段電腦輔助發音訓練系統結果，另外針對 Transformer 產生的候選結果還簡單連接(concatenated)了聲學模型分數一起作為發音模型的輸入進行實驗與測試，實驗結果如表 7 中的 N=5#所示。

實驗結果可以看到，發音模型重新選擇候選結果均能改進了發音檢測任務的各項指標。雖然採用 VGG-BiLSTM 的電腦輔助發音訓練系統在偵測任務指標表現進步幅度略小，但可以看到發音模型讓診斷錯誤的音素個數減少(diagnose error，DE)，正確診斷的音素個數增加，進而讓診斷任務的準確率有所提升。

表 7. 採用 VGG-BiLSTM 編/解碼器表現

指標	baseline	N=5
Correct Pronunciation		
PR(%)	94.57	**94.59**
RE(%)	79.53	**79.54**
F1(%)	86.4	**86.41**
Mispronunciation		
PR(%)	35.72	**35.77**
RE(%)	71.36	**71.46**
F1(%)	47.61	**47.67**
CD(音素個數)	1803	**1809**
DE(音素個數)	1120	**1118**
DIA(%)	61.68	**61.8**

表 8. 採用 Transformer 編/解碼器表現

指標	baseline	N=5	N=5 #
Correct Pronunciation			
PR	92.14	**92.16**	**92.21**
RE	91.13	**91.48**	90.98
F1	91.63	**91.65**	91.59
Mispronunciation			
PR(%)	47.95	**48.05**	47.79
RE(%)	51.24	**51.34**	**51.78**
F1(%)	49.54	**49.64**	**49.71**
CD(音素個數)	1526	**1528**	**1553**
DE(音素個數)	573	575	**568**
DIA(%)	72.7	72.66	**73.22**

在採用 Transformer 電腦輔助發音訓練系統的表現上，發音偵測的各項指標都明顯提升，尤其正確發音偵測的 recall 表現。在實務上，對正確發音的偵測性能提升，可以讓學生更願意相信並使用系統進行練習。雖然受錯誤診斷的音素個數影響，診斷錯誤率略為下降，但在更進一步的實驗中串聯聲學模型表現分數作為輸入，可以有效提升診斷準確率。正確診斷發音的音素個數明顯增加，錯誤診斷的音素個數下降，讓診斷準確率提升至 73.22 是所有實驗中表現最好的結果。實驗結果也表明在發音模型中加入更多元的資訊可以幫助電腦輔助發音訓練系統中診斷任務性能進一步有效提升。

5 結論與未來展望 (Conclusion and Future Work)

本論文實踐了二階段電腦輔助發音訓練系統，將基於端對端語音辨識的系統結合發音模型進行實驗。發音模型對候選序列重新排序，可以有助於校正第一階段辨識學習者的發音結果並提升發音檢測的指標。實驗結果顯示透過簡單模型架構，就能改進電腦輔助發音訓練系統檢測性能。未來將會加大第一階段候選者數作為發音模型輸入的實驗，也會考慮更多元的特徵與候選結果進行串聯，例如：多元的語音特徵、音素時長(duration)，甚至是學習者的發音特徵...等，來提升發音診斷的準確率。本論文僅是對發音模型進行初步的實驗，未來會持續改進發音模型，相信音素級別候選結果的重新選擇及更嚴謹的發音模型設計架構，能再讓發音檢測與診斷系統更趨完善。

參考文獻 (References)

Alex Graves, Abdel-rahman Mohamed and Geoffrey Hinton. 2013. *Speech recognition with deep recurrent neural networks*. in ICASSP 2013.

Alex Graves, Santiago Fern´andez, Faustino Gomez and J¨urgen Schmidhuber. 2016. *Connectionist temporal classification: Labelling unsegmented sequence data with recurrent neural networks*. in ICML 2006.

Eskenazi, Maxine. 2019. An overview of spoken language technology for education. in *Speech Communication*. Vol. 51, No. 10, 832–844.

Geoffrey Hinton, Li Deng, Dong Yu, George Dahl, Abdel-rahman Mohamed, Navdeep Jaitly, Andrew Senior, Vincent Vanhoucke, Patrick Nguyen, Tara Sainath, and Brian Kingsbury. 2012. Deep Neural Networks for Acoustic Modeling in Speech Recognition: The Shared Views of Four Research Groups. in *IEEE Signal Processing Magazine*, Vol. 29, No. 6, 82-97. DOI: 10.1109/MSP.2012.2205597.

Guanlong Zhao, Sinem Sonsaat, Alif Silpachai and Ivana Lucic. 2018. *L2-ARCTIC: A Non-native English Speech Corpus*. in INTERSPEECH 2018.

Hsiu-Jui Chang, Tien-Hong Lo, Tzu-En Liu and Berlin Chen. 2019. *Investigating on Computer-Assisted Pronunciation Training Leveraging End-to-End Speech Recognition Techniques*. in ROCLING 2019.

J. S. Garofolo, L. F. Lamel, W. M. Fisher, J. G. Fiscus and D. S. Pallett. 1993. DARPA TIMIT acoustic-phonetic continuous speech corpus CD-ROM. *NIST speech disc 1*-1.1. NASA STI/Recon technical report, No. 93.

Jan Chorowski, Dzmitry Bahdanau, Dmitriy Serdyuk, Kyunghyun Cho and Yoshua Bengio. 2015. *Attention-Based Models for Speech Recognition*. in NIPS 2015.

L. R. Rabiner. 1989. A tutorial on hidden Markov models and selected applications in speech recognition. in *Proceedings of the IEEE*. Vol. 77, No. 2, 257-286. DOI: 10.1109/5.18626.

Mark Gales and Steve Yang. 2018. The Application of Hidden Markov Models in Speech Recognition. in *Signal Processing*. Vol. 1, No. 3, 195–304. DOI: 10.1561/2000000004.

Mark Warschauer, Heidi Shetzer, and Christine Meloni. 2000. *Internet for English teaching.Alexandria*. VA: Teachers of English to Speakers of Other Language, Inc.

Mark Warschauer. 1995. *Virtual connections: Online activities and projects for networking language learners*. Universit y of Hawaii: SecondLanguageTeaching & Curriculum Center.

Shinji Watanabe, Takaaki Hori, Shigeki Karita, Tomoki Hayashi, Jiro Nishitoba, Yuya Unno, Nelson Enrique Yalta Soplin, Jahn Heymann, Matthew Wiesner, Nanxin Chen, Adithya Renduchintala and Tsubasa Ochiai. 2018. *ESPnet: End-to-End Speech Processing Toolkit*. in INTERSPEECH 2018.

Shinji Watanabe, Takaaki Hori, Suyoun Kim, John R. Hershey and Tomoki Hayashi. 2017. Hybrid CTC/Attention Architecture for End-to-End Speech Recognition. in *IEEE Journal of Selected Topics in Signal Processing*, Vol. 11, No. 8, 1240-1253. DOI: 10.1109/JSTSP.2017.2763455.

Suyoun Kim, Takaaki Hori, Shinji Watanabe. 2017. *Joint CTC-Attention based end-to-end speech recognition using multi-task learning*. in ICASSP 2017.

Wai-Kim Leung, Xunying Liu and Helen Meng. 2019. *CNN-RNN-CTC based end-to-end mispronunciation detection and diagnosis.* in ICASSP 2019.

Ying Qin, Yao Qian, Anastassia Loukina, Patrick Lange, Abhinav Misra, Keelan Evanini and Tan Lee. 2021. *Automatic Detection of Word-Level Reading Errors in Non-native English Speech Based on ASR Output.* in ISCSLP 2021.

The 33rd Conference on Computational Linguistics and Speech Processing (ROCLING 2021)
Taoyuan, Taiwan, October 15-16, 2021. The Association for Computational Linguistics and Chinese Language Processing

由長者語言運用預測認知彈性
Predicting elders' cognitive flexibility from their language use

汪曼穎 Man-Ying Wang
東吳大學心理學系
Department of Psychology
Soochow University
臺北市士林區臨溪路 70 號
mywang.scu@gmail.com

柯宇安 Yu-An Ko
東吳大學心理學系
Department of Psychology
Soochow University
臺北市士林區臨溪路 70 號
Kelen850408@gmail.com

黃金蘭 Chin-Lan Huang
台灣科技大學 通識教育中心
Department of Humanities & Social Sciences
National Taiwan University of
Science and Technology
臺北市大安區基隆路 4 段 43 號
chinlanhuang@gmail.com

陳俊宏 Jyun-Hong Chen
東吳大學心理學系
Department of Psychology
Soochow University
臺北市士林區臨溪路 70 號
chinlanhuang@gmail.com

丁德天 Te-Tien Ting
東吳大學資料科學系
Department of Data Science
Soochow University
臺北市士林區臨溪路 70 號
tetien@scu.edu.tw

摘要

近年開始有研究者關注語言運用與長者各種認知退化軌跡的關係，但是較少見以認知彈性為焦點的研究。本研究招募 51 位 53-74 歲的年長者，進行焦點團體討論日常生活活動，以中文 LIWC2015 資料庫 (林瑋倫等人，2020; Pennebaker et al., 2015) 分析對話文本的認知複雜度以及動態性兩個指標以及與日常生活活動相關的詞類，並分析對話過程的插話行為。結果發現，在控制教育程度、性別與年齡之後，認知彈性伴隨較多使用動態性語詞、洞察詞以及家庭詞。這些發現協助以長者日常語言運用預測其認知彈性。

Abstract

Increasing research efforts are directed towards the relationship between cognitive decline and language use. However, few of them had focused specifically on how language use is related to cognitive flexibility. This study recruited 51 elders aged 53-74 to discuss their daily activities in focus groups. The transcribed discourse was analyzed using the Chinese version of LIWC (Lin et al., 2020; Pennebaker et al., 2015) for cognitive complexity and dynamic language as well as content words related to elders' daily activities. The interruption behavior during conversation was also analyzed. The results showed that, after controlling for education, gender and age, cognitive flexibility performance was accompanied by the increasing adoption of dynamic language, insight words and family words. These findings serve as the basis for the prediction of elders' cognitive flexibility through their daily language use.

關鍵字：語言運用、認知彈性、年長者
Keywords: language use, cognitive flexibility, elders

1 緒論

老化造成生理與體能的衰弱之外，也導致認知退化以及認知衰弱(cognitive frailty) (Kelaiditi et al ., 2013; Panza et al., 2015)。認知評估有助了解認知退化及認知衰弱以進行因應，但傳統心理測驗雖為具備完善信效度的工具，但施測所需的大量資源則影響其推廣。過去研究亦曾以遊戲、電腦使用等方式進行長者認知退化的監控(Lumsden et al., 2016 ; Siraly et al., 2015)，用長期蒐集的數據發展對於個體認知狀態的預測，不過這些科技中介的資料蒐集較易受限於長者的科技識能(literacy)以及其日常使用的主動性。

相對地，語言運用在日常生活中自然形成大量數據，許多研究探討語言運用特徵與認知表現的關聯性，藉以預測輕度認知障礙(Mild Cognitive Impairment, MCI)以及失智(dementia) (Martínez-Nicolás et al., 2021)。本研究以長者日常生活對話資料進行分析，尋找對話與言談中與認知彈性(cognitive flexibility)相關的行為表現，嘗試建立基於對話資料的認知彈性預測模式。所謂認知彈性是在不同思維與行動之間轉換的能力，為執行功能(executive function)的核心，有助於個體因應新的情境需求(Buitenweg et al., 2012)，並且是日常生活功能所需的重要心智能力(Logue & Gould, 2014; Martyr & Clare, 2012)。本研究借助 LIWC 分析，以了解日常語言運用和認知彈性的關聯性。

2 文獻探討

近年許多研究嘗試運用言談(speech)的分析以區辨正常 vs.輕度認知障礙(Mild Cognitive Impairment, MCI) 與阿茲海默症(Alzheimer's Disease)病人，許多應用以 AI 的取向切入，著重於預測模式的建立(Dodge et al., 2015; Konig et al., 2018)。然而語言運用與認知表現的關聯究竟是甚麼?

Dodge 等人(2015)以長者每日對話互動總詞數(在互動總詞數中的占比)作為社交的指標，發現 MCI 病人的對話字數明顯高於正常組(控制年齡，性別等因子)，他們推測原因是因為 MCI 病人在對話過程中經歷執行控制與自我監控的困難所導致。Asgari 等人(2017)則以 LIWC2001 分析區辨 MCI 病人(vs.正常老化長者)，結果發現相對詞(指涉時間、動詞時態、空間、運動的詞)具有預測效果。

日常對話的過程涉及對於對話主題與發言順序的的理解，避免脫離主題，掌握發言時機等，這些行為展現都需要招募執行功能，以控制與調整說話的內容與行為。Polsinelli 等人 (2020) 檢視 102 位年長者(平均年齡 75.8 歲)攜帶紀錄器記錄四天(兩天為周間日，兩天為周末日) 的日常談話與執行功能的關聯，LIWC 分析結果發現工作記憶的表現與使用分析式(analytic)語言類別、較長的字、數字、個人關注、現在關注等有關，但是轉換僅與較少使用常見字有關，而抑制則沒有和任何類別的頻率有關。

認知彈性是一種重要的認知控制機制(Diamond, 2013)，涉及在不同概念或行為規則套路間轉換以支持目標導向行為，以促進個體的環境適應，並在認知老化中扮演重要角色(Hülür, Ram, Willis, Schaie, & Gerstorf, 2016)。Polsinelli 等人的研究並沒有獲得太多證據支持轉換或認知彈性與語言運用的關聯性，比較不符合預期，日常語言的運用常常需要在不同的敘事主角/時間/想法之間轉換，需要認知彈性能力的支持。可能 Polsinelli 的語言取樣架構(紀錄器每 12 分鐘紀錄 30 秒的語音)無法獲得足夠與轉換或認知彈性有關的言談內容，本研究將以不同的方式進行語料收集。

LIWC（Linguistic Inquiry and Word Count 語文探索與字詞計算）字詞分析資料庫是 Pennebaker 與同僚基於心理狀態影響語言運用行為的假設，所發展出的分析取向，針對各種詞類(諸如代名詞、情緒詞及認知詞等)的相對使用百分比，計算文本中各詞類出現頻率。許多過去研究支持這個分析取向，例如說謊者傾向使用較多的負向情緒詞、行動詞(如 arrive, car, go) (Newman et al., 2003)，而夫妻對婚姻的主觀感受與「我們」此種功能詞(function words)的使用頻率有關(Simmons et al., 2005)。LIWC 的詞類之中也有許多與認知表現有關(Weaver, 2017)，例如排除詞與區分類別歸屬有關(Tausczik & Pennebaker, 2010)，連接詞串接多種想法，用於創造連貫的敘述(Graesser, McNamara, Louwerse, & Cai, 2004)，介系詞的使用頻率則與提供更複雜、具體的訊息有關(Hartley, Pennebaker, & Fox, 2003)。黃金蘭等人(2012)以 LIWC2007 架構(Pennebaker, Booth, & Francis, 2007; Pennebaker, Chung, Ireland, Gonzales, & Booth, 2007），依照中文的語法特性修訂各詞類內容，發展中文繁體版的 CLIWC2007，後續又根據 LIWC2015 (Pennebaker et al., 2015)修訂發展 CLIWC2015 (林瑋芳等人，2020)。中文版 LIWC 且已進行各種信效度的檢驗，獲致良好的信效度表現 (黃金蘭等人，2012；林瑋芳等人，2020)，目前 CLIWC2015 對於一般的文本平均有七成以上的偵測率。

3 研究目的

認知彈性或作業轉換的表現和言談中的人際互動有關連性，例如: 輪流發言(taking turns)涉及發話者準備發言與理解目前發言內容兩種 set 之間的頻繁轉換，而如果同時有多位互動對象時，發言者也需要頻繁考量不同對象的立場與斟酌表達方式，更需要運用認知彈性的能力。本研究預期認知彈性影響長者談話表現，有助於提升談話內容的複雜性，造

成認知複雜度 (Czechowski et al., 2016)及總詞數的增加。同時，認知彈性也有助於發言者同時監控發言的準備以及他人的談話內容，在輪流發言的過程中減少各種插話的行為(包括附和及介入他人發話主題的行為)。另一方面，認知彈性可協助發話者進行敘事(narrative)的發言，考量不同時間與情節的轉換，展現在 LIWC 複合指標「動態性」(Pennebaker et al., 2014)的表現 (運用較多人稱代名詞、非人稱代名詞、助動詞、連接詞、副詞及否定詞)。

為促進發言內容及方式與認知彈性的關聯，本研究以焦點團體的方式進行，年長參與者討論其經常從事的日常活動，談話內容轉為文本之後進行 LIWC 分析。而認知彈性的測量則以路徑描繪測驗(Trail Making Test，TMT) 進行，該測驗的 A 部分反映視覺動作反應速度，B 部分則額外涉及(不同規則範疇)的轉換，B/A, B 都被認為反映轉換/認知彈性能力 (Kortte et al., 2002)，神經造影 resting state 功能性連結的研究證據也支持 B 以及(B-A)與大腦執行功能網路以及老化導致的執行功能下降有關 (Varjacic et al., 2018)。由於 TMT 的測驗任務須具備對於英文字母排序的知識，彩色路徑描繪測驗（Color Trails Test，CTT）(D' Elia et al., 1996) 以色彩取代英文字母，減少語言和文化的影響(Lee et al., 2000)。

4 方法

參與者

參與者 51 名。年齡介於 53-74 歲(M = 65.21, SD = 5.86)，36 位女性、 15 位男性，教育年數 M = 13.21，SD = 2.34。在北投及士林地區社區圖書館、鄰里活動場域張貼傳單進行招募，由參與者自行打電話報名，參與本研究可獲得 500 元參與報償。

程序

參與者依照時間狀況出席焦點團體，每場團體參與人次 2-5 人，所有場次的焦點團體均由同一主持人主持。討論內容係請參與者分享從早至晚一天大致進行的活動，以及該活動在一週內的頻率，並依該場成員狀況，挑選較具共通性的活動進行深入討論。而如理財、醫療等類型活動出現頻率較低，焦點團體參與者通常不會主動提出，所以主持人除了討論具供通性的活動外，也會視情況主動提出討論主題。

焦點團體開始之前先向參與者說明研究程序，參與者並閱覽及簽署知情同意書。焦點團體約進行 1.5-2 小時，結束之後 1-1 於另一研究空間施測彩色路徑描繪測驗(郭曉燕與花茂棽，2015)，其中第一部分參與者以筆快速依序連接數字 1-25 的圈圈，第二部分的數字 1-25 的圈圈被填上粉紅色及黃色，實施時參與者快速依數字順序跳色連接，研究者在旁紀錄完成時間以及錯誤內容。

資料登錄與分析

文本資料以參與者為單位的對談資料進行逐字稿整理，焦點團體以國語進行，對於偶而出現的閩南語則以國語登錄。另也用發言者的語音時間關係登錄每段發言是否屬於插話(interruptions)以及該插話屬於介入的(intrusive)或是附和的(cooperative)插話 (Li, 2001)。

逐字稿文本以中央研究院中文詞知識庫(CKIP)工具進行斷詞，並以 CLIWC2015 辭典(林瑋芳等人，2020)進行分析。

5 結果

本研究分析的主要依變項為彩色路徑描繪測驗的第一與第二部分完成時間 CCT1, CCT2 以及 (CCT2-CTT1)/CTT1，分別與知覺動作處理，路徑任務轉換所需時間，以及認知彈性有關。

表 1 列出 CTT1, CTT2, 認知彈性與詞類的相關，不過，認知複雜度並沒有如預期與認知彈性有顯著相關、但是表 1 也可以看出認知複雜度指標採計的詞類之一 - 洞察詞(具體詞類如:發現、瞭解、判斷)，其使用頻率與認知彈性有顯著相關，洞察詞使用頻率較多伴隨較高的認知彈性表現，表示對事件的認知處理與重新評價(Pennebaker, Mayne, & Francis, 1997)，同時認知複雜度指標採計的其他詞類(除了後置詞之外)也大致與認知彈性具有符合預期方向的相關。

認知彈性沒有和對話過程中的插話(附和或介入)行為有顯著相關，但相關的方向是符合預期的 – 高認知彈性伴隨較少的插話行為。另一方面，動態性指標與認知彈性表現有顯著相關(排除教育程度、性別與年齡的影響)，

	CTT1	CTT2	認知彈性
總詞數	-.10	-.30*	-.08
認知複雜度	-.12	-.17	-.15
差異詞	.00	.08	-.18
連接詞	-.04	-.09	-.07
洞察詞	.21	-.03	-.31*
介系詞	-.17	-.19	-.17
後置詞	-.06	.19	.24
因果詞	-.02	-.23	-.12
插話	-.22	-.22	.20
附和	-.19	-.09	.20
介入	-.19	-.23	.16
動態性	-.07	-.07	-.42**
特定人稱單數代名詞	.07	-.06	-.23
非特定人稱代名詞	.29*	.13	-.20
助動詞	-.05	.11	-.17
副詞	-.03	-.15	-.26
連接詞	-.04	-.09	-.07
助動詞	-.05	.11	-.17
否定詞	-.07	-.02	-.16

** $p < 0.01$;* $p < 0.05$，雙尾考驗

表 1.認知複雜度、插話、動態性與 CTT1, CTT2, 認知彈性的偏相關(排除教育程度、性別、年齡影響)

較高的動態性相關詞類使用，伴隨較小的轉換歷程的付出(cost)，有較高的認知彈性，而此關聯似非源於單純的知覺動作速度，因為動態性和 CTT1 或 CTT2 都無相關。動態性指標所採計使用的詞類都與認知彈性呈現符合預期方向的關聯性，其中副詞(e.g., 一般而言，無論，雖然) 和認知彈性有邊緣顯著相關。

本研究參與者討論自己日常較多從事的活動，所以可由活動相關詞了解認知彈性表現與活動的潛在關聯性，所以表 2 列出認知彈性

	CTT1	CTT2	認知彈性
家庭詞	.22	.01	-.46**
朋友詞	-.07	-.13	-.23
身體詞	-.27	-.27	-.04
健康詞	-.28	-.38**	-.01
性　詞	.36*	.11	-.12
攝食詞	-.28	-.17	.14
工作詞	.21	.37**	.17
休閒詞	-.07	-.14	.03
房屋詞	-.06	-.01	.24
金錢詞	-.23	.17	-.17
宗教詞	.01	.06	.05
死亡詞	.09	-.07	-.11

** $p < 0.01$;* $p < 0.05$，雙尾考驗

表 2. 活動相關詞類與 CTT1, CTT2, 認知彈性的偏相關(排除教育程度、性別、年齡影響)

與各種活動內容詞的相關，結果僅有家庭 (人) 詞和認知彈性的相關為顯著，發話時多用到家庭詞者伴隨較佳的認知彈性表現。而家庭詞與其他詞類的相關分析看出，家庭詞的使用伴隨較多的「我」及較少的「你」，較多的時態標定詞、比較詞、差異詞及風險詞，顯示論及家庭詞的脈絡可能常涉及家庭/家人狀態在時間(或風險)面向的比較與對照，因此與轉換/認知彈性有關。

	partial R^2	model R^2	C(p)	F	p
動態性	.10	.15	2.64	5.40	.03
洞察詞	.06	.21	1.60	3.37	.07
後置詞	.04	.25	1.60	2.28	.14

表 3. 前向選擇迴歸模型結果（無家庭詞）

接著以迴歸模型了解語言運用的認知複雜度、插話、動態性對於認知彈性的解釋與預測能力，三個控制變項先強制納入模型，並以表 1 的變項、採用前向選擇法(forward selection)建立對於認知彈性的模型。結果三

	partial R^2	model R^2	C(p)	F	p
家庭詞	.22	.27	6.18	13.87	.00
動態性	.07	.34	3.39	5.08	.03
後置詞	.03	.38	3.37	2.20	.14
非特定人稱代名詞	.04	.42	2.56	3.21	.08
洞察詞	.03	.45	2.66	2.24	.14

表 4. 前向選擇迴歸模型結果（有家庭詞）

個納入模型的變項依順序為動態性、洞察詞、後置詞 (見表 3)，模型的 $R^2 = .25$ ($F(6,44) = 2.43, p = .04$)，顯示在排除教育程度、性別、年齡的影響之後，認知彈性的表現可以由談話中這三種詞類的狀況加以預測。

如果將家庭詞納入預測變項，納入三個控制變項進行前向迴歸的結果見表 4，表 4 模型組成多出家庭詞與非特定人稱代名詞(例如:其他、那些、彼此)，後者原本就是動態性指標採計的詞類，表 4 的模型 R^2 則達.45 ($F(8,42) = 4.27, p = .0008$)。

6 討論

認知彈性協助個體在不同目標的任務或 set 之間轉換，是日常生活活動頻繁徵召的認知功能(Logue & Gould, 2014)，幫助個體面對老化過程的適應。本研究紀錄長者焦點團體討論日常活動的發言，也登錄插話行為，分析長者的認知彈性表現和其語言運用的認知複雜度、插話行為、動態性語言的關係。結果在控制教育程度、性別與年齡之後，動態性語言及洞察詞的使用皆與認知彈性表現有顯著相關，其他認知複雜度詞類以及插話行為與認知彈性的關聯雖大致符合預期方向但未達顯著。而與日常活動相關的內容詞的分析則發現家庭詞與認知彈性有顯著相關。

動態性語言指標包含助動詞，連接詞，代名詞等(見表 1)，和具有時間向度的敘事/說故事有關(Pennebaker et al., 2014)。家庭詞是一種社會關係詞，容易在描述責任(而非希望)的時候出現(Vaughn, 2019)，目前研究中家庭詞的頻率也與時態標定和比較詞等有關，顯示家庭詞涉及自己與家人關係，其運用可能與不同時間比較的脈絡有關。動態性語言與家庭詞運用涉及不同時間範疇間的轉換，可能因而都與認知彈性產生密切關聯。

另外，與認知彈性有顯著相關的洞察詞(例如:發現、瞭解、判斷)則是 LIWC(上層類別)認知歷程詞的一種，也為認知複雜度指標所採計(Czechowski et al., 2016)，代表思考或對於同一事情採取不同的思考角度，與認知彈性也有關連性。

本研究的發現顯示日常語言運用是一個洞悉認知彈性的窗口，日常對話往往與敘事或思考的表達有關，容易涉及各種時間狀態與想法的轉換並因而徵召認知彈性的機制。日常語言對於正常社區住居長者的認知彈性的預測潛能，未來可以合併其他測驗或度量，共同提供具有語言數據的實務環境進行應用。

參考文獻

Asgari, M., Kaye, J., & Dodge, H. (2017). Predicting mild cognitive impairment from spontaneous spoken utterances. *Alzheimer's & Dementia: Translational Research & Clinical Interventions, 3*(2), 219-228.

Buitenweg, J. I., Murre, J. M., & Ridderinkhof, K. R. (2012). Brain training in progress: A review of trainability in healthy seniors. *Frontiers in Human Neuroscience, 6*, 183.

D'Elia, L., Satz, P., Uchiyama, C. L., & White, T. (1996). *Color Trails Test*: PAR Odessa, FL.

Diamond, A. (2013). Executive functions. *Annual Review of Psychology, 64*, 135-168.

Graesser, A. C., McNamara, D. S., Louwerse, M. M., & Cai, Z. (2004). Coh-Metrix: Analysis of text on cohesion and language. *Behavior Research Methods, Instruments, & Computers, 36*(2), 193-202.

H Dodge, H., Mattek, N., Gregor, M., Bowman, M., Seelye, A., Ybarra, O., . . . A Kaye, J. (2015). Social markers of mild cognitive impairment: Proportion of word counts in free conversational speech. *Current Alzheimer Research, 12*(6), 513-519.

Hülür, G., Ram, N., Willis, S. L., Schaie, K. W., & Gerstorf, D. (2016). Cognitive aging in the Seattle Longitudinal Study: Within-person associations of primary mental abilities with psychomotor speed and cognitive flexibility. *Journal of Intelligence, 4*(3), 12.

Hartley, J., Pennebaker, J., & Fox, C. (2003). Abstracts, introductions and discussions: How far do they differ in style? *Scientometrics, 57*(3), 389-398.

Kelaiditi, E., Cesari, M., Canevelli, M., Van Kan, G. A., Ousset, P.-J., Gillette-Guyonnet, S., . . .

Provencher, V. (2013). Cognitive frailty: Rational and definition from an (IANA/IAGG) international consensus group. *The Journal of Nutrition, Health & Aging, 17*(9), 726-734.

Konig, A., Satt, A., Sorin, A., Hoory, R., Derreumaux, A., David, R., & Robert, P. H. (2018). Use of speech analyses within a mobile application for the assessment of cognitive impairment in elderly people. *Current Alzheimer Research, 15*(2), 120-129.

Kortte, K. B., Horner, M. D., & Windham, W. K. (2002). The trail making test, part B: Cognitive flexibility or ability to maintain set? *Applied Neuropsychology, 9*(2), 106-109.

Logue, S. F., & Gould, T. J. (2014). The neural and genetic basis of executive function: Attention, cognitive flexibility, and response inhibition. *Pharmacology Biochemistry and Behavior, 123*, 45-54.

Lumsden, J., Edwards, E. A., Lawrence, N. S., Coyle, D., & Munafò, M. R. (2016). Gamification of cognitive assessment and cognitive training: A systematic review of applications and efficacy. *JMIR Serious Games, 4*(2), e5888.

Martínez-Nicolás, I., Llorente, T. E., Martínez-Sánchez, F., & Meilán, J. J. G. (2021). Ten years of research on automatic voice and speech analysis of people with Alzheimer's disease and mild cognitive impairment: A systematic review article. *Frontiers in Psychology, 12*, 645.

Martyr, A., & Clare, L. (2012). Executive function and activities of daily living in Alzheimer's disease: A correlational meta-analysis. *Dementia and Geriatric Cognitive Disorders, 33*(2-3), 189-203.

Newman, M. L., Pennebaker, J. W., Berry, D. S., & Richards, J. M. (2003). Lying words: Predicting deception from linguistic styles. *Personality and Social Psychology Bulletin, 29*(5), 665-675.

Pennebaker, J. W., Booth, R. J., & Francis, M. E. (2007). LIWC2007:Linguistic inquiry and word count. *Austin, TX: LIWC. net, 135*.

Pennebaker, J. W., Boyd, R. L., Jordan, K., & Blackburn, K. (2015). *The Development and Psychometric Properties of LIWC2015*.

Pennebaker, J. W., Chung, C. K., Frazee, J., Lavergne, G. M., & Beaver, D. I. (2014). When small words foretell academic success: The case of college admissions essays. *PloS ONE, 9*(12), e115844.

Pennebaker, J. W., Chung, C. K., Ireland, M., Gonzales, A., & Booth, R. J. (2007). The development and psychometric properties of LIWC2007. *Austin, TX, LIWC. Net.*

Pennebaker, J. W., Mayne, T. J., & Francis, M. E. (1997). Linguistic predictors of adaptive bereavement. *Journal of Personality and Social Psychology, 72*(4), 863.

Polsinelli, A., Moseley, S., Grilli, M., Glisky, E., & Mehl, M. (2020). Natural, everyday language use provides a window into the integrity of older adults' cognitive functioning. *Innovation in Aging, 4*(Suppl 1), 623.

Simmons, R. A., Gordon, P. C., & Chambless, D. L. (2005). Pronouns in marital interaction: What do "you" and "I" say about marital health? *Psychological Science, 16*(12), 932-936.

Sirály, E., Szabó, Á., Szita, B., Kovács, V., Fodor, Z., Marosi, C., . . . Hanák, P. (2015). Monitoring the early signs of cognitive decline in elderly by computer games: An MRI study. *PloS ONE, 10*(2), e0117918.

Tausczik, Y. R., & Pennebaker, J. W. (2010). The psychological meaning of words: LIWC and computerized text analysis methods. *Journal of Language and Social Psychology, 29*(1), 24-54.

Varjacic, A., Mantini, D., Demeyere, N., & Gillebert, C. R. (2018). Neural signatures of Trail Making Test performance: Evidence from lesion-mapping and neuroimaging studies. *Neuropsychologia, 115*, 78-87.

Weaver, J. D. (2017). *Predicting employee performance using text data from resumes.* (Doctoral dissertation, Seattle Pacific University).

林瑋芳、黃金蘭、林以正、李嘉玲、James W. Pennebaker(2020)。語言探索與字詞計算詞典 2015 中文版之修訂。調查研究—方法與應用，45，73-118。

郭曉燕、花茂棽(2015)。*彩色路徑描繪測驗(中文版)指導手冊*。台北市：中國行為科學社。

黃金蘭、Cindy K. Chung、Natalie Hui、林以正、謝亦泰、Ben C.P.Lam、程威銓、Michael H. Bond、James W. Pennebaker(2012)。中華心理學期刊，*54*(2)，185-201。

The 33rd Conference on Computational Linguistics and Speech Processing (ROCLING 2021)
Taoyuan, Taiwan, October 15-16, 2021. The Association for Computational Linguistics and Chinese Language Processing

使用對話行為嵌入改善對話系統用戶訊息中提問句與閒聊句之判別
Improve Chit-Chat and QA Sentence Classification in User Messages of Dialogue System using Dialogue Act Embedding

Chi-Hsiang Chao
ChingShin Academy
Taipei, Taiwan
10835028@st.chjhs.tp.edu.tw

Xi-Jie Hou
ChingShin Academy
Taipei, Taiwan
10935020@st.chjhs.tp.edu.tw

Yu-Ching Chiu
Department of Computer Science and Information Engineering
National Central University
Taoyuan, Taiwan
crystalchiu@g.ncu.edu.tw

摘要

近年來，對話系統蓬勃發展並被廣泛應用於客服系統並取得了不錯的成效。檢視用戶與真人客服間的對話紀錄，可以發覺用戶的語句夾雜著對產品與服務的問題，以及和客服之間的閒聊。根據專業人員的經驗，在客服對話中適當地夾雜閒聊有助於提升用戶的體驗。然而，用戶提問是期望獲得解答，閒聊則是期望與客服有人與人之間的互動交流。面對這兩種意圖，對話系統必須能有效判別，以產生適當的回應。對話行為 (Dialog Act) 是語言學家將對話語句依據其作用定義出的一種分類方式。我們認為這個資訊將有助於提問句及閒聊句的區分。在本研究中，我們結合一個已公開的 Covid-19 問答資料集及一個 Covid-19 主題的閒聊資料集組成我們的實驗資料。我們基於 BERT (Bidirectional Encoder Representation from Transformers) 模型建立了一個提問句—閒聊句分類器模型。實驗結果顯示，加入對話行為嵌入 (Dialog Act Embedding) 的組態比僅使用原始語句嵌入的組態準確率高了 16%。此外，經過分析發現 ，Statement-non-opinion、Signal-non-understanding、Appreciation 等對話行為類型與提問句較相關，Wh-Question、Yes-No-Question、Rhetorical-Question 等類型則與閒聊句較相關。

Abstract

In recent years, dialogue system is booming and widely used in customer service system, and has achieved good results. Viewing the conversation records between users and real customer service, we can see that the user's sentences are mixed with questions about products and services, and chat with customer service. According to the experience of professionals, it is helpful in improving the user experience to mix some chats in customer service conversations. However, users' questions are expected to be answered, while chatting is expected to interact with customer service. In order to produce an appropriate response, the dialogue system must be able to distinguish these two intentions effectively. Dialog act is a classification that linguists define according to its function. We think this information will help distinguishing questioning sentences and chatting sentences. In this paper, we combine a published COVID-19 QA dataset and a COVID-19-topic chat dataset to form our experimental data. Based on the BERT (Bidirectional Encoder Representation from Transformers) model, we build a question-chat classifier model. The experimental results show that the accuracy of the configuration with dialog act embedding is 16% higher than that with only original statement embedding. In addition, it is found that conversation behavior types such as "Statement-non-opinion", "Signal-non-understanding" and "Appreciation" are more related to question sentences, while "Wh-Question", "Yes-No-Question" and "Rhetorical-Question" questions are more related to chat sentences.

關鍵字：對話行為、對話系統

Keywords : Dialog act classification, Dialog system

1 緒論

現今社會的客服系統多以對話系統回應用戶端，不僅能節約成本，更能在同一時間內解決大量的問題。在現實生活中，用戶與客服系統的對話中時常夾雜著「提問」和「閒聊」的語句，而這樣的對話方式有助於提升用戶的體驗。然而，提問是期望獲得解答，而閒聊則是希望與對方有所交流。因此有效的判別用戶的意圖，對於對話系統產生適當的回應十分重要。現代的對話系統大多是單一功能的系統，如：任務導向式對話系統 (Task-Oriented)、閒聊式對話系統 (Chit-Chat) 和問答

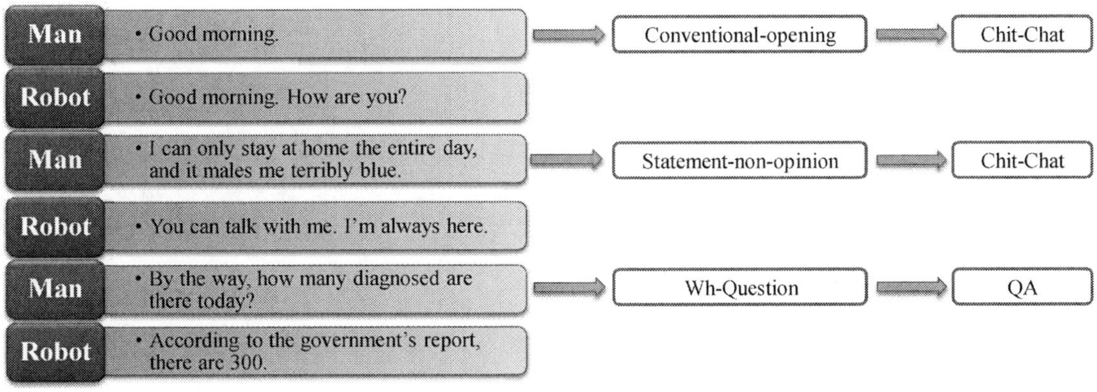

圖 1. 使用者與機器人的對話

式對話系統 (Question Answering) 等。例如：Google 助理以及 Siri 較偏向於任務式導向式對話系統，在以對話了解用戶需求後為用戶執行任務；閒聊 (Chit-Chat) 則是允許用戶與系統進行開放式聊天對話，Google 的 Meena (Adiwardana, et al., 2020)即屬之；問答式 (Question Answering) 是接收用戶端所提出的問題，從資料庫中尋找最佳的答案，再回答用戶端，IBM 的 Watson (Gliozzo, et al., 2013)即屬之。以上幾種對話系統雖然都能專精於特定領域，能提供用戶端正確的回應，但是目前對話系統的功能較為單一化，無法集上述三種對話方式於一身，使得對話系統較難運用在真實的對話場景中。為使聊天機器人通用於上述場域中，本研究引入對話行為 (Dialogue Act) (Perkoff, E Margaret, 2021)，發展辨識用戶話語意圖究竟為發問或閒聊的技術。對話行為是語言學家將對話的句子依據其作用及定義得出之分類，我們將對話行為作為分辨「問答式對話」和「閒聊式對話」的重要參考資訊，使對話系統模型能將用戶的話語導向問答模組或閒聊模組以給予回應，使兩種對話系統能合而為一，以提供更好的用戶體驗。本研究將探討是否能夠利用機器學習模型有效地藉由引入對話行為區分出問答和閒聊兩種情境的語句，以便後續利用對應的系統進行後續處理與應對。

圖 1 為使用者與對話系統之間的對話，可以看出使用者的前兩句話屬於閒聊 (Chit-Chat)，最後一句則是提問 (QA 中的 Question)。本研究探討對話行為對於模型判斷句子屬於 Chit-Chat 或 QA 是否有幫助，如同圖中的對話系統由 Conventional-opening 和 Statement-non-opinion 判斷屬於 Chit-Chat、由 Wh-Question 判斷屬於 QA 一般。

2 相關研究

2.1 Hybrid Dialogue System

大部分任務型導向對話系統與閒聊型對話系統通常單獨出現，儘管現今已有許多針對上述兩種對話系統的研究 (Hosseini-Asl, et al., 2020) (Adiwardana, et al., 2020)，然而混和這兩種對話系統的模型尚未有足夠的研究。此論文(Moirangthem, Dennis Singh, et al., 2018) 試圖以將任務導向的句子與閒聊的句子區分出來的方式，構建一個混合任務型導向對話系統與閒聊型對話系統的模型。

對話系統大多無法兼具多種功能。此篇論文 (Sun, Kai, et al., 2020) 嘗試通過添加較隨意且與上下文相關的閒聊語料增强任務導向聊天機器人的對話能力，並綜合這兩種類型的系統。目的是讓一個虛擬助理能使任務式與閒聊型的機器人合二為一，加強在兩者之間切換的能力，以及強化系統對話的趣味以及交流性，使之更像人類，藉此提升用戶的使用體驗。綜上，混合型對話系統將成為未來對話系統發展的趨勢。

2.2 Dialogue Act in Dialogue system

對話行為 (Dialogue Act)是一種從句子中抽取出來的語意抽象，表示句子在對話中的功能，即此句子背後的行為。例如：" Hi. How are you? " 的對話行為是" Greeting "，因為此句話代表的動作為「打招呼」。為了增加句子所包含的資訊，(Kumar et al., 2018) 將對話行為加入到句子中來訓練對話系統，並使其預測給使用者的回應 (next utterance selection)，對話行為反映出了對話系統與用戶之間的對話模式，對話行為提供的資訊有效改善了系統回應的表現。

在本研究中，我們將探討加入對話行為對判斷用戶語句意圖為提問或閒聊所帶來的助益，並討論不同種加入對話行為的方式對模型表現的影響。

3 方法

3.1 BERT

本文選擇訓練 BERT (Devlin, Jacob, et al., 2019) (全名為 Bidirectional Encoder Representations from Transformers) 區分 QA 及 Chit-Chat。BERT 是 Google 以無監督的方法利用大量無標註文本訓練的語言代表模型，其架構為 Transformer (Vaswani, et al., 2017)中的 Encoder。相較於其他的語言代表模型，BERT 以漏字填空(MLM)和下個句子預測 (NSP)的兩個任務訓練出一個能被廣泛用於理解自然語言的模型，再訓練此模型做 Fine-tuning 的監督式任務，來達到其目的。BERT 主要可以做四個下游任務模型，分別是單一句子分類任務、單一句子標註任務、成堆句子任務、問答任務，而本次實驗所使用的是單一句子分類任務。

3.2 DialogTag

DialogTag 是 Bhavitvya Malik 基於 38 種對話行為所製成的分類器，它能夠將輸入句子所屬的對話行為輸出。它是使用 Tensorflow 建立的一個 Transformer 模型，在 Python 中有釋出專門的模組供大家使用。它的原型是賓州大學發表的 Switchboard Corpus (雙向通話紀錄) (Godfrey, et al., 1992)，其中共分類出 42 種對話行為，DialogTag 從中抽取 38 種對話行為作為簡化過後的版本。

本研究參考了(Stolcke, Andreas, et al., 2000) 的對話行為，探討問答語句及聊天語句是否能透過對話行為進行準確的區分。我們將資料輸入 Bhavitvya Malik 所釋出的對話行為系統分類器 (DialogTag) 並分析結果，最後確認是否可以對話行為區分出問答和閒聊兩種情境。我們將句子和對話行為的嵌入表示連接成一個新的句子嵌入表示作為輸入，訓練以 BERT 為基底的二元分類模型，預測當前輸入的句子為 Chit-Chat 或是 QA，模型架構如圖 2 所示。

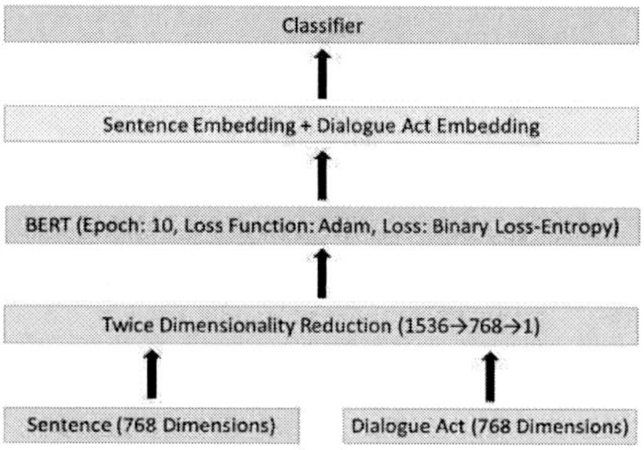

圖 2. 模型架構

4 資料集

4.1 SQuAD2.0

SQuAD2.0 (Rajpurkar, Pranav, et al., 2018) 是由超過 50000 個無法回答的問題和 2016 年 Rajpurkar 等人所發布的斯坦福問答數據集 (SQuAD (Rajpurkar et al., 2016)) 所組成的，每個問答對都有一個給定的上下文段落，成為閱讀理解任務的常用測試資料集。我們選擇 SQuAD2.0 是因為 2018 年 OpenAI-GPT 和 BERT 在使用 SQuAD2.0 做多語言任務上取得了很好的效能。它將作為問答用的資料。

4.2 Dataset for chatbot Simple questions and answers

我們使用由 Graf Stor 在 Kaggle 所釋出的 Dataset for chatbot Simple questions and answers[1]作為閒聊的資料集。此資料集是作者本人為了訓練簡單的 Seq2Seq (Sutskever, Ilya, et al., 2014) 而蒐集而成的。

[1] Stor, Graf. "Dataset for Chatbot." *Kaggle*, 14 June 2020, www.kaggle.com/grafstor/simple-dialogs-for-chatbot.

4.3 COVID-QA

我們使用由Xing Han Lu所釋出的COVID-QA[2]資料集，為關於 COVID-19 (與新聞、公共衛生和社區討論的關係較為密切) 的問答句子。此資料集是為了方便提供問答系統的建立而蒐集的 1800 多筆問答資料，因此我們將其當作問答句的資料。

4.4 COVID-19

我們所使用的是由 Moayad 釋出的 COVID-19：Audience-LiveChat[3]資料集。此資料集為有關 Covid-19 的 YouTube 影片的直播聊天室內容，共有大約 73 萬筆閒聊對話。此為閒聊資料集。

4.5 Switchboard Corpus

我們將 Switchboard Corpus 作為另一個閒聊資料的來源。它擁有大約 2400 組雙向對話紀錄與接近 260 個小時的總對話時數。

5 實驗

5.1 訓練資料、驗證資料和預測資料

這次實驗總共做了 6 個模型以判斷對話行為是否能有助於模型分辨 QA 和 Chit-Chat：BERT_General 、 BERT_General_DAC 、 BERT_General_Concatenation 、 BERT_COVID 、 BERT_COVID_DAC 與 BERT_COVID_Concatenation 。其中的「COVID」是在訓練的過程中加入較雜亂的 Chit-Chat 句子，例如「？？？？？」和「omg」，以增強模型對於 Chit-Chat 句的判斷能力。在訓練完 BERT_General 後，我們發現在 BERT_General 的輸出結果中，答錯的句子多為這類混亂的 Chit-Chat 句子，可見此模型應付這類句子的能力較低，因此我們才加入它們以提升模型的準確率。「DAC」與「Concatenation」則是將句子串接對話行為，兩者之間的差異在於串接的方式。「DAC」先將這兩部分分別轉為 e 向量後再直接連接起來，合併為一個 1536 維的向量，再送入分類器進行 Chit-Chat 與 QA 的分類。「Concatenation」則是一開始就將句子與對話行為的文字相連，再一起轉為 768 維向量並送入分類器。

表 1 為各個模型所使用的資料數量。資料來如下：(1) Chit-Chat 所用的資料集來自 Dataset for chatbot Simple questions and answers 以及 Switchboard Corpus；(2) QA 所用的資料集來自 SQuAD2.0；(3) COVID-19 相關的 Chit-Chat 資料來自 COVID-19： Audience-LiveChat；(4) COVID-19 有關的 QA 資料來自 COVID-QA。在建立三種資料集時，維持 Chit-Chat 和 QA 的數量比為 1：1，訓練資料和驗證資料的數量比為 8：2。我們最終用來測試模型的預測資料總共有 1900 筆，含有 950 筆 Chit-Chat（全部與 COVID-19 相關）以及 950 筆 QA（全部與 COVID-19 相關）。訓練資料和驗證資料所使用的資料筆數如表 1 所示，表 2 為 22 種出現在資料中的對話行為。

	Train Data			Valid Data		
	# Chit-Chat	# QA	Sum	# Chit-Chat	# QA	Sum
BERT_General	10500	10500	21000	2625	2625	5250
BERT_General_DAC	10500	10500	21000	2625	2625	5250
BERT_General_Concatenation	10500	10500	21000	2625	2625	5250
BERT_COVID	10500 (with COVID data)	10500	21000	2625 (with COVID data)	2625	5250
BERT_COVID_DAC	10500 (with COVID data)	10500	21000	2625 (with COVID data)	2625	5250
BERT_COVID_Concatenation	10500 (with COVID data)	10500	21000	2625 (with COVID data)	2625	5250

表 1. 各模型使用的資料量

Acknowledge (Backchannel), Action-directive, Appreciation, Collaborative, Conventional-closing, Conventional-opening, Declarative Yes-No-Question, Hold before Answer/Agreement, Negative, Non-no Answers, No Answer, Open-Question, Or-Clause, Other, Quotation, Repeat, Rhetorical-Question, Self-talk, Signal-non-understanding, Statement-non-opinion, Statementopinion, Wh-Question, Yes-No-Question

表 2. 出現在資料中的對話行為，共 22 種

5.2 實驗與結果

表 3 為各模型在分類 Chit-Chat 及 QA 的表現與整體的準確率，分為以下層面討論:(1)不

[2] Xhlulu. "COVID-QA." *Kaggle*, 15 Apr. 2020, www.kaggle.com/xhlulu/covidqa.

[3] Moayad. "COVID-19: Audience-LiveChat." Kaggle, 17 Apr. 2020, www.kaggle.com/moayadhn/covid19-roylablivechat.

同訓練資料的差異(2)有無加入對話行為的差異(3)不同加入對話行為方法的差異。

	QA Accuracy	Chit-Chat Accuracy	Total Accuracy
BERT_General	61.4%	45.3%	58.1%
BERT_General_DAC	76%	61.4%	68.7%
BERT_General_Concatenation	80.7%	78%	79.4%
BERT_COVID	52.5%	99.8%	76.2%
BERT_COVID_DAC	66%	99.5%	82.8%
BERT_COVID_Concatenation	85.4%	99%	92.2%

表 3. 模型準確率

5.3 不同訓練資料的差異

比較表 3 中 BERT_General 和 BERT_COVID 的數據可以看出加入較混亂的 Chit-Chat 資料大幅提升了模型判別 Chit-Chat 的能力，準確率由 45.3%上升到 99.8%，進步了 54.5%。雖然使判斷 QA 的準確率略微下降，但仍然使模型整體的準確率提升 29.4%。

5.4 有無加入對話行為的差異

由表 3 中 BERT_COVID 和 BERT_COVID_DAC 的數據比較可以看出在加入對話行為後，QA 的準確率會提升。在表中，BERT_ COVID 在 QA 上僅有 52.5%的準確率，而 BERT_COVID_DAC 則達到了 66%的準確率。在整體表現上，BERT_COVID_DAC 亦達到了 82.7%的高準確率，相較 BERT_ COVID 有 6.6%的進步，由此可見加入對話行為確實能有效的提升整體的分類準確率。

5.5 不同加入對話行為方法的差異

從表 3 的數據中可以看出不同加入對話行為的方式確實會影響模型的判斷。結果顯示 BERT_General_concatenation 的準確率比 BERT_General_DAC 高出 10.7%。BERT_COVID_Concatenation 則是比 BERT_COVID_DAC 準確 9.5%。因此，將對話行為與句子以文字方式連接擁有全部模型中最高的準確率。

5.6 資料分析

對於模型所得出的資料，我們亦以 Visual Correlation 的方式進行分析。Visual Correlation 指的是在兩組資料之間找出關聯性，並採用視覺化的方式表現。Visual Correlation 更能將數據之間的差異展現出來，比較容易讓人找出相關性高的部分。基於以上原因。我們採用 Visual Correlation 分析資料。

5.7 視覺化

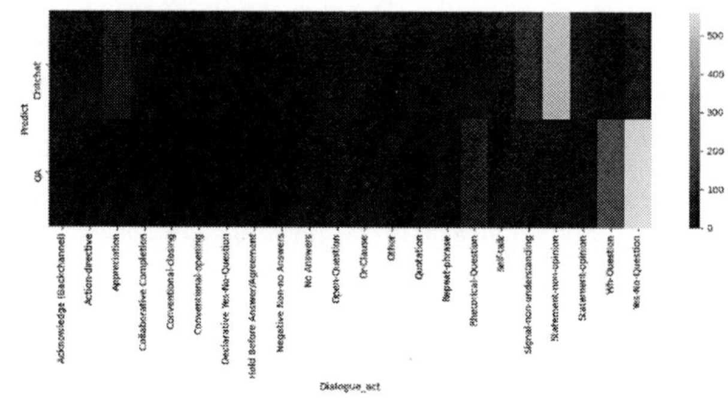

圖 3. BERT_COVID_Cocatenation 預測結果與對話行為的 Visual Correlation

Visual Correlation 指的是找出兩組數據之間的關聯性，再將其以視覺化的方式展現出來。Visual Correlation 更容易顯示出資料間的差異，也更容易找出關聯性高的項目。基於以上的原因，我們決定使用 Visual Correlation 來分析模型產出的資料。從以上的實驗，我們發現加入對話行為對於分辨閒聊與問答有所幫助。此外，我們將 Visual Correlation 套用在預測出來的資料上得到標籤（閒聊與問答）以及對話行為之間的熱圖以找出影響模型的對話行為。

圖 3 為 BERT_COVID_Cocatenation 預測結果與對話行為的 Visual Correlation，越淺色的部分相關性越高。從圖中可以發現，閒聊句與「Statement-non-opinion」高度相關，而問答句與「Yes-No-Question」和「Wh-Question」有關，其餘的對話行為則沒有顯著的相關性。因此，在以對話行為替句子分類時，若是遇到「Statement-non-opinion」，可以將句子送往閒聊機器人；反之如果是「Yes-No-Question」或「Wh-Question」則是輸入進問答機器人。

6 結論

本次研究使我們發現加入對話行為確實對於模型的準確率有所幫助。以 BERT_COVID 與 BERT_COVID_Concatenation（我們建立的模型）為例，後者比前者多了 16%的準確率，同時也比其他所有模型都優秀，達到了 92.2% 的準確率。

除此之外，我們也找出三種可以有效區別閒聊與問答的對話行為，分別是「Statement-non-opinion」、「Yes-No-Question」與「Wh-Question」。有些對話行為，例如「Appreciation」和「Rhetorical-Question」，比上述幾個的關聯性都還要低，但它們也可以提升模型的分類能力。有了對話行為的幫助，輸入句子可以被送到對應的機器人已產生適當的回應。

7 未來展望

在本論文中，我們進行處理的都是單一句子，沒有考慮前後文，這限制了我們的研究。我們的模型誤將「Answer」的對話行為判定為閒聊，但實際上這應該屬於問答的一部份。要解決這方面的問題，後續的研究可以將對話紀錄納入考量。加入對話紀錄的模型能夠透過前文與當下的句子判斷此劇屬於閒聊或是問答，特別是問答句的準確率可以大幅提升，因為在知道先前的問題下，「Answer」就會被分類為問答句。

References

D. Adiwardana, M.T. Luong, D. R. So, J. Hall, N. Fiedel, R. Thoppilan, Z. Yang, A. Kulshreshtha, G. Nemade, Y. Lu. 2020. *Towards a humanlike open domain chatbot.* arXiv preprint arXiv:2001.09977.

Alfio Gliozzo, Or Biran, Siddharth Patwardhan, Kathleen McKeown. 2013. *Semantic Technologies in IBM Watson™.* Proceedings of the Fourth Workshop on Teaching Natural Language Processing, pages 85–92

Perkoff, E Margaret. 2021. *Dialogue Act Analysis for Alternative and Augmentative Communication.* Proceedings of the 1st Workshop on NLP for Positive Impact, pages 107—114

Hosseini-Asl, Ehsan and McCann, Bryan and Wu, Chien-Sheng and Yavuz, Semih and Socher, Richard. 2020. *A simple language model for task-oriented dialogue.* arXiv preprint arXiv:2005.00796.

Dennis Singh Moirangthem and Minho Lee. 2018. *Chat Discrimination for Intelligent Conversational Agents with a Hybrid CNN-LMTGRU Network.* Proceedings of The Third Workshop on Representation Learning for NLP.

Kai Sun, Seungwhan Moon, Paul Crook, Stephen Roller, Becka Silvert, Bing Liu, Zhiguang Wang, Honglei Liu, Eunjoon Cho, and Claire Cardie. 2020. *Adding Chit-Chats to Enhance Task-Oriented Dialogues.* arXiv preprint arXiv:2010.12757.

Harshit Kumar, Arvind Agarwal, Sachindra Joshi. 2018. *Dialogue-act-driven Conversation Model: An Experimental Study.* Proceedings of the 27th International Conference on Computational Linguistics.

Jacob Devlin, Ming-Wei Chang, Kenton Lee, and Kristina Toutanova. 2019. BERT: Pre-training of Deep Bidirectional Transformers for Language Understanding. arXiv preprint arXiv:1810.04805.

Vaswani, Ashish and Shazeer, Noam and Parmar, Niki and Uszkoreit, Jakob and Jones, Llion and Gomez, Aidan N and Kaiser, Lukasz and Polosukhin, Illia. 2017. *Attention is all you need.* Advances in neural information processing systems, pages 5998--6008.

Godfrey, John J and Holliman, Edward C and McDaniel, Jane. 1992. SWITCHBOARD: Telephone speech corpus for research and development. Acoustics, Speech, and Signal Processing, IEEE International Conference on. IEEE Computer Society, pages 517--520.

Andreas Stolcke, Noah Coccaro, Rebecca Bates, Paul Taylor, Carol Van Ess-Dykema, Klaus Ries, Elizabeth Shriberg, Daniel Jurafsky, Rachel Martin, and Marie Meteer. 2000. *Dialogue Act Modeling for Automatic Tagging and Recognition of Conversational Speech.* Computational linguistics 26.3, pages 339--373.

Pranav Rajpurkar, Jian Zhang, Konstantin Lopyrev, and Percy Liang. 2016. *Squad: 100,000+ questions for machine comprehension of text.* arXiv preprint arXiv:1606.05250.

Pranav Rajpurkar, Robin Jia,and Percy Liang. 2018. *Know What You Don't Know: Unanswerable Questions for SQuAD.* arXiv preprint arXiv:1806.03822.

Ilya Sutskever, Oriol Vinyals, and Quoc V. Le. 2014. *Sequence to Sequence Learning with Neural Networks.* Advances in neural information processing systems.

Benjamin Kane, Georgiy Platonov, and Lenhart Schubert. 2020. *History-Aware Question Answering in a Blocks World Dialogue System.* arXiv preprint arXiv:2005.12501.

The 33rd Conference on Computational Linguistics and Speech Processing (ROCLING 2021)
Taoyuan, Taiwan, October 15-16, 2021. The Association for Computational Linguistics and Chinese Language Processing

語音資料增量技術應用於構音障礙輔具之效益

Data Augmentation Technology for Dysarthria Assistive Systems

朱唯中 Wei-Chung Chu
國立陽明交通大學生物醫學工程學系
Department of Biomedical Engineering
National Yang Ming Chiao Tung University
abc55169@gmail.com

洪瑛秀 Ying-Hsiu Hung
國立陽明交通大學生物醫學工程學系
Department of Biomedical Engineering
National Yang Ming Chiao Tung University
wer850718906@gmail.com

鄭惟中 Wei-Zhong Zheng
國立陽明交通大學生物醫學工程學系
Department of Biomedical Engineering
National Yang Ming Chiao Tung University
s1010654@gm.ym.edu.tw

賴穎暉 Ying-Hui Lai
國立陽明交通大學生物醫學工程學系
Department of Biomedical Engineering
National Yang Ming Chiao Tung University
yh.lai@nycu.edu.tw

摘要

以語音驅動之溝通輔具是構音障礙患者常用的方法之一。然而這類輔具需要患者大量的錄製語音來提升系統效益，而常造成使用上的困難。有鑑於此，本研究提出語音增量技術來試圖減少患者錄音負擔並提升溝通輔具辨識效益。於研究結果證明，所提出之構音障礙語音生成系統能產生類患者語音並提升溝通輔具於重複語句之辨識率。此外，於患者 Free-talk 情況下的字詞錯誤率可由 64.42%降至 4.39%。而這些成果也證實本論文提出之方法將對溝通輔具發展有所幫助。

Abstract

Voice-driven communication aids are one of the methods commonly used by patients with dysarthria. However, this type of assistive devices demands a large amount of voice data from patients to increase the effectiveness. In the meantime, this will sink patients into an overwhelming recording burden. Due to those difficulties, this research proposes a voice augmentation system to conquer the aforementioned concern. Furthermore, the system can improve the recognition efficiency. The results of this research reveal that the proposed speech generator system for dysarthria can launch corpus to be more similarities to the patient's speech. Moreover, the recognition rate, in duplicate sentences, has been improved and promoted to the higher level. The word error rate can be reduced from 64.42% to 4.39% in the case of patients with Free-talk. According to these results, our proposed system can provide more reliable and helpful technique for the development of communication aids.

關鍵字：構音障礙、溝通障礙系統、資料增量、深度學習
Keywords: dysarthria, communication assistance system, data augmentation, deep learning

一、 緒論

構音障礙為腦部(或神經)受損而導致患者無法良好的控制發聲肌肉而影響語音清晰度。根據美國語言學學會(2020)的資料顯示，全美大約有 4000 萬位溝通障礙患者，且每年還約有 100 萬人因罹患疾病而可能導致構音障礙問題。有鑑於此，我們需要投入更多研究資源來幫助患者有更好的溝通效益，進而提升他們的生活品質。

對於構音障礙患者來說，溝通輔具系統(augmentative and alternative communication, AAC)是提升溝通效率的常見方法。目前常見的 AAC 包括：溝通字板(Calculator et al., 1983)、眼動追蹤(Lin et al., 2006)等。但上述 AAC 溝通速率(約每分鐘 2~5 個字)仍遠不及透過言語驅動的方法 (約每分鐘 127±46 個字)(Murdoch & Theodoros, 2001)。換言之，以語音驅動的溝通輔具應是更有效率的方式。基於此概念並伴隨著語音訊號處理技術發展下，目前已有許多方法被提出，例如：語音轉換(voice conversion, VC)及自動語音辨識(automatic speech recognition, ASR)，來試圖改善構音障礙患者的溝通效益。

以 VC 技術用於構音障礙語音轉換來說，Yang et al.(2020)使用生成對抗網路 cycle-consistent generative adversarial network (cycle-GAN)，將構音障礙語音轉換成正常語者語音。於實驗結果證明，此方法可降低患者語音達 33.4%的字詞錯誤率(word error rate, WER)。Wang et al.(2020)提出結合文字轉語音(text-to-speech, TTS)與 knowledge distillation (KD)技術的 end-to-end VC 方法來試圖改善患者語音清析度。於實驗結果發現，此方法能讓較嚴重之構音異常患者分別降低 35.4%和 48.7%的 WER。

另一部份以 ASR 為基礎之溝通輔具也持續發展中。例如 Shor et al. (2019)提出在有限的構音障礙語音資料條件仍有準確的構音障礙語音辨識能力。於此研究中，他們先用巨量資料(1000 小時正常語者資料)來預訓練 RNN-T 模型。接著，再用 36.7 小時構音障礙語者資料進行微調(finetune)。於實驗結果顯示，在輕度和重度患者上分別降低 22.3%和 38%的 WER。Takashima et al. (2019) 透過遷移學習(transfer learning)技術來善用不同語言資料對於語音辨識模型系統之效益提升。從實驗結果也證明能使 ASR 的音素錯誤率降低(從 38.49%降至 25.69%)。

上述的多項研究顯示現今的語音訊號處理模型可以有效提升構音障礙語音的理解度，但是模型的強健度往往會受到訓練資料量和品質影響。然而對於構音障礙患者來說，要大量錄得訓練語料將十分困難且花費成本。有鑑於此，資料增量技術將顯得十分重要。目前已有許多研究嘗試使用資料增量方法來克服資料不足的問題。舉例來說， Vachhani et al. (2018)藉由調整語音速度和節奏，將正常人語音的速度調整至類患者語速作為增量資料。隨後，再將其丟入 ASR 進行訓練。由結果證明，透過提出方法能提升 ASR 系統辨識率約 3%。但在此研究中仍呈現出當患者資料產生不穩定音素情況，其生成之資料的效果仍有待加強。而 Jiao et al. (2018)使用 deep convolutional generative adversarial network 技術來設計語音轉換模型，進而將正常人語音轉換成患者語音作為增量資料。此外，他們再使用二分類網路模型來比較傳統混噪增量和上述語音轉換增量技術間的差異。於結果顯示，使用語音轉換系統作為增量手法明顯優於混噪增量方法來幫助模型學習。然而上述這些典型的資料增量技術仍無法產生高維之訓練資料分布特性，進而難以更廣泛的模擬出患者日常說出語音可能的變異性，使得以語音驅動為基礎之溝通輔具效益受到限制。

基於上述的研究結果和討論，我們假設一個具備多語者轉換能力的模型在資料增量任務中，將更能模擬出更多元之患者語音變異性，進而提升溝通輔具採用模型效益。有鑑於此，本論文將提出以多語者轉換模型為基礎之構音障礙語音生成系統，並探討生成類患者語料的品質與相似度。隨後，我們將更進一步的探討提出方法所增量之資料對於溝通輔具系統模型訓練之效益。

二、 構音障礙語音生成系統

鑒於上述討論，我們提出一個以多對多為基礎之語音轉換技術來設計構音障礙語音生成系統，稱構音障礙語音生成器(dysarthric speech generator, DSG)。於本論文提出之DSG(如圖 1)主要是使用 StarGAN-VC (Kameoka et al., 2018)作為核心模型架構，透過此模型特性來學習多位語者下轉到患者語音之模型參數，進而生成出更廣泛之患者語音特性(例如：不同語氣和語速)。此外，此提出之 DSG 將僅需患者錄製少量訓練語料(約 288 句話)來學習如何將正常語者轉換成構音障礙患者之語音，接著透過此模型來將大量正常語者語音轉成類患者語音。換言之，我們透過訓練出來之模型來將大量正常語者語音轉成大量類患者語音訓練資料，進而減少患者錄音的負擔。

StarGAN-VC 是由二類別轉換 CycleGAN-VC (Kaneko & Kameoka, 2018)所延伸出來的多類別轉換架構，在二類別轉換(CycleGAN)中若要生成k個語者類別就需要k個模型，而使用多類別轉換(StarGAN)只需要一個模型，便能大幅減少模型的訓練數目。此外，多語者特徵所訓練出的模型更具多變性，對於因為缺乏患者資料而缺少變異性的問題來說非常有幫助。StarGAN-VC 主要由三個模型組成，生成器(Generator, G)、鑑別器(Discriminator, D)和輔助分類器(Classifier, C)，其架構如圖 1 所示。x為輸入頻譜、c為語者標記類別、y為目標頻譜，生成器(G)會根據輸入的x和c輸出預測頻譜$\hat{y}$，鑑別器(D)則根據輸入的$\hat{y}$和y輸出兩者之間的相似性；輔助分類器(C)根據輸入的$\hat{y}$輸出預測類別c'。三個模型所對應的損失函數(loss function)分別為$\mathcal{L}_G(G)$、$\mathcal{L}_D(D)$和$\mathcal{L}_C(C)$，公式如下：

$$\mathcal{L}_G(G) = \mathcal{L}_{adv}^G(G) + \lambda_{cls}\mathcal{L}_{cls}^G(G) + \lambda_{cyc}\mathcal{L}_{cyc}(G) + \lambda_{id}\mathcal{L}_{id}(G) \quad (1)$$

$$\mathcal{L}_D(D) = \mathcal{L}_{adv}^D(D) \quad (2)$$

$$\mathcal{L}_c(C) = \mathcal{L}_{cls}^C(C) \quad (3)$$

$\mathcal{L}_{adv}^G(G)$和$\mathcal{L}_{adv}^D(D)$為對抗損失(adversarial loss)，藉由對抗式訓練讓模型學習x和y之間的特徵差異，使得$G(x)$的特徵趨近於y；$\mathcal{L}_{cls}^G(G)$和$\mathcal{L}_{cls}^C(C)$為類別分類器損失(domain classification loss)，$\mathcal{L}_{cls}^G(G)$越小表示分類器C對於生成器所輸出語者c的頻譜$G(x,c)$的準確度越高，$\mathcal{L}_{cls}^C(C)$越小表示分類器C對於目標語者的頻譜y的準確度越高；$\mathcal{L}_{cyc}(G)$為循環一致損失(cycle consistency loss)，確保生成器建構(construct)之後能重建(reconstruct)回語音頻譜，

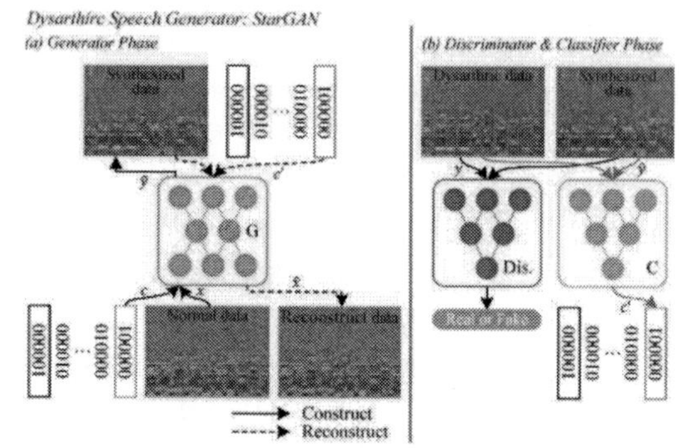

圖 1. StarGAN-VC 架構圖

強化不同語者生成器之間的特徵轉換同時也保留語音訊息。$\mathcal{L}_{id}(G)$為身分映射損失(identity loss)，當生成器(G)輸入頻譜x和其目標類別c為同一類別時，使其輸出保持不變，強化生成器(G)的語者特性。λ_{cls}、λ_{cyc}、λ_{id}為三個損失函數的權重值，本實驗的參數設定為 3、10、5。三個模型皆使用二維 gated CNN (Dauphin et al., 2017)結構，此結構中利用堆疊 sigmoid 門控單元(gated linear units, GLU)而有序列記憶的架構，並且在語言轉換任務上比起 long short-term memory (LSTM)架構有更精簡、好訓練、推算速度快等優點。

當上述轉換模型訓練完成後，我們還需要 vocoder 把聲學特徵轉換為聲音訊號。本實驗中，使用 WORLD (Morise et al., 2016)作為聲學特徵，其中包含三種特徵：基頻($F0$)、頻譜包絡線(spectral envelope, SP)、非週期參數(aperiodic, AP)。在訓練階段時，使用頻譜包絡線(SP)作為 StarGAN-VC 模型的訓練資料。在轉換階段時除了用 StarGAN-VC 轉換SP，我們也將基頻($F0$)和非週期參數(AP)用正規化線性映射轉換成目標語者的資料分布，使音調更接近目標語者。

三、 研究方法

3.1 實驗材料

我們採用 TMHINT (Huang et al., 2005)文本(共 320 句，每句 10 字)來對患者進行錄音，錄音的設定為：取樣率 16k、位元率 16bit、單聲道、wav 檔案格式。本研究共有三位構音障礙語者($D_n, n = 3$)和三位正常語者($N_m, m = 3$)，來錄製至少一套 TMHINT 語料(詳細資料如表 1)。實驗中我們也再使用 Microsoft Speech API

(Wikipedia contributors)中的 TTS 來產生輸入文本[1]之語料，進而節省患者大量錄音時間。

表 1. 資料使用表

<table>
<tr><th></th><th colspan="2">訓練資料數量與合成資料數量</th></tr>
<tr><td>原始語料總數</td><td colspan="2">D_1 (男，中風)=320 句×2 套
D_2 (女，腦性麻痺)=320 句×2 套
D_3 (女，聽力損失)=320 句×1 套
N_1 (男)=320 句×2 套
N_2 (女)=320 句×2 套
N_3 (女)=320 句×1 套
TTS (女)=320 句×1 套</td></tr>
<tr><td>訓練語料</td><td>D_{1_2}=288 句
D_{2_2}=288 句
D_3=288 句</td><td>N_{1_2}=288 句
N_{2_2}=288 句
N_3=288 句
TTS=288 句</td></tr>
<tr><td>合成語料</td><td colspan="2">N_{1_2} → D_n=320 句
N_{2_1}, N_{2_2} → D_n=640 句
N_3 → D_n=320 句
TTS → D_n=News:2880 句</td></tr>
<tr><td rowspan="2">測試語料</td><td colspan="2">重複語句測試 (Duplicate test) D_{n_1} =288 句</td></tr>
<tr><td colspan="2">外部測試 (Outside test) D_n =32 句</td></tr>
</table>

註：D_{n_b}、N_{m_a}之n、m為不同語者，a、b為各語者的第幾套語料。

3.2 實驗設計

本研究主要目的為設計一個構音障礙語音生成系統並透過以 ASR 為基礎之溝通輔具進行效益驗證。有鑑於此目標，我們透過以下實驗來證明提出系統的效益。於實驗一中，我們比較「雙語者轉換模型」和「多語者轉換模型」間所合成出之語音與構音障礙患者語音的相似度情況。我們使用 Mel-cepstral distortion (MCD)[2] (Kominek et al., 2008)來評估 CycleGAN-VC 和 StarGAN-VC 二個方法之效益。隨後，我們透過實驗二來對表現較佳之 DSG 來進行系統的實作，其完整實驗流程如圖 2 所示。

圖 2 左側為 DSG 之流程，使用的訓練語料為每位語者中同一套 TMHINT 288 句(如表 1)。在完成訓練後，我們用其生成了不同數量的患者語料。並在後續效益驗證中，使用不同倍數之增量資料各別訓練多個 ASR，觀

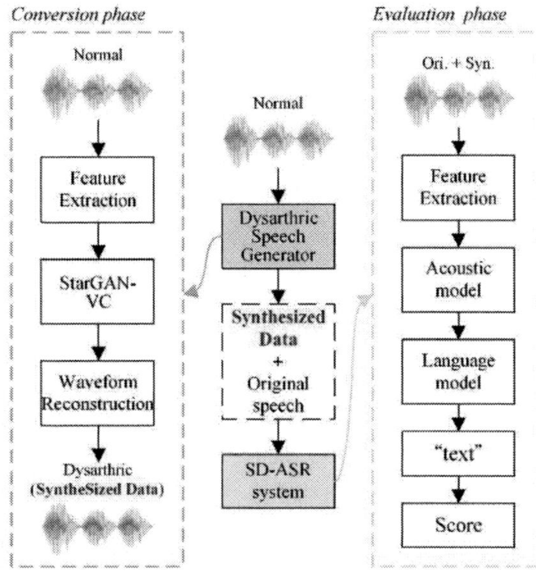

圖 2.實驗二流程圖

察增量資料對其辨識率之影響。我們使用 Kaldi ASR (Povey et al., 2011)作為驗證工具並建立每位構音障礙患者專用的 ASR，稱為 speaker dependent-ASR (SD-ASR)。而此 SD-ASR 系統是由聲學模型和語言模型組成(如圖 2 右側)，聲學模型主要學習將聲學特徵轉換為語言特徵，我們使用 time delay neural network (TDNN) (Peddinti et al., 2015)作為模型架構，聲學特徵為 MFCC，語言特徵為音素後驗機率(phonetic posteriorgrams, PPGs) (Hazen et al., 2009)。而語言模型使用 N-gram 語言概率模型，它是一種基於馬爾可夫鏈的機率統計模型，藉由統計方法推算可以在音素序列中排列出最合適的文字。在本研究使用的 N-gram 為三元模型(N=3)。

隨後我們更進一步比較，在 SD-ASR 中加入透過 DSG 轉換的合成語料與直接加入原始的正常人語音(意即未經過 DSG 轉換的正常語者語料)之差異。因為在構音障礙 ASR 系統中加入多位正常語者資料是經典的增量手法，因此本研究希望從實驗中證實合成語料比其它資料增量方法更能幫助 ASR 系統的學習。在實驗二使用之增量資料以$n\hat{Y}$、$n\widehat{W}$表示其增量資料及類別，n表示增量套數(以 TMHINT

[1] TTS 系統採用之文本為網路新聞(共 2880 句)做為 TTS 增量文本。

[2] MCD 值越小表示合成出的語音與患者越相似。

288 句為一套)，$\hat{Y}$表示真實錄音相關語料、$\widehat{W}$表示 TTS 相關語料。

四、結果與討論

實驗一結果如表 2 所示，在三位構音障礙患者語料分別使用 CycleGAN 和 StarGAN 架構建立語音轉換模型，再使用模型各別生成D_1、D_2、D_3構音障礙語音。可以觀察到在三位患者中，有兩位患者的 StarGAN 合成語料 MCD 數值較 CycleGAN 低，意即整體平均表現來看，StarGAN 的架構所轉換出之語音與患者語音較為相似。且在此實驗設計下要生成相同數量的語料，使用 CycleGAN 要比 StarGAN 多上 6 倍的模型參數和訓練時間。有鑑於上述觀察，不論是在訓練時間以及合成資料品質上，採用 StarGAN 架構做為 DSG 模型生成合成語料將是較具潛力的方法。

表 2. CycleGAN 與 StarGAN 合成語料之 MCD

MCD results of D_1 synthesized data				
	$N_1 \rightarrow D_1$(320)	$N_2 \rightarrow D_1$(640)	$N_3 \rightarrow D_1$(320)	Average
StarGAN	0.814±0.06	0.891±0.07	0.913±0.07	**0.872**
CycleGAN	0.779±0.05	1.064±0.16	1.03±0.13	0.958
MCD results of D_2 synthesized data				
	$N_1 \rightarrow D_2$ (320)	$N_2 \rightarrow D_2$ (640)	$N_3 \rightarrow D_2$(320)	Average
StarGAN	1.311±0.16	1.324±0.15	1.240±0.14	**1.292**
CycleGAN	1.516±0.50	1.348±0.19	1.168±0.17	1.344
MCD results of D_3 synthesized data				
	$N_1 \rightarrow D_3$ (320)	$N_2 \rightarrow D_3$ (640)	$N_3 \rightarrow D_3$(320)	Average
StarGAN	1.064±0.21	1.008±0.24	1.178±0.23	1.083
CycleGAN	1.039±0.19	0.974±0.18	1.069±0.15	**1.027**

接著在實驗二中的實作結果如圖 3、圖 4 所示，我們使用兩位構音障礙語者D_1、D_2訓練個人語音辨識器 SD-ASR 來驗證所提出 DSG 是否能提升溝通輔助系統的語音辨識度，並且使用字詞錯誤率(character error rate, CER)來做為評估指標。在測試資料中分為重複語句測試(duplicate test)和半外部測試(half outside test)。Duplicate test 為患者重複語句(TMHINT 語料 288 句)，資料未參與 ASR 模型訓練。Half outside test 測試語句為患者的 TMHINT 語料 32 句，資料未參與 StarGAN 訓練，也沒有放入 ASR 模型訓練，但和語料N有關。在 half outside test 結果中，當訓練資料從原始(original)資料量到增加額外 2 倍合成資料時，可將 CER 從 60%左右降至 13%左右。且後續的 4 倍、9 倍增量也都能持續降低錯誤率，最終增量至 14 倍合成資料時，分別在患者D_1、D_2的 Half outside test 中得到 3.76%與 5.02% CER。

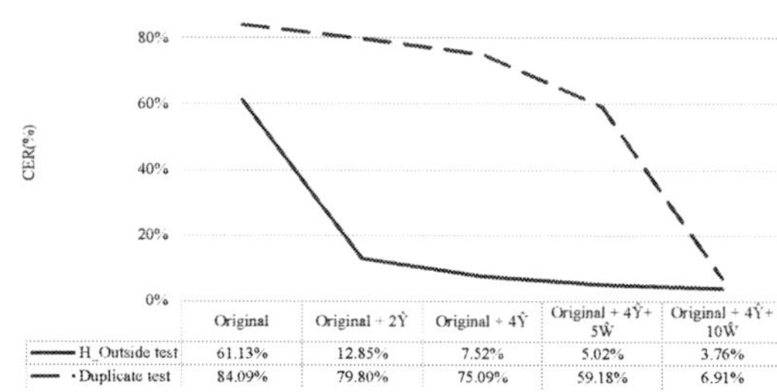

圖 3.實驗二中患者D_1之增量測試結果

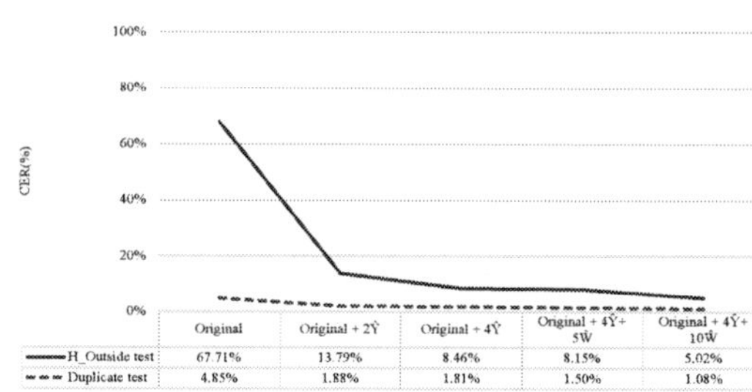

圖 4. 實驗二中患者D_2之增量測試結果

隨後，實驗二更進一步探討所提出 DSG 系統是否優於常見之增量手法(使用正常人語料作為增量資料)，而在 half outside test 中的結果如圖 5、圖 6 所示。其中可以觀察到，前 4 倍增量(4$\hat{Y}$)在兩種增量系統中皆能幫助 ASR 降低錯誤率，但使用 DSG 方法仍比直接加入正常語料的 CER 更低一些。而再加入 5~10 倍的 TTS 語料(5$\widehat{W}$、10$\widehat{W}$)，則可以從兩位語者的結果中發現，未轉換成合成語料的 TTS 會讓測試語料的 CER 有大幅度的上升現象。這是因為大量的 TTS 語料使 ASR 系統的辨識整體的偏向辨識 TTS。這也表示當加入的增量語料若未轉換成合成語料，一旦資料量增加到超越患者的原始語料量許多，會使系統辨識產生偏移。而正常人的發音與患者有著巨大的差異，若未將轉換之合成語料用於 ASR 系統，將導致系統辨識時把患者的發音誤判成正常人的發音，進而無法分類正確的音素，所以錯誤率也隨之大幅提升。而上述的實驗也再進一步的證明本論文提出之方法的效益。

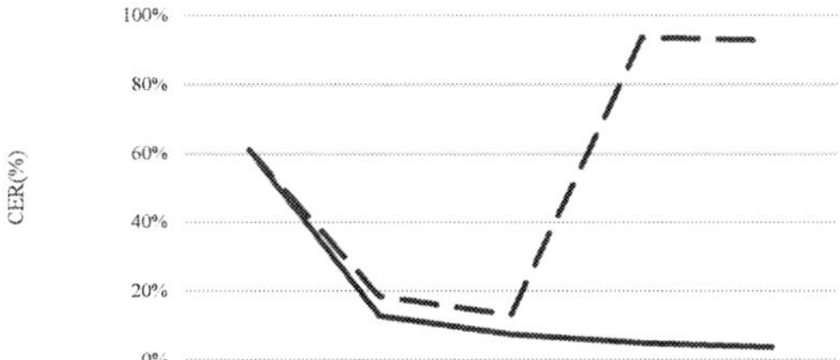

	Original	Original + 2Ŷ	Original + 4Ŷ	Original + 4Ŷ+ 5Ŵ	Original + 4Ŷ+ 10Ŵ
Synthesized	61.13%	12.85%	7.52%	5.02%	3.76%
Normal	61.13%	18.50%	13.17%	93.73%	92.79%

圖 5. 實驗二中，比較患者D_1使用合成語料與正常語料增量差異

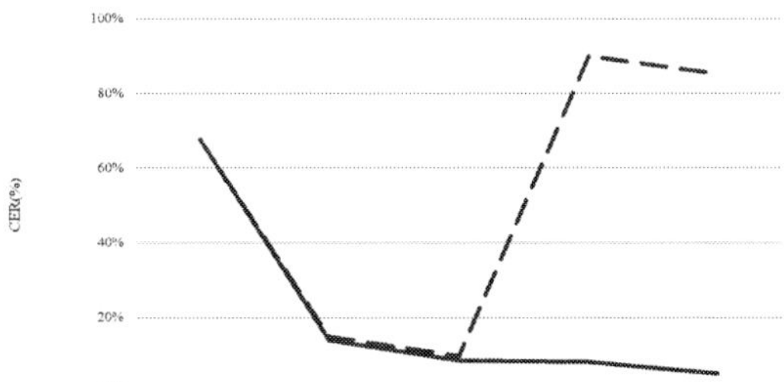

	Original	Original + 2Ŷ	Original + 4Ŷ	Original + 4Ŷ+ 5Ŵ	Original + 4Ŷ+ 10Ŵ
Synthesized	67.71%	13.79%	8.46%	8.15%	5.02%
Normal	67.71%	14.73%	9.72%	89.97%	85.27%

圖 6. 實驗二中，比較患者D_2使用合成語料與正常語料增量差異

五、 結論

本論文主要目的為探討資料增量技術對於以語音驅動為基礎之構音障礙溝通輔具的效益。於實驗結果發現，我們所提出之 DSG 系統所生成之大量患者語料能有效的提升構音障礙溝通輔具的效益。由實驗中我們也證明多語者轉換系統在生成語音質量上優於雙語者轉換技術，並且在訓練成本上有巨大的優勢。而在實驗中也證明了增量系統 DSG 應用在SD-ASR上可以明顯的降低CER，且隨著增量句數的提升可以使錯誤率持續下降。此外，比起僅加入多位正常語者來訓練模型之增量方法，本論文所提出之增量系統更能使 SD-ASR 更專注辨識單一語者。有鑑於本論文之成果，未來我們將基於 DSG 資料增量方式來生成更大量語料，進而期望幫助患者在 Free-talk 情況下有更佳之辨識效益。

Acknowledgments

本研究由科技部射月計畫(MOST110-2218-E-A49A-501)及宇康生科股份有限公司計畫(YM109J052) 支持，特此致謝。

References

American Speech-Language-Hearing Association. (2020, November 02). *Quick Facts About ASHA*. https://www.asha.org/about/press-room/quick-facts/

Calculator, S., Luchko, C. D. A. J. J. o. s., & Disorders, H. (1983). Evaluating the effectiveness of a communication board training program. *48*(2), 185-191.

Dauphin, Y. N., Fan, A., Auli, M., & Grangier, D. (2017). Language modeling with gated convolutional networks. International conference on machine learning,

Hazen, T. J., Shen, W., & White, C. (2009). Query-by-example spoken term detection using phonetic posteriorgram templates. 2009 IEEE Workshop on Automatic Speech Recognition & Understanding,

Huang, M. J. D. o. s. l. p., audiology, N. T. U. o. N., & science, H. (2005). Development of taiwan mandarin hearing in noise test.

Jiao, Y., Tu, M., Berisha, V., & Liss, J. (2018). Simulating dysarthric speech for training data augmentation in clinical speech applications. 2018 IEEE international conference on acoustics, speech and signal processing (ICASSP),

Kameoka, H., Kaneko, T., Tanaka, K., & Hojo, N. (2018). Stargan-vc: Non-parallel many-to-many voice conversion using star generative adversarial networks. 2018 IEEE Spoken Language Technology Workshop (SLT),

Kaneko, T., & Kameoka, H. (2018). Cyclegan-vc: Non-parallel voice conversion using cycle-consistent adversarial networks. 2018 26th European Signal Processing Conference (EUSIPCO),

Kominek, J., Schultz, T., & Black, A. W. (2008). Synthesizer voice quality of new languages calibrated with mean mel cepstral distortion. Spoken Languages Technologies for Under-Resourced Languages,

Lin, C.-S., Ho, C.-W., Chen, W.-C., Chiu, C.-C., & Yeh, M.-S. J. O. A. (2006). Powered wheelchair controlled by eye-tracking system. *36*.

Morise, M., Yokomori, F., Ozawa, K. J. I. T. o. I., & Systems. (2016). WORLD: a vocoder-based high-quality speech synthesis system for real-time applications. *99*(7), 1877-1884.

Murdoch, B. E., & Theodoros, D. G. (2001). Traumatic brain injury: Associated speech, language, and swallowing disorders.

Peddinti, V., Povey, D., & Khudanpur, S. (2015). A time delay neural network architecture for efficient modeling of long temporal contexts. Sixteenth annual conference of the international speech communication association,

Povey, D., Ghoshal, A., Boulianne, G., Burget, L., Glembek, O., Goel, N., . . . Schwarz, P. (2011). The Kaldi speech recognition toolkit. IEEE 2011 workshop on automatic speech recognition and understanding,

Shor, J., Emanuel, D., Lang, O., Tuval, O., Brenner, M., Cattiau, J., . . . Nollstadt, M. (2019). Personalizing ASR for Dysarthric and Accented Speech with Limited Data. *arXiv preprint arXiv:1907.13511.*

Takashima, Y., Takashima, R., Takiguchi, T., & Ariki, Y. (2019). Knowledge transferability between the speech data of persons with dysarthria speaking different languages for dysarthric speech recognition. *IEEE Access, 7*, 164320-164326.

Vachhani, B., Bhat, C., & Kopparapu, S. K. (2018). Data Augmentation Using Healthy Speech for Dysarthric Speech Recognition. Interspeech,

Wang, D., Yu, J., Wu, X., Liu, S., Sun, L., Liu, X., & Meng, H. (2020). End-to-end voice conversion via cross-modal knowledge distillation for dysarthric speech reconstruction. ICASSP 2020-2020 IEEE International Conference on Acoustics, Speech and Signal Processing (ICASSP),

Wikipedia contributors. (27 July 2021 19:52 UTC). *Microsoft Speech API.* https://en.wikipedia.org/w/index.php?title=Microsoft_Speech_API&oldid=1035806404

Yang, S. H., & Chung, M. (2020). Improving dysarthric speech intelligibility using cycle-consistent adversarial training. *arXiv preprint arXiv:2001.04260.*

The 33rd Conference on Computational Linguistics and Speech Processing (ROCLING 2021)
Taoyuan, Taiwan, October 15-16, 2021. The Association for Computational Linguistics and Chinese Language Processing

A Survey of Approaches to Automatic Question Generation: from 2019 to Early 2021

Chao-Yi Lu
Chingshin Academy
Taipei, Taiwan
chaoyilu.zoey@gmail.com

Sin-En Lu
Computer Science and Information Engineering
National Central University
Taoyuan, Taiwan
alznn@g.ncu.edu.tw

Abstract

To provide analysis of recent researches of automatic question generation from text, we surveyed 15 papers between 2019 to early 2021, retrieved from Paper with Code (PwC). Our research follows the survey reported by Kurdi et al. (2020), in which analysis of 93 papers from 2014 to early 2019 are provided. We analyzed the 15 papers from aspects including: (1) purpose of question generation, (2) generation method, and (3) evaluation. We found that recent approaches tend to rely on semantic information and Transformer-based models are attracting increasing interest since they are more efficient. On the other hand, since there isn' t any widely acknowledged automatic evaluation metric designed for question generation, researchers adopt metrics of other natural language processing tasks to compare different systems.

Keywords: Automatic question generation, Survey, Natural language processing

1 Introduction

Questions are crucial tools for assessments and providing assistance throughout the process of learning. The functions of well-designed questions include: (1) providing opportunities to practice retrieving information from memory, (2) giving learners feedback about their misconceptions, (3) focusing learners' attention on the most important material, and (4) reinforcing what learners have acquired through repeating core concepts (Thalheimer, 2003). With the rapid growth of online learning, the demand for questions has increased. However, creating questions by humans is not efficient since the process requires training and cannot produce results immediately.

Input text:
The Royal Family of Enchancia go to watch a Flying Derby race. \
Sofia states that Flying Derby is her favorite sport in the Kingdom, \
with her mother adding how Sofia used to pretend to race using their old mop as her flying horse. \
During the race, James reveals that Royal Prep has its own Flying Derby Team, and Sofia agrees to be there for the tryouts.

Questions and Answers:
answer: The Royal Family of Enchancia
question: Who watchs a Flying Derby race?

answer: flying horse.
question: What did Sofia pretend to race using their old mop?

answer: Flying Derby Team,
question: What is the name of the team that Royal Prep has?

Figure 1: An example of AQG using the model by Lopez et al. (2020). Questions and answers are provided originally as generated. Text source: Sofia the First Wiki[1]

Question generation refers to the task of generating questions from various inputs.(Rus et al., 2008). Compared with humans, automatic question generation (AQG) can produce questions in lower cost and higher efficiency. Despite the development of visual question generation (generating questions from images) is undoubtedly essential since it **combines natural language processing and computer vision** (Sarrouti et al., 2020), the focus of this survey is on AQG from texts due to its extensive usage including assessments (Stanescu et al., 2008; Ai et al., 2015), learning activities, and serving as a data augmentation approach for training Question Answering (QA) systems (Lee et al., 2020; Fabbri et al., 2020). For an example of question generation from text, please refer to Figure 1.

Hoping to compare existing AQG systems in our future works, we search the literature re-

[1] `https://sofia.fandom.com/wiki/Princess_Sofia`

viewed in this paper from Papers with Code[2] (PwC). As a survey paper, our project is concerned with reading and analyzing previous literature on AQG from text. We refer to the survey reported by Kurdi et al. (2020), which contains analysis of 93 papers from 2015 to early 2019, focusing on education. The objectives of Kurdi et al. (2020)'s review are (1) providing an overview of the AQG community and its activities, (2) summarising current QG approaches, (3) identifying the gold-standard performance in AQG, (4) Tracking the evolution of AQG since the review by Alsubait et al. (2016), which includes 81 papers published up to the end of 2014. We focus on the second objective and the evaluation of AQG systems, on the other hand, we discuss RNN-based and Transformer-based methods, both of which are classified as "statistical methods" during the procedure of transforming declarative sentences into inquisitive ones in the review proposed by Kurdi et al. (2020). Since we aim to continue their work and track the evolution of the AQG task, the papers investigated in this review range from 2019 to early 2021.

2 Background

2.1 Summary of Kurdi et al.s' Review

The work of Kurdi et al. (2020) groups the 93 papers they included together if they have at least one shared author and use the same type of AQG approach. There are a total of 72 groups, and evaluations have been made based on these groups. Not only did they provide information on AQG studies about (1) rate of publication, (2) types of papers and publication venues, and (3) research groups, but they also analyzed AQG studies based on multiple dimensions. The most crucial ones are presented in Table 1.

The results of Kurdi et al. (2020)'s evaluation on different dimensions are summarized in Table 1. Regarding "Domain", "Question format", and "Response format", the statistics are similar to the ones purposed by Alsubait et al. (2016), which implies that these aspects of AQG haven't changed much throughout the past decades. Generating domain-specific questions are more common than generating generic ones, and language learning received the most attention; wh- questions and gap-fill questions remain the most popular; multiple choice and free response are two of the most prevalent response formats. As for the development of the AQG field, Kurdi et al. (2020) found an rising tendency of publications per year and research groups, which indicates that AQG is attracting increasing interest and the community is expanding.

2.2 Data Sources

We search PwC for papers from different conferences on the question generation task and only keep papers published from 2019 to early 2021. The search queries used and results are provided in Table 2.

Using the data collecting method mentioned in the previous paragraph, we select 15 papers from conferences and journals including ACL, ICLR, EMNLP, and IJCNLP. Among the 15 papers, 3 were published in 2019 (Alberti et al., 2019; Zhang and Bansal, 2019; Cho et al., 2019a), 8 were published in 2020 (Lee et al., 2020; Pan et al., 2020b; Dhole and Manning, 2020; Fabbri et al., 2020; Chen et al., 2019; Wang et al., 2020; Qi et al., 2020; Su et al., 2020), and 4 in 2021 (Majumder et al., 2021; Pan et al., 2020a; Roemmele et al., 2021; Cho et al., 2019b).

3 Dimensions of AQG

The phrase "dimension" in our paper refers to different aspects of an AQG system. We will be providing analysis regarding (1) purpose of question generation, which is the usage of the systems purposed in review literature, (2) generation method, which stands for the approaches of understanding the input and transforming declarative sentences into inquisitive ones, and (3) evaluation, which includes the metrics and datasets the researchers used.

[2] https://paperswithcode.com/

[3] Categories that occurred three times or less are classified as "Others".

[4] Studies that do not specify any targeted field is classified as "Generic"

[5] Gap-fill questions or distract or generation are considered not having a transformation method since they only remove or select a word or phrase of the input.

[6] In their review, verbalization is defined as "**Any process carried out to improve the surface structure of questions (grammaticality and fluency) or to provide variations of questions (i.e. paraphrasing).**"

Dimension	Categories	studies	Percentage
Purpose	Assessment	40	55.56%
	Education(unspecified)	10	13.89%
	Support Learning	10	13.89%
	Self learning, self-study or self-assessment	9	12.50%
	Generate practice questions	8	11.11%
	Tutoring	5	6.94%
	Others[3]	5	6.94%
Input	Text	43	59.72%
	QuestionStem/QuestionKey	10	13.89%
	Ontology	8	8.33%
	RDFKB	5	6.94%
	Others[3]	10	13.89%
Domain	Generic[4]	33	45.83%
	Language	21	29.17%
	Math	4	5.56%
	Others[3]	13	18.06%
Generation method-Level of understanding	Semantic	60	83.33%
	Syntactic only	10	13.89%
Generation method-Procedure of transformation	Template	27	37.50%
	Rule	16	22.22%
	Statistical methods	9	12.50%
	Not having one[5]	20	27.78%
Question Format	wh-questions	22	30.56%
	Gap-fill Questions	20	27.78%
	Word Problem	4	5.56%
	Others[3]	37	51.39%
Response Format	Multiple Choice	38	52.78%
	Free Response	36	50.00%
	True/false	2	2.78%
	Sound	1	1.39%
Difficulty Controlling	Yes	14	19.44%
	No	58	80.56%
Feedback Generation	Yes	1	1.39%
	No	71	98.61%
Verbalization[6]	Yes	10	13.89%
	No	61	84.72%
	Not Clear	1	1.39%
Evaluation	Expert Review	22	30.56%
	Compare with Human-authored questions	15	20.83%
	Mock Exam	14	19.44%
	Automatic Evaluation	12	16.67%
	Student Review	10	13.89%
	Review(not clear by who)/Author Review	10	13.89%
	Crowd-sourcing	9	12.50%
	Compare with Another Generator	8	11.11%

Table 1: Results of Kurdi et al.s' review. A study may include multiple purposes and question formats

Database	Conference	Filter by Task	No. of Search Results	No. of Studies Included
PwC	ACL 2019	Question Generation	5	1
	ACL 2020	Question Generation	5	4
	NeurlPS 2019	Question Generation	1	0
	NAACL 2019	Question Generation	1	0
	NAACL 2021	Question Generation	2	2
	ICLR 2020	Question Generation	1	1
	ICLR 2021	Question Generation	2	0
	EMNLP 2020	Question Generation	4	1
	IJCNLP 2019	Question Generation	3	2
	EACL 2021	Question Generation	3	2
	Findings of the Association for Computational Linguistics 2020	Question Generation	3	2
			Total: 28	Total: 15

Table 2: Search queries and results. **No. of Search Results** shows the total papers involved with question generation. **No. of Studies Included** refer the papers are under the category we are discussing.

3.1 Purpose of Question Generation

We found out that six of our reviewed papers apply AQG for data augmentation of question answering (QA), three aim to generate clarification questions, questions that identify important and missing information in the given text, one for boosting reading comprehension, and eight papers do not have clearly-stated purpose. The result is different from that of the review reported by Kurdi et al. (2020). (Table 1). As for domain, every paper falls into the "generic" category. Despite not included, we find the cross-lingual training method proposed by Kumar et al. (2019) useful for rare languages.

3.2 Generation Method

In this section, we will discuss several approaches commonly used in AQG. In Kurdi et al. (2020)'s review, Generation methods are classified based on the level of understanding and the procedure of transformation. Regarding the level of understanding, the two categories are (1) syntactic approach, which is defined as leveraging syntactic features of the input (i.e. part of speech), and (2) semantic approach, which requires deeper understanding than lexical and syntactic information, such as contextual similarity and named entities recognition. For example, obtaining information through semantic role labeling (Màrquez et al., 2008), which means identifying the semantic relations held among a predicate and its associated properties, are considered using a semantic approach.

As for the procedure of transformation, AQG has been mainly tackled by rule-based approach, defined as template-based in this survey along with the one reported by Kurdi et al. (2020), and neural QG approach (Du et al., 2017), classified as a "statistical method" in our paper and Kurdi et al. (2020)s' work. Following the categories purposed by Kurdi et al. (2020), we adopt a more detailed classification, adding rule-based into the categories. The three categories are as following: (1) template-based, which refers to structures consisting of fixed texts and spaces that will be substituted by values, (2) rule-based, which annotates the input to navigate the selection of a suitable question type and the manipulation of the input to construct questions, and (3) statistical methods, referring to learning the transformation to inquisitive sentences from training data.

3.2.1 Level of understanding

Level of understanding discusses the extend AQG systems comprehend the input text. According to Dhole and Manning (2020), whose system takes semantic roles as the heuristic information, relying on syntactic information alone is unlikely to obtain sufficient understanding for answering complicated questions that contain multiple "wh" words. Nine studies (Lee et al., 2020; Dhole and Manning, 2020; Wang et al., 2020; Zhang and Bansal, 2019; Pan et al., 2020b; Chen et al., 2019; Fabbri et al., 2020 Cho et al., 2019b; Su et al., 2020) take advantage of both semantic and syntactic information, three systems (Alberti et al., 2019; Cho et al., 2019a; Qi et al., 2020) exploit only semantic features, and three of the included studies (Majumder et al., 2021; Pan et al., 2020a; Roemmele et al., 2021)only rely on syntactic features.

As shown in Table 1, Kurdi et al. (2020) suggests that most of the AQG studies from 2014 to early 2019 take semantic features into consideration, and we observe that the trend of performing AQG through semantic approach has become more and more prevalent among systems purposed between 2019 and early 2021.

3.2.2 Procedure of Transformation

We take the survey reported by Kurdi et al. (2020) as reference of the categories. As presented in Table 3, various statistical methods are the most popular, while the use of rules and templates each reported by one study. The results are different from that of the review by Kurdi et al. (2020)(see Table 1). Compared with rule-based and template-based techniques, which demands human effort including expert knowledge to construct guidelines and the variety of questions generated are limited, statistical approaches require far less labor and enable better language flexibility (Pan et al., 2020b; Tuan et al., 2019). We will succinctly introduce RNN-based (recurrent neural networks) and Transformer in the following section.

RNN-Based RNN-based QG models use encoder-decoder architecture to transform one sequence into another. The major drawback of RNN-based approaches is that they can only function sequentially, which makes them slow and suboptimal for longer sequences (Vaswani et al., 2017). Since Serban et al. (2016) and Du et al. (2017) applied neural-based approaches for AQG, many improvements of RNN-based

Method	Approach	Studies
Statistical methods	RNN-based	8
	Transformer	4
	Graph to sequence	1
Template	-	1
Rule	-	1

Table 3: Procedure of Transformation. **Statistical methods** refers to the approaches in which systems are trained upon massive amount of data. In our study, three approaches are reported: RNN models, Transformer, and Graph to sequence. As for **Rule-based** and **Template-based** methods, the former defines the law of the question formation, the models have to generate the whole sequence; the latter has prewritten templates, the models only need to fill in the blanks.

models have been proposed. For instance, Du et al. (2017) adopt an attention mechanism to make the models focus on certain elements of the input.

Transformer Transformer was proposed by Vaswani et al. (2017). Like Seq2Seq, Transformer converts one sequence to another one with encoder and decoder. However, instead of recurrent networks, Transformer uses self-attention mechanism instead, which can be seen as the most important feature of Transformer. In self-attention, a word is operated with every other word, including those that appear later. Furthermore, since self-attention computation has no notion of the order of the inputs, parallelization is allowed and boosts the efficiency. Since word order is an important information as it may change the meaning of the input sentences, the relative positions of the words are added to the embedded representation (n-dimensional vector) of each word.

3.3 Paper Study

After discussing the generation methods, we will move on to the overview of the AQG studies from 2019 to early 2021. In the 15 papers we reviewed, 10 papers take various approaches including reinforcement learning, encoder-decoder, knowledge graph along with RNN, semantic graph, and rule-based method to tackle QG directly; 5 researches implement QG as a method of generating datasets or gather question-answer pairs for QA training. We will mainly describe those papers focusing on QG succinctly in the following paragraphs. Zhang and Bansal (2019) apply POS and NER to deep contextualized word vectors to enrich input information, along with self-attention mechanism and reinforcement learning implemented to solve the "semantic drift" problem in QG. Two semantics-enhanced rewards, QPP and QAP were proposed, the former refers to the probability of the generated question and the ground-truth question being paraphrased, and the latter stands for the probability of the generated question being correctly answered by the given answer. The proposed mechanism were obtained from downstream question paraphrasing and question answering tasks, aiming to improve the quality of questions generated by regularizing the QG model to produce semantically valid questions.

Being aware of the fact that ignoring structure information hidden in text or excessively relying on cross-entropy loss can lead to problems such as exposure bias, inconsistency between training and test measurements, and inability to fully exploit the answer information, Chen et al. (2019) propose a reinforcement learning based graph-to-sequence model for QG. Their model includes a Graph2Seq (Xu et al., 2018) generator with an encoder based on a Bidirectional Gated Graph Neural Network, which is introduced to learn the graph embeddings from the constructed text graph effectively. Authors also proposed a hybrid evaluator with objective that combines cross-entropy and RL losses to ensure syntactic and semantical validness. The paper further introduces an effective Deep Alignment Network for incorporating the answer information into the passage at both the word and contextual levels.

The semantically one-to-many relationships between source and target sentences in QG often leads to poor performance when trying to use standard Encoder-decoder model to generate a diverse and fluent output. Cho et al. (2019a) present a method for diverse generation that separates diversification and generation stages. The diversification stage takes advantage of content selection to map the source to multiple sequences, also known as "one-to-many mapping". The generation stage uses a standard encoder-decoder model to perform one-to-one mapping by generating a target sequence given each selected content from the source. In diversification stage, a new module named SELECTOR is proposed to identify key contents to focus on during generation.

Since failing to model fact information may cause QG systems to generate irrelevant and uninformative questions, Wang et al. (2020) defines a new task of question generation in which the system is given a query in the knowledge graph of the input content. The authors further divide the task into two steps, query representation learning and query-based question generation. First, the model learns a query representation which stands for the fact information that will be mentioned in the query path, then a RNN-based generator is employed to produce corresponding questions based on these facts.The two module were trained together in an end-to-end fashion, and the interaction between these two modules is enforced in a various framework.

Pan et al. (2020b) focus on Deep Question Generation (DQG) task, which aims to generate complex questions that require reasoning over multiple pieces of input information. Authors present an innovative structure consisting of three parts: semantic graph construction, semantic-enriched document representation, and joint-task question generation. The proposed model becomes the first research to construct a semantic-level graph of the input document and encode the semantic graph by introducing an attention-based GGNN (Li et al., 2015) in QG area. After that, the document-level and graph-level representations are fused to conduct joint training on content selection and question decoding. Their method allows models to capture the global structure of the document and facilitate reasoning, which greatly reduces semantic errors, increasing the quality of generated question, and improves performance on HotpotQA (Yang et al., 2018).

Multi-hop Question Generation also requires assembling and summarizing information from multiple relevant documents. (Gupta et al., 2020). Proposed by Su et al. (2020), Multi-Hop Encoding Fusion Network for Question Generation (MulQG), features context encoding in multiple hops with Graph

Convolutional Network and encoding fusion via an Encoder Reasoning Gate. The authors claim to be the first to tackle multi-hop reasoning over paragraphs without sentence-level information. Pan et al. (2020a) propose MQA-QG, an unsupervised framework for generating human-like multi-hop QA training data. MQA-QG generates questions by first selecting relevant information from each data source and then integrating the multiple information to form a multi-hop question. Using solely the generated training data, the authors successfully train a competent multi-hop QA system.

Roemmele et al. (2021) present a system that integrates QA and QG in order to produce QA pairs that convey the content of multi-paragraph documents. They explore the impact of different training data by having one system trained on SQUAD and NEWSQA, one on the production of rule-based QG systems, and one on both kinds of data; the latter is the most outstanding. Since their model performs extractive QA, in which answers to questions are extracted directly from the given text, the evaluation focus on whether questions are answerable and relative to the input text.

Dhole and Manning (2020) consider QG as a generally simple syntactic transformation influenced by semantics. They porposed Syn-QG, a QG system, to implement their obeservation. The system includes a set of transparent syntactic rules that utilize universal dependencies, shallow semantic parsing, lexical resources, and custom rules of transforming declarative sentences into question-answer pairs. The authors apply back-translation over the rules to improve syntactic fluency and eliminate grammatical errors at a slight cost of generating irrelevant questions. The crowd-sourced evaluations result shows that thier system can generate a larger number of grammatically correct and relevant questions than previous QG systems.

Questions also serve the need of acquiring information.Majumder et al. (2021) believe that the ability to generate questions that identify useful missing information in a given context is important, and to identify these information, humans compare global view consists of previous experience with similar contexts to the given context. The authors propose a model for clarification question generation in which "what is missing" is identified first by comparing the global and the local view and then a model identifies what is useful and generate a question about it. Qi et al. (2020) dedicate their research to the scenario in which the questioner is given the shared conversation history but not the context from which answers are drawn, thus must ask questions to obtain new information. To generate pragmatic questions, the authors use reinforcement learning to optimize an informativeness metric they propose, along with a reward function which encourages more specific questions.

In this paragraph, we will briefly introduce the researches aiming to generate question-answer pairs or obtaining training data for QA. Alberti et al. (2019) introduce a novel method of generating synthetic question answering corpora by combining models of question generation and answer extraction, and filtering the results to ensure roundtrip consistency. Significant improvements were obtained after pretraining on the resulting corpora. The authors also describe a variant that does full sequence-to-sequence pretraining for question generation, obtaining outstanding performance on SQuAD 2.0 (Rajpurkar et al., 2018). Fabbri et al. (2020) demonstrate that generating questions for QA training by applying a simple template on a related, retrieved sentence rather than the original context sentence allows the model to learn more complex context-question relationships thus improves unsupervised QA. To cope with the scarcity of question-answer pairs for a specific domain with human annotation, Lee et al. (2020) propose a hierarchical conditional variational auto encoder (HCVAE) for generating QA pairs from unstructured texts given as context and maximizing mutual information between generated QA pairs to ensure consistency.

3.4 Evaluation

According to Amidei et al. (2018), currently, the evaluation of automatic question generation includes a wide variety of both intrinsic and extrinsic evaluation methodologies. Since the evaluation of AQG has no exclusive, commonly agreed metric, most literature adopts multiple evaluation metrics. The statistics of our survey are provided in Table 5. Unlike the results of the review reported by Kurdi et al. (2020) (Table 1), the most common evaluation method is comparison with manually written ground truth questions. Since there is no common framework for evaluating AQG systems, researchers use n-gram models including BLEU (Papineni et al., 2002), METEOR (Banerjee and Lavie, 2005), and ROUGE (Lin, 2004). Note that none of the mentioned metrics were created specifically for the evaluation of AQG, BLEU and METEOR were designed for evaluating machine translation, while ROUGE aims to evaluate text summarization. Nema and Khapra (2018) has delineated that the evaluation of natural language generation systems, including those of AQG, using the aforementioned n-gram based similarity metrics sometimes shows poor correlation with human judgments in terms of answerability.

On the other hand, the variety of datasets used for evaluation also makes comparison between different models more difficult (Amidei et al., 2018). We noticed that except Pan et al. (2020b) and Cho et al. (2019a), other studies included the SQuAD (Rajpurkar et al., 2016) in their evaluation datasets or used it as the only source (See Table 4 for the details). Nevertheless, SQuAD 2.0 contains unanswerable questions written by crowdworkers while SQuAD 1.1 does not, which can affect the result of evaluation. Comparison with another generator remains the second most popular. 8 of the studies compare the results of automatic evaluation with baseline models and 6 studies compare with other models through human evaluation. The most common dimensions include fluency, relevance, syntactic or grammar correctness, with occurrences of four, three, and three, respectively.

Evaluation Method	No. of Studies
Compare with manually written ground truth through automatic evaluation	8
Compare with another generator	8
Crowd sourcing	4
Human review	3

Table 4: Evaluation Methods. Multiple evaluation methods can be implemented in one study. The statistics demonstrate that using ground truth written manually for evaluation, or using the answers from other QG generator models for comparison, is the mainstream evaluating method in recent years.

4 Conclusion

In our survey, analysis of 15 AQG conference papers from PwC reported between 2019 and early 2021 is provided, taking the survey by Kurdi et al. (2020) as reference and tracking the development of the AQG field. Focusing on the purposes, methods, and evaluation of AQG, our findings are as follow:

(1) Purposes of AQG

Recent studies tend to focus on data augmentation of QA. 6 of the 15 papers we review use AQG to generate QA training data.

(2) Generation Method

When it comes to the level of understanding, most AQG systems take semantic information into consideration since it provides the systems with more understanding to answer complicated questions. Regarding the procedure of transformation, Statistical methods have become more popular for the AQG task. Since Transformer provides self-attention and parallelization thus significantly boosts accuracy and efficiency, respectively, it is attracting increasing interest.

(4) Evaluation

Despite there being no widely acknowledged evaluation metric for AQG, researchers adopt automatic evaluation metrics for other NLP tasks to compare with human-authored questions and different models.

(5) Evolvement of AQG since Kurdi et al. (2020) s' survey

The results of our review differ from that of Kurdi et al. (2020). Kurdi et al. (2020) when it comes to the purpose of using AQG and the process of creating inquisitive sentences. We found out that recent researches tend to focus on data augmentation of QA systems instead of generating assessments, and using templates to convert input text into questions is gradually replaced by implementing RNN-Based methods and Transformer.

Dataset	Source	Development method	Content	OCC
SQuAD1.1	Wikipedia	Crowdsourcing	Questions and paragraph-answer pairs	9
SQuAD2.0	Wikipedia	Crowdsourcing	SQuAD1.1 plus unanswerable questions	2
Hotpot QA	Wikipedia	Crowdsourcing	QA pairs and evidence documents	4
Natural Questions (NQ)	Search queries issued to Google search engine	Crowdsourcing	Questions corresponding Wikipedia page, a long response and a short one	2
HarvestingQA	Wikipedia	Automatic	QA pairs and Wikipedia articles	1
TriviaQA	Web, Wikipedia	Crowdsourcing	QA pairs and evidence documents	1
DROP	Wikipedia	Crowdsourcing	Questions	1
Amazon Review	Amazon.com	Not specified	Relationships between objects, an image and a category label	1
Amazon Question-answering	Amazon.com	Collecting and labeling	Questions and answers about products	1
HybridQA	Wikipedia	Crowdsourcing	Multi-hop questions, Wikipedia table and passages linked with it	1
NEWSQA	News articles from CNN	Crowdsourcing	Questions and answers	1
MS-MARCO QA	Search queries issued to Bing or Cortana, web pages	Crowdsourcing	Questions, related web pages, crowd-sourced answer and supporting information if answerable	1
QuAC	Wikimedia foundation	Crowdsourcing	Information-seeking QA dialogues	1

Table 5: Information of datasets used in reviewed studies. Of the 15 papers, a total of 13 datasets are used, including SQuAD, HotpotQA, Natural Question (Kwiatkowski et al., 2019), HarvestingQA (Du and Cardie, 2018), TriviaQA (Joshi et al., 2017), DROP (Dua et al., 2019), Amazon Review (McAuley et al., 2015), AmazonQuestion-answering (McAuley and Yang, 2016), HybridQA (Chen et al., 2020), NEWSQA (Trischler et al., 2016), MS-MARCO QA (Nguyen et al., 2016), QuAC (Choi et al., 2018). We also provide their data source, develop method, and content description of the data.

References

Renlong Ai, Sebastian Krause, Walter Kasper, Feiyu Xu, and Hans Uszkoreit. 2015. Semi-automatic generation of multiple-choice tests from mentions of semantic relations. In *Proceedings of the 2nd Workshop on Natural Language Processing Techniques for Educational Applications*, pages 26–33.

Chris Alberti, Daniel Andor, Emily Pitler, Jacob Devlin, and Michael Collins. 2019. Synthetic qa corpora generation with roundtrip consistency. *arXiv preprint arXiv:1906.05416*.

Tahani Alsubait, Bijan Parsia, and Ulrike Sattler. 2016. Ontology-based multiple choice question generation. *KI-Künstliche Intelligenz*, 30(2):183–188.

Jacopo Amidei, Paul Piwek, and Alistair Willis. 2018. Evaluation methodologies in automatic question generation 2013-2018. In *Proceedings of the 11th International Conference on Natural Language Generation*, pages 307–317, Tilburg University, The Netherlands. Association for Computational Linguistics.

Satanjeev Banerjee and Alon Lavie. 2005. Meteor: An automatic metric for mt evaluation with improved correlation with human judgments. In *Proceedings of the acl workshop on intrinsic and extrinsic evaluation measures for machine translation and/or summarization*, pages 65–72.

Wenhu Chen, Hanwen Zha, Zhiyu Chen, Wenhan Xiong, Hong Wang, and William Wang. 2020. Hybridqa: A dataset of multi-hop question answering over tabular and textual data. *arXiv preprint arXiv:2004.07347*.

Yu Chen, Lingfei Wu, and Mohammed J Zaki. 2019. Reinforcement learning based graph-to-sequence model for natural question generation. *arXiv preprint arXiv:1908.04942*.

Jaemin Cho, Minjoon Seo, and Hannaneh Hajishirzi. 2019a. Mixture content selection for diverse sequence generation. *arXiv preprint arXiv:1909.01953*.

Woon Sang Cho, Yizhe Zhang, Sudha Rao, Asli Celikyilmaz, Chenyan Xiong, Jianfeng Gao, Mengdi Wang, and Bill Dolan. 2019b. Contrastive multi-document question generation. *arXiv preprint arXiv:1911.03047*.

Eunsol Choi, He He, Mohit Iyyer, Mark Yatskar, Wen-tau Yih, Yejin Choi, Percy Liang, and Luke Zettlemoyer. 2018. Quac: Question answering in context. *arXiv preprint arXiv:1808.07036*.

Kaustubh D Dhole and Christopher D Manning. 2020. Syn-qg: Syntactic and shallow semantic rules for question generation. *arXiv preprint arXiv:2004.08694*.

Xinya Du and Claire Cardie. 2018. Harvesting paragraph-level question-answer pairs from wikipedia. *arXiv preprint arXiv:1805.05942*.

Xinya Du, Junru Shao, and Claire Cardie. 2017. Learning to ask: Neural question generation for reading comprehension. *arXiv preprint arXiv:1705.00106*.

Dheeru Dua, Yizhong Wang, Pradeep Dasigi, Gabriel Stanovsky, Sameer Singh, and Matt Gardner. 2019. Drop: A reading comprehension benchmark requiring discrete reasoning over paragraphs. *arXiv preprint arXiv:1903.00161*.

Alexander R Fabbri, Patrick Ng, Zhiguo Wang, Ramesh Nallapati, and Bing Xiang. 2020. Template-based question generation from retrieved sentences for improved unsupervised question answering. *arXiv preprint arXiv:2004.11892*.

Deepak Gupta, Hardik Chauhan, Akella Ravi Tej, Asif Ekbal, and Pushpak Bhattacharyya. 2020. Reinforced multi-task approach for multi-hop question generation. *arXiv preprint arXiv:2004.02143*.

Mandar Joshi, Eunsol Choi, Daniel S Weld, and Luke Zettlemoyer. 2017. Triviaqa: A large scale distantly supervised challenge dataset for reading comprehension. *arXiv preprint arXiv:1705.03551*.

Vishwajeet Kumar, Nitish Joshi, Arijit Mukherjee, Ganesh Ramakrishnan, and Preethi Jyothi. 2019. Cross-lingual training for automatic question generation. *arXiv preprint arXiv:1906.02525*.

Ghader Kurdi, Jared Leo, Bijan Parsia, Uli Sattler, and Salam Al-Emari. 2020. A systematic review of automatic question generation for educational purposes. *International Journal of Artificial Intelligence in Education*, 30(1):121–204.

Tom Kwiatkowski, Jennimaria Palomaki, Olivia Redfield, Michael Collins, Ankur Parikh, Chris Alberti, Danielle Epstein, Illia Polosukhin, Jacob Devlin, Kenton Lee, et al. 2019. Natural questions: a benchmark for question answering research. *Transactions of the Association for Computational Linguistics*, 7:453–466.

Dong Bok Lee, Seanie Lee, Woo Tae Jeong, Donghwan Kim, and Sung Ju Hwang. 2020. Generating diverse and consistent qa pairs from contexts with information-maximizing hierarchical conditional vaes. *arXiv preprint arXiv:2005.13837*.

Yujia Li, Daniel Tarlow, Marc Brockschmidt, and Richard Zemel. 2015. Gated graph sequence neural networks. *arXiv preprint arXiv:1511.05493*.

Chin-Yew Lin. 2004. Rouge: A package for automatic evaluation of summaries. In *Text summarization branches out*, pages 74–81.

Luis Enrico Lopez, Diane Kathryn Cruz, Jan Christian Blaise Cruz, and Charibeth Cheng. 2020. Transformer-based end-to-end question generation. *arXiv preprint arXiv:2005.01107*.

Bodhisattwa Prasad Majumder, Sudha Rao, Michel Galley, and Julian McAuley. 2021. Ask what's missing and what's useful: Improving clarification question generation using global knowledge. *arXiv preprint arXiv:2104.06828*.

Lluís Màrquez, Xavier Carreras, Kenneth C Litkowski, and Suzanne Stevenson. 2008. Semantic role labeling: an introduction to the special issue.

Julian McAuley, Christopher Targett, Qinfeng Shi, and Anton Van Den Hengel. 2015. Image-based recommendations on styles and substitutes. In *Proceedings of the 38th international ACM SIGIR conference on research and development in information retrieval*, pages 43–52.

Julian McAuley and Alex Yang. 2016. Addressing complex and subjective product-related queries with customer reviews. In *Proceedings of the 25th International Conference on World Wide Web*, pages 625–635.

Preksha Nema and Mitesh M Khapra. 2018. Towards a better metric for evaluating question generation systems. *arXiv preprint arXiv:1808.10192*.

Tri Nguyen, Mir Rosenberg, Xia Song, Jianfeng Gao, Saurabh Tiwary, Rangan Majumder, and Li Deng. 2016. Ms marco: A human generated machine reading comprehension dataset. In *CoCo@ NIPS*.

Liangming Pan, Wenhu Chen, Wenhan Xiong, Min-Yen Kan, and William Yang Wang. 2020a. Unsupervised multi-hop question answering by question generation. *arXiv preprint arXiv:2010.12623*.

Liangming Pan, Yuxi Xie, Yansong Feng, Tat-Seng Chua, and Min-Yen Kan. 2020b. Semantic graphs for generating deep questions. *arXiv preprint arXiv:2004.12704*.

Kishore Papineni, Salim Roukos, Todd Ward, and Wei-Jing Zhu. 2002. Bleu: a method for automatic evaluation of machine translation. In *Proceedings of the 40th annual meeting of the Association for Computational Linguistics*, pages 311–318.

Peng Qi, Yuhao Zhang, and Christopher D Manning. 2020. Stay hungry, stay focused: Generating informative and specific questions in information-seeking conversations. *arXiv preprint arXiv:2004.14530*.

Pranav Rajpurkar, Robin Jia, and Percy Liang. 2018. Know what you don't know: Unanswerable questions for squad. *arXiv preprint arXiv:1806.03822*.

Pranav Rajpurkar, Jian Zhang, Konstantin Lopyrev, and Percy Liang. 2016. Squad: 100,000+ questions for machine comprehension of text. *arXiv preprint arXiv:1606.05250*.

Melissa Roemmele, Deep Sidhpura, Steve DeNeefe, and Ling Tsou. 2021. Answerquest: A system for generating question-answer items from multi-paragraph documents. *arXiv preprint arXiv:2103.03820*.

Vasile Rus, Zhiqiang Cai, and Art Graesser. 2008. Question generation: Example of a multi-year evaluation campaign. *Proc WS on the QGSTEC*.

Mourad Sarrouti, Asma Ben Abacha, and Dina Demner-Fushman. 2020. Visual question generation from radiology images. In *Proceedings of the First Workshop on Advances in Language and Vision Research*, pages 12–18.

Iulian Vlad Serban, Alberto García-Durán, Caglar Gulcehre, Sungjin Ahn, Sarath Chandar, Aaron Courville, and Yoshua Bengio. 2016. Generating factoid questions with recurrent neural networks: The 30m factoid question-answer corpus. *arXiv preprint arXiv:1603.06807*.

Liana Stanescu, Cosmin Stoica Spahiu, Anca Ion, and Andrei Spahiu. 2008. Question generation for learning evaluation. In *2008 International Multiconference on Computer Science and Information Technology*, pages 509–513. IEEE.

Dan Su, Yan Xu, Wenliang Dai, Ziwei Ji, Tiezheng Yu, and Pascale Fung. 2020. Multi-hop question generation with graph convolutional network. *arXiv preprint arXiv:2010.09240*.

Will Thalheimer. 2003. The learning benefits of questions. *Work Learning Research*.

Adam Trischler, Tong Wang, Xingdi Yuan, Justin Harris, Alessandro Sordoni, Philip Bachman, and Kaheer Suleman. 2016. Newsqa: A machine comprehension dataset. *arXiv preprint arXiv:1611.09830*.

Luu Anh Tuan, Darsh J. Shah, and Regina Barzilay. 2019. Capturing greater context for question generation. *CoRR*, abs/1910.10274.

Ashish Vaswani, Noam Shazeer, Niki Parmar, Jakob Uszkoreit, Llion Jones, Aidan N Gomez, Lukasz Kaiser, and Illia Polosukhin. 2017. Attention is all you need. *arXiv preprint arXiv:1706.03762*.

Siyuan Wang, Zhongyu Wei, Zhihao Fan, Zengfeng Huang, Weijian Sun, Qi Zhang, and Xuan-Jing Huang. 2020. Pathqg: Neural question generation from facts. In *Proceedings of the 2020 Conference on Empirical Methods in Natural Language Processing (EMNLP)*, pages 9066–9075.

Kun Xu, Lingfei Wu, Zhiguo Wang, Yansong Feng, Michael Witbrock, and Vadim Sheinin. 2018. Graph2seq: Graph to sequence learning with attention-based neural networks. *arXiv preprint arXiv:1804.00823*.

Zhilin Yang, Peng Qi, Saizheng Zhang, Yoshua Bengio, William Cohen, Ruslan Salakhutdinov, and Christopher D. Manning. 2018. HotpotQA: A dataset for diverse, explainable multi-hop question answering. In *Proceedings of the 2018 Conference on Empirical Methods in Natural Language Processing*, pages 2369–2380, Brussels, Belgium. Association for Computational Linguistics.

Shiyue Zhang and Mohit Bansal. 2019. Addressing semantic drift in question generation for semi-supervised question answering. *arXiv preprint arXiv:1909.06356*.

The 33rd Conference on Computational Linguistics and Speech Processing (ROCLING 2021)
Taoyuan, Taiwan, October 15-16, 2021. The Association for Computational Linguistics and Chinese Language Processing

一個基於 BERT 與學生架構的檢索模型
A BERT-based Siamese-structured Retrieval Model

姜宏昀
Hung-Yun Chiang
國立臺灣科技大學
National Taiwan University
of Science and Technology
harrychiang0@gmail.com

陳冠宇
Kuan-Yu Chen
國立臺灣科技大學
National Taiwan University
of Science and Technology
kychen@mail.ntust.edu.tw

摘要

由於深度學習的發展，在以 Transformer 為架構的雙向編碼器 BERT 的帶領下，自然語言處理的相關任務獲得長足的進步。資訊檢索任務是從大量的文件中，尋找出與使用者查詢最相關的結果。雖然基於 BERT 的檢索模型已在許多研究中展現優異的任務成效，但這些模型通常有著計算量龐大或需要大量額外儲存空間的問題。有鑑於此，本研究提出一套基於 BERT 與學生架構的檢索模型，不僅擁有以預訓練語言模型為主體的優點，更具備了自動查詢擴增技術，與使用強化學習於模型訓練。因此，我們所提出的檢索模型不僅改善了現有方法的問題，也在三個公開的大型資料集中，驗證了它的檢索成效。

Abstract

Due to the development of deep learning, the natural language processing tasks have made great progresses by leveraging the bidirectional encoder representations from Transformers (BERT). The goal of information retrieval is to search the most relevant results for the user's query from a large set of documents. Although BERT-based retrieval models have shown excellent results in many studies, these models usually suffer from the need for large amounts of computations and/or additional storage spaces. In view of the flaws, a BERT-based Siamese-structured retrieval model (BESS) is proposed in this paper. BESS not only inherits the merits of pre-trained language models, but also can generate extra information to compensate the original query automatically. Besides, the reinforcement learning strategy is introduced to make the model more robust. Accordingly, we evaluate BESS on three public-available corpora, and the experimental results demonstrate the efficiency of the proposed retrieval model.

關鍵字：BERT、資訊檢索、學生架構、查詢擴增、強化學習

Keywords: BERT, Information Retrieval, Siamese-structured, Query Expansion, Reinforcement Learning

1 緒論

資訊檢索(Information Retrieval)是自然語言處理中一個重要的研究題目，目標是從大量的文件、段落或句子中，尋找出與使用者輸入之查詢(Query)最相關的答案。根據檢索內容的不同，資訊檢索任務又可分為文件檢索(Document Retrieval) (Yilmaz et al., 2019; Hofstätter et al., 2020; Mitra et al., 2020; Chen et al., 2020; Saar et al., 2020)與段落檢索(Passage Retrieval) (Cohen et al., 2018; Karpukhin et al., 2020; Khattab and Zaharia., 2020; Joel et al., 2020 ;Qu et al., 2021)。在過去的研究中，詞頻(Term Frequency) (Luhn, 1957)與反文件頻(Inverse Document Frequency) (Jones, 1972)是最常被使用的特徵表示法。詞頻是計算一個詞在文件中出現的次數，次數越高，通常代表這個詞在文件中是比較重要的；反文件頻則是一個詞出現在整個資料集中的文件比例之倒數，代表著這個詞的獨特性與鑑別性。藉由計算每一個詞的詞頻與反文件頻，文件與查詢可被分別表示為一組離散的特徵，藉由不同的檢索演算法，就可以計算每一篇文件

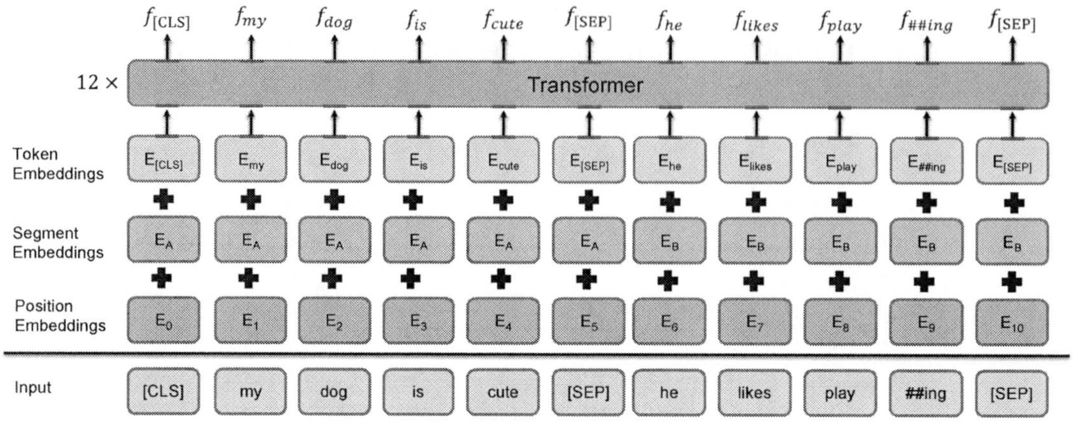

圖 1: BERT 模型架構圖。

與查詢的相關性分數，做為文件排序的依據並輸出。常見的檢索模型包含空間向量模型(Vector space model) (Salton et al., 1975)與 Okapi Best Match 25 (BM25) (Robertson et al., 1995)等。雖然這類方法簡單、快速，並且可以獲得相當的檢索成效，但僅透過關鍵詞匹配來計算相關性分數，不僅無法考慮查詢與文件的語意資訊，亦無法解決同義詞與一詞多義的問題。為此，後續有許多檢索模型紛紛提出，包含潛藏語意分析(Latent Semantic Analysis, LSA) (Deerwester et al., 1990)與主題模型(Topic Model) (Hofmann, 1999; Papadimitriou et al., 2000; Blei et al., 2003)等。

受惠於深度學習的蓬勃發展，自然語言處理的相關任務也在近期有了突破性的進展。以 Transformer (Vaswani et al., 2017)為主要架構的雙向編碼器 BERT (Bidirectional Encoder Representations from Transformers) (Devlin et al., 2019)及各種變形模型，例如 XLNet (Yang et al., 2019)、RoBERTa (Liu et al., 2019) 與 Electra (Clark et al., 2020)等，皆是以非監督式的方式訓練一個語言模型，在預訓練(Pre-trained)的語言模型完成後，針對各式下游任務，這類模型僅需以少量的標記資料進行微調(Fine-tune)，就可以在該任務中獲得相當優良的任務成效。當使用 BERT 於資訊檢索時，最常見的作法是將查詢與文件串接後，藉由 BERT 抽取一個低維度的向量做為特徵，藉由簡單的前饋神經網路與軟性最大(Softmax)激活函數，計算出此一文件與查詢的相關程度。亦有方法是以孿生(Siamese)架構基礎，利用兩個 BERT 模型分別為查詢與文件進行特徵向量的抽取後，再利用餘弦相似度或藉由各種神經網路模型進行相關性分數的計算。著名的模型包含有 DPR (Karpukhin et al,. 2020)、SentenceBERT (Reimers and Gurevych., 2019)、TwinBERT (Lu et al., 2020)與 ColBERT (Khattab and Zaharia., 2020)等。

相較於傳統的資訊檢索模型，以 BERT 為基礎的模型可以獲得相當優良的任務成效，但這些模型通常有著計算量龐大或需要大量額外儲存空間的問題，雖然已經有些方法針對這些缺點加以改善，但其成果仍有待提升。有鑑於此，本研究提出一套基於 BERT 與孿生架構的檢索模型(**BE**RT-based **S**iamese-**s**tructured Retrieval Model, BESS)，不僅繼承著以預訓練語言模型為主體的優點，更著眼於改善現有模型時間與空間複雜度過高的問題。此外，考量使用者查詢通常較短，而容易產生資訊不足的問題，我們的模型設計了一套自動的查詢擴增(Query Expansion)技術；並且，在模型訓練的過程中，我們提出了一套權重計算方式，為每一個訓練查詢，根據當前的檢索結果，計算一個權重，做為更新檢索模型參數時的比重。綜合這些改進，我們在三個公開的大型資料集中，驗證了此一檢索模型的成效。實驗結果顯示，相較於各式基礎系統，這套新穎的檢索模型 BESS 不僅獲得相當良好的檢索成效，在測試階段亦擁有可接受的時間與空間複雜度。

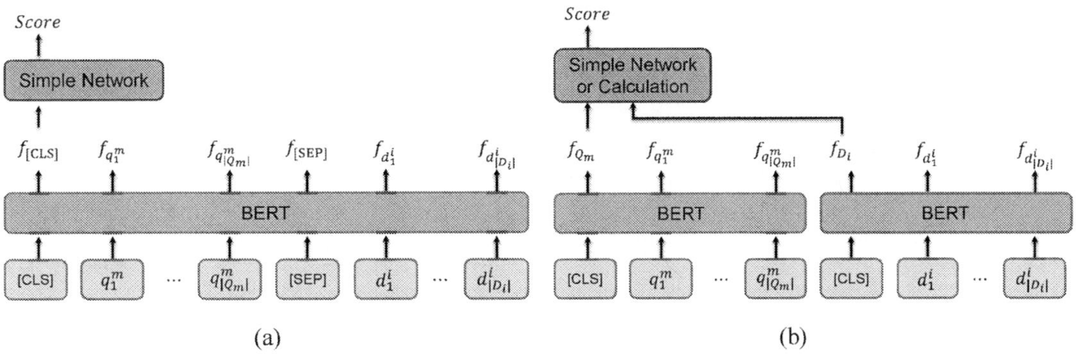

圖 2: (a) Cross-Encoder 模型架構圖。(b) TwinBERT 與 DPR 模型架構圖。

2 相關研究

2.1 BERT & Cross-Encoder

基於 Transformer 的雙向編碼器 BERT (Bidirectional Encoder Representations from Transformers)，是一個以大量文本配合非監督式學習所訓練出來的語言模型，它已被廣泛使用在自然語言處理的各項任務中，並且皆能取得良好的任務成效。BERT 語言模型的訓練目標為克漏字任務(Masked Language Model)與語句關聯性預測(Next Sentence Prediction)。在克漏字的訓練中，會隨機屏蔽訓練語句中15%的字符(Token)，並用一個特殊字符[MASK]作為代替，希望模型可以根據上下文資訊，預測此一被替換掉的字符。語句關聯性預測則是將兩段語句串接後輸入 BERT，期望模型可以準確判斷這兩個語句是否為上下文的關係。為了考量字符的順序資訊，BERT 模型引入了位置向量(Position Embeddings)與段落向量(Segment Embeddings)。位置向量是用來表示每一個字符在語句中的絕對位置，而段落向量則用於表示字符是屬於第一個輸入語句或是第二個語句。最終，每一個輸入 BERT 的字符會表示成一個加總字符相量、位置向量與段落向量的向量表示法；此外，[CLS]與[SEP]為兩個特殊的字符，通常分別插入在每個輸入語句的最前面與兩個句子之間，圖 1 為 BERT 模型的示意圖。

當 BERT 被使用於資訊檢索任務時，最起初的作法是將查詢與文件當成兩個句子，串接在一起後輸入 BERT 模型，再利用最終的[CLS]向量作為融合查詢與文件的向量表示法，藉由微調一個簡單的分類器，輸出相關性分數，作為文件排序的依據，這類方法我們統稱為為 Cross-Encoder 模型(Rodrigo and Cho, 2019 ; Qu et al., 2021)，其架構如圖 2(a)所示。雖然 Cross-Encoder 能透過 BERT 很好地得到混合查詢與文件的向量表示法，進而計算相關性分數，但對於每一個使用者輸入的查詢，Cross-Encoder 必須將查詢與資料集內的所有文件一一串接，分別輸入 BERT 獲得混合兩者資訊的向量後，再計算分數。由於資料集中的文件數量通常非常多，因此 Cross-Encoder 是非常耗費時間的。

2.2 Siamese-structured Retrieval Models

因為查詢與文件的長度、內容複雜性與表達方式等性質有著不小的差異，有研究指出，查詢與文件的向量表示法應以不同的模型進行求取，因此以孿生架構為模型基礎的檢索模型應運而生。這類模型採用兩個獨立的 BERT 作為特徵抽取器，分別輸入查詢與文件的字符序列，而最後一層的$[CLS]$向量（或是對最後一層的字符向量進行加權平均），即被用來做為查詢與文件的向量表示法，透過簡單的餘弦相似度(Cosine Similarity)計算，或藉由簡單的神經網路架構，就可以獲得文件對於查詢的相關性分數。TwinBERT (Lu et al., 2020)與 DPR (Karpukhin et al,. 2020)是這類模型經典的代表，他們的模型架構如圖 2(b)所示。以孿生架構為模型基礎的好處是系統在實際應用時，所需面對的候選文件數量通常非常巨大，可能從數十萬篇至數千萬篇，但它們的內容通常是不會再改變的。由於這些特性，我們可以事先計算每一篇文件的向量表示法，並且將這些表示法儲存起來，當使用

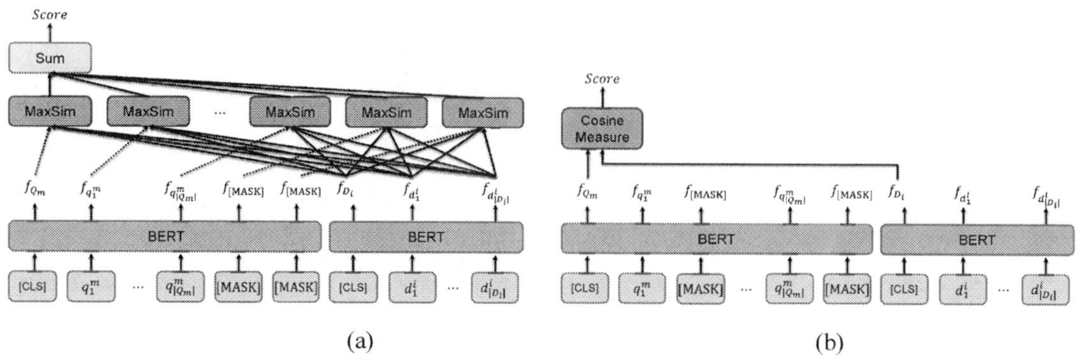

圖 3: (a) ColBERT 模型架構圖。(b) BESS 模型架構圖。

者輸入一個查詢後，我們僅需求取查詢的特徵向量表示法後，就可以跟已經算好並存儲起來的文件表示法進行相關性分數的計算，做為文件排序的依據。這樣的設計，在實際應用上，由於只需求取使用者輸入的查詢之特徵向量，並不需重複計算大量候選文件的向量表示法，因此可以大幅地減少所需的運算時間。

ColBERT (Khattab and Zaharia., 2020)同樣是以孿生架構為基礎的檢索模型，為了減少模型參數量，它的兩個 BERT 特徵抽取器的參數是共享的，為了區別查詢與文件的不同，在輸入時，將一個特別的字符$[Q]$加入在查詢的字符序列最前面，將特別字符$[D]$插入在每個文件字符序列的最前面。因此，雖然查詢與文件的特徵抽取器是參數共享的，但它依然可以區別輸入的是查詢或文件，而產生對應的向量表示法。此外，針對查詢通常遭遇資訊不足的問題，ColBERT 提出在查詢後面加入數個[MASK]字符，經過 BERT 後，這些[MASK]字符所對應的向量表示法，可以被視為是模型自動加入的查詢擴增資訊。最後，將查詢內的每一個字符向量與文件中每一個字符向量計算內積，再加總每一個查詢字符所得的最大分數，就可做為是查詢與文件的相關性分數，ColBERT 的模型架構如圖 3(a)所示。值得一提的是，雖然 ColBERT 可以預先將文件的向量表示法儲存起來，使得測試階段的速度可以較 Cross-Encoder 快，但相較於 TwinBERT 或 DPR，每篇文件僅儲存一個特徵向量，ColBERT 是將文件中所有字符的最後一層特徵向量皆儲存起來，因此 ColBERT 需要花費大量的記憶體空間。在計算相關性分數方面，由於 ColBERT 是將查詢中每一個字符向量與每一篇文件中的每個字符向量做內積計算，最後為每一個查詢中的字符留下一個最高的內積分數，加總後即為該篇文件對於查詢的相關性分數；然而，不論是 TwinBERT 或 DPR，文件的最後排序分數只要計算一個查詢特徵與一個文件特徵的內積，即是相關分數，因此 ColBERT 的計算複雜度也是 TwinBERT 或 DPR 的數千至數萬倍。

3 研究方法

3.1 模型架構

有鑑於基於 BERT 的模型已在資訊檢索任務中取得不錯的任務成效，此外，以孿生架構為基礎的模型可比 Cross-Encoder 有較佳的執行速度，因此，在本研究中，我們提出一套基於 BERT 與孿生架構之檢索模型(BERT-based Siamese-structured Retrieval Model, BESS)，模型架構如圖 3(b)所示。更明確地，當給定一個包含 M 筆資料的訓練集 $\boldsymbol{\Omega} = \langle Q_m, D_m^+, D_{m,1}^-, \dots, D_{m,N}^- \rangle_{m=1}^M$，每一筆資料包含一個長度為 $|Q_m|$ 個字符的查詢 $Q_m = [q_1^m, q_2^m, \dots, q_{|Q_m|}^m]$，一篇與 Q_m 相關的文件 D_m^+，其長度是$|D_m^+|$個字符，以及N篇非相關文件$\{D_{m,1}^-, \dots, D_{m,N}^-\}$。在基於 BERT 模型與孿生架構下，我們的模型擁有兩個參數不共享的 BERT 特徵抽取器，在查詢與文件的字符序列前後分別加上[CLS]與[SEP]後，即分別送入

特徵抽取器，並且以最後一層的[CLS]向量做為查詢或文件的特徵向量表示法 $\langle f_{Q_m}, f_{D_m^+}, f_{D_{m,1}^-}, \dots, f_{D_{m,N}^-} \rangle$。接著，模型的訓練目標函式為最大化負對數似然值(Negative Log-likelihood)：

$$\mathcal{L} = \sum_{m=1}^{M} -\log \frac{sim\left(f_{Q_m}, f_{D_m^+}\right)}{sim\left(f_{Q_m}, f_{D_m^+}\right) + \sum_{n=1}^{N} sim\left(f_{Q_m}, f_{D_{m,n}^-}\right)} \quad (1)$$

其中相似度函數$sim\left(f_Q, f_D\right)$定義為：

$$sim(f_Q, f_D) = exp\left(cos\left(f_{Q_m}, f_{D_m^+}\right)\right) \quad (2)$$

期望藉由錯誤傳遞，更新 BESS 模型的兩個特徵抽取器，使得查詢與相關文件可以擁有較相近的特徵向量，而非相關文件的特徵向量可以與查詢越不像越好。

3.2 查詢擴增

為了彌補使用者輸入的查詢通常較短，容易有資訊不足的問題，ColBERT 在查詢的字符序列後面加入多個[MASK]字符，讓檢索模型自動地為每一個查詢添加額外的資訊。在使用者給定的查詢中，名詞與形容詞往往是最為重要的資訊，並且借鑑於利用知識圖譜之BERT模型(Knowledge BERT, K-BERT) (Liu et al., 2020)的成功，我們延伸 K-BERT 模型的做法，期望能為查詢裡的名詞與形容詞添加一個自動產生的額外資訊。為了實現這個想法，我們替查詢裡的名詞與形容後面分別加入一個[MASK]字符，希望藉由訓練，BESS 可以自動地根據上下文資訊，補足名詞與形容詞資訊之不足，或是提供可能的額外資訊，使得檢索的成效可以更加提升。

3.3 強化學習

由於強化學習已在近年展現優異的成果 (Arulkumaran et al., 2017; Yang et al., 2018; Satoshi and Toshihiko, 2020; Shao et al., 2021)，因此我們採用強化學習的方式訓練 BESS。為此，我們設計了一套訓練查詢權重函式，用來調整每一個訓練查詢對模型參數更新時的貢獻度，也就是扮演著強化學習中回饋(Reward)的角色，用來動態調整模型的學習率。至於如何判斷哪些訓練查詢對模型來說比較重要呢？我們首先採用一個簡易的檢索模型為訓練集中的每個查詢進行初次檢索，並計算檢索結果，例如準確率(Precision)或排序倒數平均值(Mean Reciprocal Rank, MRR)

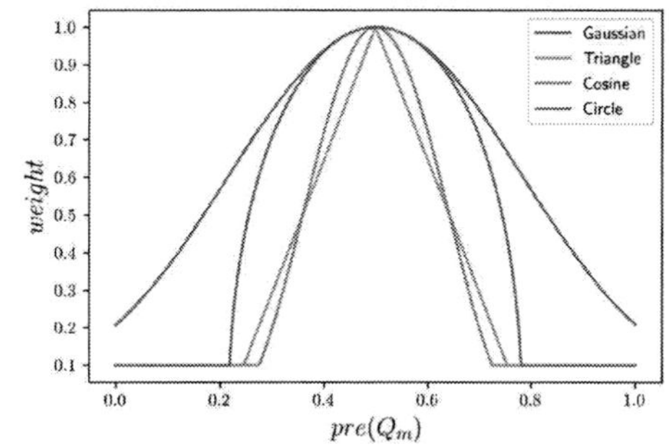

圖 4: 四種權重函式示意圖，以$\mu = 0.5$，$\sigma = 0.282$為範例。

(Hinrich et al., 2008)。有了每個訓練查詢的檢索結果後，我們提出四種不同的權重函式，包含高斯函式、三角函式、餘弦函式以及圓形函式(Lv and Zhai,. 2009)，用來計算每一個訓練查詢的權重：

- 高斯函式(Gaussian Kernel)

$$\frac{-(pre(Q_m)-\mu)^2}{2\sigma^2} \quad (3)$$

- 三角函式(Triangle Kernel)

$$\begin{cases} 1 - \frac{|pre(Q_m) - \mu|}{\sigma}, & if\ |pre(Q_m) - \mu| \le \sigma \\ 0.1, & otherwise \end{cases} \quad (4)$$

- 餘弦函式(Cosine Kernel)

$$\begin{cases} \frac{1}{2}\left[1 + cos\left(\frac{|pre(Q_m)-\mu|}{\sigma}\pi\right)\right], & if\ |pre(Q_m) - \mu| \le \sigma \\ 0.1, & otherwise \end{cases} \quad (5)$$

- 圓形函式(Circle Kernel)

$$\begin{cases} \sqrt{1 - \left(\frac{|pre(Q_m) - \mu|}{\sigma}\right)^2}, & if\ |pre(Q_m) - \mu| \le \sigma \\ 0.1, & otherwise \end{cases} \quad (6)$$

其中$pre(Q_m)$代表訓練查詢Q_m的檢索結果，μ與σ為權重函式的超參數，分別用來控制中心點與平滑程度，圖 4 為以μ =0.5 與σ =0.282 為範例的權重函式示意圖。與傳統的強化學習相較，傳統的回饋設計，通常是表現越差的訓練資料會給定較大的回饋，表現越好的資料會有較小的回饋；然而，我們認為，在使用簡易模型的檢索中，獲得良好成效的訓練查詢，不需要再對模型的訓練有較大的影響，因為這些查詢本身所蘊含的資訊與相關訊息，已被模型良好的描述與儲存，因此已可以擁有很好的檢索成果；另一方面，在簡

	Num. of Queries			Avg.	Avg. Rel.	Num. of	Avg.
	Train	Dev	Test	Tokens/Query	Passages/Query	Passages	Tokens/Passage
MovieQA	38,417	4,333	4,327	8.80	1.55	86,360	99.39
MovieQA Chinese	38,417	4,333	4,327	12.85	1.37	107,340	167.88
MS MARCO	808,731	101,093	101,092	7.46	1.05	8,841,823	74.46

表 1: MovieQA、MovieQA Chinese 與 MS MARCO 資料集統計資訊。

易模型的檢索裡，獲得較差成效的訓練查詢也不需要對模型的更新有較大的影響性，因為這些訓練查詢可能含有錯誤的標記或屬於離群資料(Outlier)，給定較高的回饋，反而會影響模型整體的準確性。綜觀這些原因，我們希望表現尚可的訓練查詢才應對模型的更新有較大的影響，因此提出四種權重函式，並且，在本研究中，我們將μ設定為所有訓練查詢的準確率平均值。最終，模型的訓練目標函式則為：

$$\mathcal{L} = \sum_{m=1}^{M} -\log \frac{weight(Q_m) sim\left(f_{Q_m}, f_{D_m^+}\right)}{sim\left(f_{Q_m}, f_{D_m^+}\right) + \sum_{n=1}^{N} sim\left(f_{Q_m}, f_{D_{m,n}^-}\right)} \quad (7)$$

其中$weight(Q_m)$表示訓練查詢Q_m的回饋，可以由任一種權重函式計算獲得。

4 實驗與討論

4.1 資料集

本研究所使用的資料集包含 MovieQA (Tapaswi et al,. 2016)、MovieQA Chinese (Tapaswi et al,. 2016)與 MS MARCO (Nguyen et al,. 2016)。MS MARCO 是一個由微軟在 2016 年推出用於閱讀理解任務的資料集，在 2018 年調整為段落檢索的資料集，包含了 880 萬個網頁中的段落，這些段落是 Bing 從 100 萬個實際的使用者查詢所收集而來，每個查詢皆對應到一個相關段落，但並沒有標註明確的非相關段落。在評量結果上，我們使用 MRR@10 與 MRR@100 來評估模型。所有實驗採用的訓練資料集是 MS MARCO small 版，並且基於官方所提供的初次檢索結果，對每一個查詢所對應的 1,000 個段落進行重新排序(Reranking)。因為該資料集的測試集沒有提供正確答案，因此在實驗中，我們隨機地切分訓練集的百分之十當做訓練時的驗證集，原始的驗證集則做為測試集使用。

MovieQA 是由多倫多大學所提供關於影片與文件的故事理解資料集，包含了 400 多部電影的相關文件，資料集中的每個問題都對應到一篇相關文件內的多個答案。我們將所有資料集中的文件切分成數個段落，每個段落大約包含 100 個單詞，因此每個查詢所對應的相關段落可能會有一至多個。為了驗證本研究所提出的方法是否可以應用在多種語言中，我們使用機器翻譯，將英文的 MovieQA 翻譯成中文，做為一套中文的資訊檢索資料集，資料前處理則與英文 MovieQA 資料集相同。與 MS MARCO 相較，在 MovieQA 與 MovieQA Chinese 資料集中，檢索模型是對所有文件進行排序，不是採用重計分的方式，僅對前幾篇文件進行重新排序。然而，因為 Cross-Encoder 所需的計算時間較長，因此我們先採用 BM25 進行初次檢索，再對前 1,000 則段落重新進行排序。在 MovieQA 與 MovieQA Chinese 資料集上，我們是以 MAP@10/50/100 進行模型的效能評估。資料集詳細的統計資訊如表 1 所示。

4.2 實驗設置

在英文的實驗中，我們使用 huggingface (Wolf et al., 2020)開源的 bert-base-uncased 模型，中文的實驗則使用 bert-base-chinese 模型。在我們所提出的檢索模型 BESS 中，查詢的字符序列長度設定為 32，文件字符序列長度設定為 384，若超過設定長度，則直接捨棄；模型訓練時的批次大小設定為 12；四種權重函式的超參數σ設定為 0.282，μ則根據資料集的不同，為 MovieQA、MovieQA Chinese 與 MS MARCO 分別設定為 0.725、0.64 與 0.364。我們的程式主要使用 pytorch 工具包，並利用 Faiss 工具包(Johnson et al., 2017)建立索引(Indexing)，與進行相關性分數的計算。

	MovieQA MAP@10/50/100	MovieQA Chinese MAP@10/50/100	MS MARCO MRR@10/100
BM25	38.4 / 39.1 / 39.2	33.3 / 34.1 / 34.2	16.7 / - (official)
Cross-Encoder	42.1 / 42.9 / 42.9	38.4 / 39.3 / 39.4	32.2 / 33.4
DPR	66.6 / 67.0 / 67.2	61.2 / 61.4 / 61.5	32.5 / 33.0
ColBERT	**70.4 / 70.9 / 71.0**	**63.5 / 63.9 / 64.0**	**33.4 / 34.3**

表 2: 基礎檢索模型於 MovieQA、MovieQA Chinese 與 MS MARCO 資料集之實驗結果。

4.3 實驗結果與討論

在第一組實驗中，我們首先探討基準系統在三個資料集的檢索成效，包含經典的 Okapi Best Match 25 (BM25) (Robertson et al., 1995)、基於 BERT 的 Cross-Encoder (Qu et al., 2021)還有屬於學生網路架構的 DPR (Karpukhin et al,. 2020)與 ColBERT (Khattab and Zaharia., 2020)，實驗結果如表 2 所示。我們可以發現，以 BERT 為基礎的 Cross-Encoder、DPR 與 ColBERT 在三個資料集中皆大幅度的超越傳統 BM25 的成效，不僅說明預訓練語言模型所帶來的好處，也驗證了當前基於神經網路的檢索系統在大型資料集中的進步。接著，我們仔細比較 Cross-Encoder、DPR 與 ColBERT，基於學生網路架構的 DPR 與 ColBERT，雖然需要花費額外的記憶體空間儲存文件的表示法，但他們不僅可以在測試階段擁有較快的運算速度，在檢索的成效上也可以獲得比 Cross-Encoder 要好的成績。最後，比較基於學生網路架構的 DPR 與 ColBERT，因為 DPR 僅為每一篇文件儲存一個向量表示法，而 ColBERT 是將文件內所有的字符向量表示法皆儲存起來，由於實驗中，我們將文件的字符序列長度設定為 384，因此 ColBERT 所需的額外儲存空間大約是 DPR 的 384 倍；此外，ColBERT 在相關分數的計算上，是將每一個查詢的字符向量與每一個文件的字符向量進行內積計算，再整合出一個最終的分數，而 DPR 只需進行一次的內積計算，就可以獲得相關分數，因此 ColBERT 的計算複雜度幾乎是 DPR 的 12,288 (32×384)倍。雖然 ColBERT 的時間與空間複雜度皆比 DPR 高出許多，但實驗結果展現了 ColBERT 優異的檢索成效！

在第二組實驗中，我們測試本研究所提出之基於 BERT 與學生架構的檢索模型 BESS 在三個資料集的檢索成效，實驗結果如表 3 所示。首先，$\text{BESS}_{\text{Gaussian}}$、$\text{BESS}_{\text{Triangle}}$、$\text{BESS}_{\text{Cosine}}$ 與 $\text{BESS}_{\text{Circle}}$ 分別表示使用四種不同權重函式的 BESS 模型，在 MovieQA 資料集中，使用高斯函式可以獲得最好的檢索成效，相較於餘弦函式，高斯函式甚至可以高出 4%的 MAP；在 MovieQA Chinese 資料集中，雖然圓形函式可以獲得最佳的檢索成效，但四種函式的效能差異不大；綜合比較 MovieQA 與 MovieQA Chinese 兩個資料集，使用餘弦函式的檢索成效皆是最差的，可能是因為餘弦函式給定的權重差異太大，即訓練查詢所獲得權重不是很大就是很小（參考圖 4），造成訓練時過分依賴部份資料而導致成效不彰的問題。接著，我們比較 BESS 與同為使用學生架構的檢索模型 DPR 和 ColBERT。觀察表 2 與表 3，除了餘弦函式外，BESS 在三個資料集裡的檢索成效皆能大幅度的領先 DPR 模型，這個結果驗證了本研究所提出之自動查詢擴增與強化學習的有效性。與 ColBERT 相較，雖然 BESS 僅能獲得小幅度的成效提升，但值得一提的是，BESS 僅為每一篇文件儲存一個向量表示法，而 ColBERT 必須將文件內所有的字符向量表示法皆儲存起來，因為在實驗中，我們將文件的長度設定為 384，所以在額外儲存空間的花費上，ColBERT 的空間複雜度大約是 BESS 的 384 倍；在計算複雜度方面，因為 BESS 僅需為一組查詢與文件計算一次餘弦相似度，然而 ColBERT 是將查詢中的所有字符與文件中的所有字符兩兩計算餘弦相似度，再為每個查詢中的字符取最大值並相加，而實驗中，查詢的長度設定為 32，文件的字符序列長度設定為 384，因此 ColBERT 所需耗費的計算時間至少是 BESS 的 12,288 倍。綜觀上述，本研究所提出的 BESS 檢索模型，不僅在時間與空間複雜度上大幅度的優於 ColBERT 模型，在檢索任務的成效上，也可以取得與 ColBERT 相當或更佳的結果，基於學生架構的設計，在

	MovieQA MAP@10/50/100	**MovieQA Chinese** MAP@10/50/100	**MS MARCO** MRR@10/100
$BESS_{Gaussian}$	**70.9 / 71.2 / 71.2**	63.4 / 63.6 / 63.6	**33.6 / 34.3**
$BESS_{Triangle}$	69.0 / 69.3 / 69.4	63.6 / 63.8 / 63.9	n/a
$BESS_{Cosine}$	66.1 / 66.7 / 66.7	62.5 / 62.7 / 62.7	n/a
$BESS_{Circle}$	70.0 / 70.2 / 70.2	**63.7 / 63.9 / 63.9**	n/a
BESS-RL	69.8 / 70.0 / 70.3	63.0 / 63.2 / 63.2	33.1 / 33.7
$BESS_{Gaussian}$-QE	70.1 / 70.3 / 70.4	62.8 / 63.0 / 63.0	32.7 / 33.3
$BESS_{Triangle}$-QE	68.8 / 69.1 / 69.2	63.1 / 63.3 / 63.3	32.4 / 33.1
$BESS_{Cosine}$-QE	65.7 / 66.0 / 66.1	62.2 / 62.4 / 62.4	32.3 / 32.6
$BESS_{Circle}$-QE	67.9 / 68.3 / 68.3	63.3 / 63.5 / 63.5	32.3 / 32.5

表 3: 本研究所提出之檢索模型 BESS 於 MovieQA、MovieQA Chinese 與 MS MARCO 資料集之實驗結果。

測試階段，BESS 也不需耗費大量的運算時間，藉由三個資料集，我們驗證了 BESS 的效率與能力！

在最後一組實驗裡，我們進行 BESS 模型的消融研究。當我們將強化學習取消，實驗結果如表 3 中 BESS-RL 所示，可以發現除了餘弦函式外，沒有使用強化學習的結果確實會讓大部分檢索的效能下降，這展現了權重函式為 BESS 的模型訓練帶來了一定的好處。此外，與 DPR 模型相較，這個實驗結果也說明了我們所提出的自動查詢擴增，在不同的資料集上，可以帶給檢索模型 1~3%的進步；接著，我們將自動查詢擴增取消，實驗結果如表 3 中的 $BESS_{Gaussian}$-QE、$BESS_{Triangle}$-QE、$BESS_{Cosine}$-QE 與 $BESS_{Circle}$-QE 所示，與 BESS 相較，缺少自動查詢擴增，不論在哪一種權重函式的使用下，皆會造成一定程度的效能損失。值得一提的是，雖然 ColBERT 與 BESS 皆有查詢擴增的設計，但由於在計算相關性分數時，ColBERT 是將查詢中所有字符的特徵向量皆與文件的每一個字符向量計算分數，因此 ColBERT 模型所擴增的查詢是直接的影響最後的排序分數，而 BESS 是只以特殊字符[CLS]向量做為查詢的特徵向量表示法，因此 BESS 模型的查詢擴增是以間接的方式改善最後的排序結果。從實驗中，我們可以說，自動查詢擴增，不論是以直接或間接的方式影響最後的排序結果，對於檢索任務的成效皆是有正向的幫助，但我們所提出的間接式方法，不僅可以提升檢索任務的成效，也不需要額外的計算負擔！

5 結論

在本研究中，我們提出了一套基於 BERT 與學生架構的檢索模型 BESS，它不僅擁有良好的檢索效能，在測試階段，也不會有過高的計算負擔。此外，自動查詢擴增與強化學習的加入，更加提升了檢索模型的成效。我們在 MovieQA、MovieQA Chinese 與 MS MARCO 三個資料集中，驗證 BESS 模型的檢索能力，實驗結果顯示，BESS 不僅可以達到最好的檢索成果，也能有較低的計算複雜度。在未來的研究裡，我們將首先改進查詢擴增方法，使其更有效率；我們也將繼續驗證 BESS 模型於其他常見且公認的各式語言資料集中；除了資訊檢索外，我們希望能將 BESS 與開放式問答(Open Domain Question Answering)系統相結合，進一步地驗證，BESS 檢索模型是否能夠提升問答系統之成效。

References

Ashish Vaswani, Noam Shazeer, Niki Parmar, Jakob Uszkoreit, Llion Jones, Aidan N. Gomez, Lukasz Kaiser & Illia Polosukhin. (2017). Attention is all you need. Advances in *Neural Information Processing Systems (p./pp. 5998--6008).*

Bhaskar Mitra, Sebastian Hofstatter, Hamed Zamani, & Nick Craswell. (2020). Conformer-Kernel with Query Term Independence for Document Retrieval. *arXiv preprint arXiv:2007.10434.*

Chenze Shao, Yang Feng, Jinchao Zhang, Fandong Meng & Jie Zhou. 2021. Sequence-Level Training for Non-Autoregressive Neural Machine Translation. arXiv preprint *arXiv:2106.08122.*

Christos H. Papadimitriou, Prabhakar Raghavan, Hisao Tamaki & SantoshVempala (2000). Latent Semantic Indexing: A Probabilistic Analysis. *Journal of Computer and System Sciences, 61*(2), 217–235.

Daniel Cohen, Liu Yang, & W. Bruce Croft (2018). WikiPassageQA: A Benchmark Collection for Research on Non-Factoid Answer Passage Retrieval. In *The 41st International ACM SIGIR Conference on Research & Development in Information Retrieval* (pp. 1165–1168). Association for Computing Machinery.

David M. Blei, Andrew Y. Ng & Michael I. Jordan. (2003). Latent Dirichlet Allocation. *J. Mach. Learn. Res., 3(null), 993–1022.*

Gerard M. Salton, Andrew Wong & Chungshu Yang (1975). A vector space model for automatic indexing. Communications of the ACM, 18(11), 613–620.

Jacob Devlin, Ming-Wei Chang, Kenton Lee & Kristina Toutanova. (2019). BERT: Pre-training of Deep Bidirectional Transformers for Language Understanding. *In Proceedings of the 2019 Conference of the North American Chapter of the Association for Computational Linguistics: Human Language Technologies, Volume 1 (Long and Short Papers) (pp. 4171–4186). Association for Computational Linguistics.*

Jeff Johnson, Matthijs Douze & Herve J ´ egou. 2017. 'Billion-scale similarity search with GPUs. *ArXiv, abs/1702.08734.*

Kai Arulkumaran, Marc Peter Deisenroth, Miles Brundage, & Anil Anthony Bharath. (2017). Deep Reinforcement Learning: A Brief Survey. *IEEE Signal Processing Magazine, 34*(6), 26–38.

Kevin Clark, Minh-Thang Luong, Quoc V. Le & Christopher D. Manning. 2020. ELECTRA: Pretraining text encoders as discriminators rather than generators. *In International Conference on Learning Representations.*

Kosugi, Satoshi & Toshihiko Yamasaki. (2020, April). Unpaired image enhancement featuring reinforcement-learning-controlled image editing software. In *Proceedings of the AAAI Conference on Artificial Intelligence* (Vol. 34, No. 07, pp. 11296-11303).

Kuzi Saar, Zhang Mingyang, Li Cheng, Bendersky Michael & Najork Marc. (2020). Leveraging semantic and lexical matching to improve the recall of document retrieval systems: a hybrid approach. *arXiv preprint arXiv:2010.01195.*

Leslie Pack Kaelbling, Michael L. Littman, & Andrew W. Moore (1996). Reinforcement Learning: A Survey. *Journal of Artificial Intelligence Research, 4*, 237–285.

Luhn, Hans Peter (1957). A Statistical Approach to Mechanized Encoding and Searching of Literary Information. *IBM Journal of Research and Development, 1*(4), 309-317.

Mackenzie Joel, Dai Zhuyun, Gallagher Luke & Callan Jamie. (2020, July). Efficiency implications of term weighting for passage retrieval. In *Proceedings of the 43rd International ACM SIGIR Conference on Research and Development in Information Retrieval* (pp. 1821-1824).

Makarand Tapaswi, Yukun Zhu, Rainer Stiefelhagen, Antonio Torralba, Raquel Urtasun & Sanja Fidler. (2016). *MovieQA: Understanding Stories in Movies through Question-Answering. 2016 IEEE Conference on Computer Vision and Pattern Recognition (CVPR)*, 4631-4640.

Nils Reimers & Iryna Gurevych. (2019). Sentence-BERT: Sentence Embeddings using Siamese BERT-Networks. *Proceedings of the 2019 Conference on Empirical Methods in Natural Language Processing and the 9th International Joint Conference on Natural Language Processing (EMNLP-IJCNLP).*

Nogueira, Rodrigo & Kyunghyun Cho. (2019). Passage Re-ranking with BERT. *arXiv preprint arXiv:1901.04085.*

Omar Khattab & Matei Zaharia. (2020). ColBERT. *Proceedings of the 43rd International ACM SIGIR Conference on Research and Development in Information Retrieval.*

Schütze Hinrich, Christopher D. Manning, & Prabhakar Raghavan. (2008). *Introduction to information retrieval* (Vol. 39, pp. 234-265). Cambridge: Cambridge University Press.

Scott Deerwester, Susan T. Dumais, George W. Furnas, Thomas K. Landaue & Richard Harshman. (1990). Indexing by latent semantic analysis. *Journal of the American Society for Information Science, 41*(6), 391–407.

Sebastian Hofstätter, Hamed Zamani, Bhaskar Mitra, Nick Craswell & Allan Hanbury. (2020). Local Self-Attention over Long Text for Efficient Document Retrieval. *Proceedings of the 43rd International ACM SIGIR Conference on Research and Development in Information Retrieval.*

Spärck Jones, K. (1972). A statistical interpretation of term specificity and its application in retrieval. *Journal of Documentation, 60*, 493-502.

Stephen E. Robertson, Steve Walker, Susan Jones, Micheline Hancock-Beaulieu & Mike Gatford. (1995). Okapi at TREC-3. *In Overview of the Third Text REtrieval Conference (TREC-3)* (pp. 109-126). Gaithersburg, MD: NIST.

Thomas Hofmann. (1999). Probabilistic Latent Semantic Analysis. *In Proceedings of the Fifteenth Conference on Uncertainty in Artificial Intelligence (pp. 289–296).* Morgan Kaufmann Publishers Inc.

Thomas Wolf, Lysandre Debut, Victor Sanh, Julien Chaumond, Clement Delangue, Anthony Moi, Pierric Cistac, Tim Rault, Remi Louf, Morgan Funtowicz, Joe Davison, Sam Shleifer, Patrick von Platen, Clara Ma, Yacine Jernite, Julien Plu, Canwen Xu, Teven Le Scao, Sylvain Gugger, Mariama Drame, Quentin Lhoest & Alexander Rush. (2020). Transformers: State-of-the-Art Natural Language Processing. *In Proceedings of the 2020 Conference on Empirical Methods in Natural Language Processing: System Demonstrations* (pp. 38–45). Association for Computational Linguistics.

Tri Nguyen, Mir Rosenberg, Xia Song, Jianfeng Gao, Saurabh Tiwary, Rangan Majumder & Li Deng. 2016. MS MARCO: A Human-Generated MAchine Reading COmprehension Dataset. (2016).

Vladimir Karpukhin, Barlas Oğuz, Sewon Min, Patrick Lewis, Ledell Wu, Sergey Edunov, Danqi Chen & Wen-tau Yih. (2020). Dense Passage Retrieval for Open-Domain Question Answering. *Proceedings of the 2020 Conference on Empirical Methods in Natural Language Processing (EMNLP).*

Wang, William Yang, Jiwei Li & Xiaodong He. (2018, July). Deep reinforcement learning for NLP. In *Proceedings of the 56th Annual Meeting of the Associationfor Computational Linguistics: Tutorial Abstracts* (pp. 19-21).

Weijie Liu, Peng Zhou, Zhe Zhao, Zhiruo Wang, Qi Ju, Haotang Deng, & Ping Wang. (2020). K-BERT: Enabling Language Representation with Knowledge Graph. *Proceedings of the AAAI Conference on Artificial Intelligence, 34*(03), 2901-2908.

Wenhao Lu, Jian Jiao & Ruofei Zhang. (2020). TwinBERT: Distilling Knowledge to Twin-Structured BERT Models for Efficient Retrieval. *Proceedings of the 29th ACM International Conference on Information & Knowledge Management.*

Xuanang Chen, Ben He, Kai Hui, Le Sun & Yingfei Sun. (2021). Simplified TinyBERT: Knowledge Distillation for Document Retrieval. *arXiv preprint arXiv:2009.07531.*

Yingqi Qu, Yuchen Ding, Jing Liu, Kai Liu, Ruiyang Ren, Wayne Xin Zhao, Daxiang Dong, Hua Wu & Haifeng Wang (2021). RocketQA: An Optimized Training Approach to Dense Passage Retrieval for Open-Domain Question Answering. In *Proceedings of the 2021 Conference of the North American Chapter of the Association for Computational Linguistics: Human Language Technologies, NAACL-HLT 2021, Online, June 6-11, 2021* (pp. 5835–5847). Association for Computational Linguistics.

Yinhan Liu, Myle Ott, Naman Goyal, Jingfei Du, Mandar Joshi, Danqi Chen, Omer Levy, Mike Lewis, Luke Zettlemoyer & Veselin Stoyanov. 2019. Roberta: A robustly optimized bert pretraining approach. *arXiv preprint arXiv:1907.11692.*

Yuanhua Lv & ChengXiang Zhai. (2009). Positional language models for information retrieval. *Proceedings of the 32nd International ACM SIGIR Conference on Research and Development in Information Retrieval - SIGIR '09.*

Zeynep Akkalyoncu Yilmaz, Wei Yang & Haotian Zhang, Jimmy Lin (2019). Cross-Domain Modeling of Sentence-Level Evidence for Document Retrieval. In *Proceedings of the 2019 Conference on Empirical Methods in Natural Language Processing and the 9th International Joint Conference on Natural Language Processing (EMNLP-IJCNLP)* (pp. 3490–3496). Association for Computational Linguistics.

Zhilin Yang, Zihang Dai, Yiming Yang, Jaime Carbonell, Ruslan Salakhutdinov & Quoc V Le. 2019. Xlnet: Generalized autoregressive pretraining for language understanding. *arXiv preprint arXiv:1906.08237.*

The 33rd Conference on Computational Linguistics and Speech Processing (ROCLING 2021)
Taoyuan, Taiwan, October 15-16, 2021. The Association for Computational Linguistics and Chinese Language Processing

MMTL: The Meta Multi-Task Learning for Aspect Category Sentiment Analysis

Guan-Yuan Chen[♠♣*] and **Ya-Fen Yeh**[♡*]
[♠]Telecommunication Laboratories, Chunghwa Telecom, Taoyuan, Taiwan
[♣]Department of Computer Science, National Tsing Hua University, Hsinchu, Taiwan
[♡]Industrial Technology Research Institute, Hsinchu, Taiwan
guanyuan@gapp.nthu.edu.tw, amilaok94@gmail.com

Abstract

Aspect Category Sentiment Analysis (ACSA), which aims to identify fine-grained sentiment polarities of the aspect categories discussed in user reviews. ACSA is challenging and costly when conducting it into real-world applications, that mainly due to the following reasons: 1.) Labeling the fine-grained ACSA data is often labor-intensive. 2.) The aspect categories will be dynamically updated and adjusted with the development of application scenarios, which means that the data must be relabeled frequently. 3.) Due to the increase of aspect categories, the model must be retrained frequently to fast adapt to the newly added aspect category data. To overcome the above-mentioned problems, we introduce a novel Meta Multi-Task Learning (MMTL) approach, that frame ACSA tasks as a meta-learning problem (i.e., regarding aspect-category sentiment polarity classification problems as the different training tasks for meta-learning) to learn an ideal and shareable initialization for the multi-task learning model that can be adapted to new ACSA tasks efficiently and effectively. Experiment results show that the proposed approach significantly outperforms the strong pre-trained transformer-based baseline model, especially, in the case of less labeled fine-grained training data.

Keywords: Aspect Category Sentiment Analysis, Meta-Learning, Multi-Task Learning

1 Introduction

Aspect-Based Sentiment Analysis (ABSA) (Pontiki et al., 2014a,b,c) is an important fine-grained task in the field of sentiment analysis, that is considerable for grasping and understanding user comments in real-world applications. ABSA contains several sub-tasks, four of which are Aspect Term Extraction (ATE), Aspect Term Sentiment Analysis (ATSA), Aspect Category Detection (ACD), and Aspect Category Sentiment Analysis (ACSA). ATE extracts and identifies the corresponding Aspect Term from the sentences of user comments and ATSA aims to predict the polarity of the sentiment toward the identified aspect terms. ACD detects the aspect categories mentioned in review sentences, and ACSA classifies the sentiments of the detected aspect categories.

Since the ATE and ATSA aim to extract the aspect terms of sentences and to predict sentiments corresponding to the extracted aspect terms, this may encounter some problems when the aspect term is not explicitly mentioned or pointed out in the sentence. For example, " 味道很棒, 很好吃" (Good-tasting). This is an example often seen in real internet reviews for a restaurant, which gives positive reviews on the taste of food but does not indicate the corresponding aspect term. To cope with the above problems, we mainly focus on the methods of ACD and ACSA (usually, the two will be combined and referred to as ACSA tasks), which dedicate to detects aspect categories of given sentences and classifying the sentiments polarities toward the detected aspect categories. For the above example, we can define suitable categories to conduct aspect-based sentiment analysis on user reviews by the ACD and ACSA approach, even the aspect term is not explicitly mentioned. For example, it may be detected as the taste of food category with positive reviews.

Since a user review may discuss more than

[*]denotes equal contribution

one aspect category and express different sentiments toward them, how to effectively detect various categories with their sentiment polarity at the same time is one of the most important research directions of ACSA. Wang et al. (2016) used the attention-based LSTM models for aspect-level sentiment classification. Cheng et al. (2017) proposed a HiErarchical ATtention (HEAT) network consisting of aspect attention and sentiment attention. Xue and Li (2018) introduced the Gated Convolutional Networks for ACSA and ATSA tasks with appropriate accuracy. Schmitt et al. (2018) used End-to-End Neural Networks which jointly model the detection of aspects and the classification of their polarity.

Recently, the transformer (Vaswani et al., 2017) based pre-trained language models such as BERT (Pre-training of Deep Bidirectional Transformers for Language Understanding) (Devlin et al., 2019), XLNet (Generalized Autoregressive Pretraining for Language Understanding) (Yang et al., 2019b), RoBERTa (A Robustly Optimized BERT Pretraining Approach) (Liu et al., 2019b), ELECTRA (Pre-training Text Encoders as Discriminators Rather Than Generators) (Clark et al., 2020) and DeBERTa (Decoding-enhanced BERT with Disentangled Attention) (He et al., 2020) have significantly improved the performance of many natural language processing (NLP) tasks on several benchmarks (Wang et al., 2019b,a; Xu et al., 2020).

In the ABSA field, some previous works have shown the promising of the pre-trained transformer models. Li et al. (2019) investigated the modeling power of contextualized embeddings from BERT to deal with End2End ABSA. Li et al. (2020) proposed a Multi-Instance Multi-Label Learning Network for ACSA tasks, and their experimental results showed that the BERT-based models significantly performed better than the non-BERT models (non-pre-trained transformer models) on the public datasets.

Despite previous studies that have demonstrated the success of deep learning models, especially, the pre-trained transformer models on the ABSA-related research and experiment setting, few works are studying and considering the crucial issues when conducting the deep ACSA models into real-world applications. In practical application, ACSA may be quite challenging and costly due to the following reasons: Firstly, Labeling the fine-grained ACSA data is often complicated and labor intensive (there may be so many aspect categories that need to detect and analyze). Secondly, the aspect categories may be dynamically updated and adjusted with the progress of application scenarios, which means that the data may need to be relabeled not infrequently. Thirdly, the model must be able to fast adapt to the newly added aspect category data, due to the increasing and changing of aspect categories.

In this paper, we propose a novel Meta Multi-Task Learning (MMTL) approach that considers ACSA tasks with various aspect categories as meta-learning and multi-task learning tasks (i.e., regarding aspect-category sentiment polarity classification problems as the training tasks for meta-learning and multi-task learning). Primary, we investigate the efficient and effective approaches for learning the well-conditioned and shareable initialization via the Model-Agnostic Meta-Learning algorithm (MAML) (Finn et al., 2017) and its variants (Nichol et al., 2018) for multi-task learning models. Different from previous MAML related works, in our case, the initialization learned through meta-learning must be shareable (parameter sharing) across the different polarity classification tasks of aspect categories with the same user review input. Because in actual applications, there will be a large number of aspect categories, and it is costly that different models are used to extract features for different aspect categories individually. Therefore, parameter (feature) sharing strategies such as multi-task learning is more appropriate. To achieve the above-mentioned goals, we introduce the new Meta Multi-Task Learning (MMTL) approach, which divides the model parameters into independent and shareable parts and uses different meta-learning objective functions for training on these two parts. For the part of parameter sharing, we employ the proximal regularization term in the objective function in the meta-learning inner loop training phase to encourage the model to learn parameters and

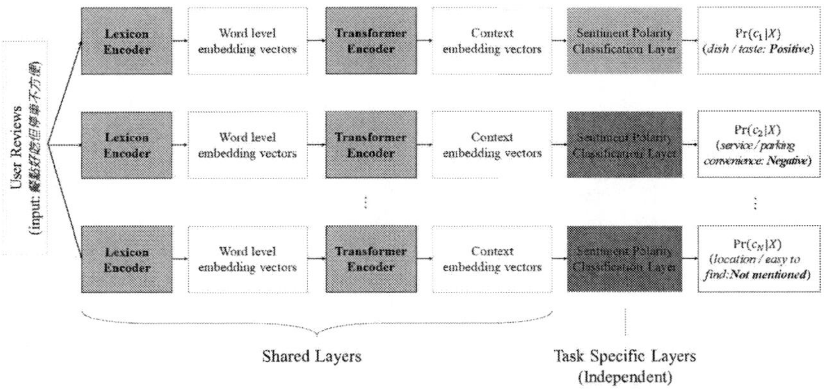

Figure 1: The architecture of the MMTL model for ACSA tasks. For each aspect category sentiment polarity classification task, most of the model parameters and features are shared, and only the parameters of the individual aspect category polarity classification layer (single layer neural network) are independent.

features that can be shared on different aspect categories tasks.

2 Related Work

Learning general representations of given text inputs for many tasks is the important goal for many Natural Language Processing (NLP) fields. The same is true for the Aspect Based Sentiment Analysis (ABSA) and its subtasks. Xue et al. (2017) proposed a multi-task learning model based on neural networks to solve the Aspect Category Classification and Aspect Term Extraction together. Yang et al. (2019a) introduced a Multi-task Learning Model for Aspect Polarity Classification and Aspect Term Extraction for Chinese-oriented tasks.

Since the transformer-based pre-trained language models have demonstrated their success in many NLP tasks, some works explored the potential of integrating the multi-task learning and pre-trained language models. Mainly, Liu et al. (2019a) presented Multi-Task Deep Neural Network (MT-DNN) learning representations by leveraging large amounts of cross-task data and obtaining state-of-the-art results on several NLU tasks.

However, there still exist some potential problems when adopting multi-task learning related algorithms into real-world applications. The most important is that multi-task learning may favor the tasks with more labeled data over the tasks with less labeled data ones. Inspired by Raghu et al. (2020); Rajeswaran et al. (2019) (they found that feature reuse is the dominant factor of the effectiveness of Model Agnostic Meta-Learning based algorithms, which means that meta-learning has the trend to learn features that can be reused in different tasks), we propose the Meta Multi-Task Learning (MMTL) approach to applying meta-learning algorithms for finding the well-conditioned and shareable initialization for multi-task learning models, such that the model can be significantly improved in the case of a small amount of data and can efficiently learn new tasks.

3 Proposed Approaches

The architecture of the Meta Multi-Task Learning (MMTL) model is shown in Figure 1. The proposed approaches are briefly described as follows. First, we treat different aspect categories of polarity classification tasks as different training tasks. Second, we apply the Model Agnostic Meta-Learning (MAML) based algorithms (Finn et al., 2017; Nichol et al., 2018) to finding the well-conditioned and shareable initialization for multi-task learning models for the different polarity classification tasks of aspect categories with the same review text. Finally, we using the multi-task learning approach with the shareable general representations and initialization to fine-tune the model on all aspect categories sentiment polarity clas-

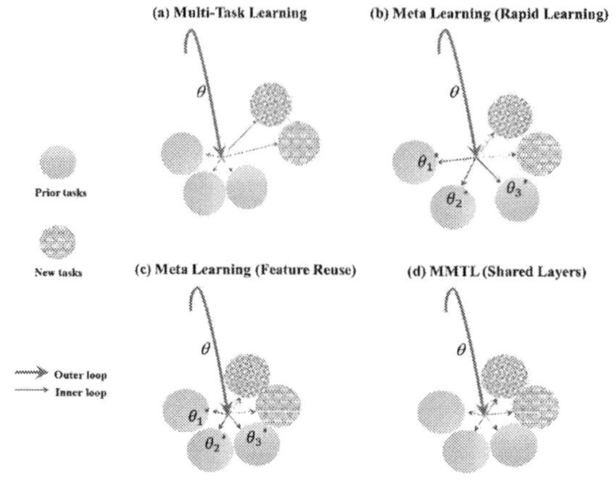

Figure 2: Differences in multi-task learning, rapid learning (meta-learning), feature reuse (meta-learning), and MMTL. (a) Multi-task learning can share the same parameter weights among different tasks, but it may favor the tasks with more data. (b) The Meta-Learning (Rapid Learning) obtains well-conditioned model initialization parameters through outer loop training, and inner loop updates result in significant task specialization. (c) The Meta-Learning (Feature Reuse) through the outer loop training to find the ideal initialization parameters of the model that can be feature reused. There are fewer differences in the updated parameters of different tasks during the inner loop training. (d) The MMTL utilizes the Meta-Learning (Feature Reuse) algorithm to find the ideal model initialization parameters that can be shared for different tasks. Then fine-tune the model through multi-task learning, so that the MMTL model can combine the advantages of multi-task learning and meta-learning, i.e. it can share most of the parameters on different tasks, and it can be adapted to new tasks with fewer training samples.

sification tasks. However, achieving the above goals is not trivial works. In particular, meta-learning and multi-task learning were regarded as two completely different methods in the past and few studies have discussed how to integrate the two methods and their respective advantages. Below, we will introduce details of the proposed method.

3.1 Meta-Learning and Multi-Task Learning

Since there are some obvious differences between meta-learning and multi-task learning, it is not trivial work to integrate these two learning algorithms with their advantages and characteristics. The differences between meta-learning and multi-task learning are shown in Figure 2. Multi-task learning trains different tasks together at the same time. This will cause multi-task learning to favor tasks with more annotated data and significantly worse performance for tasks with less annotated data. The main goal of the MAML algorithm (Finn et al., 2017) is to find good model initialization parameters such that the model can perform well to new tasks, even on tasks with fewer data. Even in many studies, it has been shown that the MAML algorithm can perform well in new tasks (especially in the case of a small amount of annotated data) (Finn et al., 2017; Gu et al., 2018; Nichol et al., 2018; Dou et al., 2019), why MAML has good learning ability in new tasks is still an issue to be analyzed. The effectiveness of MAML is mainly discussed in two different aspects (Raghu et al., 2020), 1.) Rapid Learning: There are large and effective changes in the representations, 2.) Feature Reuse: the meta-initialization containing high quality and reusable features. Since previous studies have found that MAML has the characteristics and capabilities of feature reuse, we explore ways to further impose training constraints on the model to encourage the MAML model to have the ability to share features for different tasks. Finally, we propose the novel Meta Multi-Task Learning (MMTL) algorithm to integrate meta-learning and multi-task learning algorithms. Experimental results show that the proposed MMTL algorithm can combine the advantages of meta-learning and multi-task learning, and is significantly outperform the strong pre-trained language model baseline.

3.2 The Proposed Meta Multi-Task Learning (MMTL) Model

First, we regard the ACSA tasks of different s aspect categories as a set of tasks $\{T_1, T_2, ..., T_s\}$ for meta-learning. Given a model f_θ with parameters θ and a task distribution $p(T)$ over a set of tasks $\{T_1, T_2, ..., T_s\}$. We sample a batch of tasks $\{T_b\} \sim p(T)$, and update the model parameters by k gradient descent steps for each task $\{T_b\}$ for the inner loop training of meta-learning. Where, the $k \geq 1$ and the $p(T)$ is a uniform probability distribution. For the inner loop (task specific) training of meta learning, we use the following equation to update the model parameters θ:

$$\theta_b^{(k)} = \theta_b^{(k-1)} - \beta \nabla_{\theta_b^{(k-1)}} L_b \left(f_{\theta_b^{(k-1)}} \right)$$

Where L_b is the objective function (described as follows) and β is the learning rate (a hyperparameter) of the inner loop training.

To encourage the model to have the ability to share the parameters (feature reuse) for different tasks, we divide the model into the shared layers part and the task-specific layers part. For the shared layers part, we add a proximal regularization term in the inner loop training phase. Therefore, the definition of the objective function (loss function) of the shared layers part is as follows:

$$L_b = Loss(f_{\theta_b^{(k-1)}}) + \lambda \left\| \theta_b^{(k-1)} - \theta \right\|$$

And the definition of the objective function (loss function) of the task-specific layers part is as follows:

$$L_b = Loss(f_{\theta_b^{(k-1)}})$$

Where, the $Loss$ is the Cross-Entropy Loss calculated on the inner loop training task $\{T_b\}$, the λ is a hyperparameter, and the θ is the parameter of the model. Initially, θ is the weight of the pre-trained model and is updated by the training of the outer loop of the meta-learning.

Since the original MAML algorithm (Finn et al., 2017) needs to calculate the second derivatives, resulting in excessive calculation and memory usage, we use the Reptile (a first-order gradient-based meta-learning algorithm) (Nichol et al., 2018) to update the model parameters θ for the outer loop phase.

The equation of the Reptile is defined as:

$$\theta = \theta + \gamma \frac{1}{|\{T_b\}|} \sum_{T_b \sim p(T)} \left(\theta_b^{(k)} - \theta \right)$$

Where the γ is the learning rate (a hyperparameter) of the outer loop training.

Finally, we use the model parameters trained via meta-learning as the initialization parameters, and perform multi-task learning training (fine-tuning) on the data of ACSA tasks. Overall, the training process of MMTL mainly consists of three stages: 1.) the pre-training stage as in BERT or ELECTRA, 2.) the meta-learning stage, and 3.) the multi-task learning fine-tuning stage.

The model trained by the proposed MMTL algorithm is different from the multi-task learning model (that is shown in Figure 2). Attributable to the fact that we first use meta-learning and some constraints to make the parameters of the model can be shared on different tasks and perform ideally on new tasks, even if the new task only has a relatively small amount of training data. The MMTL model is also obviously different from the meta-learning model. The meta-learning model will eventually be fine-tuned to different weights on different tasks, and it is not possible to directly share parameters for different tasks. The MMTL model can share most of the model parameters between different tasks and has obvious computational advantages on ACSA tasks with a large number of categories.

4 Experiments

We conduct experiments on the AI Challenger 2018 Sentiment Analysis Dataset[1], the large-scale Chinese fine-grained sentiment analysis dataset for the Aspect Category Sentiment Analysis (ACSA) tasks. The dataset contains 105,000 training data, 15,000 validation data, and 15,000 testing data. And the data set contains 20 categories, each of which is composed of two layers (below we define

[1]https://github.com/AIChallenger/AI_Challenger_2018

these 20 categories in the form of "The first layer/The second layer"). The 20 aspect categories are respectively 1.) "location/traffic convenience", 2.) "location/distance from business district", 3.) "location/easy to find", 4.) "service/wait time", 5.) "service/waiter' s attitude", 6.) "service/parking convenience", 7.) "service/serving speed", 8.) "price/price level", 9.) "price/cost-effective", 10.) "price/discount", 11.) "environment/decoration", 12.) "environment/noise", 13.) "environment/space", 14.) "environment/cleanness", 15.) "dish/portion", 16.) "dish/taste", 17.) "dish/look", 18.) "dish/recommendation", 19.) "others/overall experience", 20.) "others/willing to consume again". For each user review, the dataset provides the sentiment polarity label (the Positive or Neutral or Negative or Not mentioned) corresponding to the above 20 aspect categories. The goal of the model is to classify the sentiment polarity of different aspect categories.

Since the AI Challenger 2018 Sentiment Analysis Dataset does not provide annotation data for the test data, our experiment used the validation set of the original dataset to evaluate the quantitative performance of the model (as the test dataset for experiments), and we randomly split 15,000 data from the training set as the validation set.

To evaluate the performance of the model on new tasks and tasks with a small amount of data, we also perform some experimental settings on the dataset. We use the less frequently mentioned categories (also with the worst performance of the baseline models) in the dataset as new tasks ("location/distance from business district", "dish/look", "others/overall experience") and the other 17 categories are considered as prior tasks. Those are used to simulate the situation that the model encounters a new aspect category task. We also randomly sample 500, 1000, 2000 examples of the training data and test models' performance on these samples with a few-shot setting.

4.1 Model and Hyperparameter Setting

We compare our models with two strong baselines: 1.) the FastText model (Bojanowski et al., 2017; Joulin et al., 2017) and the ELECTRA model (Clark et al., 2020). For the FastText model, we used the publicly available code [2] for experiments. This code is mainly set for the AI Challenger 2018 Sentiment Analysis Dataset. Its performance is better than the SVM baseline model provided by AI Challenger 2018, and it is also more computationally efficient. For the ELECTRA model, we used the publicly available code[3] (Cui et al., 2020) for experiments. Although the ELECTRA model has larger architectures (large and base), in this experiment, we only consider the ELECTRA small model architecture. Since in actual application scenarios, transformer-based pre-training models will require more GPU computing resources, and larger models will increase the burden of computing resource costs. Therefore, we focus our experiments on smaller models that are more suitable for practical applications.

We implement our algorithms upon the ELECTRA-180g-small (Chinese) model[4]. We set the batch size to 32, the learning rate to 5e-5, and use the Adam optimizer to train the model. For the stages of meta-learning training (k is set to 5, b is set to 8, β is set to 1e-4, λ is set to 0.5 and γ is set to 1e-3) and multi-task learning fine-tuning, we train for 5 epochs individually.

5 Results

First, we use the proposed Meta Multi-Task Learning (MMTL) method to train the model on the AI Challenger 2018 Sentiment Analysis Dataset. Since the MMTL method involves three stages, 1.) the model pre-training stage (loading pre-trained model weights), 2) the meta-learning stage (using to find the optimal model initialization parameters), 3.) the fine-tuning stage of multi-task learning, we also compare the MMTL model with the results of using the pre-training model, meta-learning model, or multi-task learning model respectively.

Table 1 reports the experimental results on the test dataset (the experimental setup de-

[2] https://github.com/panyang/fastText-for-AI-Challenger-Sentiment-Analysis

[3] https://github.com/ymcui/Chinese-ELECTRA

[4] https://huggingface.co/hfl/chinese-electra-180g-small-discriminator/tree/main

F1 (macro)	FastText	ELECTRA	Multi-Task	Reptile	MMTL
Avg. of all 20 aspect categories	54.3	66.1	68.4	67.3	**68.9**
location/distance from business district	43.1	51.2	53.4	**56.6**	56.4
dish/look	43.4	54.4	55.3	57.6	**57.7**
others/overall experience	53.0	56.5	58.8	**60.3**	**60.3**

Table 1: The F1 (macro) results of the proposed models compare to the baseline. Multi-Task: The ELECTRA based model trained with the multi-task learning approach (share most of the parameters). Reptile: The ELECTRA based model trained with the mete-learning approach (no parameter sharing). MMTL: The ELECTRA based model trained with the MMTL approach (share most of the parameters). Note: the "location/distance from business district", "dish/look", and "others/overall experience" are the aspect categories that are less frequently mentioned by user reviews, and are also the aspect categories with the worst performance of the baseline models.

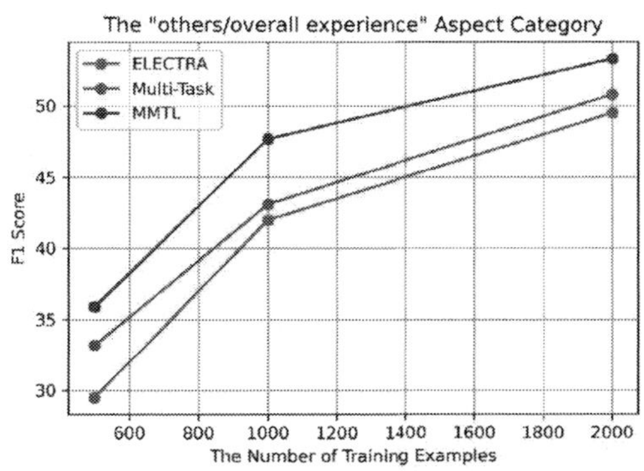

Figure 3: Results on settings for a small amount of training data (500, 1000, 2000 training samples). The target task is the sentiment polarity classification of the aspect category "others/overall experience".

tails are described in Section 4). As we can see, in general, MMTL achieves better performance than the strong baseline models. In addition, it is worth mentioning that the results of the multi-task learning and the meta-learning methods are better than pre-training models based on the same model architecture, but there are some differences in the effectiveness of the two methods.

Although multi-task learning can achieve a higher average f1 score of the 20 aspect categories than meta-learning, there is relatively little improvement in multi-task learning on categories that are less frequently mentioned by user reviews (categories with poor baseline model performance). The possible reason is that multi-task learning may favor categories with high-resource tasks over low-resource ones (Dou et al., 2019). The meta-learning model is different, it can have better performance in the above categories, but the average f1 score is lower than the multi-task learning model. In particular, the MMTL model integrates the advantages of multi-task learning and meta-learning. It performs well in both the average f1 score or the less frequently mentioned categories (more difficult categories).

Note that although it can be seen from Table 1 that the model based on meta-learning has a significant performance improvement on less-mentioned tasks, the model of meta-learning will eventually be fine-tuned to different weights for different aspect category tasks (no parameter sharing), hence it is more difficult applied to actual and real-time application scenarios (different categories require different model weights, e.g., 20 different weights are required on the AI Challenger 2018 Sentiment Analysis Dataset).

To evaluate models' performance with low-resource setting (to simulate the situation that the model encounters a new task with a new aspect category data), we also randomly sample 500, 1000, 2000 examples of the training data from the "others/overall experience" aspect category. Figure 3 shows that the proposed MMTL model significantly outperforms the multi-task learning model and the ELECTRA pre-training model when the amount of training data is small. This shows that the MMTL model that combines meta-learning and multi-task learning is helpful for new tasks (tasks with less data).

6 Conclusion

In this work, we proposed a learning approach called MMTL to combine meta-learning and multi-task learning methods for Aspect Category Sentiment Analysis (ACSA) tasks. The experimental results show that the model based on the MMTL method overall outperforms the strong baseline models of pre-trained models, meta-learning models, and multi-task learning models. And when the amount of training data is small, compared with pre-trained models and multi-tasking learning models, the MMTL model also has relatively better performance. Compared with the meta-learning model (the model of meta-learning will eventually be fine-tuned to different weights for different aspect category tasks, i.e. no parameter sharing), as a result of the MMTL can share parameters between different aspect category tasks, it has better computing efficiency and less memory usage, thus it is more suitable for deployment in practical applications.

There are many future directions worthy of further exploration, especially in addition to ACSA, the Aspect-Based Sentiment Analysis field also contains many subtasks such as Aspect Term Extraction, Opinion Term Extraction, Multi-Aspect Sentiment Analysis, and Cross-domain Aspect-based Sentiment Analysis, how to effectively share model parameters in these subtasks and achieve better performance on new tasks with less data, these are important future research directions.

References

Piotr Bojanowski, Edouard Grave, Armand Joulin, and Tomas Mikolov. 2017. Enriching Word Vectors with Subword Information. *Transactions of the Association for Computational Linguistics*, 5:135–146.

Jiajun Cheng, Shenglin Zhao, Jiani Zhang, Irwin King, Xin Zhang, and Hui Wang. 2017. Aspect-level sentiment classification with HEAT (hierarchical attention) network. In *Proceedings of the 2017 ACM on Conference on Information and Knowledge Management, CIKM 2017, Singapore, November 06 - 10, 2017*, pages 97–106. ACM.

Kevin Clark, Minh-Thang Luong, Quoc V. Le, and Christopher D. Manning. 2020. ELECTRA: pre-training text encoders as discriminators rather than generators. In *8th International Conference on Learning Representations, ICLR 2020, Addis Ababa, Ethiopia, April 26-30, 2020*. OpenReview.net.

Yiming Cui, Wanxiang Che, Ting Liu, Bing Qin, Shijin Wang, and Guoping Hu. 2020. Revisiting pre-trained models for Chinese natural language processing. In *Proceedings of the 2020 Conference on Empirical Methods in Natural Language Processing: Findings*, pages 657–668, Online. Association for Computational Linguistics.

Jacob Devlin, Ming-Wei Chang, Kenton Lee, and Kristina Toutanova. 2019. BERT: Pre-training of deep bidirectional transformers for language understanding. In *Proceedings of the 2019 Conference of the North American Chapter of the Association for Computational Linguistics: Human Language Technologies, Volume 1 (Long and Short Papers)*, pages 4171–4186, Minneapolis, Minnesota. Association for Computational Linguistics.

Zi-Yi Dou, Keyi Yu, and Antonios Anastasopoulos. 2019. Investigating meta-learning algorithms for low-resource natural language understanding tasks. In *Proceedings of the 2019 Conference on Empirical Methods in Natural Language Processing and the 9th International Joint Conference on Natural Language Processing (EMNLP-IJCNLP)*, pages 1192–1197, Hong Kong, China. Association for Computational Linguistics.

Chelsea Finn, Pieter Abbeel, and Sergey Levine. 2017. Model-agnostic meta-learning for fast adaptation of deep networks. In *Proceedings of the 34th International Conference on Machine Learning, ICML 2017, Sydney, NSW, Australia, 6-11 August 2017*, volume 70 of *Proceedings of Machine Learning Research*, pages 1126–1135. PMLR.

Jiatao Gu, Yong Wang, Yun Chen, Victor O. K. Li, and Kyunghyun Cho. 2018. Meta-learning for low-resource neural machine translation. In *Proceedings of the 2018 Conference on Empirical Methods in Natural Language Processing*, pages 3622–3631, Brussels, Belgium. Association for Computational Linguistics.

Pengcheng He, Xiaodong Liu, Jianfeng Gao, and Weizhu Chen. 2020. Deberta: Decoding-enhanced BERT with disentangled attention. *CoRR*, abs/2006.03654.

Armand Joulin, Edouard Grave, Piotr Bojanowski, and Tomas Mikolov. 2017. Bag of tricks for efficient text classification. In *Proceedings of the 15th Conference of the European Chapter of the Association for Computational Linguistics: Volume 2, Short Papers*, pages 427–431, Valencia, Spain. Association for Computational Linguistics.

Xin Li, Lidong Bing, Wenxuan Zhang, and Wai Lam. 2019. Exploiting BERT for end-to-end aspect-based sentiment analysis. In *Proceedings of the 5th Workshop on Noisy User-generated Text (W-NUT 2019)*, pages 34–41, Hong Kong,

China. Association for Computational Linguistics.

Yuncong Li, Cunxiang Yin, Sheng-hua Zhong, and Xu Pan. 2020. Multi-instance multi-label learning networks for aspect-category sentiment analysis. In *Proceedings of the 2020 Conference on Empirical Methods in Natural Language Processing (EMNLP)*, pages 3550–3560, Online. Association for Computational Linguistics.

Xiaodong Liu, Pengcheng He, Weizhu Chen, and Jianfeng Gao. 2019a. Multi-task deep neural networks for natural language understanding. In *Proceedings of the 57th Annual Meeting of the Association for Computational Linguistics*, pages 4487–4496, Florence, Italy. Association for Computational Linguistics.

Yinhan Liu, Myle Ott, Naman Goyal, Jingfei Du, Mandar Joshi, Danqi Chen, Omer Levy, Mike Lewis, Luke Zettlemoyer, and Veselin Stoyanov. 2019b. Roberta: A robustly optimized BERT pretraining approach. *CoRR*, abs/1907.11692.

Alex Nichol, Joshua Achiam, and John Schulman. 2018. On first-order meta-learning algorithms. *CoRR*, abs/1803.02999.

Maria Pontiki, Dimitris Galanis, John Pavlopoulos, Harris Papageorgiou, Ion Androutsopoulos, and Suresh Manandhar. 2014a. SemEval-2014 task 4: Aspect based sentiment analysis. In *Proceedings of the 8th International Workshop on Semantic Evaluation (SemEval 2014)*, pages 27–35, Dublin, Ireland. Association for Computational Linguistics.

Maria Pontiki, Dimitris Galanis, John Pavlopoulos, Harris Papageorgiou, Ion Androutsopoulos, and Suresh Manandhar. 2014b. SemEval-2014 task 4: Aspect based sentiment analysis. In *Proceedings of the 8th International Workshop on Semantic Evaluation (SemEval 2014)*, pages 27–35, Dublin, Ireland. Association for Computational Linguistics.

Maria Pontiki, Dimitris Galanis, John Pavlopoulos, Harris Papageorgiou, Ion Androutsopoulos, and Suresh Manandhar. 2014c. SemEval-2014 task 4: Aspect based sentiment analysis. In *Proceedings of the 8th International Workshop on Semantic Evaluation (SemEval 2014)*, pages 27–35, Dublin, Ireland. Association for Computational Linguistics.

Aniruddh Raghu, Maithra Raghu, Samy Bengio, and Oriol Vinyals. 2020. Rapid learning or feature reuse? towards understanding the effectiveness of MAML. In *8th International Conference on Learning Representations, ICLR 2020, Addis Ababa, Ethiopia, April 26-30, 2020*. OpenReview.net.

Aravind Rajeswaran, Chelsea Finn, Sham M Kakade, and Sergey Levine. 2019. Meta-learning with implicit gradients. In *Advances in Neural Information Processing Systems*, volume 32. Curran Associates, Inc.

Martin Schmitt, Simon Steinheber, Konrad Schreiber, and Benjamin Roth. 2018. Joint aspect and polarity classification for aspect-based sentiment analysis with end-to-end neural networks. In *Proceedings of the 2018 Conference on Empirical Methods in Natural Language Processing*, pages 1109–1114, Brussels, Belgium. Association for Computational Linguistics.

Ashish Vaswani, Noam Shazeer, Niki Parmar, Jakob Uszkoreit, Llion Jones, Aidan N. Gomez, Lukasz Kaiser, and Illia Polosukhin. 2017. Attention is all you need. In *Advances in Neural Information Processing Systems 30: Annual Conference on Neural Information Processing Systems 2017, December 4-9, 2017, Long Beach, CA, USA*, pages 5998–6008.

Alex Wang, Yada Pruksachatkun, Nikita Nangia, Amanpreet Singh, Julian Michael, Felix Hill, Omer Levy, and Samuel R. Bowman. 2019a. Superglue: A stickier benchmark for general-purpose language understanding systems. In *Advances in Neural Information Processing Systems 32: Annual Conference on Neural Information Processing Systems 2019, NeurIPS 2019, December 8-14, 2019, Vancouver, BC, Canada*, pages 3261–3275.

Alex Wang, Amanpreet Singh, Julian Michael, Felix Hill, Omer Levy, and Samuel R. Bowman. 2019b. GLUE: A multi-task benchmark and analysis platform for natural language understanding. In *7th International Conference on Learning Representations, ICLR 2019, New Orleans, LA, USA, May 6-9, 2019*. OpenReview.net.

Yequan Wang, Minlie Huang, Xiaoyan Zhu, and Li Zhao. 2016. Attention-based LSTM for aspect-level sentiment classification. In *Proceedings of the 2016 Conference on Empirical Methods in Natural Language Processing*, pages 606–615, Austin, Texas. Association for Computational Linguistics.

Liang Xu, Hai Hu, Xuanwei Zhang, Lu Li, Chenjie Cao, Yudong Li, Yechen Xu, Kai Sun, Dian Yu, Cong Yu, Yin Tian, Qianqian Dong, Weitang Liu, Bo Shi, Yiming Cui, Junyi Li, Jun Zeng, Rongzhao Wang, Weijian Xie, Yanting Li, Yina Patterson, Zuoyu Tian, Yiwen Zhang, He Zhou, Shaoweihua Liu, Zhe Zhao, Qipeng Zhao, Cong Yue, Xinrui Zhang, Zhengliang Yang, Kyle Richardson, and Zhenzhong Lan. 2020. CLUE: A Chinese language understanding evaluation benchmark. In *Proceedings of the 28th International Conference on Computational Linguistics*, pages 4762–4772, Barcelona, Spain (Online). International Committee on Computational Linguistics.

Wei Xue and Tao Li. 2018. Aspect based sentiment analysis with gated convolutional networks. In *Proceedings of the 56th Annual Meeting of the Association for Computational Linguistics (Volume 1: Long Papers)*, pages 2514–2523, Melbourne, Australia. Association for Computational Linguistics.

Wei Xue, Wubai Zhou, Tao Li, and Qing Wang. 2017. MTNA: A neural multi-task model for aspect category classification and aspect term extraction on restaurant reviews. In *Proceedings of the Eighth International Joint Conference on Natural Language Processing (Volume 2: Short Papers)*, pages 151–156, Taipei, Taiwan. Asian Federation of Natural Language Processing.

Heng Yang, Biqing Zeng, Jianhao Yang, Youwei Song, and Ruyang Xu. 2019a. A multi-task learning model for chinese-oriented aspect polarity classification and aspect term extraction. *CoRR*, abs/1912.07976.

Zhilin Yang, Zihang Dai, Yiming Yang, Jaime G. Carbonell, Ruslan Salakhutdinov, and Quoc V. Le. 2019b. Xlnet: Generalized autoregressive pretraining for language understanding. In *Advances in Neural Information Processing Systems 32: Annual Conference on Neural Information Processing Systems 2019, NeurIPS 2019, December 8-14, 2019, Vancouver, BC, Canada*, pages 5754–5764.

The 33rd Conference on Computational Linguistics and Speech Processing (ROCLING 2021)
Taoyuan, Taiwan, October 15-16, 2021. The Association for Computational Linguistics and Chinese Language Processing

應用對抗式 Reptile 於家電產品網路評論之研究
Home Appliance Review Research Via Adversarial Reptile

甘岱融 Tai-Jung Kan
中央大學資訊工程學系
j7400660@gmail.com

張嘉惠 Chia-Hui Chang
中央大學資訊工程學系
chia@csie.ncu.edu.tw

莊秀敏 Hsiu-Min Chuang
國防大學理工學院資訊工程學系
showmin1205@gmail.com

摘要

對於生產家電廠品的廠商來說，收集及分析產品在社群平台上被討論及喜好程度是企業長久經營相當重要的部份。本論文探討家電產品的評論分析方法，尤其是提及產品不同面向的優劣，是產品設計改良時很好的指標。在本篇論文中，我們將家電產品評論分析分成三個子任務：產品名稱辨識、意見標的面向種類擷取、以及情緒分類。我們首先以 BERT 爲基礎的模型，做爲三項任務的基本效能。其次在情緒分類的任務中，嘗試針對不同的意見目標面向訓練任務導向的模型。此部分我們結合遷移式學習中的 Reptile 演算法、以及對抗式訓練的概念，組成對抗式 Reptile 演算法。研究結果顯示，在多模型的基礎上，使用了對抗式 Reptile 架構訓練後的模型，其 Macro-F1 達到 70.3%，較原始數值 (68.6%) 有些微提升，統計 p 值爲 0.04，獨立樣本檢定爲顯著差異，顯示遷移式學習有助於情緒分類任務提升其效能。

Abstract

For manufacturers of home appliances, the Studying discussion of products on social media can help manufacturers improve their products. Opinions provided through online reviews can immediately reflect whether the product is accepted by people, and which aspect of the product are most discussed . In this article, we divide the analysis of home appliances into three tasks, including named entity recognition (NER), aspect category extraction (ACE), and aspect category sentiment classification (ACSC). To improve the performance of ACSC, we combine the Reptile algorithm in meta learning with the concept of domain adversarial training to form the concept of the Adversarial Reptile algorithm. We find show that the macro-f1 is improved from 68.6% (BERT fine tuned model) to 70.3% (p-value 0.04).

關鍵字：意見目標情緒分析、意見面向擷取、元學習、遷移式學習

Keywords: aspect-based sentiment analysis, aspect category classification, meta-learning, transfer learning

1 緒論

網路社群媒體發展蓬勃，造成社群平台上眾多不同類型的討論，龐大的討論資料是輿情分析最佳資訊來源。以實體商品爲例，產品製造商除了最基本的廠牌名稱以及產品名稱之外，也需要知道該評論針對該產品的何種面向進行討論。然而對於不同類型的商品，通常會有各自不同的討論面向。例如，對於家電產品來說，功能可以視作一種討論標的面向，但在討論美食時，就不會存在功能這個討論標的。

在本研究中，我們將商品種類限定在「家電產品」，並且將網路評論分析分成廠牌、產品名稱、討論標的、蘊含情緒等四種不同資訊。舉例來言，「不推日立除濕機，雖然耐用但很吵。」，該句話包含的廠牌及產品名稱分別爲日立、除濕機，而對於該產品的評論有兩個面向：「耐用」在目標種類中可以歸類爲品質，屬於正向評價、「很吵」歸類爲音量，屬於負向評論。我們可將上述三種資訊簡單分類成三種不同的任務。首先，針對產品名稱以及廠牌名稱，可以作爲命名實體辨識 (Name Entity Recognition, NER) 進行識別；而對於判定產品的目標種類可以視爲是面向種類擷取 (Aspect Category Extraction, ACE)；情緒辨識則是基於某產品的某目標種類的情緒表，，可以看成基於目標種類的情感分類 (Aspect Category Sentiment Classification, ACSC) 任務。

我們首先使用 BERT 爲基礎的表示法，對命名實體辨識 (NER)、面向類別擷取 (ACE)、基於目標種類的情感分類 (ACSC) 三種任務建構基礎模型、得出這些任務的基準效能。對於 NER 任務我們採用 BERT-BiLSTM-CRF 序

列標記架構，針對廠牌及產品分別得到 94.2% 及 93.6%F1 效能。而在 ACE 及 ACSC 兩個任務上，我們參考了 Sun(Sun et al., 2019b) 等人的做法，在輸入方式改成以輔助句進行分類，在 ACE 任務上得到 68.1% Micro F1，另外在 ACSC 任務上效能僅有 73.6% F1。

為改善 ACSC 效能，我們分析了不同的意見標的面向的情感分析效能。由於同一字詞在不同意見標的面向有不同情緒的標籤，例如「高」這個字在品質面向是代表正向情緒，但在音量面向上就會是負面情緒。因此在不同的意見標面向，其文字敘述都有一定程度的差異。針對此問題，我們嘗試為不同的意見標的面向，訓練各自專屬的情緒偵測模型。同時由於某些意見面向的訓練資料過少，因此我們試著藉助其他不同領域的情感分類資料來做遷移式學習 (Transfer Learning)。我們選用適合做少樣本學習的元學習 (Meta Learning) 方法，並採用其中的 Reptile 演算法 (Nichol and Schulman, 2017)，結合對抗式學習 (Ganin et al., 2016) 的概念，提出了對抗式 Reptile(Adversarial Reptile) 的訓練架構。

首先比較使用單模型，無任何遷移式學習訓練的模型效能作為基礎，觀察使用對抗式 Reptile 的架構在多模型的基礎上訓練後的模型是否能提升效能，在 Macro-F1 由 68.6% 提升至 70.3%，並且統計 p 值為 0.04，低於 0.05，獨立樣本檢定為顯著差異。接著比較 Reptile、DANN 兩者與對抗式 Reptile 的消融實驗，發現對抗式 Reptile 在計算上的貢獻主要幾乎都來自於 Reptile 演算法。

雖然目前元學習在諸多領域都有相關的研究，但在自然語言處理上的發展仍較少，因此本論文藉由元學習探討其在 ACSC 任務上的發展也提供了未來若有人想要在自然語言上應用元學習的相關依據。

2 相關研究

2.1 意見分析

線上評論分析是一種意見擷取最主要的應用，其目的在一段話中找出其中我們關注的資訊，例如 Amazon 的書評 (Aashutosh Bhatt, 2015; A. Mounika, 2019)、旅館評論分析 (Walter Kasper, 2011)、航空公司評論 (Ayat Zaki Ahmed, 2020) 等等。意見擷取中最基本的任務即是情感分析 (Sentiment Analysis)，情感分析又可依據情感對象的不同分成文件層級、句子層級、以及意見目標層級三種。文件層級是分析一個文本的情感，句子層級則是判斷每個句子的情感，意見面向情感分析 (Aspect Based Sentiment Analysis, ABSA) 則是針對句子中不同的面向給出相對應的情感分析。

意見面向情感分析依據是否額外參考意見標的詞，又可分為基於面向的目標詞情感分析 (Targeted-ABSA, TABSA) 以及意見面向類別情感分析 (Aspect Category Sentiment Analysis, ACSA)。當文中沒有具體提及意見目標，而是以隱式表達某件事物的角度時，我們定義意見面向類別 (Aspect Category)，目的在判別出句子中提及的目標面向類別，再對這些類別進行情感辨識，因此稱此為目標類情感分類問題 (Aspect Category Sentiment Classification, ACSC)。在 TABSA 的任務中，則是給定句中可能會出現的目標詞 (Target Word)，判斷文句對於意見目標的目標種類及其正、負或中立情感意見。TABSA 與 ACSA 兩者最大的差距在於，TABSA 是針對句子中的給定目標詞進行分析，但 ACSA 則是針對整個句子進行分析。

在 TABSA 的任務中，目前最知名的訓練方式是應用 BERT 中對於句子對優異的預測效能，使用輔助句子 (Auxiliary Sentences) 協助預測 (Sun et al., 2019b)，該篇論文將輔助句子依照句子類型及輸出模式，提出四種輔助句子。句子類型分為句子推論 NLI(Natural Language Inference)、問答 QA(Question-Answer) 兩種：NLI 類型的句子為虛擬句子，僅包含關鍵字，不具有實際上的語句意義；而 QA 則是問句類型的句子。輸出則分為二元 (Binary)、多元 (Multiple) 兩種，二元輸出的輔助句子包含所有資訊 (目標詞、目標種類)，任務是要判斷該輔助句子所意涵的資訊是否正確；多元輸出的輔助句子資訊僅包含目標詞及目標種類，目標是希望判別何種情緒。依上述各二的分類可以組合成四種不同的輔助句子：NLI-M、NLI-B、QA-M、QA-B。

2.2 遷移式學習

遷移式學習的概念是將一個領域學習到的知識模型應用到其他不同但相關的問題。當訓練資料不足，需要藉助其他相似的任務來輔助學習時，遷移式學習的模型架構、訓練方式可以做為模型效能提升的解決方法。在遷移式學習中，通常會分成來源領域及目標領域 (Target Domain)，根據來源領域及目標領域各有無標記資料的情況，有不同的遷移式學習的方法。當來源領域及目標領域都有標記資料時，最常使用的方法有兩種，分別是微調 (Fine-Tuning) 及多任務學習 (Multi-Task)(Caruana, 1998)。微調是將模型在來源領域上訓練完之後，再放到目標領域上進行訓練，做參數的調整，由於概念簡單，所以在各種不同的領域

上都有應用 (Sun et al., 2019a; Nguyen et al., 2020)。而多任務學習的方法就是將不同來源領域及目標領域的資料放在一起學習，在模型中不同領域或任務會對應到不同的輸出，但其中會有部分的參數或網路層是兩個領域共享的，較知名的例子是多語言的同步翻譯 (Huang et al., 2013)。

當目標領域沒有標記資料時，例如來源領域與目標領域資料分佈不同時，最常使用的方法爲領域對抗學習 (Domain-Adversarial Training of Neural Networks, DANN)(Ganin et al., 2016)。雖然缺少目標領域標記資料，但是由於知道來源領域與目標領域兩種資料，相當於多一個自我標記的資訊。因此 DANN 的設計即是再額外訓練一個領域判別器 (Domain Discriminator)，專門用來判別每筆資料是來自什麼領域。從架構上來說，DANN 的模型架構先將輸入資料進行特徵擷取，也就是相當於資料的特徵擷取器 (Feature Extractor)，再利用聯合學習 (Joint Learning) 機制，分別進行原始來源任務、以及領域分類兩種任務的最佳化。DANN 的核心概念是在特徵擷取器的輸出與領域分類任務中間接上梯度反轉層 (Gradient Reversal Layer)，這樣的設計可以迫使特徵擷取器找出其他眞正幫助原始來源任務的特徵，而非是幫助領域判別器結果的特徵，也就是說應用梯度反轉層來確保找出對兩個領域都共有的特徵，使得領域分類器盡可能無法區分資料來源域。

除了上述幾種經典的遷移式學習方法外，近幾年也出現了一個新的分支: 元學習 (Meta Learning)。元學習並不將來源領域與目標領域一起訓練，而是在來源領域上學習出一個學習能力強的模型，再放到目標領域上重新訓練。假設來源領域有多種不同的任務，而目標領域是一種在來源領域並未出現過的任務，元學習的目標即是透過來源領域的不同任務學習到一個能夠適應不同任務的模型，再將這個模型放入目標領域中進行學習，期許能在較少量資料的情況下學習出一個效能強的模型，近期研究也證實元學習對於這種小樣本學習 (Few-shot Learning) 的問題有相當好的成效。簡言之，元學習的核心思想是讓機器「學習如何學習」。

近年來在不同的任務上也出現不少元學習的相關演算法，而絕大多數的元學習算法都可以歸納成雙層優化問題 (Bilevel Optimization)。其包含了兩層迴圈：Inner-loop 及 Outer-loop，分別進行不同目標的優化。在元學習中，模型主要分成個別任務模型 (Base-Learner) 以及元模型 (Meta-Learner) 兩種，而這兩種模型的架構都長得一樣，差別在於優化目標不同。在 Inner-loop 中，首先會對於來源領域的每個任務訓練其個別任務模型，訓練完成後在 Outer-loop 中利用前訓練的模型結果更新元模型的參數，再將原模型的參數重新賦予給每個個別任務模型進行初始化，之後進入下一次迭代，迭代完成的元模型即是該元學習算法得出的結果。多數的元學習算法就是在 Inner-loop 及 Outer-loop 的參數更新或優化方式進行更改。

3 家電評論意見資料集

我們從生活網站論壇「Mobile01」中，與家用電器有關的五個版下載其中的發文及討論串內容，作爲原始文章。並從經濟部網站中蒐集家電產品名稱、廠牌相關種子進行篩選及段落裁切，共擷取出 7,195 個段落，並隨機抽取 2,000 份進行人工標記。人工標記的項目包含「產品名稱」、「廠牌名稱」、「目標種類」、「目標情緒」，其中目標種類分爲功能、品質、外觀、音量、售後、價位、配件、其他，以上八項；情緒則分爲正向、負向、中立三種。而在段落中對於某特定產品的其中一個目標種類敘述標記，則稱爲一個「關係」。

資料標記由兩人進行獨立標記，再評估兩份標記結果的一致性，以確保資料標記的可靠度，在計算一致性時，我們採用 Cohen Kappa(McHugh, 2012) 值進行一致性計算。在我們標記資料中的 Kappa 值計算需要分成兩部分：一是對於標記實體的 Kappa 值計算，此所述實體包含了標記項目中的產品名稱、廠牌名稱；二是對於標記類別的 Kappa 值計算，包含目標種類、目標情緒兩類。通常在 Kappa 值大於 0.6 時便認爲是有較高的一致性，而低於 0.6 則認爲一致性較低。

對於實體類型的 Kappa 值計算，Alex 等人 (Brandsen et al., 2020) 認爲，若是基於字元進行 Kappa 值計算會出現過多的負向標記，很容易高估實際的一致性。而若是基於標記實體進行計算反倒因爲不存在兩人皆未標註的實體資訊，而缺少負向標記的資料，而在計算結果上嚴重低估其實際一致性。因此我們嘗試在實體基礎的算法上添加負向標記的資料。我們根據該實體的平均字元長度以及目前段落長度去預估該段落存在的所有實體數量，並將預估數量減去有標記的實體數量，作爲負向標記的實體資訊。按照上述方法算出的產品名稱及廠牌名稱標記 Kappa 值分別爲 0.959 及 0.965，屬於高度一致性。

對於目標種類及目標情緒的 Kappa 值計算會比單純的實體計算需要更清楚的定義，由於兩者標記是綁定關係的，對於不同標記人員標記的關係需要一套直觀可以對照的方式。對此，我們依照標記的邏輯分別對目標種類及目標情緒做出對應的定義。目標種類可以由其標記的產品名稱及廠牌名稱作爲關鍵詞組，若兩標記人員在某關係上標記的產品名稱及廠牌名稱相同，則可視爲兩者是在敘述同一件商品，進而可以對應到關係的標記結果；而目標情緒的對應則是若是兩個標記人員標記關係的結果，在產品名稱、廠牌名稱、目標種類相同的情況下，則可以進行目標種類的一致性比較。經上述方法匹配後，目標種類及目標情緒計算出的 Kappa 值分別爲 0.691 及 0.724，皆高於 0.6，落在可接受範圍。

4 家電評論意見分析

4.1 資料處理

根據相關研究可知，在諸多不同的任務中，TABSA 是與我們標記的資料形式最爲相近的，TABSA 也可再細分爲 ACE、ACSC 兩個子任務。因爲標記有產品名稱、產品廠牌、目標種類、目標情緒四項，我們可以很直觀地將四個標記項目分成三個子任務，產品名稱、廠牌名稱對應 NER，目標種類相當於 ACE 任務，目標情緒可用於 ACSC。在進行不同資料的處理前，先將標記的 2,000 個段落隨機切成等分的訓練及測試資料各 1,000 個段落，後續對於不同的任務中的訓練及測試資料，均是從此部分切出的段落生成的。

在 NER 的任務中，我們使用 BIEOS 做爲詞語標籤。針對兩標記組別，由於廠牌名稱及產品名稱的一致性非常高，因此我們將兩組在廠牌名稱及產品名稱標記結果取聯集，避免有漏標的情況發生。而針對 ACE 任務，必須先定義目標詞是什麼。由於根據我們資料標記的形式，直接套用的目標詞會是產品名稱及廠牌名稱的組合。但此時會面臨到的問題是，不一定所有的關係標記都同時標有產品名稱及廠牌名稱，因此我們要將問題目標詞簡化。在觀察後發現，大部分的評論都是針對特定產品，進行單個或多個廠牌的比對，因此我們可以將目標詞縮減成廠牌名稱。定義目標詞後，便要進行兩標記資料合併，我們將兩標記人員標記同樣的廠牌名稱及目標種類進行合併。在 ACSC 任務的部分則是將兩標記人員標記相同的廠牌名稱、目標種類及目標情緒進行合併。最後三項任務合併後的資料數量如表 2，其中 NER 數量單位以段落數爲單位。

4.2 命名實體辨識與情緒分析

在 NER、ACE、ACSC 這三個任務上。我們均採用 BERT 爲基底的模。NER 使用 BERT-BiLSTM-CRF 的模型架構；ACE 及 ACSC 均使用 BERT 的分類模型。對於 ACE 及 ACSC，我們參考 Su(Sun et al., 2019b) 的做法，應用輔助句子分別訓練三個模型。若按照原論文的方法將 ACE、ACSC 照 TABSA 格式產生輔助句子資料共同訓練，會產生過多的無意義輔助句子，因此在實驗中我們將兩者分別訓練。ACE 任務的輔助句子給定資訊僅有廠牌名稱，而 ACSC 任務的輔助句子給定資訊則有廠牌名稱、目標種類。在建立的輔助句子中，我們以僅用廠牌名稱做爲輔助句的輸入作爲基本效能，兩種任務的範例輔助句如表 1。

Table 1: 輔助句子範例

輔助句類型	ACE	ACSC
僅廠牌名稱	三星	三星
NLI-M	三星	三星-品質
QA-M	敘述三星產品的什麼面向	三星產品的品質面向有什麼情感
NLI-B	三星-品質	三星-品質-正向
QA-M	敘述三星產品的品質面向	三星產品的品質面向有正向情感

Table 2: 個別任務資料量

任務	NER	ACE	ACSC
訓練資料	1,000	1,001	1,345
測試資料	1,000	1,045	1,422

在三個任務中，我們均使用 Micro-F1 做爲評估效能好的指標。而對於 ACSC 任務，爲了要考慮在不同目標種類下可能的效能影響，因此在某些實驗中，該任務中也會使用 Macro-F1 作爲指標參考，該 Macro-F1 的定義爲將每個目標情緒中 ACSC 任務的 Micro-F1 效能計算出來後取平均。

在 NER 的實驗結果中，產品名稱及廠牌名稱的的 F1 分別爲 93.6% 及 94.2%，顯示在簡易的 BERT 模型架構上，在識別產品名稱、廠牌已有相當好的成果。ACE 及 ACSC 的任務結果如表 3。首先比較多元分類 (NLI-M、QA-M) 及二元分類 (NLI-B、QA-B) 的結果，可發現無論是在 ACE 或是 ACSC 上，多元分類的任務形式表現都比二元分類好上許多。而比較 NLI-M 及 QA-M 兩種輔助句子的形式，在 ACE 的任務上 NLI-M 高了 0.9%，而在 ACSC 的任務上兩者的表現則是相同。接著與只用廠牌名稱作爲輔助句子的基本效能比較，在 ACE 的任務上其與 NLI-M 因輸入形式相同因此效能一樣，故不多提。而在 ACSC 任務中，可發現與 NLI-M 或 QA-M 比起來，有 6% 的效能差距，兩者在輔助句子最大的差別就是在於目標種類資訊的有無，因此可知目標種類的資訊是有助於 ACSC 任務的。

Table 3: ACE 及 ACSC 效能 (Micro-F1)

輔助句類型	ACE	ACSC
僅廠牌名稱	**68.1%**	67.6%
NLI-M	**68.1%**	**73.6%**
QA-M	67.2%	**73.6%**
NLI-B	58.4%	69.3%
QA-B	62.0%	70.3%

接著針對 ACSC 的任務進行更深入的分析，分別比較不同目標種類的訓練資料量與效能的關係 (圖 1)，以及每個目標種類的情緒分布與效能的關係 (圖 2)。圖 1，可發現在不同的目標種類下，ACSC 的任務效能差異甚大，從不到 60% 到超過 80% 的結果都有，不同的目標種類的訓練資料有著極大的數量差異，而效能確實會因爲訓練資料少而較低。圖 2呈現出不同目標種類的三種情緒分布都不一樣，但較難直接看出情緒分布與效能之間的關係。

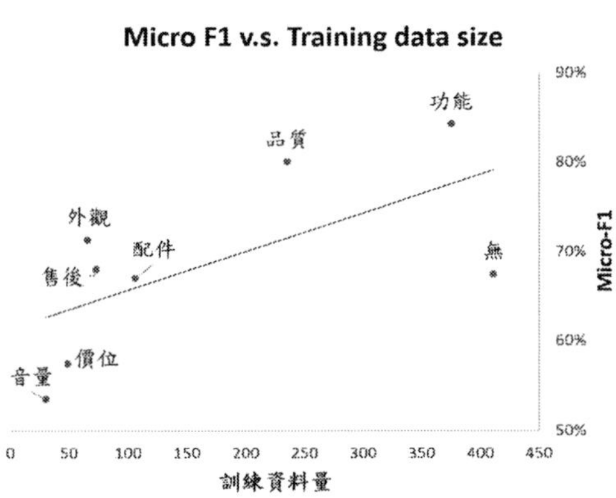

Figure 1: 訓練資料數量與效能關係圖

4.3 多模型方法實驗

由於在不同的目標種類中，情緒的資料存在著不小的差異。因此若能針對各個目標種類都訓練屬於他們自己的 ACSC 模型，說不定能有助於提升效能。所以我們把八個目標種類依照其訓練及測試資料各自訓練 ACSC 模型並評估其效能，而由於在這樣的情況下每個模型都只有包含一個目標種類，所以在輔助句子的建構只需要使用廠牌名稱即可。原先對於所有的種類資練訓練一個模型的方式我們簡稱爲單

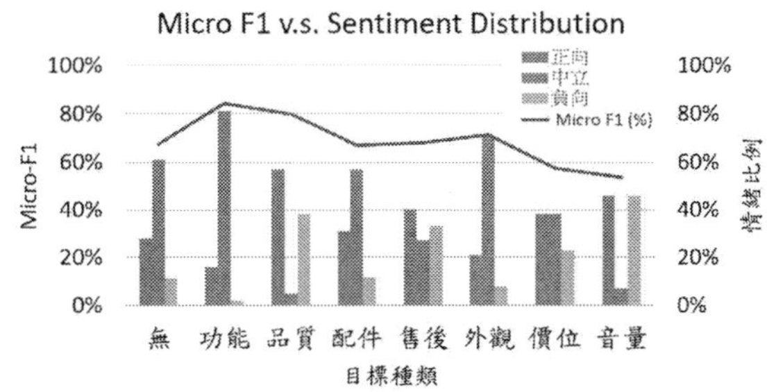

Figure 2: 情緒分布與效能關係圖

模型 (Single Model)，而對於不同目標種類訓練多個模型的方式我們稱爲多模型 (Multiple Models)，各目標種類訓練結果比較如圖 3，可以明顯看出多模型的訓練方式在幾乎所有目標種類上都是輸給單模型的，而多模型的總體效能，Micro-F1 及 Macro-F1 分別 60.1% 與 69.2%，比起單模型的 68.6%、73.6% 低了 8.5% 及 4.4%。在訓練資料特別少的幾個目標種類 (如價位、音量) 成效差距更是超過 10%。由此結果可以推知，多模型的方法在部分目標種類會因爲訓練資料不足而難以得出好的效能，接下來的目標便是要如何提升多模型方法的成效。

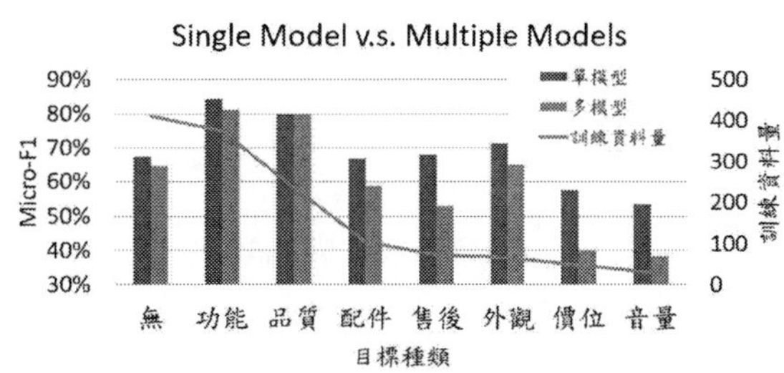

Figure 3: 單模型與多模型效能比較

5 遷移式學習於意見面向分析之應用

在上一個章節中，提到部分的目標種類由於訓練資料過少導致模型效能不好，因此在本章節我們嘗試借助其他的情緒分類資料集，探討其他資料集是否能夠對於我們資料集的訓練有幫助。

5.1 來源資料

遷移式學習除了原始的目標資料集外，也需要來源資料集。由於 ABSA 任務的中文的公開資料集並不多，我們參考 (邱威誠, 2020) 使用的歌手情緒分析資料集，也另外也參考 (Pontiki et al., 2014) 所使用的有關餐廳及筆

Algorithm 1 Reptile

Initialize θ
1: **for** iteration = 1,2,... **do**
2: Sample tasks $\tau_1,\tau_2,...,\tau_n$
3: **for** $i = 1,2,...,n$ **do**
4: Compute $\theta_i = SGD(L_{\tau_i}, \theta, \alpha, k)$
5: **end for**
6: Update $\theta \longleftarrow \theta + \beta \frac{1}{n} \sum_{i=1}^{n} (\theta_i - \theta)$
7: **end for**

電的英文評論資料集。前者本質上是 ABSA 任務，但是探討的對象都是歌手；而後者由於是英文評論，因此我們使用 Google 提供的翻譯 API 將其翻譯成中文。而翻譯的資料由於可能產生同樣字詞在不同上下文而有不同翻譯結果的情況，造成文句中的目標詞與實際目標詞不一致的情況，恐會影響訓練，因此在翻譯的過程時我們便把這類的資料剔除，餐廳評論刪除了 47.1% 的資料筆電評論則是刪除 47.6% 的資料。蒐集的統計資料如表 4。

Table 4: 來源資料統計

資料集	正向	負向	中立	資料總數
歌手	28%	50%	22%	8,425
餐廳	59%	17%	24%	1,908
筆電	43%	18%	39%	1,220

5.2 方法

在前個章節遇到的問題中，部分目標種類的訓練資料過少，可視爲是一種小樣本問題，而元學習對於小樣本學習在過去的實驗上有良好的效能。

以元學習中的 Reptile 演算法 (演算法1) 爲例，在最一開始需先初始化元模型的參數 θ，第一、三行分別代表 Outer-loop 及 Inner-loop。在每次進入 Outer-loop 的迭代時，會隨機抽取 n 個任務，再進入 Inner-loop。而 Inner-loop 就會針對每個抽取出的任務計算並以元模型的參數爲初始值更新各自任務模型的參數，其中參數選定更新 k 次後的結果。待每個任務的模型參數更新後結束 Inner-loop，最後更新元模型的參數，更新方向則是取 Inner-loop 中所有訓練過的模型參數與元模型的參數差異平均，更新元模型的參數後再進入下一次的迭代。最終演算法的輸出即是元模型的參數 θ。

我們提出的方法以 Reptile 演算法爲核心，由於來源資料來自不同的領域，甚至不同的語系，撇除不同領域上的資料分布差異，在語言轉換的過程中也可能導致資料分布的改變，因此爲了減少不同來源域的資料差異，我們參

Algorithm 2 Adversarial Reptile

Input: $\alpha, \beta, \lambda, k, D = \{D_1, ..., D_n\}$
Output: θ^0, ϕ^0
1: Initialize θ, ϕ, γ as $\theta^0, \phi^0, \gamma^0$
2: **for** iteration = 1,2,... **do**
3: **for** $i = 1,2,...,n$ **do** // each source D_i
4: Compute $(\theta_i', \phi_i', \gamma^0) = SGD(D_i, \theta^0, \phi^0, \gamma^0, \alpha, k)$
5: **end for**
6: $\theta^0 \longleftarrow \theta^0 + \beta \frac{1}{n} \sum_{i=1}^{n} (\theta_i' - \theta^0)$
7: $\phi^0 \longleftarrow \phi^0 + \beta \frac{1}{n} \sum_{i=1}^{n} (\phi_i' - \phi^0)$
8: **end for**

Algorithm 3 SGD (Update base learner)

Input: $D_i, \theta_0, \phi_0, \gamma^0, \lambda, \alpha, k$
Output: $\theta_k, \phi_k, \gamma^0$
1: Sample $\tau_0, ..., \tau_{k-1}$ from D_i
2: **for** j = 0,1,...,$k-1$ **do**
3: Compute decoder loss $L^{dec}(\tau_j)$
4: Compute discriminator loss $L^{dis}(\tau_j)$
5: $\theta_{j+1} \longleftarrow \theta_j - \alpha \nabla_\theta (L^{dec}(\theta_j, \phi_j) - \lambda L^{dis}(\theta_j, \gamma^0))$
6: $\phi_{j+1} \longleftarrow \phi_j - \alpha \nabla_\phi L^{dec}(\theta_j, \phi_j)$
7: $\gamma^0 \longleftarrow \gamma - \alpha \nabla_\gamma L^{dis}(\theta_j, \gamma^0)$
8: **end for**

考 (Ganin et al., 2016) 搭配對抗式學習的概念，組合成對抗式 Reptile 演算法 (Adversarial Reptile)。由於元學習是基於任務的演算法，在多數使用元學習的環境中會有多個不同的任務。但目前我們要解決的只有 ACSC 任務，因此將元學習演算法中，對於不同任務的定義改變成不同的來源域 (Li et al., 2020)，也就是將每個來源域都視爲是一個任務。在此我們將 BERT 做爲編碼器 (特徵擷取器)，參數爲 θ；分類的輸出層做爲解碼器，參數爲 ϕ；而此外照 (Ganin et al., 2016)，添加了領域判別器，參數爲 γ。解碼器及領域分類器的損失函數皆使用 Categorical Cross-Entropy。

對抗式 Reptile 的演算法如 Algorithm2、3所示，元 (目標任務) 模型的參數以上標 0 表示，如 θ^0；個別任務模型的參數以下標 i 再加上上標撇表示，如 θ_i'。演算法分爲兩部分，第一部分 (演算法2) 爲外層主要演算法的更新，架構大致上與 Reptile 相同，但在元模型更新時，僅針對編碼器及解碼器進行更新，如演算法2的第 6-7 行，β 代表更新的學習率。領域判別器由於對於所有的個別任務模型都是共用的，因此會在內部迴圈 (第 3-5 行) 更新時進行。

第二部分 (演算法3) 是對於個別任務模型的更新，基本是採用 SGD(Stochastic Gradient Descent) 的更新方式。由於是使用對抗式學習，因此在編碼器及領域判別器中間有一層梯度反轉層。編碼器在更新時的目標即是讓其在確保提升解碼器效能時，同時要混淆領域判別

器，使得編碼器的輸出不會因爲輸入的來源域不同而有過多的差異。如演算法3的第 5 至第 7 行 (α 爲更新的學習率)。領域判別器的參數由於不是在該演算法中主要學習的重點，且所有的個別任務模型都共用同一個領域判別器，因此在此時便會直接更新整個領域判別器的參數。

5.3 實驗

此小節的實驗分成兩個部分，首先比較我們提出的對抗式 Reptile 與前一節單一模型的效能，接著進行消融實驗，由於對抗式 Reptile 可以拆解成 Reptile 及對抗式訓練兩部分，因此我們將其與 Reptile 及 DANN 模型效能進行比較。而本章節的所有實驗結果均是五次實驗數據的平均值。

5.3.1 與原始效能比較

此小節將比較對抗式 Reptile 藉由來源域進行訓練後，所得模型參數在家電產品資料集上使用多模型方式進行微調訓練後得出的效能，與上一節使用單模型方式訓練 (Baseline) 的基礎效能進行比較。各目標種類的效能表現如圖 4，藍色爲 Baseline 效能，橘色爲對抗式 Reptile 效能，可發現除功能及外觀外，在其餘的目標種類，F1 的表現都是對抗式 Reptile 表現較爲優異。因此在加上遷移式學習的方法後，在多模型的效能上確實是可以超越未加入遷移式學習的單模型方法。

而由於圖 4有不少項目是兩者效能極度相近的，因此在每個類別效能的統計檢定比較中，我們檢定兩種方法得出效能差距是否在統計上顯著。使用假設檢定的虛無假設爲兩種方法計算出的效能平均值相等，計算出 p 值並判斷是否小於 0.05，若小於則拒絕假設 (以星號粗體表示)，代表效能差距顯著，反之則接受虛無假設，代表效能差距不顯著。統計結果如表 5所示，其中我們爲每個細部的效能加上其正負兩個標準差的結果，表示其在 95% 的信賴區間中的效能範圍。結果顯示，兩者效能在功能、品質、售後、Macro-F1 四項指標 p 值皆小於 0.05，因此拒絕虛無假設，效果差距顯著，值得一提的是，在功能的部分反倒是原始效能顯著高於我們所提出的模型效能，推測可能的原因是由於在功能層面的敘述上比較沒有特別的固定用詞，情緒也多爲中立，因此在同模型具有較多訓練資料的單一模型訓練環境中就較具優勢；而在配件、外觀、價位、音量四項目標種類可能是因爲 baseline 的效能標準差過大而接受虛無假設；無、Micro-F1 則可能因爲兩者平均效能差距過小而導致差異不顯著。

Table 5: 對抗式 Reptile 效能統計檢定

F1(%)	Baseline	對抗式 Reptile	p 值
無	67.5 ± 2.5	68.3 ± 1.3	0.25
功能	84.3 ± 1.1	82.5 ± 1.8	**0.005***
品質	80.0 ± 5.1	83.9 ± 3.1	**0.02***
配件	67.0 ± 8.1	67.2 ± 4.0	0.91
售後	68.0 ± 9.4	75.6 ± 4.4	**0.01***
外觀	71.3 ± 3.8	70.1 ± 3.3	0.33
價位	57.5 ± 11.1	59.7 ± 2.8	0.40
音量	53.5 ± 7.0	55.1 ± 9.0	0.54
Macro	68.6 ± 5.9	70.3 ± 1.0	**0.04***
Micro	73.6 ± 3.8	74.3 ± 1.1	0.22

Table 6: 消融實驗

多模型	Macro-F1	Micro-F1
DANN	60.7%	69.7%
Reptile	70.0%	74.1%
對抗式 Reptile	**70.3%**	**74.3%**

5.3.2 消融實驗

本節比較的對象是針對對抗式 Reptile 做架構拆解，分爲 Reptile 及對抗式學習的部分，而對抗式學習是 DANN 架構 (Ganin et al., 2016) 的訓練，因此會比較單獨使用 Reptile 演算法及 DANN 兩者模型與對抗式 Reptile 的效能差異。效能如表 6所示。可以明顯看出 Reptile 與對抗式 Reptile 的效能是差不多的，對抗式 Reptile 在兩項指標上只領先 Reptile 不到 0.5%。而兩者皆勝過 DANN 不少，在 Macro-F1 上差距約 10%，Micro-F1 約 5%。因此我們可以得知對抗式 Reptile 在效能上的主要貢獻是來自於其 Reptile 的演算架構，而加上對抗式學習的概念後並未在效能指標上有顯著的成長。

6 結論

在本研究中，我們設計了一份家電產品的資料，可用於 NER、ACE、ACSC 等任務。我們在資料標記完成後也進行了一致性的比對，並確認最終用於實驗的資料是具有較高一致性，品質夠高的。在第一部份的實驗中，對於 NER、ACE、ACSC 三個不同的子任務以 BERT 爲基底模型給出了基礎效能，F1 在 NER 任務的效能平均達到 93.9%，ACE 達到 68.1%，而 ACSC 則有 73.6% 左右的效能。接著針對 ACSC 的任務進行更深入的討論，發現在不同的目標種類之中，ACSC 預測的成效高低不定，細究後推測可能是因爲不同的資料大小或情緒分布導致。因此我們嘗試針對不同的目標種類去各自訓練他們的 ACSC 任務模

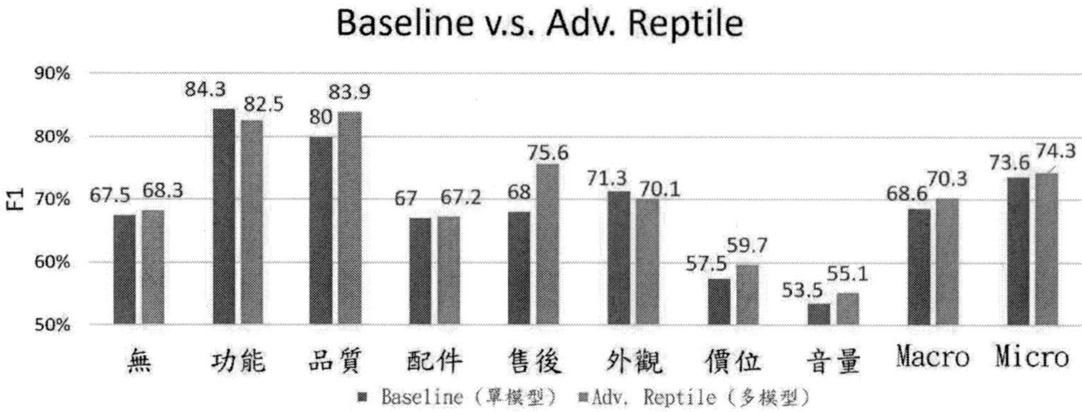

Figure 4: 對抗式 Reptile 與基本效能比較

型，但多模型的方式初始訓練成效遠不如單模型，尤其對於部分目標種類的訓練資料過少，難以訓練出好的效能。接下來的目標是多模型的基礎上提升 ACSC 任務的效能，嘗試使用不同的資料集協助。

而採用不同的資料集協助預測，便會運用到遷移式學習的方法。在此部分的研究，由於元學習對於少樣本資料的訓練相當有效，因此我們在元學習的 Reptile 演算法基礎上，再加上了對抗式訓練的結構，提出了對抗式 Reptile 的模型。在實驗中，對抗式 Reptile 的模型效能在多模型的基礎上可以超越單模型的基準值；在消融實驗中，則觀察到在對抗式 Reptile 的算法中，其架構主要貢獻都是來自於 Reptile，對抗式學習在其中並沒有起到非常大的作用。

元學習在 NLP 相關領域的研究目前資源還比較少，因此本論文藉由元學習探討其在 ACSC 任務上的發展也提供未來 NLP 應用元學習方法的一個方式，期望未來元學習在 NLP 上的發展能更有突破。

References

Dr. S. Sarawathi A. Mounika. 2019. Classification of book reviews based on sentiment analysis: A survey. *IJRAR*, 6.

Harsh Chheda Kiran Gawande Aashutosh Bhatt, Ankit Patel. 2015. Amazon review classification and sentiment analysis. *IJCSIT*, 6:5107–5110.

Manuel Rodriguez-Diaz Ayat Zaki Ahmed. 2020. Significant labels in sentiment analysis of online customer reviews of airlines. *MDPI*.

Alex Brandsen, Suzan Verberne, Milco Wansleeben, and Karsten Lambers. 2020. Creating a dataset for named entity recognition in the archaeology domain. In *Proceedings of The 12th Language Resources and Evaluation Conference*, pages 4573–4577.

R. Caruana. 1998. Multitask learning. In *Encyclopedia of Machine Learning and Data Mining*.

Yaroslav Ganin, E. Ustinova, Hana Ajakan, P. Germain, H. Larochelle, F. Laviolette, M. Marchand, and V. Lempitsky. 2016. Domain-adversarial training of neural networks. *ArXiv*, abs/1505.07818.

Jui-Ting Huang, J. Li, Dong Yu, L. Deng, and Y. Gong. 2013. Cross-language knowledge transfer using multilingual deep neural network with shared hidden layers. *2013 IEEE International Conference on Acoustics, Speech and Signal Processing*, pages 7304–7308.

Jing Li, Shuo Shang, and Ling Shao. 2020. Metaner: Named entity recognition with meta-learning. *Proceedings of The Web Conference 2020*.

Mary McHugh. 2012. Interrater reliability: The kappa statistic. *Biochemia medica : časopis Hrvatskoga društva medicinskih biokemičara / HDMB*, 22:276–82.

Quoc Thai Nguyen, Thoai Linh Nguyen, N. Luong, and Quoc Hung Ngo. 2020. Fine-tuning bert for sentiment analysis of vietnamese reviews. *2020 7th NAFOSTED Conference on Information and Computer Science (NICS)*, pages 302–307.

Alex Nichol and John Schulman. 2017. Reptile: a scalable metalearning algorithm. In *Proceedings of the 34th International Conference on Machine Learning*, volume 70 of *Proceedings of Machine Learning Research*, pages 1126–1135. PMLR.

Maria Pontiki, Dimitris Galanis, John Pavlopoulos, Harris Papageorgiou, Ion Androutsopoulos, and Suresh Manandhar. 2014. SemEval-2014 task 4: Aspect based sentiment analysis. In

Proceedings of the 8th International Workshop on Semantic Evaluation (SemEval 2014), pages 27–35, Dublin, Ireland. Association for Computational Linguistics.

C. Sun, Xipeng Qiu, Yige Xu, and X. Huang. 2019a. How to fine-tune bert for text classification? *ArXiv*, abs/1905.05583.

Chi Sun, Luyao Huang, and Xipeng Qiu. 2019b. Utilizing BERT for aspect-based sentiment analysis via constructing auxiliary sentence. In *Proceedings of the 2019 Conference of the North American Chapter of the Association for Computational Linguistics: Human Language Technologies, Volume 1 (Long and Short Papers)*, pages 380–385. Association for Computational Linguistics.

Mihaela Vela Walter Kasper. 2011. Sentiment analysis for hotel reviews. *Computational Linguistics-Applications Conference*, pages 45–52.

邱威誠. 2020. 應用歌手辨識及情感分析於目標情感偵測與分析之研究. Master's thesis, National Central University, Taiwan.

The 33rd Conference on Computational Linguistics and Speech Processing (ROCLING 2021)
Taoyuan, Taiwan, October 15-16, 2021. The Association for Computational Linguistics and Chinese Language Processing

Unsupervised Multi-document Summarization for News Corpus with Key Synonyms and Contextual Embeddings

Yen-Hao Huang[1], Ratana Pornvattanavichai[2], Fernando Henrique Calderon Alvarado[3], Yi-Shin Chen[*]
Institute of Information Systems and Applications[12]
Department of Computer Science[*]
National Tsing Hua University, Hsinchu, Taiwan
Social Networks and Human-Centered Computing Program[3]
Institute of Information Sciences, Academia Sinica, Taipei, Taiwan
{yenhao0218[1], fhcalderon87[3], yishin[*]}@gmail.com, trp3110@hotmail.com[2]

Abstract

Information overload has been one of the challenges regarding information on the Internet. It is no longer a matter of information access, instead, the focus has shifted towards the quality of the retrieved data. Particularly in the news domain, multiple outlets report on the same news events but may differ in details. This work considers that different news outlets are more likely to differ in their writing styles and the choice of words, and proposes a method to extract sentences based on their key information by focusing on the shared synonyms in each sentence. Our method also attempts to reduce redundancy through hierarchical clustering and arrange selected sentences on the proposed orderBERT. The results show that the proposed unsupervised framework successfully improves the coverage and coherence, while also reducing the redundancy for a generated summary. Moreover, due to the process through which the dataset is obtained, a data refinement method is proposed to alleviate the problem of undesirable texts, which result from the process of automatic scraping.

1 Introduction

Text summarization is defined as the act of expressing the most important facts or ideas about something or someone in a short and clear form. The two most common types of summarizations are classified by their output types, known as extractive summarization and abstractive summarization. The first extracts sentences from the original document, then aggregates the extracted salient text units together to output a summary. Meanwhile, abstractive summarization is the act of paraphrasing to generate a summary that still maintains the main idea of the original document. Summarization can also be classified by the number of source documents they utilize, namely, single document and multi-document summarization. In this research, we are focusing on extractive summarization of multi-document news articles aiming to provide generic summaries.

Although single and multi-document summarization share common challenges which are coverage, the amount of main ideas are being covered in the summary, and coherence, the connection and consistency of the content in the extracted summary, there is an additional challenge that multi-document summarization has to address, redundancy. Redundancy occurs when a piece of information is being expressed more than once in the summary, especially for multi-document tasks. A good summary should not contain sentences that repeat the same ideas. Therefore, we propose a framework to address the problem of coverage and redundancy explicitly, then integrate them together to ensure coherence in the final step.

Our contributions to address the problems of coverage, redundancy, and coherence in multi-document summarization can be summarized as follows:

- We propose an unsupervised framework to construct a sentence-level graph with shared synonyms to address coverage.
- The redundancy level of the extracted summary is reduced by utilizing hierarchical clustering on BERT embeddings.
- Our experiment shows that the proposed orderBERT provides better coherence than original position ordering for

[*]The corresponding author.

news corpus.

2 Related Work

There are several well-known approaches for multi-document extractive summarization. Details are introduced in following sections.

2.1 Frequency-based Methods

One of the most well-known and explainable method in summarization is to utilize the term frequency of the content. Early researches on multi-document summarization focused on extracting words and their lexical characteristics to solve content selection. Some approaches to maximize coverage of the content utilized a classifier (Conroy et al., 2004; Ramanujam and Kaliappan, 2016; Hennig et al., 2008) or directly assigned a score to sentences (Schiffman et al., 2002; Lin and Hovy, 2002; Meena and Gopalani, 2014) to identify the importance of those sentences. Other works introduced "concept" (Schluter and Søgaard, 2015) or "event" (Filatova and Hatzivassiloglou, 2004) to represent the important text unit that best covers the main idea of the source documents. SumBasic (Nenkova and Vanderwende, 2005) was based on the relation of words frequency in a document cluster and human summaries. The study showed that the higher the frequency in the document cluster, the higher the probability of the word to appear in the human summary. Despite the different detailed approaches, one thing these methods have in common is utilizing the term frequency of the content. However, with the nature of multiple source documents, the limitation to word frequency is their lexical form. If only the lexical form is considered, we would be limited to capturing only some part of the information.

2.2 Greedy-algorithm Methods

A greedy-algorithm is an intuitive algorithm that is used in optimization problems. The process is to make the optimal choice at each step in order to find the overall optimal way to solve the whole problem. Some works integrated submodularity (Dasgupta et al., 2013) and minimum dominating set (Shen and Li, 2010) with the algorithm to solve the text summarization task. Other work such as the KLSum (Haghighi and Vanderwende, 2009) focused on minimizing the divergence between the true distribution and the approximating distribution. One of the most well-known method is the Maximal Marginal Relevance(MMR) (Carbonell and Goldstein, 1998) which tried to reduce redundancy while maintaining relevance in the retrieved text unit. The method performs well for the task of information retrieval where the task is to retrieve documents related to a user's query. However, for the task of multi-document summarization, there is no user's query labelled which means that further determination of the reference needs to be made. Moreover, Takamura and Okumura (2009) also stated that although relevance and redundancy are taken into consideration, no global viewpoint is given. We found that these methods do address redundancy in nature, but not explicitly.

2.3 Graph-based Methods

Sentence-level graph-based extractive summarization generally assigns each sentence to the nodes and determine the edges of them depending on their relationship. The centroid-based method (Radev et al., 2004b), MEAD (Radev et al., 2004a), TextRank (Mihalcea and Tarau, 2004), and LexRank (Erkan and Radev, 2004) are some of the common graph-based methods in previous works. However, the limitation to the nodes connections are that they either rely on whole sentence similarity which needs a defined threshold to determine their connection, or only considers the lexical form of the words that overlap between sentences.

3 Methodology

This work aims to overcome the three main challenges introduced in Section 1 and proposes a framework toward coverage, redundancy, and coherence as shown in Figure 1.

3.1 Data Refinement

In our work, we utilized the Multi-News dataset (Fabbri et al., 2019), a large multi-document news dataset consisting of 56, 216 news clusters, obtained through automatic scraping. According to Kryściński et al. (2019), manual inspection of data is impractical and expensive and mostly limited to removing only markup structure and obvious noises. Despite the fact that the authors of

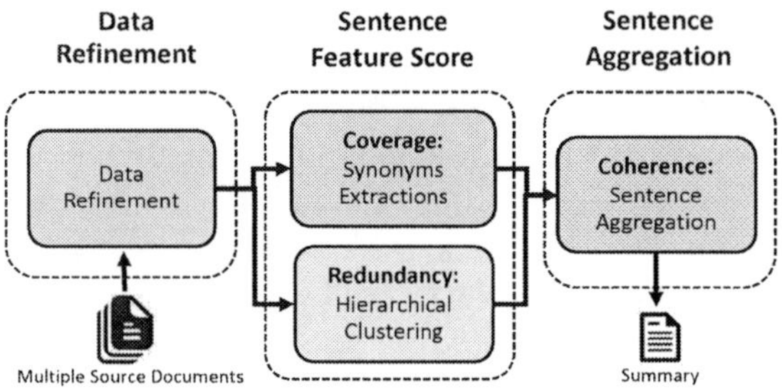

Figure 1: Overall Framework

Multi-News have provided an updated version of their dataset, we can still detect some unrelated source documents throughout the dataset. Therefore, in the process to refine data quality, we have divided noises into two categories: retrieval noises and content noises. **Retrieval noises** are error texts from the process of content retrieval. These texts are found to be duplicated within their own clusters and across different clusters. There are two major retrieval noises: (1) *Duplicated source documents within the same news clusters*, that are possibly result from a news service supplied articles to more than one outlets. As some news outlets have limited resources, they rely on information supplied by other news service instead. As a result, news articles from different outlets may be identical and ensure that the dataset does not unintentionally allow more weight to a specific document. (2) *Duplicated source documents across different news clusters*, which are generally the result of scraping error messages. We found that the same error messages appear throughout multiple documents. Therefore, regardless of the news clusters, there are risks that these error messages can appear as one of the source documents. With a list of scraping error messages, source documents in the list are removed at the end. **Content noises** refers to the source documents' lengths and the semantic similarity of source documents within their own clusters. (1) *Single sentence source document* are undesirable news articles. They are more likely to be error messages generated when scraping data from the website. Although they sometimes share the same words with other source documents within the cluster, but are entirely unrelated or can not provide enough information to be considered an independent source document. (2) *Discrepancy between source documents* of the same news cluster are also undesirable characteristics of source documents that needs elimination. In order to ensure that the remaining source documents are related to the reference summary but not totally identical, we compare the similarity of each source document by embedding them utilizing Sentence-BERT(Reimers and Gurevych, 2019) and compare the cosine similarity of all source documents within the same news clusters. We empirically set to filter unqualified news clusters that contain 2 source documents with cosine similarity less than 0.5 or equal to 1.0.

To comply with the task of multi-document summarization, after refining all the unrelated source documents, we finally eliminated news clusters with only one source document.

3.2 Sentence Feature Score

There are two components for sentence score features designed for coverage and redundancy factors, respectively.

3.2.1 Coverage Factor: Synonyms Extractions

This component aims to capture the overlapping content despite the lexical differences. Documents written by different authors are likely to be different in the writing styles and the word usage. Within the same news clusters, despite the different words, authors still have to deliver the same information. Therefore, this work considers that synonym is the key to identify the overlapping information between documents where different words are used. To extract synonyms of different source documents, a two-step approach is proposed and described as follow:

Wordnet Synonyms Extractions. WordNet (Miller, 1995) is a large lexical database links nouns, verbs, adjectives, and adverbs to sets of synonyms, known as synsets. Synsets are linked by their conceptual-semantic and lexical relations, resulting in a network of related words and concepts. To identify the overlapping content, we utilized the synonymy semantic relations from WordNet to capture the common word senses and their meaning between sentences.

First, the part-of-speech (POS) tagging was adopted to categorize words into their syntac-

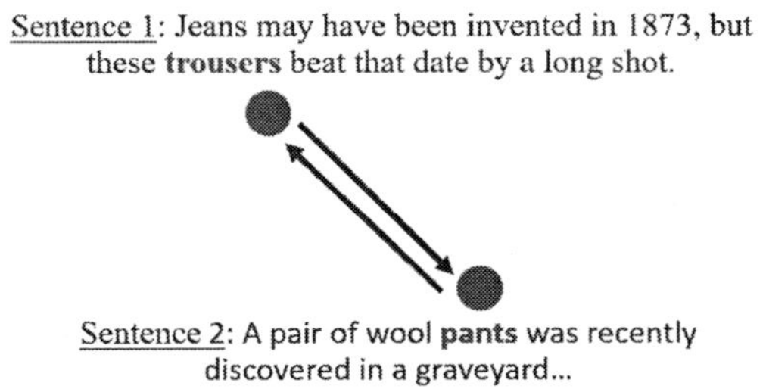

Figure 2: An Example of Sentences Connection.

tic category: nouns, verbs and adjectives. To determine which syntactic category to include, this work considers the journalistic questions when readers read news articles. In general, we assumed that what readers are most interested in an article is the "Who" did "What" in the article. According to the two questions, candidate answers usually result with nouns and a combination of other POS such as verbs and adjectives. Then, we performed synonym extractions by utilizing NLTK for WordNet.

Graph-based Sentence Scoring. With the list of synonyms for each word, a sentence graph was constructed where each individual sentence is the vertex and sentences were connected if there was any shared synonyms. The sentence graph is formally defined in Definition 1.

Definition 1 (Sentence Graph). *Let D, S denote a set of source documents and sentences in documents D, respectively, such that $D = \{d_i\}$, $S = \{s_j\}$. The directed graph for each news cluster is denoted as:*

$$G_D = (S, E) \tag{1}$$

where S represents all the sentence vertices in D, E denotes the edges between two sentences that shared common synonyms.

To construct a sentence graph G_D, originally, one edge was constructed for each synonym; however, each undirected edge was further converted to two directed edges toward each sentence. Figure 2 shows an example of the connection between sentences.

After constructing a graph for each news cluster, PageRank (Page et al., 1999) algorithm was adopted to calculate the score of each vertex as in Equation 2.

$$PR(s_i) = (1 - \delta) + \delta * \sum_{s_j \in In(s_i)} \frac{PR(s_j)}{|Out(s_j)|} \tag{2}$$

where $PR(s_i)$ is the score of $(s_i) \in S$, δ is a parameter usually set to 0.85 by default, $In(s_i)$, $Out(s_i)$ are the inbound link and outbound link of sentence vertex s_i, respectively. The PageRank score $PR(s)$ was treated as the final sentence scores, which determines the level of coverage for each sentence.

3.2.2 Redundancy Factor: Hierarchical Clustering

To minimize redundancy, sentences S were first embed by Sentence-BERT (Reimers and Gurevych, 2019) to retrieve the contextual embeddings $X \in R^{|S| \times dim}$ where dim is the hidden size of Sentence-BERT. The agglomerative hierarchical clustering was adopted at sentence level for each news cluster with sentence embeddings X. The metrics of hierarchical clustering were set as the group average similarity, which takes into consideration all sentence features within the cluster as in Definition 2.

Definition 2 (Sentence Group Similarity). *Let C_1, C_2 denote two sentence group, their corresponding features are presented as X_{C_1}, X_{C_2}. The sentence group similarity could be calculated by Equation 3.*

$$sim(C_1, C_2) = \sum sim(X_i, X_j)/|X_{C_1}| * |X_{C_2}| \tag{3}$$

where X_i and X_j are sentence features, s_i belongs to group C_1 and s_j belongs to group C_2.

In the process of clustering, we evaluated the quality of the clustering utilizing two cluster validity indices, Silhouette Score and DB Index or Davies—Bouldin Index as shown below.

The calculation of Silhouette Score is defined in Equation 4.

$$silh(s) = \frac{dis_{inter}(s) - dis_{intra}(s)}{max\{dis_{intra}(s), dis_{inter}(s)\}} \tag{4}$$

where $silh(s)$ is the Silhouette Score of the sentence s, $intra_d(s)$ is the average Euclidean distance on sentence feature $x \in X$ between sentence s and all the other sentences in the cluster $C, s \in C$, $inter_d(s)$ is the minimum average distance from sentence s to all clusters $\{\check{C} | s \notin \check{C}\}$. The score ranges from -1 to 1. The higher values indicate that objects within the cluster are more similar to their own clusters and less similar to other clusters.

For DB index DB, it was calculated as follows:

$$DB = \frac{1}{k} \sum_{m=1}^{k} \max_{m \neq n} R_{m,n} \tag{5}$$

where $R_{m,n}$ is the within-to-between cluster distance ratio for the ith and jth clusters

$$R_{m,n} = \frac{dis_m + dis_n}{dis_{m,n}} \tag{6}$$

dis_m is the average Euclidean distance between each sentence in the mth cluster and the centroid of the mth cluster. dis_n is the average distance between each point in the nth cluster and the centroid of the nth cluster. $dis_{m,n}$ is the distance between the centroids of the mth and nth clusters. The minimum value of DB Index is 0. The lower value indicate that objects are less dispersed.

With the combination of the two indices, the optimal threshold for clustering is then able to obtained by selecting a threshold that can get the highest Silhouette score and the lowest value for DB index. Finally, sentence cluster label l_s was retrieved for each sentence s, which determines which sentences are semantically similar.

3.3 Sentence Aggregation

Sentence aggregation takes two input, namely, the sentence score $PR(s)$ and the sentence cluster label l_s. Both of the values were used as the criteria to select and rearrange sentences in this phase.

3.3.1 Sentence Selection

The goal of this step was to select top-N representative sentences, where $N = 9$ is the average number of sentences in the reference summary. To reduce redundancy, we first grouped the sentences by l_s. For each cluster, a candidate sentence was selected which had the highest $PR(v)$. By utilizing both the coverage indicating value (sentence score), and the redundancy grouping (sentence cluster label), we considered that the selected sentences were the top salient and least redundant sentences.

In cases that there were more than N clusters within the news cluster, the top-N sentences with the least position value in their original documents were selected.

3.3.2 Sentence Ordering

News content are known for their lead sentences bias where the main content and the flow are based on the first few sentences of the articles. However, for multi-document summarization, the common method leveraging original position of the sentences might not give the best fluent order for a summary.

Hence, we proposed to fine-tuned BERT for a modified next sentence prediction task (Devlin et al., 2019) with the extracted top-N sentences, namely orderBERT. Specifically, inverse-order sentences within source article are added as false samples. In the original paper, BERT was trained to predict whether the observed sentences come from the same or distinct documents, but not to manage the orders. Meanwhile, the orderBERT was trained to predict whether the second sentence is next order to the first sentence. The higher the *continuation value* (CV) output from orderBERT, the more continuity the given 2 sentences are.

For reordering, an *anchor sentence* was initialized as the least original position value sentence among top-N sentences. If there were many sentences at first position, the one with the highest $PR(s)$ was selected. The *anchor sentence* was further paired with all the other top-N sentences for orderBERT to obtain the corresponding CVs. The sentence with the highest CV was assigned as next anchor sentence and continue throughout the remaining top-N sentences. This algorithm generally take $O(N^2)$ time complexity; however, as the N is small, it was not too time consuming.

4 Experiment

4.1 Dataset

This work experiments on a multi-document news corpus, namely Multi-News (Fabbri et al., 2019). The dataset contains the reference summary obtained from Newser website [1] and multiple source documents of the

[1] `www.newser.com`

same news story. The total number of source documents per news story ranges from 2 to 10 documents per reference summary. The data refinement process is conducted as mention in Section 3.1. The statistics of the original and refined dataset are shown in Table 1.

Source #	Original	Refined
2	3049/3072/23894	2843/2854/22298
3	1565/1574/12707	1521/1531/12367
4	608/624/5022	583/586/4764
5	223/206/1873	198/188/1656
6	113/82/763	86/64/657
7	38/41/382	34/32/330
8	15/14/209	12/11/163
9	10/7/89	7/7/61
10	1/2/33	1/0/19
Total	**56,216**	**52,873**

Table 1: Data Statistics (test/validation/train)

4.2 Experimental Setup

To evaluate the performance, as our methods are unsupervised, we have experimented on our refined dataset with five other unsupervised baselines including *common extractive summarization baseline*: (1) **Lead-3** sentences, which takes first 3 sentences of each source documents to aggregate as the extracted summary; *frequency-based*: (2) **SumBasic** (Haghighi and Vanderwende, 2009) computes the probability distribution over the input words. For each input sentences, a weight equal to the average probability of the words are assigned as the sentence score. With top score sentences selected, the words probability are updated for additional sentence selection until a designated summary length is reached; *greedy algorithm*: (3) **KLSum** (Nenkova and Vanderwende, 2005) selects sentences by minimizing the divergence between the true distribution in the original document and the approximating distribution in the summary; *graph-based*: (4) **LexRank** (Erkan and Radev, 2004) is sentence-level graph algorithm where edges between the nodes are assigned when the node pair exceeds a cosine similarity threshold, in our work 0.1 according to the best performance LexRank experiment. When calculating the weight of the edges, their idf value is also taken into consideration; and (5) **TextRank** (Mihalcea and Tarau, 2004), for the task of extracting salient sentences, is sentence-level graph algorithm. The weighted edges are calculated by dividing the overlapping words of two sentences with the length of each sentence. For LexRank and TextRank, Equation 2 is applied to obtain the final sentence score. Finally, all the algorithms were limited to select Top-$N = 9$ sentences as generated summary, which is the average sentence number in the reference summary.

The settings to implement the proposed method are illustrated below. As shown in Figure 3, the highest value for Silhouette score and the lowest value for DB index equation indicate that the best cosine similarity threshold was found at 0.9 and set as the ultimate parameter. The final number of selected sentence is 9 as baselines. To finetune the orderBERT proposed in Section 3.3.2, a pretrained base version of BERT is selected to optimize the next sentence prediction objective with batch size set as 32 for 5 epochs.

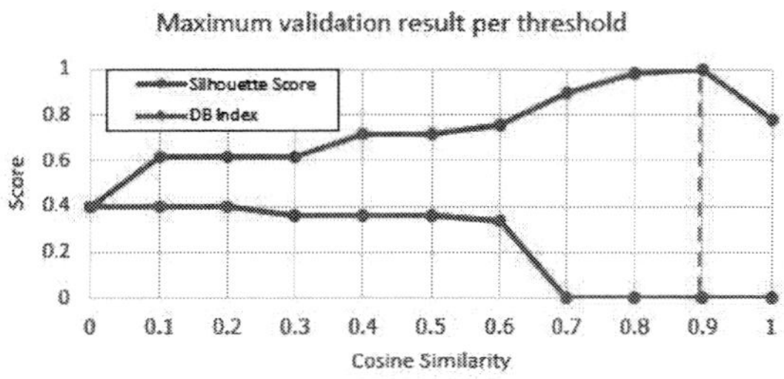

Figure 3: Optimal threshold from Silhouette Score and DB Index values

5 Results and Analysis

For the experimental results, this work carefully evaluates our main focuses separately in the following sections, which are coverage, redundancy, and coherence.

5.1 Coverage

To evaluate coverage, ROUGE score was selected by comparing 4 combinations of the different POS settings with our method as shown in Table 2. There are 3 different ROUGE scores adopted, which are ROUGE-1 (R-1), ROUGE-2 (R-2), ROUGE-SU (R-SU) for evaluating uni-gram, bi-gram overlaps and skip/uni-gram co-occurrence, respectively.

Method	Refined All			Refined Testing			Original Testing		
	R-1	R-2	R-SU	R-1	R-2	R-SU	R-1	R-2	R-SU
Lead-3	0.4114	0.1215	0.1545	0.4098	0.1210	0.1536	0.3964	0.1071	0.1406
LexRank	0.4174	0.1247	0.1620	0.4179	0.1253	0.1624	0.4154	0.1247	0.1611
TextRank	0.3963	0.1272	0.1446	0.3954	0.1271	0.1438	0.4016	0.1186	0.1494
SumBasic	0.3749	0.1020	0.1218	0.3769	0.1028	0.1231	0.3775	0.1041	0.1242
KLSum	0.3665	0.1012	0.1200	0.3672	0.1018	0.1203	0.3669	0.1027	0.1207
N. Syn.	**0.4272**	**0.1304**	**0.1680**	0.4268	**0.1315**	0.1681	**0.4218**	**0.1321**	**0.1663**
N.+V. Syn.	0.4266	0.1300	0.1674	0.4262	0.1310	0.1675	0.4209	0.1318	0.1655
N.+Adj. Syn.	0.4246	0.1291	0.1664	**0.4278**	0.1312	**0.1684**	0.4213	0.1319	0.1659
N.+V.+Adj. Syn.	0.4265	0.1299	0.1673	0.4275	0.1310	0.1681	0.4207	0.1317	0.1653
PG-ORIGINAL	Supervised Methods			*			0.4185	0.1291	0.1646
PG-BRNN							0.4280	0.1419	0.1675
CopyTransformer							0.4357	0.1403	0.1737
Hi-MAP							0.4347	0.1489	0.1741

Table 2: ROUGE Evaluation. Note that "Refined All" denotes the results from entire Multi-News dataset with refinement for all unsupervised methods; whereas, "Refined Testing" reports the results from only testing set with refinement, and "Original Testing" shows the results from testing set without refinement.

5.1.1 Performance

As observed from the results, our proposed methods that adapts synonyms to find sentence connections can help improve ROUGE score and outperform all unsupervised baselines. This implies that there are connections that are added when considering synonyms. We also found that within the each document itself, the author might utilize synonyms when talking about the same subject. Therefore, utilizing synonyms not only contribute to capturing connections between documents but within each document itself.

In addition to the unsupervised baselines, we also compare to supervised approaches, which are PG-ORIGINAL (Lebanoff et al., 2018), PG-BRNN (Gehrmann et al., 2018), CopyTransformer (Gehrmann et al., 2018), and Hi-MAP (Fabbri et al., 2019). It is worth mentioning that their results are obtained from Hi-MAP's paper for a fair comparison. Although our method can not outperform the supervised baselines, with data refinement, we can achieve comparable results to PG-BRNN. The possibles reasons are: first, our method is fully unsupervised; second, they summarize in an abstractive manner, which is suitable for multi-document tasks. These strengths will be further considered in our future work.

5.1.2 POS Connections Analysis

For different combinations of POS, we observe that utilizing only synonyms that are nouns performed the best. However, in the case of verbs and adjectives, we might need to consider the subject or object that is doing the action or being described. In order to improve the usage of verbs and adjectives, further improvements could focus on the noun that is directly associated with them.

5.1.3 Necessity of Data Refinement

Since we have proposed data refinement as part of our methodology to emphasize the importance of refined data, we analyse the results in comparison to other methods with the original dataset by the author. We compare our method before and after the refinement. Noted that we found some source documents without refinement to be about the same length or even shorter than the reference (golden) summary. For the mentioned instances, we utilize all sentences in the source document as the extracted summary for comparison. The results are shown in Table 2. We can observe that the proposed refinement could successfully improve most of the results on ROUGE including all the proposed methods. Only TextRank and SumBasic slightly decrease on their partial scores.

5.2 Redundancy

To evaluate performance of our hierarchical clustering method which is designed to address redundancy issues, we first test the redundancy reducing performance and study the ablation effects for the clustering on the coverage. Detailed analyses are discussed in below.

Method	Average Word #	
	max.	mean.
Lead-3	12.6	1.37
LexRank	19.75	1.50
TextRank	25.32	1.47
SumBasic	19.96	1.29
KLSum	14.06	1.42
N. Syn.	**9.54**	1.36
N. + V. Syn.	11.20	1.36
N. + Adj. Syn.	19.69	1.38
N. + V. + Adj. Syn.	11.20	**1.02**

Table 3: Redundancy Analysis

5.2.1 Hierarchical Clustering Influence on Reducing Redundancy

The maximum and mean value of the average occurrences for distinct words are calculated for generated summaries from each method with stopwords removed. The lower the redundancy, the fewer the word occurs in the summary. The results are shown in Table 3.

As observed from the table, the proposed methods (named with Syn.) generally have lower word occurrence for each distinct word, especially for our method with N.+V.+Adj. Syn. which has a lowest 1.02 on average. Although the other combinations of our methods did not have such big gaps as the N.+V.+Adj. Syn. approach, their occurrences are generally lower than the other baselines. This result implies that with the hierarchical clustering step, the extracted sentences for summaries contains less words that are redundant.

5.2.2 Hierarchical Clustering Influence on Boosting Coverage

Besides word occurrences, an ablation study of our methodology with/without hierarchical clustering was conducted with its evaluation based on ROUGE. As shown in Table 4, we found that hierarchical clustering not only helps reduce redundancy but also helps increase coverage. Results without hierarchical clustering are lower than with clustering. Without the clustering, the selected sentences may have high score but cover duplicated topics and contain redundant information. Therefore, reducing redundancy also contributes to the coverage of summaries.

5.2.3 Different Hierarchical Clustering Technique and their Performance

In addition to agglomerative hierarchical clustering, we also experimented with another common clustering technique, K-means, with the other settings remains the same. The performance of the 2 techniques in terms of coverage and redundancy is as shown in Table 5.

Method	ROUGE-1	
	w. Cluster.	w/o. Cluster.
N. Syn.	**0.4272**	0.4173
N.+ V. Syn.	**0.4266**	0.4187
N.+ Adj. Syn.	**0.4246**	0.4187
N.+ V.+ Adj. Syn.	**0.4265**	0.4167

Table 4: Ablation Study for Clustering on ROUGE

Technique	ROUGE-1	Average Word #
Hierarchical	0.42684	**1.48**
K-Means	0.42108	1.49

Table 5: Clustering Techniques Comparison

According to the result, we found that utilizing hierarchical clustering performs better than utilizing K-means in both coverage and redundancy performance. We found that the lower performance of K-means is most probably due to the pre-defined number of clusters. The limited number of clusters influence the degree in which sentences can be clustered. As for the agglomerative hierarchical clustering, the number of clusters are jointly decided by Silhouette Score and DB Index.

5.3 Coherence

For the coherence evaluation of our proposed orderBERT reordering, we conduct human evaluation with 14 participants to compare to other 2 ordering methods. The extracted sentences are obtained from our noun synonym method. Given an original article and three summaries generated by different reordering mechanisms, our questionnaire asks to respondents to answer two questions: (1) rate the fluency for each summary individually; and (2) rank the fluency from all summaries.

In Table 6, original position method has the most vote for score 5, which is 8% more than ours. However, considering score 4 and 5, the proposed orderBERT reordering method have totally 64% of vote that over original position's 43%. For average rating and ranking score in Table 7, the orderBERT reordering achieve top score over the other two methods. The above results show that the proposed method outperforms the common methods which reference to sentences' original position. Over-

Method	Rating Score				
	1	2	3	4	5
orderBERT	0%	7%	29%	**43%**	**21%**
Original Position	7%	21%	29%	14%	**29%**
Random	7%	29%	29%	**29%**	7%

Table 6: Coherence Rating Evaluation Result (1 is the least coherent, 5 is the most coherent rating)

Method	Avg. Score	
	Rate	Rank
orderBERT	**3.86**	**2.43**
Original Position	3.43	1.86
Random	3.07	1.71

Table 7: Coherence Rating and Ranking Score

all, orderBERT predicts the next sentence regarding the content of the reference sentence so that the flow of the whole content is consistent. The method takes into consideration the connectivity that the anchor sentence can transfer to the next sentence.

6 Conclusion and Future Work

In our research, we assume different authors write who write news articles for different outlets, are very likely to utilize a variety of words. With this intuition, the synonyms are adapted to connected sentences among multi-documents. Results showed that identifying synonyms shared between sentences can successfully help to capture the content both within and across documents. In addition to coverage, we were also able to reduce redundancy through hierarchical clustering and improve coherence of the final summary using the proposed orderBERT. Moreover, although our entire framework are fully unsupervised, we are able to achieve comparable result than the supervised methods. In future work, we would like to combined supervised objective in our algorithm and focus on the compression rate which is also another challenging task for multi-document summarization.

Acknowledgments

We would like to thank members of the IDEA Lab and the anonymous reviewers for the helpful feedback. This research is supported in part by Ministry of Science and Technology in Taiwan (Program No. MOST 110-2221-E-007-085-MY3, MOST 108-2221-E-007-064-MY3).

References

Jaime Carbonell and Jade Goldstein. 1998. The use of mmr, diversity-based reranking for reordering documents and producing summaries. In *Proceedings of the 21st annual international ACM SIGIR conference on Research and development in information retrieval*, pages 335–336.

John M Conroy, Judith D Schlesinger, Jade Goldstein, and Dianne P O' leary. 2004. Left-brain/right-brain multi-document summarization. In *Proceedings of the Document Understanding Conference (DUC 2004)*.

Anirban Dasgupta, Ravi Kumar, and Sujith Ravi. 2013. Summarization through submodularity and dispersion. In *Proceedings of the 51st Annual Meeting of the Association for Computational Linguistics (Volume 1: Long Papers)*, pages 1014–1022.

Jacob Devlin, Ming-Wei Chang, Kenton Lee, and Kristina Toutanova. 2019. Bert: Pre-training of deep bidirectional transformers for language understanding. In *Proceedings of the 2019 Conference of the North American Chapter of the Association for Computational Linguistics: Human Language Technologies, Volume 1*, pages 4171–4186.

Günes Erkan and Dragomir R Radev. 2004. Lexrank: Graph-based lexical centrality as salience in text summarization. *Journal of artificial intelligence research*, 22:457–479.

Alexander R Fabbri, Irene Li, Tianwei She, Suyi Li, and Dragomir R Radev. 2019. Multi-news: A large-scale multi-document summarization dataset and abstractive hierarchical model. *arXiv preprint arXiv:1906.01749*.

Elena Filatova and Vasileios Hatzivassiloglou. 2004. Event-based extractive summarization.

Sebastian Gehrmann, Yuntian Deng, and Alexander M Rush. 2018. Bottom-up abstractive summarization. *arXiv preprint arXiv:1808.10792*.

Aria Haghighi and Lucy Vanderwende. 2009. Exploring content models for multi-document summarization. In *Proceedings of human language technologies: The 2009 annual conference of the North American Chapter of the Association for Computational Linguistics*, pages 362–370.

Leonhard Hennig, Winfried Umbrath, and Robert Wetzker. 2008. An ontology-based approach to text summarization. In *2008 IEEE/WIC/ACM International Conference on Web Intelligence and Intelligent Agent Technology*, volume 3, pages 291–294. IEEE.

Wojciech Kryściński, Nitish Shirish Keskar, Bryan McCann, Caiming Xiong, and Richard Socher. 2019. Neural text summarization: A critical evaluation. *arXiv preprint arXiv:1908.08960*.

Logan Lebanoff, Kaiqiang Song, and Fei Liu. 2018. Adapting the neural encoder-decoder framework from single to multi-document summarization. *arXiv preprint arXiv:1808.06218*.

Chin-Yew Lin and Eduard Hovy. 2002. Automated multi-document summarization in neats. In *Proceedings of the Human Language Technology Conference (HLT2002)*, pages 23–27. San Diego, CA, USA.

Yogesh Kumar Meena and Dinesh Gopalani. 2014. Analysis of sentence scoring methods for extractive automatic text summarization. In *Proceedings of the 2014 international conference on information and communication technology for competitive strategies*, pages 1–6.

Rada Mihalcea and Paul Tarau. 2004. Textrank: Bringing order into text. In *Proceedings of the 2004 conference on empirical methods in natural language processing*, pages 404–411.

George A Miller. 1995. Wordnet: a lexical database for english. *Communications of the ACM*, 38(11):39–41.

Ani Nenkova and Lucy Vanderwende. 2005. The impact of frequency on summarization. *Microsoft Research, Redmond, Washington, Tech. Rep. MSR-TR-2005*, 101.

Lawrence Page, Sergey Brin, Rajeev Motwani, and Terry Winograd. 1999. The pagerank citation ranking: Bringing order to the web. Technical report, Stanford InfoLab.

Dragomir R Radev, Timothy Allison, Sasha Blair-Goldensohn, John Blitzer, Arda Celebi, Stanko Dimitrov, Elliott Drabek, Ali Hakim, Wai Lam, Danyu Liu, et al. 2004a. Mead-a platform for multidocument multilingual text summarization.

Dragomir R Radev, Hongyan Jing, Małgorzata Styś, and Daniel Tam. 2004b. Centroid-based summarization of multiple documents. *Information Processing & Management*, 40(6):919–938.

Nedunchelian Ramanujam and Manivannan Kaliappan. 2016. An automatic multidocument text summarization approach based on naive bayesian classifier using timestamp strategy. *The Scientific World Journal*, 2016.

Nils Reimers and Iryna Gurevych. 2019. Sentence-bert: Sentence embeddings using siamese bert-networks. *arXiv preprint arXiv:1908.10084*.

Barry Schiffman, Ani Nenkova, and Kathleen McKeown. 2002. Experiments in multidocument summarization.

Natalie Schluter and Anders Søgaard. 2015. Unsupervised extractive summarization via coverage maximization with syntactic and semantic concepts. In *Proceedings of the 53rd Annual Meeting of the Association for Computational Linguistics and the 7th International Joint Conference on Natural Language Processing (Volume 2: Short Papers)*, pages 840–844.

Chao Shen and Tao Li. 2010. Multi-document summarization via the minimum dominating set. In *Proceedings of the 23rd International Conference on Computational Linguistics (Coling 2010)*, pages 984–992.

Hiroya Takamura and Manabu Okumura. 2009. Text summarization model based on maximum coverage problem and its variant. In *Proceedings of the 12th Conference of the European Chapter of the ACL (EACL 2009)*, pages 781–789.

The 33rd Conference on Computational Linguistics and Speech Processing (ROCLING 2021)
Taoyuan, Taiwan, October 15-16, 2021. The Association for Computational Linguistics and Chinese Language Processing

基於參數生成網路的遷移學習進行情感分析和歌手命名識別
Aspect-Based Sentiment Analysis and Singer Name Entity Recognition using Parameter Generation Network Based Transfer Learning

曾筱雯 Hsiao-Wen Tseng
中央大學資訊工程學系
wen80187@g.ncu.edu.tw

張嘉惠 Chia-Hui Chang
中央大學資訊工程學系
chia@csie.ncu.edu.tw

莊秀敏 Hsiu-Min Chuang
國防大學理工學院資訊工程學系
showmin1205@gmail.com

摘要

當訓練資料有限時，如何應用已標記的訓練資料，幫助目標任務的模型快速建構，是遷移式學習 (Transfer Learning) 的重要議題。在本論文中，以多任務學習 (Multi-task Learning) 的方式進行中文歌手命名實體辨識 (Name Entity Recognition, NER) 和基於面向的情感分析 (Aspect-Based Sentiment Analysis, ABSA) 的任務。我們應用參數生成網路 (Jia et al., 2019) 結合梯度反轉層 (Gradient Adversarial Layer, GRL)(Ganin and Lempitsky, 2015) 架構來建立模型，並且使用 Tie/Break 規則進行標記，動態調節權重的機制 (Dynamic Weight Average, DWA) (Liu et al., 2019)，依據每個任務的損失變化率來調整任務權重。實驗結果顯示，我們的擴展參數生成網路模型 (Extended Parameter Generation Network, E-PGN)，在僅考慮 NER 任務時，F1 可以達到 90%，和 IBHB 效能 86% 相比，有所改善，加入 ABSA 任務後，平均 F1 能夠達到 78%，和 IBHB(Chiu, 2020) 效能相差了 22%，明顯的大幅成長。

Abstract

When we are interested in a certain domain, we can collect and analyze data from the Internet. The newly collected data is not labeled, so the use of labeled data is hoped to be helpful to the new data. We perform name entity recognition (NER) and aspect-based sentiment analysis (ABSA) in multi-task learning, and combine parameter generation network (Jia et al., 2019) and DANN architecture (Ganin and Lempitsky, 2015) to build the model. In the NER task, the data is labeled with Tie, Break, and the task weight is adjusted according to the loss change rate of each task using Dynamic Weight Average (DWA) (Liu et al., 2019). This study used two different source domain data sets. The experimental results show that Tie, Break can improve the results of the model; DWA can have better performance in the results; the combination of parameter generation network and gradient reversal layer can be used for every good learning in different domain.

關鍵字： 參數生成網路、梯度反轉層、命名實體辨識、目標情緒分析、多任務學習。

Keywords: Parameter Generation Network, Gradient Adversarial Layer, Named Entity Recognition and Aspect-Based Sentiment Analysis

1 簡介

自從網路進入 Web2.0 時代，各種部落格及社交平台的興起，人們主動地將他們的想法、意見發布在網路上，讓我們更容易在網路上得知目前討論的熱門話題、流行趨勢。這些使用者原創內容 (User Generated Content, UGC) 變成爲輿情分析的消息來源。當我們對某個主題有興趣時，便可以蒐集這些資料，並透過分析文本提到的目標，以及對目標的情緒來進行進一步的分析。

命名實體辨識 (Named Entity Recognition, NER) 是資訊抽取 (Information Extraction, IE) 技術的任務之一，目標是識別文本中的實體 (Entities)。然而，社群網路上的文章由於是廣大使用者所分享的想法與意見，所以這類的資料與報章雜誌相較下，文句較無正規的的文法，且經常包含有表情符號、火星文、注音文等非正規寫法，在用字遣詞上，常有用户自創的詞彙。本論文所使用的目標任務資料集是從批踢踢實業坊 (Ptt.cc) 所爬取音樂相關的評論，因此在文本分析上更具挑戰性。

情感分析 (Sentiment Analysis) 則是判別文句的情感極性，表示作者對意見目標的正向、反向或中立的立場。本研究主要結合命名實體辨識與情感分析，即意見目標擷取與情感分析兩項任務。本論文的情感分析問題屬於基於面向的情感分析 (Aspect-Based Sentiment Analysis, ABSA) 任務，ABSA 旨在辨別文句中面向 (Aspect) 的情感極性。這個議題對於不少企業來說相當重要。由於更爲細粒度 (Fine-grained) 分析其產品在不同面向的網路評價，更有助於產品的持續改善。

然而在標記資料有限時，如何應用現有其他領域已標記的訓練資料幫助加速目標任務的模型建構，是一項重要的研究議題，也是遷移式學習 (Transfer learning) 主要解決的問題。換言之，遷移式學習是借用來源域 (Source Domain) 中的知識遷移到目標域 (Target Domain)，提高模型在目標域的表現，這樣便可以減少大量目標域訓練資料的依賴，同時提升模型在目標域的表現。

在本論文中，我們使用遷移式學習來改善歌手名稱辨識及情感分析模型的效能，結合參數生成網路 (Parameter Generation Network, PGN)(Jia et al., 2019) 和梯度反轉層 (Gradient Adversarial Layer, GRL)(Ganin and Lempitsky, 2015) 的模型，分別針對語言模型 (Language Model, LM)、命名實體辨識和面向的情感分析三個任務進行多任務學習 (Multi-task Learning)。由於多任務學習在計算整體損失 (Loss) 時，有多個子任務損失，每個任務的資料數量大小不一，因此在參數的設定上，我們參考了動態計算權重 (Dynamic Weight Average, DWA)(Liu et al., 2019) 的方式，以達到最好的效能。在資料集的標記準備上，爲了能有效分隔中文詞彙，有別於常見的 BIEOS 標記，我們採用 Tie/Break 的標記方式 (Shang et al., 2018)，表達中文字與字之間是否連結在一起，再預測每個連結的詞是否爲命名實體。

實驗結果顯示，我們提出的擴展參數生成網路模型 (Extended Parameter Generation Network, E-PGN)，在使用新聞人名資料做爲來源域時 (Chou et al., 2016)，在僅考慮歌手 NER 任務和語言模型任務時，則 NER 效能可以達到 90% 的 F1，相比 IBHB 效能 86% 改進了 4.65%；若是加入 ABSA 任務一起考慮時，則在歌手 NER 任務上達到 85.5%，相較 IBHB 效能 87.4% 雖略有下降，但在 ABSA 任務可以達到 78% 的 F1 效能，相較 IBHB(Chiu, 2020) 效能 56% 相差 22% 是相當大的突破，即使新聞人名資料並不包含 ABSA 標記資訊。

2 相關研究

遷移式學習強調來源域和目標域中的領域 (Domain) 和任務 (Task) 的概念。Pan and Yang (2010) 定義了領域和任務。領域 $D = \{X, P(X)\}$ 是由特徵空間 X 和特徵空間上的邊際機率分布 $P(X)$ 組成。$X = \{x_1, x_2, ..., x_n\} \in X$，$X$ 是一個文本資料，x_i 則是文本中對應的第 i 個字的向量。一般來說，如果兩個域不同，那他們大多是具有不同的特徵空間或是不同的邊際機率分布。任務 $T = \{Y, P(y|x)\}$ 由標籤空間 Y 和目標預測函數 $P(y|x)$，$Y = \{y_1, y_2, ..., y_n\} \in Y$，$Y$ 是一個文本資料 X 的標籤，y_i 則是文本中對應的第 i 個字的標籤。透過來源域 D_S 和來源域任務 T_S 中的知識來改進目標域 D_T 中目標預測函數 $P(y|x)$ 的學習，其中 $D_S \neq D_T$, 或 $T_S \neq T_T$。

在 ABSA 任務上，使用不同領域的資料來建立模型的像是Hu et al. (2019) 專注於提取領域不變特徵，He et al. (2019) 引入了消息傳遞架構，並使用不同領域的文本級資料建立模型，Li et al. (2019) 將選擇性對抗學習作爲領域適應方法引入到模型中，Zhang et al. (2019) 基於 LSTM 的交互式註意力轉移網路，實現跨領域的 ABSA。

2.1 參數生成網路 (Parameter Generation Network, PGN)

Jia et al. (2019) 在進行跨域的命名實體辨識實驗中，設計了一種新的參數生成網路 (PGN)，使用了領域嵌入 (Domain Embedding) 的方式，對不同領域進行處理。透過領域和任務之間的相似性，來學習領域和任務相關性和領域及任務嵌入 (Task Embedding)。

參數生成器 主要的模型是使用了 BiLSTM-CRF，透過領域嵌入和任務嵌入生成 BiLSTM 參數 $\theta^{d,t}_{LSTM}$，以達到在不同領域、不同任務上轉移知識的目的。

$$\theta^{d,t}_{LSTM} = W \otimes I^D_d \otimes I^T_t \tag{1}$$

式 1 中，d 表示來源域和目標域，t 表示命名實體辨識和語言模型兩個任務，$I^D_d \in R^U$ 是領域嵌入，U 是領域嵌入大小，$I^T_t \in R^V$ 是任務嵌入，V 是任務嵌入的大小，W 是由 $P^{(LSTM)*V*U}$ 組成的三維張量，$P^(LSTM)$ 則是 LSTM 的參數數量，使用 $\otimes$ 來進行張量縮減 (Tensor contraction)。

2.2 神經網路的域對抗訓練

Ganin and Lempitsky (2015) 提出 DANN 模型，DANN 是受生成對抗網路（Generative Adversarial Network, GAN）所啓發的對抗技術，生成和訓練資料集分佈一致的資料。使用對抗層辨別特徵的來源，當對抗網路的表現不佳時，表示來源域和目標域的特徵只存在細微差異，可遷移性更好，反之亦然。

DANN 的模型架構，由以下三個部分組成：

特徵提取器 將來源域和目標域的資料都映射到特徵空間上，混合兩個域的資料後，並提取後續網路需要完成任務所需要的特徵。

標籤分類器 標籤分類器的資料爲來源域帶有標籤的資料，並對特徵空間來源域的資料進行分類，分辨出正確的標記，協助特徵提取器所提取的特徵是能夠用來做分類。

域分類器 對特徵空間的資料進行域分類，分辨出數據是來自哪個領域，是由不帶標籤的來源域和目標域的資料組成。

域分類器和標籤分類器的輸入都是來自特徵提取器，不過域分類器的目標是最大化域分類損失，混淆來源域和目標域的資料；標籤分類器的目標則是最小化分類損失，讓標籤可以精準的被分類。

爲了解決兩個分類器的目標不同，Ganin and Lempitsky (2015) 提出了梯度反轉層，在反向傳遞的過程中，梯度方向自動相反，在前向傳遞過程中恆等變換。也就是在域分類器損失的梯度反向傳遞到特徵提取器的參數之前，自動加一個負號，如此便實現了和生成對抗網路相似的對抗損失。

3 模型架構

本論文的模型架構主要是基於 PGN (Jia et al., 2019) 模型架構進行擴展，因此本研究的模型命名爲 Extended Parameter Generation Network，簡稱爲 E-PGN。

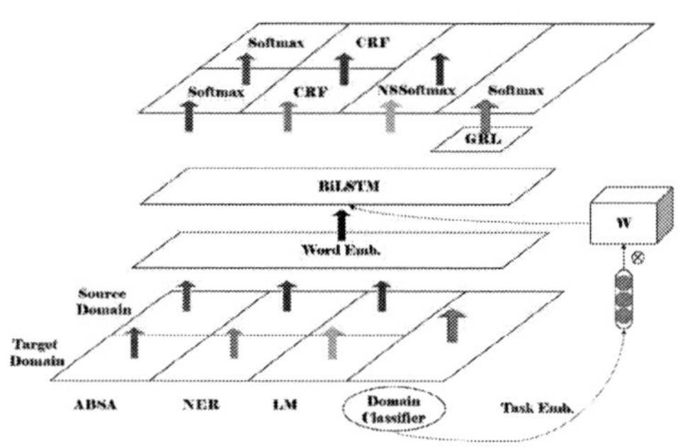

Figure 1: E-PGN 模型架構圖

模型架構如圖 1，在原 PGN 模型基礎上，保留任務參數生成的架構，且除了命名實體辨識及語言模型任務外，增加了 ABSA 任務；另外在領域參數生成的部份，則不使用 Domain Embedding，而改以領域對抗式 (Domain Adversarial) 架構，結合梯度反轉層，增加一個混淆領域分類的損失函數。我們在後面小節中分別詳述本模型的各層功能。

3.1 輸入層

輸入層共有七個資料集，每個資料集在輸入資料時，皆是以句子的字元 (Character-based) 爲單位。NER 和 ABSA 任務的來源域表示爲 $S_{NER/ABSA} = \{x_i, y_i\}_{i=1}^{m}$ 和目標域 $T_{NER/ABSA} = \{x_i, y_i\}_{i=1}^{n}$，LM 任務的來源域和目標域分別表示爲 $S_{LM} = \{x_i\}_{i=1}^{m}$, $T_{LM} = \{x_i\}_{i=1}^{n}$，領域分類任務表示爲 $D_{Dom} = \{x_i, y_i\}_{i=1}^{m+n}$。其中 x 代表句子內的第 i 個字，y 代表句子內第 i 個標記，m, n 表示爲資料集的第 m, n 個句子。

3.2 嵌入層

從輸入層得到的字元，在嵌入層轉換爲數值向量，本論文使用 GloVe (Global Vectors for Word Representation)(Pennington et al., 2014)，將 GloVe 模型預先訓練的詞向量表示爲 V_c，並使用查表的方式映射，找到該字元所表示的向量。映射函數寫爲

$$v_i = V_c(X_i) \tag{2}$$

其中 X_i 是輸入的字元在 V_c 中的第 i 個，v_i 則表示通過 GloVe 所得到的詞向量且 $v_i \in R^D$，D 爲向量維度。

3.3 參數產生層

參數產生器可以讓不同領域間知識能夠傳遞，動態地生成 θ_{LSTM}^{t} 參數，不同於原 PGN 的設計，在 θ_{LSTM}^{t} 部分，我們只保留了任務嵌入。

$$\theta_{LSTM}^{t} = W \otimes I_t \tag{3}$$

式 3 中，t 表示爲任務，可以爲語言模型、命名實體辨識、ABSA、域分類四種任務。$I_t \in V$ 表示爲任務嵌入，V 是任務嵌入的大小，$W \in P^{(LSTM)*V}$ 是由 BiLSTM 的參數數量和任務嵌入的大小組成。最後 W 和 I 使用 $\otimes$ 計算得到 θ，$\otimes$ 用來進行張量的縮減 (Tensor Contraction)。

3.4 雙向長短記憶網路層

雙向長短記憶網路 (Bi-directional Long Short-Term Memory, BiLSTM) 由前向 LSTM 與後向 LSTM 組合而成。爲了最大化考量文章中上下文的資訊，本論文採用 BiLSTM 的方式來進行實驗，使用雙向的訊息傳遞 $\overrightarrow{h_i^{d,t}}$ 和 $\overleftarrow{h_i^{d,t}}$，表示如式 4。

$$\overrightarrow{h}_i^{d,t} = LSTM(\overrightarrow{h}_{i-1}^{d,t}, v_i, \overrightarrow{\theta}_{LSTM}^{d,t}) \tag{4a}$$

$$\overleftarrow{h}_i^{d,t} = LSTM(\overleftarrow{h}_{i+1}^{d,t}, v_i, \overleftarrow{\theta}_{LSTM}^{d,t}) \tag{4b}$$

3.5 輸出層

本論文所提出的 E-PGN 模型，採多任務學習，因此在輸出層時同時進行語言模型、命名實體辨識、ABSA、領域分類四種任務結果輸出。

語言模型 LM 語言模型任務預測採用了 NSSoftmax (Negative Sampling Softmax) (Mikolov et al., 2013) 作爲預測前後字的模型。前向 LSTM 計算 $x_{1:i}$ 的下一個字 x_{i+1} 的機率，表示爲 5a。後向 LSTM 計算 $x_{1:i}$ 的上一個字 x_{i-1} 的機率，表示爲 5b。

$$P^f(x_{i+1}|x_{1:i}) = \frac{1}{Z} exp\{w_{\#x_{i+1}}^{\mathsf{T}} \overrightarrow{h_i} + b_{\#x_{i+1}}\} \tag{5a}$$

$$P^b(x_{i-1}|x_{1:n}) = \frac{1}{Z} exp\{w_{\#x_{i1}}^{\mathsf{T}} \overleftarrow{h_i} + b_{\#x_{i-1}}\} \tag{5b}$$

其中 $\#x$ 代表目標字 x 的在字典中的序號。$w_{\#x}$ 和 $b_{\#x}$ 分別是目標字的向量和目標字的偏差。Z 則是通過計算的標準化項。

損失函數則定義爲式 6，其中 $D_{LM} = \{(x^n)\}_{n=1}^N$。

$$L_{LM} = -\frac{1}{2|D_{LM}|} \sum_{n=1}^{N} \sum_{t=1}^{T} \{\log(p^f(x_{t+1}^n|x_{1:t}^n)) + \log(p^b(x_{t-1}^n|x_{t:T}^n))\} \tag{6}$$

命名實體辨識 NER 命名實體辨識的序列預測使用傳統 CRF 模型，將 $\overrightarrow{h_i^{d,t}}$ 和 $\overleftarrow{h_i^{d,t}}$ 相加得到 h_i。因此給定輸入句子 x，預測標籤序列 $y = l_1, l_2, ..., l_i$ 的輸出機率 $P(y|x)$，如式7。

$$P(y|x) = \frac{exp\{\sum_i (w_{CRF}^{l_i} \cdot h_i + b_{CRF}^{(l_{i-1}, l_i)}\}}{\sum_{y'} exp\{\sum_i (w_{CRF}^{l'_i} \cdot h_i + b_{CRF}^{(l'_{i-1}, l'_i)})\}} \tag{7}$$

其中 y' 表示任意標籤序列，$w_{CRF}^{l_i}$ 是特定於 l_i 的模型參數，而 $b_{CRF}^{(l_{i-1}, l_i)}$ 則爲特定於 l_{i-1} 和 l_i 的偏差值。

損失函數定義爲式 8，$D_{ner} = \{(x^n, y^n)\}_{n=1}^N$。

$$L_{ner} = -\frac{1}{|D_{ner}|} \sum_{n=1}^{N} \log(p(y^n|x^n)) \tag{8}$$

基於面向情感分析 ABSA ABSA 任務使用 Cross-Entropy 進行情感分類，將 BiLSTM 的 $\overrightarrow{h}$ 和 $\overleftarrow{h}$ 相加得到 v_s，輸入到 softmax，如式 9

$$y = softmax(W_x v_s + b_s) \tag{9}$$

損失函數如式 10，其中 $\hat{y}_i, y_i \in \{0, 1\}$ 分別表示文本 i 的眞實和預測的情感類別。

$$L_{ABSA} = -\frac{1}{N_s} \sum_{i=1}^{N_s} (\hat{y}_i \ln y_i + (1 - \hat{y}_i) \ln(1 - y_i)) \tag{10}$$

域分類器 Domain Classifier 首先將 BiLSTM 輸出的向量視爲域分類的文檔，表示爲 v_d，在 v_d 輸入到 Softmax 之前，先通過梯度反轉層。在數學上，將梯度反轉層視爲一個僞函數 (pseudo-function)，在反向傳遞時，梯度反轉層從後續層獲取梯度 (Gradient)，並且乘上-λ 後，傳遞給前一層。

$$R_\lambda(x) = x \tag{11a}$$

$$\frac{\partial R_\lambda(x)}{\partial x} = -\lambda I \tag{11b}$$

我們可以透過式 11 描述前向和後向傳遞的行爲。最後利用式 12 進行預測。

$$d = softmax(W_d \hat{v}_d + b_d) \tag{12}$$

損失函數如式 13

$$L_{dom} = -\frac{1}{N_s + N_t} \sum_{i=1}^{N_s + N_t} \hat{d}_i \ln d_i + (1 - \hat{d}_i) \ln(1 - d_i) \tag{13}$$

其中 $\hat{d}_i, d_i \in \{0, 1\}$ 分別是文本 i 的眞實和預測領域，N_s, N_t 則代表來源域和目標域的資料數量。

整體損失計算 由於 E-PGN 模型採用多任務學習，整體損失函數表示如式 14，將兩個域的三個任務和域分類器的損失，共七個損失函數進行加總。

$$L_{total} = \sum_{d,t} \lambda_t^d L_t^d + \lambda_{dom} L_{dom} \tag{14}$$

因爲每個域任務的資料集大小不一，我們使用 DWA(Liu et al., 2019) 來動態地調整不同損失函數間的 λ 大小。在 DWA 中，每個任務先計算前一個 Epoch 對應的損失比，如式 15。

$$w_k(t-1) = \frac{L_k(t-1)}{L_k(t_2)} \tag{15}$$

再將結果代入式 16，得到任務 k 的權重，並除以常數 T，得到每次 Epoch 任務 k 的權重 λ。

$$\lambda_k(t) := \frac{k exp(w_k(t-1)/T)}{\sum_i exp(w_i(t-1)/T)} \tag{16}$$

t 為 Epoch，T 是一個常數，代表了任務間的鬆散程度，如果 T 值越大，λ 會越接近 1，也就是說各任務間權重差異較小。

4 實驗

本論文使用的資料集共有三種，分別是使用於目標域的歌手文章，來源域的新聞、家電評論，以下將分別介紹這三個資料集的訓練與測試資料數量及標記策略。

歌手文章 歌手文章是本論文的目標域資料集，擷取自『批踢踢 PTT 實業坊』論壇與音樂相關的 97 個版，標記方式參考 Chiu (2020) 所使用的資料集，標記人員會依照段落的敘述，來判斷該段落的實體，以及對實體表達的情感極性，情感極性有三種類別，分別爲正向、負向、中立，資料比例分別爲 28%、22%、50%，詳如表 1。

		實體	情感		
	段落數量	歌手	正向	負向	中立
訓練資料	4,000	6,715	1,834	1,475	3,406
測試資料	1,000	1,710	489	382	839

Table 1: 歌手文章的訓練與測試資料集

新聞 新聞資料作爲來源域的資料集，針對各種不同的新聞網站，將提及人名實體的文章進行蒐集。標記方式參考 Chou et al. (2016) 所使用的資料集，是透過自動標記的方式，一共標記了訓練和測試資料分別 15,000 句與 500 句，共 20,000 句，如表 2。

	句子數量	人名實體個數
訓練資料	15,000	3,723
測試資料	500	155

Table 2: 新聞的訓練與測試資料集

家用電器評論 家用電器評論的資料集作爲本論文的另外一個來源域，取自『Mobile01』與家用電器有關的五個版，使用者的發文及文章底下的討論串，作爲我們的資料集。標記方式參考 Kan (2021) 的人工標記，共使用了 2,000 個句子的家電評論，其中訓練和測試資料分別爲 1,500 句與 500 句，具有產品廠牌 (Product Name, PN) 以及產品名稱 (Brand Name, BN) 的情感標記，情感類別包括正向、負向、中立等三種，如表 3。

效能評估與參數設定 在命名實體辨識任務上，我們採用完全比對 (Exactly Match) 的方式來進行評估。ABSA 任務亦同，也就是情感

		實體		情感		
	句子數量	PN	BN	正向	負向	中立
訓練資料	1,500	2,075	2,538	968	484	186
測試資料	500	650	820	373	187	260

Table 3: 家電評論的訓練與測試資料集

標記的數量、極性必須和實體完全一致，才會納入計算。

表 4 爲本論文 E-PGN 模型的參數設置，在這個設定下，可以得到最佳的效能。

#of words per sentence	128	Batch size	30
Word Embedding	100	Dropout	0.5
Task embedding	8	Learning rate	1e-3
BiLSTMLayer	2	L2-regularization	1e-8
Hidden	200	Optimizer	SGD

Table 4: 參數設定

標記策略 在命名實體辨識任務上，我們參考 AutoNER (Shang et al., 2018) 的 Tie/Break 的標記方式。並使用 CKIP Tagger (Li et al., 2020) 對中文資料進行斷詞。

Token	吳	亦	凡	到	數	與	你	的	時	間	距	離
Chunk	B	T	T	B	T	B	B	B	B	T	B	T
Type	A			N		N	N	N	N		N	
Sentiment	Neu	Neu	Neu	N	N	N	N	N	N	N	N	N

Figure 2: 標記範例

圖 2 中，Chunk 爲 CKIP 斷詞後的結果，B 表示 Break，與前字無關，T 表示 Tie，可與前字合爲一個詞。Type 代表是否爲實體，A 表示 Artist，N 表示 None。Sentiment 代表實體的情感極性，分爲正向 (Pos)、負向 (Neg)、中立 (Neu)、無 (N)。

模型效能 本論文的目標域爲歌手文章，依據來源域的不同，分成兩個部分 (家用電器評論、新聞)，並在不同的來源域的實驗下，再分別進行輸入資料爲兩個任務 (LM, NER) 以及三個任務 (LM, NER, ABSA) 的實驗。爲了提高實驗的準確性，每個實驗皆執行五次後計算平均值。

4.1 來源域爲家用電器評論

兩個任務 (LM, NER) 這個實驗使用的輸入資料只有命名實體辨識和語言模型兩個資料集，並進行 BIESO 與 Tie/Break 標記的比較。

圖 3 可以看到，使用 Tie/Break 標記可以得到 0.85 的 F1，相較於 BIESO 標記效能 (0.83) 相差了 2%，但和 BaseLine(Chiu, 2020) 相比，還有一點成長的空間。從結果可以得知

使用 Tie/Break 標記，有助於模型效能，因此後續實驗皆使用 Tie/Break 的標記方式。

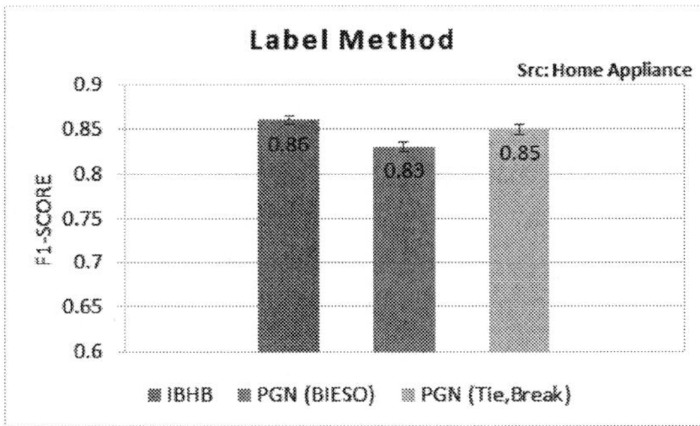

Figure 3: BIESO 和 Tie/Break 比較 (src: 家電評論)

三個任務 (LM, NER, ABSA) 這個實驗新增了 ABSA 任務，因此輸入資料有三個任務的資料集，並比較固定 (Fixed) 和動態 (DWA) 的兩種計算 Loss 權重的方式。

圖 4 顯示，在命名實體辨識任務上，較沒有兩個任務時的效能來的好，和 Baseline 相比，Fixed 和 DWA 皆略有下降。但在 ABSA 任務上，不論是 Fixed 或是 DWA，均顯著優於 BaseLine，且使用 DWA 優於 Fixed，在三種情緒的平均值分別相差了 8%、18%。另外也可以從圖中看出來，使用 DWA 的五次實驗的標準差也比 Fixed 的標準差小。另外不論是 Fixed 或是使用 DWA，兩個不同的實驗，五次實驗的結果差距皆不大，只相差了 0.06。因此在後續的實驗中，皆以 DWA 的計算方式來進行。

4.2 來源域爲新聞

兩個任務 (LM, NER) 在來源域有大量的標記資料下，可以從圖 5 看到，BIESO 和 Tie/Break 標記的效能皆優於 BaseLine，相差了 2% 和 4%。因此根據實驗結果，在 PGN 來源域的資料多於目標域資料時，可以得到不錯的效能。

三個任務 (LM, NER, ABSA) 加上 ABSA 任務後，比較使用領域嵌入和梯度反轉層的效能，圖 6 所示。在命名實體辨識任務上僅有微小的差距，E-PGN 的 F1 達到 85.5%，PGN 則是 85.2%，雖然在命名實體辨識任務上沒辦法優於 BaseLine 的效能 87.4%，但在 ABSA 任務有顯著的成長，PGN 的 SA 平均 F1 爲 70%，E-PGN 爲 78%，和 BaseLine 的效能 56% 相比，有大幅的成長。因此在領域的處理上，和領域嵌入相比，使用梯度反轉層對模型有明顯的幫助。

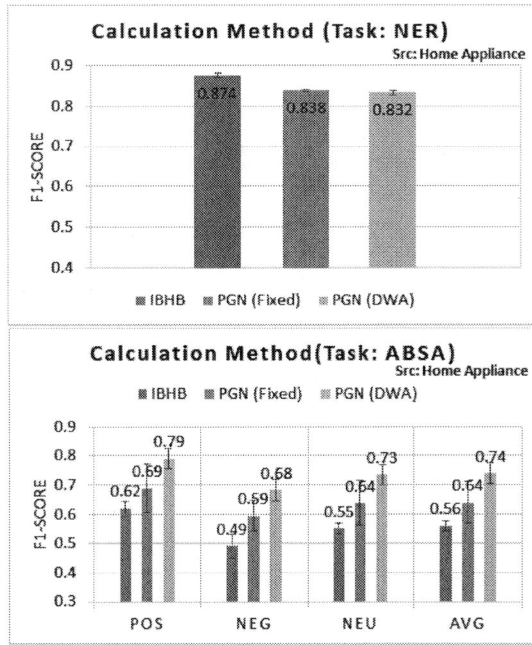

Figure 4: Fixed 和 DWA 比較 (src: 家電評論) (上)NER 任務 (下)ABSA 任務

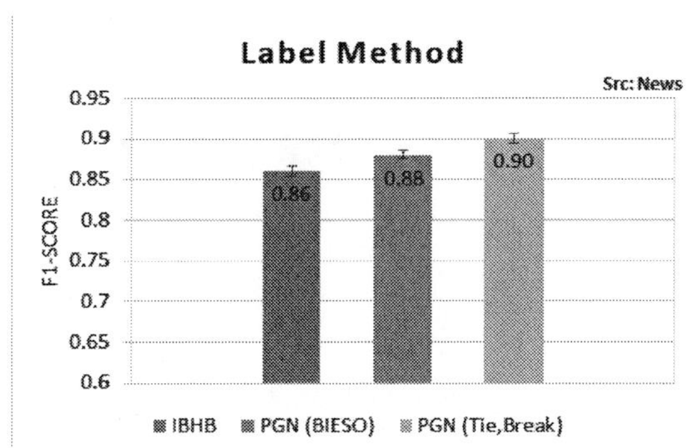

Figure 5: BIESO 和 Tie/Break 比較 (src: 新聞)

詞嵌入 (Word Embedding) 比較 本實驗比較了使用 GloVe 和 BERT 的結果，圖7 可以看到，不論在 ABSA 或是命名實體辨識任務上，使用 BERT 時，效能皆低於使用 GloVe。因此認爲模型在使用 BERT 時，會產生太多的參數，反而造成模型無法得到較好的效能。

5 結論

爲了有效辨識社群網路上歌手的網路聲量，本論文參考了參數生成網路 (Jia et al., 2019) 與 DANN 模型 (Ganin and Lempitsky, 2015)，提出擴展參數生成網路 (E-PGN) 的遷移學習方法來達成跨領域的命名實體辨識和 ABSA 任務，並解決目標域訓練資料不足的問題。由

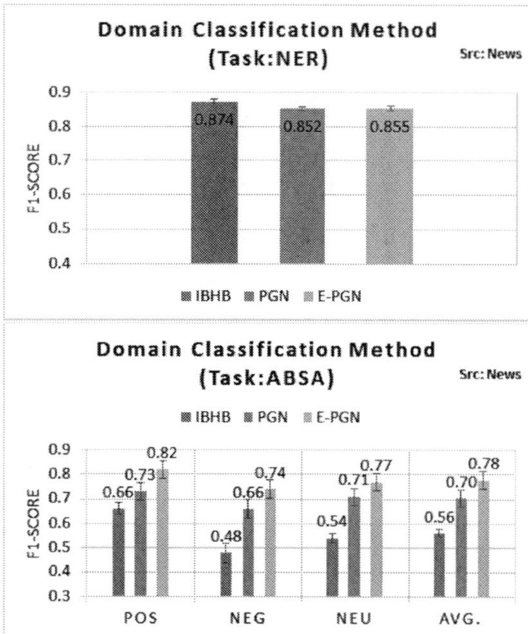

Figure 6: Domain Emb. 和 GRL 比較 (src: 新聞) (上)NER 任務 (下)ABSA 任務

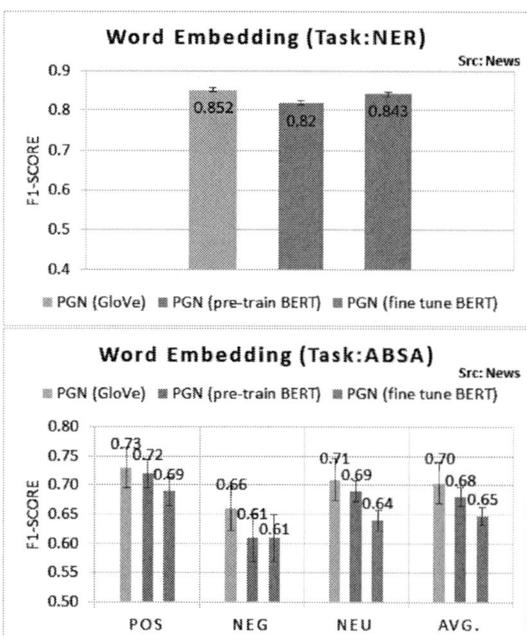

Figure 7: Word Emb 比較 (src: 新聞) (上)NER 任務 (下)ABSA 任務

於採用多任務學習 (Multi-task Learning) 進行命名實體辨識和 ABSA 的任務，因此在訓練過程中會產生大量的參數。不同於原 PGN 模型，我們移除了領域嵌入，並改用了梯度反轉層 GRL 進行領域分類，並且在計算整體損失函數的部分引用態動態調節權重的機制 (Liu et al., 2019)，有效進行權重設定。

實驗結果顯示，使用 Tie/Break 標記可以提升模型辨識效能；在權重設定的比較中，使用 DWA 動態設定權重，確實能有效提升模型效能。在家電評論作爲來源域的實驗中，雖然家電評論只有少量資料，但模型效能仍可在 ABSA 任務上有顯著的成長。在目標域資料不足下，本論文展現了 E-PGN 模型較原 PGN 仍能獲得良好的效能。

References

Wei-Cheng Chiu. 2020. Joint learning of aspect-level sentiment analysis and singer named recognition from social networks. In *International Conference on Technologies and Applications of Artificial Intelligence (TAAI)*.

Chien-Lung Chou, Chia-Hui Chang, and Ya-Yun Huang. 2016. Boosted web named entity recognition via tri-training. *ACM Trans. Asian Low-Resour. Lang. Inf. Process.*, 16(2).

Yaroslav Ganin and Victor Lempitsky. 2015. Unsupervised domain adaptation by backpropagation. In *Proceedings of the 32nd International Conference on International Conference on Machine Learning - Volume 37*, ICML'15, page 1180—1189. JMLR.org.

Ruidan He, Wee Sun Lee, Hwee Tou Ng, and Daniel Dahlmeier. 2019. An interactive multi-task learning network for end-to-end aspect-based sentiment analysis. In *Proceedings of the 57th Annual Meeting of the Association for Computational Linguistics*, pages 504–515.

Mengting Hu, Yike Wu, Shiwan Zhao, Honglei Guo, Renhong Cheng, and Zhong Su. 2019. Domain-invariant feature distillation for cross-domain sentiment classification. In *Proceedings of the 2019 Conference on Empirical Methods in Natural Language Processing and the 9th International Joint Conference on Natural Language Processing, EMNLP-IJCNLP 2019, Hong Kong, China, November 3-7, 2019*, pages 5558–5567.

Chen Jia, Xiaobo Liang, and Yue Zhang. 2019. Cross-domain NER using cross-domain language modeling. In *Proceedings of the 57th Annual Meeting of the Association for Computational Linguistics*, pages 2464–2474. Association for Computational Linguistics.

Tai-Jung Kan. 2021. Home appliance review research via adversarial reptile. Master's thesis, National Central University.

Peng-Hsuan Li, Tsu-Jui Fu, and Wei-Yun Ma. 2020. Why attention? analyze bilstm deficiency and its remedies in the case of ner. In *AAAI*.

Zheng Li, Xin Li, Ying Wei, Lidong Bing, Y. Zhang, and Qiang Yang. 2019. Transferable end-to-end aspect-based sentiment analysis with selective adversarial learning.

Shikun Liu, Edward Johns, and A. Davison. 2019. End-to-end multi-task learning with attention. *2019 IEEE/CVF Conference on Computer Vision and Pattern Recognition (CVPR)*, pages 1871–1880.

Tomas Mikolov, Ilya Sutskever, Kai Chen, Greg Corrado, and Jeffrey Dean. 2013. Distributed representations of words and phrases and their compositionality. In *Proceedings of the 26th International Conference on Neural Information Processing Systems - Volume 2*, NIPS'13, page 3111—3119. Curran Associates Inc.

Sinno Jialin Pan and Qiang Yang. 2010. A survey on transfer learning. *IEEE Transactions on Knowledge and Data Engineering*, 22(10):1345–1359.

Jeffrey Pennington, Richard Socher, and Christopher D Manning. 2014. Glove: Global vectors for word representation. In *EMNLP*, volume 14, pages 1532–1543.

Jingbo Shang, Liyuan Liu, Xiang Ren, X. Gu, Teng Ren, and Jiawei Han. 2018. Learning named entity tagger using domain-specific dictionary. In *EMNLP*.

Kai Zhang, Hefu Zhang, Qi Liu, Hongke Zhao, Hengshu Zhu, and Enhong Chen. 2019. Interactive attention transfer network for cross-domain sentiment classification. *Proceedings of the AAAI Conference on Artificial Intelligence*, 33(01):5773–5780.

The 33rd Conference on Computational Linguistics and Speech Processing (ROCLING 2021)
Taoyuan, Taiwan, October 15-16, 2021. The Association for Computational Linguistics and Chinese Language Processing

以注入情緒構面的雙向長短期記憶模型應用於社群媒體產品評論之情感分析
Using Valence and Arousal-infused Bi-LSTM for Sentiment Analysis in Social Media Product Reviews

Yu-Ya Cheng[1], Wen-Chao Yeh[2], Yan-Ming Chen[3], Yung-Chun Chang[*]
[1]Professional Master Program in Data Science, Taipei Medical University, Taipei, Taiwan
[2]Institute of Information Systems and Applications, National Tsing Hua University, Hsinchu, Taiwan
[3,*] Graduate Institute of Data Science, Taipei Medical University, Taipei, Taiwan
[1,3,*]{ i906108009, m946109002, changyc}@tmu.edu.tw
[2]wyeh@m109.nthu.edu.tw

摘要

現今是網際網路普及的時代，社群媒體平台擔任私人企業與大眾間相互溝通的橋樑角色。本研究之目的是透過解析不同領域的產品評論資料獲取用戶對於產品的心得。我們提出一個具有更細膩詞彙情感資訊的 BiLSTM (Bi-directional Long-Short Term Memory) 模型，不只能預測文字中最小詞素「詞彙」的情緒構面 Valence & Arousal，也能加入詞彙間的依存關係。實驗結果顯示，本研究在預測詞彙之 Valence & Arousal 可以達到良好的效能。而且，經由融合 VA (Valence & Arousal) 及詞彙間依存關係至 BiLSTM 模型更可以對於社群文字情感分析做出優異表現，驗證此模型對於產品評論留言的情感預測準確性。

Abstract

With the popularity of the current Internet age, online social platforms have provided a bridge for communication between private companies, public organizations, and the public. The purpose of this research is to understand the user's experience of the product by analyzing product review data in different fields. We propose a BiLSTM-based neural network which infused rich emotional information. In addition to consider Valence and Arousal which is the smallest morpheme of emotional information, the dependence relationship between texts is also integrated into the deep learning model to analyze the sentiment. The experimental results show that this research can achieve good performance in predicting the vocabulary Valence and Arousal. In addition, the integration of VA and dependency information into the BiLSTM model can have excellent performance for social text sentiment analysis, which verifies that this model is effective in emotion recognition of social medial short text.

關鍵字：情感分析、情緒構面、社群媒體、產品評論

Keywords: Sentiment Analysis, Valence & Arousal, Social Media

1 研究動機與目的

隨著人們越來越依賴不斷發展的網路科技，各種便利的網路購物平台及社群平台如雨後春筍般興盛，不只轉換人們散佈及獲取資訊的管道，也改變現代人的生活型態。例如：可以從 Google 地圖中看到不同地標的評論，而這些評論也確實影響大多數人在行動前會先參考其他顧客的意見作為考量。但是，累積越來越多的評論卻使人們無法迅速的閱讀到關鍵資訊。情感分析技術能夠對這些資料進行有效地分析與挖掘，並識別出情感傾向，成為自然語言處理 (Natural Language Processing, NLP) 領域中最活躍的研究主題之一。

分析產品評論是瞭解群眾意見相當重要的一環，透過分析留言內容可掌握評論的情感傾向與趨勢。情感分析已有許多相當先進的研究，因此本論文著重於目前的先進研究上做出突破，計畫應用預測詞彙的情緒構面

(Valence-Arousal) 來提取出社群媒體上的輿論情感。除了分析句子的詞彙情感外，句子中各詞彙間的依存關係也是組成句子的重要參考依據。充分考量詞彙間的關聯性可獲得更細膩的分析資料，本研究在多種領域的產品評論資料上使用有別於以往的特徵方法進行情感分析任務。

2 相關研究探討

隨著近幾年網路普及與社群網站平台的盛行，網際網路已經成為分享訊息的重要場域。人們透過諸如 Facebook 、 Instagram 等社交平台發表個人意見或討論當前的公眾議題。如何從大量的評論留言抓取重點與關鍵表達，更成為資料科學的熱門研究主題。近年來，透過情感分析 (sentiment analysis) 技術從社群媒體文本中檢測和提取主觀信息 （例如：觀點和態度） 在眾多不同領域的應用相當廣泛 (Liu, B., 2012) ，尤其在政治 (Shakeel and Karim, 2020) 、 產品 (Zhang et al., 2012) 與電影 (Yenter and Verma, 2017) 等領域上都有傑出的表現。

在語法的架構單位上，Turney (2002) 提出以文檔級別的情感分類任務方法，接續有其他研究提出以更小單位對此進行分類任務，至今發展成可以句子級別 (Hu et al., 2004) 、短語級別 (Agarwal et al., 2009) 與詞彙級別 (Sayeed, Asad, et al., 2012) 進行分類任務。本研究將採用最小語素的詞彙級別進行情感預測實驗，並將詞彙情感預測延伸為每則留言的情感分類任務，進而以此探討產品評論的情感層級。本論文提出有別以往的方法，從預測詞彙情感的結果去追朔原評論內容，並探討群眾意見之情感面向。

情感分析的研究領域基本作法是先將情感區隔表示成數個類別 (例如：正面、負面) ，但僅以情感類別來分類將無法呈現各種情感的高低程度。情緒構面 (Valence-Arousal, VA) (Yu, Liang-Chih, et al., 2015) 為使用雙維度來表示情感的類別及程度，藉由預測詞彙的 Valence & Arousal 來清楚辨識該詞彙的情感類型及呈現出來的強弱程度。其中， Valence 為表示情感程度分級，以 1 至 9 的連續數值代表情緒由負面到正面。Arousal 為情緒激動程度，由 1 至 9 的連續數值代表，其數值由高到低分別代表情緒由激動到平靜。Valence-Arousal 能清楚辨識詞彙的極性分數也可以有效提升情感分析的效能 (Chang et al.,2019; Cheng, Yu-Ya, et al., 2021) ，因此本研究將情緒構面融合至雙向長短期記憶神經網路於分析文本情感，並應用在中文評論留言上以證明其有效性。

此外，依存句法分析 (Dependency Parsing) 是將句子解析成一棵依存句法樹，描述句子中詞彙與詞彙間的依存關係。本研究採用哈爾濱工業大學的 LTP 自然語言處理套件 Pyltp 進行文本依存句法關係探討。透過分析語言單位內成分間的依存關係來揭示其句法結構：文本句法結構為詞彙與詞彙間的修飾關係，兩個詞彙間連接一個依存關係，而依存關係包含許多類型。例如：主謂關係 (SBV) 、動賓關係 (VOB) 等。近年來有許多相關研究使用到 LTP 的依存句法分析皆獲得良好的效能 (Zhai, Pengjun, et al., 2020; Qidi, Jiao., 2021) ，證明加入句子結構特徵可增強語意信息的表達能力，進而幫助提升模型學習能力。

3 研究方法

首先將經由社群媒體產生的大量非結構化輿論文字資料施行預處理，進而預測詞彙之情緒構面向量，基於 BiLSTM 模型建構情感分類之預測機制來推論出文字之最小語素「詞彙」的情感資訊：Valence 與 Arousal，再將之融合進深度學習模型中，更細膩地分析社群文本之情感表現。

本節將依序介紹 VA 預測方法以及將 VA 當作特徵來預測多個產品領域的情感分類任務。

3.1 情緒構面預測

計畫透過更細粒度的情感分析預測詞彙的情感極性分數，並加入特徵信息提升模型推論表現。以下將依序介紹所使用到的特徵：

1. POS: 先以正體中文語料訓練出來的 MONPA[1] (Hsieh, Yu-Lun, et al., 2017) 斷詞套件取得每條句子中各個中文詞彙的詞性標註，再將這些詞性轉

1 https://github.com/monpa-team/monpa

化為具 50 維的表示向量，作為後續預測詞彙情感的重要特徵。

2. NTUSD: 參考台大中文情感極性詞典 (NTUSD)[2] 將文本詞彙進行情感正負面分類，例如：正面中文詞彙包含「開心、大方、公平」等；負面中文詞彙包含「反感、可怕、失望」等。若該詞彙出現在正面詞典列表，類別表示為 1，詞彙位於負面詞典，則將類別表示為 -1。當詞彙未被 NTUSD 詞典收錄，則使用餘弦相似度 (cosine similarity) 對其進行排序，藉此挑選出前五個在 NTUSD 有收錄最相近的詞彙，並以多數決選擇所屬類別 (Chang, Yung-Chun, et al., 2019) ，以此詞彙分類方法取得情緒特徵。

3. E-HowNet: E-HowNet 是基於 HowNet拓展出的知識本體，依據詞彙的語義將其轉換為概念 (Chen, Wei-Te, et al., 2010) ，例如：「一去不返」的概念是「消失」、「一心一意」的概念是「誠心」，透過 E-HowNet 將相同概念的 VA 值取平均，當作該詞彙的語義特徵。如未能找到相同概念的詞彙，就利用餘弦相似度 (cosine similarity) 找到最相近的概念，並取其 VA 平均值。透過以上方法可以得到兩維的詞彙語義特徵。

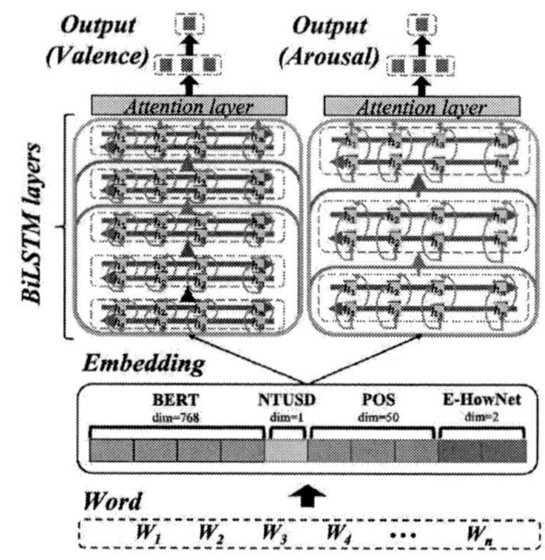

圖 1. 基於深度神經網路之 V & A 預測模型

本研究採用由 Devlin et al. (2018) 提出的 BERT (Bidirectional Encoder Representations from Transformers) 從文本資料中提取語言特徵向量表示作為嵌入向量表示，將其與上述經由 POS、NTUSD 與 E-HowNet 等方法取得之特徵向量做串聯得到該詞彙完整向量表示，如圖 1 的 Embedding 所示，共 821 維。

雙向長短期記憶 (BiLSTM) 除了解決較長距離的依賴性外，藉由組合前向和後向的 LSTM 可以更好捕獲雙向語意特徵，疊加 Attention Layer 對輸入的每個部分賦予不同權重 (Vaswani, Ashish, et al., 2017) 。近年來，集成學習方法已被廣泛用於提高分類性能 (Moreno, Jose G., 2020; Gomes, Heitor Murilo, et al., 2017; Dong, Xibin, et al., 2020) ，因此本研究將使用集成學習的方法透過組合不同級別的模型來得到更好的表達情感輸出。圖 1 是集成學習模型預測 V & A 的架構。

2 http://academiasinicanlplab.github.io/

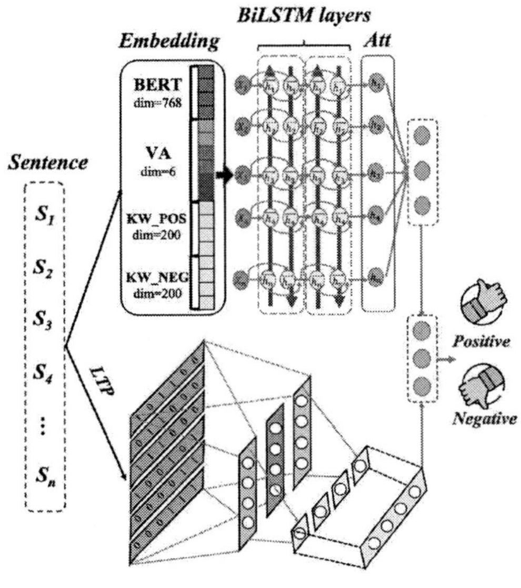

圖 2. 社群留言情感預測模型 (BLV-depCNN)

3.2 社群留言情感預測

圖 2 為基於情緒構面之社群留言情感分析模型架構圖，將上下兩部分的預測輸出合併成最終分類結果。圖 2 上半部分，先將社群留言以 MONPA 套件斷詞並移除 Stop Words，再以 3.1 節所述取得所有詞彙的 Valence 與 Arousal，結合句子語義特徵後丟進深度學習模型，得到該留言的情感傾向，依序介紹所使用的特徵：

1. 情緒關鍵詞特徵：本研究透過對數似然比 (Log Likelihood Ratio, LLR) 擷取出正面和負面的關鍵詞彙。公式 (1) 可獲取假設的可能性，為有利於選擇關鍵單詞特徵的方法。其 $\boldsymbol{PS}$ 表示訓練樣本(句子)中肯定句子的集合；$\boldsymbol{N(PS)}$ 和 $\boldsymbol{N(\neg PS)}$ 表示正樣本和負樣本的數量；$\boldsymbol{N(w\wedge PS)}$ 表示包含正面詞 w 的正面句子的數量。經最大似然估計來獲得概率 $\boldsymbol{p(w)}$、$\boldsymbol{p(w|PS)}$ 和 $\boldsymbol{p(w|\neg PS)}$，具有較高 LLR 的詞彙視為與特定情感具有較高的聯繫。選出正負面各 200 個關鍵詞進行特徵表示，分別將原始句子的詞彙對應到正負面關鍵詞列表中，並將所對應到的詞彙以權重數字取代，其他則以「0」表示，因此會形成正面 200 維與負面 200 維，共 400 維的特徵向量。

$$-2log\left[\frac{p(w)^{N(w\wedge PS)}(1-p(w))^{N(PS)-N(w\wedge PS)}}{p(W|PS)^{N(w\wedge PS)}(1-(W|PS))^{N(PS)-N(w\wedge PS)}}\right]\times\left[\frac{p(w)^{N(w\wedge\neg PS)}(1-p(w))^{N(\neg PS)-N(w\wedge\neg PS)}}{p(W|\neg PS)^{N(w\wedge\neg PS)}(1-(W|\neg PS))^{N(\neg PS)-N(w\wedge\neg PS)}}\right] \quad (1)$$

2. 情緒構面特徵：透過上述 LLR 關鍵詞去對應原文的 VA，只選取權重最高的前三名，將其 Valence 和 Arousal 作為特徵表示。若不足三組則選擇原文中極性最高的 Valence 和 Arousal 補足到三組，因此共可獲得共 6 維的特徵表示。將 BERT 文字向量表示法與上述的 LLR 與 VA 特徵向量合併後獲得 1,174 維的向量，投入 BiLSTM + Attention Layer 的推論模型。

3. 依存關係特徵：圖 2 下半部分為加入句子語義特徵。使用 LTP 套件中的依存句法分析 (Dependency Parsing) 獲得句子中各詞彙的依存關係，如圖 3 所示。箭頭連接兩詞彙表示含有依存關係，紅色字體顯示兩者的依存關係類型，將兩詞彙間的關係轉換為矩陣形式。如圖 3，詞彙間有關係以「1」表示，無依存關係則以「0」表示。考量每句話的詞彙數量可能不相等，將所有矩陣長度都轉換為最長句子的長度。例如，此資料集最長句子長度為 145，就將所有矩陣大小轉換成 [145x145] 後投入卷積神經網絡 (Convolutional Neural Network, CNN) 模型。

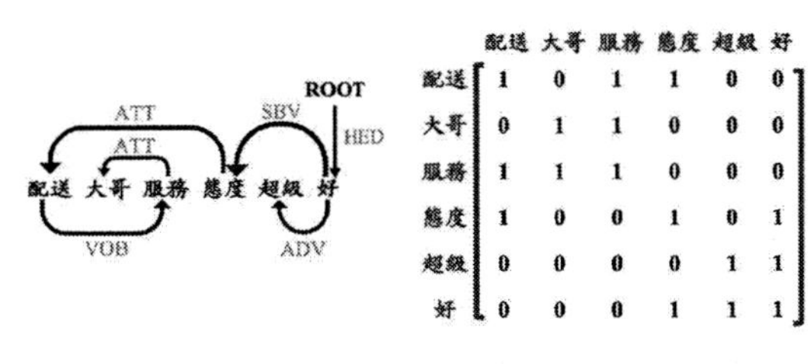

圖 3. 依存分析樹與句子關係矩陣之範例

最後，結合 BERT 文字向量表示法、VA 以及 LLR 的 BiLSTM 加上 Attention Layer 之推論模型的輸出與考慮詞彙間依存關係的矩陣特徵放入 CNN 模型，使用 concat layer 進行合併。concat layer 的功能為將兩個通道 (Channel) 進行拼接，這有利於在向量表示上具有更多特徵並提高分類性能，經過兩層全連接層 (Dense Layer) 取得二元分類預測結果。命名為 BLV-depCNN 模型，用來分析文本情感傾向。

4 實驗結果與討論

實驗分成兩部分，第一部分運用 VA 預測模型取得以多維度連續數值方式來精確表達情感的詞彙 VA 。第二部分則是延用第一部分的結果當成特徵進行情感分類任務。實驗結果皆優於以往的方法，確認本模型架構的價值。

4.1 情緒構面預測之效能評估

資料集來自於 2017 年 IJCNLP 的共享任務：中文短語的維度情感分析 (Dimensional Sentiment Analysis for Chinese Phrases, DSA_P) ，稱為 CVAW 3.0。訓練資料有 2,802 筆，測試資料為 750 筆，共 3,552 筆具有 VA 等級分數的中文維度型情感詞典，所有中文詞彙皆為人工標註 Valence 和 Arousal 的數值。將所有矩陣大小轉換成 [145x145] 後投入超參數設置 batch_size 為 64、optimizer 為 Adam、dropout rate 為 0.2。

本實驗之評估指標比照 DSA_P 預測任務之平均絕對誤差 (Mean Absolute Error, MAE) 及皮爾森相關係數 (Pearson Correlation Coefficient, PCC) 進行評估，如以下公式：

$$\text{MAE:} \quad \mathbf{MAE} = \frac{1}{n}\sum_{i=1}^{n} |\mathbf{A_i} - \mathbf{P_i}| \tag{2}$$

$$\text{PCC:} \quad \boldsymbol{r} = \frac{1}{n-1}\sum_{i=1}^{n} \left(\frac{A_i - \bar{A}}{\sigma_A}\right)\left(\frac{P_i - \bar{P}}{\sigma_P}\right) \tag{3}$$

其中，n 代表測試資料個數，A_i 表示人工註釋的 V 值和 A 值，P_i 表示預測出的 V 值和 A 值，$\bar{A}$ 和 $\bar{P}$ 分別為 A 和 P 的算術平均數，σ_A 和 σ_P 分別為 A 和 P 的標準差。

本研究使用三種不同的嵌入方法，將 BERT 文字向量表示法與 Word2Vec 和單字向量嵌入 (Character Embedding, CE) 相比，分別加入深度神經網路 (Deep Neural Network, DNN) 後的結果如表 1 所示。BERT 在 Valence 與 Arousal 的平均絕對誤差 (MAE) 與皮爾遜相關係數 (PCC) 相較於其他嵌入方法明顯獲得最好的效能。因為 Word2Vec 的每個詞彙表示一個固定的向量，CE 則是每個單詞表示一個固定的向量，兩者皆與單詞出現的上下文無關，而 BERT 生成的向量特徵表示是有考慮上下文的關係及位置關係，因此所生成的向量表示較具有優勢，從而提高模型的效能。

表 1. 嵌入方法之性能比較

Embedding	Valence		Arousal	
	MAE	PCC	MAE	PCC
CE	0.824	0.710	0.936	0.535
Word2Vec	0.947	0.662	1.194	0.138
BERT	**0.687**	**0.831**	**0.878**	**0.634**

表 2 為本研究方法 (Our method 欄位) 與 VA 預測任務前三名 (Wu, Chuhan, et al., 2017; Zhou, Xin, et al., 2017; Li, Peng-Hsuan, 2017) 以及疊加不同特徵的效能比較。本研究方法與基於 BERT 疊加多個特徵向量 (BERT+POS 與 BERT+POS+NTUSD) 可以發現考慮越多的特徵可有效提高模型預測能力，凸顯出在 NTUSD 的特徵中將詞彙分成正負兩類可有效幫助模型判斷 Valence 值可能落點區間，而 E-HowNet 的特徵原理是將相似概念的詞彙獲得一樣的特徵表示，可增加模型學習能力，因此可說明考慮越多基於詞彙特徵可有效提升模型效能。

表 2. 嵌入方法之性能比較

Group	Valence		Arousal	
	MAE	PCC	MAE	PCC
THU_NGN	**0.509**	**0.908**	0.864	0.686
Our method	0.543	0.887	**0.855**	**0.689**
AL_I_NLP	0.545	0.892	0.857	0.678
CKIP	0.602	0.858	0.949	0.576
BERT + POS + NTUSD	0.605	0.869	0.875	0.617
BERT + POS	0.646	0.837	0.883	0.615

本論文所提出之方法在預測中文單詞的情感維度方面表現出眾，媲美排名最高的 THU_NGN。由於本研究充分考慮詞彙間的特性，疊加三種不同特徵以增加模型訓練，且使用考慮單詞向量也考慮上下文及位置關係的 BERT，而能提升模型效能。對於 Valence 的預測結果中 MAE 為 0.543，PCC 增至 88.7%，

這表明本模型預測與正確值之間具有非常高的相關性；對於 Arousal 的預測結果中 MAE 大幅降低至 0.855，PCC 增至 68.9%，證明本模型之優勢。

4.2 社群文本情感預測之效能評估

第二個實驗將利用 VA 預測模型的輸出，集成到混合的深度神經網路模型，對社交媒體評論的整體情緒進行分類。資料集來自於 2014 年 NLPCC 競賽的共享任務「Sentiment Classification with Deep Learning」，以下簡稱為 SCDL。該資料集由中文及英文的產品評論網站上收集得出，此數據來自多個產品領域，包含書籍、DVD 和電子產品等多個領域。資料標籤區分為正面與負面兩個類別，各有 6250 筆。訓練集包含 5,000 筆正面資料以及 5,000 筆負面資料。測試資料包含 1,250 筆正面資料以及 1,250 筆負面資料。為了證明所提出模型的泛化能力，我們選用電子商務服務評論數據集 (ECSR) 以及外送平台用戶評論數據集 (URDP) 進行比較實驗。ECSR 數據集包括從電子商務網站收集的電視產品和發行服務的評論，在該數據集中每個評論都帶有一個情感標籤：正面或負面，數據總共包含 4,212 條評論，其中 1883 條為正面，2329 條為負面。URDP 數據集為某外送平台收集的用戶評論，每則評論皆帶有一個情感標籤：正面或負面，數據集總共包含 6000 筆對於外送餐點、外送員以及平台使用相關評論，正面與負面筆數皆為 3000 筆，是相當平衡的資料。

情感分類任務將使用 precision、recall 和 F_1-score 進行評估。本論文將與 SCDL 數據集的最新系統 (NNLM) (Wang, Yuan, et al., 2014) 以及近年來使用相同資料集的 CNN-SVM (Cao, Yuhui, 2015) 方法進行比較，在 ECSR 和 URDP 數據集上使用 Naïve Bayes Classifier、XGBoost 等機器學習模型以及 BiLSTM 作為 Baseline 方法進行基準比較，結果如表 3 所示。

Bi-LSTM 模型較機器學習方法可獲得更好的效能，因為通過雙向處理文本來學習過去和將來的上下文信息。此外，並非所有單詞對文本的情感分析做出相同的貢獻，注意力機制 (Attention Mechanism) 能夠根據單詞註釋權重對句子含義的重要性來對它們進行改組，可以發現基於注意力的 Bi-LSTM(Bi-LSTM+Att) 比沒有注意力機制的 Bi-LSTM(Bi-LSTM) 效能更高，這是因為注意力機制 (Attention Mechanism) 可以從眾多信息中選擇出對當前任務目標更關鍵的信息，進而增強模型學習的能力。從結果得出在每個類別中本研究之方法 (BLV-depCNN) 表現皆較優，在 SCDL、ECSR 和 URDP 數據集上，BLV-depCNN 模型可以分別達到 80%、94% 和 86% 的 F_1-score。使用注意力機制將情感的 Valence 與 Arousal 注入到 Bi-LSTM，也考慮了單詞與單詞間的關係，並利用 CNN 模型完整的學習文本間的單詞的兩兩關聯性，增強了情感信息和語義信息的表達能力，從而有效地增強正確識別商品評論情緒的能力。

表 1. 嵌入方法之性能比較

Data	Method	Positive	Negative
		Precision, Recall, F_1-score	
NLPCC 2014	Naïve Bayes	0.723/0.741/0.732	0.732/0.713/0.722
	XGBoost	0.754/0.754/0.754	0.754/0.754/0.754
	Bi-LSTM	0.748/0.729/0.738	0.736/0.754/0.745
	Bi-LSTM+Att	0.741/0.772/0.756	0.762/0.729/0.745
	NNLM	0.758/0.789/0.773	0.780/0.748/0.764
	CNN-SVM	0.766/0.806/0.785	0.795/0.754/0.774
	BLV-depCNN	**0.814/0.796/0.804**	**0.786/0.813/0.799**
ECSR	Naïve Bayes	0.772/0.788/0.780	0.826/0.811/0.818
	XGBoost	0.861/0.857/0.858	0.873/0.792/0.831
	Bi-LSTM	0.858/0.824/0.841	0.862/0.890/0.876
	Bi-LSTM+Att	0.852/0.842/0.847	0.873/0.881/0.877
	BLV-depCNN	**0.946/0.925/0.935**	**0.937/0.954/0.945**
URDP	Naïve Bayes	0.861/0.783/0.827	0.797/0.867/0.822
	XGBoost	0.864/0.753/0.804	0.775/0.879/0.823
	Bi-LSTM	0.864/0.779/0.819	0.802/0.874/0.836
	Bi-LSTM+Att	0.847/0.841/0.843	0.841/0.849/0.844
	BLV-depCNN	**0.881/0.833/0.856**	**0.840/0.891/0.864**

根據以上實驗結果，本研究之方法確實可以藉由提供更多詳細的情感知識來提高情感

分類器的分類有效性，在不同類型的情感分類數據集中也表現出色的性能。

5 結論與未來展望

隨著越來越多人在線上購物，顧客與購物網站之間的交流也越趨頻繁，2020 年台灣網路資訊中心 (TWNIC)10[3] 網路報告統計當年度 59.6% 的民眾有網購的經驗。顧客留下包含帶有不同情感色彩和個人語義信息的產品評論。大量產品評論已成為潛在客戶的關鍵信息來源，面對來自網際網路上大量的資訊，很難快速掌握到產品評論的關鍵重點。所以，本研究利用社群媒體上的短文本，提出一個具有細粒度情感特徵的深度神經網路模型，同時考慮詞彙情感特徵與句子結構特徵，利用 LTP 套件的依存句法分析短文本中詞彙間的依存特性，並整合 BERT 文字向量表示法以及 VA 預測模型訓練出具有價值的情感類別預測模型並應用於電子商務服務平台、外送平台、書籍、DVD 和電子產品等領域皆獲得良好的效能。證明情感特徵可有效幫助模型學習，也顯示出本研究之貢獻。

如何妥善處理大量資料並有效地轉為知識是相當重要的議題，產品評論分析的目的在於萃取出消費者對於產品的評價，以獲得重要的資訊，不僅對於潛在消費者、企業、製造商與零售商等都是相當有價值的資訊。在產品評論分析中將眾多評論進行情感分類，包含二元分類 (Binary Classification) 、多元分類 (Multi-Class Classification) 以及基於觀點的情感分析 (Aspect Based Sentiment Analysis, ABSA) 。未來，可開發一個多種分析評論系統幫助企業快速掌握用戶對於產品的回饋，提供評論情感傾向以及資訊視覺化。節省閱讀與統整人力時間，快速且有效的分析萃取重要的顧客知識與商品的優缺點以提供企業有價值的資訊，針對網路平台上豐富的留言意見可以幫助企業改善產品品質、提供後續產品設計依據、規劃行銷策略以及促銷方案等，以達到更好的業績。

References

Liu, B. 2012. Sentiment analysis and opinion mining. *Synthesis lectures on human language technologies, 5*(1), 1-167.

Shakeel, M. H., and Karim, A. 2020. Adapting deep learning for sentiment classification of code-switched informal short text. In *Proceedings of the 35th Annual ACM Symposium on Applied Computing*, pages 903-906.

Zhang, W., Xu, H., and Wan, W. 2012. Weakness Finder: Find product weakness from Chinese reviews by using aspects-based sentiment analysis. *Expert Systems with Applications, 39*(11), 10283-10291.

Yenter, A., and Verma, A. 2017. Deep CNN-LSTM with combined kernels from multiple branches for IMDb review sentiment analysis. In *2017 IEEE 8th Annual Ubiquitous Computing, Electronics and Mobile Communication Conference (UEMCON)*, pages 540-546.

Turney, P. D. 2002. Thumbs up or thumbs down? Semantic orientation applied to unsupervised classification of reviews. *arXiv preprint cs/0212032*.

Hu, M., and Liu, B. 2004. Mining and summarizing customer reviews. In *Proceedings of the tenth ACM SIGKDD international conference on Knowledge discovery and data mining*, pages 168-177.

Agarwal, A., Biadsy, F., and Mckeown, K. 2009. Contextual phrase-level polarity analysis using lexical affect scoring and syntactic n-grams. In *Proceedings of the 12th Conference of the European Chapter of the ACL (EACL 2009)*, pages 24-32.

Sayeed, A., Boyd-Graber, J., Rusk, B., and Weinberg, A. 2012. Grammatical structures for word-level sentiment detection. In *Proceedings of the 2012 Conference of the North American Chapter of the Association for computational Linguistics: Human language technologies*, pages 667-676.

Yu, L. C., Wang, J., Lai, K. R., and Zhang, X. J. 2015. Predicting valence-arousal ratings of words using a weighted graph method. In *Proceedings of the 53rd Annual Meeting of the Association for Computational Linguistics and the 7th International Joint Conference on Natural Language Processing (Volume 2: Short Papers)*, pages 788-793.

Chang, Y. C., Yeh, W. C., Hsing, Y. C., and Wang, C. A. 2019. Refined distributed emotion vector representation for social media sentiment analysis. *Plos one, 14*(10), e0223317.

Cheng, Y. Y., Chen, Y. M., Yeh, W. C., and Chang, Y. C. 2021. Valence and Arousal-Infused Bi-

3 https://report.twnic.tw/2020/index.html

Directional LSTM for Sentiment Analysis of Government Social Media Management. *Applied Sciences, 11*(2), 880.

Zhai, P., Huang, X., Zhang, B., and Fang, Y. 2020. Relation extraction based on fusion dependency parsing from chinese EMRs. *Scientific Programming.*

Qidi, J. 2021. Research on Topic Mining of Medical Surgical Mask Reviews Sold on E-commerce Platform. In *Journal of Physics: Conference Series* (Vol. 1820, No. 1, p. 012182). IOP Publishing.

Hsieh, Y. L., Chang, Y. C., Huang, Y. J., Yeh, S. H., Chen, C. H., and Hsu, W. L. 2017. MONPA: Multi-objective named-entity and part-of-speech annotator for Chinese using recurrent neural network. In *Proceedings of the Eighth International Joint Conference on Natural Language Processing (Volume 2: Short Papers)*, pages 80-85.

Chang, Y. C., Yeh, W. C., Hsing, Y. C., & Wang, C. A. 2019. Refined distributed emotion vector representation for social media sentiment analysis. PLoS One, 14(10), e0223317.

Chen, W. T., Lin, S. C., Huang, S. L., Chung, Y. S., and Chen, K. J. 2010. E-HowNet and automatic construction of a lexical ontology. In *Coling 2010: Demonstrations*, pages 45-48.

Vaswani, A., Shazeer, N., Parmar, N., Uszkoreit, J., Jones, L., Gomez, A. N., ... and Polosukhin, I. 2017. Attention is all you need. *arXiv preprint arXiv:1706.03762.*

Moreno, J. G., Boros, E., and Doucet, A. 2020. TLR at the NTCIR-15 FinNum-2 Task: Improving Text Classifiers for Numeral Attachment in Financial Social Data. In *Proceedings of the 15th NTCIR Conference on Evaluation of Information Access Technologies, Tokyo Japan*, pages 8-11.

Gomes, H. M., Barddal, J. P., Enembreck, F., and Bifet, A. 2017. A survey on ensemble learning for data stream classification. *ACM Computing Surveys (CSUR)*, *50*(2), 1-36.

Dong, Xibin, et al. 2020. A survey on ensemble learning. Frontiers of Computer Science 14.2, pages 241-258.

Wu, Chuhan, et al. 2017. Thu_ngn at ijcnlp-2017 task 2: Dimensional sentiment analysis for chinese phrases with deep lstm. In *Proceedings of the IJCNLP 2017, Shared Tasks*, pages 47-52.

Zhou, Xin, et al. 2017. Alibaba at IJCNLP-2017 Task 2: A Boosted Deep System for Dimensional Sentiment Analysis of Chinese Phrases. In *Proceedings of the IJCNLP 2017, Shared Tasks*, pages 100-104.

Li, Peng-Hsuan, Wei-Yun Ma, and Hsin-Yang Wang. 2017. CKIP at IJCNLP-2017 Task 2: Neural Valence-Arousal Prediction for Phrases. In *Proceedings of the IJCNLP 2017, Shared Tasks*, pages 89-94.

Wang, Yuan, et al. 2014. Word vector modeling for sentiment analysis of product reviews. *CCF International Conference on Natural Language Processing and Chinese Computing.* Springer, Berlin, Heidelberg.

Cao, Yuhui, Ruifeng Xu, and Tao Chen. 2015. Combining convolutional neural network and support vector machine for sentiment classification. *Chinese national conference on social media processing*. Springer, Singapore.

The 33rd Conference on Computational Linguistics and Speech Processing (ROCLING 2021)
Taoyuan, Taiwan, October 15-16, 2021. The Association for Computational Linguistics and Chinese Language Processing

基於依存關係感知能力的深度學習模型進行金融推文之數值關係檢測
Numerical Relation Detection in Financial Tweets using Dependency-aware Deep Neural Network

Yu-Chi Liang[1], Min-Chen Chen[2], Wen-Chao Yeh[3], Yung-Chun Chang[*]
[1, 2, *]Graduate Institute of Data Science, Taipei Medical University, Taipei, Taiwan
[3] Institute of Information Systems and Applications, National Tsing Hua University, Hsinchu, Taiwan
[1, 2, *]{ m946108001, m946109001, changyc}@tmu.edu.tw
[3]wyeh@m109.nthu.edu.tw

摘要

近年來，許多研究是以金融文本資料進行分析，然而，我們發現在這些文本資料中的數字亦包含值得探討的豐富資訊。本論文藉由分析金融議題相關之推特文章，探討文本中目標數字與目標標籤是否具有關聯性。本研究採用基於變換器的雙向編碼器表示式作為模型架構之主要表示機制，並將依存關係作為特徵轉成依存關係矩陣後放入卷積神經網路中，使模型透過依存關係學習到文本中詞與詞間的關聯性。根據實驗結果顯示，本研究採用之方法對於此任務有良好之預測能力，其 Macro-averaging F1 Score 為 71.05%。

Abstract

Machine learning methods for financial document analysis have been focusing mainly on the textual part. However, the numerical parts of these documents are also rich in information content. In order to further analyze the financial text, we should assay the numeric information in depth. In light of this, the purpose of this research is to identify the linking between the target cashtag and the target numeral in financial tweets, which is more challenging than analyzing news and official documents. In this research, we developed a multi model fusion approach which integrates Bidirectional Encoder Representations from Transformers (BERT) and Convolutional Neural Network (CNN). We also encode dependency information behind text into the model to derive semantic latent features. The experimental results show that our model can achieve remarkable performance and outperform comparisons.

關鍵字：金融社交媒體、基於變換器的雙向編碼器表示技術、卷積神經網路、依存語法
Keywords: Financial Social Media, BERT, CNN, Dependency Grammar

1 Introduction

隨著人工智慧的蓬勃發展，各行業正在研究如何將技術應用在產業實務上。金融服務業拓展一個新穎的研究領域，稱為金融科技 (Financial Technology, FinTech)。目前 FinTech 已融入自然語言處理 (Natural Language Processing, NLP) 技術，透過機器學習與文字探勘分析財務數據來獲取許多與財務相關的有用訊息。例如，財務情緒分析可以獲得專家對於股票市場趨勢的意見讓客戶能夠做出更好的決策 (Sohangir et al., 2018)；透過銀行員工和客戶之間聯繫過程的歷史紀錄分析產業關聯以及決定當地產業之信心水準 (Sakaji et al., 2019)。

以往分析財務文本資料時，主要是針對文字部分做探索分析；然而要瞭解金融資料的細節，不僅須要分析文字內容還須依靠數字資訊。若能取得財務資料中數字所包含的意義可以更快速的掌握關鍵內容。隨著網際網路的發展，人們透過社交媒體表達自己意見的頻率隨之增高，也直接讓社交媒體平台成為當今訊息的主要來源之一。Vilas 等人研究推特用戶對金融市場相關事件的影響，分析結果顯示儘管推特只是社交媒體而非專業金融論壇，但推文內容對於金融事件仍具影響

力 (Vilas et al., 2019) ，若善加利用社交媒體上的文章並加以分析，相信可以獲得對於市場和客戶都有幫助的相關資訊。相較於新聞文章，經由社交媒體產生的資料並無固定格式，內容可能包含表情符號、連結網址和網路用語。因此，在使用自然語言處理技術分析社交媒體數據時需考慮到比較複雜的情況，如何掌握數據中的關鍵訊息成為一項具挑戰性的任務 (Farzindar and Inkpen, 2015) 。考量文本中可能包含多個數字或是多個目標標籤，因此需決定推特文章中特定數字與特定附加目標之間是否具有關聯性。如圖 1 的例子，當目標標籤為股票「BAC」時，數字「3」表示股票「BAC」每一股的現金支出為3。因此，數字「3」是表示股票「BAC」，而數字「2009」表示年份，它與股票「BAC」並無直接關聯性。此為二元分類任務，透過金融推文判斷文本中目標數字與目標標籤之間是否具關聯性：「1」表示目標數字與目標標籤間具有關聯性，而「0」則是目標數字與目標標籤間沒有關聯性。本研究計畫藉由依存句法分析應用在深度學習模型上來探討與金融事件相關之推特文章中目標數字與目標標籤之間是否存在相關性。

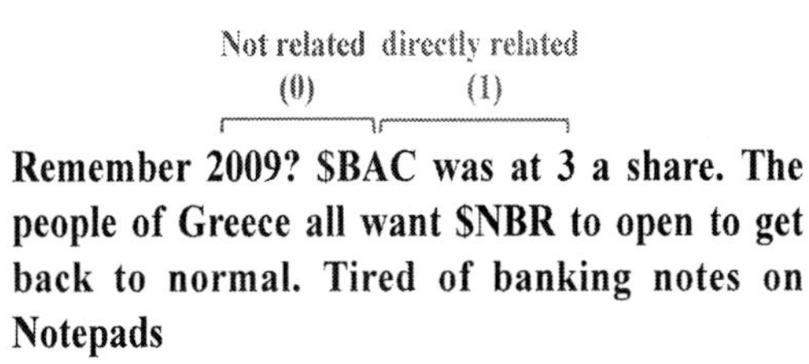

圖 1. 推文中數字與股票代碼間之關係示意圖

2 Related Work

使用自然語言處理技術進行數值分析任務之應用相當廣泛，其中包含臨床醫學領域、科學領域、新聞領域等。然而，隨著 FinTech 議題逐漸受到重視，有許多任務著重在如何將自然語言處理技術應用於金融領域，像是語義評估工作坊 (International Workshop on Semantic Evaluation, SemEval) 於 2017 年舉辦之金融微博和新聞的情緒分析(Cortis et al., 2017) 、耶拿大學語言和訊息工程實驗室舉辦之第一屆經濟學和自然語言處理研討會 (1st Workshop on Economic and Natural Language Processing, ECONLP 2018) (Hahn et al., 2018) 、 國際資訊檢索評估會議 (NII Testbeds and Community for Information access Research, NTCIR) 第十四屆的理解金融推文中的數字 (Fine-Grained Numeral Understanding in Financial Tweets, FinNum) 任務 (Chen et al., 2019) 以及第十五屆金融推文的數字附件 (Numeral Attachment in Financial Tweets, FinNum-2) 任務 (Chen et al., 2020) 。

FinNum 是一項理解金融社交媒體文本資料中數字屬性的任務。當我們實際執行 FinNum 任務時，發現一項值得探討的主題：金融社交媒體中的資料通常包含多組數字，在進行數值分類任務前應先判別數字是否與股票文字代碼有關聯性。適逢 NTCIR 第十五屆提出新的任務以改善 FinNum 任務實際應用時所遇到的問題，任務名稱為 FinNum-2。FinNum-2 是一項二元分類任務，主要是探討金融社交媒體數據中已標註完成的目標數字與目標標籤之間是否具有關聯性。主辦單位共提供兩組比較基準 (Baseline)，其中 Baseline-Majority 是將全部資料都視為數字和目標標籤之間存在關聯性之實驗結果。Baseline-Caps-m 則是合併單詞的嵌入向量 (Token embedding) 、字元嵌入向量 (Character Embedding) 、單詞的位置嵌入向量 (Position Embedding) 以及單詞的幅度嵌入向量 (Magnitude Embedding) ，並放入膠囊網路中進行訓練 (Chen et al., 2019) 。除了上述由主辦單位提供之比較基準組外，

- TLR-3：採用基於變換器的雙向編碼器表示技術 (Bidirectional Encoder Representations from Transformers, BERT) 與 Robustly optimized BERT approach (RoBERTa) 進行集成學習 (Ensemble learning) 並根據預測機率最小值選出預測結果 (Moreno et al., 2020) 。

- CYUT-2： 針對預訓練 XLM-RoBERTa 模型進行微調 (Jiang et al., 2020)

- MIG-2：在 BERT 預訓練模型後添加雙向長短期記憶模型 (Bi-directional Long Short-Term Memory, BiLSTM) 並

將損失函數權重設為 0.8 與 0.2 (Chen et al., 2020)。

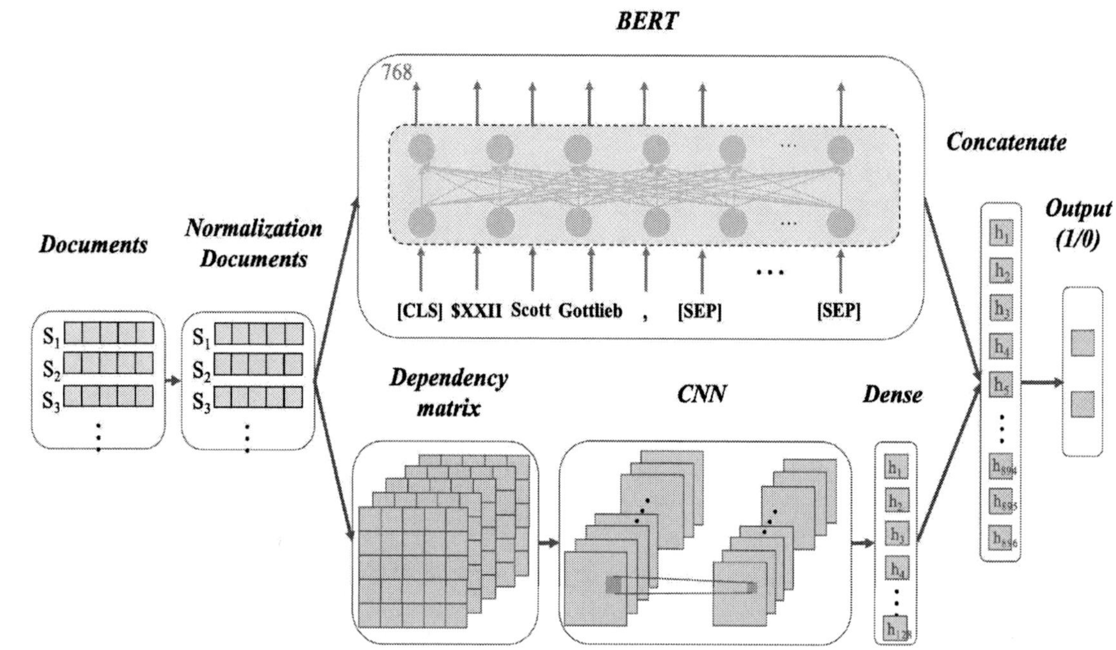

圖 2. Dependency Grammars-infused BERT-CNN Model 架構圖

- TMUNLP-1：取出 BERT 產生之向量表達式，將之放入 BiLSTM 模型並續接一層注意力機制 (Attention) (Liang et al., 2020)。

- WUST：透過 TF-IDF 生成文本表示法再放入支援向量機 (Support Vector Machine, SVM) 模型進行分類預測 (Xia et al., 2020)。

3 Methodology

本研究之模型架構稱為 Dependency Grammars-infused BERT-CNN Model，如圖 2。先將金融短文本經預處理步驟後放入 BERT 模型學習完整之短文本內容，並將短文本轉為向量後取出備用。同時，將金融短文本進行依存句法分析 (Dependency parsing) 並將結果
轉換成依存關係矩陣 (Dependency matrix)。依存關係矩陣將做為卷積神經網路 (Convolutional Neural Network, CNN) 輸入特徵，並將 CNN 模型輸出結果使用全連接層 (Dense Layer) 來降低維度。最後，將上述兩個輸出結果合併後放入全連接層進行最終分類預測，判斷文本中股票代碼與數字間是否具關聯性。

預處理步驟旨在標註目標標籤與目標數字，作法為在目標標籤與目標數字的前後皆分別使用「£」與「§」符號標註單詞。透過此法標註所有文本讓模型於訓練時能學習到文本中的目標標籤與目標數字，進而獲取更多目標標籤與目標數字之訊息。BERT 模型是由 Transformer 中的編碼器訓練而成 (Devlin et al., 2018)，可由 BERT 官方網站 下載預訓練模型。本研究採用 BERT-Base Uncased 模型，包含 12 層 Transformer 區塊、 768 維度之隱藏層尺寸。使用 Uncased 模型能一併將文本中大寫英文字母轉為小寫以及移除文本中之重音符號。將金融短文本放入此模型訓練後取出第一個 [CLS] 產出之 768 維度向量，與依存關係矩陣向量結合並進行最終預測。

圖 3 為文本輸入 BERT 模型至產出向量之流程。首先將文本加入特殊標籤後放入 BERT 模型，即為變換器 (Transformer) 模型之編碼器 (Encoder) 架構。BERT 模型會根據選用的預訓練模型將文本中每個文字皆輸出成大小與隱藏層尺寸相同之向量，在此步驟中選用第一個單詞 [CLS] 產出之向量，續接依存句法向量進行最終模型訓練。

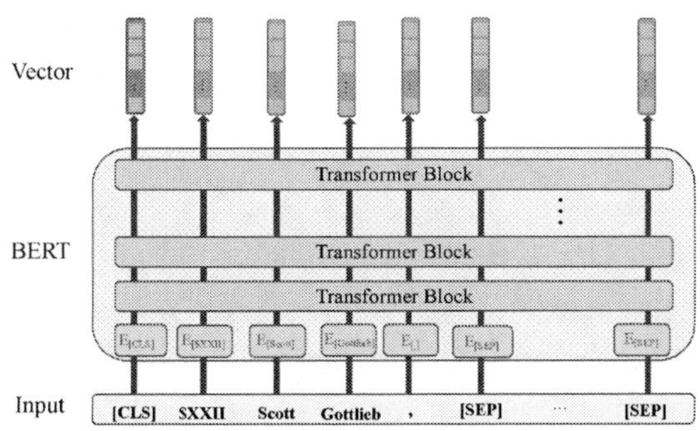

圖 3. 文本表示法生成圖

依存句法分析 (Dependency Parsing) 為 NLP 一項關鍵技術，本研究使用 StanfordCoreNLP 套件進行依存句法分析。Stanford CoreNLP 是由史丹佛 (Stanford) 大學自然語言處理實驗室提出之自然語言分析套件，除了依存句法分析外亦包含其他多種功能；例如，分詞 (Tokenization)、詞形還原 (Lemmatization)、命名實體識別技術 (Named Entity Recognition, NER) 與詞性標註 (Part-Of-Speech, POS) 等。從 3.5.2 版本開始，Stanford CoreNLP 預設參照 Universal Dependencies v1 (Nivre et al., 2016) 輸出語法關係 (Schuster and Manning, 2016)，此文檔一共包含 40 種不同之依存關係。圖 4 上半部為使用 StanfordCoreNLP 生成依存句法之範例，箭頭連接之兩分詞表示含有依存關係，箭頭旁之文字顯示兩者依存關係。統整文本放入依存句法分析產生之依存關係種類並將依存關係進行編號，以供後續產生依存關係矩陣使用。

圖 4 下半部為依存關係矩陣範例，其縱軸與橫軸皆以文本表示，在含有依存關係兩個分詞之對應位置放入相對應的依存關係編號，若是分詞之對應位置並無依存關係則在對應位置中填入「0」。舉例如下，在分詞「$DPW」與「Glad」之間具有依存關係「acl:relcl」且此關係編號為「12」，在進行依存關係矩陣轉換時便會在縱軸為「$DPW」且橫軸為「Glad」以及縱軸為「Glad」且橫軸為「$DPW」兩處皆放上「12」。另考量每一個文本之長度可能不同且為因應後續接 CNN 模型時輸入特徵圖需為固定尺寸之向量，故需先判斷全部資料中各單一文本的單詞數量。以各文本中單詞數量最大者為依存關係矩陣之固定長度 N。若是尺寸小於 N 的文本則以 0 填補長度不足處，於是可將依存關係矩陣尺寸皆處理成大小為 $N \times N$ 矩陣。

CNN 模型是以深度神經網路為基礎架構再增添兩種新的神經元，分別為卷積層 (Convolutional Layer) 與池化層 (Pooling Layer) (Murugan, 2017)。CNN 不只被廣泛應用於影像辨識與聲音辨識等任務上，也被發現可在自然語言處理上有良好效能。我們將文本轉為固定尺寸之依存關係矩陣後便放入 CNN 模型中訓練並將經由平坦層輸出之向量透過全連接層轉為 128 維度之向量。

將上述由依存句法分析產生之特徵向量與 BERT 模型產生之文本表示法進行串連 (Concatenate) 後放入全連接層進行最終預測。

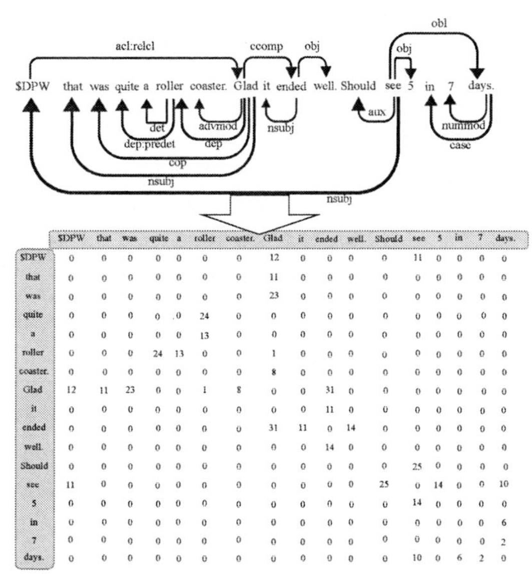

	$DPW	that	was	quite	a	roller	coaster.	Glad	it	ended	well.	Should	see	5	in	7	days.
$DPW	0	0	0	0	0	0	0	12	0	0	0	0	11	0	0	0	0
that	0	0	0	0	0	0	0	11	0	0	0	0	0	0	0	0	0
was	0	0	0	0	0	0	0	23	0	0	0	0	0	0	0	0	0
quite	0	0	0	0	0	24	0	0	0	0	0	0	0	0	0	0	0
a	0	0	0	0	0	13	0	0	0	0	0	0	0	0	0	0	0
roller	0	0	0	24	13	0	0	1	0	0	0	0	0	0	0	0	0
coaster.	0	0	0	0	0	0	0	8	0	0	0	0	0	0	0	0	0
Glad	12	11	23	0	0	1	8	0	0	31	0	0	0	0	0	0	0
it	0	0	0	0	0	0	0	0	0	11	0	0	0	0	0	0	0
ended	0	0	0	0	0	0	0	31	11	0	14	0	0	0	0	0	0
well.	0	0	0	0	0	0	0	0	0	14	0	0	0	0	0	0	0
Should	0	0	0	0	0	0	0	0	0	0	0	0	25	0	0	0	0
see	11	0	0	0	0	0	0	0	0	0	0	25	0	14	0	0	10
5	0	0	0	0	0	0	0	0	0	0	0	0	14	0	0	0	0
in	0	0	0	0	0	0	0	0	0	0	0	0	0	0	0	0	6
7	0	0	0	0	0	0	0	0	0	0	0	0	0	0	0	0	2
days.	0	0	0	0	0	0	0	0	0	0	0	0	10	0	6	2	0

圖 4. 生成依存句法與依存關係矩陣範例圖

4 Result and Discussion

本研究使用 NTCIR 第十五屆會議的金融推文數字探討 (Numeral Attachment in Financial Tweets, FinNum-2) 任務之 NumAttach 資料集，探討與金融事件相關之推特文章 (Tweets) 中數字和目標標籤間是否存在相關性。此資料集包含推特文章 (tweet) 、目標數字 (target number)、目標標籤 (target cashtag)、關係 (relation) 以及目標數字位置 (offset) 共五個欄位。參考表 1，整體資料集包含 10,340 句短文本，切分 70% (7,187 句) 做為訓練資料集、10% (1,044 句) 為開發資料集以及 20% (2,109 句) 為測試資料集。本研究採用 macro F1 分數作為實驗評估效能標準。

表 1. NumAttach 資料集分佈

資料集	具關聯性	不具關聯性	總和
訓練集	5,827	1,360	7,187
開發集	850	194	1,044
測試集	1,721	388	2,109
總和	8,398	1,942	10,340

表 2 為採用三種不同方式表達依存句法分析特徵並比較三者實驗結果與未添加依存句法分析特徵之實驗結果。

- BERT：指不使用任何依存句法分析特徵僅將原句經預處理後放入 BERT 模型中。
- BERT+Dep (SDP) 、 BERT+Dep (OHM)以及 Our Method 分別表示將上述三種依存句法分析特徵分別放入 CNN 模型中並與 BERT 模型之結果合併，其中 Our Method 即為本論文所提出之 Dependency Grammars-infused BERT-CNN Model。

「Dep (SDP)」為透過目標標籤與目標數字間最短依存關係路徑 (Shortest Dependency Path, SDP) 並整理出依存關係進行編號，而後將 SDP 透過編號轉為 10 維向量，若 SDP 之長度大於 10 則取出前 5 個以及後 5 個依存關係，若 SDP 之長度小於 10 則是使用 0 將向量擴充至長度為 10。

「Dep (OHM)」是將依存句法分析特徵轉為 One-Hot 矩陣 (One-Hot Matrix, OHM) 後放入 CNN 模型， One-Hot 矩陣是先將矩陣之橫軸與縱軸皆以原句表示並逐一比對兩單詞間是否具有依存關係，若兩單詞間具有依存關係則以「1」表示，反之，「0」表示單詞間不具有依存關係。

表 2. 金融推文探討數字之依存句法分析實驗比較

Method	Macro F_1 score (%)
BERT	70.20%
BERT + Dep (SDP)	58.74%
BERT + Dep (OHM)	64.25%
Our Method	**71.05%**

比較 BERT + Dep (SDP) 、 BERT + Dep (OHM) 以及 Our Method 三組實驗結果可看出，使用最短依存關係路徑產生 10 維向量以及 One-Hot 矩陣皆比僅採用 BERT 模型之效能差，前者之效能減少 11.46%，後者則是減少 5.95%。BERT + Dep (SDP) 在找尋最短路徑時是透過計算空白字元得到句子的最短依存關係路徑，然而目標數字可能包含著其他符號使得句子無法找出最短依存關係路徑僅能使用全句替代，此特徵設計方式未能良好表達出目標數字與目標標籤之間依存關係。

將依存關係特徵設計成 One-Hot 矩陣時，僅能表達出單詞間有無依存關係但無法學習到依存關係種類，使得模型未能透過學習 Dependency parsing 特徵來增加識別推特文章中的目標標籤與數字間關聯性的能力。

本論文所提出之 Dependency Grammars-infused BERT-CNN Model 效能為 71.05%，不僅相較 BERT 模型效能略高 0.62%。且為全部實驗中最具辨識能力之模型。此結果顯示使用編號之方式表達依存句法分析特徵能夠完整表達出句子中所有依存關係及種類，此特徵設計方式有助於模型學習到每一句話中單詞之間不同種類之依存關係，加入此特徵亦能幫助模型對於推特文章中的目標標籤與數字間關聯性有更好之辨識能力。

表 3 為本研究提出之模型架構 (Our Method) 與兩組 Baseline、五組參賽模型之實驗結果比較。Our Method 於 NTCIR FinNum-2 任務中排名第三，且明顯高於第四名。雖非最優異之效能，但在預測與金融事件相關之推特文章

中數字和目標標籤之間是否存在相關性方面已表現出眾。Baseline-Majority 之方式未經模型訓練僅將全部資料皆視為有關聯性，故此 Baseline 於此比賽中效能排最後。WUST 使用 TF-IDF 生成文本表示法並搭配 SVM 模型訓練，文本經過模型訓練有助於辨識沒有關聯性之文本，因此，此模型之效能較 Baseline-Majority 提升約 10%。Baseline-Caps-m 考量四種詞嵌入並放入膠囊網路中，不僅學習到常見之單詞的嵌入向量，同時學習了字元嵌入向量 (Character Embedding)、單詞的位置嵌入向量 (Position Embedding) 以及單詞的幅度嵌入向量 (Magnitude Embedding)，因此相較於 WUST 採用 TF-IDF 生成文本表示法，此方法學習到較多資訊且在放入膠囊網路中可以更有效地學習資訊中的特徵。因此，此模型相較於 WUST 之模型效能提升約 10%。

TMUNLP-1 使用 BiLSTM 模型架構，在文本訓練上，BiLSTM 模型可以學習到句子雙向的語義關係，對於內容主要為辨識句子中兩單詞間是否具關聯性之任務來說，BiLSTM 模型可以獲取良好之效能，此模型較 Baseline-Majority 提升約 1.4%。與 TMUNLP-1 不同的是 MIG-2 之模型架構是經過完整之 BERT 預訓練模型再訓練而非僅採用 BERT 產生之文本表示法，因此在模型 Macro F_1 Score 效能上 MIG-2 比 TMUNLP-1 提升約 4%。Our Method 考量依存關係編號矩陣特徵且使用符號分別標注目標數字和目標標籤，上述之方式皆有助於模型學習辨識文本中的目標數字與目標標籤，在模型效能上，此方式較 MIG-2 提升 2.33%。CYUT-2 雖未考慮使用特徵添加至模型中但他們所使用之方式是針對 XLM-RoBERTa 模型中之學習率進行微調，XLM-RoBERTa 模型中每一層皆使用不同且與該層最合適之學習率，此舉可以提升 XLM-RoBERTa 模型整體之效能，比本論文所提出之模型架構略為提升 0.85%。TLR-3 分別同時訓練 BERT 模型與 Robustly optimized BERT approach (RoBERTa) 模型，而後根據預測出之機率選出結果，此方式可以集合兩個模型之結果，此外，因資料分布不平衡關係，透過選擇預測出機率的最小值可以更好地辨識目標數字和目標標籤之間不具有關聯性之文本，所以此方法較 CYUT-2 提升約 2%，同時，此模型架構亦為比賽中辨識任務最優異之模型。

本研究採用 BERT 模型添加依存關係編號矩陣特徵之方式，與第一名 (TLR-3) 需訓練兩個模型並採用集成學習之方法以及第二名 (CYUT-2) 針對 XLM-RoBERTa 模型進行微調之方式相比；本論文之模型訓練時間相對較短且對於電腦硬體設備要求相對較低。本研究提出的方法可以在相對較低的能耗時間情況下獲取與前二名近似之預測效能，顯示出此模型對於辨識任務內容具有貢獻度。

表 3. 嵌 FinNum-2 任務模型效能比較

Method	Macro F_1 score (%)
TLR-3	73.95%
CYUT-2	71.90%
Our Method	71.05%
MIG-2	68.72%
TMUNLP-1	64.76%
Baseline-Caps-m	63.37%
WUST	54.43%
Baseline-Majority	44.93%

5 Conclusion

近年來隨著網際網路的蓬勃發展，人們逐漸改由在社交媒體上表達自己對於某事件的看法，因此針對從社交媒體上獲取之文本使用自然語言處理技術之研究也逐年上升。然而，過去在分析文本時大多都是著重於分析文字部分，往往容易忽略文本中的數字其實包含相當重要之資訊；尤其針對金融方面之資料，瞭解文本中數字之含義對於決策者如何根據數字結果做出適當決策更是有深遠的影響。

本論文嘗試由推特上所獲取與金融議題相關之短文資料集進行探討，計畫透過演算法辨別文章中的目標數字與目標標籤之間是否具有關聯性以助於日後瞭解文本中數字所具有之含義。本研究是以 BERT 模型為主要基礎架構並將依存句法分析所得結果轉為依存關係矩陣作為特徵放入 CNN 後，再與 BERT 串連進行最終預測。與常見進行相關任務使用之方法不同之處在於以往在設計特徵時會選用一維之方式呈現，本研究採用二維之方式呈現依存關係，透過二維矩陣搭配依存關係編號方式能夠完整表達出每一個詞與詞間之依存關係，使整體模型對於辨識社交媒體短文本中的特定兩單詞之間是否具關聯性之效能往上提升。

考量取得完整依存關係之重要性，未來或可嘗試使用 Tweebo parser 等以推特文章訓練而成的套件 (Kong et al., 2014)，期待能對寫作格式不受拘束之社交媒體短文本提取出更完整的依存關係。希望透過微調技術提升 BERT 模型架構之辨識能力，進而讓整體模型對於社交媒體短文本中的特定兩單詞之間是否具關聯性之辨識能力獲得更進一步提升之可能。

Acknowledgments

本研究承蒙科技部計畫 MOST 109-2410-H-038 -012 -MY2 之補助。

References

Sohangir, S., Wang, D., Pomeranets, A., and Khoshgoftaar, T. M. 2018. Big Data: Deep Learning for financial sentiment analysis. *Journal of Big Data*, 5(1): 1-25.

Sakaji, H., Kuramoto, R., Matsushima, H., Izumi, K., Shimada, T., and Sunakawa, K. 2019. Financial text data analytics framework for business confidence indices and inter-industry relations. *In Proceedings of the First Workshop on Financial Technology and Natural Language Processing*, pages 40-46.

Vilas, A. F., Redondo, R. P. D., Crockett, K., Owda, M., and Evans, L. 2019. Twitter permeability to financial events: an experiment towards a model for sensing irregularities. *Multimedia Tools and Applications*, 78(7): 9217-9245

Farzindar, A. and Inkpen, D. 2015. Natural language processing for social media. *Synthesis Lectures on Human Language Technologies*, 8(2): 1-166.

Cortis, K., Freitas, A., Daudert, T., Huerlimann, M., Zarrouk, M., Handschuh, S., and Davis, B. 2017. Semeval-2017 task 5: Fine-grained sentiment analysis on financial microblogs and news. *Association for Computational Linguistics (ACL)*

Hahn, U., Hoste, V., and Tsai, M. F., 2018. Proceedings of the First Workshop on Economics and Natural Language Processing. *In Proceedings of the First Workshop on Economics and Natural Language Processing.*

Chen, C. C., Huang, H. H., Takamura, H., and Chen, H. H., 2019. Overview of the ntcir-14 finnum task: Fine-grained numeral understanding in financial social media data. *In Proceedings of the 14th NTCIR Conference on Evaluation of Information Access Technologies*, pages 19-27.

Chen, C. C., Huang, H. H., Takamura, H., and Chen, H. H., 2020. Overview of the NTCIR-15 FinNum-2 Task: Numeral Attachment in Financial Tweets. *Development*, 850(194): 1-44.

Chen, C. C., Huang, H. H., and Chen, H. H., 2019. Numeral attachment with auxiliary tasks. *In Proceedings of the 42nd International ACM SIGIR Conference on Research and Development in Information Retrieval*, pages 1161-1164.

Moreno, J. G., Boros, E., and Doucet, A., 2020. TLR at the NTCIR-15 FinNum-2 Task: Improving Text Classifiers for Numeral Attachment in Financial Social Data. *In Proceedings of the 15th NTCIR Conference on Evaluation of Information Access Technologies*, pages 8-11.

Jiang, M. T. J., Chen, Y. K., and Wu, S. H., 2020. CYUT at the NTCIR-15 FinNum-2 Task: Tokenization and Fine-tuning Techniques for Numeral Attachment in Financial Tweets. *In Proceedings of the 15th NTCIR Conference on Evaluation of Information Access Technologies*, pages 92-96.

Chen, Y. Y. and Liu, C. L., 2020. MIG at the NTCIR-15 FinNum-2 Task: Use the transfer learning and feature engineering for numeral attachment task. *In Proceedings of the 15th NTCIR Conference on Evaluation of Information Access Technologies.*

Liang, Y. C., Huang, Y. H., Cheng, Y. Y., and Chang, Y. C., 2020. TMUNLP at the NTCIR-15 FinNum-2. *In Proceedings of the 15th NTCIR Conference on Evaluation of Information Access Technologies.*

Xia, X., Wang, W., and Liu, M., 2020. WUST at NTCIR-15 FinNum-2 Task. *In Proceedings of the 15th NTCIR Conference on Evaluation of Information Access Technologies.*

Devlin, J., Chang, M. W., Lee, K., and Toutanova, K., 2018. Bert: Pre-training of deep bidirectional transformers for language understanding. *arXiv preprint arXiv:1810.04805.*

Nivre, J., De Marneffe, M. C., Ginter, F., Goldberg, Y., Hajic, J., Manning, C. D., ... and Zeman, D., 2016. Universal dependencies v1: A multilingual treebank collection. *In Proceedings of the Tenth International Conference on Language Resources and Evaluation (LREC'16)*, pages 1659-1666.

Schuster, S. and Manning, C. D. 2016. Enhanced english universal dependencies: An improved representation for natural language understanding tasks. *In Proceedings of the Tenth International Conference on Language Resources and Evaluation (LREC'16)*, pages 2371-2378.

Murugan, P. 2017. Feed forward and backward run in deep convolution neural network. *arXiv preprint arXiv:1711.03278.*

Kong, L., Schneider, N., Swayamdipta, S., Bhatia, A., Dyer, C., and Smith, N. A., 2014. A dependency parser for tweets. *In Proceedings of the 2014 Conference on Empirical Methods in Natural Language Processing (EMNLP)*, pages 1001-1012.

The 33rd Conference on Computational Linguistics and Speech Processing (ROCLING 2021)
Taoyuan, Taiwan, October 15-16, 2021. The Association for Computational Linguistics and Chinese Language Processing

Aggregating User-Centric and Post-Centric Sentiments from Social Media for Topical Stance Prediction

Jenq-Haur Wang
Department of Computer Science and Information Engineering,
National Taipei University of Technology
Taipei, Taiwan
jhwang@ntut.edu.tw

Kuan-Ting Chen
Joint Credit Information Center
Taipei, Taiwan
rabbitcgt@gmail.com

Abstract

Conventional opinion polls were usually conducted via questionnaires or phone interviews, which are time-consuming and error-prone. With the advances in social networking platforms, it's easier for us to automatically collect and aggregate the overall topical stance for a specific topic. In this paper, we propose to predict topical stances by aggregating user-centric and post-centric sentiments from social media. Firstly, related posts of a given topic are collected from social media and clustered by word embeddings, where major keywords are extracted as the expanded concepts. Then, machine learning methods are used to train sentiment lexicon with word embeddings. Finally, the sentiment scores from user-centric and post-centric views are aggregated as the total stance on the topic. In the experiments on data from online forums, the proposed approach can obtain the best performance with a mean absolute error (MAE) of 0.52% for stance prediction of 2016 Taiwan Presidential Election. This shows the effectiveness of our proposed approach in topical stance aggregation and prediction. Further investigation is needed to evaluate the performance of the proposed method in larger scales.

Keywords: Topical stance detection, Sentiment analysis, Word embeddings, Document clustering

1 Introduction

People usually express their opinions in social occasions with friends and to the public. To know what the general public think about a specific topic, it usually takes much human efforts in designing questionnaires, collecting feedbacks and analyzing them. It's time-consuming and error prone. Depending on the participation of people, there could be not too many effective responses. With the advances of social networking platforms, it's very easy to post articles and reply with comments. For example, Twitter, Facebook, and Instagram are among the most popular social networking sites with different functions. This facilitates users to make online discussions in an immediate way. Given huge amount of social opinions, it would be useful if we can automatically collect and aggregate the general stances from them.

There are some challenges to the problem. Firstly, given the very diverse contents in social media, it would be difficult to obtain the most relevant contents from huge amount of data. Secondly, people might express their opinions in different ways. It would be difficult to extract what they really think about specific topics from very short texts in social media.

Content in a short text is usually limited in scope. Without explaining the ideas and referencing related documents, we might only obtain fragmented terms or named entities just from the sole content of a single post. It might even contain emotional feelings or noises that cannot help us clarify the main idea.

On the other hand, users have different types of activities in addition to posting. For example, most social networking platforms provide mechanisms for making friends, following people or topics that you are interested in, and expressing agreement or disagreement, replying, or commenting on others' posts. These social relations, both explicit and implicit, provide useful clues for understanding what people really think, in addition to what they explicitly mention in post contents. This makes it possible to analyze user opinions by extracting social relations and discovering the major concepts.

In this paper, we propose to aggregate user-centric and post-centric stances for topical stance prediction. Firstly, given the simple topical keyword, we expand the concepts by clustering topic-related posts and comments by their word embeddings, and extract major keywords from each group using word segmentation and named entity recognition methods. Then, given word embeddings, sentiment classification is done by machine learning methods including Naïve Bayes (NB) and Extreme Learning Machines (ELMs) (Huang, 2015). Finally, we aggregate topical stances using both post-centric and user-centric sentiments. In post-centric views, the more positive feedbacks a post gets, the more positive it is regarding the topic. In user-centric views, the more positive comments a user gives, the more positive the user is regarding the topic. By aggregating both post-centric and user-centric sentiments, we are able to analyze the influences of user posts from broader aspects.

In the experiments, we collected data from the most popular online discussion forum in Taiwan called PTT. For sentiment analysis on short texts, we found inconsistent sentiment between user ratings and post contents. After adjustment, ELMs are more stable in sentiment classification performance than Naïve Bayes classifiers. By aggregating stances on three groups of candidates in the 2016 Taiwan Presidential Election to predict the election result, the best performance can be obtained for ELMs with the MAE of 0.52%. This shows the potential of our proposed approach in stance prediction. Further investigation is needed for different types of social media in larger scales.

2 Related Work

Sentiment classification is one of the major techniques for social media analysis and opinion mining. Documents are classified by overall sentiment instead of topic. For example, Pang et al. (2002) first utilized machine learning techniques in learning classifiers for positive and negative movie reviews. They found features as important factors in social media sentiment classification. Conventional bag-of-words models do not distinguish between word orders. Word n-gram models such as bigrams simply consider consecutive words as a unit for representing documents. It's only limited in the local context of words. Nowadays, word embedding models such as Word2Vec (Mikolov et al., 2013) or GloVe (Pennington et al., 2014) have been used as a more suitable representation of documents, especially for short texts in social media. They utilize neural networks to learn the semantics of words in different contexts. Furthermore, different deep learning methods have been used to automatically learn the features in sentiment classification. For example, Recurrent Neural Networks (RNNs) and their variants such as Long Short-Term Memory (LSTM) and Gated Recurrent Units (GRUs) are often used to capture long-term dependency in sequential data. They have been successfully applied in sentiment classification of tweets (Wang et al., 2018). Convolutional Neural Networks (CNNs) were originally used in image recognition. With suitable representation of word embeddings in documents, CNNs were also found effective in sentiment classification of tweets (Severyn and Moschitti, 2015).

Based on sentiment classification of a single review or post, it's useful to further determine the *stance* that indicates whether the author is in favor of or against a specific target entity. For example, Mohammad et al. (2017) created the first stance dataset in Twitter, and proposed a stance detection system using Support Vector Machine (SVM) classifiers with character and word n-grams and word embedding features. But the target entity needs to be specified before determining the stance, and it's only based on the tweet content. It's closely related to aspect-based sentiment analysis tasks in SemEval 2014 (Pontiki et al., 2014) and SemEval 2015 (Pontiki et al., 2015).

In addition to the typical stance detection of texts, social media data are often used in determining the polarization in political opinions (Conover et al., 2011) and predicting voting intentions or outcomes in elections (Tumasjan et al., 2010). Instead of detecting the stance of a single user on a specific target, it's useful to derive the stance from the general public on a topic, which we called *topical stance*. For example, in SemEval 2016 topical stance detection contest, MITRE (Zarrella and Marsh, 2016) used LSTM with Word2Vec word embeddings. DeepStance (Vijayaraghavan et al., 2016) used CNN models, while Du et al. (2017) used attention models. Dey et al. (2018) developed a two-phase solution to topical stance detection for Twitter including subjectivity detection and sentiment classification using LSTM with attention. Samih and Darwish (2021) proposed user-level stance detection using only a few tweets for users by fine-tuning contextualized embedding. As mentioned in the literature (ALDaye and Magdy, 2021), there are usually two levels of stance detection: statement-level, which is simply based on text content, and user-level, which is to predict the stance of a user on the target. Also, there could be three different types of stance detection according to targets: target-specific stance, multi-related target stance, and claim-based stance. In addition to stance detection, research on stance prediction is usually concerned with detecting stances before the event. Most previous studies investigated the micro-level prediction, which estimates the individual user's viewpoint toward a target. For example, Dong et al. (2017) considers joint modeling of content and social interactions for user stance prediction. Darwish et al. (2017) used content and user interactions to calculate user similarity for stance prediction. In this paper, we propose a macro-level approach to stance prediction by aggregating topical stances from post-centric and user-centric views in social media, based on sentiment classification results on very short texts using word embedding features and machine learning methods.

3 The Proposed Method

There are three major modules in the proposed approach: concept expansion, opinion analysis, and stance aggregation. The overall architecture of the proposed approach is illustrated in Fig. 1:

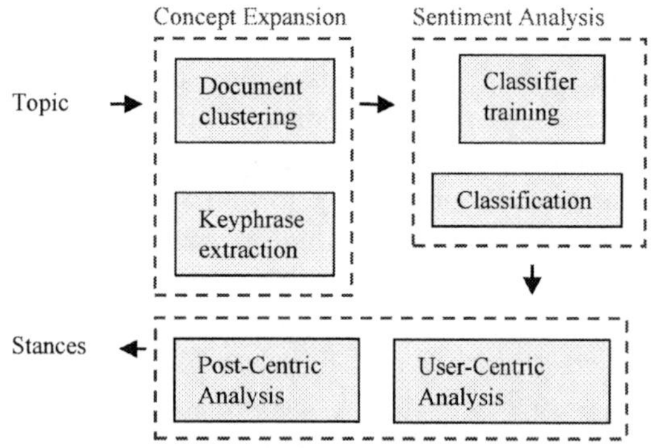

Figure 1. The system architecture of the proposed approach.

As a preprocessing step, given the topical keyword, topic-relevant posts and comments are collected and represented by word embeddings. First, concept expansion is done by clustering the topic-relevant posts and comments, and extracting the keyphrases in each cluster. Then, machine learning methods are utilized to train the classifiers for sentiment classification. Sentiment orientation is then used to calculate the corresponding stances from both post-centric and user-centric points of view. Finally, the stances are aggregated by their linear combination. In the following subsections, we will explain the details.

3.1 Data Representation

Social media contents might be very diverse and noisy. To facilitate more efficient analysis, we routinely crawled all data from the target source media and extracted the corresponding structures from the post-centric and user-centric views and stored in a search engine called Apache Solr for efficient search and analysis. The two different views are described as follows.

In post-centric views, each post consists of the major content and responses from others including replies (or comments), ratings (such as like/dislike), and sharing (such as forwarding, or retweeting, depending on the social platform). These various responses constitute how people think about this post. Generally, the more positive feedbacks a post gets, the more positive it is regarding the topic.

In user-centric views, each user might post an article, and respond to other users' posts, including replies, ratings, and sharing. From these posts and responses, we might be able to observe what he or she thinks about a topic. The more positive comments a user gives, the more positive the user is regarding the topic.

Since we focus on the analysis of text contents and users, we need to correctly identify person names and the concepts of different entities. In this step, we utilize word segmentation and word embedding for the representation of documents.

Word Segmentation: The feature units of documents usually include segmented words or word *n*-grams. In the case of Chinese documents, the definition of words depends on the result of word segmentation since there's no space characters between Chinese characters in a sentence. Usually there are two major problems in word segmentation: ambiguity and unknown words. To resolve the issues, lexicon-based and machine learning methods are often used. The size and quality of the lexicon determines the accuracy of the words segmented.

In this paper, we utilize a popular open source tool called Ansj [1] for word segmentation. It's a word-based generative model based on a bi-gram model which is a first-order Markov chain. That is, each character is assumed to be dependent on it previous character. The word candidate that generates the maximum union probability will be selected. Since the first-order Markov chain model might not be able to achieve high recalls for unknown words, a Hidden Markov Model (HMM)-based method (Zhang et al., 2003) is used for identifying out-of-vocabulary words. From our observation, this model can generate better segmentation results for person names.

Word Embedding: After feature units are identified by word segmentation technique, we need to find an appropriate representation for documents. Conventional bag-of-words model is not efficient due to the following reasons. Firstly, it's high dimensional and very sparse. Secondly, word orders are completely ignored, which generates ambiguous semantic meanings. In order to better capture semantics in documents, we utilize word embedding models such as Word2Vec. Through the training of contexts from large amounts of documents, we can better predict the contexts of a word or predict a word from its context. Also, it's fixed dimensional which make the machine learning algorithms easier to calculate. Specifically, we represent a document d_j by its component words $w_1, \ldots, w_n$ after word segmentation as follows.

$$V(d_j) = \frac{\sum_{i=1}^{n} V(w_i)}{n} \quad (1)$$

where $V(w_i)$ is the vector representation of each word w_i.

3.2 Concept Expansion

People might describe the same idea in different terms. Given a single term, the semantics are usually limited. For example, people searching for information about "presidential election" might be interested in the candidates, their names, and election results. To understand what people think about a topic, we need to collect their opinions on all related concepts. In this paper, we utilize document clustering and keyword extraction for concept expansion. Firstly, initial topic was used to collect related documents and grouped into clusters. Then, keywords are extracted from each cluster and the top-frequent keywords are kept as the major concepts. In order to improve the informativeness of the concepts extracted, we repeat the same process by using these keywords to collect related documents for augmenting the keywords until it converges to the number of concepts we need.

Document Clustering: To obtain all related concepts, we first start with the topic word t. By using search engines such as Google, we get the search result pages $P(t)$. Then, we use the same word embedding models to represent each document p_i in its vector form $V(p_i)$, from which K-means clustering algorithm is used to separate them into K groups. These correspond to the different groups of documents for different concepts. The selection of K depends on how many possible concepts might be related to this topic. In the example of presidential election, the number of clusters K might correspond to the different groups of candidates in the election.

Keyword Extraction: After documents are grouped by their embeddings, the next issue is how to identify the corresponding concepts for each group. Firstly, we apply the same word segmentation technique Ansj on all documents in each cluster to identify the corresponding keywords. Then, we need to discover the named entities since they are often the most important candidates for the major concepts. In this paper, we use Stanford Named Entity Recognizer (Finkel et al., 2005) which employed conditional random fields (CRFs) to recognize the named entities in probabilistic ways.

3.3 Sentiment Analysis

To understand the opinion orientation of each post, we first train the sentiment lexicon from our training data. Then, we use ELMs (Huang, 2015) to classify the sentiment into positive, neutral, and negative, and compare with a simple baseline Naïve Bayes classifier.

The structure of ELMs is a neural network with single hidden layer. The major difference of ELMs from common neural networks is its lack of back

[1] https://github.com/NLPchina/ansj_seg

propagation phase to reduce training errors. Thus, it's much faster than conventional neural networks. The architecture of ELMs is shown in Figure 2.

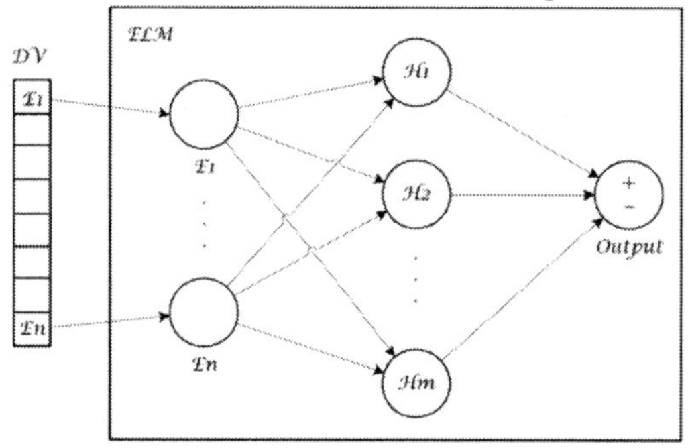

Figure 2. The architecture of Extreme Learning Machines (ELMs).

As shown in Figure 2, ELMs need numeric data as input just like common neural networks, we apply the word embedding models such as Word2Vec on each document. The number of neurons in input layer corresponds to the dimension of word embeddings. The number of neurons in output layer is one, which simply classifies each document as positive or negative. In this paper, the number of neurons in the hidden layer is set as 200.

User ratings might not reflect the actual sentiment orientation of users, for example, in the case of sarcasm. From our observation, people are more proactive in negative ratings, and they might give negative replies or comments with a positive rating. This is possible in some cases where people respond to some people or events instead of the document itself. It was also indicated in related work (Heath, 1996). In order to fix this phenomenon, we adjust the user ratings by combining with sentiment classification of replies or comments as follows.

$$Class(d_j) = \begin{cases} 1 & if\ r(d_j) > 0\ and\ Sent(d_j) > 0 \\ 0 & if\ r(d_j) = 0 \\ -1 & othrwise \end{cases} \quad (2)$$

Where $r(d_j)$ is the user rating such as like or dislike, and $Sent(d_j)$ is the sentiment orientation of the document.

3.4 Stance Aggregation

Given user input topic t and the number of concepts K, we obtain related concepts $Q_1, \ldots, Q_K$. For each concept Q_i, we obtain the set of all the related documents D_i and the set of all the related users U_i. Then, we conduct analyses in two different views as follows.

Post-Centric Stance: For a given concept Q_i, we have the set of all related documents D_i. For each document d_j in D_i, instead of using the sentiment orientation defined previously, we first calculate the aggregate score from all the comments.

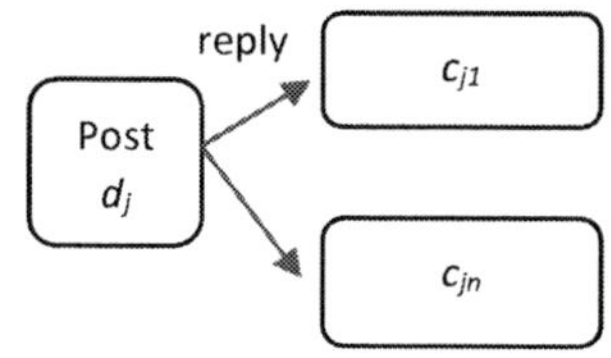

Figure 3. The idea of post-centric stance.

The idea is that: the orientation of a post is determined by the orientation of its comments.

$$S_{post}(d_j) = \sum_{p_k \in Comm(d_j)} class(p_k) \quad (3)$$

Where $Comm(d_j)$ denotes all the comments p_k for post d_j, and $class(p_k)$ is defined as in Eq.(2). The higher the score, the more positive people judge on this post.

To accumulate all the scores into the overall post stance for the concept Q_i, we define the *post-centric stance* as follows:

$$Stance_{post}(Q_i) = \frac{|\{d_j \in D_i | S_{post}(d_j) > 0\}|}{|\{d_j \in D_i | S_{post}(d_j) != 0\}|} \quad (4)$$

where D_i is the set of all documents related to concept Q_i.

User-Centric Stance: For a given concept Q_i, we also have the set of all related users U_i who posted or comments on posts in related concepts. For each user u_j in U_i, we consider the aggregate score from all the posts generated by him or her.

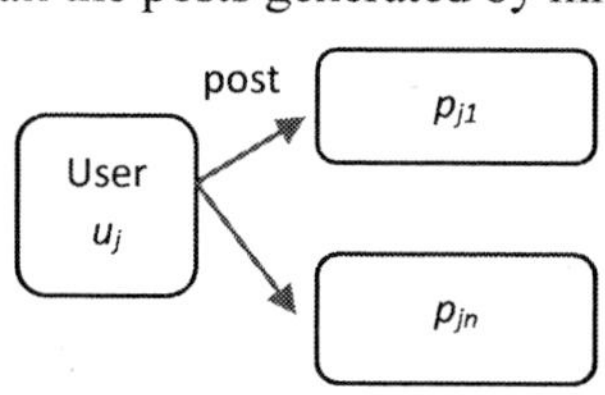

Figure 4. The idea of user-centric stance.

The idea is that: the stance of a user is determined by the orientation of his/her posts.

$$S_{user}(u_j) = \sum_{p_k \in Posts(u_j)} class(p_k) \quad (5)$$

Where *Posts(u_j)* denotes all the posts p_k by user u_j, and *class(p_k)* is defined as in Eq.(2). The higher the score, the more positive people judge on this user.

To accumulate all the scores into the overall user stance for the concept Q_i, we define the *user-centric stance* as follows:

$$Stance_{user}(Q_i) = \frac{|\{u_j \in U_i | S_{user}(u_j) > 0\}|}{|\{u_j \in U_i | S_{user}(u_j) != 0\}|} \quad (6)$$

where U_i is the set of all users related to concept Q_i.

Aggregate Stance: For each given concept Q_i, the data size might be different in terms of related posts and users. To give a more balanced aggregation, we can further consider the weights for posts and users as follows.

$$w_{post}(Q_i) = \frac{|D_i|}{\sum_{j=1}^{K} |D_j|} \quad (7)$$

Where D_i is the set of all documents related to concept Q_i.

$$w_{user}(Q_i) = \frac{|U_i|}{\sum_{j=1}^{K} |U_j|} \quad (8)$$

Where U_i is the set of all users related to concept Q_i. Thus, the weighted post-centric and user-centric stances for a given concept Q_i can be defined as follows:

$$WS_{post}(Q_i) = w_{post}(Q_i) * Stance_{post}(Q_i) \quad (9)$$

$$WS_{user}(Q_i) = w_{user}(Q_i) * Stance_{user}(Q_i) \quad (10)$$

Since we calculate the post-centric and user-centric stances individually, to further allow for the relative importance between the two views, we finally assign a weight α for linear combination for the total stance as follows.

$$Stance_{total}(Q_i) = \alpha * WS_{user}(Q_i) + (1 - \alpha) * WS_{post}(Q_i) \quad (11)$$

The idea is that: the higher the total stance for a concept, the more positive people give feedbacks to this concept.

4 Experiments

In our experiments, we designed our customized crawler in Telnet to collect data from the most popular online discussion forum called PTT. During Feb. 2015 an Jun. 2016, a total of 881,322 documents in Chinese was collected in the discussion board of "Gossip". The number of users participated in these posts is 60,018.

4.1 The Effects of Concept Expansion

To verify the effects of concept expansion, we selected a number of topics. The results of concept expansion are as follows:

Topic	Initial Concepts	Added Concepts
Presidential election (總統大選)	Chu Li-luan (朱立倫)、Tsai Ing-wen (蔡英文)、Soong Chu-yu (宋楚瑜)、Chen Chien-Jen (陳建仁)	Tsai-Chen ticket (英仁配)、Soong-Hsu ticket (宋瑩配)、Chu-Wang ticket (朱玄配)
Ma-Xi meeting (馬習會)	Ma Ying-jeou (馬英九)、Tsai Ing-wen (蔡英文)、Xi Jinping (習近平)、Ma-Xi meeting (馬習會)	Chu Li-luan (朱立倫)、Zhang Zhijun (張志軍)、Hsia Li-yan (夏立言)

Table 1: Example results of concept expansion.

As shown in Table 1, we can see more relevant concepts can be extracted. For example, for 2016 presidential election, the candidates and the running mates can also be discovered. In the case of Ma-Xi meeting, the major participants from both sides including the Minister of the Mainland Affairs Council Hsia Li-yan and Taiwan Affairs Office Director Zhang Zhijun. Also, the KMT chairman Chu Li-luan met Xi the year before in the 2015 Xi-Chu meeting (朱習會). From these examples, we can see more related concepts are helpful to the representation of documents.

4.2 The Effects of Sentiment Analysis

After concept expansion, we need to conduct sentiment analysis for text documents. We selected a number of concepts to test the performance. The ground truth is taken from user ratings such as likes or dislikes in each comment. The results of sentiment analysis using Naïve Bayes are as follows:

Concept	Recall	Precision	F-score	Accuracy
Tsai Ing-wen (蔡英文)	0.717	0.982	0.829	0.728
Chu Li-luan (朱立倫)	0.860	0.464	0.603	0.696

Soong Chu-yu (宋楚瑜)	0.780	0.921	0.845	0.799
Average	0.786	0.789	0.759	0.741

Table 2: Example results of sentiment analysis using Naïve Bayes.

As shown in Table 2, we can see a good average accuracy of 0.741 and F-score of 0.759 for Naïve Bayes. However, since data is imbalanced, the precision value of some concepts are as low as 0.464. This is not stable. Next, we show the results of sentiment analysis using ELMs.

Concept	**Recall**	**Precision**	**F-score**	**Accuracy**
Tsai Ing-wen (蔡英文)	0.744	0.811	0.776	0.686
Chu Li-luan (朱立倫)	0.629	0.651	0.640	0.636
Soong Chu-yu (宋楚瑜)	0.667	0.792	0.724	0.643
Average	0.680	0.751	0.713	0.655

Table 3: Example results of sentiment analysis using ELMs.

As shown in Table 3, we can see an average accuracy of 0.655 and F-score of 0.713 for ELMs. Comparing to Naïve Bayes, we can see lower accuracies, but more stable precision values and F-measures across different concepts. Given more training data, NB is able to learn the probabilistic distributions. ELM cannot reduce the error with back propagation, which gives much lower recalls. The precision values are only slightly affected. We will analyze the reasons as follows.

There are several possible reasons for the mismatch between user ratings and post content sentiments.

The first possible case of incorrect classification is a "false positive". There are many cases when the post content explains the support of one new candidate, but the opinions are against the current officers. That's why we see positive user ratings (for the new candidate), but negative content sentiments (against the current officers). If we conduct sentiment analysis on the contents, they are correctly classified as negative, which is different from the ground truth of positive.

The second example case of misclassification is when a government agency post content criticizing candidate Tsai. Users gave negative ratings against this government post, but positive content in favor of the candidate. That's another type of mismatch for "false negatives".

To show the effects of these misclassification, we selected a part of the posts from the same concepts and manually adjust the labels of two types of misclassified instances.

Method	**Recall**	**Precision**	**F-score**	**Accuracy**
NB	0.961	0.695	0.807	0.680
NB-adj	0.722	0.851	0.781	**0.782**
ELM	0.972	0.738	0.839	0.728
ELM-adj	0.570	0.910	0.701	0.646

Table 4: Performance comparison of NB and ELM before and after adjustment of Type-1 errors.

As shown in Table 4, we can observe the performance improvement for NB in terms of accuracy. Specifically, since false positives are greatly reduced for both NB and ELM, precision values are greatly improved. At the same time, false negatives are increased much more for ELM, which gives lower recall. The best performance can be seen for NB after adjusting Type-1 errors.

Method	**Recall**	**Precision**	**F-score**	**Accuracy**
NB	0.174	0.923	0.293	0.389
NB-adj	0.986	0.723	**0.834**	**0.716**
ELM	0.193	0.846	0.314	0.495
ELM-adj	0.982	0.596	0.742	0.589

Table 5: Performance comparison of NB and ELM before and after adjustment of Type-2 errors.

As shown in Table 5, we can observe the performance improvement for both NB and ELM. Specifically, since false negatives are greatly reduced for both NB and ELM, recall values are greatly improved. At the same time, false positives are increased, which gives lower precision. Although ELM can also be improved, the best performance can be seen for NB after adjusting Type-2 errors.

These results are simply sampled from selected topics, it could not reflect the overall performance. But we can see the advantage of adjusting Type-1 and Type-2 errors, which are very common in social media posts, especially for the discussion forum PTT. The sarcastic phenomenon on political issues among social network users have much impact on the sentiment analysis results.

4.3 The Effects of Post-centric vs. User-centric Stance Detection

In this experiment, we want to verify the effects of post-centric and user-centric stance detection. Here, we focus on the prediction of 2016 presidential election in Taiwan by the two views of stance detection using NB and ELM classifiers and manually adjusted ratings, which are denoted as Post-NB, Post-ELM, User-NB, User-ELM, respectively. Then, we have two baselines: Post-Baseline, and User-Baseline, which simply use statistics of user ratings as the baseline for post-centric and user-centric, respectively.

In this experiment, the topic “presidential election” can be expanded into the three candidates, who got the percentages of final votes: Chu-Wang (31.04%), Tsai-Chen (56.12%), and Soong-Hsu (12.84%). These are considered as the ground truth. Firstly, we compared the mean absolute error (MAE) as follows.

Method	**MAE -Tsai**	**MAE -Chu**	**MAE-Soong**	**MAE -avg.**
Post-Baseline	6.45	10.14	3.69	6.76
Post-NB	6.12	9.76	3.63	6.50
Post-ELM	1.25	2.99	4.24	**2.83**
User-Baseline	8.01	8.33	0.33	5.56
User-NB	0.38	0.81	1.19	**0.79**
User-ELM	0.58	2.01	1.43	1.34

Table 6: Performance comparison of election result prediction for both post-centric and user-centric views.

As shown in Table 6, we can see the best post-centric result is Post-ELM with a MAE of 2.83%, and the best user-centric result is User-NB with a MAE of 0.79%. For each method, we can obtain better performance for user-centric views.

4.4 The Effects of Stance Aggregation

Next, we further determine the stance aggregation using different weights for post-centric and user-centric results. We compared the better results as shown previously with the aggregated results. From our observation, better MAE values can be obtained when α is 0.7-0.9, we show the result when $\alpha = 0.7$ as follows.

Method	**MAE -Tsai**	**MAE -Chu**	**MAE-Soong**	**MAE -avg.**
Aggregate-Baseline	7.54	8.88	1.34	5.92
Aggregate-NB	2.10	2.36	0.26	1.57
Aggregate-ELM	0.78	0.51	0.27	**0.52**

Table 7: Performance comparison of election result prediction when $\alpha = 0.7$ in stance aggregation.

As shown in Table 7, we can observe the best performance for ELMs in predicting the percentage of votes for three candidates. Specifically, when aggregating stances using ELMs, the best MAE of 0.52% can be obtained. This shows the potential of the proposed approach to topical stance aggregation from post-centric and user-centric sentiments.

5 Discussions

From our experimental results, there are some observations:

- Firstly, from our observations on sentiment classification of PTT data, we found Type-1 and Type-2 errors that frequently occurred in posts. Users might give positive ratings with negative contents, or vice versa. After adjusting these errors, the performance of sentiment classification can be improved for both ELM and NB.

- Secondly, we consider two different views of stance detection: post-centric and user-centric. User-centric stance detection works better than post-centric, especially for Naïve Bayes.

- Finally, we validated the effects of stance aggregation by the weighted sum of both user-centric and post-centric stances. The best prediction performance with MAE of 0.52% can be obtained. It shows the potential of our proposed approach to stance prediction.

6 Conclusions

In this paper, we have proposed to aggregate post-centric and user-centric sentiments from social media for stance detection. Firstly, we performed concept expansion to obtain the related concepts for the given topic. Secondly, we trained classifiers such as Naïve Bayes and Extreme Learning Machines for sentiment classification. Finally, we proposed a potential way of calculating the individual influences from comments for posts and posts from each user, and aggregating to obtain the total stance for the topic. From our experimental results, we can see a good performance with the best MAE of 0.52% when we aggregate stances estimated using ELMs. This shows the potential of our proposed approach in topic-specific opinion mining and stance detection. Further investigations are needed to evaluate our proposed approach in different topic domains.

Acknowledgments

The authors would like to thank the partial funding support from Ministry of Science and Technology (MOST), Taiwan under the grant numbers MOST109-2221-E-027-090 and MOST110-2221-E-027-099.

References

Abeer ALDaye, Walid Magdy, 2021. Stance detection on social media: State of the art and trends, *Information Processing & Management*, 58(4).

Michael Conover, Jacob Ratkiewicz, Matthew R. Francisco, Bruno Goncalves, Filippo Menczer, and Alessandro Flammini. 2011. Political polarization on Twitter. In *Proceedings of the International AAAI Conference on Weblogs and Social Media*, pp. 89–96.

Kareem Darwish, Walid Magdy, Tahar Zanouda, 2017. Improved Stance Prediction in a User Similarity Feature Space. In *Proceedings of the 2017 IEEE/ACM International Conference on Advances in Social Networks Analysis and Mining (ASONAM 2017)*, pp.145–148.

Kuntal Dey, Ritvik Shrivastava, and Saroj Kaushik. 2018. Topical Stance Detection for Twitter: A Two-Phase LSTM Model Using Attention, In *Proceedings of the 40th European Conference on Information Retrieval (ECIR 2018)*, pp. 529–536.

Rui Dong, Yizhou Sun, Lu Wang, Yupeng Gu, Yuan Zhong, 2017. Weakly-Guided User Stance Prediction via Joint Modeling of Content and Social Interaction. In *Proceedings of the 2017 ACM on Conference on Information and Knowledge Management (CIKM 2017)*, pp.1249–1258.

Jiachen Du, Ruifeng Xu, Yulan He, Lin Gui. 2017. Stance classification with target-specific neural attention networks. In *Proceedings of the Twenty-Sixth International Joint Conference on Artificial Intelligence (IJCAI 2017)*, pp. 3988–3994.

Jenny Rose Finkel, Trond Grenager, and Christopher Manning. 2005. Incorporating Non-local Information into Information Extraction Systems by Gibbs Sampling. In *Proceedings of the 43nd Annual Meeting of the Association for Computational Linguistics (ACL 2005)*, pp. 363-370.

Chip Heath, 1996. Do People Prefer to Pass Along Good or Bad News? Valence and Relevance as Predictors of Transmission Propensity. *Organizational Behavior and Human Decision Processes*, 68 (2): 79–94.

Guang-Bin Huang, 2015. What are extreme learning machines? Filling the gap between Frank Rosenblatt's dream and john von Neumann's puzzle. *Cognitive Computation*, 7(3): 263–278.

Tomas Mikolov, Kai Chen, Greg Corrado, Jeffrey Dean, 2013. Efficient estimation of word representations in vector space. In *Proceedings of the International Conference on Learning Representations 2013 Workshop*.

Saif M. Mohammad, Parinaz Sobhani, and Svetlana Kiritchenko, 2017. Stance and Sentiment in Tweets, *ACM Transactions on Internet Technology*, 17(3):26.

Bo Pang, Lillian Lee, Shivakumar Vaithyanathan, 2002. Thumbs up? Sentiment Classification using Machine Learning Techniques, In *Proceedings of the 2002 Conference on Empirical Methods in Natural Language Processing (EMNLP 2002)*, pp.79-86.

Jeffrey Pennington, Richard Socher, Christopher D. Manning, 2014. GloVe: global vectors for word representation. In *Proceedings of the 2014 Conference on Empirical Methods in Natural Language Processing (EMNLP 2014)*, pp. 1532–1543.

Maria Pontiki, Dimitrios Galanis, Haris Papageogiou, Suresh Manandhar, and Ion Androutsopoulos. 2015. SemEval-2015 Task 12: Aspect based sentiment analysis. In *Proceedings of the International Workshop on Semantic Evaluation*.

Maria Pontiki, Dimitrios Galanis, John Pavlopoulos, Harris Papageorgiou, Ion Androutsopoulos, and Suresh Manandhar. 2014. SemEval-2014 Task 4: Aspect based sentiment analysis. In *Proceedings of the International Workshop on Semantic Evaluation*.

Younes Samih and Kareem Darwish, 2021. A Few Topical Tweets are Enough for Effective User Stance Detection, In *Proceedings of the 16th Conference of the European Chapter of the Association for Computational Linguistics*, pp. 2637–2646.

Aliaksei Severyn, Alessandro Moschitti, 2015. Twitter Sentiment Analysis with Deep Convolutional Neural Networks, In *Proceedings of the 38th International ACM SIGIR Conference on Research and Development in Information Retrieval (SIGIR 2015)*, pp.959–962.

Andranik Tumasjan, Timm O. Sprenger, Philipp G. Sandner, Isabell M. Welpe, 2010. Predicting Elections with Twitter: What 140 Characters Reveal about Political Sentiment, In *Proceedings of the Fourth International AAAI Conference on Weblogs and Social Media (ICWSM)*, pp.178-185.

Prashanth Vijayaraghavan, Ivan Sysoev, Soroush Vosoughi and Deb Roy, 2016. DeepStance at SemEval-2016 Task 6: Detecting Stance in Tweets Using Character and Word-Level CNNs, In *Proceedings of the 10th International Workshop on Semantic Evaluation (SemEval-2016).*

Jenq-Haur Wang, Ting-Wei Liu, Xiong Luo, and Long Wang, 2018. An LSTM Approach to Short Text Sentiment Classification with Word Embeddings, In *Proceedings of the 30th annual Conference on Computational Linguistics and Speech Processing (ROCLING 2018)*, pp.214-223.

Guido Zarrella and Amy Marsh, 2016. Mitre at SemEval-2016 Task 6: Transfer Learning for Stance Detection. In *Proceedings of the 10th International Workshop on Semantic Evaluation (SemEval-2016).*

Hua-Ping Zhang, Hong-Kui Yu, De-Yi Xiong, Qun Liu, 2003. HHMM-based Chinese lexical analyzer ICTCLAS, In *Proceedings of the second SIGHAN workshop on Chinese language processing (SIGHAN 2003)*, pp.184–187.

Meishan Zhang, Yue Zhang, Duy-Tin Vo, 2016. Gated Neural Networks for Targeted Sentiment Analysis, In *Proceedings of the Thirtieth AAAI Conference on Artificial Intelligence (AAAI-16)*, pp.3087-3093.

The 33rd Conference on Computational Linguistics and Speech Processing (ROCLING 2021)
Taoyuan, Taiwan, October 15-16, 2021. The Association for Computational Linguistics and Chinese Language Processing

使用低通時序列語音特徵訓練理想比率遮罩法之語音強化
Employing low-pass filtered temporal speech features for the training of ideal ratio mask in speech enhancement

Yan-Tong Chen, 陳彥同
National Chi Nan University
國立暨南國際大學
s109323508@mail1.ncnu.edu.tw

Zi-Qiang Lin, 林子強
National Chi Nan University
國立暨南國際大學
a0979959806@gmail.com

Jeih-weih Hung, 洪志偉
National Chi Nan University
國立暨南國際大學
jwhung@ncnu.edu.tw

摘要

在諸多基於深度學習之語音強化法中，遮罩式 (masking-based) 強化法求取一個遮罩與雜訊語音之時頻圖相乘、藉此使所得乘積之新時頻圖所含雜訊成分降低、以重建相對乾淨的語音訊號。在用以訓練遮罩之深度模型其輸入特徵的選取上，許多長期以來用以語音辨識的特徵、如梅爾倒倒頻譜、振幅調變時頻圖、感知線性估測係數等都是適合的選擇、可使訓練所得的遮罩達到有效的語音強化效果。另外，傳統上若將語音特徵之時序列作低通濾波處理，可以抑制雜訊所帶來的失真，因此，在本研究中，我們嘗試將各種語音特徵時序列，藉由離散小波轉換的方式加以低通濾波，再用它們來訓練語音遮罩的深度模型，探究其是否能使所學習之遮罩能對於原始雜訊語音之時頻圖有更佳的語音強化效果。在我們的初步實驗裡，在人聲雜訊環境中，我們發現上述之低通濾波所得之特徵序列、相較於原始特徵序列而言所學習而得的深度模型，能更有效地提升測試語音之品質與可讀性。

Abstract

The masking-based speech enhancement method pursues a multiplicative mask that applies to the spectrogram of input noise-corrupted utterance, and a deep neural network (DNN) is often used to learn the mask. In particular, the features commonly used for automatic speech recognition can serve as the input of the DNN to learn the well-behaved mask that significantly reduce the noise distortion of processed utterances. This study proposes to preprocess the input speech features for the ideal ratio mask (IRM)-based DNN by lowpass filtering in order to alleviate the noise components. In particular, we employ the discrete wavelet transform (DWT) to decompose the temporal speech feature sequence and scale down the detail coefficients, which correspond to the high-pass portion of the sequence. Preliminary experiments conducted on a subset of TIMIT corpus reveal that the proposed method can make the resulting IRM achieve higher speech quality and intelligibility for the babble noise-corrupted signals compared with the original IRM, indicating that the lowpass filtered temporal feature sequence can learn a superior IRM network for speech enhancement.

關鍵字：語音強化、特徵時序列、低通濾波、理想比例遮罩法、小波轉換

Keywords: speech enhancement, temporal feature sequence, lowpass filtering, ideal ratio mask, wavelet transform

1 簡介

深度類神經模型與相關之學習演算法的高度發展，引發許多科技研究的空前突破與創新，過往的許多技術開發，常是基於解釋思維、在多次試錯之後找到一個可行方案，再對此可行方案賦予人們專業的解釋，然而深度學習則普遍基於統計思維、並不著重於方法在解釋上的合理性，而是嘗試將大量觀察（輸入）和對應結果（輸出）的關聯性藉由深度類神經網路加以詮釋，以期對於新的觀察能精準預測出對應的結果。而在語音處理的領域中，近年來基於深度學習所開發出的演算法也琳瑯滿目，且因訓練資料的可取得性越來越高，這些演算法在學習與預測結果的能力也隨之增強。以本研究著重的語音強化法為例，基於深度類神經模型之各式語音強化架構其表現常超越經典且富有高度理論根據的演算法，或是以後者的演算法的原型 (prototype) 出發，但配合深度類神經網路來有效學習該演算法的各項參數，使其語音強化效果更佳。

根據文獻 (Wang et al., 2014)，許多基於深度學習之語音強化法根據其訓練目標大致可以分為兩大範疇：對映式 (mapping) 與遮罩式 (masking)，前者直接求取一個對映函

數，使此對映函數之理想輸出為乾淨語音的呈現式 (特徵)，如時域訊號波形、時頻圖 (spectrogram) 或耳蝸時頻譜圖 (cochleagram)，後者是求取一個遮罩 (mask)，用以與原始輸入訊號或特徵呈現作點對點的相乘，使相乘後的訊號呈現式能趨近乾淨時的狀態。簡單來說對映式所求取的函數，對於輸入訊號特徵的運算可以是任意由所使用之深度學習模型定義的非線性運算，而遮罩式所求取的函數運算，則簡化或限制為對輸入訊號特徵作乘法 (即加權運算)。二者各擅勝場。以遮罩式為例，相關的演算法包括了理想二元遮罩 (ideal binary mask, IBM) (Wang et al., 2014; Srinivasan et al., 2006)、理想比例遮罩 (ideal ratio mask, IRM) (Srinivasan et al., 2006)、頻譜強度遮罩 (spectral magnitude mask, SMM) (Wang et al., 2014)、複數理想比例遮罩 (complex ideal ratio mask, cIRM) (Williamson et al., 2016)、相位敏感型遮罩 (phase-sensitive mask, PSM) (Erdogan et al., 2015) 等。

在本研究中，主要是針對上述之遮罩式語音強化法加以改進，我們提出對於訓練遮罩模型的輸入雜訊語音的特徵時序列作簡單的預處理 (pre-processing)，使其包含的雜訊失真較低，以期在之後的訓練遮罩步驟能更加精確。而使用的預處理方法，是透過簡易的一階離散小波轉換 (discrete wavelet transform, DWT)(Mallat, 2008)，將特徵時序列分為高低兩調變頻帶 (modulation frequency bands)，然後藉由一權重的相乘來降低高調變頻帶之序列的振幅，將其與原始低調變頻帶序列搭配、透過一階反離散小波轉換 (inverse discrete wavelet transform, IDWT) 重建特徵序列，再使用此特徵序列來訓練遮罩模型。上述低通濾波之處理，主要是基於先前諸多學者所提出的觀察 (Vuuren and Hermansky, 1998; Chen and Bilmes, 2007)：乾淨語音特徵時序列主要分布頻率在 1 Hz 至 16 Hz 之間，以一般的音框取樣率 100 Hz 而言，特徵序列可包含的（調變）頻帶為 [0,50 Hz]，因此後半頻帶鮮少包含語音成分，抑制此頻帶不會對語音造成明顯失真，但可有效抑制雜訊的干擾。另外，基於文獻 (Wang et al., 2018) 所述，使用小波轉換分解語音特徵時序列、消除其細節係數 (detail coefficients，相當於調變高頻成分) 後重建之語音特徵，在雜訊環境下有明顯進步的語音辨識率，我們參照這樣的做法來實現前述之語音特徵序列的低通濾波處理，期許它對應的遮罩深度模型能得到更佳的語音強化效果。

2 提出的新方法

在本研究中，我們選擇加以研究改進的是理想比例遮罩 (ideal ratio mask, IRM) 法，此法通常是求取語音之一般時頻圖 (spectrogram) 或耳蝸時頻圖 (cochleagram) 對應的理想遮罩值：

$$M(m, f) = \frac{|s(m, f)|^2}{|s(m, f)|^2 + |d(m, f)|^2} \qquad (1)$$

其中，$|s(m, f)|^2$ 與 $|d(m, f)|^2$ 分別代表了雜訊語音其時頻圖或耳蝸時頻圖在音框時間 m 與頻率 f 之時頻單位 (time-frequency unit, T-F unit) 所對應的乾淨語音與純雜訊的能量，在人造訓練雜訊語句的準備上，由於事先可得知其乾淨語音及純雜訊的成分，因此可根據式1計算其理想比例遮罩的值，作為 IRM 深度模型的訓練目標。

在我們構思的新方法中，嘗試將用以訓練 IRM 深度模型所使用的語音特徵時序列，加以低通濾波處理、藉此抑制其調變高頻的成分，再使用處理後的語音特徵來求取 IRM 深度模型，預期此 IRM 模型相對於原始特徵對應之 IRM 模型，能求取更佳的遮罩來抑制雜訊對語音時頻圖上的失真。值得一提的是，我們使用離散小波轉換 (discrete wavelet transform, DWT) 來執行上述的低通濾波處理，部分原因是在 DWT 其分解與重建的濾波器彼此互補，在分解與重建的過程中不會造成序列相位的失真，此相較於一般的低通濾波器而言存在優勢。以下，我們敘述此新方法的步驟：

訓練階段：

1. 將訓練集 (training set) 中的任一雜訊干擾的語音 $x[n]$，經音框化 (framing) 與窗化 (windowing) 切割成個別音框訊號 $x_m[n]$ 後（m 為音框索引），再將個別音框訊號轉換成語音特徵，如 amplitude modulation spectrogram (簡稱 AMS), relative spectral transformed perceptual linear prediction coefficients (簡稱 RASTA-PLP), mel-frequency cepstral coefficients (簡稱 MFCC) 及 Gammatone filterbank power spectra(簡稱 GF) 等。我們將對應的 D 維語音特徵向量以 $\mathbf{x}_m$ 表示，$\mathbf{x}_m$ 為一 $D \times 1$ 的行向量，假設該語句共切割成 M 個音框，則其對應的語音特徵矩陣可表示為：

$$X = [\mathbf{x}_0 \ \mathbf{x}_1 \ \ldots \ \mathbf{x}_{M-1}], \qquad (2)$$

其尺寸為 $D \times M$。

2. 上述之特徵矩陣 X 的任一第 d 個橫列向量

$$[X(d,0)\ X(d,1)\ ...\ X(d,M-1)], \quad (3)$$

以 $X_d[m]$ 代表之，其稱作 X 的第 d 維特徵時序列，尺寸為 $1 \times M$，其中 $1 \le d \le D$。我們將任一維特徵時序列 $X_d[m]$ 以一階離散小波轉換加以分解如下：

$$[cA_d[m], cD_d[m]] = \mathbf{DWT}(X_d[m]), \quad (4)$$

其中 $\mathbf{DWT}(.)$ 代表離散小波轉換 (discrete wavelet transform, DWT)、$cA_d[m]$ 與 $cD_d[m]$ 分別為轉換分解而得的近似係數 (approximation coefficients) 與細節係數 (detail coefficients)，其可視為原始序列 $X_d[m]$ 之低通成分與高通成分，二者頻寬均約等於原始序列頻寬的一半，且點數減半。

3. 我們將上一步驟所得的細節係數 $cD_d[m]$ 乘上一個小於 1 的權重 α，再與原近似係數相組合、經過反離散小波轉換重建第 d 維特徵時序列，表示如下：

$$\tilde{X}_d[m] = \mathbf{IDWT}([cA_d[m], \alpha \times cD_d[m]], \quad (5)$$

其中 $\mathbf{IDWT}(.)$ 代表反離散小波轉換，$\tilde{X}_d[m]$ 為更新的特徵時序列，相較於原始特徵時序列 $X_d[m]$，$\tilde{X}_d[m]$ 包含較低的高通成分，因此應當包含較少雜訊造成的失真。

4. 參照一般 IRM 深度模型的訓練法，我們改以新的特徵序列 $\{\tilde{X}_d[m], 1 \le d \le D\}$ 作為輸入，以理想 IRM 遮罩值為目標輸出，訓練 IRM 深度模型。值得注意的是，若式 (5) 中的權重 $\alpha = 1$，則所訓練的 IRM 模型與原始（即使用原始特徵訓練）IRM 模型完全一致。

測試階段：

將測試之語句如同訓練語句之處理的前三個步驟、求取低通濾波之特徵時序列，將其通過訓練完成的 IRM 模型求取遮罩值，將遮罩值與原設定之對應的時頻圖作點乘積 (dot product)，即可得強化後的時頻圖，經由適當的反轉換重建成強化版的時域訊號。

3 實驗設定

參照文獻 (Williamson et al., 2016) 所提供的程式碼 (Jitong Chen, 2016)，我們使用了 TIMIT 資料庫的部分語句 (取樣頻率為 16 kHz) 來實驗評估我們所提出的方法，其中，訓練集包含了 5 位語者、每人 10 句共 50 個語句，而測試集則包含了與訓練集不同的 3 位語者、每人 10 句共 30 個語句。我們將訓練與測試語句摻入 babble 雜訊，訓雜比 (signal-to-noise ratio, SNR) 固定為-2 dB。在訓練與測試 IRM 之深度模型上，輸入特徵的種類包含了 AMS、RASTA-PLP、MFCC 與 GF 四種，同時，我們將左右相鄰的 5 個音框 (frames) 串接成一個長向量，作為深度模型的輸入單位，深度模型之架構為全連結層 (densely connected layers) 網路，共包含 4 層隱藏層，每個隱藏層由 1024 個神經元 (neurons) 構成。目標是求取語音之耳蝸時頻圖 (cochleagram) 的遮罩，其每個音框設有 64 維，相當有 64 個頻道 (channel)。在我們所提的新 IRM 訓練法上，對於輸入特徵之時序列之細節係數（高頻係數）所給予的權重 α，分別設定為 0, 0.25, 0.50, 0.75，藉此觀察細節係數之壓抑程度對於 IRM 效果之影響（原始 IRM 所對應之權重 $\alpha = 1$）。在使用的離散小波轉換與反轉換中，我們使用 db2 小波函數。在評估效能上，我們使用了 PESQ 分數 (Rix et al., 2001) 作為語音品質 (quality) 的客觀指標、STOI 分數 (Taal et al., 2011) 作為語音可讀性 (intelligibility) 的客觀指標，PESQ 分數介於-0.5 與 4.5 之間，STOI 分數介於 0 與 1 之間，分數越高代表語音的品質/可讀性越佳。

4 實驗結果與分析

在我們的評估實驗上，我們將分為三部分來呈現並討論，第一部分是對應於使用所有種類之輸入特徵組合所訓練及測試之 IRM 模型，第二部分是對應於使用單一種類之輸入特徵所訓練及測試之 IRM 模型，我們將在這兩部分中，探究所提新方法之低通濾波特徵時序列對於 IRM 效能的改變，第三部分則是藉由時頻圖的展示，觀察原始與更新之 IRM 所強化的語音訊號的差異。

4.1 使用所有種類之輸入特徵所得的 IRM 效能分析

首先，表 1 列出了測試雜訊語句在處理前、經由理想 IRM（遮罩直接由乾淨語音與摻雜之雜訊求得）及原始 IRM（使用原始輸入特徵訓練，並可能額外加入差量特徵）處理後所對應的 PESQ 與 STOI 的平均值。從此表中，我們可以看到：

1. 雜訊語句經過理想 IRM 處理後，在 PESQ 與 STOI 都得到了大幅的提升。

	未處理語音	理想 IRM	原始 IRM_1	原始 IRM_2
STOI	0.6130	0.9004	0.6763	0.6658
PESQ	1.6081	2.6408	1.7755	1.7748

表 1: 未處理語音與經過理想 IRM、原始 IRM_1（使用原特徵求取）、原始 IRM_2（使用原特徵與其差量特徵求取）處理後對應的 STOI 與 PESQ 平均分數，原特徵由四種特徵 (AMS, RASTA-PLP, MFCC, GF) 排列而得

	原始 IRM_1	不同權重 α 抑制調變高頻之 IRM			
		$\alpha = 0$	$\alpha = 0.25$	$\alpha = 0.50$	$\alpha = 0.75$
STOI	0.6763	0.6767	0.6728	**0.6799**	0.6789
PESQ	1.7755	**1.7844**	1.7612	1.7717	1.7760

表 2: 未處理語音與經過理想 IRM、原始 IRM_1（使用原特徵求取）、不同權重 α 抑制調變高頻之 IRM（未搭配差量特徵）處理後對應的 STOI 與 PESQ 平均分數。原特徵由四種特徵 (AMS, RASTA-PLP, MFCC, GF) 排列而得

	原始 IRM_2	不同權重 α 抑制調變高頻之 IRM			
		$\alpha = 0$	$\alpha = 0.25$	$\alpha = 0.50$	$\alpha = 0.75$
STOI	0.6658	0.6639	0.6671	0.6615	**0.6682**
PESQ	1.7748	1.7819	1.7916	1.7589	**1.7996**

表 3: 未處理語音與經過理想 IRM、原始 IRM_2（使用原特徵與其差量特徵求取）、不同權重 α 抑制調變高頻之 IRM（有搭配差量特徵）處理後對應的 STOI 與 PESQ 平均分數。原特徵由四種特徵 (AMS, RASTA-PLP, MFCC, GF) 排列而得

STOI 分數	原始 IRM_2	不同權重 α 抑制調變高頻之 IRM			
		$\alpha = 0$	$\alpha = 0.25$	$\alpha = 0.50$	$\alpha = 0.75$
AMS	**0.6472**	0.6430	0.6435	0.6458	0.6466
RASTA-PLP	0.6559	0.6600	0.6607	**0.6611**	0.6556
MFCC	0.6740	0.6771	**0.6772**	0.6761	0.6770
GF	0.6695	**0.6698**	0.6667	0.6672	0.6692
combo	0.6658	0.6639	0.6671	0.6615	**0.6682**

表 4: 單一種類特徵的 STOI 分數比較，未處理語音與經過理想 IRM、原始 IRM_2（使用原特徵與其差量特徵求取）、不同權重 α 抑制調變高頻之 IRM（有搭配差量特徵）處理後對應的 STOI 平均分數，其中"combo" 表示四類特徵之組合

PESQ 分數	原始 IRM_2	不同權重 α 抑制調變高頻之 IRM			
		$\alpha = 0$	$\alpha = 0.25$	$\alpha = 0.50$	$\alpha = 0.75$
AMS	1.6721	1.6705	1.6712	**1.6731**	1.6758
RASTA-PLP	1.7463	**1.7634**	**1.7634**	1.7630	1.7426
MFCC	1.7966	1.7870	1.7916	1.7946	**1.7977**
GF	1.7641	**1.7791**	1.7669	1.7635	1.7633
combo	1.7748	1.7819	1.7916	1.7589	**1.7996**

表 5: 單一種類特徵的 PESQ 分數比較，未處理語音與經過理想 IRM、原始 IRM_2（使用原特徵與其差量特徵求取）、不同權重 α 抑制調變高頻之 IRM（有搭配差量特徵）處理後對應的 PESQ 平均分數，其中"combo" 表示四類特徵之組合

2. 原始 IRM 雖然也能帶來顯著的改進，但效果明顯與理想 IRM 有差距，這代表了藉由雜訊語音（特徵）中估測乾淨語音與雜訊成分之精準度仍有很大的進步空間。

3. 差量特徵的有無並未對於訓練而得 IRM 在 STOI 與 PESQ 的表現上有大幅影響，額外使用差量特徵甚至使 IRM 得到較低的 STOI 分數。

接下來，我們開始評估所提之新 IRM 訓練法，表 2 列出了在不使用差量特徵時，給定輸入特徵之時序列之高頻係數不同的權重 α，經訓練之 IRM 所對應的 STOI 與 PESQ 分數，從此表中，我們有以下的發現：

1. 當使用低通濾波之 IRM 時，權重 $\alpha < 1$ 之設定都得到了更佳的 STOI 與 PESQ 值（$\alpha = 0.25$ 在 STOI 分數除外，$\alpha = 0.25, 0.50$ 在 PESQ 分數除外），此初步驗證了此方法對於訓練更佳 IRM 模型、以抑制雜訊干擾有更好的效果。

2. 全然移除（設定 $\alpha = 0$）或少量移除（設定 $\alpha = 0.75$）調變高頻成分似乎是較佳選項，二者至少皆可使 PESQ 與 STOI 值提升，$\alpha = 0$ 得到最佳的 PESQ 值，而 $\alpha = 0.75$ 則使 STOI 進步最大。

其次，表 3 列出了在額外使用差量特徵時，給定輸入特徵之時序列之高頻係數不同的權重 α，經訓練之 IRM 所對應的 STOI 與 PESQ 分數，從此表中，我們有以下的發現：

1. 相較於原始 IRM 而言，使用較大權重 α (0.75) 在 STOI 與 PESQ 上都有較明顯的改進，其他較小值的 α 設定值則並未一致性地得到明顯進步的效果，這可能原因是，當使用差量特徵時，差量特徵本身就已經抑制原始特徵的調變高頻成分，因此此時用較大的 α 值再對原始特徵的調變高頻成分小幅抑制，即可達到預期之進步效果。

2. 若我們將表 2 與表 3 的數據同時比較，發現達到最佳 STOI 值 (0.6799) 的是「不使用差量特徵、使用 $\alpha = 0.50$ 之抑制調變高頻」的 IRM 法，而達到最佳 PESQ 值 (1.7996) 的則是「使用差量特徵、使用 $\alpha = 0.75$ 之抑制調變高頻」的 IRM 法。

4.2 使用個別種類之輸入特徵所得的 IRM 效能分析

在前一節中，我們已經呈現綜合四類特徵所得之 IRM 的效果，並初步驗證將特徵時序列低通濾波可以進一步強化 IRM。在本節裡，我們想進一步觀察各個類別的特徵（包含 AMS, RASTA-PLP, MFCC, GF）對於 IRM 效能之影響，同時我們也使用低通濾波來處理其序列、進而比較濾波前與濾波後對於 IRM 效能的影響，表 4 與表 5 分別列出各種不同特徵搭配低通濾波對應之 IRM 所得之測試語句的 STOI 與 PESQ 分數，為了使整體效能優化起見，這裡我們把差量特徵一併加入，同時，我們將前一節四類特徵的組合（以 “combo” 表示）之結果列在表的最下一列，以供比較。從這兩個表之數據，我們有以下幾點的觀察與討論：

1. 對於語音可讀度指標 STOI 而言，不使用低通濾波之四類特徵中，以 MFCC 表現最佳(0.6740)，甚至超越了組合特徵的結果（0.6658)，然而，當配合低通濾波時，MFCC 可以達到更佳的 STOI 值，例如當使用 $\alpha = 0.25$ 的權重時，MFCC 對應之 STOI 值可以進一步提升至 0.6772。此外，低通濾波處理並非對每一種特徵都能帶來改進，例如對於 AMS 特徵而言，不使用低通濾波所對應的原始 IRM 表現最好。

2. 對於語音品質指標 PESQ 而言，在不使用低通濾波之四類特徵中，MFCC 仍表現最佳（1.7966），超越了組合特徵（1.7748)，而 AMS 特徵表現較不好，只有 1.6721 之 PESQ 值。然而，當配合低通濾波時，各種類特徵皆可以達到更佳的 PESQ 值，例如當使用 $\alpha = 0.75$ 的權重時，MFCC 對應之 PESQ 值可以進一步提升至 1.7977。然而，獲得 PESQ 最佳之特徵是組合特徵配合 $\alpha = 0.75$ 之低通濾波法，可達 1.7996。

根據以上觀察，四類特徵的組合未必在 STOI 表現上優於單類特徵，而在 PESQ 表現上只能些許超越個別單類特徵，這可能原因在於某類特徵（如 AMS）在表現上與其他特徵差異較大，即使後端的深度模型在學習中理應能淡化這類特徵的負面影響，但是從測試結果上，多類特徵組合並未發揮顯著的加成性。

4.3 使用時頻圖演示結果

最後在這一小節，我們使用語音訊號的強度時頻圖 (magnitude spectrogram)，來檢視原始 IRM 與我們提出之低通濾波特徵之 IRM 的強化效能，圖 1-5 為一語句在各種狀態下所對應的強度時頻圖，首先，我們比較圖 1 與圖 2，發現雜訊對於語音在時頻圖上產生顯著的失真，接著，比較圖 2 與圖 3 可看出，理想的 IRM 可帶來顯著的語音強化效果，最後，觀察原始 IRM 與低通濾波特徵之 IRM 所對應的圖 4 與圖 5，相對於圖 2，雜訊所造成的失真明顯降低，但效果並不如理想 IRM 所對應的圖 3，例如在時間 0.1-0.2 秒之間的頻譜強度並未有效重建（在紅色框所標示區域），然而圖 5 的在此區域的頻譜重建程度稍優於圖 4，根據此比較結果，我們似乎可看出，低通濾波特徵之 IRM 在此語句的處理上略優於原始 IRM。

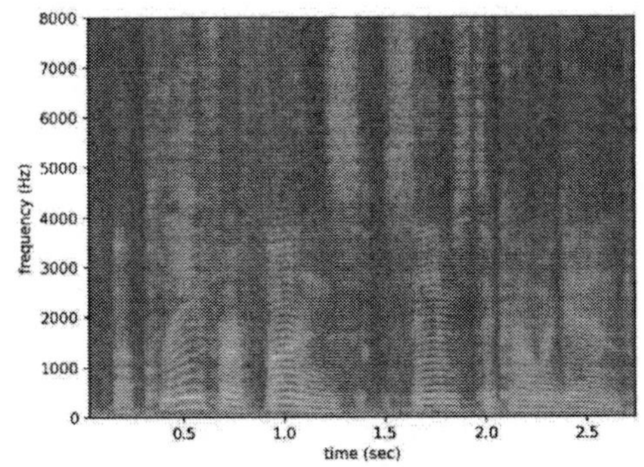

圖 1: 原始乾淨語音時頻圖

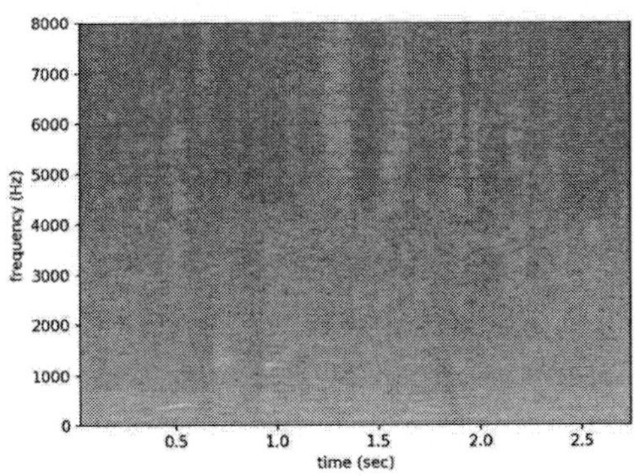

圖 2: 摻入-2 dB SNR 之 babble 雜訊之語音時頻圖

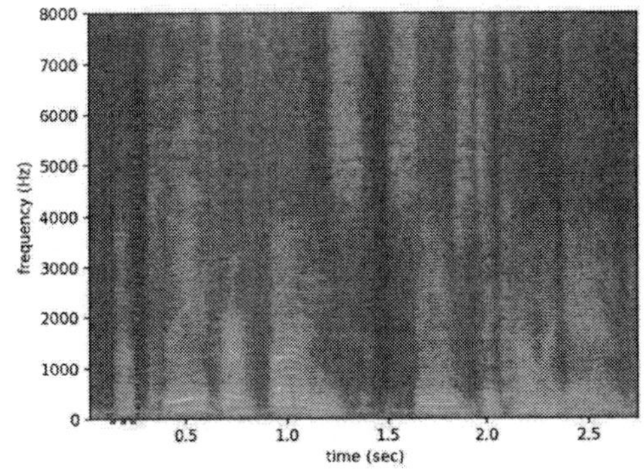

圖 3: 雜訊語音經由理想 IRM 處理後之時頻圖

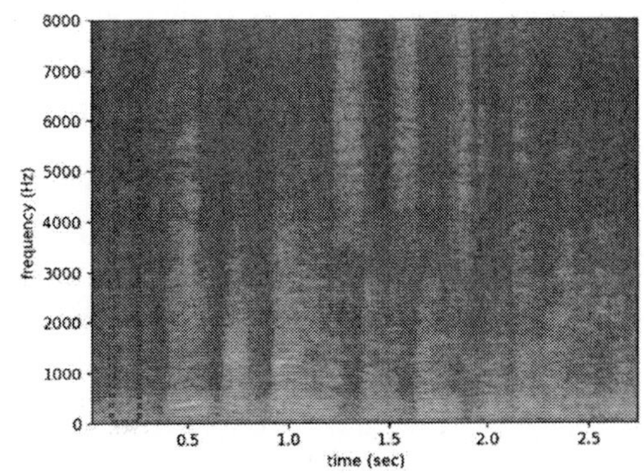

圖 4: 雜訊語音經由原始 IRM 處理後之時頻圖

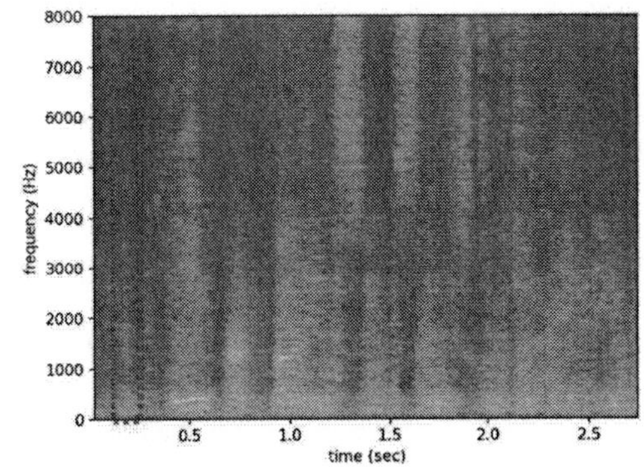

圖 5: 雜訊語音經由低通濾波 IRM 處理後之時頻圖

5 結論與未來展望

在本研究中，我們提出並初步驗證了當理想比例遮罩 (IRM) 之深度模型使用低通濾波之語音特徵時序列來訓練時，相較於使用原特徵時序列訓練，可以得到更佳的語音強化效果。我們使用小波轉換來實現低通濾波的處理，其執行簡易但效果明顯，在未來工作上，我們初步規劃將此低通濾波的時序列處理用在訓練其他種類的語音強化深度模型之特徵上，檢視其是否也能更有效改進該模型的效能、提升語音之品質與可讀性。

References

Chia-Ping Chen and Jeff A. Bilmes. 2007. Mva processing of speech features. *IEEE Transactions on Audio, Speech, and Language Processing*, 15(1):257–270.

Hakan Erdogan, John R. Hershey, Shinji Watanabe, and Jonathan Le Roux. 2015. Phase-sensitive and recognition-boosted speech separation using deep recurrent neural networks. In *2015 IEEE International Conference on Acoustics, Speech and Signal Processing (ICASSP)*, pages 708–712.

Yuzhou Liu Jitong Chen, Yuxuan Wang. 2016. Matlab toolbox for dnn-based speech separation. http://web.cse.ohio-state.edu/pnl/DNN_toolbox/. Accessed: 2021-08-06.

Stphane Mallat. 2008. *A Wavelet Tour of Signal Processing, Third Edition: The Sparse Way*, 3rd edition. Academic Press, Inc., USA.

A.W. Rix, J.G. Beerends, M.P. Hollier, and A.P. Hekstra. 2001. Perceptual evaluation of speech quality (pesq)-a new method for speech quality assessment of telephone networks and codecs. In *2001 IEEE International Conference on Acoustics, Speech, and Signal Processing. Proceedings (Cat. No.01CH37221)*, volume 2, pages 749–752 vol.2.

Soundararajan Srinivasan, Nicoleta Roman, and DeLiang Wang. 2006. Binary and ratio time-frequency masks for robust speech recognition. *Speech Communication*, 48(11):1486–1501. Robustness Issues for Conversational Interaction.

Cees H. Taal, Richard C. Hendriks, Richard Heusdens, and Jesper Jensen. 2011. An algorithm for intelligibility prediction of time - frequency weighted noisy speech. *IEEE Transactions on Audio, Speech, and Language Processing*, 19(7):2125–2136.

Sarel Vuuren and Hynek Hermansky. 1998. On the importance of components of the modulation spectrum for speaker verification. In *The 5th International Conference on Spoken Language Processing, Incorporating The 7th Australian International Speech Science and Technology Conference, Sydney Convention Centre, Sydney, Australia, 30th November - 4th December 1998*. ISCA.

Syu-Siang Wang, Payton Lin, Yu Tsao, Jeih-Weih Hung, and Borching Su. 2018. Suppression by selecting wavelets for feature compression in distributed speech recognition. *IEEE/ACM Transactions on Audio, Speech, and Language Processing*, 26(3):564–579.

Yuxuan Wang, Arun Narayanan, and DeLiang Wang. 2014. On training targets for supervised speech separation. *IEEE/ACM Transactions on Audio, Speech, and Language Processing*, 22(12):1849–1858.

Donald S. Williamson, Yuxuan Wang, and DeLiang Wang. 2016. Complex ratio masking for monaural speech separation. *IEEE/ACM Transactions on Audio, Speech, and Language Processing*, 24(3):483–492.

The 33rd Conference on Computational Linguistics and Speech Processing (ROCLING 2021)
Taoyuan, Taiwan, October 15-16, 2021. The Association for Computational Linguistics and Chinese Language Processing

Hidden Advertorial Detection on Social Media in Chinese

Meng-Ching Ho[1*], Ching-Yun Chuang[2*], Yi-Chun Hsu[1*], Yu-Yun Chang[1]
[1]Graduate Institute of Linguistics
[2]Master's Program in Digital Content and Technologies (DCT)
National Chengchi University
109555006@g.nccu.edu.tw, 109462007@g.nccu.edu.tw,
109555003@g.nccu.edu.tw, yuyun@nccu.edu.tw

Abstract

Nowadays, there are a lot of advertisements hiding as normal posts or experience sharing in social media. There is little research of advertorial detection on Mandarin Chinese texts. This paper thus aimed to focus on hidden advertorial detection of online posts in Taiwan Mandarin Chinese. We inspected seven contextual features based on linguistic theories in discourse level. These features can be further grouped into three schemas under the general advertorial writing structure. We further implemented these features to train a multi-task BERT model to detect advertorials. The results suggested that specific linguistic features would help extract advertorials.

Keywords: advertorial, linguistic feature, discourse, advertisement, machine learning

1 Introduction

Advertisements on social media are changing, and the vague boundary between advertising and editorial lead to an emergence of a new type of advertising strategy (Keach, 2012). Advertorial is a way of combining advertisement with editorial content. This innovative and hybrid type of discourse involves promotional and journalistic genres, specifically advertisements along with editorials (Deng et al., 2021). Figure 1 is an online

Figure1: An example of online advertorials posted by an Instagramer, *@imjennim*, on date June 3, 2021.

advertorial. This kind of posts often contain advertising cues such as 品牌合作 'paid partnership' and hashtags (e.g., *#ad*) in the editorials. In addition, utilizing different type sizes and fonts in the layout arrangement are also part of the advertorial tactics (Kim et al., 2001).

According to Keach's (2012) investigation, people who saw the post through a friend's recommendation were 24% more likely to view the sponsor positively. Additionally, BuzzFeed, a popular Internet news company, said that advertisements on its site get an average of 40% additional views from people sharing them on social media and that readers are between 10 to 20 times more likely to click on them than on an average banner advertisement (Keach, 2012).

* These three authors contributed equally.

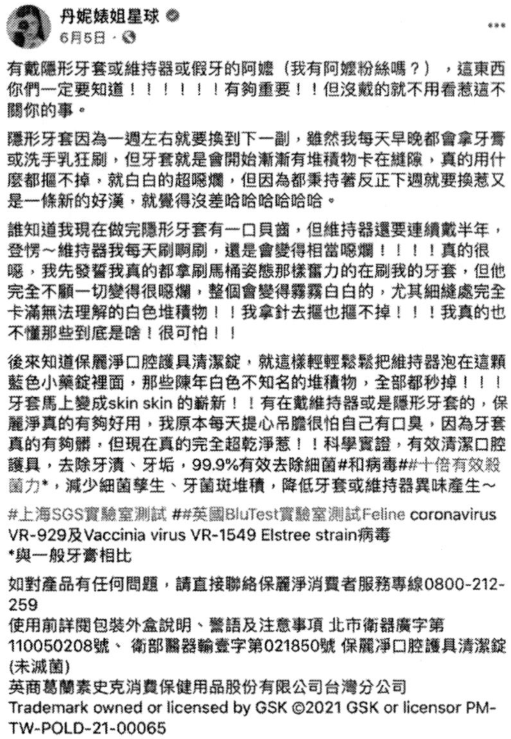

丹妮婊姐星球
6月5日 ·

有戴隱形牙套或維持器或假牙的阿嬤（我有阿嬤粉絲嗎？），這東西你們一定要知道！！！！！！有夠重要！！但沒戴的就不用看惹這不關你的事。

隱形牙套因為一週左右就要換到下一副，雖然我每天早晚都會拿牙膏或洗手乳狂刷，但牙套就是會開始漸漸有堆積物卡在縫隙，真的用什麼都摳不掉，就白白的超噁爛，但因為都秉持著反正下週就要換惹又是一條新的好漢，就覺得沒差哈哈哈哈哈哈。

誰知道我現在做完隱形牙套有一口貝齒，但維持器還要連續戴半年，登愣～維持器我每天刷啊刷，還是會變得相當噁爛！！！！真的很噁，我先發誓我真的都拿刷馬桶姿態那樣奮力的在刷我的牙套，但他完全不顧一切變得很噁爛，整個會變得霧霧白白的，尤其細縫處完全卡滿無法理解的白色堆積物！！我拿針去摳也摳不掉！！！我真的也不懂那些到底是啥！很可怕！！

後來知道保麗淨口腔護具清潔錠，就這樣輕輕鬆鬆把維持器泡在這顆藍色小藥錠裡面，那些陳年白色不知名的堆積物，全部都秒掉！！！牙套馬上變成skin skin 的嶄新！！有在戴維持器或是隱形牙套的，保麗淨真的有夠好用，我原本每天提心吊膽很怕自己有口臭，因為牙套真的有夠髒，但現在真的完全超乾淨惹！！科學實證，有效清潔口腔護具，去除牙漬、牙垢，99.9%有效去除細菌#和病毒##十倍有效殺菌力*，減少細菌孳生、牙菌斑堆積，降低牙套或維持器異味產生～

#上海SGS實驗室測試 ##英國BluTest實驗室測試Feline coronavirus VR-929及Vaccinia virus VR-1549 Elstree strain病毒
*與一般牙膏相比

如對產品有任何問題，請直接聯絡保麗淨消費者服務專線0800-212-259
使用前詳閱包裝外盒說明、警語及注意事項 北市衛器廣字第110050208號、衛部醫器輸壹字第021850號 保麗淨口腔護具清潔錠(未滅菌)
英商葛蘭素史克消費保健用品股份有限公司台灣分公司
Trademark owned or licensed by GSK ©2021 GSK or licensor PM-TW-POLD-21-00065

Figure 2: An example of online hidden advertorials posted by a Facebooker, @*丹妮婊姐星球*, on date June 5, 2021.

Although it is suggested by Guidelines for Editors and Publishers (American Society of Magazine Editors, 2014) that an advertorial should include advertising labels such as "Advertisement", "Advertising" and "Special Advertising Section", and the labels should be clearly printed at the page or advertising unit. However, more and more people have ignored and violated the advertising guidelines through time (Ju-Pak et al., 1995). With the lack of these executional cues (e.g., advertisement label, type sizes, and fonts) that act as a way of distinguishing advertorial content from editorial content, we should focus on how advertorials could be identified as such in their contents (Kim et al., 2001). These advertorials that are not clearly labeled are called "hidden advertorials", and they are contents paid for by advertisers but not identified by viewers. Figure 2 is an example of a hidden advertorial retrieved from Facebook. This advertorial looks like an experience-sharing article, which was hard to be identified at first sight, and does not include clear advertising labels mentioned above.

To the best of our knowledge, little research focused on Chinese advertorial detection, especially hidden advertorial detection. Due to the overflow of hidden advertorials on social platforms, and the difficulty in distinguishing advertorials from editorials, we aim to observe contextual features from linguistic perspective in discourse level, and apply machine learning models to detect hidden advertorials.

In the study, two research questions are listed in the following: (1) what contextual features are involved in advertorials in Chinese text and their underlying linguistic meanings? and (2) are these contextual features suitable for the classifiers to detect hidden advertorials in Chinese social media?

2 Literature review

Hidden advertorials might mislead the public, and the partial and subjective information would influence consumer behaviors. According to a study of Kim et al. (2001), unlabeled advertorials are more likely to be recognized as an editorial material.

Hidden advertising would decrease journalistic quality and cause questioning of the media's ability to provide the society with reliable and diverse information (Rožukalne, 2010; Rožukalne, 2012). If advertorials are not clearly distinguishable from editorial content in format and tone, legitimate journalism will lose its integrity, and the advertising business could be perceived as a negative image (Ellerbach, 2004). Furthermore, it has been argued that advertorials confuse readers into thinking they are a part of editorial content (Cameron & Haley, 1992). This may indicate that the presence of a label for an advertorial is desired in preventing potential consumer confusion. Therefore, advertising positioned as news must be labeled as "advertorial" to ensure that the readers understand that the message is impartial (Tuten & Perotti, 2019).

To identify advertorials, some relevant studies of features in advertorials are discussed. Persuasive Linguistic Tricks (PLT) (Stepaniuk & Jarosz, 2021) are commonly observed in advertorials. PLT includes strategies such as problems and solutions, which persuades consumers by presenting a solution to a common problem (Stepaniuk & Jarosz, 2021). For instance, hidden advertorials that promote health products and services in magazines usually begin with a life-style problem or a seasonal illness and lead to a problem-solution structure (Kovacic et al., 2012).

Zhou (2012) mentioned advertorials usually employ the strategy into the writing structure, by raising an existing problem in society in the beginning, and then promoting a solution with the technique of product placement to the problem.

Another feature of advertorials are the frequent use of gradable words and expressions (e.g., 非常 'extremely', and 很 'very') that evaluate the products, and take a positive stance toward the sponsors by using positive appreciations (Zhou, 2012). Advertorials usually express positive emotions, hedonic mood and also a great deal of superlative adjectives and nouns to help present a positive image of the sponsors (Zhou, 2012; Burton et al, 2020). Therefore, in advertorials, repetition of positive adjectives and positive verbs are observed. Advertorials also sometimes contain words such as "love" and phrases like "my favorite" to show more assurance from celebrities (Forbes, 2016).

Advertorials also involve some lexical features. The study from Kovacic et al. (2011) combined a textual analysis, in-depth interviews and observations to examine unlabeled advertorials in magazines. The researchers investigated the phenomenon of over-lexicalization in the advertorials, which include several synonymous or near-synonymous terms. Similarly, a linguistic style that measures preciseness is based on whether or not an author uses various terms to describe a single concept (Short & Palmer, 2008). And preciseness would influence the potential to capture viewers (Lee & Theokary, 2021).

In addition, from a large majority of analyzed advertorials, it is observed that advertorials tend to address readers directly. That is, the pronoun "you" is commonly used in advertorials in order to close a 'discursive gap' (Fowler, 1991). This constant appearance of "you" is analyzed as the generic use of "you" linguistically, which refers to 'a specific person the author tries to address to' or 'people in general'. The generic use of "you" (henceforth, generic-you) might function as a linguistic nudge that carries persuasive force, which may influence viewers' behaviors (Orvell et al., 2019).

The study of Labrador et al. (2014) reveals that e-commerce texts typically have two main elements: one to identify the product and the other one to describe it. The latter element includes objective features (e.g., size and weight) and also focuses on persuading the potential customer. Besides, advertorials often describe the details of the product design, and give advice about their specific use of the product, which allows authors to demonstrate helpfulness and attract more consumers (Forbes, 2016).

Lee's (2018) investigation based on China market mentioned that hunger-marketing would not only increase customers' curiosity but also fulfill their conformity. Therefore, one of the PLTs, "uniqueness" (e.g., products or services that are in limited edition), can make the product more desirable by promoting limited editions of the product (Stepaniuk & Jarosz, 2021).

According to a research of Cheung (2010), the discourse strategy, discourse structure and linguistic choices in the sales genre have increased localization. For instance, compared to English advertisements, the results indicated that Chinese advertisements tended to use the strategy, "setting the scene", which describes the situation and background of the posts, to achieve the social purpose of persuasion more often. Another common persuasive strategy in Chinese advertisements is "offering incentives". Incentives involved gifts, discounts, free trial or free tests and games. Therefore, aside from the studies of advertorials mentioned above, we intended to focus on advertorials in Taiwan Mandarin Chinese.

3 Methodology

This section will be introducing our data collection, feature observation, data preprocessing, and model training.

3.1 Data collection

Our dataset was collected from three online social platforms, which are Dcard, Facebook and Instagram. The dataset consisted of 1,040 articles, and we manually labeled them into 463 advertorials and 577 non-advertorials. The 463 advertorials contained both hidden advertorials and explicit advertorials (with clear advertising labels). Hidden advertorials include posts which are not clearly labeled as advertisements or commercial cooperation, but are authors' own experiences that involve marketing purposes, and can be classified as advertorials based on previous studies and our own observations. The dataset was separated into 70% as a training set (728 posts), 15% as a validation set (156 posts), and 15% as a test set (156 posts). All the articles were in Taiwan

Mandarin Chinese. The reason that we collected articles from three social platforms was that online posts from different platforms may have various advertorial writing styles.

For example, Facebook and Instagram are mostly posted by influencers, and are usually more well-structured. Moreover, sponsors always provide the influencers with special discount codes which can attract more consumers. *#AD, #Brand name* are common hashtags that label the posts as advertorials on Facebook and Instagram. Dcard usually offers users a free trial of a sponsored product, and users are required to write a review article and share their experience on the platform. Through these review articles, the sponsored products can gain more publicity. Therefore, keywords such as 開箱大使 'unboxing ambassador' and 此文為官方合作文 'this post is a collaborative article' are observed in these review articles which are actually advertorials.

3.2 Feature observation

This section introduces the seven features observed in the dataset, which can be further divided into three schemas based on the general advertorial writing structure: background description, product-related information, and building connections with viewers. Features and their related schemas are shown in Table 1.

3.2.1 Background description

Referring to previous studies (Zhou, 2012; Cheung 2010; Kovacic et al., 2012; Stepaniuk & Jarosz, 2021), "setting the scene" is listed as an important feature in our model training. "Setting the scene" includes problem solving and scenario simulation. For instance, skin and hair care problems or social-related issues are commonly seen in collected advertorials.

To identify the posts with the feature "setting the scene", we extracted posts with keywords such as 問題 'problem', 困擾 'problem' and 煩惱 'worries' and posts that mentioned special events. For instance, 敏感肌問題都跑到臉上作客了嗎？ 'Do you have sensitive skin problems?' and 即將開學，穿搭行頭準備好了嗎？ 'Have you prepared your new semester clothing?'

3.2.2 Product-related information

Another significant feature is that these advertorials usually contained very detailed information about the product, which matches the study of Forbes (2016). The detailed information not only includes many technical terms but also elaborated descriptions of the products. Additionally, advertorials related to cosmetics and hair products sometimes includes tutorials and clear steps of how to use the product. This kind of advertorials disguise themselves as instructional content that helps viewers learn how to put on makeup or do hair care routines. There are also some features that we observed from the dataset. Authors often present comparisons of before and after using the product to show the differences and highlight the benefits of the product. In our data processing, we searched for words such as 對比 'comparison' and 前後 'before and after' to filter out the advertorials that implied the effects of the products.

Uniqueness is also a frequent PLT found in our advertorials. In our collected data, keywords like 期間限定 'limited time offer' and 卡友限定 'Dcard users only' which may limit the products to a specific time or group of customers appeared constantly. In our dataset, sponsors often offer free samples and sometimes exclusive discount codes in advertorials, and these incentives have more persuasive potential (Cheung, 2010). Advertisers often raise a ruffle which requires the viewers to leave their comments or tag their friends to boost the reach of the post.

3.2.3 Building connections with viewers

Previous studies showed the influence of positive words in advertorials (Zhou, 2012; Burton, 2020). In the dataset, authors also use exaggeration tones, excessive exclamation marks and various emojis to express their favor and positive appreciation of the products. Two advertorials with this feature are shown in Figure 3 and 4. Furthermore, the direct address of using pronoun 'you' may simulate a conversational and relatively personal relationship (Fowler, 1991; Orvell et al, 2019). Additionally, the use of generic-you, which does not refer to a specific person but the general readers, is commonly used in our dataset.

Schemas of writing structure	Features
Background description	(a) setting the scene (including problem solving and scenario simulating)
Product-related information	(b) product-related activities (including ruffles, limited products and free gifts)
	(c) the comparison of before and after using the product
	(d) detailed product information
	(e) product tutorials
Building connections with the viewers	(f) positive and exaggeration tone
	(g) the use of generic-you

Table 1: The seven contextual features grouped into three schemas under advertorial writing structure for model training.

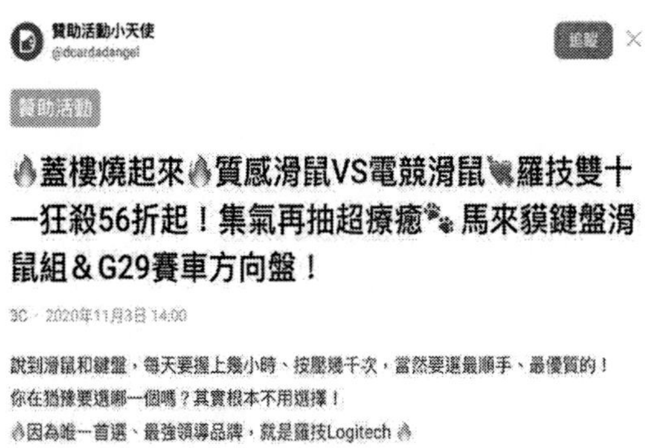

Figure 3: An example of online advertorials using exaggeration tone from Dcard, *@dcardangel*, on date November 3, 2020.

Figure 4: An example of online advertorials using exaggeration tone from Dcard, *@fingerlick*, on date April 23, 2021.

For example,說到仙境傳說，**你**會想到什麼？ 'What will you think of when it comes to Ragnarok Online Game?' and IKEA 聽到**你**的心願了！ 'IKEA is going to fulfill your dream!'[1]

3.3 Data preprocessing and model training

We manually annotated each article with 7 features. We applied one-hot encoding to feature labeling.

We used multi-task learning on Bidirectional Encoder Representations from Transformers (multi-task BERT) referred to Liu et al. (2019) to inspect the effectiveness of the seven features in advertorial detection. Figure 5 shows the architecture of the multi-task BERT model. Multi-task learning is expected to be more beneficial to detect advertorials compared to single task learning. Based on the architecture of multi-task BERT model, we focused on examining the features. We assumed the 7 features as separate classification tasks, and applied multi-task learning on BERT to assess the effectiveness of the features in advertorial detection.

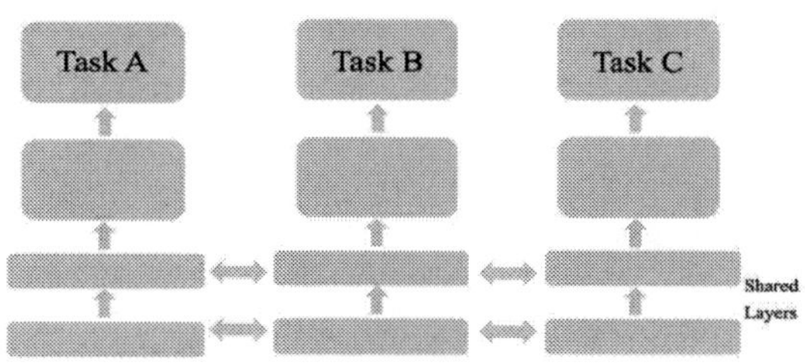

Figure 5: The multi-task BERT model

BERT is a language model based on transformer networks and pre-trained on large corpora. The model uses several multi-head attention layers to learn bidirectional embeddings for input tokens. Some input tokens are masked and the task is to predict a masked word given its context. BERT summed together with positional and segment embeddings using word pieces that passed through an embedding layer (Vaswani et al., 2017; Devlin et al., 2019).

The pre-trained embeddings we used was Chinese-based BERT model (12-layer, 768-hidden, 12-heads, 103M parameters). The model was trained with 10 epochs, with a learning rate set as 5e-5. The loss weight of a linguist task $w \in \{0.1, 0.2, 0.3, 0.4, 0.5, 0.6, 0.7, 0.8, 0.9, 1\}$. After fine-tuning, models have higher performance when w is in the range of [0.3, 0.4]. The performance of the model without involving linguistic features was set as a baseline.

4 Results

Model performances were evaluated with accuracy, precision, recall, and macro F1 score. The comparison of task performances is shown in Table 2.

We applied all the seven contextual features into the model and the result slightly outperforms the baseline. In order to investigate the effectiveness of each contextual feature to the model performance, we further train the model with seven features respectively.

To compare the model performances of adding various contextual features, different statistical measures (e.g., accuracy, precision, recall, and F1-score) are presented in Table 2. The results indicated that all seven features helped improve the performance of the model. Among all the features, (a) setting the scene, (b) product-related activities, (c) the comparison of before and after using the product, (d) detailed product information, (e) product tutorials, and (g) the use of generic-you appeared to be more effective with F1-score higher than 0.90. Moreover, (g) the use of generic-you had the most significant improvement. On the other hand, (f) positive and exaggeration tone did help advertorial detection but were comparatively less effective than the above mentioned. The results indicated that features would have various degrees of different effectiveness influences on model training.

5 Discussion

The results revealed that the features (a) setting the scene, (b) product-related activities, (c) the comparison of before and after using the product, (d) detailed product information, (e) product tutorials, and (g) the use of generic-you may be more effective in advertorial detection. On the

[1] Generic-you are marked in bold type.

Model	Accuracy	Precision	Recall	F1-score
Baseline	0.87	0.87	0.87	0.87
All features	0.88	0.87	0.88	**0.88**
(a) Setting the scene	0.90	0.90	0.91	**0.90**
(b) Product-related activities	0.90	0.90	0.89	**0.90**
(c) The comparison of before and after using the product	0.90	0.91	0.90	**0.90**
(d) Detailed product information	0.90	0.91	0.90	**0.90**
(e) Product tutorials	0.90	0.90	0.90	**0.90**
(f) Positive and exaggeration tone	0.88	0.89	0.87	**0.88**
(g) The use of generic-you	0.91	0.91	0.91	**0.91**

Table 2: The comparison of task performances before and after adding contextual features in model training (Boldfaced numbers represented that F1 scores of the features were higher than baseline.)

other hand, (f) positive and exaggeration tone seems to have less effectiveness in identifying advertorials.

Seven features that are categorized into three schemas will be discussed in the following paragraphs. In the schema *background description,* for the feature (a) setting the scene, advertorials usually set up a scene or simulate a scenario in contrast to non-advertorials which express users' experiences only. This may help build connections between the viewers and the authors, which is consistent with previous studies from Cheung (2010), Zhou (2012), and Stepaniuk and Jarosz (2021).

As to the second schema, *product-related information,* which often requires advertorials to provide sufficient information of products, the feature (b) product-related activities can help distinguish advertorials by involving exclusive information and discounts which are seldom seen in non-advertorials. Another feature (c) the comparison of before and after using the product would be a significant feature to distinguish advertorials. Sponsors especially on Dcard usually recruit users to actually try the products and write review articles. These advertorials often contain the comparison of using the products or not. This kind of comparison can enhance credibility. Other features, (d) detailed product information and (e) product tutorials, can reduce knowledge gaps by effectively communicating this knowledge to the viewers (Burton et al., 2020). Besides, the higher degree of professional knowledge which conveys clear information to their audience can help build credibility and make the information more convincing. The advice about the specific use of the product may aid consumers and allow authors to demonstrate helpfulness and attract more consumers (Forbes, 2016).

Under the third schema, *building connections with the viewers,* the feature (g) the use of generic-you is also commonly seen in advertorials; therefore, it might be a suitable feature to differentiate advertorials from other posts. Generic-you is often used to set a scene or raise a question to build relations with viewers. On the contrary, non-advertorials usually express the authors' own opinions only, which seldom connect to the viewers by using generic-you. This feature is in accordance with previous studies (Fowler, 1991; Kovacic et al., 2011; Orvell et al., 2019). However, the less effective feature (f) positive and exaggeration tone also belongs to the schema *building connections with the viewers.* Positive and exaggerated tone may extract viewers' attention, and the high frequency of emojis and exclamation marks may express the excitement of the authors and thus influence viewers' attitude toward the products. However, people nowadays prefer using lots of emojis to express their emotions even in non-advertorials. Moreover, in the advertorials we collected, to disguise their advertising intentions, the advertorials often avoid using excessive exaggeration tones to be noticed. Therefore, (f) positive and exaggeration tone might be a comparatively less effective feature.

Although in this study, the model trained with all features does not have a higher performance, this might lead to the implementation of the shared layer in the model architecture. Wu et al., (2019) mentioned that since shared features in the shared layer are equally distributed to multi-tasks without filtering, this would introduce noise to the learning process.

We also applied the McNemars' statistical test to compare the performances of the models. It should be noted that the McNemars' test is sensitive to number of counts, and only 156 posts are included in the test set which might bias the result. Although the McNemars' test did not present any significance in our models, the F1-score of the models still indicated that all these independent features may help the model in identifying hidden advertorials.

6 Conclusion

This research has attempted to discover the linguistic features in discourse level which can help identify hidden advertorials in Taiwan Mandarin Chinese. We trained a multi-task BERT model with contextual features based on previous studies and our observations. In general, all the seven contextual features under three schemas mentioned above have enhanced advertorial detection with different degrees of effectiveness.

For future works, larger datasets and other types of genres such as product reviews which are especially difficult to be distinguished from hidden advertorials can be included. Thus, more discourse-level contextual features can be inspected and implemented into machine learning models. Furthermore, different combinations of linguistic features based on schemas can be employed into the models to detect advertorials.

References

American Society of Magazine Editors. (2014). ASME Guidelines for Editors and Publishers. In ASME.

Burton, J. L., Mosteller, J. R., & Hale, K. E. (2020). Using linguistics to inform influencer marketing in services. *Journal of Services Marketing.*

Cameron, G. T., & Haley, J. E. (1992). Feature advertising: Policies and attitudes in print media. *Journal of Advertising, 21*(3), 47-55.

Cheung, M. (2010). The globalization and localization of persuasive marketing communication: A cross-linguistic socio-cultural analysis. *Journal of Pragmatics,42*(2), 354–376.

Cocker, H., Mardon, R., & Daunt, K. L. (2021). Social media influencers and transgressive celebrity endorsement in consumption community contexts. European Journal of Marketing.

Deng, L., Laghari, T., & Gao, X. (2021). A genre-based exploration of intertextuality and interdiscursivity in advertorial discourse. *English for Specific Purposes (New York, N.Y.), 62*, 30–42.

Devlin, J., Chang, M. W., Lee, K., & Toutanova, K. (2018). Bert: Pre-training of deep bidirectional transformers for language understanding. *arXiv preprint arXiv:1810.04805.*

Ellerbach, J. (2004). The advertorial as information pollution. *Journal of information ethics*, 61.

Forbes, K. (2016). Examining the beauty industry's use of social influencers. *Elon Journal of Undergraduate Research in Communications,* 7(2), 78-87.

Fowler, R. (1991). Language in the News. London, New York: Routledge.

Keach Hagey. (2012). Media: The Advertorial's Best Friend --- BuzzFeed Site Relies on

Sponsored Content Shared by Visitors on Social Media. *The Wall Street Journal. Eastern Edition.*

Kim, B. H., Pasadeos, Y., & Barban, A. (2001). On the deceptive effectiveness of labeled and unlabeled advertorial formats. *Mass Communication & Society*, *4*(3), 265-281.

Kovacic, M. P., Erjavec, K., & Stular, K. (2011). Unlabelled advertorials in Slovenian life-style press: A study of the promotion of health products. *Communication & medicine*, *8*(2), 157.

Labrador, B., Ramón, N., Alaiz-Moretón, H., & Sanjurjo-González, H. (2014). Rhetorical structure and persuasive language in the subgenre of online advertisements. English for Specific Purposes (New York, N.Y.), 34(1), 38–47. https://doi.org/10.1016/j.esp.2013.10.002

Liu, X., He, P., Chen, W., & Gao, J. (2019). Multi-task deep neural networks for natural language understanding. *arXiv preprint arXiv:1901.11504*.

Orvell, A., Kross, E., & Gelman, S. A. (2019). "You" and "I" in a foreign land: The persuasive force of generic-you. *Journal of Experimental Social Psychology*, *85*, 103869–. https://doi.org/10.1016/j.jesp.2019.103869

Rožukalne, A. (2012). Significance of hidden advertising of the media business models in Latvia. *Media transformations, 2012, vol. 8, p. 126-150.*

Ruder, S. (2018, October 24). An Overview of Multi-Task Learning for Deep Learning. Sebastian Ruder. https://ruder.io/multi-task/

Stepaniuk, K., & Jarosz, K. (2021). Persuasive linguistic tricks in social media marketing communication—The memetic approach. *PloS One*, *16*(7), e0253983–.

Tuten, T., & Perotti, V. (2019). Lies, brands and social media. Qualitative Market Research: An International Journal.

Vaswani, A., Shazeer, N., Parmar, N., Uszkoreit, J., Jones, L., Gomez, A. N., ... & Polosukhin, I. (2017). Attention is all you need. In *Advances in neural information processing systems* (pp. 5998-6008).

Wu, L., Rao, Y., Jin, H., Nazir, A., & Sun, L. (2019). Different absorption from the same sharing: Sifted multi-task learning for fake news detection. arXiv preprint arXiv:1909.01720.

Zhou, S. (2012). 'Advertorials': A genre-based analysis of an emerging hybridized genre. *Discourse & Communication*, *6*(3), 323-346.

李东昆. (2018). 基于消费心理的饥饿营销策略研究. 中国集体经济, *2*, 66–67.

The 33rd Conference on Computational Linguistics and Speech Processing (ROCLING 2021)
Taoyuan, Taiwan, October 15-16, 2021. The Association for Computational Linguistics and Chinese Language Processing

Automatic Extraction of English Grammar Pattern Correction Rules

Kuan-Yu, Shen
Institute of Information Systems and Applications
National Tsing Hua University
kyshen@nlplab.cc

Yi-Chien, Lin
Department of Foreign Languages and Literature
National Tsing Hua University
nicalin@nlplab.cc

Jason S. Chang
Department of Computer Science
National Tsing Hua University
jason@nlplab.cc

Abstract

We introduce a method for creating error-correction rules for grammar pattern errors in a given annotated learner corpus. In our approach, annotated edits in the learner corpus are converted into edit rules for correcting common writing errors. The method involves automatic extraction of grammar patterns, and automatic alignment of the erroneous patterns and correct patterns. At run-time, grammar patterns are extracted from the grammatically correct sentences, and correction rules are retrieved by aligning the extracted grammar patterns with the erroneous patterns. Using the proposed method, we generate 1,499 high-quality correction rules related to 232 headwords. The correction rules are tested and about 36% of the essays are improved by applying these rules. The method can be used to assist ESL students in avoiding grammatical errors, and aid teachers in correcting students' essays. Additionally, the method can be used in the compilation of collocation error dictionaries and the construction of grammar error correction systems.

Keywords: grammar patterns, edit rules, pattern alignment, pattern extraction

1 Introduction

The importance of using correct grammar patterns is directly associated with the proficiency level of a language learner. English proficiency tests aiming at learners of English as a second language (ESL) such as TOEIC and TOEFL both include questions that require the examinee to have accurate knowledge on grammar patterns.

However, grammar patterns pose a great barrier to ESL learners for its inconsistency. For instance, "*talk about an issue*" is a grammatically correct phrase, while "*discuss about an issue*" is grammatically incorrect and should be corrected into "discuss an issue" . Hence, researches on the detection and correction of grammar pattern errors have been conducted with computational approaches.

Grammar patterns are rules that describe how words are used. A grammar pattern tells us the correct combination of a clause or phrase with a given verb, noun, or adjective. For instance, the verb discuss could be used with a prepositional phrase with with (*discuss with the manager*) or with a one noun phrase (*discuss the issue*).

Our goal is to convert the erroneous sentence into edit rules in the form of part of speech tags. For the example above, the correction of "*discuss about an issue*" to "*discuss an issue*" would be express as "*V about n* $\rightarrow$ *V n*" . By leveraging an annotated learner corpus Education First - Cambridge Open Language Database (EFCAMDAT) Geertzen et al. (2013) Huang et al. (2018), we retrieve the editing process and the frequency of the error being made. We automatically extract the grammar patterns from the sentences, which patterns are provided by Collins Dictionary of Grammar Patterns.

This paper focuses on the algorithm of converting sentences with verb grammar pattern errors into edit rules. Our method successfully extracts 1,499 common grammar pattern errors over 232 headwords with a basic threshold of frequency above 10.

Comparing to the corpus of Longman Dictionary of Common Errors (Turton and Heaton, 1996), our result specifically focuses on the errors of grammar pattern and express the correction rules in a cleaner format. The correction rules constructed by our method are being experimented in a situation mimicking a teacher correcting a learner' s essay. The result shows that about 36% of the essays contain errors that could be corrected by the rules.

The remaining of this paper would be organized as follows: Section 2 gives a background of previous works related to grammar pattern error correction. Section 3 presents our proposed method and the corpus used. Section 4 shows our experimental results and evaluation among other methods. Finally, section 5 provides a conclusion and insights for future studies.

2 Related Works

Grammatical error correction is an extensively studied topic. Numerous works have been conducted through rule-based and statistical approaches, specifically focus on the correction of prepositional errors written by ESL learners.

For rule-based approaches, Eeg-Olofsson and Knutsson (2003) defines a set of rules for detecting word, phrase, and prepositional errors in Swedish text. Bender et al. (2004) develops strategies regarding syntactic rules to reconstruct erroneous sentences into correct sentences. These approaches rely heavily on designed rules which require the time and labor of linguistic experts.

Statistical methods have been widely used due to the emerging of large text databases. Researchers apply statistical methods to correct prepositional errors in articles written by ESL learners. Sun et al. (2007) builds a classifier to identify erroneous and correct sentences. The features of the classifier, Labeled Sequential Patterns, are common patterns that indicate the errors or correctness of a sentence, which are closely related to grammar patterns. Brockett et al. (2006) uses phrasal Statistical Machine Translation (SAT) techniques to identify and correct writing errors made by learners. The proposed model maps small phrasal *"treelets"* generated by dependency parsing to grammatically correct strings, allowing the input erroneous sentence to be slightly ungrammatical, which is a typical feature of ESL learners.

Combining rule-based and statistical approaches, Chodorow et al. (2007) combines maximum entropy classifier and rule-based filters to detect preposition errors of student essays. The classifier is trained with contextual features regarding the Part-Of-Speech tags adjacent to the prepositions.

Recently, Huang et al. (2010) describes a framework to extract correction rules by calculating Levenshtein distance between correct and erroneous sentences. The framework is language independent and does not take linguistic features into account. Chen et al. (2017) considers grammar pattern and the semantic category of noun phrases while extracting the correction rules, establishing a writing suggestion system for language learners.

3 Method

Since we are interested in the edit rules for grammar pattern errors, we utilize a learner corpus with annotated edit process EFCAMDAT. The annotations of the corpus are corrections made by English experts. The corpus provides 2,300,000 sentences with annotations. We obtain the original sentences and the corrected sentences from the corpus, in which the former are assumed to be grammatically incorrect, and the latter to be grammatically correct. Since we are interested in grammar pattern errors, among all the edit tags that show the error type, we reserve only the ones with *XC (change of word)*, *D (deletion of word)*, *IS (insertion of word)*, *MW (missing of word)*, *PR (prepositional error)*, or *WC (word choice error)* tags. These tags are chosen for they are more relevant to grammar patterns (Geertzen et al., 2013) (Huang et al., 2018).

Our method could then be divided into two parts: Grammar pattern extraction and optimal alignment. After achieving the pairwise edit rules, a threshold could be set to improve the quality.

3.1 Extracting grammar patterns

Our grammar pattern data are taken from Collins COBUILD of Grammar Patterns[1], which provides up to 145 grammar patterns for verb. Collins COBUILD of Grammar Patterns is based on corpus research carried out by lexicographers, which lists all the grammar patterns used in English, and all the words regularly used with a given pattern.

We extract grammar patterns from the grammatically correct sentences. First, we merge each noun phrase into one single token by constituency parsing, and then perform part-of-speech tagging on all the tokens. We convert the tags of the tokens into a simplified form that adapts to our grammar pattern data. The conversion rules are manually written to adapt to the tool used for part-of-speech tagging and the grammar pattern data, which, in our experiment, SpaCy and Collins COBUILD of Grammar Patterns are used.

Grammar patterns are detected by sequence matching. The tokens of the grammatically correct sentence are iterated, and multiple patterns could be detected in a single phrase. An example of the whole process of grammar pattern extraction is provided (Table 1).

3.2 Aligning original and edited patterns

Since we had the edited grammar patterns of a given sentence, we then need to retrieve its unedited form to obtain the common grammar pattern errors. We use a dynamic programming approach *pairwise sequence alignment* to retrieve the unedited forms.

In pairwise sequence alignment algorithm, two sequences are aligned with the least cost (or highest score). In our approach, the first sequence is the extracted grammar pattern, while the other is a 5-gram phrase extracted from the unedited sentence, starting from the location of the grammar pattern's headword.

[1]https://grammar.collinsdictionary.com/grammar-pattern

Three conditions occurred in pairwise sequence alignment algorithm: gap, mismatch, and match. A gap indicates that a token of a sequence does not align to any token of another sequence. A mismatch indicates that a token of a sequence does align to a token of another sequence, but the two tokens are not identical. A match indicates that a token of a sequence is aligned to a token of another sequence, and the two tokens are identical. In our approach, gaps or mismatches acquire no score, and a match acquires 1 score. Pairwise sequences with scores below 2 are discarded.

After alignment, to ensure only one editorial occurred in a pairwise rule, tokens of both sequences are iterated simultaneously. This time, gaps or mismatches acquires -1 score, and a match acquires 1 score. We retrieve the pairwise pair with the highest score at the maximum length possible.

4 Results & evaluation

Using EFCAMDAT and Collins COBUILD as our reference data, our method successfully achieves 1,499 correction rules over 232 headwords with the basic threshold of frequency above 10. The usage of grammar pattern ensures the extracted patterns to be correct and meaningful. Threshold and reference data could be adjusted as needed. Table 2 shows part of our result.

Edit rules achieved from our method are pairwise, consist of common grammar pattern errors and their corrections. Our result clearly gives the headword, frequency, and examples of the edit rules.

Comparing to the Longman Dictionary of Common Errors, the rules are more explicit and concise and with much more examples, which could be utilized conveniently for further research and applications. Additionally, our result focuses on grammar pattern errors, while the Longman Dictionary of Common Errors covers all sorts of common errors, including word choice, spelling errors, and tense errors.

We examine the correction rules by providing the rules as suggestions for the corrector while correcting the essays written by ESL learners. The essays are provided by the ETS Corpus of Non-Native Written English, Lin-

Original sentence	Give	the elegant present	to	Tom	.
Merging noun-phrase	Give	<NP>	to	<NP>	.
POS tagging	VB	NNP	PREP	NNP	.
Simplifying the tags	V	N	to	N	.
Extracted pattern	(give, V n to n, 0), (give, V n, 0)				

Table 1: Process of grammar pattern extraction. Two grammar patterns are extracted for the given phrase. The three columns of the final output indicate the headword, the grammar pattern, and the location of the headword in the original sentence

Headword	Edit Rule	Freq.
graduate	V at n → V from n	124
graduate	V n → V from n	482
graduate	V in n → V from n	295
call	V to n → V n	390
call	V for n → V n	101
call	V n → V for n	12
ask	V n → V for n	533
ask	V for n → V n	138
ask	V to n → V n	303
talk	V with n → V to n	256
talk	V to n → V on n	217
talk	V n → V to n	385
talk	V n → V on n	156
talk	V n → V about n	119
introduce	V n for n → V n to n	45
introduce	V n n → V n to n	63
discuss	V about n → V n	144
discuss	V with n → V n	17
thank	V for n → V n	118
thank	V for n → V n for n	89
thank	V quote n → V n	61

Table 2: Example of our result.

guistic Data Consortium (LDC). Learners are divided into three categories due to their English proficiency level. We randomly select ten essays for each category and let our English expert correct these essays with the help of our correction rules, aiming to mimic the situation of a teacher correcting students' essays.

For low proficiency level, 50% of the essays contain errors that are correctable by our correction rules, 20% for medium, and 40% for high proficiency level respectively. In general, 36% of essays are correctable by using our correction rules. Our result shows that the correction rules extracted by our method assist the process of correcting learners' essays.

Few of the corrected sentences from the high proficiency level category are shown below:

- **Original sentence:** They cannot attend *to* the social events or community services which generally take place in the cities.
- **Corrected sentence:** They cannot attend the social events or community services which generally take place in the cities.

The sentence above applies the rule *"attend, V to N → V N"*, while the following sentence applies the rule *"spend, V N for N → V N on N"*.

- **Original sentence:** Moreover, students now have to spend too much time *for* preparing for this hard education in order to be successful.
- **Corrected sentence:** Moreover, students now have to spend too much time *on* preparing for this hard education in order to be successful.

5 Conclusion

Our method could be easily adjusted to adapt on different reference data. By combining various annotated learner corpus, the quantity and quality of correction rules could be larger and higher. The result could be used to assist ESL students in avoiding grammatical errors, and aid teachers in correcting students' essays. Additionally, it could be used in the compilation of collocation error dictionaries and the construction of grammar error correction systems. Our pattern extraction algorithm could be used independently for corpus researches (Lin and Shen, 2021). From linguistic aspect of view, the choice of preposition usually depends on the semantic category of the following noun. Future works could be conducted to investigate the relationship between prepositions and the semantic category of adjacent nouns and verbs.

References

Emily Bender, Dan Flickinger, Stephan Oepen, Annemarie Walsh, and Timothy Baldwin. 2004. Arboretum: Using a precision grammar for grammar checking in call.

Chris Brockett, William Dolan, and Michael Gamon. 2006. Correcting esl errors using phrasal SMT techniques.

Jhih-Jie Chen, Jim Chang, Yang Ching-Yu, Mei-Hua Chen, and Jason S. Chang. 2017. Extracting formulaic expressions and grammar and edit patterns to assist academic writing. In *Proceedings of EUROPHRAS 2017, Computational and Corpus-based Phraseology: Recent advances and interdisciplinary approaches*, pages 95–103, London, UK. Tradulex.

Martin Chodorow, Joel Tetreault, and Na-Rae Han. 2007. Detection of grammatical errors involving prepositions. In *Proceedings of the Fourth ACL-SIGSEM Workshop on Prepositions*, pages 25–30, Prague, Czech Republic. Association for Computational Linguistics.

Jens Eeg-Olofsson and Ola Knutsson. 2003. Automatic grammar checking for second language learners —the use of prepositions.

J. Geertzen, T. Alexopoulou, and A. Korhonen. 2013. Automatic linguistic annotation oflarge scale l2 databases: The ef-cambridge open language database(efcamdat). In *Selected Proceedings of the 31st Second Language Research Forum (SLRF)*, Cascadilla Press, MA.

Anta Huang, Tsung-Ting Kuo, Ying-Chun Lai, and Shou-de Lin. 2010. Identifying correction rules for auto editing. In *ROCLING 2010 Poster Papers*, pages 251–265, Nantou, Taiwan. The Association for Computational Linguistics and Chinese Language Processing (ACLCLP).

Y. Huang, A. Murakami, T. Alexopoulou, and A. Korhonen. 2018. Dependency parsing of learner english. international journal of corpus linguistics. In *International Journal of Corpus Linguistics*.

Fu-Ying Lin and Kuan-Yu Shen. 2021. Features of the spoken academic english (of MOOCs): take the grammar patterns of verbs as an example. In *Corpus Linguistics International Conference 2021*.

Guihua Sun, Xiaohua Liu, Gao Cong, Ming Zhou, Zhongyang Xiong, FGFH EWR, and Chin-Yew Lin. 2007. Detecting erroneous sentences using automatically mined sequential patterns. In *Annual Meeting-Association for Computational Linguistics*, volume 45.

ND Turton and JB Heaton. 1996. *Longman Dictionary of Common Errors (New Ed)*. Longman, England.

The 33rd Conference on Computational Linguistics and Speech Processing (ROCLING 2021)
Taoyuan, Taiwan, October 15-16, 2021. The Association for Computational Linguistics and Chinese Language Processing

運用超圖注意力網路於中文幽默文本多標籤分類
Multi-Label Classification of Chinese Humor Texts Using Hypergraph Attention Networks

高浩銓 [1] Hao-Chuan Kao[1], 洪滿珍 [1] Man-Chen Hung[1],
李龍豪 [1] Lung-Hao Lee[1], 曾元顯 [2] Yuen-Hsien Tseng[2]
[1] 國立中央大學 電機工程學系
[2] 國立臺灣師範大學 圖書資訊學研究所
[1]Department of Electrical Engineering, National Central University
[2]Graduate Institute of Library & Information Studies, National Taiwan Normal University
{108521098, 109521068}@ncu.edu.tw, lhlee@ee.ncu.edu.tw, samtseng@ntnu.edu.tw

摘要

我們運用超圖注意力網路 (HyperGAT) 模型來辨識中文幽默文本的多重類別，文本以超圖表示，並用順序超邊和語意超邊構建超邊結構，接著使用注意力機制取得語境資訊，最後預測文本的多標籤分類。我們在中文幽默多標籤資料集比較模型效能，無論哪個評測指標，HyperGAT 模型皆優於其他基於序列 (CNN, BiLSTM, FastText) 和基於圖形 (Graph-CNN, TextGCN, Text Level GNN) 的深度學習模型。

Abstract

We use Hypergraph Attention Networks (HyperGAT) to recognize multiple labels of Chinese humor texts. We firstly represent a joke as a hypergraph. The sequential hyperedge and semantic hyperedge structures are used to construct hyperedges. Then, attention mechanisms are adopted to aggregate context information embedded in nodes and hyperedges. Finally, we use trained HyperGAT to complete the multi-label classification task. Experimental results on the Chinese humor multi-label dataset showed that HyperGAT model outperforms previous sequence-based (CNN, BiLSTM, FastText) and graph-based (Graph-CNN, TextGCN, Text Level GNN) deep learning models.

關鍵字：超圖神經網路、幽默辨識、多重分類
Keywords: hypergraph neural networks, humor recognition, multi-label classification.

1 介紹

幽默是指令人感到好笑、高興或滑稽的言行舉止，有助於幫助化解敵意、緩和摩擦與安慰他人，也是人際交往的重要溝通的元素。在商業應用中，幽默的溝通可以消除用戶的抱怨 (Bellegarda, 2014; Binsted, 1995)。在教育方面，Bryant & Zillmann (1989) 和 Mcghee & Frank (2014) 研究發現課堂上適當的使用幽默，可以吸引學生的注意力並改善課堂互動，幫助學生在樂趣中能夠有更好的學習成效。在高壓的環境下，像是在公共場合發表演講時，幽默可以幫助演講者減輕焦慮並提升他們的表現。除此之外，廣告、娛樂等商業領域也是幽默應用的領域。

幽默的內容可能包含挑戰社會規範或禁忌、攻擊或嘲諷人或事物，又或是用來安慰他人的元素。這些內容可以引發不同的情感 (例如：釋放自我約束，或是增加個人優越感)，從而化解內部壓力並產生愉悅感。隨著科技進步，人類的對話系統介面或聊天機器人變得更廣泛使用，將幽默引入人機交流之中變得非常重要。因此，我們運用機器學習來辨識人類產生幽默的話語。

幽默辨識 (humor recognition) 本質上是一個多標籤分類問題，因為一則笑話可能屬於多個意向或動機，也可能屬於多個建構類別。因此，我們運用 Kaize et al. (2020) 所提出的超圖注意力神經網路模型 (Hypergraph Attention Network, HyperGAT) 來辨識人類幽默文本的多重類別。藉由超圖注意力網路找出字詞與

句子的關聯，並用超邊聚合結構與邊層級注意力，建構超邊與獲得上下文信息，用以預測文本的多標籤結果。在中文幽默多標籤資料集 (Tseng et al., 2020)，我們採用的 HyperGAT 模型可以達到 Macro F1-score 0.2419 、Micro F1-score 0.4695、Weighted F1-score 0.4084 與 Subset Accuracy 0.1215，整體效能皆優於其他相關研究模型。

本文章節如下，第二章探討相關研究，第三章敘述我們使用的超圖神經網路模型架構，第四章為模型效能評估，最後是結論。

2 相關研究

2.1 中文幽默種類

在創造笑話時會運用一些幽默的技巧， Chen et al. (2017) 研究發現大多數建構笑話的方法類別與心理學上的不協調有關。建構笑話的方法分為八種，分別是雙重含義、誇飾法、擬人化、聯繫性推論、缺乏邏輯、諷刺、模仿和其他技巧。說明如下：

(1) 雙重含義：雙重意味著不只一種解釋文本的方法，其中一種是隱藏在普遍能意會到的解釋方式，而一旦發現另一個解釋方式，就會產生一種幽默的感覺。雙重含義有同音異義詞、雙關語、語義學、語法和短語等類型。例如：女員工：「老闆，您必須幫我加薪，已經有三家公司在找我了！」老闆：「哪三家？」員工：「自來水公司，台電，天然氣公司。」

(2) 誇飾法：是指將情境或描述的層次最大化，以打動人們或表達創造力。例如：某醫生在家接到同事電話：「打麻將，三缺一！」醫生說：「我馬上來！」妻子在旁邊問：「情況嚴重嗎？」醫生嚴肅地說：「很嚴重，已有三位醫生在那了。」

(3) 擬人化：是指將人類的特徵套用在非人事或事件上的解釋。例如：「0 認為自己是一個優雅的人。當她遇見 8 時，她批評 8 是一個戴腰帶的假胖子。」

(4) 聯繫性推論：隱含著不同角度的關聯，以有趣的方式用哏給讀者/聽眾帶來驚喜。例如：妻子：「你很少在外面喝酒，你為什麼在家喝很多酒？」丈夫：「有人告訴我酒精讓我勇敢。(沒有酒精而要面對妻子太可怕了。)」

(5) 不合邏輯：在錯誤的情況下，使用合乎邏輯的方式，來嘲笑一個人的愚蠢或行為。例如：「我的妻子總是鼓勵我盡力而為，所以我盡我所能使她放棄讓我做所有的家務。」

(6) 諷刺：描述與預期相反的消極/積極的情況。例如：「我窮得只剩下錢。」

(7) 模仿：按照設置情景的邏輯來做一個相似的情景。例如：「一個好的配偶是你在暴風雨中休息的港灣；糟糕的配偶是港口的暴風。」

(8) 其他技巧：不能歸入以上七類的，像是俗諺或語錄。例如：「什麼手術可以把眼睛變成耳朵？(讀唇技術)」

另外，根據 Chen et al. (2017) 所提出的觀點，笑話的意圖可以分為六類，分別為親和力、自我提升、攻擊、自我抑鬱、禁忌和其他動機。介紹如下：

(1) 親和力：扭轉局面，用友好和善的話語擺脫尷尬，使別人感到安慰，或是說一些有趣和輕鬆的事情，讓彼此更親近或緩解團隊中的衝突。例如：「大家都希望有個和平的世界，但我只想要你的世界。」

(2) 自我提升：接受糟糕的情況並改變觀點或自我鼓勵，讓自己打起精神來面對問題，這是一種幽默的應對方式。例如：「如果長得好看是一種罪，那我就是有罪。」

(3) 攻擊：透過嘲笑別人的缺點讓自己開心，說別人的缺點或刁難的話，或是讓別人感到不舒服使其降低自己在群體的地位。例如：「我已經等了一個小時的餐點了，廚師是睡著了嗎？」

(4) 自我抑鬱：用自嘲的方式來取悅他人，例如：「我無意犯下天生醜陋的罪刑。」

(5) 禁忌：嘲笑與性、死亡、排泄物、被禁止的行為或思想有關的事物。例如：「18 歲少女 20 年前離奇失蹤。」

(6) 其他意圖：不能歸入上述五類的。

2.2 多標籤文本分類

多標籤文本分類 (Multi-Label Text Classification) 是一種多重分類，各文本可能同時屬於幾個預先定義的標籤。不同於多元文本分類任務 (Multi-Class Text Classification) 標籤是互斥的，多標籤分類的每個標籤可以來自不同的分類任務，而標籤在某種程度上是相關的。

近年來，各種基於神經網路的模型被用於多標籤文本分類任務中。卷積神經網路 (Convolutional Neural Network, CNN) 最早使用於圖像分類，運用卷積濾波器 (filters) 提取圖片特徵，可以同時將不同核 (kernel) 定義的卷積應用於序列的多個區塊，大大提升了影像辨識的表現。CNN 應用於文字上是將輸入文本的詞向量拼接成矩陣，再將矩陣送入卷積層(convolution layer)，該層包含多個不同維度的濾波器。最後，卷積層的輸出經過池化層 (pooling layer) 將池化結果拼接起來，得到文本的最終向量表示，並預測文本歸屬的標籤。Yoon Kim (2014) 所提出的 TextCNN 模型使用無偏差值 (bias) 的 CNN，它可以通過一層卷積，更好地決定最大池化層中有區別性的詞語，並將詞向量保持靜態以學習除了詞向量之外的超參數。

長短期記憶 (Long Short Term Memory, LSTM) 模型加入了遺忘閘、更新閘、輸出閘三個控制閘來強化記憶的儲存與使用，提升了其在長期記憶中的表現。但是利用 LSTM 對句子進行模型的運算，無法編碼從後到前的語意資訊，雙向長短期記憶 (Bidirectional LSTM, BiLSTM) 模型，便是由前向 LSTM 與後向 LSTM 組合而成，通過前後的結合可以捕獲更好的雙向語義依賴。

FastText (Joulin et al., 2016) 是一個開源資料庫，由 Facebook 人工智能研究實驗室開發，它的目標是簡單且快速地完成文本分類任務，並且有詞向量的訓練生成。它的結構類似於 Word2Vec 中的 CBOW 架構，通過一個全連接層將句子特徵映射到向量空間，再直接對詞向量進行平均進行預測。模型當中使用 Huffman 演算法建立用於表徵類別的樹形結構以加速運算，並用 n-gram 的特徵加強句子的表達。

Graph-CNN (Defferrard et al., 2016) 利用柴比雪夫多項式 (Chebyshev polynomials) 來近似擬合卷積核，來解決起初基於拉普拉斯 (Laplace) 及傅立葉 (Fourier) 的圖形卷積網路 (Graph Convolutional Network, GCN) 的缺點。

TextGCN (Yao et al., 2019) 是使用圖卷積神經網路 (GCN) 為整個資料集建構了一個基於文本和詞的異質 (heterogeneous) 圖，可以用來取得全局詞的共現信息，使 GCN 能夠對文本進行半監督分類。

Text Level GCN (Huang et al., 2019) 為每個輸入的文本建構獨立，但具有全局參數共享的圖，而不是為整個訓練、測試語料庫建立一個巨大的單圖，並透過滑動窗口 (sliding-window) 來構建圖形，當中可以設定 n 元語法 (n-gram) 的數量，用以提取更多的局部特徵，並減少大量的計算資源，這也是使圖神經網路能夠從已有的資料中歸納出模式，並應用於新的資料與任務。

總而言之，基於序列的方法 (sequence-based methods) 有 CNN、LSTM、BiLSTM 和 FastText。而基於圖形的方法 (graph-based methods)有 Graph-CNN, TextGCN 和 Text-Level-GNN。我們採用的超圖注意力網路，也是一種圖神經網路模型。

3 實驗方法

我們使用的模型架構是超圖注意力網路 (Hypergraph Attention Netwoks, HyperGAT) (Kaize et al., 2020)，在此章節之中，我們會介紹如何將文本以超圖表示，並用兩種方式構建超邊結構，接著使用注意力機制在超邊與節點上，捕獲文本上下文信息，最後預測文本的多標籤分類結果。

3.1 圖表示

超圖 (hypergraph) 是一種圖的結構，可以將其定義為G： = (N, E)，N = $\{n_1, n_2, \ldots, n_v\}$ 為超圖中的節點 (node)，E = $\{e_1, e_2, \ldots, e_m\}$ 為超圖中的超邊 (hyperedge)，其中對於每個超邊 e，可以連結兩個或兩個以上的節點 n，即 $\sigma(e) \geq 2$。超圖 G 中的拓樸結構 (topological structure) 亦可以表示為關聯矩陣(Incidence matrix) A ∈ $R^{v \times m}$，其中 v 是節點數量，m 是超邊數量，定義如下：

$$A_{ij} = \begin{cases} 1, if\ n_i \in e_j \\ 0, if\ n_i \notin e_j \end{cases} \quad (1)$$

我們將實驗資料中每一篇文本，建立成獨立的超圖結構，為了考慮超圖結構中每個單一節點的屬性，把文本中的單詞 (token) 作為超圖中的節點後，需要先初始化節點的屬性。

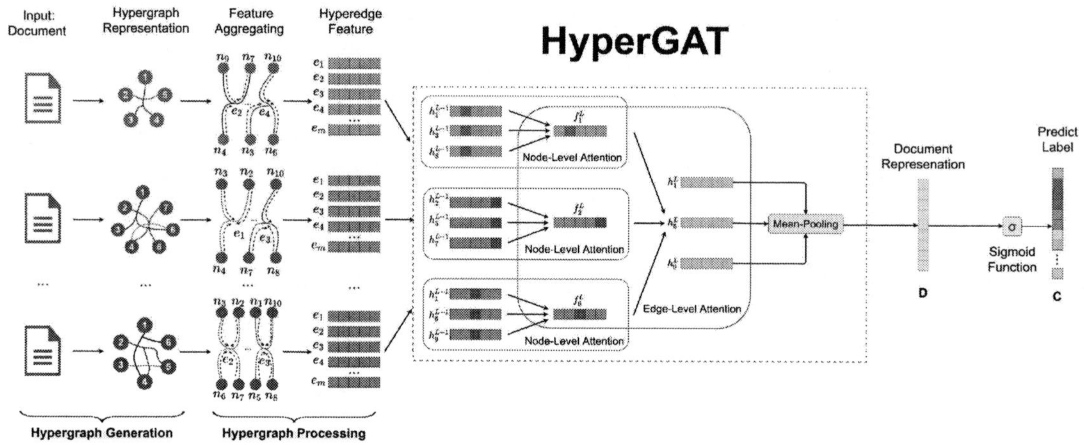

圖 1: 超圖注意力網路 (HyperGAT) 模型架構

將每個節點定義成維度 d 的向量，並以矩陣 $X = [x_1, x_2, \ldots, x_n]^T \in R^{n \times d}$ 來表示所有的節點屬性，其中 n 是節點數量，d 是節點屬性之維度，並以 $G = (A, X)$ 表示整個超圖結構。

3.2 超邊聚合結構

為了捕獲文本之中，高階全局之上下文信息，我們使用兩種多關係超邊，分別是順序超邊跟語意超邊。

3.2.1 順序超邊 (sequential hyperedge)

文本中的語句是有順序性的，透過上下文我們可以知道文字之間，局部共同出現的語言特徵。為了利用每個詞的順序信息，我們需要為資料中的每個文本建構順序超邊：將每個文本中的句子，使用標點符號分隔，並將其視為超邊，此超邊結構稱為順序超邊，它連接了句子中的所有詞，如此一來，能使模型捕獲整個文本每個句子的結構信息。

3.2.2 語意超邊 (semantic hyperedge)

除了文本的順序信息，我們也希望能找到詞的語意信息。在本模型中，我們使用隱含狄利克雷分布 (Latent Dirichlet allocation, LDA) (Blei et al., 2003) 去建構語意超邊，將文本文檔中的潛在主題 T 找出之後，每個主題 $t_i = (\theta_1, \theta_2, \ldots, \theta_w\}$ 可以表示成單詞的機率分佈，w 為詞彙量的大小。接著我們將每個主題中機率最大的前 K 個單詞連接成語意超邊，通過這些與主題相關的超邊，取得單詞與主題的相關性，能夠豐富每個詞彙的語意訊息。

3.3 超圖注意力網路層

為了有效的聚合文本超圖中的超邊與節點，我們使用超圖注意力網路層訓練模型。本層使用兩種不同的注意力聚合方法，分別是節點層級注意力 (node-level attention) 以及邊層級注意力 (edge-level attention)。$AGGR^l_{node}$ 是節點聚合函數，將節點的特徵聚合到超邊；$AGGR^l_{edge}$ 是另一個聚合函數，將超邊的特徵聚合到節點。兩種注意力聚合方式的定義如方程式(2)和(3)：

$$\mathrm{f}^l_j = AGGR^l_{node}(\{h^{l-1}_k | \forall n_k \in e_j\}) \quad (2)$$

$$\mathrm{h}^l_i = AGGR^l_{edge}(h^{l-1}_i, \{f^l_j | \forall e_j \in E_i\}) \quad (3)$$

其中，E_i 為連接到節點 n_i 的超邊集合、f^l_j 是超邊 e_j 在 l 層中的表示、 h^l_i 是節點 i 在 l 層的節點表示，一般將初始化向量 x_i 作為首層 h^0_i 之節點特徵。方程式(2)與(3)的細項分別於 3.3.1 小節與 3.3.2 小節做介紹。

3.3.1 節點層級注意力

我們將特定的節點標示為 n_i、超邊標示為 e_j，並將所有的超邊集合表示為 $e_j \in E_i$，由於每個超邊中的節點對超邊的重要程度不盡相同，我們使用注意力機制來強調那些對超邊意義較為重要的節點，將其聚合 (aggregate) 之後計算超邊表示 f^i_j：

$$f_j^i = \sigma(\sum_{n_k \in e_j} \alpha_{jk} W_1 h_k^{l-1}) \tag{4}$$

其中 σ 是非線性函數 ReLU、 W_1是可以訓練的權重矩陣、α_{jk}為節點 n_k 與超邊 e_j的注意力參數，並用以下方式去做計算：

$$\alpha_{jk} = \frac{\exp(a_1^T u_k)}{\sum_{n_p \in e_j} \exp(a_1^T u_p)} \tag{5}$$

$$u_k = \text{LeakyReLU}(W_1 h_k^{l-1}) \tag{6}$$

其中 a_1^T是權重向量，亦可以說是上下文向量。注意力當中使用的激勵函數為 LeakyReLU。

3.3.2 邊層級注意力

將節點信息傳遞至超邊後，為了強調那些較具有資訊的超邊，我們將所有超邊 $\{f_j^l | \forall e_j \in E_i\}$ 應用邊層級的注意力 (edge-level attention) 機制，將信息繼續傳播給下一層節點 n_i。過程如下：

$$h_i^l = \sigma(\sum_{e_j \in E_i} \beta_{ij} W_2 f_j^l) \tag{7}$$

其中 h_i^l 是節點 n_i的輸出表示、 W_2是可以訓練的權重矩陣、 β_{ij}為超邊e_j與節點 n_i的注意力參數，並用以下方式去做計算：

$$\beta_{ij} = \frac{\exp(a_2^T v_j)}{\sum_{e_p \in E_i} \exp(a_2^T v_p)} \tag{8}$$

$$v_j = \text{LeakyReLU}([W_2 f_j^l || W_1 h_i^{l-1}]) \tag{9}$$

其中， a_2^T 是另一個權重(上下文)向量用以計算超邊的重要程度，而「‖」符號為串接(concatenation)的操作。注意力當中使用的激勵函數為 LeakyReLU。

以上提出的雙重注意力機制，可以使超圖注意力網路層不僅能取得單詞間的交互關係，還可以在節點表示的學習過程中，強調顯示不同精細度的關鍵信息。

3.4 歸納文本分類

對於每個文本，經過單個超圖注意力網路層後，我們能夠計算構建的文本超圖上的所有節點表示。然後，我們將學習到的節點表示使用均值池化 (mean-pooling) 的操作，以獲得文本表示 z，並將其饋送到 sigmoid 層進行多標籤文本分類：

$$\hat{y} = \text{sigmoid}(W_c z + b_c) \tag{10}$$

其中 W_c 是將文檔表示映射到輸出空間的參數矩陣，b_c是偏差(bias)。 $\hat{y}$ 表示預測的標籤機率。最後，多標籤文本分類的損失函數定義為交叉熵損失：

$$L = \sum_{c=1}^{C} y^c \log(\sigma(\hat{y}^c)) + (1 - y^c) \log(1 - \sigma(\hat{y}^c)) \tag{11}$$

其中 C 為標籤數，我們假設文本的真實標籤是 $y \in R^C$，其中 $y^i = \{0, 1\}$ 表示第 i標籤是否存在。

我們使用的 HyperGAT 模型，對於新加入的測試文本可以直接將它們對應生成的文本超圖，提供給先前訓練好的模型預測它們的標籤，解決了訓練期間需要對測試文本的強制訪問，讓模型可以用歸納 (inductive) 的方式處理新添加的數據，而不是重新訓練模型。

4 效能評估

4.1 實驗資料

我們使用的實驗資料為中文幽默多標籤資料集 (Tseng et al., 2020)，資料來源為網路蒐集的笑話，經由人工標記類別標籤後分別是：雙關、誇飾、擬人化、僑介推論、法則誤用、悖理、模仿、其他技巧、親和、自我提昇、攻擊、自我貶抑、 禁忌以及其他意圖，總共有 14 個標籤。資料集文本總數是 3,365 則笑話，平均字數是 114.47、平均詞數是 76.98，標籤總數是 7,227，每篇文章平均 2.15 個標籤。

4.2 實驗設定

在將資料輸入進模型前，我們先將笑話以 ckiptagger 系統進行斷詞，並將斷詞後的結果作為模型的輸入。每個實驗會執行 k-fold cross-validation (k 值取 5) 以確保模型訓練的可信度，我們使用的 HyperGAT 模型參數值設置如下：潛在主題抽取 T 為標籤數量 14；而機率最大的前 K 個單詞設定為 10；批次大小 (batch size) 的大小設定為 8；學習率 (learning rate) 設定為 0.005；epoch 取 10；文本表示起

Method	Macro F1-score	Micro F1-score	Weighted F1-score	Subset Accuracy
CNN (Yoon, 2014)	13.95	45.83	32.30	7.88
BiLSTM (Liu et al., 2016)	12.42	46.29	33.28	8.50
FastText (Joulin et al., 2016)	21.92	46.20	40.50	13.16
Graph-CNN (Defferrard et al., 2016)	21.27	40.64	39.54	8.44
TextGCN (Yao et al., 2019)	21.27	38.78	37.33	9.45
Text Level GNN (Huang et al., 2019)	22.42	44.48	40.55	12.78
Our used model (HyperGAT)	**24.19**	**46.95**	**40.84**	**12.15**

表 1: 中文幽默多標籤分類資料集的實驗結果

始向量是 300 維的隨機向量而文本表示之最後一層隱藏層維度為 100；L2 正規化懲罰 (L2 penalty) 參數設定為 1e-6；dropout rate 設定為 0.3 以防止過擬合 (overfitting)。

4.3 評估方法

多標籤文本分類的結果是一篇文本不僅僅只有單一標籤，無法單純的以二元的方法評估。目前主要的評估方法需要計算出每一個類別的 F1-score，根據不同的方式綜合各個標籤的 F1-score 以評估多標籤分類器的效能。其中最常見的是 Macro F1-score，將所有標籤視為平等，計算方式是將各標籤的 F1-score 先計算出來之後，再取其平均值，此評估方法提升樣本數較少的類別對分類器性能評估之影響。Micro F1-score 先計算所有類別加總的 Precision 和 Recall，然後再計算兩者的調合平均 F1，此評估方法會使樣本數較多之類別對性能評估的影響較大。Weighted F1-score 也是需要先將各標籤的 F1，根據每個標籤真實樣本的數量，賦予每個標籤不同的權重，是一種類似加權平均的 F1-score。最後，Subset Accuracy 是最嚴格的指標，表示所有標籤都正確的樣本百分比，舉凡有一個標籤分類錯誤，則 Subset Accuracy 不將其判斷為正確結果。

4.4 模型比較

表 1 為的實驗結果。 在基於序列的方法之中，CNN 表現比 BiLSTM 來得好。CNN 以不同的核定義的卷積，來抽取序列單詞中的多個區塊信息，並透過池化層將結果拼接起來，可以得到比 BiLSTM 模型較好的文本表示結果。FastText 是繼 Word2Vec (Mikolov et al.,2013) 與 GloVe (Pennington et al., 2014) 之後，較為新穎的單詞表示模型，在執行文本分類的同時也會輸出由文本訓練的詞嵌入向量，其 Macro-F1 score 比基於序列的方法提升。接著，比較基於圖形的方法可以發現 TextGCN 雖然比 Graph-CNN 新穎，但表現上沒有差距太多。由於 TextGCN 為整個實驗資料建構了一個基於文本和詞的巨大圖結構，訓練時會消耗大量的記憶體空間，以及每次測試時都需要重新訓練分類器，因此沒辦法執行在線測試 (online testing)。Text Level GNN 改善了記憶體需求過多的問題，並使用滑動窗口取得文本相對位置，比 TextGCN 模型的 Macro F1-score 高出 1.15%。我們採用的 HyperGAT 模型為文本建立超圖建構，使用兩個不同的超邊抓取句子順序信息與語意信息，用注意力機制取得文本的特徵，以上優勢是一般圖神經網路架構模型無法獲得的。由實驗結果得知，無論哪個效能指標，HyperGAT 皆比其他基於序列和圖形的深度學習方法好。

4.5 錯誤分析

我們想要找出測試資料當中，哪些標籤容易被我們使用的 HyperGAT 模型混淆，具體作法是將各標籤的 FN (False Negative) 算出之後，

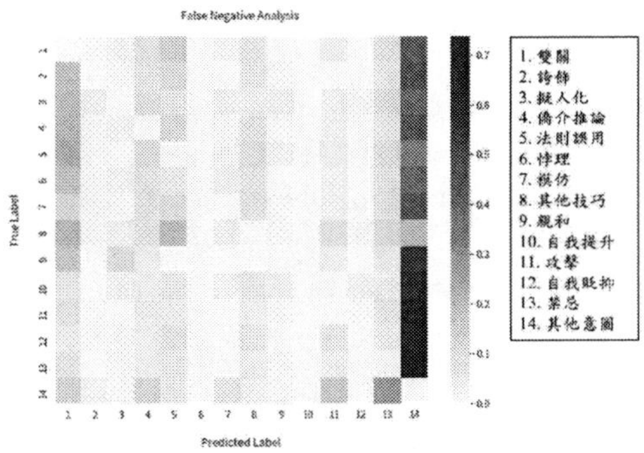

圖 2: HyperGAT 模型錯誤分析

再將與其他標籤的 FP (False Positive) 重疊的索引統計成表格，並用視覺化的方法將數值的大小以顏色深淺作為表達，若顏色越深，表示當某特定標籤無法被正確預測時，模型更傾向歸類出此標籤。

圖 2 為錯誤分析結果。首先，可以發現對角線顏色皆為空白，數值皆為 0 表示其標籤無法被正確預測。本模型的錯誤分析可以歸納以下幾點發現：1) 當標籤沒有被判斷正確時，容易誤判成標籤最多的「其他意圖」，這是因為模型傾向分類到標記數量多的標籤。2) 幽默技巧中，標籤「其他意圖」之直行方格的顏色較深是因為標籤的 FN 數量較小，因此誤判後所占比例較高。 3) 在沒有判斷出「其他意圖」這個標籤時，分類器會將標籤分到「攻擊」和「禁忌」。

5 結論

本研究我們運用一種新的基於超圖結構的深度學習方法，解決中文幽默多標籤文本分類問題，透過超圖找出更好的文本表示，我們使用的超圖注意力神經網路模型，效能優於其他基於序列和基於圖形的深度學習模型，達到 Macro F1-score 0.2419、Micro F1-score 0.4695、Weighted F1-score 0.4084 與 Subset Accuracy 0.1215。

未來研究方向，我們將持續改善 HyperGAT 提升模型的表現，並且應用在其他領域，例如：健康照護和醫療問題等。

致謝

This work was partially supported by the Ministry of Science and Technology, Taiwan under the grant MOST 108-2218-E-008-017-MY3 and MOST 109-2410-H-003-123-MY3.

參考文獻

Jerome Bellegarda. 2014. Spoken Language Understanding for Natural Interaction. In *Proceedings of the SIGDIAL 2013 Conference, page 203.*https://aclanthology.org/W13-4033.pdf.

Kim Binsted. 1995. Using humour to make natural language interfaces more friendly. *Paper presented at the AI, ALife and Entertainment Workshop, Montreal, Canada.* https://www2.hawaii.edu/~binsted/papers/BinstedIJCAI1995.pdf.

David M. Blei, Andrew Y. Ng, and Machael I. Jordan. 2003. Latent dirichlet allocation. *The Journal of machine Learning research, vol. 3, pages 993-1022,* https://dl.acm.org/doi/10.5555/944919.944937.

Jennings Bryant and Dolf Zillmann. 1989. Chapter 2: Using Humor to Promote Learning in the Classroom. *Journal of Children in Contemporary Society, 20(1-2), pages 49-78.* https://doi.org/10.1300/J274v20n01_05.

Hsueh-Chih Chen, Yu-Chen chan, Ru-Huei Dai, Yi-Jun Liao, and Cheng-Hao Tu. 2017. Neurolinguistics of Humor. *In S. Attardo (Ed.), The Routledge Handbook of Language and Humor, pages 282-294.* https://doi.org/10.4324/9781315731162.

Michaël Defferrard, Xavier Bresson, and Pierre Vandergheynst. 2016. Convolutional neural networks on graphs with fast localized spectral filtering. In *Proceedings of the 30th International Conference on Neural Information Processing SystemsDecember 2016, pages 3844–3852.* https://doi.org/10.5555/3157382.3157527.

Jacob Devlin, Ming-Wei Chang, Kenton Lee, and Kristina Toutanova. 2019. BERT: Pre-training of Deep Bidirectional Transformers for Language Understanding. In *Proceedings of the 2019 Conference of the North American Chapter of the Association for Computational Linguistics: Human Language Technologies, Volume 1 (Long and Short Papers). Human Language Technologies, pages 4171-4186.* https://doi.org/10.18653/v1/N19-1423.

Kaize Ding, Jianling Wang, Jundong Li, Dingcheng Li, and Huan Liu, 2020. Be More with Less: Hypergraph Attention Networks for Inductive Text Classification. In *Proceedings of the 2020 Conference on Empirical Methods in Natural*

Language Processing, pages 4927–4936. https://doi.org/10.18653/v1/2020.emnlp-main.399.

Dan Gusfield. 1997. Algorithms on Strings, Trees and Sequences. *Cambridge University Press, Cambridge, UK.* https://doi.org/10.1017/CBO9780511574931.

James Goodman, Andreas Vlachos, and Jason Naradowsky. 2016. Noise reduction and targeted exploration in imitation learning for abstract meaning representation parsing. In *Proceedings of the 54th Annual Meeting of the Association for Computational Linguistics (Volume 1: Long Papers). Association for Computational Linguistics, pages 1–11.* https://doi.org/10.18653/v1/P16-1001.

Mary Harper. 2014. Learning from 26 languages: Program management and science in the babel program. In *Proceedings of COLING 2014, the 25th International Conference on Computational Linguistics: Technical Papers. Dublin City University and Association for Computational Linguistics, page 1.* http://aclweb.org/anthology/C14-1001.

Sepp Hochreiter and Jurgen Schmidhuber. 1997.Long short-term memory. *Neural computation, vol. 9, no. 8, pages 1735-1780.* https://www.bioinf.jku.at/publications/older/2604.pdf.

Lianzhe Huang, Dehong Ma, Sujian Li, Xiaodong Zhang, and Houfeng WANG. 2019. Text level graph neural network for text classification. In *Proceedings of the 2019 Conference on Empirical Methods in Natural Language Processing and the 9th International Joint Conference on Natural Language Processing, pages 3444–3450.* https://aclanthology.org/D19-1345.pdf.

Armand Joulin, Edouard Grave, Piotr Bojanowski, and Tomas Mikolov. 2017. Bag of tricks for efficient text classification. In *Proceedings of the 15th Conference of the European Chapter of the Association for Computational Linguistics (Volume 2, Short Papers). Association for Computational Linguistics, pages 427-431.* https://aclanthology.org/E17-2068.

Yoon Kim, 2014. Convolutional Neural Networks for Sentence Classification , In *Proceedings of the 2014 Conference on Empirical Methods in Natural Language Processing (EMNLP) , page 1746–1751.* https://doi.org/10.3115/v1/D14-1181.

Pengfei Liu, Xipeng Qiu, and Xuanjing Huang, 2016. Recurrent neural network for text classification with multi-task learning. In *Proceedings of the Twenty-Fifth International Joint Conference on Artificial IntelligenceJuly 2016, pages 2873–2879.* https://doi.org/10.5555/3060832.3061023.

Paul E. Mcghee. 1989. Humor and Children's Development: A Guide to Practical Applications. *Oxford, UK: Routledge*.

Tomas Mikolov, Kai Chen, Greg Corrado, and Jeffrey Dean. 2013. Efficient Estimation of Word Representations in Vector Space. https://arxiv.org/pdf/1301.3781.pdf.

Jeffrey Pennington, Richard Socher, and Christopher D. Manning. 2014. GloVe: Global Vectors for Word Representation. In *Proceedings of the 2014 Conference on Empirical Methods in Natural Language Processing (EMNLP), pages 1532–1543.* https://aclanthology.org/D14-1162.pdf.

Yuen-Hsien Tseng, Wun-Syuan Wu, Chia-Yueh Chang, Hsueh-Chih Chen, and Wei-Lun Hsu. 2020. Development and Validation of a Corpus for Machine Humor Comprehension. In *Proceedings of the 12th Conference on Language Resources and Evaluation (LREC 2020), pages 1346–1352.* https://aclanthology.org/2020.lrec-1.168.

Liang Yao, Chengsheng Mao, and Yuan Luo. 2019. Graph convolutional networks for text classification. In *Proceedings of the AAAI conference on artificial intelligence, 2019, vol. 33, no. 01, pages 7370-7377.* https://doi.org/10.1609/aaai.v33i01.33017370.

The 33rd Conference on Computational Linguistics and Speech Processing (ROCLING 2021)
Taoyuan, Taiwan, October 15-16, 2021. The Association for Computational Linguistics and Chinese Language Processing

結合領域知識之語言轉譯器於中文醫療問題多標籤分類
Incorporating Domain Knowledge into Language Transformers for Multi-Label Classification of Chinese Medical Questions

陳柏翰 Po-Han Chen, 曾昱翔 Yu-Xiang Zeng, 李龍豪 Lung-Hao Lee
國立中央大學 電機工程學系
Department of Electrical Engineering, National Central University
{108521106, 109521127}@ncu.edu.tw, lhlee@ee.ncu.edu.tw

摘要

我們提出知識導入語言轉譯器模型架構，將弱監督層級資料視為知識來源，由其上下文推理並預測出被遮罩的焦點與面向，藉以捕獲相關領域知識。有鑑於當前缺乏公開的中文醫療問題多標籤分類資料集，因此我們從網路上蒐集醫療問題，並且人工標記 1,814 則問句，橫跨 8 個問題類別：原由、疾病、檢驗、醫療資訊、營養補充、人物機構、症狀、以及治療，標籤總數是 2,340，每則問題平均 1.29 個標籤。我們以百度醫學百科當作領域知識來源，比較 BERT 和 RoBERTa 兩個轉譯器的效能差異，實驗結果得知我們的知識導入機制，在不同的評測指標 Macro F1、Micro F1、Weighted F1 及 Subset Accuracy 都能有效提升效能 。

Abstract

In this paper, we propose a knowledge infusion mechanism to incorporate domain knowledge into language transformers. Weakly supervised data is regarded as the main source for knowledge acquisition. We pre-train the language models to capture masked knowledge of focuses and aspects and then fine-tune them to obtain better performance on the downstream tasks. Due to the lack of publicly available datasets for multi-label classification of Chinese medical questions, we crawled questions from medical question/answer forums and manually annotated them using eight predefined classes: persons and organizations, symptom, cause, examination, disease, information, ingredient, and treatment. Finally, a total of 1,814 questions with 2,340 labels. Each question contains an average of 1.29 labels. We used Baidu Medical Encyclopedia as the knowledge resource. Two transformers BERT and RoBERTa were implemented to compare performance on our constructed datasets. Experimental results showed that our proposed model with knowledge infusion mechanism can achieve better performance, no matter which evaluation metric including Macro F1, Micro F1, Weighted F1 or Subset Accuracy were considered.

關鍵字：文本分類、領域知識擷取、預訓練語言模型、生醫資訊學
Keywords: text classification, domain knowledge extraction, pretrained language models, biomedical informatics.

1 介紹

近年來深度學習技術的興起，預訓練語言模型在許多自然語言處理任務皆有著亮眼的表現。在文本分類任務中，轉譯器 (transformer) 網路架構為最廣泛使用的主流模型，通過大規模無標記資料，進行自監督之預訓練，這些模型捕獲了廣域語意資訊與結構句法，並利用這些知識進一步微調下游任務。例如：專有領域之語言模型 BioBERT (2020)，通過遮罩語言模型 (Masked Language Modeling, MLM) 在生物醫學語料庫進行預訓練，該訓練機制旨在捕獲隨機遮罩之標記與其上下文之語意關係。

隨著科技的進步，人類壽命延長的同時，對健康照護的意識也逐漸抬升，許多媒體及報

章雜誌都在談論相關議題，人民也時常在網路上的尋求問題的答案。例如：一般民眾可以在醫聯網 (https://med-net.com/) 上提出健康相關的醫療疑問，專科醫生則在這個平台上根據問題回答。除了由專家或社會大眾回答問題之外，開發自動問答 (Question Answering, QA) 系統讓電腦回答人類問題，也是人工智慧時代的發展重點之一。無論是由人類或者是機器回答問題，要先能理解問題，例如：「請問血栓溶解劑與心悸跟心肌炎有關嗎？」，問題理解上可以歸納成與「治療」和「症狀」這兩個類別有關。

因此，本研究關注中文醫療問題的多標籤分類問題。我們提出知識導入 (Knowledge Infusion, KI) 機制預訓練語言模型，從百度醫學百科蒐集的弱監督層級資料，由其上下文推理並預測出被遮罩之焦點與其面向，藉以捕獲醫療相關知識。有鑑於當前缺乏公開的中文資料集，我們從網路論壇平台上，蒐集醫療相關問題，並且人工標記 1,814 則問句，橫跨 8 個問題類別：原由、疾病、檢驗、醫療資訊、營養補充、人物機構、症狀、以及治療，標籤總數是 2,340，每則問題平均 1.29 個標籤。實驗結果得知，我們的知識導入機制，在四個評測指標 Macro F1、Micro F1、Weighted F1 及 Subset Accuracy，都能有效提升效能 。

本文章節如下，第二章探討相關研究，第三章敘述我們提出的知識導入機制，第四章為實驗結果與分析，最後是結論。

2 相關研究

Zhang et al. (2019) 提出一種能同時在知識圖譜及大規模語料庫上預訓練語言模型的方法，名為 ERNIE，其架構分為抽取知識信息與訓練語言模型，與 BERT 類似，隨機遮罩經知識圖譜匹配之命名實體，並訓練模型從知識圖譜中選擇適合的實體進行預測，實現將其知識化的語言表徵模型。

Liu et al. (2019) 提出 K-BERT 模型將知識圖譜三元組作為領域知識注入句子中，引入 soft-position embedding 與可視化矩陣，搭配 BERT 來解決因為過多知識，導致句子偏離其正確意涵之知識噪聲 (knowledge noises) 問題，研究發現雖然 BERT 在經過預訓練後，語言模型可以從大規模語料獲取語言結構信息，但在需要知識驅動的問題時，仍然無法有效發揮。K-BERT 在搭配知識圖譜三元組時，可以輕鬆將特定領域知識注入模型中，後續實驗證明在金融、法律及醫學上之下游任務，相較於 BERT 更亮眼的表現。

Lee et al. (2020) 在英文文本上延續了 BERT，在自挖掘之大規模生物醫學語料進行預訓練，並運用 WordPiece Tokenization ，解決專有領域之詞條無法在詞庫表查找的新詞(Out-Of-Vocabulary, OOV)問題，後續實驗證明在生物醫學的下游任務，例如：命名實體識別、關係抽取及問答系統等的效能表現，刷新了排行榜，成為最先進的 (state-of-the-art, SOTA) 模型。

Xiong et al. (2020) 發現目前的預訓練語言模型通常是字符級別，並沒有以實體為中心的知識建模，因此提出了一項新的弱監督 (weakly supervised) 知識學習目標函數，訓練語言模型區分文本中正確的實體與被隨機選擇替換的其他實體。進行實體替換時，通過匹配維基三元組知識庫，選擇將被匹配之實體替換成該類型的其他實體，進一步訓練語言模型，實驗發現從非結構化文本，直接學習實體知識，在下游任務上有顯著的成長。

Wang et al. (2021) 提出了一種知識嵌入 (knowledge embedding) 和預訓練語言嵌入表示，模型名為 Kepler，作者將實體的描述與預訓練語言模型作為嵌入進行編碼與訓練，實驗結果在各項自然語言處理任務上都有更好的效能表現，為知識嵌入研究帶來新的基準。

He et al. (2020) 將維基中與疾病相關的知識，注入到 BERT 中並進行預訓練，在消費者健康問答、醫學語言推理及疾病命名實體識別上都取得了更好的效果。

本研究以預訓練語言模型做為基礎，有別於 He et al. (2020) ，我們加入了以疾病、症狀、治療方法、檢測方式、藥物、食品等為焦點，以及從焦點出發相應延伸的不同面向，以弱監督層級資料作為預訓練時之遮罩目標，使醫療健康照護特徵資訊能夠充分完整。

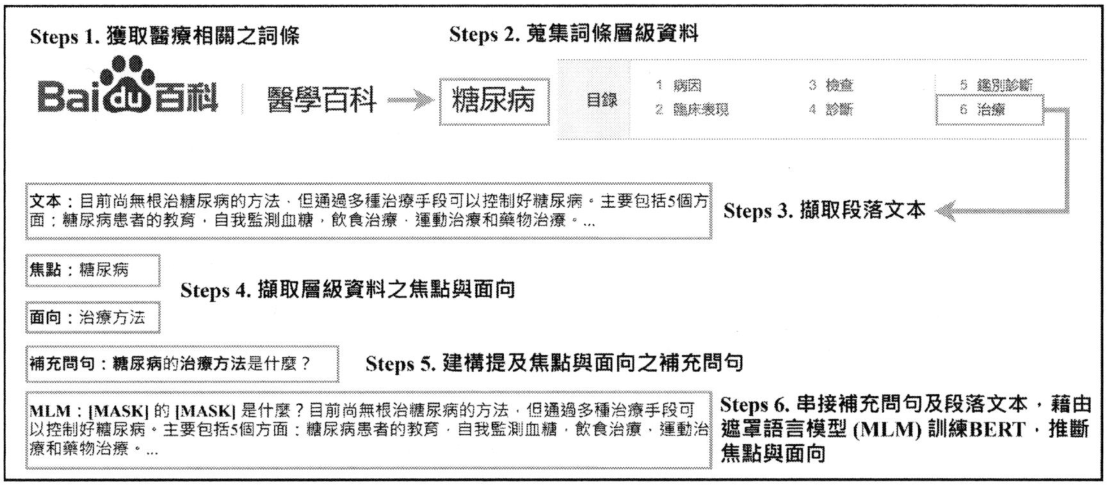

圖 1: 知識來源：百度醫學百科

3 知識導入語言轉譯器模型

3.1 知識來源

臨床文獻與生物醫學網站的文章通常包含多個疾病、症狀及診療技術等，導致難以判別原文焦點及面向，且經醫學專家協助標註通常是昂貴且費時的，諸如英文的 MeSH (Medical Subject Heading) 與 SNOMED CT 都提供了醫學術語供查詢。

我們選擇百度醫學百科 (如圖 1)，作為弱監督層級知識來源。以糖尿病為例，該目錄包含了以糖尿病為焦點衍伸出的多個面向，我們接續提取對應於各面向的段落文本。假設我們將糖尿病視為焦點，治療方法視為面向，可以由層級資料特徵建立事先定義好的制式的補充問句：「[焦點] 的 [面向] 是什麼？」，制式補充問句的優點是當模型在預測被遮罩的標記時，因為各個面向都使用了相同的制式補充問句，所以不會提供模型線索，強迫其根據段落文本學習。我們然後將制式補充問句與提取的段落文本串接起來，建構出問題形式的文本，用新的損失函數L，進行遮罩語言模型 (MLM) 訓練。

3.2 知識導入機制

我們提出一個知識導入 (Knowledge Infusion, KI) 機制，假設補充問句中焦點的字序列為 $X = [x_1, x_2, x_3, \dots, x_T]$，補充問句中焦點之交叉熵損失函數如方程式(1)，$passage$ 為補充問句及段落文本建構出之問題形式的文本，$p(x_t|passage)$為條件機率如方程式(2)，其中 z_t 為 x_t 之未歸一化的對數機率分布 (unnormalized log probabilities)，β 為平衡 L_{focus} 因 z_t 數值過小之補償參數，a 為面向種類，方程式(3)中的L_{aspect} 為其損失函數，模型在訓練過程中透過降低總損失函數L如方程式(4)，捕獲醫學百科知識。

$$L_{focus} = -\sum_{t=1}^{T} log\, p\,(x_t|passage) + \frac{\beta}{\sum_{t=1}^{T} z_t} \tag{1}$$

$$p(x_t|passage) = \frac{exp\,(z_t)}{\sum_{z\epsilon V} exp\,(z)} \tag{2}$$

$$L_{aspect} = -\, log\, p\,(a|passage) \tag{3}$$

$$L = L_{focus} + L_{aspect} \tag{4}$$

圖 2 為模型架構，使用了 BERT 作為模型的基礎架構。在預訊練 (pre-training) 階段，輸入的文本經 WordPiece tokenization 處理後，Token Embedding 層將 [CLS] 插入結果的開頭，[SEP]插入第一句結尾與第二句結尾，並轉換為固定維度之向量。Position Embedding 層賦予各個字序列順序的信息。Segment Embedding 層能夠處理輸入句子對之分類任務，前一向量把 0 賦予給第一個句子中之各個字，

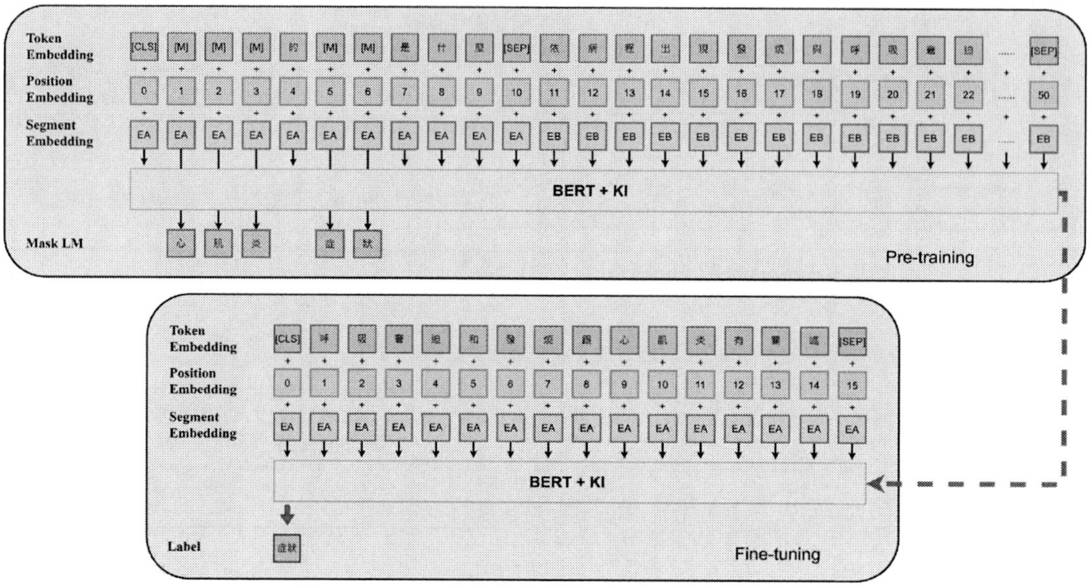

圖 2: 知識導入語言轉譯器模型架構

後一向量把1賦予給第二個句子中之各個字。

在微調 (fine-tuning) 階段，Transformer 中的自注意力機制允許 BERT 建模於自定義的下游任務上，BERT 根據 [CLS] 標記生成一代表句的特徵向量，並通過一層全連接層進行微調，損失函數根據任務設計，由於是多標籤分類任務，我們使用 Sigmoid 與 Binary Cross Entropy Loss (BCELoss)。

BERT 加上我們的知識導入機制，藉由上下文語意正確預測出被遮罩的焦點與對應的面向，更有效率地學習領域語意資訊。例如：圖一的預訊練階段學習到心肌炎相關症狀，在微調階段能更好理解呼吸窘迫與發燒為心肌炎的症狀，從而在微調時，正確地預測出標籤種類。

4 模型效能評估

4.1 資料集

由於缺乏公開的中文醫療問題分類資料集，我們透過爬蟲將醫聯網 (https://med-net.com/) 的問答紀錄擷取下來，一共有 1,814 則醫療問題。經由歸納整理，總共有 8 個問題類型，其定義和例子如表 1。參與標記的人員一共有三位師大中文系的大學生，對於每個中文句子做人工斷詞及問題類型標註，最終標籤總數是 2,340，每則問題平均 1.29 個標籤。

4.2 實驗設定

我們透過爬蟲蒐集百度醫學百科做為知識來源，資料經過過前處理，濾除字序列長度過短與對應至焦點數量低於 500 則之面向種類，最後包含 103,225 句，焦點包含疾病與症狀、中醫、治療與檢查、以及藥物，相對應的面向如表 2。

我們比較以下兩個轉譯器模型，以及加入我們的知識導入機制後的模型效能差異。(1) BERT (Devlin et al., 2019)：以字作為基礎當作輸入，基於轉譯器的雙向編碼器表示技術，使用中文維基百科語料庫當作訓練資料。(2) RoBERTa-wwm-ext (Cui et al., 2019)：提出中文全詞遮罩模型，使用中文維基百科語料庫與外部資源當作訓練資料。

4.3 評測指標

多標籤文本分類的結果是一篇文本不僅僅只有單一標籤，無法單純的以二元的方法評估。目前主要的評估方法需要計算出每一個類別的 F1 分數，根據不同的方式綜合各個標籤的 F1 分數以評估多標籤分類器的效能。我們採用以下幾種效能指標：(1) Macro F1：將所有標籤視為平等，計算方式是將各標籤的 F1 先計算出來之後，再取其平均值。(2) Micro

問題類型	定義	範例
原由 (Cause)	事情的緣起與由來	請問報告中的雙側肺尖輕度肋膜增厚原因為何？
疾病 (Disease)	詢問是否為何種疾病	用力深呼吸時，腰部兩側有輕微的疼痛，這是僵直性脊椎炎嗎 ？
檢驗 (Examination)	詢問做哪一類型的檢查	請問 CA125 檢測值高達 150 是否需要進行什麼其他檢測呢？
醫療資訊 (Information)	詢問檢測、疾病、症狀、醫療保健等的醫療資訊與建議	請問同時染上愛滋病或其他性病的 機率有多大呢
營養補充 (Ingredient)	關係食品或補給品的問題	醣尿病患者可以喝白蘭氏雞精？
醫療資訊 (Information)	詢問疾病科別、醫療機關或人物	請問猝睡症哪裡有權威醫師？
人物機構 (Person & Org.)	對身體產生之影響與狀況或併發症引起其他症狀	我的 r 一麩胺酸轉化酶偏低，請問會有什麼影響嗎？
治療 (Treatment)	管理或照顧患者以對抗疾病或病症	有椎間盤突出症狀一定必須要靠手術治療嗎？

表 1: 問題類型定義及範例

焦點	面向	數量
疾病與症狀	病因、臨床表現、檢查、診斷、鑑別診斷、治療、簡介、預防、併發症、預後	40,821
中醫	簡介、入藥部位、性味、歸經、功效、主治、相關配伍、用法用量、相關論述、形態特徵、生長環境、病因、治法、採集加工	8755
治療與檢查	簡介、正常值、臨床意義、注意事項、檢查過程、相關疾病、相關症狀	10,765
藥物	成份、性狀、功能主治、規格、用法用量、不良反應、禁忌、注意事項、貯藏、簡介、藥物相互作用、適應症、藥理毒理	42884

表 2: 焦點與面向的定義及數量

F1: 先計算所有類別加總的 Precision 和 Recall，然後再計算兩者的調合平均 F1。(3) Weighted F1：先將各標籤的 F1，根據每個標籤真實樣本的數量，賦予每個標籤不同的權重，是一種類似加權平均的 F1。(4) Subset Accuracy：這是最嚴格的指標，表示所有標籤都正確的樣本百分比，舉凡有一個標籤分類錯誤，則不將其判斷為正確結果。

4.4 實驗結果

表 3 為模型效能評估結果，RoBERTa-wwm-ext 比 BERT 使用了更長的時間、更大的 batch size 和更多元的數據進行訓練，並去掉了 BERT 中之 NSP (Next Sentence Prediction) 訓練機制和採用了全詞遮罩，從實驗結果得知 RoBERTa-wwm-ext 相較於 BERT 提升了 5.55%的 Macro F1、1.49%的 Micro F1、1.89%的 Weighted F1 與 0.01%的 Subset Accuracy，證實了使用全詞遮罩訓練更多元及序列更長的數據，對下游任務的效果更好。我們提出的知識導入(KI) 機制無論哪個效能指標，相對於 BERT 與 RoBERTa-wwm-ext 模型都能有效提升效能。BERT + KI 相較於 BERT 提升了 3.89%的 Macro F1、1.36%的 Micro F1、1.83%的 Weighted F1

Model	Macro F1	Micro F1	Weighted F1	Subset Accuracy
BERT (Devlin et al., 2019)	0.6979	0.7576	0.7560	0.6082
BERT + KI (ours)	**0.7251**	**0.7679**	**0.7698**	**0.6165**
RoBERTa-wwm-ext (Cui et al., 2019)	0.7366	0.7689	0.7703	0.6083
RoBERTa-wwm-ext + KI (ours)	**0.7386**	**0.7750**	**0.7763**	**0.6220**

表 3: 模型效能評估結果

與 1.36%的 Subset Accuracy。RoBERTa-wwm-ext + KI 相較於 RoBERTa-wwm-ext 提升了 0.27%的 Macro F1、0.79%的 Micro F1、0.78%的 Weighted F1 與 2.25%的 Subset Accuracy。

5 結論

我們提出由百度醫學百科作為弱監督知識來源，藉由知識導入機制，繼續訓練微調語言模型的作法。從實驗結果證實，知識導入機制能更準確地完成醫療問題多標籤分類任務標籤，在 Macro F1、Micro F1、Weighted F1 和 Subset Accuracy 都能有效提升效能 。

致謝

This work was partially supported by the Ministry of Science and Technology, Taiwan under the grant MOST 108-2218-E-008-017-MY3

參考文獻

Yiming Cui, Wanxiang Che, Ting Liu, Bing Qin, Ziqing Yang, Shijin Wang, Guoping Hu. 2019. Revisiting Pre-Trained Models for Chinese Natural Language Processing, In *Proceedings of the 2020 Conference on Empirical Methods in Natural Language Processing: Findings*, pages 657-668. https://arxiv.org/abs/2004.13922

Jacob Devlin, Ming-Wei Chang, Kenton Lee, Kristina Toutanova. 2019. BERT:Pre-training of Deep Bidirectional Transformers for Language Understanding. In *Proceedings of the 2019 Conference of the North American Chapter of the Association for Computational Linguistics: Human Language Technologies, Volume 1 (Long and Short Papers)*, pages 4171–4186. https://doi.org/10.18653/v1/N19-1423

Yun He, Ziwei Zhu, Yin Zhang, Qin Chen, James Caverlee. 2020. Infusing Disease Knowledge into BERT for Health Question Answering, Medical Inference and Disease Name Recognition, In *Proceedings of the 2020 Conference on Empirical Methods in Natural Language Processing (EMNLP)*, pages 4604–4614. https://doi.org/10.18653/v1/2020.emnlp-main.372

Jinhyuk Lee, Wonjin Yoon, Sungdong Kim, Donghyeon Kim, Sunkyu Kim, Chan Ho So, and Jaewoo Kang. 2020. Biobert: a pre-trained biomedical language representation model for biomedical text mining. *Bioinformatics*, 36(4): 1234-1240. https://doi.org/10.1093/bioinformatics/btz682

Weijie Liu, Peng Zhou, Zhe Zhao, Zhiruo Wang, Qi Ju, Haotang Deng, and Ping Wang. 2019. K-bert: Enabling language representation with knowledge graph. In *Proceedings of the AAAI Conference on Artificial Intelligence*, pages 2901-2908. https://doi.org/10.1609/aaai.v34i03.5681

Xiaozhi Wang, Tianyu Gao, Zhaocheng Zhu, Zhengyan Zhang, Zhiyuan Liu, Juanzi Li, Jian Tang.2021.KEPLER: A Unified Model for Knowledge Embedding and Pre-trained Language Representation. *Transactions of the Association for Computational Linguistics,* 2021(9):176-194. http://doi.org/10.1162/tacl_a_00360

Wenhan Xiong, Jingfei Du, William Yang Wang, Veselin Stoyanov. 2020. Pretrained Encyclopedia: Weakly Supervised Knowledge-Pretrained Language Model. In *Proceedings of the 2020 International Conference on Learning Representations*, https://arxiv.org/abs/1912.09637

Zhengyan Zhang, Xu Han, Zhiyuan Liu, Xin Jiang, Maosong Sun, and Qun Liu. 2019. Ernie: Enhanced language representation with informative entities. In *Proceedings of the 57th Annual Meeting of the Association for Computational Linguistics*, pages 1441–1451. http://doi.org/10.18653/v1/P19-1139

The 33rd Conference on Computational Linguistics and Speech Processing (ROCLING 2021)
Taoyuan, Taiwan, October 15-16, 2021. The Association for Computational Linguistics and Chinese Language Processing

What confuses BERT? Linguistic Evaluation of Sentiment Analysis on Telecom Customer Opinion

Cing-Fang Shih
National Taiwan University
r08142004@ntu.edu.tw

Yu-Hsiang Tseng
National Taiwan University
seantyh@gmail.com

Ching-Wen Yang
National Taiwan University
b06102020@ntu.edu.tw

Pin-Er Chen
National Taiwan University
cckk2913@gmail.com

Hsin-Yu Chou
National Taiwan University
r10142008@ntu.edu.tw

Lian-Hui Tan
National Taiwan University
b06102036@ntu.edu.tw

Tzu-Ju Lin
National Taiwan University
b05102085@ntu.edu.tw

Chun-Wei Wang
Chunghwa Telecom Laboratories
chriswang@cht.com.tw

Shu-Kai Hsieh
National Taiwan University
shukaihsieh@ntu.edu.tw

Abstract

Ever-expanding evaluative texts on online forums have become an important source of sentiment analysis. This paper proposes an aspect-based annotated dataset consisting of Chinese telecom reviews on social media. We introduce a data category called implicit evaluative texts, *impevals* for short, to investigate how the deep learning model works on these implicit reviews. We first compare two models, BertSimple and BertImpvl, and find that while both models are competent to learn simple evaluative texts, they are confused when classifying *impevals*. To investigate the factors underlying the correctness of the model's predictions, we conduct a series of analyses, including qualitative error analysis and quantitative analysis of linguistic features with logistic regressions. The results show that local features that affect the overall sentential sentiment confuse the model: multiple target entities, transitional words, sarcasm, and rhetorical questions. Crucially, these linguistic features are independent of the model's confidence measured by the classifier's softmax probabilities. Interestingly, the sentence complexity indicated by syntax-tree depth is not correlated with the model's correctness. In sum, this paper sheds light on the characteristics of the modern deep learning model and when it might need more supervision through linguistic evaluations.

Keywords: Linguistic Evaluation, Sentiment Analysis, Implicit Evaluative Text, Deep Learning

1 Introduction

In recent years, social networking has revolutionized ways of communication and information exchange. People nowadays are allowed to express their feelings and views instantly online. With their immediate and ubiquitous nature, online reviews have become a valuable source of information extraction. To process crucial information, natural language processing (NLP) is applied to analyze textual data. Sentiment Analysis/Opinion Mining is an important branch of NLP to achieve the goal of opinion mining and social listening. Among all the related tasks such as *Opinion holder detection*, *Subjectivity Analysis*, Aspect-based Sentiment Analysis (ABSA) on short texts has been extensively explored, which specifies the polarity of each aspect in a sentence, providing comprehensive data for sentiment classification.

As neural models prosper, deep learning approaches are widely used in sentiment analysis. The participation of pre-trained models has promoted the accuracy of sentiment detection. Although deep learning models perform well in many circumstances, there are still some unresolved problems. The main concern lies in the model's tendency of learning explicit features while overlooking implicit ones, such as sarcasm, common sense, and deep reasoning. These limitations could hinder the models from making progress in recognizing sentiment. Considering the complexity of language, we aim to find out what linguistic features affect text classification accuracy of BERT (Devlin et al., 2018), the current state-of-the-art NLP model.

This paper is organized as follows. Section 1 provides the introduction and brings about the research question. Section 2 briefly reviews related literature. Annotation methods and details of the model will be explained in section 3. Subsequently, empirical evaluation is discussed in section 4. Section 5 analyzes the results. Finally, section 6 concludes the paper.

2 Literature Review

According to Liu (2012), sentiment analysis can be classified into three levels, namely the document level, the sentence level, and the aspect level. The document-level sentiment analysis assumes that there is only one topic in one document. Similarly, the sentence level extracts sentiment polarity based on one single sentence. However, in real-life social media comments, there could be several topics within only one sentence or document. ABSA thus solves the issue by indicating the polarity of each aspect in a sentence. It has received recognition and has become an important research field in computational linguistics.

Different approaches have been used in sentiment analysis. For instance, Pang and Lee (2009) presented a task utilizing traditional machine learning methods for document-level sentiment analysis. Tsytsarau and Palpanas (2012) later proposed four different approaches for document-level polarity prediction, namely machine learning-based, dictionary-based, semantic-based, and statistical-based respectively. As for ABSA, Schouten and Frasincar (2015) introduced a machine learning technique including aspect extraction and classification. Lately, as neural models flourish, deep learning-based sentiment analysis has become prominent in the research community. Zhou et al. (2019) provided an in-depth analysis of the deep learning-based aspect-level sentiment classification (ASC). Although the neural model is undoubtedly a practical approach in ASC, Zhou et al. (2019) pointed out its limitation of learning explicit emotional expression exclusively. Implicit emotional expressions such as irony, deep reasoning, and common sense were still too complicated for the recent neural networks (Zhou et al., 2019).

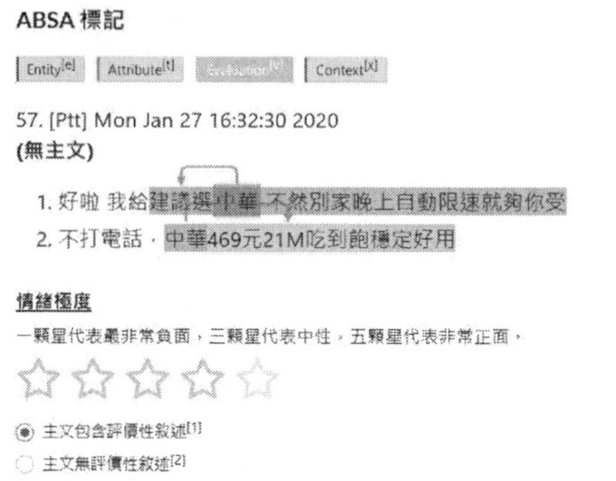

Figure 1: Annotation interface built with Label-Studio. The evaluative text number 1 says "Alright, I suggest choosing CHT, otherwise you will be fed up with other telecoms' automatic speed limit at night." Number 2 says "If you are not calling, the 469 NTD plan with 21M unlimited data offered by CHT is stable and handy." The star signs allow annotators to rate the polarity. One is for the most negative, three is for neutral, and five is for the most positive.

Many attempts have been made to fill in the missing piece of the puzzle. Cui et al. (2020) conducted a quantitative analysis to test the performance of BERT solving the CommonsenseQA task and concluded that with fine-tuning, BERT was able to make use of common sense features on higher layers. Baruah et al. (2020) challenged BERT's ability of context-aware sarcasm detection. They found out that contextual information slightly improved the performance of the Twitter data set, but not the Reddit data set. Ways to utilize the context and its features to improve the model performance is still a debated topic in the research community.

3 Data Annotation

This paper concentrates on the public customer reviews of the telecommunications service. To reflect the realistic opinion of customers, all of the data regarding service providers were extracted from popular anonymous forums, including PTT, Dcard, and Mobile01 to name a few. Comments without evaluative information, such as reposted news or special offers promotion, were eliminated in this task. If a thread contained an evaluation, its aspect tuple would then be annotated. All of the data were annotated by six linguistic-trained students from National Taiwan University. The annotation interface was built with LabelStudio (Tkachenko et al., 2020-2021) (see Figure 1 for the interface screenshot).

There are three elements in an aspect tuple: (i) an entity, (ii) an attribute, and (iii) an evaluation text. (i) The entity in this task refers to the service provider, and (ii) the attribute refers to the service. To improve the annotation, domain-specific information such as aliases of different providers and types of services are provided by the Department of Customer Service at Chunghwa Telecom. Finally, (iii) the evaluation text is a phrase including a customer's evaluative review of a certain provider or service. In other words, the evaluation text is usually where the sentiment cues appear. An example of a comment thread is demonstrated in (1).

(1) 平常生活圈自用中華網路都蠻順的

píngcháng shēnghuóquān zìyòng
daily living.sphere personal.use
zhōnghuá wǎnglù dōu mán
Chunghwa.Telecom internet always pretty
shùn de
smooth MOD

'For daily personal use in the living sphere, the internet provided by Chunghwa Telecom is always pretty smooth.'

In (1), the entity is the service provider *zhōnghuá* 'Chunghwa Telecom', the attribute is the feature of service *wǎnglù* 'internet', and the evaluation is the phrase *mán shùn de* 'pretty smooth'.

In some cases, there is more than one entity or attribute in a comment, as shown in (2). This is when aspect-based annotation proves useful. All of the entities, attributes, and evaluations found in an opinion thread as well as their corresponding relationship would be annotated.

(2) 中華網路穩定但費用貴

zhōnghuá wǎnglù wěndìng dàn
Chunghwa.Telecom internet stable but
fèiyòng guì
fee expensive

'The internet of Chunghwa Telecom is stable, but the fee is expensive.'

In (2), the entity is *zhōnghuá* 'Chunghwa Telecom'. The mixed feeling appears in the two evaluative adjectives *wěndìng* 'stable' and *guì* 'expensive', which points to two different attributes, *wǎnglù* 'internet' and *fèiyòng* 'fee', respectively.

The rating of the sentiment polarity came right after the annotation of the aspect tuple. Annotators rated the polarity as positive, neutral, or negative according to the sentiment conveyed in the comment thread.

There are some cases that even if a thread does not include a complete aspect tuple, it still conveys evaluative opinion. The sentiment cues may be triggered by certain linguistic constructions or syntactic patterns, as exemplified in (3).

(3) 只有遠傳才有距離

zhǐyǒu yuǎnchuán cái yǒu
only Far.EasTone.Telecom only have
jùlí
distance

'Only Far EasTone Telecom has distance.'

The comment thread in (3) only specifies *yuǎnchuán* 'Far EasTone Telecom' as an entity. Both the attribute and the evaluation text are missing. However, the thread still encodes a negative polarity since it is known as the parody of a catchy slogan, 只有遠傳沒有距離 'Only Far EasTone Telecom has no distance'. In this situation, instead of determining the three elements, the whole thread is annotated as an 'impeval' and is given negative polarity. The flowchart of the annotation task is presented in Figure 2.

We were intrigued by the case that a comment thread could express sentiment even if the information was incomplete. Therefore, a BERT classification task was designed to test its performance of predicting sentiment polarity of these impevals. Since there was a wide variety of sentimental expressions in impevals, we assumed that the addition of impevals should improve the model accuracy if BERT could learn from its linguistic features.

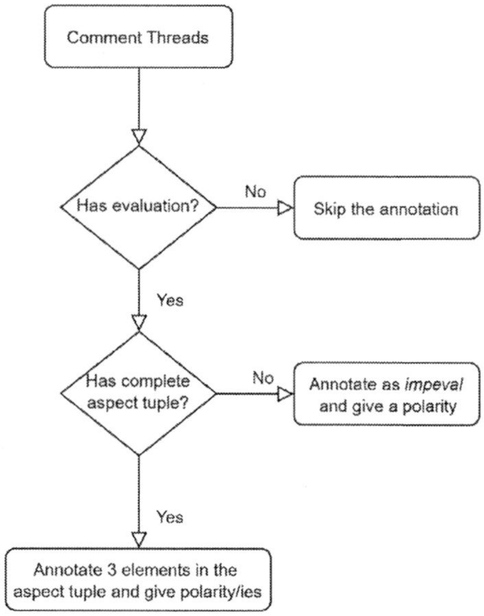

Figure 2: A flowchart presenting the process of the annotation

Dataset	Train ratio	Test ratio	Total
Evaluation	0.8 (1362)	0.2 (341)	1.0 (1703)
Impevals	0.8 (465)	0.2 (117)	1.0 (582)

Note: the number in the bracket indicates the dataset size.

Table 1: The ratio split and data number of each dataset

base model	bert-base-chinese
batch size	32
training epoch	10
learning rate	1.00e-05
weight decay	5.00e-03
optimizer	AdamW
random seed	0

Table 2: Model settings of the sentiment classification

4 Classification model

Two models are trained to compare their performances on simple evaluation texts and impevals. These two models are the same in architecture: they are both fine-tuned sequence classification models based on pretrained Chinese BERT. They are also identical in terms of the number of parameters. The only difference is the first model, BertSimple, only has evaluation texts as its training data. In contrast, the second model, BertImpvl, is trained with both evaluation texts and impevals. The comparison aims to show that impevals are intrinsically different from evaluation texts, as suggested by the annotation guidelines. Therefore, the hypothesis is that the model is less likely to transfer the knowledge it learns from evaluation texts to impevals. Furthermore, the regularities underlying the impevals may be more difficult to capture for the current model.

To train the models, we first split the annotated data into two groups, which were the evaluation dataset and the impeval dataset. In each dataset, training and testing sets were separated with an 8:2 ratio, which is demonstrated in Table 1 (denoted by {ratio}_{dataset_type}, i.e. 0.8_eval, 0.8_impeval, 0.2_eval, 0.2_impeval). To ensure equal label proportion in training and testing distributions, the train-test split was done along with stratification with respect to polarities. We then built two models for further analysis: BertSimple and BertImpvl. The base model is "bert-base-chinese" and its setting is specified in Table 2. While sharing the same architecture and parameters, the only difference between BertSimple and BertImpvl is their experience. BertSimple was trained on 80% of the evaluation dataset (0.8_eval), while BertImpvl was trained on the combination of 80% of the evaluation dataset and 80% of the impeval dataset (0.8_eval+0.8_impeval). It should be noted that since the training set was relatively small after the 8:2 train-test split, no validation set was used during the training phase.

The respective model accuracies of BertSimple and BertImpvl are shown in Table 3. The training accuracies are always very high for both models, which both exceed .98. The model BertSimple, which is only trained with evaluation texts, has validation accuracy of .927 in the evaluation text but only .709 in the impevals. The difference is arguably due to the lack of impevals in the training data. However, the BertImpvl model, trained with impevals, only gains a .06 benefit on the validation accuracy in impevals. It is also worthy to note that the evaluation text accuracy of BertImpvl is .909, which is a slight drop compared with the one of BertSimple.

	Training	Validation	
		Eval	Impevals
BertSimple	0.984	0.927	0.709
BertImpvl	0.981	0.909	0.769

Table 3: Model performance

The overall results are consistent with our hypothesis. Evaluation texts alone are readily learned by transformer-based models, such as BERT. In contrast, impevals are more difficult for the model. Adding the impevals in training data helps, but the model cannot perform as well as it does in evaluation texts. Admittedly, modeling/training-related factors may be responsible for the low accuracy, e.g., inappropriate model architecture, insufficient data size, sub-optimal training parameters, etc. However, evaluation texts and impevals are all linguistic expressions that are used to communicate evaluation polarities. They have similar *functions*, yet their *forms* are different enough so that the same model/training scheme can not readily transfer the regularities between the two. Therefore, it is at least interesting to ask what makes the model confused when classifying the impevals. In the next section, we will try to investigate and show the underlying factors that make the predictions challenging.

5 Linguistic Evaluation on Model Correctness

To investigate the factors underlying the true correctness of model predictions, we follow a three-step analysis scheme. First, we conduct an error analysis against model predictions on impevals. This step serves as an exploratory method to examine possible factors involve in the model's errors. Secondly, we hand-annotated some of the linguistic features in the first step, which are difficult to extract automatically. Once these features are annotated, we could test the relationship between the features and the model's true correctness. Thirdly, we automatically extract the rest of the linguistic features found in step 1. We then show that these features are indeed correlated with the model's correctness of predictions.

5.1 Error Analysis

We conduct an error analysis on the model's predictions of impevals. The model we choose to analyze is BertSimple, which is only exposed to simple evaluation text. With this constraint, we can observe how well the experience of simple evaluations performs on implicit ones. Although having slightly lower accuracy on impevals, it shows a clearer contrast on how models classify impevals based solely on simple evaluation text. We first select all the model's prediction errors and observe, qualitatively, possible factors influencing the predictions. Then, the observations are summarized into 6 categories, as shown in Table 4.

Among the categories identified in error analysis, we aim to find factors that systematically influence the model's correctness. The correctness of the model is conceptually related but distinct from the accuracy metric, which is the proportion of the model's correctness in each item. Some factors are complex, at least not from the off-the-shelf package, to extract automatically, namely, sarcasm and rhetorical questions. We further annotate these factors and explore their relations with model correctness in section 5.2. In contrast, some factors are readily operationalized with automatic NLP tools, such as number of entities, number (and types) of transitions, number of symbols. These factors are further investigated in section 5.3.

5.2 Annotated linguistic features

Rhetorical questions and sarcasm are complex linguistic expressions known to be thorny topics in sentiment classification (Maynard and Greenwood, 2014). Indeed, ongoing studies focus on exploiting the intricacies of linguistic features and developing more flexible model architectures to better detect and weave them into sentiment analysis (Joshi et al., 2017; Seo et al., 2020; Zhuang and Riloff, 2020). However, rhetorical questions and sarcasm are still tricky to handle, and they may still be the contributing factors to why impevals have lower accuracy than simple evaluative texts. Therefore, we try to show that these known-to-be difficult phenomena are still pertinent to the impevals observed in our dataset.

Rhetorical questions and sarcasm expres-

Category	Examples
Sarcasm	只有遠傳，才有距離 Only FET has distance.
Rhetorical question	你看中華吃到飽有限制上網流量嗎？玩不起就不要推出吃到飽 Have you seen CHT unlimited data plan imposing a bandwidth cap? You shouldn't sell the plan if you are not up to it.
Multiple entities	之前遠傳有時收不到，現在中華還算穩定 couldn't get the signal with FET before, but it's stable now with CHT
Transitions	以前爆快但最近有點慢 It's amazingly fast before but slow now.
Symbols	......, >>>, QQ
Others	我用手機連居然不曾斷過 Surprisingly I never lose the signal with my cell.

Table 4: Error analysis of model's predictions on impevals

	Coeff	*SE*	*z*	*p*
(Intercept)	1.18	0.10	11.54	<0.0001
Rhe. ques.	-0.72	0.07	-1.84	0.0653
Sarcasm	-0.88	0.03	-2.12	0.0342

Table 5: Logistic regression analysis of sarcasm and rhetorical question

sions are manually annotated on each impeval by two annotators. They are both native speakers with linguistics-related majors. Considering the correlation structures among the independent variables, the annotation results were analyzed with a logistic regression model to determine their effect on model correctness. The statistical results are shown in Table 5.

The results show that rhetorical questions and sarcasm are still difficult for the model to capture. BERT tends to mispredict rhetorical questions and sarcasm. Since their actual meanings are usually the opposite of their literal meanings, the prediction becomes even more challenging. This observation is consistent with the statistical results of the significant effect of sarcasm and the negative effect, while not significant, of the rhetorical question. Hence, these complicated linguistic expressions are still challenging for the transformer-based model.

5.3 Automatically extracted linguistic features

5.3.1 Feature extraction

Multiple factors observed in error analysis (section 5.1) can be extracted automatically. These factors include number of entities, number of symbols, and transitions. Transitions are especially pertinent in sentiment classification, since they may suggest contrasting evaluations presented in impevals. Therefore, we further analyze the transitions with their dependency structures.

To begin with, each of the impevals was passed through the spaCy dependency parser (Honnibal et al., 2020) to provide syntactic information, which follows the Penn Treebank tag set. The tags and dependencies generated would later be utilized in extracting features. Additionally, dependency tree's maximum depth of each sentence was computed. It was used as an indicator of the complexity of the syntactic structure of the sentences. Finally, we used transition word lists in the literature to see if certain words influence the model performance.

Intending to provide a detailed observation of the impevals, we made efforts to create more variables. Aside from descriptive features such as the number of entities and special characters, tags and dependencies were utilized to build the features of transition. A transition

	Transition dependency 1	Transition dependency 2
Tag after the transition	CD, NN, NT, P, PN, VV, JJ	VC
Dependency after the transition	auxmod, advmod, case, compound:nn, dep, dobj, nsubj, nmod:tmod, nmod:range, ROOT	cop

Table 6: Details of the three transition features

can be found in words such as *dànshì* 'however' and *zhǐbùguò* 'no more than', indicating the change of the speaker's attitude. A transition word is often tagged with AD, which refers to an adverb, or CS, which refers to subordinating conjunction. Based on this constraint, two transition features were created by specifying the properties of the token right after the transition, as shown in Table 6.

We distinguished two transitional features with the help of dependency structures. Transition dependency 1 was defined by observing the actual impeval data. An example could be found in 遠傳至少還有 LM 可以在雙十一出來應戰 'at least Far EasTone Telecom still got LM (Line Mobile) to compete with others on Double Eleven Day'. In this example, the transition was *zhìshǎo* 'at least' with the tag 'AD'. The word next to it was *hái* 'still', with a tag 'NN' and the dependency 'dep'.

Another important transitional feature was the situation that some transitions were not followed by a noun but a copula *shì* 'is', Transition dependency 2 aimed to find out all the *shì* 'is' as a copula. It was found in 我家反而是亞太沒信號 'instead, Asia-Pacific has poor reception at my house'. The transition word here was *fǎnér* 'instead', and the word next to it was *shì* 'is', with a tag 'VC' and the dependency 'cop'.

In addition to transitional features constructed with dependency parsing, we also included 'transition with word list' feature based on Chang's (2018) research to see if the data contained any transition words. Another word list consisting of *chúle*, *chúfēi*, and *chúwài* was used to build the 'exception' construction.

To serve as a baseline, we additionally computed the model's prediction probabilities to indicate the model *confidence*. In past studies, it was shown deep learning models are not necessarily "well-calibrated" so that their confidences matched the actual correctness (Guo et al., 2017). Specifically, we evaluated the full impeval dataset with BertSimple and used the probabilities of the predicted class as the model's confidence.

5.3.2 Evaluation Results & Discussion

We include 8 features in the final logistic regression model. The statistical results are shown in Table 7. First, the significance coefficient of the model `confidence` shows that the model tends to be correct when it is confident. It is not always the case since past studies suggest deep learning models may not be confidence-calibrated (Guo et al., 2017). The effect indicates that although BertSimple is only trained on simple evaluation texts, it nevertheless learns, to an extent, the relation between evaluative language and its sentiment. It is just that impevals involve additional factors than what the model captures.

These additional factors are what we try to describe with linguistic features. From the statistical results, the number of entities and `exception` features significantly reduce the model's correctness. In contrast, the number of symbols and Transition dependency 1 slightly increase the model's correctness. One possible pattern that emerged from the results is that the model tends to be confused with local, focused features when these features potentially involve a "global revision" of the whole sentence's representation. This revision needs to occur when multiple entities occur, which may imply a comparison, and multiple evaluations need to compete for the evaluating entities. In the case of "exception", the prominent transition word signals an evaluation that could have complex relations with the main sentence. This observation is consistent with other positive effects of the number of symbols and Transition dependency 1. That is, as long as there's contextual information for the model to learn, the model could do better in these circumstances. This argu-

	Coeff	*SE*	*z*	*p*
Intercept	-3.22	0.72	-4.46	<0.0001
confidence	5.27	0.70	7.56	<0.0001
complexity	-0.08	0.08	-0.98	0.3271
No. entities	-0.43	0.13	-3.29	0.0010
No. symbols	0.36	0.17	2.08	0.0373
Exception	-2.08	0.68	-3.08	0.0021
Trans. words	-0.51	0.36	-1.40	0.1615
Trans. dep. 1	0.44	0.22	1.97	0.0493
Trans. dep. 2	-0.32	0.45	-0.71	0.4798

Table 7: Logistic regression analysis of all features

ment is also in line with recent studies that the transformer layers operate to help model mixing and capturing relations among input data (Lee-Thorp et al., 2021; Bronstein et al., 2021). Consistently and interestingly, the sentence complexity itself is not a problem for the model, as seen by the non-significant coefficient of the `tree depth` variable.

Finally, the contribution of linguistic features is independent of the model's prediction confidence. It is supported by the likelihood ratio test between two models: a base model, which only includes model confidence, and the full model described above. The likelihood ratio test is significant, $\chi^2(7) = 28.11$, $p < 0.0005$. The statistical result indicates that even though model confidence is highly correlated with the model's true correctness, the linguistic features complement the factors that the model is confused about.

6 Conclusion

Sentiment analysis has been an ongoing popular topic among the NLP community. This paper compiles an aspect-based annotated dataset consisting of social media comment threads about telecommunication services. To fully describe the versatility of evaluative texts, we distinguish between simple evaluation texts and implicit evaluation texts, *impevals*. As deep learning becomes more and more crucial in the field of computational linguistics, interpreting deep learning models is essential to understand how they come to a result and when they could possibly fail.

In particular, we focus on BERT, the current NLP state-of-the-art, and build two models: BertSimple and BertImpvl, to test BERT's knowledge about impevals. We find that the model learns a little about impevals, but not as well compared to simple evaluations. Hence, we conduct a series of qualitative and quantitative analyses on the factors that make impevals difficult. The overall results show that local features that require a global representation update confuse the model, such as multiple target entities, transitional words, sarcasm, and rhetorical questions. Consistently, the sentence complexity does not affect the model's correctness. It is also worthy to note although the model is predominantly trained with simple evaluations, the model confidence does reflect its correctness on impevals. However, the linguistic features complement the model confidence. That is, they together better explain when the model will be less accurate in each instance. To sum up, we expect that the linguistic evaluations of sentiment classification with BERT could help us understand more the characteristics of the model and when it might need more supervision with the help of linguistic feature analysis.

References

Arup Baruah, Kaushik Das, Ferdous Barbhuiya, and Kuntal Dey. 2020. Context-aware sarcasm detection using bert. In *Proceedings of the second workshop on figurative language processing*, pages 83–87.

Michael M Bronstein, Joan Bruna, Taco Cohen, and Petar Veličković. 2021. Geometric deep learning: Grids, groups, graphs, geodesics, and gauges. *arXiv preprint arXiv:2104.13478*.

Li-Li Chang. 2018. The formation of the modal adverbs occurring frequently in adversative clauses. 成大中文學報, (63):191–230.

Leyang Cui, Sijie Cheng, Yu Wu, and Yue Zhang. 2020. Does BERT solve commonsense task via commonsense knowledge? *arXiv preprint arXiv:2008.03945*.

Jacob Devlin, Ming-Wei Chang, Kenton Lee, and Kristina Toutanova. 2018. Bert: Pre-training of deep bidirectional transformers for language understanding. *arXiv preprint arXiv:1810.04805*.

Chuan Guo, Geoff Pleiss, Yu Sun, and Kilian Q Weinberger. 2017. On calibration of modern neural networks. In *International Conference on Machine Learning*, pages 1321–1330. PMLR.

Matthew Honnibal, Ines Montani, Sofie Van Landeghem, and Adriane Boyd. 2020. spaCy: Industrial-strength natural language processing in python.

Aditya Joshi, Pushpak Bhattacharyya, and Mark J Carman. 2017. Automatic sarcasm detection: A survey. *ACM Computing Surveys (CSUR)*, 50(5):1–22.

James Lee-Thorp, Joshua Ainslie, Ilya Eckstein, and Santiago Ontanon. 2021. Fnet: Mixing tokens with fourier transforms. *arXiv preprint arXiv:2105.03824*.

Bing Liu. 2012. Sentiment analysis and opinion mining. *Synthesis lectures on human language technologies*, 5(1):1–167.

Diana Maynard and Mark Greenwood. 2014. Who cares about sarcastic tweets? investigating the impact of sarcasm on sentiment analysis. In *Proceedings of the Ninth International Conference on Language Resources and Evaluation (LREC'14)*, pages 4238–4243, Reykjavik, Iceland. European Language Resources Association (ELRA).

Bo Pang and Lillian Lee. 2009. Opinion mining and sentiment analysis. *Comput. Linguist*, 35(2):311–312.

Kim Schouten and Flavius Frasincar. 2015. Survey on aspect-level sentiment analysis. *IEEE Transactions on Knowledge and Data Engineering*, 28(3):813–830.

Seungwan Seo, Czangyeob Kim, Haedong Kim, Kyounghyun Mo, and Pilsung Kang. 2020. Comparative study of deep learning-based sentiment classification. *IEEE Access*, 8:6861–6875.

Maxim Tkachenko, Mikhail Malyuk, Nikita Shevchenko, Andrey Holmanyuk, and Nikolai Liubimov. 2020-2021. Label Studio: Data labeling software. Open source software available from https://github.com/heartexlabs/label-studio.

Mikalai Tsytsarau and Themis Palpanas. 2012. Survey on mining subjective data on the web. *Data Mining and Knowledge Discovery*, 24(3):478–514.

Jie Zhou, Jimmy Xiangji Huang, Qin Chen, Qinmin Vivian Hu, Tingting Wang, and Liang He. 2019. Deep learning for aspect-level sentiment classification: survey, vision, and challenges. *IEEE access*, 7:78454–78483.

Yuan Zhuang and Ellen Riloff. 2020. Exploring the role of context to distinguish rhetorical and information-seeking questions. In *Proceedings of the 58th Annual Meeting of the Association for Computational Linguistics: Student Research Workshop*, pages 306–312, Online. Association for Computational Linguistics.

The 33rd Conference on Computational Linguistics and Speech Processing (ROCLING 2021)
Taoyuan, Taiwan, October 15-16, 2021. The Association for Computational Linguistics and Chinese Language Processing

運用混合注意力生成對抗網路於科學論文引用意圖分類
Generative Adversarial Networks based on Mixed-Attentions for Citation Intent Classification in Scientific Publications

王昱翔 Yuh-Shyang Wang, 陳昭沂 Chao-Yi Chen, 李龍豪 Lung-Hao Lee
國立中央大學電機工程學系
Department of Electrical Engineering
National Central University
{107521135, 107501543}@ncu.edu.tw, lhlee@ee.ncu.edu.tw

摘要

我們提出一個基於混合力的生成對抗網路模型 (簡稱 maGAN)，應用於科學論文引用分類任務。我們先選擇合適的領域訓練資料，透過提出的混合注意力機制，以及生成對抗網路架構，先預訓練語言模型，然後微調至多元分類任務。我們用 SciCite 資料集比較模型效能，由實驗結果得知 maGAN 模型得到最好的 Macro-F1 0.8532。

Abstract

We propose the mixed-attention-based Generative Adversarial Network (named maGAN), and apply it for citation intent classification in scientific publication. We select domain-specific training data, propose a mixed attention mechanism, and employ generative adversarial network architecture for pre-training language model and fine-tuning to the downstream multi-class classification task. Experiments were conducted on the SciCite datasets to compare model performance. Our proposed maGAN model achieved the best Macro-F1 of 0.8532.

關鍵字：注意力機制、預訓練語言模型、引用意圖、科學論文

Keywords: attentions, pretrained language models, citation intents, scientific publications.

1 緒論

近年來科學論文出版量大幅成長，透過自然語言處理的方法，分析探討這些資料變得相當重要，目前以深度神經網路為主要方向，但這需要大量標記的資料，大規模數據通常是交由群眾外包 (crowdsourcing) 的方式獲得，但要對科學文本進行手動標註，標記人員須要具備專業知識，導致蒐集標記成本極高。ELMo (Peters et al., 2018)、GPT (Radford et al., 2018) 和 BERT (Devlin et al., 2019) 等這些語言模型在大型語料庫上進行無監督預訓練，為許多的自然語言處理任務帶來顯著的提升。以 BERT 為例，BERT 訓練時不需要額外的標記資料，只以訓練文本中挑選兩句辨識是否為前後文。這類無監督預訓練的方法對於像科學、醫學這些無法獲得大量標記的領域變得相當重要。

SciCite (Cohan et al., 2019) 是艾倫人工智慧研究所提供的資料集，來源為 Semantic Scholar 語料庫 (Ammar et al., 2018)，標註關於科學論文的引用意圖分類，對於論文的引用可以分為背景知識、方法和結果比較，每筆論文引用屬於三種類別其中之一。現有的方法以使用 SciBERT (Beltagy et al., 2020) 或 BERT 進行微調為主，並以 Macro-F1 作為評分標準。

本研究使用 SciCite 作為評估預訓練模型效果的測試資料。我們透過使用科學文本 S2ORC 資料集 (Lo et al., 2020) 訓練出的基於混合注意力(mixed-attention, ma)的生成對抗網路

(Generative Adversarial Network, GAN)，模型簡稱 maGAN，在 SciCite 資料集上獲得的 Macro-F1 為 0.8532，比 BERT 的 0.844 和 SciBERT 的 0.8499 更高。

本文章節如下，第二章探討相關研究，第三章敘述我們提出的 maGAN 模型，第四章為實驗結果與分析，最後是結論。

2 相關研究

預訓練語言模型 (pretrained language models) 是透過大規模未標記語料訓練模型，接著在下游任務上微調模型。最初的語言模型以學習單獨的單詞表示為主，例如：Word2Vec (Mikolov et al., 2013) 以及 GloVe (Pennington et al., 2014)。後來藉由 LSTM (Hochreiter and Schmidhuber, 1997) 為基底，建立了 CoVe (McCann et al., 2017) 和 ELMo (Peters et al., 2018) 這類包含上下文資訊的單詞表示方式。近年來，基於多頭注意力(multi-head attention) 的 Transformer (Vaswani et al., 2017) 架構，在許多自然語言處理任務中，表現得比 LSTM 來得更好。GPT 採用 Transformer 作為主架構，加入生成訓練的概念，在下游任務有不錯的提升。Google 於 2019 年提出的 BERT 模型架構基於多層雙向的 Transformer，訓練過程中不採用傳統由左到右的語言建模方式，而是在兩個任務上進行訓練：遮罩語言模型 (Masked Language Model, MLM) 以及下一句預測(Next Sentence Prediction, NSP)。MLM 是將句子中的片段遮起來，預測遮蔽處應填入的字詞，NSP 則是判斷兩個句子當中，第二句是否為第一句在原始文本中的下一句。由於 NSP 需要輸入兩段文字作為訓練資料，需要的訓練資源較高，ELECTRA (Clark et al., 2020) 提出元素替換檢測 (replaced token detection)，透過模型將輸入文句的部分元素做替換，再判斷文句是否經過替換，降低訓練成本，也提升訓練效果。後續研究也有對注意力進行改良，ConvBERT (Jiang et al., 2020) 則是基於 ELECTRA 架構，加入卷積的概念收集區間訊息。

語言模型在下游任務的表現，與其所使用的訓練文本涵蓋領域高度相關，大部分的 BERT 相關模型，都是通用語料庫如 Wikipedia、Common Crawl 中訓練，因此在特定領域的任務表現相對較差。目前有許多特定領域的預訓練模型，比方說在生物醫學領域的 BioBERT (Lee et al., 2020)、使用臨床診斷書和出院報告的 Clinical-BERT (Alsentzer et al., 2020)，以及使用科學論文的 SciBERT (Beltagy et al., 2020) 等等。這些預訓練模型，都在與該領域相關的任務中獲得良好的表現。

本研究採用的預訓練資料為 SciBERT 團隊於 2020 年提出的開放研究語料庫 (The Semantic Scholar Open Research Corpus, S2ORC) (Lo et al., 2020)，該語料庫的建立是使用 Semantic Scholar 的文獻語料庫 (Ammar et al., 2020)，包含來自 MAG (Shen et al., 2018)、arXiv 及 PubMed 等約 811 萬篇來自各領域的英文論文，其中占比最多的三個領域為藥學、生物學及化學。

3 研究方法

3.1 注意力機制

Bahdanau et al. (2014) 提出注意力機制，為解決使用 Seq2Seq 模型時，編碼輸入越長的句子，越前面的資訊越容易丟失的問題，注意力機制將上下文以及位置資訊也一併傳遞下去，如此即便是模型末段，也能獲得在序列前端的重要資訊。

自注意力(self-attention) 如圖 1 (a)。計算過程如方程式 (1) 到 (4) ，由輸入序列 A 產生三個矩陣 Q (Query), K (Key), V (Value)，先對 Q 跟 K 進行點積，相當於計算 Q 跟 K 的相似度，再將其降低 d_k 維度，並透過 softmax 轉換為機率分布，最後再乘上 V 獲得注意力權重。雖然自注意力具有學習非局部資訊的特色，但是仍有相當比例的注意力頭 (head) 是在學習局部依賴性，如果只採用部分注意力頭，反而會提升表現 (Kovaleva et al., 2019)。

$$Q = W_q A \quad (1)$$

$$K = W_k A \quad (2)$$

$$V = W_v A \quad (3)$$

$$SelfAttention(Q, K, V) = softmax(\frac{QK^T}{\sqrt{d_k}})V \quad (4)$$

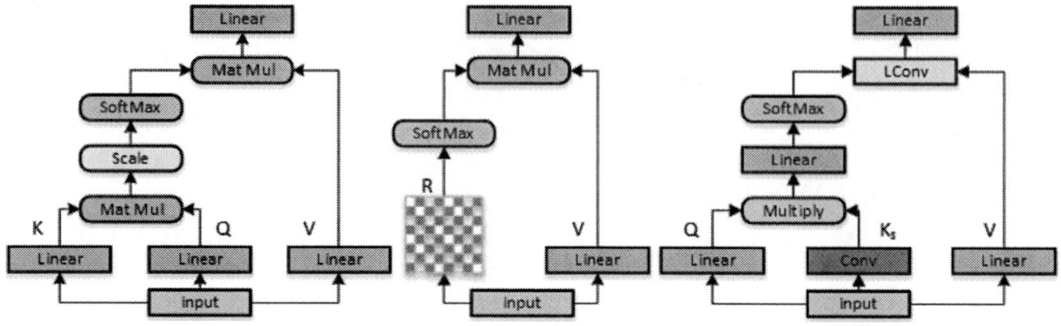

(a) self attention (b) random synthesized attention (c) span-based dynamic convolution

圖 1: 三種注意力機制

隨機合成注意力(random synthesized attention) (Tay et al., 2020) 是 synthesized attention 的一種如圖 1 (b)。計算過程如方程式 (5) 與 (6)，透過一個完全不受輸入 token 影響、隨機初始化的矩陣 R 進行訓練，矩陣 R 經過 softmax 得到機率分布後，再與由輸入序列產生的矩陣 V 相乘，獲得注意力權重。

$$V = W_v A \quad (5)$$

$$Random\,Synthesized\,Attention(R, V) = softmax(R)V \quad (6)$$

跨度動態卷積 (span-based dynamic convolution) 是由 ConvBERT (Jiang et al., 2020) 提出的注意力提取方式，如圖 1 (c) 所示。計算方式如方程式 (7) 與 (8)，該研究觀察到多頭注意力中，有些頭 (head) 只需要局部資料，便能完成注意力。因此，建立了局部依賴機制，藉此減少不必要運算量，但這種設計會在獲取全局資訊上表現較差。使用由 MobileNets 提出的深度分離卷積 (depthwise separable convolution) (Howard et al., 2017) 產生 K_s，再與 Q 做點積、降維、softmax 後，再與輸入序列產生的矩陣 V，一起經過輕量卷積 (light-weight convolution) (Wu et al., 2019)，就能得到跨度動態卷積的注意力權重，計算方式如方程式 (7) 與 (8)，其中 W 為 CNN 的卷積核。
由於不同注意力機制各有優缺點，若能結合長處並填補短處，便能更有效的提取資訊。因此，我們提出的混合注意力 (mixed-attention) 是由三個區塊所組成，包含自注意力、隨機合成注意力及跨度動態卷積，透過多頭注意力 (multi-head attention)，將自注意力機制 (SA)、隨機合成注意力(RSA)及跨度動態卷積 (SDConv)，三者以不同頭數獲得的注意力權重連接起來，並獲得新的注意力權重，如方程式 (9)。

$$LConv(X, W, i) = \sum_{j=1}^{k} W_j \cdot X_{i+j-\lceil\frac{k+1}{2}\rceil} \quad (7)$$

$$SDConv() = LConv(V, softmax\left(W_f(Q \odot K_s)\right), i) \quad (8)$$

$$MixAttention() = Concate(SA(), RSA(), SDConv()) \quad (9)$$

3.2 模型架構

我們提出的混合注意力生成對抗網路 (mixed-attention-based Generative Adversarial Network, maGAN) 模型，使用大量科學論文 S2ORC 資料集 (Lo et al., 2020) 作為預訓練語料，以 ELECTRA 架構 (Clark et al., 2020) 為基底，並採用改良的混合注意力機制訓練語言模型，預訓練 (pre-training) 架構如圖 2 (a)，分為兩個主要部分：生成器 (Generator)、判別器 (Discriminator)。生成器的功能是將輸入句中的遮罩部分進行替換，產生新的句子，並作為判別器的輸入。而判別器則是判斷輸入句

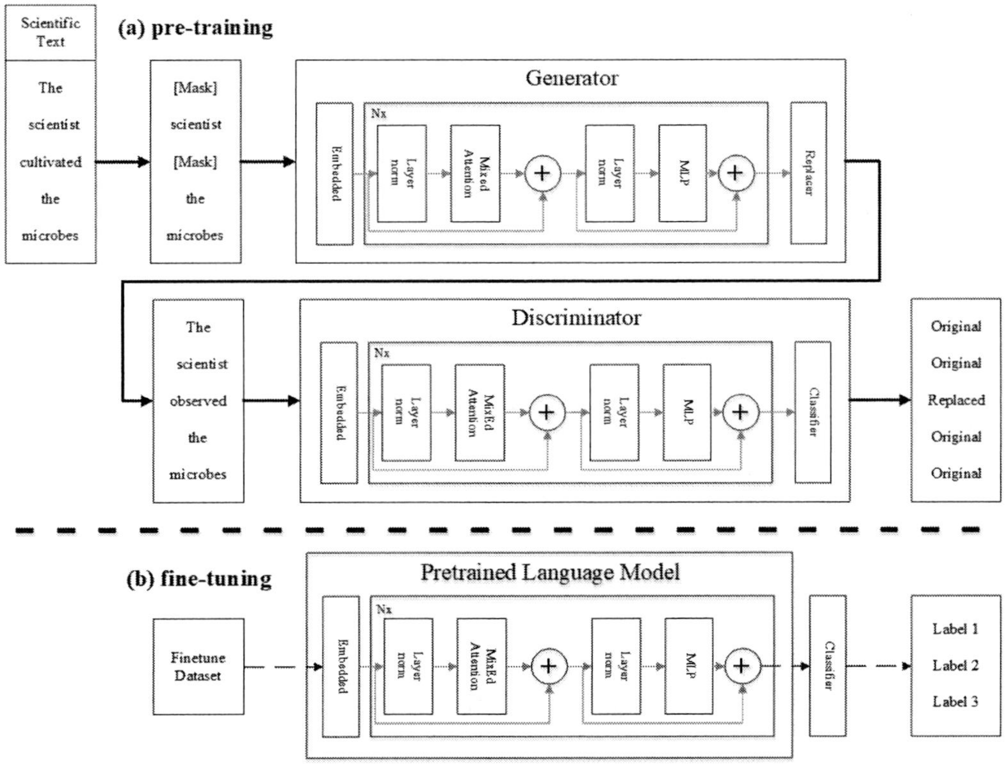

圖 2: 混和注意力生成對抗網路模型架構

中的字詞是否被生成器所替換。生成器和判別器架構相似都是透過其中的詞嵌入層 (embedding layer) 將輸入文字序列轉為固定詞向量，輸入編碼器 (transformer encoder)，藉由注意力機制獲取語意資訊，經過 N 層編碼器後，產生帶有語境的詞向量。

與 ELECTRA 架構不同的是，此處的注意力機制改用我們所提出的混合注意力 (mixed-attention)，而不是原來的多頭自注意力 (multi-head attention) 。生成器提取資訊後，將資訊輸入到替換器 (replacer) ，將文句進行替換，並輸出經替換的文句交由判別器；判別器完成資訊提取後，輸入到分類器中，判斷是否有元素被替換。

在圖 2 (b) 的微調 (fine-tuning) 階段，將下游任務的資料，藉由已完成訓練的判別器進行資訊提取，再連接符合任務需求的分類器進行訓練，微調過後的分類器，最後用來預測類別標籤 (label)。

4 模型評估

4.1 資料集

實驗資料來自 SciCite 資料集 (Cohan et al., 2019)，將科學論文的引用意圖分為三類：背景知識 (background information)、方法 (method) 與結果比較 (result comparison) ，類別定義與範例如表 1 所示。其中訓練集含有 8,243 筆、發展集有 916 筆，而測試集包含 1,861 筆。

4.2 實驗設定

模型參數設定均與 ELECTRA-BASE 相同，只有 Batch size 礙於硬體需求降為 64。而模型中採用的混合注意力機制中，三種注意力 SA : RSA : SDConv 各自頭數以 3:3:1 的方式組合。

效能指標如同公開的效能評測排行榜 (leaderboard)，以 Macro-F1 作為主要的評分依據，先計算各個類別的 Precision 及 Recall，然後算其調和平均數 F1-score，再將各類別的 F1 平均，即可獲得 Macro-F1。

意圖類別	定義	範例
背景知識 Background information	引文提供有關問題、概念、方法或重要性的背景信息	Recent evidence suggests that co-occurring alexithymia may explain deficits [12]. Locally high-temperature melting regions can act as permanent termination sites [6-9]. One line of work is focused on changing the objective function (Mao et al., 2016).
方法 Method	使用方法、工具或數據集	Fold differences were calculated by a mathematical model described in [4]. We use Orthogonal Initialization (Saxe et al., 2014)
結果比較 Result comparison	論文的結果或發現與相關研究的比較	Weighted measurements were superior to T2-weighted contrast imaging which was in accordance with former studies [25-27] Similar results to our study were reported in the study of Lee et al (2010)

表 1: 引用意圖類別與範例

Model	Macro F1
BiLSTM-Attention+ELMo	82.6
Structural-scaffolds	84.0
SciBERT	84.99
maGAN (ours)	85.32

表 2: 模型效能評估結果

預測分類 \ 實際分類	背景知識	方法	結果比較
背景知識	884	93	25
方法	44	489	1
結果比較	69	23	233

表 3: 錯誤分析混肴矩陣

4.3 效能分析

實驗結果如表 2。其他模型效能取自公開的效能評測排行榜[1]，除了 SciBERT 外，其他模型為 Cohan et al. (2019) 提出資料集的同時所提出的方法，BiLSTM-Attention+ELMo 使用 ELMo 為詞嵌入並藉由 BiLSTM 提取注意力，而 Structural-scaffolds 則是基於前者同時訓練多個任務，我們的 maGAN 模型獲得了 Macro-F1 85.32 目前是最好的成績。

表 3 為錯誤分析的混肴矩陣，最容易辨識錯誤的狀況為「方法」類別辨別為「背景知識」(佔全部錯誤的 36.4%)，其次是將「背景知識」分辨為「結果比較」(佔 27%)。根據我們的觀察，有部分錯誤是因為缺乏全文資訊而導致誤判，若是額外將論文前後文加入微調訓練中，有機會正確判斷分類。

[1] https://paperswithcode.com/sota/citation-intent-classification-on-scicite

5 結論

本研究針對科學論文引用分類任務，提出一個基於混和注意力的生成對抗網路模型，透過選擇合適的領域訓練語料，提出混和注意力機制，透過生成對抗網路架構，先預訓練語言模型，然後微調至分類任務，在 SciCite 測試資料獲得 0.8532 的 Macro-F1，目前是表現最好的模型。

致謝

This work was partially supported by the Ministry of Science and Technology, Taiwan under the grant MOST 108-2218-E-008-017-MY3.

参考資料

Emily Alsentzer, John R. Murphy, Willie Boag, Wei-Hung Weng, Di Jin, Tristan Naumann, and Matthew B. A. McDermott. 2019. Publicly Available Clinical BERT Embeddings. *arXiv Preprint*, https://arxiv.org/abs/1904.03323

Waleed Ammar, Dirk Groeneveld, Chandra Bhagavatula, Iz Beltagy, Miles Crawford, Doug Downey, Jason Dunkelberger, Ahmed Elgohary, Sergey Feldman, Vu Ha, et al. 2018. Construction of the literature graph in semantic scholar. In *Proceedings of NAACL-HLT'18, (Industry Papers)*. pages 84–91.

Dzmitry Bahdanau, Kyunghyun Cho, and Yoshua Bengio. 2014. Neural machine translation by jointly learning to align and translate. *arXiv Preprint*, https://arxiv.org/abs/1409.0473

Iz Beltagy, Kyle Lo, and Arman Cohan. 2019. SciBERT: A Pretrained Language Model for Scientific Text. In *Proceedings of EMNLP-IJCNLP'19*, pages 3615-3620.

Kevin Clark, Minh-Thang Luong, Quoc V. Le, and Christopher D. Manning. 2020. Electra: Pre-training text encoders as discriminators rather than generators. *arXiv Preprint*, https://arxiv.org/abs/2003.10555

Arman Cohan, Waleed Ammar, Madeleine van Zuylen, and Fiels Cady. 2019. Structural scaffolds for citation intent classification in scientific publications. *arXiv Preprint*, https://arxiv.org/abs/1904.01608

Jacob Devlin, Ming-Wei Chang, Kenton Lee, and Kristina Toutanova. 2018. BERT: Pre-training of Deep Bidirectional Transformers for Language Understanding. *arXiv Preprint*, https://arxiv.org/abs/1810.04805

Sepp Hochreiter and Jürgen Schmidhuber. 1997. Long short-term memory. *Neural computation*, *9*(8):1735-1780.

Andrew G. Howard, Menglong Zhu, Bo Chen, Dmitry Kalenichenko, Weijun Wang, Tobias Weyand, Marco Andreetto, and Hartwig Adam. 2017. Mobilenets: Efficient convolutional neural networks for mobile vision applications. *arXiv Preprint*, https://arxiv.org/abs/1704.04861

Zihang Jiang, Weihao Yu, Daquan Zhou, Yunpeng Chen, Jiashi Feng, and Shuicheng Yan. 2020. ConvBERT: Improving BERT with Span-based Dynamic Convolution. *arXiv Preprint*, https://arxiv.org/abs/2008.02496

Olga Kovaleva, Alexey Romanov, Anna Rogers, and Anna Rumshisky. 2019. Revealing the dark secrets of BERT. *arXiv Preprint*, https://arxiv.org/abs/1908.08593

Jinhyuk Lee, Wonjin Yoon, Sungdong Kim, Donghyeon Kim, Sunkyu Kim, Chan Ho So, and Jaewoo Kang. 2020. BioBERT: a pre-trained biomedical language representation model for biomedical text mining. *Bioinformatics*, *36*(4):1234-1240.

Kyle Lo, Lucy Lu Wang, Mark Neumann, Rodney Kinney, and Daniel Weld. 2020. S2ORC: The Semantic Scholar Open Research Corpus. In *Proceedings of ACL'20*, pages 4969-4983.

Bryan McCann, James Bradbury, Caiming Xiong, and Richard Socher. 2017. Learned in translation: Contextualized word vectors. *arXiv Preprint*, https://arxiv.org/abs/1708.00107

Thomas Mikolov, Ilya Sutskever, Kai Chen, Greg Corrado, and Jeffrey Dean. 2013. Distributed representations of words and phrases and their compositionality. In *Proceedings of NIPS'13*, pages 3111-3119.

Jeffrey Pennington, Richard Socher, and Christopher D. Manning. 2014. GloVe: Global Vectors for Word Representation. In *Proceedings of EMNLP'14*, pages 1532-1543.

Matthew E. Peters, Mark Neumann, Mohit Iyyer, Matt Gardner, Christopher Clark, Kenton Lee, and Luke Zettlemoyer. 2018. Deep contextualized word representations. In *Proceddings of NAACL'18*, pages 2227-2237.

Alec Radford, Karthik Narasimhan, Tim Salimans, and Ilya Sutskever. 2018. Improving language understanding by generative pre-training.

Zhihong Shen, Hao Ma, and Kuansan Wang. 2018. A Web-scale system for scientific knowledge exploration. In *Proceedings of ACL'18, System Demonstrations*, pages 87-92.

Yi Tay, Dara Bahri, Donald Metzler, Da-Cheng Juan, Zhe Zhao,and Che Zheng. 2021. Synthesizer: Rethinking Self-Attention for Transformer Models. In *Proceedings of ICML'21*, PMLR 139:10183-10192.

Ashish Vaswani, Noam Shazeer, Niki Parmar, Jakob Uszkoreit, Llion Jones, Aidan N. Gomez, Łukasz Kaiser, and Illia Polosukhin. 2017. *Attention is all you need.* In *Proceeding of NIPS'17*, pages 5998-6008.

Felix Wu, Angela Fan, Alexei Baevski, Yann N. Dauphin, and Michael Auli. 2019. Pay less attention with lightweight and dynamic convolutions. *arXiv Preprint*, https://arxiv.org/abs/1901.10430

The 33rd Conference on Computational Linguistics and Speech Processing (ROCLING 2021)
Taoyuan, Taiwan, October 15-16, 2021. The Association for Computational Linguistics and Chinese Language Processing

A Corpus for Dimensional Sentiment Classification on YouTube Streaming Service

Ching-Wen Hsu
Department of Big Data Management,
Soochow University, Taipei, Taiwan
06170139@gm.scu.edu.tw

Chun-Lin Chou
Department of Big Data Management,
Soochow University, Taipei, Taiwan
07370005@gm.scu.edu.tw

Hsuan Liu
Department of Big Data Management,
Soochow University, Taipei, Taiwan
06170114@gm.scu.edu.tw

Jheng-Long Wu
Department of Data Science,
Soochow University, Taipei, Taiwan
jlwu@gm.scu.edu.tw

Abstract

The streaming service platform such as YouTube provides a discussion function for audiences worldwide to share comments. YouTubers who upload videos to the YouTube platform want to track the performance of these uploaded videos. However, the present analysis functions of YouTube only provide a few performance indicators such as average view duration, browsing history, variance in audience's demographics, etc., and lack of sentiment analysis on the audience's comments. Therefore, the paper proposes multi-dimensional sentiment indicators such as YouTuber preference, Video preferences, and Excitement level to capture comprehensive sentiment on audience comments for videos and YouTubers. To evaluate the performance of different classifiers, we experiment with deep learning-based, machine learning-based, and BERT-based classifiers to automatically detect three sentiment indicators of an audience's comments. Experimental results indicate that the BERT-based classifier is a better classification model than other classifiers according to F1-score, and the sentiment indicator of Excitement level is quite an improvement. Therefore, the multiple sentiment detection tasks on the video streaming service platform can be solved by the proposed multi-dimensional sentiment indicators accompanied with BERT classifier to gain the best result.

Keywords: Sentiment Analysis, Text Classification, Machine Learning, Deep Learning, Streaming Service

1 Introduction

Due to the rapid rise of new media and the popularization of mobile phone networks, audiences' viewing habits have shifted from TV to online social media platforms. Now people can watch videos on different platforms such as Facebook, Dailymotion, and YouTube anytime and anywhere. YouTube has 16 million active users in Taiwan monthly, and nearly 93% of users have visited YouTube. In addition, YouTube has become ubiquitous and played an increasingly important role in modern life and entertainment. Also, YouTube provides a discussion function for audiences to express their opinion by clicking like or dislike bottom or leaving comments. Therefore, comprehensive sentiment analysis for comments of the audience on YouTube is necessary.

It is verified that public views, comments, and attitudes towards many events can be analyzed through social media (Heredia et al., 2016). Public reviews on Amazon were used to evaluate users' opinions and determine the audience's preference by classifying opinions into negative, positive, and neutral (Bhatt et al., 2015). Another research investigated the popularity of videos by indicators such as the number of likes, dislikes, and views (Chelaru et al., 2013). Social media, especially YouTube. is considered the largest video sharing site, and the platform has developed into a leading marketing tool. (Schwemmer and Ziewiecki, 2018) Inspired by the above analysis tasks and the rapid growth status of YouTube, we propose the multi-dimensional sentiment indicators to analyze comments on YouTube, which aim to help YouTubers check their videos' performance uploaded on the YouTube platform.

In general, sentiment analysis focuses on determining the positive, negative, or neutral emotions in many pieces of research (Cunha et al., 2019). Even if Keith et al. (2016) extend the emotional detection, which includes highly positive, optimistic, neutral, negative, and highly damaging, the emotional variance may have a different dimension, such as excitement which expresses the audience's fluctuating emotion. So, we also propose detecting the audience's excitement level on YouTube because excitement more precisely determines how much the audience likes Youtubers or videos.

To obtain comprehensive sentiment indicators, we design three indicators: YouTuber preference, Video preference, and Excitement level to analyze a multi-dimensional aspect of the audience's comments. In the experiment, these three sentiment indicators also represent three detection tasks that aim to detect the audience's motivations behind a myriad of comments.

Various models deal with text-based sentiment classification tasks. Machine learning-based models are used to address the text classification task (Sun et al., 2019). Other deep learning models have been used for sentiment analysis and obtained acceptable performances (Hassan & Mahmood, 2017). Recently, it has refreshed the best performance of using pre-trained language models as soon as it appears. ELMo (Peters et al., 2018) and BERT (Radford et al., 2018) have been effective because pre-trained models have learned by detecting other tasks from a larger corpus which capture more linguistic structure.

This paper's objectives are: (1) to create a corpus for multi-dimensional sentiment indicators, which include YouTuber preference, Video preferences, and Excitement level; (2) train an automatic sentiment detection model, including machine learning-based, deep learning-based, and BERT-based models. Overall, the contributions of this paper are: (1) We establish a benchmark dataset of dimensional sentiment classification for analyzing comments on YouTube. (2) Successfully using different models to deal with sentiment classification issues.

2 Related Work

More and more researchers undertook experiments on YouTube as the data source. The purpose is to obtain an understanding of the community commenting behavior. Severyn et al. (2016) showed that although most audiences present their opinions as comments, some abuse this mechanism by posting links to external web pages or posting disruptive, false, or offensive comments to fool and provoke other users. Based on the result of the above research, this paper's dataset eliminates non-relative comments such as links that guide people to external web pages and advertisements that have no relation to video content. Schultes et al. (2013) work on YouTube video comments, likes, and dislikes to show that it genuinely influences users' perceptions of like or dislike towards videos when reviewing valuable comments.

Moving to some purposes of text classification used nowadays, Turney (2002) did sentiment analysis by establishing an unsupervised classifier to judge the positivity or negativity of product reviews (cars, banks, and tourist destinations) and movie reviews. Another paper presented an approach based on a clustering of comment content, leading to appropriate video categories (Leung et al., 2009). Machine learning approaches are then introduced to automatically classify comments according to their usefulness (Bhavitha et al. 2017). As the above papers show, comments can achieve various objectives by using different technical methods.

There are currently two approaches to address sentiment analysis: (1) lexicon-based techniques (2) algorithm-based techniques. Lexicon-based techniques rely on predefined words and rules to guide the sentence towards the tendency of emotion. Algorithm-based techniques can be divided into two groups: machine learning-based models s and deep learning-based models.

Zhang and Zheng (2016) discussed machine learning methods for sentiment analysis. Dang et al. (2020) employed deep-learning approaches with word embedding and TF-IDF to solve sentiment analysis problems. As a result, the best behavior when using the word embedding method against TF-IDF of all models has been proved. Another research used pre-trained word embedding as an important component for it downstream models. (T. Miyato, A. M. Dai, et al., 2017) Thus, we identify that word embedding is in conjunction with deep learning-based models in our experimental and pre-trained word embedding offer significant improvement over embedding learned from scratch. Moreover, due to the effectiveness of pre-trained language models, adding one additional output layer can fine-tuned models and accelerating the accuracy of classification problems. Sun et al. (2019) fine-tuned with Bidirectional Encoder Representations from the Transformers (BERT) model and achieved state-of-the-art results using comments. Liat Ein-Dor et al. (2020) using BERT based models for binary classification tasks

To deal with sentiment analysis tasks, these papers all share some commons. Firstly, comments in nowadays social media, especially YouTube, are of great value and even thoroughly necessary. Secondly, despite different methods that are conducted, comments do reflect users' opinions on social media. The above works are similar to this paper, all using comments as data sources but a different way to solve the task; we reference the above methods and determine to use all the methods, including deep learning-based, machine learning-based, and BERT-based classifiers. However, each method has been experimented with separately so as to carry out a comparative study. Also, the difference is that we focus our experiment on multi-class text classification.

3 Methodology

Figure 1 shows the proposed method for sentiment analysis and classification processes as follows: Firstly, we collected the audience's comments from YouTube platform and subsequently labeled these comments to provide meaningful and informative labels such as three sentiment indicators for model training. Data preprocessing works are conducted to clear text. Next, all comment's texts need to be converted into vectors to serve as the model's input. And then, machine learning and deep learning models propose to train detection models for our proposed sentiment indicators. Finally, by the experiment stage, we evaluate the performance of each classifier in three detection tasks and discuss a comparative study.

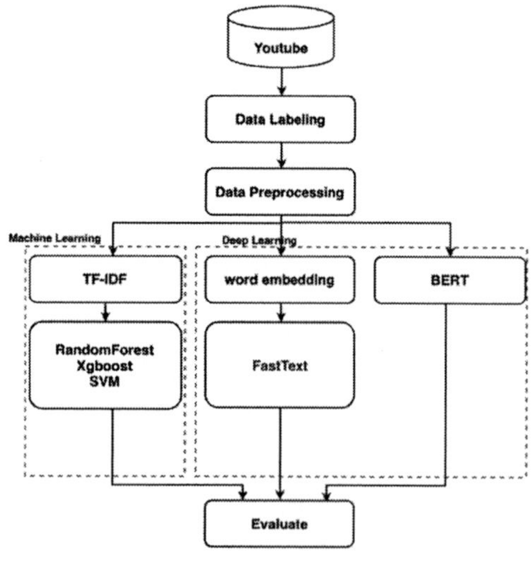

Figure 1: The process of the proposed sentiment analysis in this paper.

3.1 Comment Collection

To properly fit data with our analysis targets and cover the diversity of YouTube channels, we select different YouTube channels as our dataset, including 25 YouTuber channels. The composition of the selected videos' film creation types which game with 1%, education 4%, DIY with 4%, science and technology with 5 %, comedy 9%, entertainment with 28%, and blog with 49%. Through these selecting channels, we then filter five videos from each channel that have been highly popular or controversial since 2019 because people imminently show their interest in new tread and debatable topics. Therefore, a total of 25 videos were selected as our data sources. In this way, more controversial and polarizing comments are generated, and it becomes easier to determine the sentimental tendency of comments. However, to avoid different accumulated numbers of comments in each video, we randomly remain 100 pieces of comments from each video. Thus, a total of 12500 pieces comments is taking into consideration.

3.2 Definition of Sentiment Indicators for Comment of YouTube

We design three indicators, including YouTube preference, Video preference, and Excitement level, to investigate different aspects of the audience's comment. Each sentiment indicator and the detailed definition is as following:

- **YouTuber preference**: Comments can roughly divide into non-relative and relative towards YouTubers. However, YouTubers may be more concerned about relative comments because these comments help improve YouTubers' behaviors, so we subdivide relative comments into three attitudes towards YouTubers: unlike, neutral, and like. For example, comments not containing YouTuber's name or affair will be labeled as non-relative, and the rest of the labels can determine the audience's tendency of their preferences. Overall, the indicator, YouTuber preference, is categorized as non-relative, unlike, neutral, and like.

- **Video preference**: The indicator, Video preference, is classified into four parts as YouTuber preference. Non-relative, unlike, neutral, and like are four categories used to judge Video preference. For example, if comments did not contain video content or talk about YouTuber's affair, then comments are be labeled as non-relative comments. In contrast, comments discussing videos, whether showing their preference, may be labeled as one of unlike, neutral, or like towards video.

- **Excitement level**: The Excitement level, which shows the audience's emotional ups and downs, is designed into five categories, classifying the audience's speaking tone from no emotion to extreme emotion state step by step. Moreover, we consider emojis a judgment in this indicator because of the audience's switching habit in leaving comments. People use a variety of emojis as an emotional expression nowadays, and thus emojis are highly accompanied by texts. Thus, a higher number of emojis containing in comments, a larger Excitement level and sentiment are expressed. For example, the number 0 stands for barely excited emotion contained in comments, while the number 4 represents hyper excited emotion.

3.3 Sentiment Indicator Labeling

In this paper, there are three experts to annotate sentiment indicators. All experts possess the background of using YouTube for an extended period and use the YouTube platform frequently. During the annotation process, we eliminate some non-relative comments, such as advertisements, comments that not using Mandarin, comments that post links to external web pages, and merely timestamps in the comments, to optimize the availability of the dataset. Also, to address semantic comprehension gaps between each annotator, we even provide an annotation guideline to consistently label the audience's comments. Table 1 is a guideline of annotation for the Excitement level indicator. When marking indicator of Excitement Level, sentences with emojis must not be allow to mark as 0 points. Besides, watching the videos is also required before labeling comments; in this way, annotators might resonate powerfully with the audience's opinions.

Excitement level	**Definition**
Barely excited	No emoji
Slightly excited	One type of emoji
Excited	Speak confidently and contain two types of emojis
Fairly excited	Emojis are highly repetitive or over three types emojis
Hyper excited	A lot of rhetoric and a series of emojis

Table 1: Annotation guideline to Excitement level.

In Table 2, we show the result of annotation agreement scores using three assessments, including Krippendorff's Alpha, Fleiss's Kappa, and Cronbach's Alpha. With Krippendorff's Alpha method, due to the reason that values smaller than 0.667 represent as discard data, so our three indicators are shown not up to the standard. Fleiss's Kappa method stands for fair and moderate data because values between 0.21 to 0.6 are considered acceptable levels. Cronbach's Alpha method evaluates three indicators as outstanding labeling work because a value higher than 0.7 may show annotation agreement, let alone we get 0.9 on Excitement level. Therefore, two of the methods were qualified as acceptance results, and thus we provide an adequately labeled dataset to train and assess a given model.

	YouTuber preference	**Video preference**	**Excitement level**
Krippendorff's Alpha	0.5829	0.4545	0.3898
Fleiss's Kappa	0.5840	0.4594	0.3928
Cronbach's Alpha	0.8520	0.7264	0.900

Table 2: Annotation agreement scores for each indicator.

3.4 Text Preprocessing

To deal with a few variances in our annotated results, we use the majority decision to filter out inconsistent labels unless each comment annotation is marked as the same point. This objective is to provide a 'ground truth,' a properly labeled dataset, to train and assess a given model. As we mentioned in section 3.3, we consider emojis emotional expressions, so dealing with rich emojis is our priority. We transfer emojis to text by the package called "emojiswitch." Then, we establish a user-defined dictionary to recognize specific words. For example, we establish the names of the lead actors/actresses and the supporting actors/actresses from our selected videos. Additionally, texts transferred from emojis are also defined as unique objects and be part of our defined dictionary. In this way, we can increase the accuracy of word tokenization. After executing the above two steps, we use the current state-of-art word tokenization tool created by the Chinese Knowledge and Information Processing (CKIP) Group. This tool is available for dealing with tokenization in Mandarin. Through these processes, every word may contain the same meaning as we do data labeling job.

3.5 Text Classification

To verify dimensional sentiment classification that we propose several classifiers to learn and detect sentiment indicators. There are three series classifiers and describe:

- **Machine learning-based classifiers**: RandomForest, Xgboost, and SVM (Amrani et al., 2018) are used as methods for experiments. We transform comments into numerical vectors by using TF-IDF to represent each word related to the entire corpus and serve as inputs to fit models.

- **Deep learning-based classifiers**: We utilize FastText, which is bought with word-embedding in our experiment stage. Because of the lack of a myriad of training Chinese corpus, we take advantage of pre-trained word embeddings based on the 2021 Wikipedia Chinese corpus to transform our data into vectors and use them as inputs to train deep learning-based algorithms. Such a massive corpus may get better feature learning than we train word vectors from our dataset.

- **BERT-based classifier**: Using the pre-trained models (Devlin et al., 2018): We select "distilbert-base-multilingual-cased" and "bert-base-multilingual-cased" as our models. According to the mechanism of pre-trained tokens, the inputs are the output of transferring text using a pre-trained corpus, with 21 thousand words in size. However, not using the word-embedding method as model training, only adding a unique embedding ([CLS]) before the first word of tokens.

3.6 Classification Tasks

We apply three methods, six models, to train classifiers and analyze three targets to capture comprehensive sentiment on the comment of the audience. The following elaborates the meaning of three tasks for our experiment.

- **T1**: The audience's sentiment towards YouTubers is an extended issue from an indicator of YouTuber preference. We exclude non-relative comments and remain comments of unlike, neutral, and like from the indicator. Like and dislike can serve as a hallmark for YouTubers to check the performance of his or her channel. Also, YouTubers can know what attractive they own or what causes them to make a nuisance.

- **T2**: The audience's sentiment towards videos excludes non-relative comments from the indicator of Video preference and remains the rest of the comments, including comments of unlike, neutral, and like, just like T1 does. Even if watching the same channel, the different themes will captivate and engage different audiences. Therefore, this task may help YouTubers understand their audience's preferences within a specific channel.

- **T3**: Corresponding to the indicator of Excitement level, T3 aims to analyze the audience's emotional ups and downs, which can firmly confirm the degree of support from different audiences and affirm the audience's attitude towards specific issues.

4 Experiment

4.1 Dataset

After excluding the non-relative dataset from the indicator of YouTuber preference, most rest comments are labeled as like in the audience's sentiment towards YouTubers. Next, the composition of comments towards Video preference shows that 60 percent of comments are neutral attitudes. T3 applies the result of the indicator of Excitement level, revealing that the audience could express their happiness and wrath by commenting. Table 3 shows the proportion of data to our three tasks.

Task	Class	Number
T1	Unlike	287 (10%)
	Neutral	784 (28%)
	Like	1,705 (61%)
T2	Unlike	659 (7%)
	Neutral	5,842 (60%)
	Like	3,274 (33%)
T3	Barely excited	2,788 (30%)
	Slightly excited	2,478 (27%)
	Excited	2,341 (25%)
	Fairly excited	1,136 (12%)
	Hyper excited	471 (5%)

Table 3: Distribution of five tasks.

4.2 Experiment design

In this section, we introduce the process of building multiple classifiers. Multiple models are shown in Table 4 and are conducted with different parameters. Through experiments, we configure the best parameters on each model to predict different aspects of sentiment analysis.

Model	Description
M1	BERT model using *bert-base-multilingual-cased* pre-trained model.
M2	BERT model using *distilbert-base-multilingual-cased* pre-trained model.
M3	RandomForest + TF-IDF
M4	Xgboost + TF-IDF
M5	SVM + TF-IDF
M6	FastText + embedding

Table 4: There are six models use to solve three tasks.

We use 5-fold cross-validation to ensure the performance for all models. By fixedly set k=5 to our dataset, 80% of the data for training and 20% for testing in each fold. After conducting experiments, we evaluate and interpret the performances of different models through the suitable metrics used for classification problems: overall accuracy and F1-score. These tasks are all be performed by Google Colab GPU.

Selecting the correct parameters is vital to attain maximizing model performance. A set of experimented parameters based on their influence on the models are conducted in our paper. In deep learning and BERT experiments, parameters such as batch sizes (32 and 64), dropout rates (0.1 and 0.5), and learning rates (0.001 and 0.005) are considered.

By experimenting with numerous combinations of parameters, finally, we configure the best parameter for each algorithm and use it to predict the test dataset. However, the classification in each indicator may not be equally distributed, so accuracy is not efficiently reflecting the model's performance. Thus, we also use F1-score to measures models' performance.

4.3 Results

Figure 2 shows the result of the audience's sentiment towards YouTubers. The threshold of model performance is set as 0.5 according to the performance of machine learning-based algorisms. BERT-based classifiers and deep learning-based classifier have similar outcomes, and thus are all better than the machine learning-based classifiers.

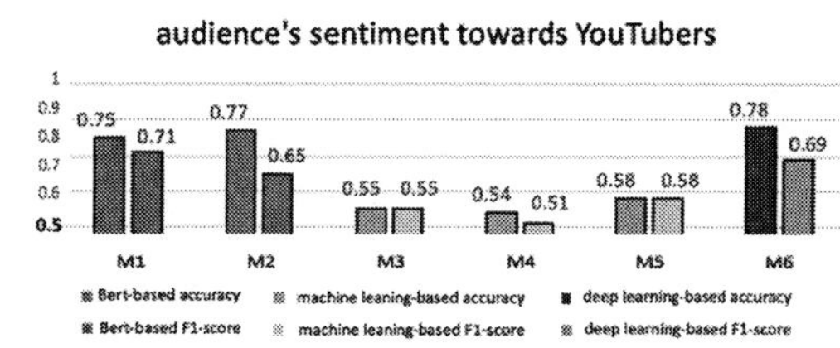

Figure 2: Performance of models on audience's sentiment towards YouTubers (T1).

Figure 3 is the result of predicting the audience's sentiment towards videos. We set the threshold of 0.5 according to the performance of machine learning-based algorisms. M3, M4, and M5 achieve the same score in each of their accuracy and F1-score. However, BERT and deep learning-based methods show the same tendency: accuracy is 10% higher than F1-score. It proves that whether models the F1-score of machine learning-based algorisms can highly perform as the accuracy.

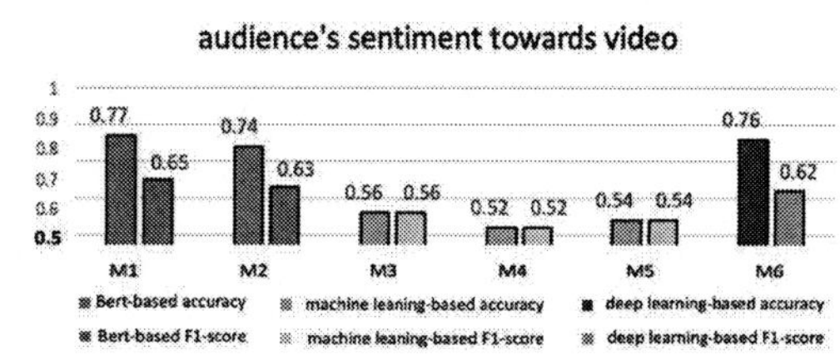

Figure 3: Performance of models on audience's sentiment towards videos (T2).

As Figure 4, we set the threshold as 0.3 to be the baseline of our models' performance. Compared with the above two tasks, predicting the audience's emotion differs significantly in each method. Nevertheless, this task is relatively the best to distinguish the performance of different methods. For example, scores of machine learning-based classifiers reduce significantly compared with detecting the audience's sentiment towards videos, nearly 20% decrease in accuracy and F1-score. Although BERT and deep learning-based models also drop their performance compared with detecting the audience's sentiment towards videos by 10%, these two methods have the better efficacy of dealing with a multi-classification problem.

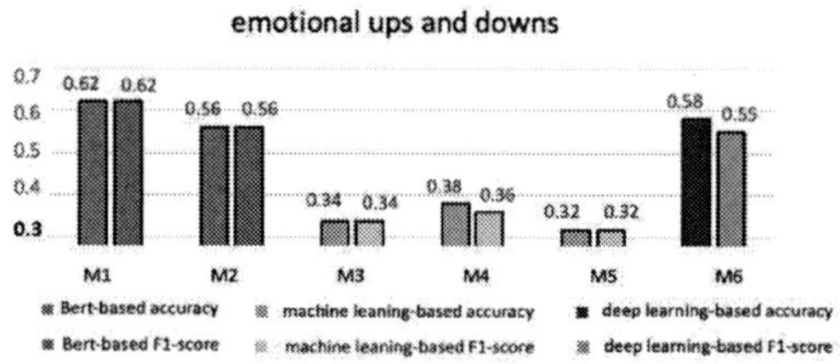

Figure 4: Performance of models on emotional ups and downs (T3).

4.4 Discussion

In summary, three findings follow (1) Within three sentiment detection tasks for comments on YouTube, machine learning-based classifiers cannot achieve performances compared with other methods. (2) When comparing three methods' performance in each detection task, it shows that the performance of the deep learning-based models evenly matched the score with BERT-based models. However, a slight variance exists in F1-score. (3) BERT slightly outperforms other models in three tasks according to the F1-score, and F1-score also achieves its accuracy, which stands for the minority of dataset's categories that are taken into consideration during model predicting.

Nevertheless, the task of the audience's sentiment indicators prediction has solved by this paper, and the BERT model has obtained a significant difference which has 0.62 F1-score improvement over these machine learning-based models. We can also highlight that most comments in the indicator of Excitement level are labeled as barely excited or slightly excited as our training dataset; only a few comments are labeled as having hyper excited. However, few labels obtain nearly the same recall as the majority of labels in our result. Therefore, the BERT-based models have learned some sentiment patterns from comments of the audience's extreme emotions. Moreover, the experimental result presents that the TF-IDF method has not obtained good performance, because the context of comment is a very important factor but TF-IDF does not handle that.

5 Conclusion

This paper focuses on sentiment analysis using the core of BERT pre-trained language models and accompanied by one deep learning-based model and three machine learning-based models. After conducting experiments, the method of deep learning and BERT perform better than the machine learning method. We also show that BERT can deal with sentiment polarity by determining the audience's likes or dislikes towards YouTubers. Finally, BERT is perfectly addressing the multi-classification problem. Before utilizing these classifiers, introducing related labeling jobs as a prerequisite is vital to getting a reliable dataset. Through these methods, we genuinely fill the gaps between human semantic comprehension.

Analyzing the public's perception of YouTubers and the influence of their videos is a challenging task for researchers so far. Proposing different sentiment indicators and utilizing different classifiers has been done in this paper, but there still is a long way to overcome some problems. In this paper, we have emphasized the following problems in order to make our results improve. (1) Informal language styles such as sparse emojis used by the audiences may impede models from capturing linguistic structure. (2) the semantic comprehension gap among annotators needs to be reduced to improve annotation consistency.

In the future, we may explore other techniques for optimizing multiple-dimensional sentiment analysis tasks, such as training YouTubers' names as embedding before utilizing different models. In this way, perhaps models can precisely filter out non-relative comments towards YouTubers. In addition, others indicators, such as whether the comments contain an ironic statement or whether the comments are erotic, can be added for analyzing other aspects of the audience's comments. The latter proposed indicator may serve as a guard for children users, and the former indicator may prevent YouTubers from getting into conflict with their fans.

References

Ain, Q. T., Ali, M., Riaz, A., Noureen, A., Kamran, M., Hayat, B., & Rehman, A. (2017). Sentiment analysis using deep learning techniques: a review. *Int J Adv Comput Sci Appl, 8*(6), 424-433.

Al Amrani, Y., Lazaar, M., & El Kadiri, K. E. (2018). Random forest and support vector machine based hybrid approach to sentiment analysis. *Procedia Computer Science, 127*, 511-520.

Bhatt, A., Patel, A., Chheda, H., & Gawande, K. (2015). Amazon Review Classification and Sentiment Analysis. *International Journal of Computer Science and Information Technologies, 6*(6), 5107-5110.

Bhavitha, B., Rodrigues, A.P., & Chiplunkar, N.N. (2017, March). Comparative study of machine learning techniques in sentimental analysis. In *2017 International Conference on Inventive Communication and Computational Technologies (ICICCT)* (pp. 216-221). Coimbatore, India: IEEE.

Cunha, A.A.L., Costa, M.C., & Pacheco, M.A.C. (2019, June) Sentiment Analysis of YouTube Video Comments Using Deep Neural Networks. In *International Conference on Artificial Intelligence and Soft Computing (ICAISC)* (pp. 561-570). Zakopane, Poland: Springer.

Dang, N. C., Moreno-García, M. N., & Prieta, F. D. L. (2020). Sentiment Analysis Based on Deep Learning: A Comparative Study. *Electronics, 9*(3), 483-512.

Devlin, J., Chang, M. W., Lee, K., & Toutanova, K. (2018). BERT: Pre-training of deep bidirectional transformers for language understanding. https://arxiv.org/abs/1810.04805

Keith Norambuena, B., Lettura, E. F., & Villegas, C. M. (2019). Sentiment analysis and opinion mining applied to scientific paper reviews. *Intelligent Data Analysis, 23*(1), 191-214.

Hassan, A., & Mahmood, A. (2017, April). Deep learning approach for sentiment analysis of short texts. In *2017 3rd international conference on control, automation and robotics (ICCAR)* (pp. 705-710). Nagoya, Japan: IEEE.

Heredia, B., Khoshgoftaar, T. M., Prusa, J., & Crawford, M. (2016, July). Cross-domain sentiment analysis: An empirical investigation. In *2016 IEEE 17th International Conference on Information Reuse and Integration (IRI)* (pp. 160-165). Pittsburgh, PA, United States: IEEE.

Leung, J. K.-W., Li, C.H., & Ip, T. K. (2009). Commentary-based Video Categorization and Concept Discovery. In *Proceedings of the 2nd ACM workshop on Social web search and mining (SWSM '09)* (pp. 49-56). New York, United States: Association for Computing Machinery.

Dor, L. E., Halfon, A., Gera, A., Shnarch, E., Dankin, L., Choshen, L., ... & Slonim, N. (2020, November). Active learning for BERT: An empirical study. In *Proceedings of the 2020 Conference on Empirical Methods in Natural Language Processing (EMNLP)* (pp. 7949-7962).

Pandey, A.C., Rajpoot, D.S., & Saraswat, M. (2017). Twitter sentiment analysis using hybrid cuckoo search method. *Information Processing & Management, 53*(4), 764-779.

Peters, M. E., Neumann, M., Iyyer, M., Gardner, M., Clark, C., Lee, K., & Zettlemoyer, L. (2018). Deep contextualized word representations. https://arxiv.org/abs/1802.05365

Schultes, P., Dorner, V., & Lehner, F. (2013). Leave a Comment! An In-Depth Analysis of User Comments on YouTube. *Wirtschaftsinformatik, 42*, 659-673.

Schwemmer, C., & Ziewiecki, S. (2018). Social Media Sellout: The Increasing Role of Product Promotion on YouTube. *Social Media + Society. 4*(3). https://doi.org/10.1177/2056305118786720

Severyn, A., Moschitti, A., Uryupina, O., Plank, B., & Filippova, K. (2016). Multi-lingual opinion mining on YouTube. *Information Processing & Management, 52*(1), 46-60.

Siersdorfer, S., Chelaru, S., Pedro, J. S., Altingovde, I. S., & Nejdl, W. (2014). Analyzing and mining comments and comment ratings on the social web. *ACM Transactions on the Web (TWEB), 8*(3), 1-39.

Sun, C., Huang, L., & Qiu, X. (2019). Utilizing BERT for aspect-based sentiment analysis via constructing auxiliary sentence. https://arxiv.org/abs/1903.09588

T.Miyuto,A. M.Dai, and I. Goodfellow, "Adversarial training methods for semi-supervised text classification," in The 5th International Conference on Learning Representation (ICLR 2017), 2017.

Turney, P. D. (2002). Thumbs up or thumbs down? Semantic orientation applied to unsupervised classification of reviews. https://arxiv.org/abs/**0212032**

Zhang, X., & Zheng, X. (2016, July). Comparison of text sentiment analysis based on machine learning. In *2016 15th international symposium on parallel and distributed computing (ISPDC)* (pp. 230-233). Fuzhou, China: IEEE.

The 33rd Conference on Computational Linguistics and Speech Processing (ROCLING 2021)
Taoyuan, Taiwan, October 15-16, 2021. The Association for Computational Linguistics and Chinese Language Processing

Improved Text Classification of Long-term Care Materials

范姜頤 Yi Fan Chiang
國立政治大學語言學研究所
Graduate Institute of Linguistics
National Chengchi University
vianne6@gmail.com

李季陵 Chi-Ling Lee
國立政治大學華語文教學碩博士學位學程
Master's & Doctor's Program in Teaching Chinese as a Second Language
National Chengchi University
19940818jillian@gmail.com

廖恒佳 Heng-Chia Liao
國立政治大學華語文教學碩士學位學程
Master's Program in Teaching Chinese as a Second Language
National Chengchi University
106161011@nccu.edu.tw

蔡宜庭 Yi-Ting Tsai
國立政治大學語言學研究所
Graduate Institute of Linguistics
National Chengchi University
109555005@nccu.edu.tw

張瑜芸 Yu-Yun Chang
國立政治大學語言學研究所
Graduate Institute of Linguistics
National Chengchi University
yuyun@nccu.edu.tw

Abstract

Aging populations have posed a challenge to many countries including Taiwan, and with them come the issue of long-term care. Given the current context, the aim of this study was to explore the hotly-discussed subtopics in the field of long-term care, and identify its features through NLP. Texts from forums and websites were utilized for data collection and analysis. The study applied TF-IDF, the logistic regression model, and the naive Bayes classifier to process data. In sum, the results showed that it reached a F1-score of 0.92 in identification, and a best accuracy of 0.71 in classification. Results of the study found that apart from TF-IDF features, certain words could be elicited as favorable features in classification. The results of this study could be used as a reference for future long-term care related applications.

Keywords: long-term care, natural language processing (NLP), text classification, Chinese

1 Introduction

Long-term care, by the definition of Ministry of Health and Welfare[1], refers to "the living support, assistance, social participation, care and relevant healthcare services in accordance with the needs of any individual whose mental or physical incapacity has lasted or is expected to last for six months or longer".

As for long-term care services, according to Harris-Kojetin et al. (2019), include assistance with activities of daily living (abbreviated as ADLs, which includes activities such as dressing, bathing, and toileting), instrumental activities of daily living (abbreviated as IADLs, which includes activities such as medication management and housework), and health maintenance tasks. Long-term care services assist people to improve or maintain an optimal level of physical functioning and quality of life, which can include help from other people and special equipment or assistive devices.

According to National Development Council (2020)[2], driven by a low birth rate of 1.2 and an all-time high life expectancy in 2020, senior citizens (people aged 65 or older) will account for over 20 percent of Taiwan's total population by 2025, indicating Taiwan will step into a super-aged society. Within the context, how long-term care services can meet the escalating demand is absolutely critical.

While extensive long-term care studies have been conducted, few of them are from the perspective of caregivers, especially family caregivers. Chen (2013) pointed out that long-term care system in Taiwan lacked support services for the caregivers.

For most family caregivers, they provided ADLs and IADLs for their family members. Sometimes, they might get stuck when being confronted with several care problems. Lu (2005) showed that their needs included respite care services, psychological and educational support programs, and financial subsidies. Among psychological and educational support programs, caring skills and consulting services were what the caregivers desperately wanted while taking care of their family members.

In the course of caring, emergencies could happen. Caregivers might need timely help but lack sufficient time to search and browse – for an appropriate answer to their question. Besides, caregivers might be in need when it was late at night and had no one to turn to. Despite the abundant resources on the Internet, not every piece of information is suitable for caregivers, let alone those irrelevant discussions. Still, they had to filter.

To bridge the gap, this study aimed to explore features useful to identify (1) long-term care and unrelated texts (2) long-term care topics that generate intensive discussion, so that the application could be designed more user-friendly, and caregivers could get the needed information more efficiently.

At present, despite the fact that there are many online long-term care platforms, their manner and principles of classification are not based on caregivers' needs. This study intended to fill this gap by collecting authentic materials, adjusting its categories manually and processing them with caregiver-oriented topics.

This study sought to answer the following research questions:

1. What are the topics that the caregivers have been hotly discussing?
2. How to provide caregiver-oriented information through NLP?

2 Literature Review

In terms of much-discussed topics, according to a global overview study by Fu et al. (2019), the simultaneous analysis of both references and keywords revealed that common long-term care hot topics included 'dementia care', 'quality of care', 'prevalence and risk factors', 'mortality', and 'randomized controlled trial'.

Back in Taiwan, Lee et al. (2019) had studied about what topics in an online blog would readers (including family caregivers or others) mainly follow. The study suggested that out of the eight categories, the most commonly read and discussed topics were 'family relationships', 'caregiving experiences', 'caregiving stress', 'physical, psychological, and social adaptation', and 'seniors care issues'. The left ones were 'long-term care

1 https://www.mohw.gov.tw/mp-2.html

2 National Development Council. 2020. Population Projection in ROC (from 2020 to 2070) (ISBN : 978-986-5457-22-8). Retrieved from: https://pop-proj.ndc.gov.tw/upload/download/中華民國人口推估(2020至2070年)報告.pdf

policies', 'the ups and downs in caring', and 'special caregiver groups' – such as male caregivers and former caregivers.

In order to find appropriate features, this paper applied TF-IDF, which was consulted from studies by Phetkrachang and Kittiphattanabawon (2019) and Paik (2013). They both applied TF-IDF weighting in their research.

3 Methodology

The procedure of this research could be presented as Figure 3.1.

Firstly, data from three platforms were collected and separated into caregiver-oriented ones and non-caregiver-oriented ones. Secondly, a task of annotation was done to appropriately classify relevant data into eight categories. Thirdly, by appling TF-IDF, the logistic regression model, and the naive Bayes classifier, features were extracted. Afterwards, manually obtained features were also taken into consideration. Lastly, with the model, it was hoped to be beneficial to different applications, such as chatbot development or website-building. It could help website designers to build a more caregiver-friendly platform.

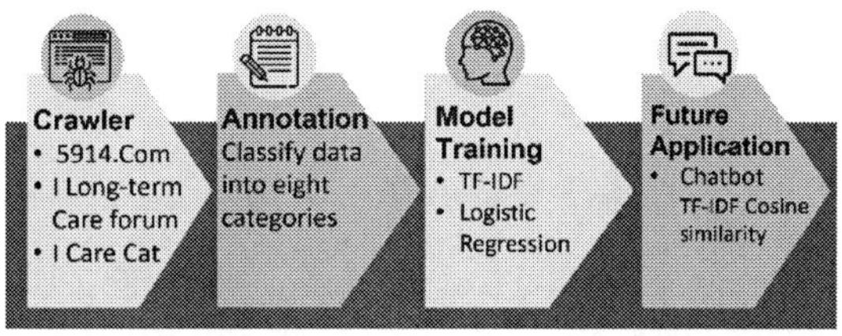

Figure3.1: Main procedure of this study

3.1 Data Collection

To investigate topics that spark widespread discussion in long-term care, 800 articles were collected from three online platforms, which included 長照喵 'long-term care cat'[3], 愛長照 'love long-term care'[4], and 呼叫醫師 'call for doctor'[5]. In the field of long-term care, all of these platforms are considered to be the most representative ones in Taiwan. First, 長照喵 'long-term care cat' is a website which mainly shares articles about long-term care information, health knowledge, and activities of long-term care. The website straightforwardly categorize these articles into two types: 找活動 'Activities' and 找知識 'Knowledge'. 找活動 'Activities' includes lectures or activity information about long-term care, whereas 找知識 'Knowledge' contains the practical knowledge or experience sharing on long-term care. In the research, we collected the articles of 找知識 'Knowledge', since the information of 找活動 'Activities' were time-sensitive – data collected went out-of-date or expired soon. Second, 愛長照 'love long-term care' is a website for caregivers to seek resources and advice. The platform also provides plenty of articles about long-term care. In addition, there is an online forum for users to ask questions or discuss long-term care issues. In the forum, the posts are classified into 16 categories, which are 居家服務 'home services', 照顧機構 'care institutions', 外籍看護 'foreign nursing workers', 我要找幫手 'find helpers', 照顧技巧 'care skills', 輔具 'assistive devices', 飲食營養 'diet and nutrition', 補助 'subsidy', 失智症 'dementia', 疾病 'diseases', 安寧 'palliative care', 照顧尊嚴 'dignity', 照顧苦水 'complaint', 健康保健 'health care', 生活/課程 'life and lessons', and 其他 'others'. This research obtained all posts and comments in this forum, and consulted the topic categorization to find the hot issues about long-term care. Last, 呼叫醫師 'call for doctor' is an online platform for people to talk to doctors directly. Doctors would professionally answer the questions posted online. The discussion field involves long-term care, which provides the data needed of the research.

To analyze the main topics discussed online, the language materials were first collected from websites mentioned above. Although articles were taken from long-term care websites, some of the materials were time-sensitive activities or advertisements. Therefore, the first task of the research was to identify the target articles. The relevant articles and the irrelevant ones were marked manually afterwards. Finally, 400 were annotated as long-term care articles and 400 articles were classified as irrelevant ones. This dataset was designed as the gold-standard data in the identification task.

[3] Long-term care cat: icarecat.com

[4] Love long-term care: https://www.ilong-termcare.com/

[5] Call for doctor: https://www.5914.com.tw/

In the course of inspecting the articles between caregiver-oriented and irrelevant articles, we found that the words used were quite similar. For instance, (3-1) is an article section from 'long-term care cat'; however, the content of it is about the requirements of long-term care worker, which is not suitable for long-term caregivers. This kind of articles contain the words which frequently show up in caregiver-oriented articles such as 照顧'look after' or 長照 'long-term care'. Therefore, the research first tried to build a model which identifies the articles between caregiver-oriented writings and irrelevant articles.

(3-1) Q1、成為 「照顧服務員」需要
Q1, become 'care worker' need

什麼 資格 ?
what qualification?

'Q1,What qualifications are needed to become a "care worker"? '

有 以下 資格 之 一
have below qualification of one

就 可以 成為 照顧服務員
and can become 'care worker'

'Having one of the following qualifications could become a care worker.'

受訓 參加 「照顧 服務員 專業
train participate 'care worker professional

訓練 課程」 取得 結業 證書
train course' obtain graduation certification

'participate the training of "Professional Training Course for Care Workers" and obtain a certification'

To find out the hot topics for long-term care discussion, the forum categories in the 'love long-term care' forum and the studies by Lee et al. (2019) and Fu et al. (2019) were consulted. Based on the data collected, categories in 'love long-term care' forum and the above-mentioned studies, the topics of our collected data were re-categorized manually into 8 categories. The topics of 'home services', 'care institutions', 'foreign nursing workers', 'find helpers' were merged into 'care manpower'. Besides, the topics of 'palliative care' and 'dignity' were merged into 'dignity' as one of the 'social issues'. The 'subsidy' posts were eliminated in this research. For one thing, articles in 'subsidy' included too many details about long-term care policies, statics (Lee et al., 2019) shown that caregivers were less interested in them. For another, most contents were time-sensitive. Besides, the original topic 'health care' overlapped issues of many topics. As a result, the articles under this topic were re-classified into topics of 'diet and nutrition' and 'care skills'. To sum up, the eight categories in the study are as follows – 失智症 'dementia', 疾病 'diseases', 照顧技巧 'care skills', 照顧苦水 'complaint', 照顧尊嚴 'dignity', 輔具 'assistive devices', 飲食營養 'diet and nutrition' and 照顧人力 'care manpower'. Figure 3.2 demonstrates the article counts of each category. The definitions of these categories are shown in Table 3.1. The second language model in the research would be employed to automatically characterize all the articles accordingly.

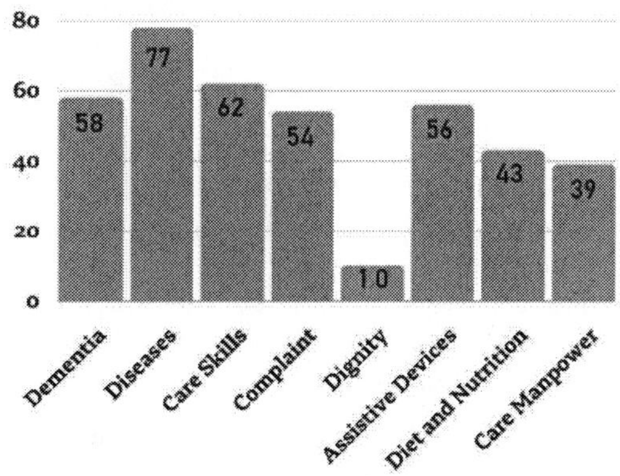

Figure 3.2: Counts on each topics of articles

category	content
失智症 'dementia'	Discussion about dementia
疾病 'diseases'	Discussion about diseases other than dementia
照顧技巧 'care skills'	Topics about caring skills and details
照顧苦水 'complaint'	Complaint about caring patients.
照顧尊嚴 'dignity'	Topics about how to treat patients with dignity, e.g., palliative care, good death
輔具 'assistive devices'	Discussion about Assistive devices, e.g., wheelchair
飲食營養 'diet and nutrition'	Details about patients' nutrition and diet
照顧人力 'care manpower'	Topics about foreign nursing workers and long-term care institutions

Table 3.1: Category definitions of topics on long-term care

3.2 Model

Before training, the data cleaning processes were implemented in advance. The punctuations and English characters were removed before training. Besides, the articles were segmented with *jieba*[6] package for the purpose of further data training.

The first model training is to identify the long-term care contents. We employ the trained TF-IDF model provided by jieba to help identify topic-related features for each category. To find the features of long-term care articles, TF-IDF scores were calculated to find the common and recurring keywords through the whole topics of the long-term care contexts. Each topic filtered out 20 keywords. Some of the keywords overlapped among categories. For finding the common features of long-term care, the words which repeated above three times were selected as common features. Moreover, for the purpose of gathering target articles more comprehensively, the top two keywords of each topic were added up as features for identifying the long-term care articles. All of the features for identifying long-term care contexts were 照顧 'look after', 因為 'because', 我們 'we', 照護 'care', 問題 'problem', 他們 'they', 治療 'treatment', 輪椅 'wheelchair',失智症 'dementia', 失智 'dementia', 藥物 'medicine', 醫療 'medical', 安寧 'palliative care', 輔具 'assistive devices', 服務 'service', 飲食 'diet', and 營養 'nutrition'[7]. With these features, the logistic regression model was applied to identify the long-term care articles. In the collected dataset, there were 400 articles with care-giver centered topics, and the other 400 articles discussed other topics. The entire dataset was split into 70% for training and 30% for testing.

The second step of model training was to classify the articles on long-term care into eight categories. The training model was also based on the logistic regression model.

4 Results

4.1 Model

Regarding the identification model based on the logistic regression model and TF-IDF features, the best f1-score was 0.72. The average was 0.65.

To further examine the model, 56 articles were collected from PTT 銀髮族板 'the Elderly board on PTT'[8]. This was the most relevant board to discuss long-term care on PTT. When the dataset was composed of PTT Elderly posts solely, the f1-score was 0.92.

In the identification phase, the features of the articles were extracted from the TF-IDF scores.

4.2 Text classification

First, to distinguish whether articles were related to long-term care, the TF-IDF weighting helped us in doing so. The features we got from the calculation of articles associated with long-term care were shown in table 4.2.1.

Category	Features
Dementia	失智症 'dementia'、失智 'dementia'、我們'we'、他們 'they'、認知'cognition'
Diseases	治療'treatment'、藥物 'medicine'、症狀'symptom'、用藥'medication'、障礙 'barrier'
Care Skills	我們'we'、治療'treatment'、訓練'training'、運動 'exercise'、活動'movement'
Complaint	我們'we'、悲傷'sadness'、自己'self'、一個'one'、他們 'they'
Dignity	醫療'medical care'、病人 'patient'、灌食'tube feeding'、痛苦'pain'、生命 'life'
Assistive Devices	輪椅'wheelchair'、輔具 'assistive devices'、我們 'we'、補助'subsidy'、支撐 'support'
Diet and Nutrition	飲食'diet'、營養'nutrition'、攝取'take in'、建議 'suggestion'、食物'food'
Care Manpower	服務'service'、單位 'affiliation'、居家'home'、照護'care'、機構'institution'

Table 4.2.1: Main TF-IDF features of topics on long-term care

[6] Jieba : https://github.com/fxsjy/jieba

[7] These features, as a part of the research outcome, would be further discussed in the result section.

[8] The Elderly board on PTT: https://www.ptt.cc/bbs/elderly/index.html

Then, some of the distinctive TD-IDF features of long-term care articles were picked, along with some manually obtained features. The adjustment was as follows. In sum, the best f1-score under such arrangement was 0.71. The average was 0.67.

TF-IDF features	Manually obtained features
Dementia 失智症	
失智症 'dementia'、失智 'dementia'、認知 'cognition'	阿滋海默症 'Alzheimer's disease'
Diseases 疾病	
治療 'treatment'、症狀 'symptom'、藥物 'medicine'、用藥 'medication'	疾病 'diseases'
Care Skills 照顧技巧	
訓練 'training'、運動 'exercise'、活動 'movement'	指甲 'nails'、技巧 'skills'、練習 'practices'
Complaint 照顧苦水	
悲傷 'sadness'、自己 'self'	媳婦 'daughter-in-law'、體會 'relate to'、加油 'hang in there'、累 'tired'、辛苦 'You've worked hard'、溝通 'communicate'
Dignity 照顧尊嚴	
灌食 'tube feeding'	鼻胃管 'nasogastric tube'、安寧 'palliative'、尊嚴 'dignity'、臨終 'hospice'、善終 'good death'
Assistive Devices 輔具	
輔具 'assistive devices'、輪椅 'wheelchair'、補助 'subsidy'	電動 'electric'、扶手 'handrail'、拐 'crutch'、杖 'walking stick'
Diet and Nutrition 飲食營養	
飲食 'diet'、營養 'nutrition'、攝取 'take in'	東西 'things'、牙口 'teeth'、維他命 'vitamin'
Care Manpower 照顧人力	
服務 'service'、單位 'affiliation'、居家 'home'、機構 'institution'	仲介 'agency'、雇主 'employer'

Table 4.2.2: Features of each category on long-term care

5 Discussion

In the previous section, several high-frequency features were retrieved from the dataset, including 照顧 'look after', 因為 'because', 治療 'treatment', 我們 'we', and 照護 'care'. All of these words occurred over three times among the 8 categories.

Among these features, 我們 'we' was the most impressive one. It was not a long-term care related word, but it had such a high weight compared with the other features that were directly associated with long-term care. One possible explanation for this is that articles related to long-term care topics sometimes offer information and suggestions with empathy. With this inclusive title, those readers as caregivers might feel a special closeness and feel understood.

Another finding was about a less frequent feature 他們 'they'. Both the type 失智症 'dementia' and 照顧苦水 'complaint' obtained the feature 他們 'they'. To explore this phenomenon, we compared where they occurred in posts of these two categories, and in posts of 疾病 'diseases'.

失智症 'dementia' and 疾病 'diseases' were both diseases. From our observation, when it came to diseases, narrators of the articles often talked about their symptoms and the corresponding treatments. However, when an article's topic is 失智症 'dementia', hardly would the narrator suffer from dementia. In general, narrators under this topic view people who have dementia as 'the constitutive other', and thus use the title 他們 'they' in particular.

On the whole, with these articles and features of various types, our observations could be roughly divided into two kinds. For the first kind, features indicated relationships, as mentioned above. Besides, features sometimes consisted of identities, such as 媳婦 'daughter-in-law'. These articles tended to express personal experience, and mostly were under topics such as 照顧苦水 'complaint'.

When articles with family titles were categorized into the complaint type, they often described care experiences from the perspective of caregivers themselves. Moreover, apart from 照顧苦水 'complaint', in articles under topics of 照顧技巧 'care skills' and 輔具 'assistive devices', the feature 我們'we' almost topped the TF-IDF list. Although articles of this kind were not solely written from caregivers' perspectives, it reflected the fact that when offering advice from the clinical experiences, the doctors or specialists tended to use 我們'we' often.

The second kind of features belonged to objective things, instead of showing relationships and communications. They are closely related to symptoms and treatments, or associated affiliations and services on long-term care.

While features approximately reflect the content of every type of topic, certain features stood out for their good performance in discrimination.

The TF-IDF weighting indicated the feature 輔具 'assistive devices' was a favorable feature in identify long-term care articles. Besides, the feature 牙口 'teeth' also played an important role in distinguishing 飲食營養 'diet and nutrition' posts from others.

In the course of classification, we found articles under 照顧技巧 'care skills' were the hardest to be classified. This was because 'care skills' posts usually mention the diseases first, then the techniques and suggestions. The suggestions might contain reminders on diets, and if the situation went severe, the narrator might provide suggestions on corresponding assistive devices. These made the classification of 照顧技巧 'care skills' challenging.

Limitation for the present study was that it was a relatively small dataset for analyzing. More contents on long-term care may help refine the categories and enrich the features.

6 Conclusions and Future Work

The results of this study could have broad applications in the future. For example, chatbot, search engine, or Q&A keywords.

One possible application is a long-term care chatbot. The chatbot could be designed to classify the topic of the question or inputs, and give the answer accordingly. The TF-IDF Cosine similarity model of sklearn[9] could be applied to find the most appropriate answer to the input question.

Since our study focused on long-term caregivers, specialists could optimize their services to caregivers. Thus, caregivers would get suitable advice more efficiently. They could save time on browsing and filtering information on the Internet.

7 References

Zheng-Fen Chen. 2013. 我國長期照顧體系欠缺的一角：照顧者支持服務 (a missing piece of Taiwan's long-term care system: caregiver support services) [in Chinese]. *Community Dev J*, 141: 203-213.

Li-Ping Fu, Zhao-Hui Sun, Lan-Ping He, Feng Liu, and Xiao-Li Jing. 2019. Global long-term care research: A scientometric review. *International journal of environmental research and public health*, 16(12): 2077. https://doi.org/10.3390/ijerph16122077

Lauren Harris-Kojetin, Manisha Sengupta, Jessica P. Lendon, Vincent Rome, Roberto Valverde, and Christine Caffrey. 2019. Long-term care providers and services users in the United States, 2015-2016. *DHHS Publication No. 2019–1427, National center for health statistics*. https://www.cdc.gov/nchs/data/series/sr_03/sr03_43-508.pdf

Mun-Sim Lai, and An-Chi Tung. 2015. Who supports the elderly? The changing economic lifecycle reallocation in Taiwan, 1985 and 2005. *The Journal of the Economics of Ageing*, 5: 63-68. https://doi.org/10.1016/j.jeoa.2014.10.012

I Lee, Chii-Jun Chiou, and Yueh-Feng Lu. 2019. 應用網路部落格倡導家庭照顧者議題 (lessons learned from developing web-based educational support blogs for family caregivers in Taiwan) [in Chinese]. *The Journal of Long-Term Care in Taiwan*, 23(3): 217-230.

Pau-Ching Lu. 2005. 支持家庭照顧者的長期照護政策之構思 (toward a more family caregiver-responsive long-term care policy) [in Chinese]. *National Policy Quarterly*, 4(4): 25-40. https://doi.org/10.6407/NPQ.200512.0025

Jiaul H. Paik. 2013. A novel TF-IDF weighting scheme for effective ranking. In *Proceedings of the 36th international ACM SIGIR conference on Research and development in information retrieval*, pages 343-352.

Ketsara Phetkrachang and Nichnan Kittiphattanabawon. 2019. Fuzzy TF-IDF Weighting in Synonym for Diabetes Question and Answers. In *Proceedings of the 15th International Conference on Computing and Information Technology*, pages 59–68.

Hsiu-Hung Wang, and Shwn-Feng Tsay. Elderly and long-term care trends and policy in Taiwan: Challenges and opportunities for health care professionals. *The Kaohsiung journal of medical sciences*, 28(9): 465-469.

[9] Sklearn: https://scikit-learn.org/stable/

The 33rd Conference on Computational Linguistics and Speech Processing (ROCLING 2021)
Taoyuan, Taiwan, October 15-16, 2021. The Association for Computational Linguistics and Chinese Language Processing

Learning to Find Translation of Grammar Patterns in Parallel Corpus

Kai-Wen Tuan[1], **Yi-Jyun Chen**[1], **Yi-Chien Lin**[1], **Chun-Ho Kwok**[1], **Hai-Lun Tu**[2], **Jason S. Chang**[1]
[1]Department of Computer Science, National Tsing Hua University
[2]Department of Library and Information Science, Fu Jen Catholic University
{kevintuan,yijyun,nicalin,isaackch,helen.tu,jason}@nlplab.cc

Abstract

We introduce a method for assisting English as Second Language (ESL) learners by providing translations of *Collins COBUILD* grammar patterns (GP) for a given word. In our approach, bilingual parallel corpus is transformed into bilingual GP pairs aimed at providing native language support for learning word usage through GPs. The method involves automatically parsing sentences to extract GPs, automatically generating translation GP pairs from bilingual sentences, and automatically extracting common bilingual GPs. At run-time, the target word is used for lookup GPs and translations, and the retrieved common GPs and their example sentences are shown to the user. We present a prototype phrase search engine, *Linggle GPTrans*[1], that implements the methods to assist ESL learners. Preliminary evaluation on a set of more than 300 GP-translation pairs shows that the methods achieve 91% accuracy.

Keywords: Grammar Pattern, ESL Learning, Parallel Corpus

1 Introduction

In an era of globalization, English fluency becomes an increasingly important asset, and an increasing number of online services specifically target English as Second Language (ESL) learners. Dictionaries, thesauri, online English courses, and editorial tools are just a few examples. However, few if any of those services take into consideration the important relationship between grammar patterns (GPs) and word meanings. We expand upon the idea "one sense per collocation" proposed by Yarowsky (1993) and assume each GP would have only one word sense. For example, the word "keep" has multiple meanings: it meas "to delay or prevent" in the GP **V n from n** (e.g."keep candy from kids") and it means "to continue" in the GP **V -ing** (e.g."keep moving").

[1]https://linggle.com/

Figure 1: An example *GPTrans* search query *keep* : GPs, and Chinese translations

We focus our research on verbal GPs as linguistic researches identify verb phrases are particularly difficult for learners to understand. Moreover, verb phrase is a prominent component of sentence structure and lack of such knowledge often leads to grammatical errors.

We present a system, *Linggle Grammar Pattern Translator* (*Linggle GPTrans*), that automatically matches input words to corresponding GPs and relevent translations. Figure 1 shows the GPs and translations for the input word "keep." This system would help users to learn meanings of each word, in relation to its GPs.

2 Related Works

Language skills in English has proved indispensable along with the development of globalization. As a result, ESL learning has become an area of active research and many researches have worked on autonomous language learning (e.g., Kormos and Csizer (2014)).

Many researches show that, for non-native language learners, verbs are particularly difficult to learn compared to nouns (e.g., Hirsh-Pasek and Golinkoff (1999); Waxman and Booth (2001); Gleitman (1990); Gentner (1982); Imai et al. (2008)). In our system, we interactively provide the bilingual verb GP pairs to improve learning experience and efficiency.

In the past few decades, a large number of bilingual corpus resources have made statistical machine translation more and more feasible. In the 1990s, bilingual sentence alignment technology developed rapidly (Gale and Church (1991); Gale and Church (1993), Brown et al. (1991); Simard et al. (1993); Chen (1993)). Early research are aimed toward finding the corresponding bilingual sentences from bilingual corpus (Debili and Sammouda (1992); Kay and Roscheisen (1993)). Some studies use statistical models to improve the word correspondence generated by automatic alignment, such as Hidden Markov Model (HMM) (Brown et al. (1991)), log-likelihood ratio (Gale and Church (1991); Gale and Church (1993)) and K-Vec algorithm (Fung and Church (1994)). Based on the previous results, Melamed (1999) proposed the Smooth Injective Map Recognizer (SIMR), which regards bilingual phrase alignment as the best distribution of x-axis and y-axis in two-dimensional space. SIMR uses a greedy algorithm to calculate the best distribution of two-dimensional space as the calculation unit.

More recent researches concentrate on learning word translation and extracting bilingual word translation pairs from bilingual corpus, and then calculate the degree of mutual relationship between word pairs in parallel sentences, thereby deriving the precise translation (Catizone et al. (1989); Brown et al. (1990); Gale and Church (1991); Wu and Xia (1994); Fung (1995); Melamed (1995); Moore (2001)). Previously, we utilize statistical model in *Linggle* (Boisson et al., 2013), a linguistic search engine based on *Google Web 1T*. In our system, we focus on using statistical methods to extract translations of verbal GPs extracted from *Collin COBUILD Grammar Dictionary* (Cobuild et al., 2005).

(1) Parse sentences and extract grammar patterns
(Section 3.1)
(2) Extract translations of words
(Section 3.2)
(3) Count and filter headword translations for grammar patterns (Section 3.3)
(4) Extract Chinese pattern for grammar patterns
(Section 3.4)

Figure 2: Identification process

In the area of phrase alignment, Ko (2006) proposed a method for verb phrase translation. For specific verb fragments (e.g. *make a report to police*), automatic alignment is applied to calculate the collocation relationship across two language (e.g. when *make* and *report* appear together, *report* often corresponds to "報案" (bau an)), then word and phrase correspondences are generated (e.g. *make a report to police* correspond to "向警察報案" (shiang jing cha bau an)), to tally translations and counts. Chen et al. (2020) focus on the translation of noun+prepositional collocations. Using statistical methods to extract translations of nouns and prepositions from bilingual parallel corpora with sentence alignment, and then adjust the translations with additional information of Chinese collocations extracted from a Chinese corpus.

3 Methods

We attempt to identify the senses and translations of verbs in various GPs in *Collins COBUILD Dictionary.* Our identification process is shown in Figure 2.

3.1 Parsing Sentences and Extracting Grammar Patterns

In the first stage of the identification process (Step (1) in Figure 2), we parse each sentence and extract grammar patterns for each verb in each sentence. For example, the sentence "*we will charge him with a crime.*" contains the verb *charge*, our goal is to extract the grammar pattern (GP) **V n with n** for the verb *charge* in the sentence, where **V** denotes the headword *charge*.

The input to this stage is English sentences from bilingual parallel corpora. We parse each

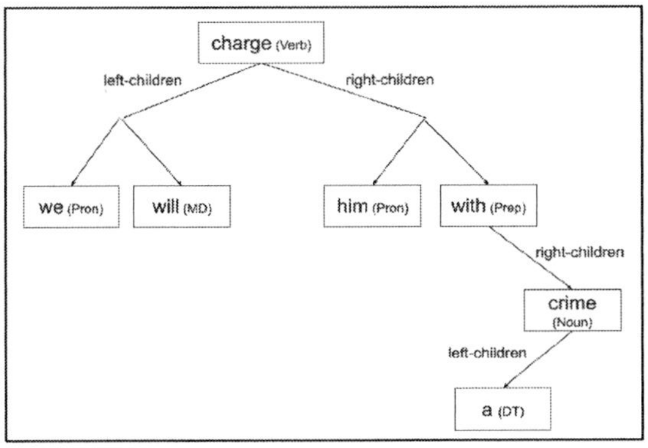

Figure 3: The structure of "we will charge him with a crime"

sentence into a tree structure to reveal the dependency of words in the sentence. For example, the sentence "*we will charge him with a crime*" will be parsed into a structure shown in Figure 3.

We use a recursive approach to extract GPs from the parse tree. We identify each verb, and consider all its right-children. We replace these words with their corresponding part of speech to form the GPs. Note that prepositions and specific function words (e.g. *out*, *up*, *down*) are not replaced. For example, in the sentence in Figure 3, the verb *charge* generate **charge n**. Then, the same process is then applied to the prepositions and other function words. The patterns generated from this process are then added to the partial GP to form a complete GP. For example, the prepositions *with* in Figure 3 generate a pattern **with n**. **with n** is then added to form a complete pattern, **charge n with n**. Note that there are some GPs with multiple word elements that can not be handle by the method described, such as **V wh-to-inf** and **V wh**. To handle these GPs, we design special rule to deal with these elements (e.g., **V wh-to-inf**).

Finally, we convert the generated GPs into the form consistent with *Collins COBUILD Dictionary*. In addition to replacing the headword in patterns as **V**, we also shorten the patterns that are too long to match GPs in *Collins Dictionary*.

The output of this stage is GPs which are in *Collins COBUILD Dictionary* of each verb in each English sentence.

3.2 Extracting Translations of Words

In the second stage of the identification process (Step(2) in Figure 2), we extract Chinese translations of each English verb. The input to this stage is English and Chinese sentences in bilingual parallel corpora with word alignment.

We use the method of extracting word translations in (Chen et al., 2020). For each English word, we consider its forward-correspondence to Chinese words and reverse-correspondence of these Chinese words, to filter out translations of the English word.

The output to this stage are Chinese translations for each English word. Sample translations of the word "charge" and the word " keep" are shown in Table 1.

3.3 Counting and Filtering Translations

In the third stage of the identification process (Step (3) in Figure 2), we count and filter Chinese translation of headword for each grammar pattern(GP) and verb. For example, the verb *charge* has the GP **V n with n**. Our goal is to obtain the common translations such as " 控告" (kung kao, means "accuse") or " 指控"(jhih kong, also means "accuse") for *charge* in **V n with n**.

The input to this stage is English and Chinese sentences in bilingual parallel corpora with word alignment, GPs of each verb extracted from each English sentence in the first stage (Step(1) in Figure 2), and word translations extracted in the second stage (Step(2) in Figure 2).

For each GP of each verb, we compute the frequency of each translation as shown in Table 2. We than calculate the average and standard deviation in relation to other translation of the same GP. We filter and identify translations more frequent than average by 1 standard deviation.

To retain some less common translations which are correct (e.g., "跟上" (ken sheng, means "keep up with") for V n of *keep*), we also compute the frequency of translations of verbs in each grammar pattern as shown in Table 5 and calculate the average and standard deviation. We filter and identify gram- mar patterns that are more frequent than average

Word	Translations
charge	主管 (1222), 負責 (599), 收費 (506), 押記 (358), 控罪 (324), 掌管 (280), 電荷 (266), 費用 (260), 收取 (258), 指控 (114), 充電 (66), 控告 (47), 罪名 (38), 檢控 (35), 徵收 (33), 控 (18), 指責 (11), 衝鋒 (11), 起訴 (6)
keep	保持 (1681), 維持 (312), 繼續 (304), 備存 (297), 不斷 (246), 保留 (236), 一直 (154), 儲存 (137), 保存 (61), 持續 (46), 保守 (42), 防止 (40), 不停 (39), 保管 (37), 留 (37), 保住 (36), 留住 (32), 阻止 (29), 存備 (12), 記錄 (11), 跟上 (11),

Table 1: Translations and count of "charge" and " keep"

Word	GP*	Trans*	Count	Std	Example
keep	V n	保持	1669	**4.88**	keep space (保持距離)
keep	V n	維持	356	0.72	keep peace (維持和平)
keep	V n	備存	316	0.60	keep record (備存記錄)
keep	V n	繼續	147	0.06	keep a close watch (繼續密切留意)
keep	V n	記錄	52	-0.23	keep track of expenses (記錄支出)
keep	V n	飼養	33	-0.32	keep animal (飼養動物)
keep	V n	跟上	24	-0.33	keep pace (跟上步伐)

Table 2: Count the number of each translation for grammar pattern **V n** of "*keep*" .

by 1 standard deviation, and add the translation into the translation list of these grammar patterns for the verb.

The output of this stage is translations for each grammar pattern for each verb. For example, translations for each GP for the word *keep* and the word *charge* are shown in Table 4. After filter grammar patterns from each translation for each verb and add the translation into the translation list of these grammar patterns, we can extract translations that are relatively un- common such as "跟上" (ken sheng, means "keep up with") or "飼養" (ssu yang, means "bread") for "keep" .

3.4 Extracting Chinese patterns

In the forth and final stage of the identification process (Step(4) in Figure 1), we filter Chinese patterns for each English of each verb. For example, the verb "*use*" has the GP **V n as n**, and our goal is to derive the Chinese pattern such as " 使用 $\mathbf{n_1}$ 作爲 $\mathbf{n_2}$" where "$\mathbf{n_1}$" and "$\mathbf{n_2}$" represent Chinese words corresponding to the first and second "**n**" in **V n as n**.

The input to this stage is English-Chinese sentence pairs in a word-aligned bilingual parallel corpus, grammar pattern for each verb in each English sentence we extracted in the first stage (Step(1) in Figure 1), and translations of verbs in their GP we extracted in the third stage (Step(3) in Figure 1).

For each grammar pattern and verb, we extract Chinese counterparts of the English grammar pattern in all sentence pairs, and convert them into Chinese patterns. For example, the GP **use n as n** in the sentence "*we use computer as a tool*", corresponds to " 使用電腦作爲工具" according to the word alignment, where the headword "**use**" corresponds to " 使用"(shih yong), the first "**n**" corresponds to " 電腦"(dian nao), "**as**" corresponds to " 作爲"(zuo wei), and the second "**n**" corresponds to " 工具"(gong jyu). " 使用" and " 作爲" which correspond to "**V**" and "**as**" and convert " 電腦" and " 工作" which correspond to the first "**n**" and the second "**n**" to "$\mathbf{n_1}$" and "$\mathbf{n_2}$" respectively . Therefore, Chinese pattern " 使用 $\mathbf{n_1}$ 作爲 $\mathbf{n_2}$" is generated.

After generating Chinese patterns for each sentence, we count the number of each Chinese pattern for each English headword and GP as shown in Table 5, and calculate the average and standard deviation. We filter and identify Chinese patterns more frequent than average by 1 standard deviation.

The output of this stage is Chinese patterns for each English headword and GP.

4 Run-Time Interactive System

The system *Linggle GPTrans* is build on the foundation of *Linggle*, an linguistic search en-

Word	Trans	GP	Count	Std	Example
keep	跟上	**V n**	24	**3.32**	keep pace (跟上步伐)
keep	記錄	**V n**	52	**3.31**	keep track of expenses (記錄支出)
keep	記錄	V -ing	1	-0.24	-
keep	飼養	**V n**	26	**3.08**	keep animal (飼養動物)
keep	備存	**V n**	316	**3.29**	keep record (備存記錄)
keep	備存	V n -ing	7	-0.27	-
keep	備存	V n -ed	4	-0.29	-

Table 3: Count the number of each grammar pattern for each translation of "*keep*"

Word	Grammar pattern	Translations (Sorted by count)
charge	V n	收取 (212), 收費 (182), 徵收 (67), 指控 (20), 費用 (16), 起訴 (11), 檢控 (5), 落案 (2)
charge	V n n	收取 (29), 收費 (10)
charge	V to-inf	收費 (10), 收取 (4)
charge	V n with n	控告 (30), 指控 (11)
charge	V n for n	收取 (25), 收費 (14)
charge	V n to n	收取 (3)
keep	V n	保持 (1669), 維持 (356), 備存 (316), 保留 (241), 繼續 (147), 儲存 (121), 保存 (78), 保管 (55), 保住 (54), 記錄 (52), 留 (44), 留住 (40), 一直 (36), 保守 (33), 飼養 (26), 跟上 (24), 存備 (24), 阻止 (22), 持續 (13)
keep	V n form n	防止 (50), 阻止 (28), 保持 (16)
keep	V -ing	繼續 (233), 不斷 (163), 一直 (75), 不停 (59), 持續 (17), 下去 (13)
keep	V n -ed	保持 (31)
keep	V form n	阻止 (2), 保持 (2)
keep	V n -ing	保持 (42), 繼續 (19), 維持 (15)
keep	V to n	保持 (24), 維持 (13)
keep	V n to n	維持 (9), 保持 (8)
keep	V n as n	維持 (8), 保持 (7)

Table 4: Translations for each grammar pattern for "*charge*" and " *keep*"

Word	Trans	GP	Chinese Pattern	Count
use	使用	V n as n	使用 n_1 作爲 n_2	35
use	使用	V n as n	使用 n_1 作 n_2	5
use	使用	V n as n	n_1 作爲 n_2 使用	3
use	使用	V n as n	使用 n_1	3
use	使用	V n as n	n_1 使用	1

Table 5: The Chinese patterns for the grammar pattern **use n as n** when translated as " 使用"

gine. *Linggle* indexes and retrieves common phrases in *Google Web 1T*. In addition to phrases, *Linggle* also provides example sentences extracted from *Google Books*.

We transform GPs to corresponding *Linggle* queries according to a phrase table (e.g. the notation **to-inf** is adjusted to **to v.**, and **pron-refl** is adjusted to **pron.** to fit our system). Additional adjustments are also made to make the patterns compatible to our system. Specifically, noun phrases in GP are translated into queries that retrieve pronouns, determiners, and nouns with leading adjectives. The symbol **wh** is transformed into question words (i.e. where, when, how, etc.). Specific verb tenses are identified by matching the corresponding suffix (i.e. -ing, -ed, etc.). For simplicity, we ignore light verb in our system since their meaning are heavily influenced by their objects. Table 6 shows sample queries for various GPs.

Generally, each GP of the head word has many translations, and some translations may have similar meanings. To avoid redundancy, we perform pairwise word vector similarity of the Chinese translations. Among the pairwise similarities of the Chinese translations, if a subset of translations have the similarity above 0.5, we drop the translation with lower ranking according to Section 3.3. To keep the system interface simple and information concise, we only display the top three translations for each GP.

We show the screenshot of the our system in Figure 4. The user input the word "keep" and the system presents the many GPs and relevant translations. One search result, "keep n from n" and their example sentences, are shown in Figure 4. We also provide a video demo of our system online.[2]

5 Evaluation

The purpose of *GPTrans* system is to allow users to retrieve the translation of GPs for the better understanding of a target pattern.The system automatically returns the translations for each GP of verbs to the users. Therefore, in this section, we report the results of preliminary evaluations on the extraction of GPs and their corresponding translations. The evaluation process was conducted on a set of verbs along with their GPs and translations of the GP.

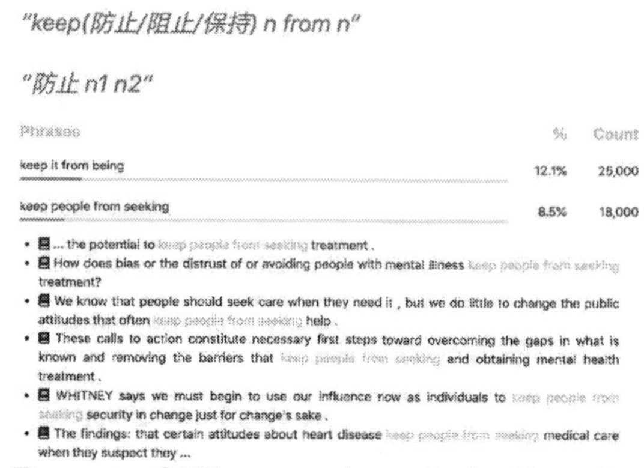

Figure 4: GPTrans search results for the pattern "keep n from n"

5.1 Experimental setting

The bilingual parallel corpora we used are the *Minutes of Legislative Council of the Hong Kong Special Administrative* from the legislative council of Hong Kong, and the *UM-corpus* from university of Macau. We used CKIP(Ma and Chen, 2003) which is a Chinese knowledge and information processing system developed by academic sinica to process Chinese word segmentation and used fast-align(Dyer et al., 2013) to process word alignment of bilingual parallel sentences.

We used Spacy(Honnibal and Montani, 2017) to parse English sentences and generated GPs for each verb in sentences as we described in section 3.1. Then, we extracted Chinese translations of each English word as we describe in section 3.2. Finally, we count and filter translations for each GP of each verb as we describe in section 3.3.

5.2 Evaluation Metrics

The output of our method are translations for each GP of all verbs in Collins dictionary. To evaluate our approach, we randomly selected 16 verbs with totally 126 GPs (388 items). The translations of each GP are evaluated by two linguists. Note that the verb *be* and light verbs were excluded from our evaluation since their senses usually depend on collocates. Among the selected sentence pairs, some English sentences are incorrectly parsed by SpaCy. That is, the target pattern of the verb does not exist

[2] `https://youtu.be/PQ-u07A5qM8`

GP Tag	Linggle query
n	n./det._?adj._n./pron./pron._n.
wh	where/when/how/which/why/what
to-inf	to v.
-ing	$ing
-ed	$ed

Table 6: Partial phrase table for translation GP to Linggle queries

Word	Accuracy	Word	Accuracy
ask	93%	feel	90%
know	93%	make	81%
look	97%	train	88%
end	80%	agree	84%
argue	100%	answer	100%
save	96%	deal	66%
predict	100%	hang	100%
figure	0%	elect	88%

Table 7: Accuracy of each verbs.

in the English sentence. In such cases, these sentences pairs were removed from our evaluation set, resulting in the removal of 28 items and leaving 360 items in our evaluation. Then, we evaluated the average accuracy of translating each verb (shown in Table 7) and the overall accuracy. The overall accuracy is 91%.

5.3 Discussion

The result of evaluation shows that most of the translations generated by our method are correct. We observes that incorrect translations may be due to the incorrect parsing and incorrect part-of-speech (POS) tagging. Incorrect parsing may arises from tokenization of Chinese text which further leads to misalignment. POS errors occurs when one word can be multiple POS. For example, "walk" could be a verb that denotes "to move on foot" or a noun meanings "a journey one make by walking." Since grammar patterns are essentially verb phrases and noun phrases, incorrect POS tag would lead to erroneous results.

In addition, some training sentences are in passive voice, which lead to the detection of incorrect GPs. The GP in *COBUILD* are generally in active voice. The lack of passive voice GPs in predetermined rule patterns lead to detection of incorrect GPs.

Finally, GPs with consecutive noun phrases such as **V n n** are much more complicated to deal with since the two noun phrases are hard to distinguish from one another.

Looking at the results of our evaluation, the 0% accuracy for "figure" stands out as an anomaly. After going through the testing data, we found out there are two reasons for the result. First of all, *COBUILD* treats the most common GP for "figure", **figure out n.** as a phrasal verb. Our system is build on the assumption that the verb would be a single word, thus dropping phrasal verbs in the process. Other than phrasal verbs, another reason for the result is incorrect POS tagging. Our system marks some occurrences of "figure" as verbs when they are nouns in reality.

6 Conclusion and Future Work

Many avenues exist for future research and improvement of our system. We identify our system's inability to process phrasal verbs during evaluation and plan to rectify this issue. One possible extension of our work is to utilize word embedding to consolidate translations with similar meanings but different wordings as one translation. We are also interested in extending our research outside of verbal grammar patterns and evacuating whether similar method would be effective for adjectives and nouns.

In summary, we discussed a method to provide translation of English grammar patterns for ESL learners and implemented a search system that shows the resulting translation. Our result presents nuanced translations for different GPs of the same word and helps ESL learners avoid common preposition errors. Our system utilized predetermined rule patterns and simple statistical models to identify the correct translation for each GP. This approach not only negates some of the reliance machine training models on training data size but also provides accurate translation results.

References

Joanne Boisson, Ting-Hui Kao, Jian-Cheng Wu, Tzu-Hsi Yen, and Jason S Chang. 2013. Linggle: a web-scale linguistic search engine for words in context. In *Proceedings of the 51st Annual Meeting of the Association for Computational*

Linguistics: System Demonstrations, pages 139–144.

Peter F Brown, John Cocke, Stephen A Della Pietra, Vincent J Della Pietra, Frederick Jelinek, John Lafferty, Robert L Mercer, and Paul S Roossin. 1990. A statistical approach to machine translation. *Computational linguistics*, 16(2):79–85.

Peter F Brown, Jennifer C Lai, and Robert L Mercer. 1991. Aligning sentences in parallel corpora. In *29th Annual Meeting of the Association for Computational Linguistics*, pages 169–176.

Roberta Catizone, Graham Russell, and Susan Warwick. 1989. Deriving translation data from bilingual texts. In *Proceedings of the First International Lexical Acquisition Workshop*, pages 1–7.

Stanley F Chen. 1993. Aligning sentences in bilingual corpora using lexical information. In *31st Annual Meeting of the Association for Computational Linguistics*, pages 9–16.

Yi-Jyun Chen, Ching-Yu Helen Yang, and Jason S. Chang. 2020. Improve word alignment for extraction phrasal translations. *International Journal of Computational Linguistics Chinese Language Processing*, 25(2):37–54.

Collins Cobuild et al. 2005. *Collins Cobuild English Grammar.* Collins Cobuild.

Fathi Debili and Elyès Sammouda. 1992. Aligning sentences in bilingual texts french-english and french-arabic. In *COLING 1992 Volume 2: The 15th International Conference on Computational Linguistics*.

Chris Dyer, Victor Chahuneau, and Noah A Smith. 2013. A simple, fast, and effective reparameterization of ibm model 2. In *Proceedings of the 2013 Conference of the North American Chapter of the Association for Computational Linguistics: Human Language Technologies*, pages 644–648.

Pascale Fung. 1995. A pattern matching method for finding noun and proper noun translations from noisy parallel corpora. *arXiv preprint cmp-lg/9505016*.

Pascale Fung and Kenneth Church. 1994. K-vec: A new approach for aligning parallel texts. *arXiv preprint cmp-lg/9407021*.

William A Gale and Kenneth Church. 1991. Identifying word correspondences in parallel texts. In *Speech and Natural Language: Proceedings of a Workshop Held at Pacific Grove, California, February 19-22, 1991*.

William A Gale and Kenneth Church. 1993. A program for aligning sentences in bilingual corpora. *Computational linguistics*, 19(1):75–102.

Dedre Gentner. 1982. Why nouns are learned before verbs: Linguistic relativity versus natural partitioning. *Center for the Study of Reading Technical Report; no. 257.*

Lila Gleitman. 1990. The structural sources of verb meanings. *Language acquisition*, 1(1):3–55.

Kathy Hirsh-Pasek and Roberta M Golinkoff. 1999. *The origins of grammar: Evidence from early language comprehension.* MIT press.

Matthew Honnibal and Ines Montani. 2017. spacy 2: Natural language understanding with bloom embeddings, convolutional neural networks and incremental parsing. *To appear*, 7(1):411–420.

Mutsumi Imai, Lianjing Li, Etsuko Haryu, Hiroyuki Okada, Kathy Hirsh-Pasek, Roberta Michnick Golinkoff, and Jun Shigematsu. 2008. Novel noun and verb learning in chinese-, english-, and japanese-speaking children. *Child development*, 79(4):979–1000.

Martin Kay and Martin Roscheisen. 1993. Text-translation alignment. *Computational linguistics*, 19(1):121–142.

M. H. Ko. 2006. Alignment of Multi-word Expressions in Parallel Corpora. Master's thesis, National Tsing Hua University, Taiwan.

Judit Kormos and Kata Csizer. 2014. The interaction of motivation, self-regulatory strategies, and autonomous learning behavior in different learner groups. *Tesol Quarterly*, 48(2):275–299.

Wei-Yun Ma and Keh-Jiann Chen. 2003. Introduction to ckip chinese word segmentation system for the first international chinese word segmentation bakeoff. In *Proceedings of the second SIGHAN workshop on Chinese language processing*, pages 168–171.

I Dan Melamed. 1995. Automatic evaluation and uniform filter cascades for inducing n-best translation lexicons. *arXiv preprint cmp-lg/9505044*.

I Dan Melamed. 1999. Bitext maps and alignment via pattern recognition. *Computational Linguistics*, 25(1):107–130.

Robert C Moore. 2001. Towards a simple and accurate statistical approach to learning translation relationships among words. In *Proceedings of the ACL 2001 Workshop on Data-Driven Methods in Machine Translation*.

Michel Simard, George F Foster, and Pierre Isabelle. 1993. Using cognates to align sentences in bilingual corpora. In *Proceedings of the 1993 conference of the Centre for Advanced Studies on Collaborative research: distributed computing-Volume 2*, pages 1071–1082.

Sandra R Waxman and Amy E Booth. 2001. Seeing pink elephants: Fourteen-month-olds' interpretations of novel nouns and adjectives. *Cognitive psychology*, 43(3):217–242.

Dekai Wu and Xuanyin Xia. 1994. Learning an english-chinese lexicon from a parallel corpus. In *Proceedings of the First Conference of the Association for Machine Translation in the Americas*.

David Yarowsky. 1993. One sense per collocation. Technical report, PENNSYLVANIA UNIV PHILADELPHIA DEPT OF COMPUTER AND INFORMATION SCIENCE.

The 33rd Conference on Computational Linguistics and Speech Processing (ROCLING 2021)
Taoyuan, Taiwan, October 15-16, 2021. The Association for Computational Linguistics and Chinese Language Processing

Keyword-centered Collocating Topic Analysis

Yu-Lin Chang
National Taiwan University
b06701146@g.ntu.edu.tw

Yongfu Liao
National Taiwan University
liao961120@gmail.com

Po-Ya Angela Wang
National Taiwan University
diff@cmgsh.tp.edu.tw

Mao-Chang Ku
National Taiwan University
d08142002@ntu.edu.tw

Shu-Kai Hsieh
National Taiwan University
shukaihsieh@ntu.edu.tw

Abstract

The rapid flow of information and the abundance of text data on the Internet have brought about the urgent demand for the construction of monitoring resources and techniques used for various purposes. To extract facets of information useful for particular domains from such large and dynamically growing corpora requires an unsupervised yet transparent ways of analyzing the textual data. This paper proposed a hybrid collocation analysis as a potential method to retrieve and summarize Taiwan-related topics posted on Weibo and PTT. By grouping collocates of 臺灣 'Taiwan' into clusters of topics via either word embeddings clustering or Latent Dirichlet allocation, lists of collocates can be converted to probability distributions such that distances and similarities can be defined and computed. With this method, we conduct a diachronic analysis of the similarity between Weibo and PTT, providing a way to pinpoint when and how the topic similarity between the two rises or falls. A fine-grained view on the grammatical behavior and political implications is attempted, too. This study thus sheds light on alternative explainable routes for future social media listening method on the understanding of cross-strait relationship.

Keywords: Social Media Listening, Collocation Analysis, Grammatical Collocation, Topic Modeling, Unsupervised Methods

1 Introduction

Social Media Listening (Social Media Monitoring) is a modern data science technique to the monitoring of social media. With the advances of NLP and text analytics, social mentions, i.e., keyword of key phrases referring to brand and product name, trending topic, etc., can be constantly tracked and analyzed in real-time.

The potentials of social media listening do not appear explicitly only in commercial and marketing domain, but also in other political agenda, and national security sphere. For instance, Taiwan and PRC are long known for their political rivalry since 1949. The tension of this rivalry changes from time to time and could be observed from news and social media. With the advent of the Internet, information flows instantly on social media. Monitoring corpora could thus be built to record and detect the latest issues hotly discussed on the web. The rivalry between Taiwan and mainland China demands applications that monitor tensions between the two political regimes. Since text data on the web accumulate rapidly, and only a subset of text data is relevant to particular applications, various methods need to be deployed to retrieve relevant information from the texts in an unsupervised yet transparent manner. One of such methods is collocation analysis.

Collocation analysis has been adopted in studies about how "Muslim" is represented in news media (Li and Zhang, 2021; Baker et al., 2013). These studies have shown that implicit political images of "Muslim" in news media can be revealed by analyzing the word choices, or collocates, around the target word. Collocates are not random companies but indicators of the context of the target word since collocations are the result of "mutual expectations" (Firth, 1957) between the two words. This expectation includes compatibility between the two units in grammatical aspects, semantic aspects, and knowledge about reality. Collocates can be further categorized according to their semantic information (Li and Zhang,

2021; Baker et al., 2013), and can be used to understand how a concept is described in the media. The original concept of collocation, which only captures associated word pairs occurring close in positions, could be extended. Grammatical collocations capture associated word pairs of a particular grammatical relationship. For example, Pearce (2008) has identified that "woman" often plays as the subject of verbs about annoyance.

In this study, we explore the potential of leveraging (grammatical) collocation analysis to monitor Taiwan-related topics that are posted on social media in mainland China and Taiwan. As a preliminary step, we compare text data collected from two representative social media, Weibo and PTT, aiming to provide a sketch of the differences and similarities between the two sources.

2 Data

To monitor changes over time, we construct two comparable corpora from Weibo and PTT respectively, using web crawlers to collect posts published between 2020-05-01 and 2020-10-01 (ranged 153 days). Posts with the word 臺灣 'Taiwan' and its form variants on Weibo and PTT are extracted respectively with weibo-search[1] and PTT corpus (Liu, 2014). Since the data collected from PTT is larger than that of Weibo, we balance the size of the two corpora by reducing the size of PTT corpus with random sampling of posts. Then, each of the corpora is split into nine time-sliced subcorpora, with each subcorpus containing post data spanning about 17 days. The resulting time-sliced subcorpora each contains about 0.4 to 1.25 million tokens. The corpora are word segmented with jieba[2]. After word segmentation, simplified Chinese are converted to traditional Chinese via OpenCC[3]. In addition, usage variations between Taiwan and mainland China, such as 台灣/臺灣, are normalized. These corpora are then used for collocation extraction and dependency relation parsing, which are described in Section 3 and 4 respectively.

[1]https://github.com/dataabc/weibo-search
[2]https://github.com/fxsjy/jieba
[3]https://github.com/BYVoid/OpenCC

3 Exploring Collocating Topic of "Taiwan"

In this study, we are interested in exploring potential methods that could be applied to monitor topics discussed on different social media sources. As an exploratory step, we extract collocates of the term 臺灣 from different times on Weibo and PTT. This would allow us to compare these collocates across different dimensions (time and sources). These collocates could be seen as hints that provide information about what is being discussed about Taiwan. In addition to extracting collocates, we also need a (semi-)automatic method to cluster these collocates into meaningful groups to better interpret the results. To achieve this, we explored two different methods—the first uses word embeddings of the collocates to cluster them into discrete groups, and the second uses Latent Dirichlet allocation to derive topics from the corpora such that each collocate could be given a vector of weights across topics. Section 3.2 and 3.3 further describe the two methods respectively. Section 3.1 describes the procedure of collocation extraction.

3.1 Collocation Extraction

We focus here only on word pairs occurring in a running window of two (i.e., bigrams) as candidates of collocations. Since we are interested only in collocates of 臺灣, collocation extraction here is equivalent to finding word pairs containing 臺灣 and showing strong associations. To measure the strength of association between word pairs, we adopt a measure known as Log Likelihood (Dunning, 1993). Log Likelihood has several advantages over another widely used measure, mutual information (MI), in that (1) it is less subject to low-frequency bias, (2) it takes sampling variations into account, and (3) it best approximates Fisher's exact test, which is considered the most appropriate significance test for collocation contingency table (Evert, 2009). Equation (1) below shows how Log Likelihood and MI are calculated for a word pair. O_{ij} corresponds to the observed frequency and E_{ij} to the expected frequency of a cell in the contingency table. MI simply measures the log ratio of the observed frequency of a word pair (O_{11}) to its expected frequency (E_{11}). Log Likelihood takes into account all four cells in the contingency table.

$$Log\ Likelihood = 2\sum_{ij} O_{ij} log \frac{O_{ij}}{E_{ij}}$$
$$MI = log_2 \frac{O_{11}}{E_{11}} \quad (1)$$

By using the Log Likelihood measure (a.k.a, G^2), we extract 20 collocates of 臺灣 that have the largest G^2 values for each of the time-sliced subcorpus, resulting in 18 lists of collocates. In the next two sections, we describe how we convert these lists of collocates into probability distributions over topics.

3.2 Deriving a distribution of topics with word embeddings

We use the Weibo corpus and the PTT corpus to obtain three sets of word embeddings. The first and second sets were derived from the Weibo and PTT corpus respectively, and the third set is derived from data combined from both sources. The word embeddings were trained using the Word2Vec algorithm (Mikolov et al., 2013) implemented in gensim (Řehůřek and Sojka, 2010). The hyperparameters for the three sets are set to identical values—the window size is set to 5, the minimum frequency of occurrence is set to 5, and the resulting dimension of the word vectors is set to 100. Since during training, initializations of the Word2Vec models are random, the resulting vector spaces of the models need to be rotated and aligned before one can compute semantic distances across different models. We used orthogonal Procrustes, introduced in Hamilton et al. (2016), to align the first (Weibo) and second (PTT) model against the third model (Weibo + PTT).

We then assign word vectors from the Weibo and PTT models to the collocates[4] extracted from the time-sliced subcorpora. The vectors of the collocates could then be treated as a matrix. Principal component analysis is performed on the matrix to reduce the dimension of the word vectors from 100 to 4. K-Means clustering is then performed on the matrix to cluster the collocates into discrete groups. We tested different cluster numbers (k) by calculating the resulting *inertia* of each clustering. *Inertia* is defined as the sum of squared distance of the data points to their closest cluster center. Since there is an inverse relationship between *inertia* and k, and since we want both of them to be low, we adopt the elbow method by plotting *inertia* against k and look for the place where the decrease in *inertia* starts to slow down. Using this method, we arrive at an optimal k of 10.

Given these clusters of collocates, we could then derive a frequency distribution from a list of collocates. The idea is to assign each collocate in the list to its belonging cluster in order to obtain a frequency distribution of the clusters. Figure 1 contrasts the distribution of collocate clusters between Weibo and PTT. The cluster labels are generated by using the six closest words to the cluster center in each cluster. The distributions in Figure 1 leave out the time dimension and use collocates across all time steps to provide an overview of the topics discussed on Weibo and PTT. Contrasts considering the time dimension are discussed in Section 3.4, in which we will also consider distributions derived from another method—Latent Dirichlet allocation (Blei et al., 2003). We describe how distributions are derived with Latent Dirichlet Allocation next.

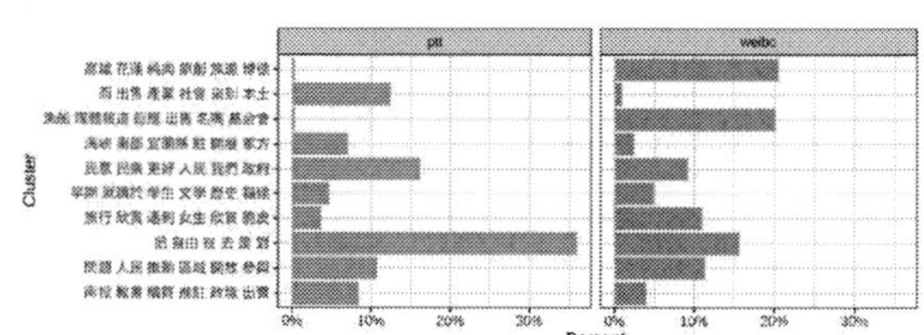

Figure 1: Distribution of collocate topics derived from word embeddings.

3.3 Deriving a distribution of topics with Latent Dirichlet Allocation

Topic modeling is a good unsupervised choice to explore unstructured data. Various topic models have been developed (Zhao et al., 2015), including Latent Semantic Indexing (LSA), Probabilistic Latent Semantic Analysis (PLSA), and Latent Dirichlet Allocation (LDA). Latent Dirichlet Allocation (LDA) is one of the models popularly employed in mod-

[4] A word occurring in two different sources is treated as two different collocates.

eling topics of unorganized textual data. The purpose of adopting Latent Dirichlet Allocation (LDA) as another method to derive topic distributions is that, compared to "hard" clustering, LDA is more flexible in how it can be used to assign topics to a given word. Since a topic is a mixture of words weighted by probabilities, we can go in another direction and define a word as a mixture of topics, using relative probabilities of the word across all topics to derive a distribution.

Thus, we trained a single LDA model with all of the corpus data (Weibo + PTT). Words with frequencies below 5 are discarded and the number of topics is set to 20[5]. After obtaining the topics, two annotators independently assigned labels to the topics. Inconsistency between assigned labels were further discussed and resolved. The resulting labels for the twenty topics are shown in Table 1.

Given the topics generated from LDA, we are able to assign each occurrence of a word in the corpus a probability distribution. The remainder of this section describes the rationale behind this procedure. Suppose that we would like to assign a vector of topic probabilities to a word w_i, in vector form, this would be:

$$\begin{aligned}&\left[p(T_1|w_i), p(T_2|w_i), \cdots, p(T_{20}|w_i)\right]\\&= \left[\frac{p(T_1 \cap w_i)}{p(w_i)}, \frac{p(T_2 \cap w_i)}{p(w_i)}, \cdots, \frac{p(T_{20} \cap w_i)}{p(w_i)}\right]\end{aligned} \quad (2)$$

Since we are interested in arriving at a probability distribution (i.e., a vector summing to one), we can discard the denominator $p(w_i)$, which gives us:

$$\left[p(T_1 \cap w_i), p(T_2 \cap w_i), \cdots, p(T_{20} \cap w_i)\right] \quad (3)$$

From the LDA model, we can obtain $p(w_i|T_j) = p(T_j \cap w_i)\, p(T_j)$. Plugging this into the equation gives us:

$$\left[p(w_i|T_1)p(T_1), p(w_i|T_2)p(T_2), \cdots, p(w_i|T_{20})p(T_{20})\right] \quad (4)$$

Finally, making the assumption that the marginal probability of all topics are equal $p(T_1) = p(T_2) = \ldots = p(T_{20})$ allows us to arrive at

$$\left[p(w_i|T_1), p(w_i|T_2), \cdots, p(w_i|T_{20})\right] \quad (5)$$

Normalizing the vector above such that it sums to one would then give us the probability distribution we want for each occurrence of a word. Thus, given a list of collocates with their frequencies of occurrence, we can sum the distribution derived from each occurrence together to arrive at a distribution of topics. For instance, Figure 2, which can be compared to Figure 1, contrasts the distribution of collocate topics between Weibo and PTT by adopting LDA to derive the distributions.

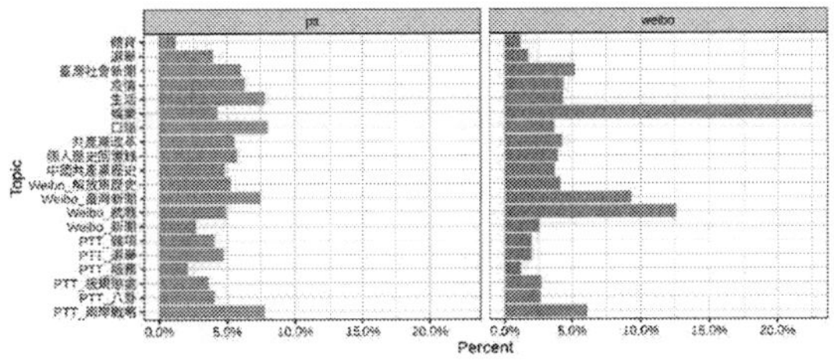

Figure 2: Distribution of collocate topics derived from Latent Dirichlet allocation.

3.4 Quantitative analysis of collocate topic distributions

Based on the distribution extraction methods described in previous sections, we are able to quantify the distance (or similarity) between Weibo and PTT across different dimensions. One of such dimensions is *time*. By splitting the corpus into time-sliced subcorpora, we could retrieve a list of collocates for each time step. These lists of collocates are then converted to distributions and thus can be compared directly using quantitative metrics.

For the first analysis, we look at topical variations *within* a source. This analysis allows us to notice, for instance, whether there are particular times when the topic distribution deviated from the grand mean, either on Weibo or PTT. To achieve this, for each of the nine time steps and each of the sources (Weibo and PTT), we extract 20 collocates of 臺灣. This results in 18 distributions (9 for PTT and 9 for Weibo). The mean distribution for each of the sources is calculated by summing up the

[5]The number of topics (k) is determined through the elbow method described in Section 3.2. We test LDA with different values of k and compute corresponding values of perplexity and arrive at an optimal k of 20 with the elbow method.

Table 1: Labels assigned to the 20 topics generated by Latent Dirichlet allocation.

Topic	Translation	Topic	Translation
PTT 選舉	PTT election	PTT 版務	PTT affairs
口語	Spoken terms	PTT 板規懲處	PTT Regulations
中國共產黨歷史	History of Chinese Communist Party	生活	Daily life
Weibo 統戰	Weibo Cross-Strait unification	選舉	Election in Taiwan
Weibo 臺灣新聞	News about Taiwan on Weibo	Weibo 新聞	News on Weibo
PTT 兩岸戰略	Cross-Strait Military strategy	娛樂	Entertainment
臺灣社會新聞	Social News in Taiwan	PTT 八卦	PTT Gossiping
共產黨改革	Chinese Communist Party reform	個人歷史回憶錄	Personal memoir
Weibo 解放軍歷史	History of People's Liberation Army	體育	Sports
PTT 雜項	Miscellaneous topics on PTT	疫情	Coronal virus

nine time-step distributions and normalizing it to a probability distribution. The distance between a particular time step and the mean then is defined as the cosine distance between the two distributions:

$$CosDist = 1 - CosSim(Distr_t, Distr_{mean})$$
$$CosSim(\vec{x}, \vec{y}) = \frac{\vec{x} \cdot \vec{y}}{|\vec{x}||\vec{y}|} \tag{6}$$

This would give us nine distance measures for each source, indicating how deviated the topic discussed is from the mean in a particular time step. Figure 3 shows the results derived from both word embedding clustering (Section 3.2) and LDA (Section 3.3). A quick glance at the plots shows that topic variations on Weibo are larger compared to PTT. This seems to result from certain topics bursting in particular time steps on Weibo, as evident in Figure 4.

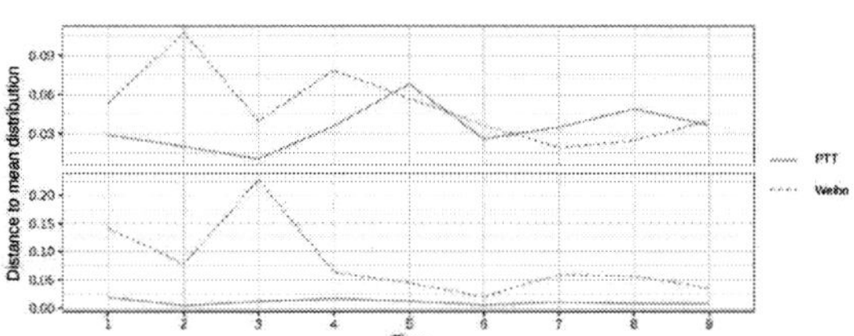

Figure 3: Topical variation with a source. The plot on the top results from adopting word embedding clusters to derive distributions for distance calculations; the plot on the bottom results from adopting LDA to derive distributions for distance calculations.

The second analysis directly compares Weibo and PTT across time. With the same set of distributions, we could calculate the similarity between Weibo and PTT for each time step. This allows us to notice, for instance, when the topics discussed are similar and when the topics seem to deviate between the two sources. The results are shown in Figure 5.

4 Dependency Relations

To provide a finer-grained view of discussions of Taiwan-related topics, we resort to a more linguistically-involved dependency relation analysis. As mentioned in Section 3.1, it has been widely attested that Log Likelihood (G^2) is a better association measure of collocates, as it always provides higher precision values at the same recall percentage. However, it is also found that for some specific types of grammatical collocation, other measures might work better (Uhrig et al., 2018). For instance, while G^2 provides the best performance for almost all relations (such as verb-object, adverb-adjective, etc), t-score surpasses it for adjective-noun collocation. Based on BNC, Uhrig et al. also did a comprehensive evaluation of different dependency parser and annotation schemes as a filter on the collocation candidate extraction task, and show that SpaCy (Honnibal et al., 2020) is a robust parser with good results on all grammatical relations. So in this study, we utilize SpaCy as the syntactic dependency parser to further extract grammatical collocations of the verb-directObject pairs, with all verbs that take 臺灣 'Taiwan' as the direct object in both PTT and Weibo subcorpora across different time-sliced periods.

For the sake of brevity, we only consider verbs that consist of two or more characters, and the minimum frequency is set to 2. After collecting the verbs, we compute G^2 values for every verb, extract the top 10 verbs that have the highest G^2 values in each time step, and

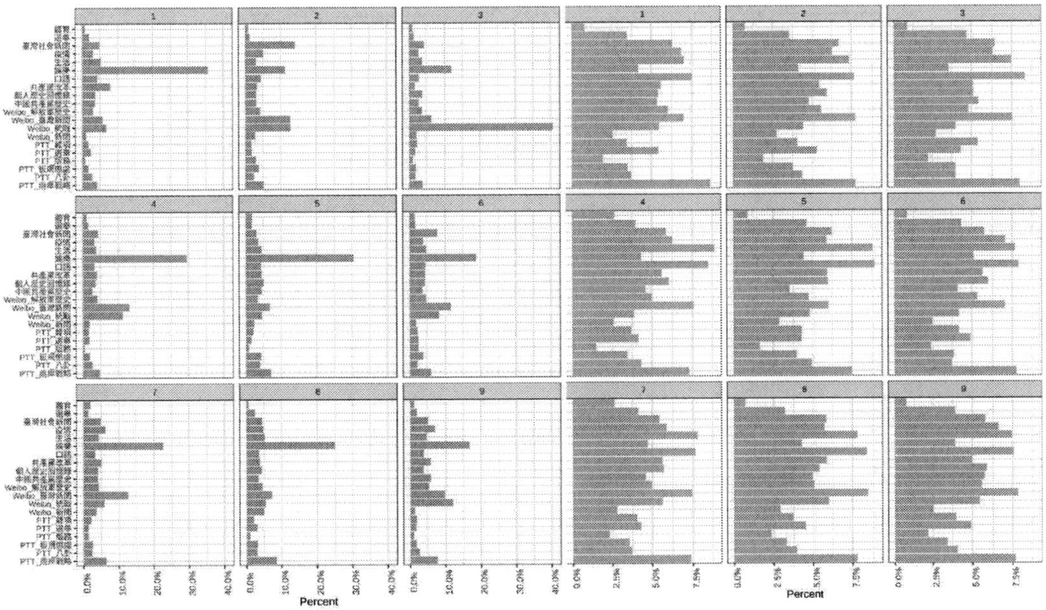

Figure 4: Distributions of topics across time using topics derived from LDA. The left part plots the results of Weibo and the right part plots the results of PTT.

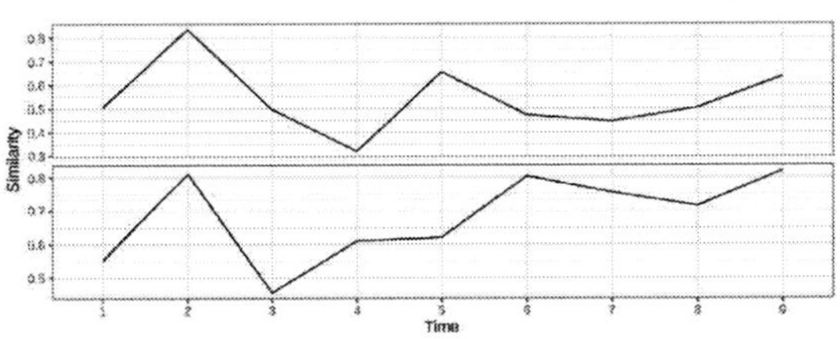

Figure 5: Similarity of topic distributions between Weibo and PTT across time. The top row results from word embedding clustering; the bottom row results from LDA.

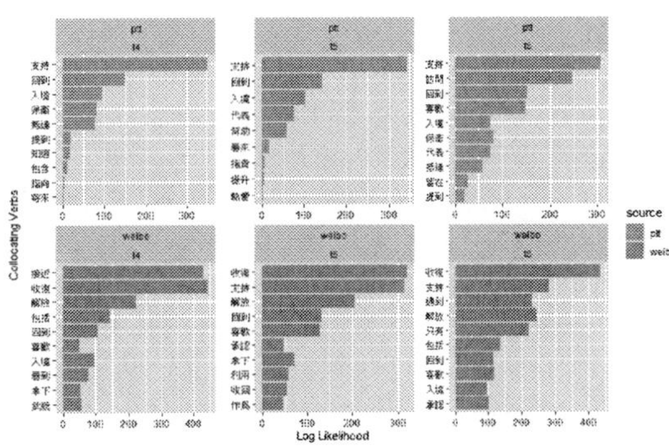

Figure 6: Collocating Verbs of the Direct Object 臺灣 'Taiwan'

finally rank them in descending order. The charts in Figure 6 demonstrate the results of dependency relations from time step 4 to 6 in the two corpora respectively. It is shown that compared with PTT, Weibo users frequently choose military terms such as 收復 'recapture' and 解放 'liberate'. PTT users, in contrast, consistently use Taiwan-oriented verbs, e.g. 入境 'enter', 回到 'return', and 抵達 'arrive'.

5 Discussion

In Section 3.2 and 3.3, two different methods are used to derive collocate topic distributions of 臺灣 'Taiwan'. The two methods each have advantages and drawbacks. The word embedding clustering method is fully automatic, in that labels of the clusters are generated from picking out the words that are closest to the cluster center. In addition, compared to LDA, word embedding clustering is more computationally efficient, which may be a crucial property for developing large-scale monitoring applications since the corpus data are subject to frequent updates in such applications. On the other hand, results generated from the LDA method match human intuition more since the labels of the topic are manually given and word topic distributions can be interpreted easily due to inherent properties of LDA. Below, we focus the discussion on the results of distributions derived from LDA across time.

The distributions of topics across nine time

steps on Weibo and PTT are summarized in Figure 4. The most prominent distinction between the two sources is that distributions from PTT are flat whereas distributions from Weibo often peak in particular topics. This shows that in general, the focuses of discussion of Taiwan on PTT seems to be more widespread, whereas, on Weibo, discussions of Taiwan are focused on particular topics such as Entertainment (time step 1 and 4~9), Cross-Strait unification (time step 2~4 and 9), and News about Taiwan (time step 2, 4, 7). The focus-shifting on Weibo seems to be the primary force that drives the fluctuation in the similarity between Weibo and PTT. As evident in the bottom part of Figure 5, the sharp drop in similarity at time step 3 corresponds to Weibo's extreme focused discussion about Cross-Strait unification, which is estimated to account for roughly 40% of the top-ranked collocates of Taiwan. On the other hand, the peaking of similarity at time step 2, 6, and 9 corresponds to a flatter distribution of topics on Weibo, where the focuses of the discussion seem much less prominent.

In addition to utilizing simple co-occurrence in texts to extract collocates (Section 3), incorporating grammatical relations also shows promising results. In Section 4, by narrowing down the collocates of Taiwan to verbs only, we are able to see some interesting contrasts between Weibo and PTT. Since a verb often expresses *intentions* toward its object, we could immediately spot that most of the top collocating verbs of Taiwan on Weibo exhibit intentions to assault, whereas such intentions are absent in the top collocating verbs on PTT. This points to a direction for future research, in which clustering methods (Section 3.2 and 3.3) may be applied to these collocating verbs, and the annotation of the resulting clusters could focus on the intentions of the verbs. This could potentially facilitate the development of monitoring applications that focus more on sensitive topics (e.g., whether there may be a rise in political or military tensions between mainland China and Taiwan).

6 Conclusion

In this study, we adopted collocation analysis as a method to explore Taiwan-related topics posted on social media. To summarize a large number of extracted collocates, we utilized clustering and topic modeling to derive a probability distribution over topics from a list of collocates. Similarities between Weibo and PTT across time were characterized in terms of these distributions. Finer-grained analysis of grammatical collocates hints on future work to apply clustering methods to verbal collocates, which may reveal details such as intentions toward the object.

References

Paul Baker, Costas Gabrielatos, and Tony McEnery. 2013. Sketching Muslims: A Corpus Driven Analysis of Representations Around the Word 'Muslim' in the British Press 1998—2009. *Applied Linguistics*, 34(3):255–278.

David M. Blei, Andrew Y. Ng, and Michael I. Jordan. 2003. Latent dirichlet allocation. *Journal of Machine Learning Research*, 3(null):993–1022. Number of pages: 30 Publisher: JMLR.org tex.issue_date: 3/1/2003.

Stefan Evert. 2009. Corpora and collocations. In Anke Lüdeling and Merja Kytö, editors, *Volume 2*, pages 1212–1248. De Gruyter Mouton.

John Rupert Firth. 1957. *A Synopsis of Linguistic Theory, 1930-1955.*

William L. Hamilton, Jure Leskovec, and Dan Jurafsky. 2016. Diachronic Word Embeddings Reveal Statistical Laws of Semantic Change. In *Proceedings of the 54th Annual Meeting of the Association for Computational Linguistics (Volume 1: Long Papers)*, pages 1489–1501, Berlin, Germany. Association for Computational Linguistics.

Matthew Honnibal, Ines Montani, Sofie Van Landeghem, and Adriane Boyd. 2020. spaCy: Industrial-strength natural language processing in python.

Ke Li and Qiang Zhang. 2021. A corpus-based study of representation of Islam and Muslims in American media: Critical Discourse Analysis Approach. *International Communication Gazette*, page 1748048520987440. Publisher: SAGE Publications Ltd.

Tsun-Ju Liu. 2014. PTT Corpus: Construction and Applications. Master's thesis, National Taiwan University, Taipei, Taiwan, January.

Tomas Mikolov, Kai Chen, Greg Corrado, and Jeffrey Dean. 2013. Efficient estimation of word representations in vector space.

Michael Pearce. 2008. Investigating the collocational behaviour of man and woman in the BNC using Sketch Engine. *Corpora*, 3(1):1–29.

Peter Uhrig, Stefan Evert, and Thomas Proisl. 2018. Collocation candidate extraction from dependency-annotated corpora: Exploring differences across parsers and dependency annotation schemes. In Pascual Cantos-Gómez and Moisés Almela-Sánchez, editors, *Lexical collocation analysis: Advances and applications*, pages 111–140. Springer, Cham.

Weizhong Zhao, James J. Chen, Roger Perkins, Zhichao Liu, Weigong Ge, Yijun Ding, and Wen Zou. 2015. A heuristic approach to determine an appropriate number of topics in topic modeling. *BMC Bioinformatics*, 16(13):S8.

Radim Řehůřek and Petr Sojka. 2010. Software framework for topic modelling with large corpora. In *Proceedings of LREC 2010 workshop new challenges for NLP frameworks*, pages 46–50, Valletta, Malta. University of Malta.

The 33rd Conference on Computational Linguistics and Speech Processing (ROCLING 2021)
Taoyuan, Taiwan, October 15-16, 2021. The Association for Computational Linguistics and Chinese Language Processing

利用文本分類技術於刑事判決書之沒收物辨識
Confiscation Detection of Criminal Judgment Using Text Classification Approach

史軒慈 Hsuan-Tzu Shih
School of Big Data Management,
Soochow University, Taiwan
dollyshih39@gmail.com

邱鈺臻 Yu-Cheng Chiu
School of Big Data Management,
Soochow University, Taiwan
jean199925@gmail.com

陳筱詩 Hsiao-Shih Chen
School of Big Data Management,
Soochow University, Taiwan
kellywithchen@ gmail.com

吳政隆 Jheng-Long Wu
Department of Data Science,
Soochow University, Taiwan
jlwu@gm.scu.edu.tw

摘要

在沒收制度日漸完善時，掌握法院實際宣告沒收之種類分布將能更瞭解趨勢變化，除可協助立法者制定法律外，亦可提供外界瞭解沒收制度實際運作之情況。為了使人工智慧技術能夠自動化辨識沒收物，降低以人工方式進行判讀所耗費之人力及時間成本。本研究之目的為建立自動化沒收辨識模型，能快速且準確辨識沒收之多標籤類別，提供各界對於沒收資訊之需求，以利後續法條修正或裁量。本研究以刑事第一審判決書為主要實驗數據，根據現行法條規範將沒收物分為違禁物、犯罪工具及犯罪所得三種類別，並進行多重標籤辨識。本研究將採用 Term Frequency－Inverse Document Frequency （TF-IDF）及 Word2Vec 演算法作為特徵萃取演算法並搭配隨機森林分類器進行建模。另也採用 CKIPlabBERT 預訓練模型進行建模與辨識。實驗結果顯示，採用 CKIPlabBERT 預訓練模型進行沒收物辨識訓練與預測下，在僅依據判決書中所提及沒收字詞之句子時，可獲得最佳的辨識效果，以案件沒收為任務時，Micro F1 分數可高達 96.2716%，以被告沒收為任務時，Micro F1 分數高達 95.5478%。

Abstract

As the system of confiscation becomes more and more perfect, grasping the distribution of the types of confiscations actually announced by the courts will enable you to understand changing of the trend. In addition to assisting legislators in formulating laws, it can also provide other people with an understanding of the actual operation of the confiscation system. In order to enable artificial intelligence technology to automatically identify the distribution of confiscation, and consumes a lot of manpower and time costs of manual judgment. The purpose of this research is to establish an automated confiscation identification model that can quickly and accurately identify the multiple label categories of confiscation, and provide the needs of all social circles for confiscation information, so as to facilitate subsequent law amendments or discretion. This research uses the first instance criminal cases as the main experimental data. According to the current laws, the confiscation is divided into three categories: contrabands, criminal tools and criminal proceeds, and perform multiple label identification. This research will use Term Frequency－Inverse Document Frequency (TF-IDF) and Word2Vec algorithm as the feature extraction algorithm, with random forest classifier, and CKIPlabBERT pretrained model for training and identification. The experimental results show that under the CKIPlabBERT pretrained model, the best identification effect can be obtained when only use sentences with confiscated words mentioned in the judgment. When the task is case confiscation, the Micro F1 Score can be as high as 96.2716%, and when the task is defendant confiscation, the Micro F1 Score is as high as 95.5478%.

關鍵字：刑事判決、沒收、文本分類、機器學習、預訓練模型、多標籤分類
Keywords ： Criminal Cases, Confiscation, Text Mining, Machine Learning, Pretrained model, Multi-label Detection

1 緒論

我國刑法沒收制度在 105 年有了重大變革，沒收對象擴大到第三人，不再僅限於犯罪行為人，販售黑心食品之不肖業者，其違法行為所獲得之不當得利，國人期待以法律剝奪之。此外，違禁物，如毒品，同樣需由法律加以沒收。依內政部警政署統計，12 歲至 23 歲之

毒品嫌疑人，108 年共 5,676 人，顯示毒品潛入校園，戕害青少年身心健康程度不低。而施用毒品所衍生之犯罪問題亦不容忽視。沒收件數於 99 年至 104 年間平均每年約 3.1 萬件，105 年沒收制度變革後，則大幅上升，105 至 108 年間平均每年約 4.3 萬件。顯示修法後，刑事案件宣告沒收之件數大幅提高。

無法以名詞與沒收物類別有對照關係，因為相同之物品，若被告所犯罪名不同，則會有不同之沒收分類，故無法僅以對照表對沒收物進行分類，仍需視判決書內容而定。本研究沒收物之分類是以刑法第 38 條及第 38 條之 1 作為分類基準，若特別法有規定，則從特別法之規定。為了使本研究所建立的模型可使法官撰寫判決書時能作參考依據，故將採用刪除判決書中有關法條之文字，亦即在不知道法條的前提下，進行沒收物之分類。

近年法學上利用機器學習、文字探勘技術與 BERT 模型進行之研究，多集中在量刑因子、量刑系統等方面，尚無應用在沒收物之研究上，目前僅能以人工方式研讀判決書並做標記，其處理效率不佳。若能將文本分類技術應用在沒收物之分類上，便能改善沒收物辨識的人工成本，及提升沒收物統計之效率。此外自動化辨識能更進一步瞭解沒收物種類與所犯罪名之相關性，故掌握沒收物分類之分布，可幫助立法者針對沒收較多之種類，制定更完善的法律規範。本文將以司法院法學資料檢索系統公開之判決書作為資料，透過文字特徵萃取演算法與機器學習模型來建立沒收物多標籤分類模型。另也採用深度學習模型中最新進的 BERT 模型進行建模，期望所建構的模型可以有效辨識沒收物多標籤分類，使非結構化之判決書能夠自動辨識出沒收物類型。本研究將達成以下貢獻：（1）因本研究是將判決書中有關法條之文字先予刪除，再進行分類，故可提供法官於判決書正本完成前，先行檢視所引法條是否正確，避免事後修正及增加行政成本，亦可提升民眾對司法之信任。（2）違禁物可能有銷毀之必要，因此可視違禁物之多寡進行更精準之預算編列，犯罪工具或犯罪所得，除法律有規定者外，可進行拍賣或繳庫，本研究可幫助外界瞭解沒收對國庫之貢獻。

2 文獻探討

2.1 我國沒收制度

105 年 7 月以前，刑法第 38 條將沒收物之種類分為因犯罪所生或所得之物、供犯罪所用或犯罪預備之物及違禁物，且刑法從刑之種類分為：褫奪公權、沒收、追徵、追繳或抵償。所謂從刑就是須依附於主刑，主刑存在時，從刑才會存在，也才能宣告沒收，且對於第三人之財產不得進行沒收，亦即沒收主體僅限犯罪行為人。林宗志（2014）建議以三種面向改進：建立沒收物之保全機制，避免事先轉移，無法執行沒收；建立第三人參與訴訟機制，保障第三人權益；沒收程序不以定罪為必要。

105 年 7 月起，刑法沒收新制上路，新法讓沒收具獨立性，無須依附主刑，得單獨宣告沒收，且對第三人之財產同樣可執行沒收。惟新法將沒收擴大解釋後，可能產生罰金刑與沒收重複剝奪犯罪所得的疑慮（陳贈吉，2017），及沒收金額之計算是否應扣除成本問題。有學者認為應視該法人是否有過失而定（陳偉倫，2018），劉韋汝（2019）則認為可能被宣告沒收之當事人，若已具備程序上主體地位，皆可能成為本案參與人，不應由實體法的角度判定是否屬於第三人，如此才能確實保障第三人應有之訴訟權利。惟若第三人捨棄參與此項訴訟權利，林宜潔（2020）認為效力僅及於聽審權，法院仍可對其宣告沒收，且該第三人亦喪失救濟之權利，對於沒收之判決不得提起上訴。

除了沒收行為人之犯罪所得外，如有其他來源不明且可能源自不明違法行為之所得，亦可宣告沒收。林秉衡（2020）認為我國沒收制度之設計，應分為二元體制，分別係犯罪物沒收與利得沒收，其目的分別為危險防衛及犯罪預防，其中犯罪物沒收又含違禁物及犯罪工具產物，然本研究將犯罪工具產物簡稱為犯罪工具，且沒收物之分類依據刑法第 38 條第 1 項、第 2 項及第 38-1 條分為三類。

2.2 文字特徵萃取

TF（Term Frequency）演算法（Luhn，1957）是計算一個字詞在一篇文章中被提及的次數，但為避免不同文章間做比較時，篇幅較長之文章，字詞出現的頻率必較短篇文章多，因此演算法做了修正，再除以一篇文章的總字詞數。IDF（Inverse Document Frequency）演算法（Spärck Jones,1972）是計算一個字詞，在一群文章中所占的篇幅數，若字詞在較少的文章被提及，則該字詞較能代表那篇文章的分類特性。Term Frequency–Inverse Document Frequency（TF-IDF）為兩者之乘積，用以表示一個字詞出現之頻率及其重要度。謝知庭（2020）以 2014 年至 2020 年有關實驗教育之碩博士論文及期刊為研究文本，利用 TF-IDF 進行字詞權重分析，利用潛在狄利克雷分配（Latent Dirichlet Allocation，LDA），分別研究各年度代表關鍵字並建立主題模型，提出實驗教育三項法規自公布以來，學者研究分析之主題趨勢。梁家徹（2020）針對筆記型電腦研發過程中，需對過程所遇問題排列優先處理程序，因此利用實際發問紀錄，以 TF-IDF 篩選特徵值並建立預測模型，最後搭配類神經網路模型獲得最佳實驗結果，召回率（Recall）高達 85%。鍾育東（2019）以台灣旅遊論壇「背包客棧」不同地區之討論內容，以 TF-IDF 方法找出背包客最常討論的內容，提供旅遊業者推出符合旅客期待的行程。謝宛芷及胡雅涵（2014）為了自動分類資安問題及預測問題嚴重度，利用資訊安全相關新聞進行斷詞，並將字詞給予不同的權重，研究結果顯示使用詞頻加權與類神經網路分類器之 F-Measure 為 97.6%，為所有方法中之最佳。

詞嵌入（Word Embedding）技術能將文本資訊嵌入於向量中，用於表達所訓練過的文本語意，Word2Vec 演算法（Tomas Mikolov 等人，2013），是詞嵌入的其中一種作法，目的是將文字轉換為向量數值，供後續機器學習模型使用。Word2Vec 又可分為 Skip-gram 及 CBOW（Continuous Bag of Word）兩種模式，兩者的差別在於 Skip-gram 是給定中間字詞，預測前後文字，而 CBOW 則是給定前後文字，預測中間文字。陳克威（2020）應用於論文推薦系統，在 TF-IDF 及 Word2Vec 兩種方法比較下，Word2Vec 更能推薦潛在的相關性論文，維度低於 100 時，TF-IDF 優於 Word2Vec，當維度逐漸提高，Word2Vec 的表現越來越好，該研究建議維度設定於 200 至 300 間效果最好。林祥慶（2018）使用 TF-IDF、Word2Vec 及人工篩選特徵搭配線性迴歸，施用一級毒品之預測刑期與實際月數平均差 3.08 個月，F1 Score 為 86%，施用二級毒品則平均差 1.60 個月，F1 Score 為 88%，但是運用到較複雜的案件，例如販賣毒品時，則較難準確預測刑期。

2.3 文字探勘在判決書上之應用

目前以刑度預測相關研究為大宗，林琬真等人（2012）以 TF-IDF 作為文字重要度，以文字出現之頻率來表示，進行文字加權，其所犯罪名特別選用強盜罪與恐嚇取財罪者，並達到改善案件分類之效果。黃玉婷（2012）以智慧財產案件為例，利用正規表示法找出量刑因子之段落，發現文字探勘所產出之因子與人為標記之因子相差無幾。王安定（2016）則以毒品相關判決為例，利用 TF-IDF 和 N-gram 解析判決書字詞，並使用線性迴歸及神經網路進行量刑模型之建立，發現線性迴歸用來預測量刑的效果優於神經網路。姜晴文（2019）以過往之研究及其判決書樣本特性建立若干欄位，手動標記欄位及親權歸屬，且均依照法官撰寫之裁判書內容作為標記基礎，並使用對數機率迴歸、決策樹（Decision Trees）、隨機森林（Radom Forest）、梯度型推進決策樹及類神經網路分類器，實驗結果發現五種分類器在預測裁判結果上，準確率均可達 95.5%以上。

2.4 文本分類模型之應用

黃馨慧（2013）以靜態影像訓練臉部表情識別模型、郭家妏（2014）建立河流水位即時通報系統、陳時仲（2015）評估隨機森林與迴歸模型之效力。葉子維（2018）以決策樹、線性判別分析及隨機森林為模型，尋找行動銀行之潛在客戶、蔡宗諺（2019）藉由決策樹及隨機森林模型，訓練禪定與休息狀態下之腦電波分類。以上研究均在使用隨機森林演算法時，獲得較好之成效。王厚勛（2020）使用 DistilBERT 搭配隨機森林分類器以及 BERT 搭配支援向量機（SVM）開發了一款以通訊軟體為基礎的聊天機器人用於金融防詐騙，協助民眾判別其遭遇的情境是否為詐騙，並提供相對應的處理建議。翁嘉嫻（2020）使用 BERT 預訓練語言模型來識別網路上的虛假評論，實驗結果顯示 BERT 模型的識別效果較傳統基於靜態特徵向量之模型要來得精準。曾浚宥（2020）透過網路爬蟲蒐集食品廣告違規案例以建立食品廣告違規識別所需的訓練資料，並將訓練資料用以訓練 BERT 模型，其研究結果顯示可以有效地識別食品廣告中的違規詞。

3 研究方法

本研究以文本分類技術作為自動化沒收物辨識系統，主要是針對判決書的文本內容進行斷詞、文字萃取、清整、建模及分類評估等處理，其中本研究採機器學習分類模型以及 CKIPlabBERT 預訓練模型進行沒收物案例學習，以利建立判決書有關沒收物種類的自動化多重標籤辨識模型，其整體流程如圖 1 所示。

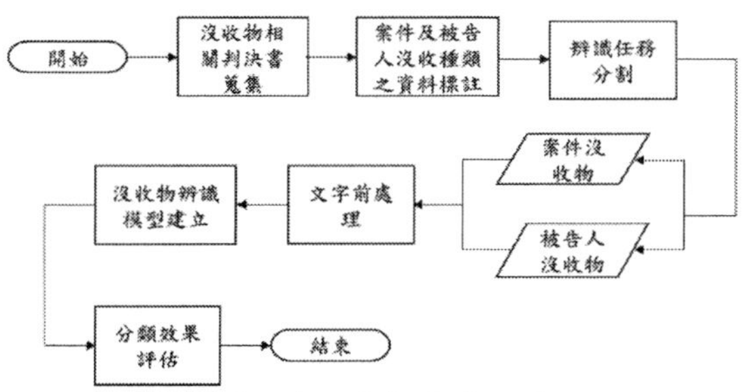

圖 1：本研究方法流程圖

3.1 資料收集

3.1.1 判決書擷取

本研究使用之資料為地方法院刑事第一審判決，且有宣告沒收之判決文本，不使用未宣告沒收之判決文係因是否宣告沒收屬主文應記載事項，若未於主文明確載明宣告沒收，原則上該案件即無沒收適用，因此無須再由分類模型判斷是否沒收，可逕予剔除未宣告沒收之案件。為了獲得本研究所需與刑事沒收相關的裁判書，於是採用司法院法學資料檢索系統之裁判書，搜尋刑事判決中主文中包含「沒收」關鍵字，透過網路爬蟲技術抓取判決書，其中資料欄位含法院別、裁判字號、主文及全文等內容。依刑事訴訟法第 308 條規定，判決書之內文僅規定須分別記載其裁判之主文與理由；有罪之判決書並應記載犯罪事實，且得與理由合併記載，並無明文規定法官撰寫判決書之撰寫格式，因此本研究所使用的資料屬於非結構化數據。

3.1.2 沒收物標記

本研究根據判決書引用之法條，沒收種類分為違禁物、犯罪工具及犯罪所得[1]。上訴所引用之條以外之判決書，則依判決書中沒收段落之描述，以專業法律從業人員進行專業判斷，獲得最終沒收物之歸類。本研究是以判決書引用之法條為標記沒收物種類之準則，因此法條與沒收種類存有一對一之對應關係。為符合分類模型訓練之合理性，以及輔助法官在撰寫判決書時，可作為檢查之用，故訓練分類模型時，所有判決書皆刪除判決書所提到的法律名稱及其法律條號。

3.2 資料分割

本研究依據判決書之特性，將資料集分為兩大任務及三種角度，各自獨立進行實驗，其中兩大辨識任務分別為案件沒收及被告沒收。（1）案件沒收：係指取全部被告沒收物種類之聯集，作為該案之沒收物標記；（2）被告沒收：係以人為單位，分別標記各被告之沒收物種類，例如一案有兩名被告，被告A被沒收違禁物，被告B被沒收犯罪工具。詳細標記結果如表 1 所示，以案件沒收物標記，分別為違禁物及犯罪工具；以被告沒收物標記，被告 A 標記違禁物，被告 B 標記犯罪工具。另一情況，如案件僅有 1 位被告被宣告沒收，則案件沒收與被告沒收標記結果相同。

標記方式	被告人	違禁物	犯罪工具	犯罪所得
案件	-	1	1	0
被告	被告 A	1	0	0
	被告 B	0	1	0

表 1：案件沒收與被告沒收標記方式，以 110 年度訴字 20 號為例

一般情況下，判決書字數非常多，這將導致模型訓練不易，且多數段落在於描述事實與理由等，因此擷取不同段落之文字，將可能提升辨識精準度，本研究採用三種角度進

[1] 屬違禁物者，係指判決書引用刑法第 38 條第 1 項:「違禁物，不問屬於犯罪行為人與否，沒收之。」；若引用刑法第 38 條第 2 項：「供犯罪所用、犯罪預備之物或犯罪所生之物，屬於犯罪行為人者，得沒收之。但有特別規定者，依其規定。」，則歸為犯罪工具；若引用刑法第 38-1 條：「犯罪所得，屬於犯罪行為人者，沒收之。但有特別規定者，依其規定。」，則歸為犯罪所得。

行擷取，分述如下：（1）主文：僅使用主文之文字，判決書其餘文字皆不採用。（2）沒收句：使用判決書中所有提到「沒收」之句子，若主文有使用沒收文字，則位於主文段之該句亦屬沒收句資料範圍。（3）全文：使用所有判決書之文字進行後續實驗，不刪除任一文字，文字量為三個角度中最多。

再者分別將三個角度資料集，依裁判日期先後排序，分割成70%作為訓練資料，用於訓練模型；10%作為驗證資料，用於超參數與模型選擇之使用；剩餘20%作為測試資料，用於評估辨識效果。此外若同一裁判日期有數份判決書，則手動調整該筆資料，讓相同裁判日期之判決書分屬相同資料集。根據實驗顯示，需手動調整之資料筆數不超過 10 件，故影響狀況相當小，仍維持約 70%、10%、20%之訓練資料、驗證資料及測試資料。

3.3 文字前處理

因判決書為正式公文，所以撰寫之句型與結構相當完整，故本研究以正規表示式（Regular Expression）去除相關法律名稱與條號，刪除前後之文字及標點符號。

3.4 建立模型分類器

3.4.1 建立隨機森林模型

採用 Jieba[2]中文斷詞工具進行文本斷詞，以利後續單詞特徵化模型進行轉換。由於斷詞前已將法律名稱及條號相關字串移除，故輸入後續分類模型之文本並未包含任何與法律名稱及條號相關之字串，便利於幫助法官於撰寫判決書時，作為條號引用之輔助工具。

為使機器能夠學習判決書的文本，本研究根據訓練資料集的單詞，採用 TF-IDF 方法產生各判決書之特徵值，利用訓練之資料來獲得必要之特徵，即所有訓練資料中的單詞。再者依訓練所建立之特徵，計算訓練集、驗證資料集及測試資料集之各篇判決書之 TF-IDF 值，並藉由在訓練資料的單詞出現頻率，調整特徵數量多寡，以獲得最佳之特徵數量。

此外，本研究亦使用另一詞嵌入模型進行特徵計算，主要是採用最具規模與應用範圍的 Word2Vec 模型作為詞嵌入演算法，其中以 CBOW 模式進行訓練資料集的學習。本研究亦透過調整詞嵌入的維度大小，產生不同向量大小的詞向量。而在轉換文字至向量詞，本研究採用各篇判決書所採用的文字取得向量平均值，並作為該判決書的特徵向量，相同的轉換過程應用於訓練、驗證及測試資料集。提供後續機器學習模型使用。本研究兩大任務及三種角度均係獨立實驗，因此獨立產生之特徵詞，無論是在 TF-IDF 或詞嵌入皆為獨立計算。

採用 TF-IDF 與 Word2Vec 計算後的特徵與特徵值，並使用機器學習模型進行判決書之沒收物辨識之學習與訓練，以最常見的隨機森林演算法進行建模，建立隨機森林模型，而模型學習目標以沒收物多重標籤為主，預測每一篇判決書時需辨識數個沒收物種類。本研究將針對每個沒收物類別分別獨立訓練一個二元分類器，再以驗證資料實驗結果，選擇最好的參數數據作為最終模型，以進行測試資料之預測，其預測結果將作為最終模型之評估指標。

3.4.2 建立 BERT 模型

由於本研究針對的判決書之內文為繁體中文，所以將使用中央研究院所開發的繁體中文之 BERT 預訓練模型，命名為 CKIPlabBERT[3]，並進行沒收物種類辨識模型訓練。CKIPlabBERT 是以標準 BERT 作為網路結構，以字作為訓練單位，因此對文字的前處理不同於傳統的文字特徵轉換法，將每個字轉換成 CKIPlabBERT 模型中 Token 編號，並將每個輸入的長度都填充至最長序列，然後使用 CKIPlabBERT 預訓練模型以進行判決書之沒收物辨識之訓練，接著預測驗證資料集及測試資料集之沒收物種類，最後將其預測結果作為模型之評估指標。

[2] 中文分词工具，採用精準模式進行斷詞。來源：https://github.com/fxsjy/jieba

[3] CKIP LAB 所開發之 CKIP Transformers 為繁體中文的 transformers 模型，預訓練模型名稱為 ckiplab/bert-base-chinese。網址：https://huggingface.co/CKIP_lab

4 實驗結果與評估

4.1 實驗資料

本研究從司法院法學資料檢索系統擷取裁判日期介於107年1月1日至107年12月31日，且有宣告沒收者，共計擷取了41,971篇判決書。資料分布筆數如表2所示，沒收種類表示一件判決書總計被沒收的種類。本實驗數據中僅有1種沒收物之比率為70.17%最多，有2種沒收物之比率為27.50%次之，3種沒收物皆有之比率則為2.33%，經分割後之各資料集分布情形也大致相同。由於資料是由人工標記之，而107年所擷取的判決書就已高達四萬多篇，故僅使用107年之資料。

沒收種數	總計件數	訓練集	驗證集	測試集
總計件數	41,971	29,502	4,694	7,775
1種	29,453	20,674	3,338	5,441
2種	11,540	8,169	1,256	2,115
3種	978	659	100	219

表2：沒收種類占各資料集之分布情形

當一篇判決書中僅宣告沒收1種類別時，如表3所示以犯罪所得為大宗，占44.49%，違禁物次之，占28.57%，犯罪工具占比最低，為26.94%。雖犯罪所得最多，惟其占比僅占四成四，其餘兩類亦有近三成之比例，因此資料分布尚非偏頗，又由表3顯示大部分資料均僅沒收1種類別，幸而任一類別之占比差距不大，因此不影響後續實驗效果。

沒收種類	總計件數	訓練集	驗證集	測試集
總計件數	29,453	20,674	3,338	5,441
違禁物	8,415	5,860	996	1,559
犯罪工具	7,934	5,627	810	1,497
犯罪所得	13,104	9,187	1,532	2,385

表3：一種沒收物之分布情形

當一篇判決書中僅宣告沒收2種類別時，如表4所示違禁物與犯罪工具、犯罪工具與犯罪所得之組合為多，各占57%及43%，違禁物與犯罪所得之組合最少。而一篇判決書中3種類別均同時宣告沒收之分布情形如表4最末列所示，占總件數之20%。

沒收種類	訓練集	驗證集	測試集
總計件數	8,169	1,256	2,115
違禁物+犯罪工具	4,615	731	1,178
違禁物+犯罪所得	70	4	15
犯罪工具+犯罪所得	3,484	521	922

表4：二種沒收物之分布情形

4.2 實驗設計

本研究所使用之硬體配備相關規格如下：作業系統為 Ubuntu 18.04.5，CPU 為 Intel i7 950 3.07GHz，記憶體為 DDR3 22GB，以及 GPU 為 RTX 3060。本研究使 TF-IDF 及 Word2Vec 兩種方法進行文字轉特徵，在超參數設定上，TF-IDF 設定字詞數量 100 至 5,000 個字詞為主，1,000 字詞，每次間格 100，超過每次間格 500。而 Word2Vec 之向量維度則設定 50 至 1,000，固定每次間格 50。另隨機森林分類演算法，設定決策樹數量為 1,000。CKIPlabBERT 模型部分則採用最大 512 個字，學習率為 5e-5，訓練跌代次數為 10 次。

4.3 評估指標

本研究採用分類問題中的 Accuracy 及 F1-Score 進行分類效果評估，本研究目標是多標籤分類，故最後採用各沒收類別的二元分類評估指標的平均值為最終分類效果，即選擇平均 F1-Score 作為模型評估之指標，而平均 Macro-F1 容易受單一類別的影響，故本研究也採用平均 Micro-F1 作為模型評估指標。

4.4 隨機森林模型之分類效果分析

將各實驗於驗證集中表現的最佳結果整理為表 5 和表 6，顯示在驗證集中，不論是採用 TF-IDF 或是 Word2Vec 的方法，驗證資料集之 Macro-F1 分數多數大於分數 Micro-F1。實驗結果顯示六個實驗中，各評估指標皆大於 89%以上，顯示本研究所提出的方法可以在驗證集中獲得非常優秀的多標籤分類效果。

在案件沒收方面，如表5所示，以 TF-IDF 特徵萃取法在驗證集中效果較佳，不論輸入之文字量多寡，均優於 Word2Vec 演算法；在資料的選擇上，以沒收句效果表現最好，這是因為使用主文會因為資訊量不足，不容易辨識沒收物之種類，而使用全文又因資訊量過多，雜訊也較多，反而影響分類效果，但沒收句是整篇判決書中所有提到沒收的句子，因此較不會受影響。沒收物結合 TF-IDF 可獲得 Micro-F1 分數至高達 96.7038%，Macro-F1 分數亦達 96.8168%。

文本	特徵法	Macro-F1	Micro-F1
主文	TF-IDF	95.0185	94.9128
	Word2vec	92.6038	92.4377
沒收句	TF-IDF	96.8168	96.7038
	Word2vec	93.9458	93.7520
全文	TF-IDF	96.1669	96.0110
	Word2vec	90.6409	90.4168

表 5：案件沒收任務於驗證集之隨機森林模型評估

在被告沒收方面，如表6所示，以TF-IDF特徵萃取法在驗證集中效果較佳。在資料的選擇上，仍是以沒收句效果表現最好。沒收物結合 TF-IDF 可獲得 Micro-F1 分數至高達 96.6757%，Macro-F1 分數亦達 96.8123%。

文本	特徵法	Macro-F1	Micro-F1
主文	TF-IDF	95.3112	95.1939
	Word2vec	92.8588	92.6777
沒收句	TF-IDF	96.8123	96.6757
	Word2vec	94.0070	93.7603
全文	TF-IDF	96.3717	96.1613
	Word2vec	89.7311	89.3409

表 6：被告沒收任務於驗證集之隨機森林模型評估

4.5 CKIPlabBERT 模型之分類效果分析

在案件沒收的部分，各個實驗在驗證集效果顯示於表 7，其分類的效果在資料的選擇上，皆以沒收句之效果為最佳。其 Micro-F1 分數至高達 96.5796%，Macro-F1 分數亦達 96.6243%。

文本	Macro-F1	Micro-F1
主文	93.4420	93.3244
沒收句	96.6243	96.5796
全文	96.0123	95.9777

表 7：案件沒收任務於驗證集之 BERT 模型評估

在被告沒收的部分，各個實驗在驗證集效果顯示於表 8，其 Micro-F1 分數至高達 96.2059%，Macro-F1 分數亦達 96.3096%。

文本	Macro-F1	Micro-F1
主文	92.2302	92.3913
沒收句	96.3096	96.2059
全文	94.1776	94.0444

表 8：被告沒收任務於驗證集之 BERT 模型評估

整體而言，BERT 模型預測之結果與隨機森林模型在驗證集所得之分析結果大致相同，仍是沒收句資料範圍得到最佳效果。

4.7 隨機森林模型與 CKIPlabBERT 模型之分類效果比較

本研究所採用的隨機森林與 CKIPlabBERT 模型預將用於辨識測試集之效果，其結果統整於表 9，評估結果顯示在案件沒收任務時，CKIPlabBERT 模型之分類效果較機器學習模型佳，兩者之 Micro-F1 分數相差 0.0739%和 Accuracy 分數相差 0.6688%，但 Macro-F1 分數較差，相差 0.0579%；標記方式為被告沒收時，在三個評估指標上，都是隨機森林模型之分類效果較 CKIPlabBERT 模型佳。由此實驗結果可得知，刑事案件之沒收物辨識，無論是以案件為單位還是被告為單位，都能夠有著相當良好的多標籤分類效果。

任務	模型	評估指標		
		Accuracy	Macro-F1	Micro-F1
案件沒收	隨機森林	90.7653	96.3269	96.1977
	CKIPlabBERT	91.4341	96.2690	96.2716
被告沒收	隨機森林	90.4517	96.2679	96.0950
	CKIPlabBERT	88.8603	95.6722	95.5478

表 9：隨機森林模型與 CKIPlabBERT 模型在測試集之比較

5 結論

本研究所提出的自動化沒收辨識模型確實可有效辨識多標籤任務且獲得相當良好的效果。無論以案件沒收或被告沒收為任務時，在隨機森林和 CKIPlabBERT 模型均證實可獲得 95%至 96%左右的 F1 分數。而隨機森林模型採用特徵萃取演算法方面，可得知 TF-IDF 演算法獲得比 Word2Vec 演算法還要好的分類效果，其約有3%至5%差距。本研究所提出之模型可以提供法院於判決正本製作前，檢視沒收引用之法條是否有錯誤情況，這樣的輔助辨識下，可提升民眾對司法之信任，並協助立法者瞭解沒收物種類之分布，成為往後修訂相關法律之依據，藉由沒收之宣判，有效降低犯罪率，達到預防犯罪之目的。此外司法院法學資料檢索系統基於保護當事人隱私原則，並非所有判決書都會公開於網路供大眾檢索，因此模型缺少特定類型判決書之訓練，故降低模型分類效果。另一方面，為了使判決書易於理解，司法院於 108 年 5 月鼓勵法官減少使用艱澀字詞，因此或有裁判書因簡化內容或改變用字遣詞，這將有可能影響模型分類準確度。但因無法確切證實法官所撰寫之判決書是否有艱澀字詞或用字遣詞的簡化，這仍需要待確認後，再行本研究所提模型以進行驗證，這樣才能夠知曉該限制影響模型分類準確度的程度為何。未來研究可考慮使用更符合長篇文章的 BERT 模型，以獲得更全面的字詞，避免因 BERT 模型的字數限制而錯失更具辨識度的字詞。

參考文獻

H. P. Luhn, 1957. A statistical approach to mechanized encoding and searching of literary information. IBM *Journal of Research and Development*, 1(4):309-317.

S. Jones, K. 1972. A statistical interpretation of term specificity and its application in retrieval. *Journal of Documentation*, 28(1):11-21.

T. Mikolov, K. Chen, G. Corrado, and J. Dean. 2013. Efficient estimation of word representations in vector space. CoRR abs/1301.3781.

王安定，2016，判決書之探勘分析與量刑迴歸模型之建立~以法院毒品判決書為例。*臺北市立大學資訊科學系碩士在職專班碩士論文*，台北市。

林宗志，2014，犯罪所得沒收與保全制度之研究-以程序規範為中心。*輔仁大學法律學系碩士論文*，新北市。

林宜潔，2020，犯罪所得之第三人沒收程序。*國立臺北大學法律學系碩士論文*，新北市。

林秉衡，2020，犯罪物沒收之研究。*國立政治大學法律學系碩士班碩士學位論文*，台北市。

林祥慶，2018，基於判決文之量刑系統設計與實作。*國立中正大學資訊工程研究所碩士論文*，嘉義縣。

林琬真、郭宗廷、張桐嘉、顏厥安、陳昭如、林守德，2012，利用機器學習於中文法律文件之標記、案件分類及量刑預測。*中文計算語言學期刊*, 17(4) P49-P67。

姜晴文，2019，法律資料分析的優化與應用：以離婚後未成年子女親權酌定的裁判為素材。*國立臺灣大學法律學系法律學研究所碩士論文*，台北市。

郭家妏，2014，隨機森林在河川水位即時預報之應用。*國立成功大學水利及海洋工程研究所碩士論文*，台南市。

陳克威，2020，基於 Word2Vec 的學術論文推薦系統。國立東華大學資訊工程學系碩士論文，花蓮縣。

陳時仲，2015，隨機森林模型效力評估。*國立交通大學統計學研究所碩士論文*，新竹市。

陳偉倫，2018，沒收制度之變革—以法人沒收為中心。*東吳大學法律學系碩士班碩士論文*，台北市。

陳贈吉，2017，刑法新修正沒收規定之檢討。*國立臺灣大學法學院法律學研究所碩士論文*，台北市。

黃玉婷，2012，以文字探勘技術產製求量刑因子之研究—以我國智慧財產權法律為中心探討。*東吳大學法律學系碩士在職專班科技法律組碩士論文*，台北市。

黃馨慧，2013，以隨機森林架構結合臉部動作單元辨識之臉部表情分類技術。*國立清華大學電機工程學系碩士論文*，新竹市。

葉子維，2018，顧客消費行為分析及行動銀行使用預測-決策樹、隨機森林與判別分析之比較。*國立臺北大學統計學系碩士論文*，新北市。

劉韋汝，2019，沒收特別程序參與主體之探討。*國立清華大學科技法律研究所碩士論文*，新竹市。

蔡宗諺，2019，隨機森林應用於禪定與放鬆休息腦電波之頻率空間特性分類。*國立交通大學電控工程研究所碩士論文*，新竹市。

謝宛芷、胡雅涵，2014，文字探勘技術用於資安事件之自動化分類。*電腦稽核期刊*，第 29 期，P92－101。

王厚勛，2020，以 BERT 搭配機器學習研發反詐騙聊天機器人。*國立中興大學資訊管理研究所碩士論文*，台中市。

翁嘉嫻，2020，使用 BERT 預訓練模型識別網路上之虛假評論。*國立中興大學資訊管理學系所學位論文*，台中市。

曾浚宥，2020，訓練 BERT 模型以識別食品廣告中的違規詞。*淡江大學資訊工程學系碩士班學位論文*，新北市。

The 33rd Conference on Computational Linguistics and Speech Processing (ROCLING 2021)
Taoyuan, Taiwan, October 15-16, 2021. The Association for Computational Linguistics and Chinese Language Processing

整合語者嵌入向量與後置濾波器於提升個人化合成語音之語者相似度
Incorporating speaker embedding and post-filter network for improving speakersimilarity of personalized speech synthesis system

Sheng-Yao Wang, Yi-Chin Huang
National Pingtung University
mike456852@gmail.com, ychuangnptu@mail.nptu.edu.tw

摘要

近年來在語音合成的研究之中，單一語者的合成系統已經有著高音質的表現，但對於多語者系統來說，合成語音的品質與語者相似度仍是一大挑戰，本研究針對合成語音的品質與語者相似度，透過兩個面向來建立出一套可合成多語者之文字轉語音系統，首先針對於多語者的議題，並盡量達成透過少量樣本 (zero-shot) 來達成語者轉換，我們透過探討兩類語音嵌入向量 (speaker embedding) 對於多語者語音合成系統較爲合適，我們比較了用於語者辨識 (speaker verification) 以及單純用於語音轉換 (voice conversion) 的語者嵌入向量。接著，爲了提升合成的語者相似度以及語音品質，我們嘗試置換類神經網路架構中，作爲提升頻譜的 post-net 的部分，在此處我們使用了一個後置濾波器的網路來取代，且比較和 post-net 所產生的頻譜差異以及探討其模型參數量之差異性。實驗結果表明，透過疊加性注意力機制來整合語者嵌入向量進入到類神經網路架構的語音合成系統的確能夠有效地產生具有目標語者的合成語音，並且在加入後置濾波器網路後能夠比傳統透過 post-net 的方式來強化合成語音的語者特性以及合成語音的語音品質，且合成一般長度語音句的時間約爲 2 秒鐘，已接近即時合成個人化語音之成果。未來將進一步探討如何產生可控制語速或情緒之個人化語音。

Abstract

In recent years, speech synthesis system can generate speech with high speech quality. However, multi-speaker text-to-speech (TTS) system still require large amount of speech data for each target speaker. In this study, we would like to construct a multi-speaker TTS system by incorporating two sub modules into artificial neural network-based speech synthesis system to alleviate this problem. First module is to add speaker embedding into encoding module for generating speech while a large amount of the speech data from target speaker is not necessary. For speaker embedding method, in our study, two main speaker embedding methods, namely speaker verification embedding and voice conversion embedding, are compared to deciding which one is suitable for our personalized TTS system. Second, we substituted the conventional post-net module, which is adopted to enhance the output spectrum sequence, to further improving the speech quality of the generated speech utterance. Here, a post-filter network is used. Finally, experiment results showed that the speaker embedding is useful by adding it into encoding module and the resultant speech utterance indeed perceived as the target speaker. Also, the post-filter network not only improving the speech quality and also enhancing the speaker similarity of the generated speech utterances. The constructed TTS system can generate a speech utterance of the target speaker in fewer than 2 seconds. In the future, we would like to further investigate the controllability of the speaking rate or perceived emotion state of the generated speech.

關鍵字：多語者語音合成、語音轉換、語者識別、少量樣本、後置濾波器

Keywords: Multi-speaker Text-to-Speech, Voice Conversion, Speaker Verification, Zeor-shot, Post-Filter

1 緒論

就單一語者的語音合成技術來看，其合成技術已經能夠合成出逼眞且自然的語音，並且不需要太多的語音數據及訓練時間，而爲了擴展到其他語者，常見的方法有語音轉換和模型自適應兩種方法，語音轉換透過更換不同的語者訊息來達成目標，有基於 GAN 的 StarGAN (Kameoka et al., 2018) 和 CyCleGAN (Kaneko et al., 2020) 等方法，也有基

The 33rd Conference on Computational Linguistics and Speech Processing (ROCLING 2021)
Taoyuan, Taiwan, October 15-16, 2021. The Association for Computational Linguistics and Chinese Language Processing

於 AutoEncoder 的 AdaIN-VC (Chou et al., 2019) 和 AutoVC (Qian et al., 2019) 等方法，它們都有相當不錯的效果，唯一個侷限就是僅能更換語者而不能更改內容；而模型自適應主要是在 TTS 系統中加入 Speaker ID Table 來使模型能夠依照 Speaker ID 生成不同語者的聲音，它既能更換內容也能更換語者，但是需要大量不同語者的語音數據以及較多的訓練時間來達成目標，且無法擴展到沒看過的語者，因此，有 (Chien et al., 2021) 和 (Jia et al., 2018) 等研究，將語音轉換與模型自適應兩種方法結合，或是引入語者辨識取代模型自適應裡的語者編號以此擴展到沒看過的語者。

近年來各種語音合成的神經網路模型被提出，但是自回歸模型的 Tacotron 2(Shen et al., 2018) 仍然有著很大的討論空間，它將文字轉換爲一序列的 Embedding 表示，並對每個音框的梅爾頻譜建立注意力對齊，這使每個文字與特定時間單位的頻譜建立一種映射關係，上一個音框推測出下一個音框使得生成的頻譜更有連續性。FastSpeech 2(Ren et al., 2020) 或是 Transformer TTS(Vaswani et al., 2017) 等非自回歸模型，因爲加入了 Self-Attention，使得文字或梅爾頻譜間有著跨時間單位的連接，這減輕了 Tacotron 2 使用 LSTM 作爲文字編碼輸出層或是頻譜解碼輸出層因爲序列長度所帶來的記憶門壓力，如 (Wang et al., 2019) 所述。

Tacotron 2 使用 Local Sensitive Attention 作爲文字與梅爾頻譜間建立映射關係的方法，對於現在的 TTS 系統來說，訓練速度慢且對於較長的語句可能會發生漏字、重複發音等現象，該問題已由 Google 使用 Dynamic Convolution Attention 改善 (Battenberg et al., 2020)。也有如 Glow TTS(Kim et al., 2020) 使用單調函數來限制 Attention 只能向前對齊的方式來解決訓練速度慢以及重複發音的問題。

最後，Tacotron 2 經過文字轉換成序列、序列與頻譜建立映射關係，再透過 LSTM 解碼輸出之後，還會經過 Post-net 層，其目的是要解決解碼輸出後的頻譜過於平滑的問題，現在很多 TTS 架構的 Post-Net 都是採用該架構。

鑑於 Tacotron 2 有著明確的合成步驟，使得許多研究都在其系統上完成，例如多語者 TTS 系統。目前合成語音品質較好的多語者系統是在 Tacotron 2 內部建立 Speaker ID Table，但它無法擴展到沒看過的語者，於是語者識別和語音轉換的方法被加入到語音合成系統裡。

在本研究中，我們提出了一個多語者語音合成的系統，它基於 Tacotron 2 的架構並加入語者驗證及語音轉換的方法以擴展到沒看過的語者，也加入了 Self-Attention 減輕訊息長距離的傳播所造成的負擔，最重要的是我們引入了一種後處理的方式，使我們的系統有著良好的語音品質以及語者相似度，我們也期望透過該後處理方式減輕多語者系統所需要的大量語音數據以及訓練時間。

接下來，我們在第二章節說明本研究所提出的多語者語音合成系統，並於第三章節說明實驗過程與結果，第四章則是說明我們的結論。

2 提出的系統架構

在此章節，我們將多語者語音合成分成四個部份:

- Speaker Embedding：該部份我們比較語音轉換及語者驗證所提取的 Speaker Embedding 何者對於我們的模型較有幫助。
- Text Encoding：該部份目的是將中文字轉換成一種 Embedding 表示，其輸出作爲 Decoding 的輸入。
- Decoding：該部份目的是將 Text Encoding 的輸出與梅爾頻譜建立映射關係，其輸出爲梅爾頻譜。
- Post-Net：該部份目的是增強 Decoding 輸出的梅爾頻譜的特性。

我們的系統運作的順序如 Figure 1。

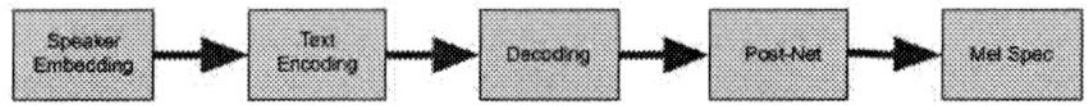

Figure 1: 系統運作順序

2.1 Speaker Embedding

我們引入語音轉換和語者驗證的方式來取代多語者 Tacotron 2 中的 Speaker ID Table，以使我們能擴展到沒看過的語者。

語音轉換的模型採用 (Chou et al., 2019) 的架構，其架構是一種 Variational AutoEncoder，它能夠將來源語音分解成語者編碼跟內容編碼，透過更換語者編碼的方式來達到語音轉換的效果，其模型能夠用於資料外的語者，這正是我們所考慮的。

語者驗證的模型採用 (Cooper et al., 2020) 的架構，其架構是一種 ResNet34(He et al.,

2016) 的改進，該模型於語者驗證中的性能可與 X-Vector(Snyder et al., 2018) 相比，在多語者語音合成系統中，是優於 X-Vector 的，因此我們選擇使用它。

2.2 Text Encoding

我們將輸入的中文字透過 pypinyin 轉換爲羅馬拼音作爲輸入，一樣經過 3 層 Conv Layer 和雙向 LSTM 作爲 Encoding，我們在這邊做了一個改動，爲了減輕 LSTM 必須依照順序傳播訊息所產生的高負擔，我們實現了 (Cooper et al., 2020) 與 (Wang et al., 2019) 等人提出的改進，在雙向 LSTM 輸出後降維並加入 Self-Attention 作爲另一個 Encoding 輸出，透過 Self-Attention 可以連接遠處的訊息狀態這點特性，有效的減輕 LSTM 的負擔，且在 Decoding 的部份能夠更快的與梅爾頻譜建立映射關係。

因此，Text Encoding 將會有兩個輸出，我們分別取名爲 Text Information 及 Long-distance Text Information，同時這兩個個輸出都會與語音轉換所提取的語者嵌入向量串接，架構如 Figure 2所示：

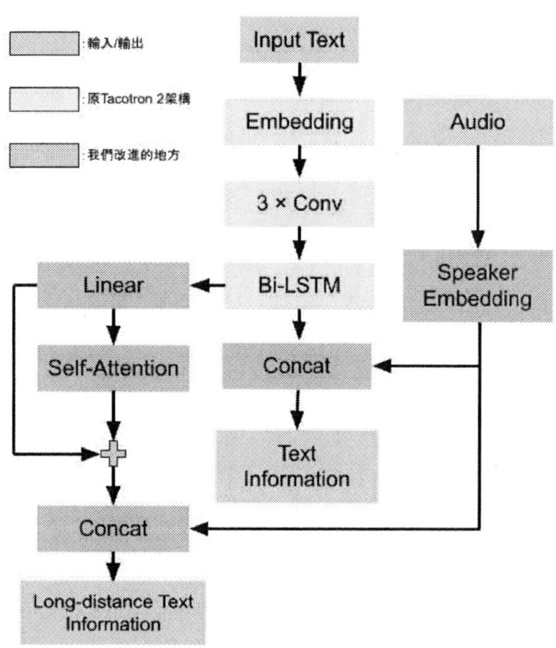

Figure 2: Text Encoding 架構

2.3 Decoding

由於 Text Encoding 層有兩個輸出，因此我們引入了兩個 Attention 機制：Dynamic Convolution(DCA) 與 Bahdanau Attention。

Text Information 使用 DCA 與梅爾頻譜建立映射關係，改善原本 Tacotron 2 因舊有的 Attention 導致漏字、重複發音現象，且 DCA 訓練速度上也比較快，如 (Battenberg et al., 2020) 所述；而 Long-distance Text Information 則使用 Bahdanau Attention 與梅爾頻譜建立映射關係，這是早期的一種 Additive Attention(Bahdanau et al., 2014)，是 Local Sensitive Attention 的簡化版，使用原因是爲了讓 Self-Attention 所學得的長距離訊息能夠簡單幫助 DCA 快速建立映射關係，該 Attention 無須與梅爾頻譜建立良好的映射關係。

另外，爲了加強語者嵌入向量的效果，這邊同樣實現 (Cooper et al., 2020) 和 (Wang et al., 2019) 等人提出的改進，在梅爾頻譜通過 Pre-Net 層之前與語者嵌入向量相加，這能夠有效的使語者嵌入向量影響梅爾頻譜。

以及，最後一層 LSTM 解碼輸出的時候，同樣引入 Self-Attention 幫助 LSTM 減輕訊息傳播的負擔，架構如 Figure 3所示：

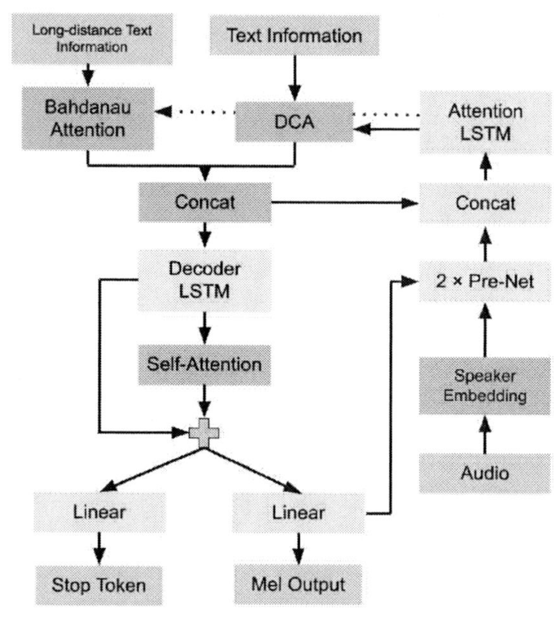

Figure 3: Decoding 架構

2.4 Post-Net

原本的 Post-Net 是爲了改善頻譜過度平滑導致生成的聲音過於低沉，但我們研究發現該 Post-Net 架構仍無法有效解決頻譜平滑的問題，我們受到 (Kaneko et al., 2017a) 和 (Kaneko et al., 2017b) 的啓發，設置了一個 Post-Filter，透過添加噪音的方式補齊與目標頻譜間的差距，我們發現這種方式增強了合成聲音的品質之外，還增強了語者的相似度，使得生成音檔更接近目標語者，並且，這種修改

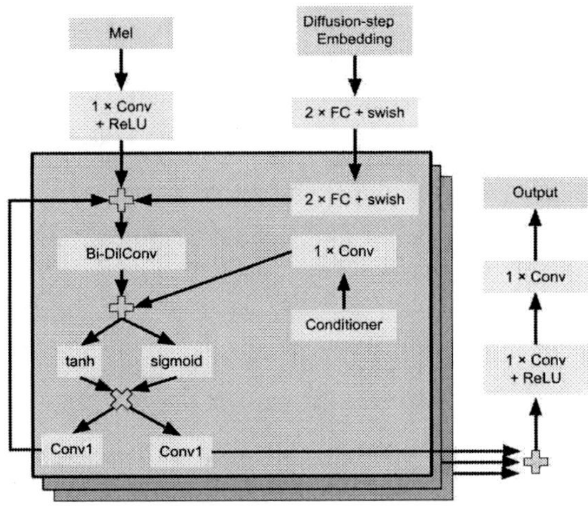

Figure 4: Diffwave 架構

並不會使模型參數有所增加。

爲了改善 Tacotron 2 的 Post-Net，我們使用 Diffwave(Kong et al., 2020) 模型作爲一個 Post-Filter 取代 Post-Net。

Diffwave 是基於降噪機率擴散 (Ho et al., 2020) 所提出的一種聲碼器模型，該擴散概率透過指定步驟的馬可夫鏈與可控條件逐漸將白噪音轉換爲波形訊號，其結構如 Figure 4所示。

我們將輸入改爲與 Decoding 輸出的頻譜相同形狀的噪音，可控條件爲 Decoding 輸出的頻譜，透過指定的步驟來將噪音逐步消除，這裡值得注意的是，與聲碼器需要生成出乾淨的波形訊號不同，我們適當減少了步驟的次數，期望該 Post-Filter 生成的頻譜保留部份噪音來減少與眞實頻譜的差距。

3 實驗過程與結果

3.1 實驗設置

我們使用 AISHELL-3(Shi et al., 2020) 作爲本次實驗的中文語料庫，該語料庫具有 218 位語者，取 173 位語者每位語者 100 個音檔作訓練集 (語者數約佔整體 75%，其餘語者作爲 Unseen 測試模型性能。)，並將所有音檔下採樣至 22050Hz，並取出 80 維梅爾頻譜作爲訓練 Tacotron 2 與語音轉換的輸入，其音框長度爲 1024 個採樣點，音框移動的距離爲 256 個採樣點，音高的頻率範圍爲 20Hz 至 8000Hz。

爲了比較我們所提出的方法優劣，我們訓練了四個多語者 Tacotron 2，分別爲：

- Tacotron 2 + 語者驗證
- Tacotron 2 + 語音轉換
- Tacotron 2 + 語者驗證 + Self-Attention + Post-Filter (Our propose A)
- Tacotron 2 + 語音轉換 + Self-Attention + Post-Filter (Our propose B)

另外，爲了方便撰寫，在後續的內文中如果沒有提起語者驗證或語音轉換，則代表兩者性能是一致的。

3.2 實驗過程

我們使用 AISHELL-3 的語料庫來訊練語音轉換與語者驗證的模型，其訓練設置皆依照 (Chou et al., 2019) 和 (Cooper et al., 2020) 所提供，取出的語者嵌入向量維度數皆設置 128，且我們將各個語者提取的語者嵌入向量取平均，依照 AISHELL-3 的語者數我們共提取出 218 個語者嵌入向量。

再來是多語者 Tacotron 2，在 Text Encoding 的部份，我們將語者嵌入向量做相同維度的 Linear 與 ReLU，使它與我們的模型匹配，另外，我們在通過 Bi-LSTM 之後還添加了 Linear + Self-Attention 作爲另一個輸出，其輸出維度爲 128。

Decoding 的部份只有 Pre-Net 需要注意，我們將上一個音框降維度至 256，語者嵌入向量則升維至 256 並以 Softsign 激活後才做相加，其輸出才通過 Pre-Net。

最後的 Post-Net 部份，我們將 Decoding 輸出的頻譜直接通過 Diffwave Post-Filter 取代了原本 Tacotron 2 的 Post-Net，並且其輸出結果不需要再做殘差連接。

Diffwave Post-Filter 的模型是於 Tacotron 2 訓練完後才訓練的，因爲我們需要 Tacotron 2 的輸出作爲 Post-Filter 的訓練集。

我們在下方的 Table 1 中提供了模型的訓練時間作爲參考，由於多語者 TTS 僅訓練 72 個小時，因爲訓練時間不夠長的關係導致其輸出音質還未達到最佳狀態，但我們透過 Post-Filter 增強了音質與語者相似度，可以在下方連結試聽我們的樣本[1]。

Model	Batch Size	Total Step
語音轉換	32	1M
語者驗證	32	1M
Tacotron 2	64	99k
Our propose A/B	64	99k
Post-Filter	16	320k

Table 1: 模型訓練參數

[1] `https://babaili.github.io/tacotron2_samples/`

3.3 實驗結果

本來於上方有提到我們訓練了四個系統，但由於 Tacotron 2 沒有 Self-Attention 的幫助，訓練了 72 小時仍未有良好的對齊線，因此在下方僅討論 Our propose A/B 的結果。

我們比較了原音檔與 Our propose A/B 的頻譜，請看 Figure 6，依圖像來看，我們可以發現 Post-Filter 距離原音檔的頻譜仍有一大段距離，最明顯變化的地方是雜訊的部份多了橫向的雜訊。我們將上述頻譜拿去做語者相似度分析，採用 Resemblyzer 分析器[2]來投影語者空間，該分析器是 (Wan et al., 2018) 的實現，其結果如 Figure 5，由於 AISHELL-3 大部分語者的性別是女性（佔整體語料庫 80%）的關係，所以對於合成男性聲音區分度沒有如女性一樣明顯。

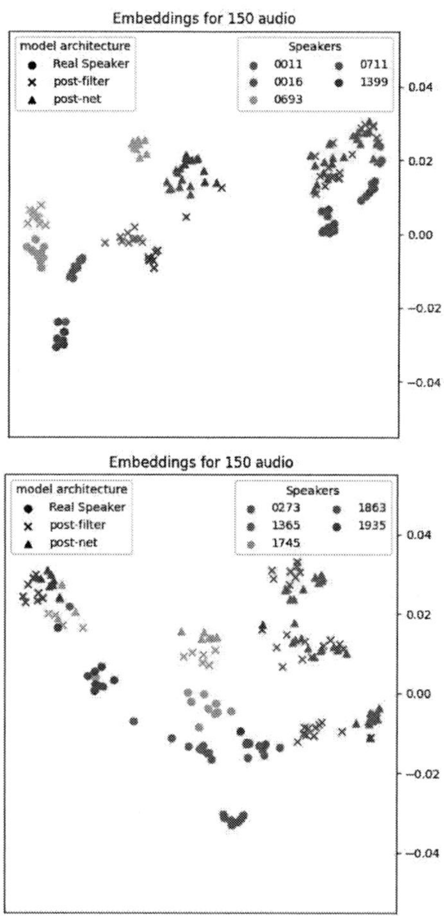

Figure 5: 透過 Resemblyzer 分析，上圖爲女性，下圖爲男性。

接著我們使用客觀評測與主觀評測來證實實驗結果，首先，使用 Mel Cepstral Distortions

Model	MCD
VC-Post-Filter	9.62±0.42
VC-Post-Net	10.16±0.53
SV-Post-Filter	9.29±0.85
SV-Post-Net	10.29±0.72

Table 2: MCD 客觀評測，數值越低越好。VC: 語音轉換，SV: 語者驗證

Model	Quality
VC-Post-Net	2.67±0.35
VC-Post-Filter	3.75±0.71

Table 3: MOS 主觀評測，比較 Post-Net 和 Post-Filter 音質。

(MCD) 作爲客觀評測的方法，我們隨機取 5 個語者各 10 個眞實音檔，共 50 個眞實音檔，並用四個系統分別合成對應的 50 個音檔，總共 250 個音檔，接著將音檔用 World 分析器取出頻譜資訊，再透過 SPTK 工具轉換成梅爾廣義倒頻譜後才計算 MCD，結果如 Table 2。

再來是使用 Mean Opinion Score(MOS) 作爲主觀評測的方法，我們針對語音轉換和語者辨識做音質的比較，兩者皆用 Post-Net 進行 MOS 主觀評測，我們在語音轉換上獲得了 2.67 的分數，在語者辨識上獲得了 2.54 的分數，我們發現語音轉換比語者驗證還來得好，於是我們接著比較語音轉換在 Post-Net 和 Post-Filter 的音質差異，其結果如 Table 3，接著我們對語者相似度進一步的比較，其結果如 Table 4。

我們也提供 Tacotron 2、Post-Net 及 Post-Filter 的模型參數，如 Table 5，也大略測試了生成頻譜、Post-Filter 推論和頻譜轉換成波形的時間，如 Table 6。

實驗結果證明，Post-Filter 確實可以取代 Tacotron 2 的 Post-Net，我們可以看到 Post-Filter 的參數甚至比 Post-Net 還小，這樣更換所付出的成本僅僅是多了 6 個小時的訓練時間。在推理合成音頻上，因爲 Diffwave 模型是透過大量迴圈來進行降噪的，它的推理時間比 Tacotron 2 還多了大概 0.2 秒，這樣的付出我們認爲是值得的，如同我們所展示的音頻，Post-Filter 對於音質和語者相似度的提昇是可見的。

4 結論

本研究提出了一種多語者的 Tacotron 2 架構，修改了 Encoding、Decoding 層的架構，使得語者嵌入向量的效果更加明顯，同時，我們

[2]https://github.com/resemble-ai/Resemblyzer

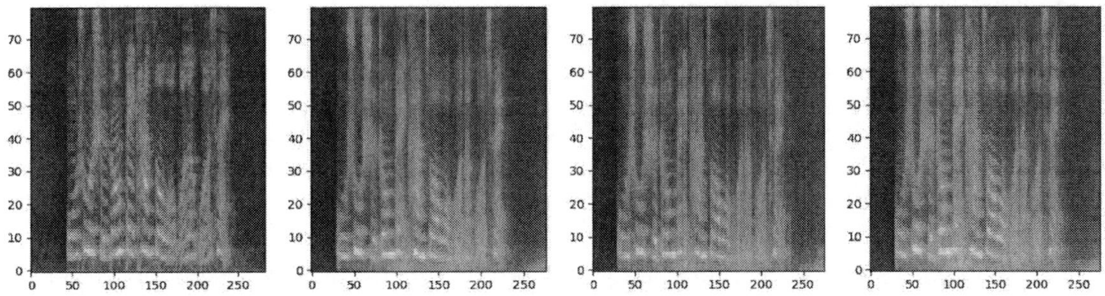

Figure 6: 第 1 張：原始頻譜、第 2 張：Tacotron 2 Linear、第 3 張：Tacotron 2 Post-net、第 4 張：Tacotron 2 Post-Filter，以『武術始終被看作我國的國粹』爲例。

Model	Similarity
VC-Post-Net	2.70±0.41
VC-Post-Filter	3.75±0.71
SV-Post-Net	2.31±0.18
SV-Post-Filter	3.51±0.32

Table 4: MOS 主觀評測，VC 和 SV 的語者相似度

Model	Parameters
Baseline	29M
Our propose	45M
Post-Net	4M
Diffwave Post-Filter	2M

Table 5: 模型參數量

也使用 Diffwave 作爲 Post-Filter 取代原本 Tacotron 2 的 Post-net，我們實驗證明，這種取代不但能夠提昇合成的音質，還加強了語者的特性，使得合成出來的頻譜與目標語者更爲接近，且模型的參數也不會因爲這種改動而大幅度增加。

Model	Time
Text Encoding + Decoding	0.4 s
Post-Filter	0.6 s
Diffwave Vocoder	0.9 s

Table 6: 模型推論所花費時間，以『武術始終被看作我國的國粹』爲例，總合成時間約爲 2 秒。

References

Dzmitry Bahdanau, Kyunghyun Cho, and Yoshua Bengio. 2014. Neural machine translation by jointly learning to align and translate. *arXiv preprint arXiv:1409.0473*.

Eric Battenberg, RJ Skerry-Ryan, Soroosh Mariooryad, Daisy Stanton, David Kao, Matt Shannon, and Tom Bagby. 2020. Location-relative attention mechanisms for robust long-form speech synthesis. In *ICASSP 2020-2020 IEEE International Conference on Acoustics, Speech and Signal Processing (ICASSP)*, pages 6194–6198. IEEE.

Chung-Ming Chien, Jheng-Hao Lin, Chien-yu Huang, Po-chun Hsu, and Hung-yi Lee. 2021. Investigating on incorporating pretrained and learnable speaker representations for multi-speaker multi-style text-to-speech. In *ICASSP 2021-2021 IEEE International Conference on Acoustics, Speech and Signal Processing (ICASSP)*, pages 8588–8592. IEEE.

Ju-chieh Chou, Cheng-chieh Yeh, and Hung-yi Lee. 2019. One-shot voice conversion by separating speaker and content representations with instance normalization. *arXiv preprint arXiv:1904.05742*.

Erica Cooper, Cheng-I Lai, Yusuke Yasuda, Fuming Fang, Xin Wang, Nanxin Chen, and Junichi Yamagishi. 2020. Zero-shot multi-speaker text-to-speech with state-of-the-art neural speaker embeddings. In *ICASSP 2020-2020 IEEE International Conference on Acoustics, Speech and Signal Processing (ICASSP)*, pages 6184–6188. IEEE.

Kaiming He, Xiangyu Zhang, Shaoqing Ren, and Jian Sun. 2016. Deep residual learning for image recognition. In *Proceedings of the IEEE conference on computer vision and pattern recognition*, pages 770–778.

Jonathan Ho, Ajay Jain, and Pieter Abbeel. 2020. Denoising diffusion probabilistic models. *arXiv preprint arXiv:2006.11239*.

Ye Jia, Yu Zhang, Ron J Weiss, Quan Wang, Jonathan Shen, Fei Ren, Zhifeng Chen, Patrick Nguyen, Ruoming Pang, Ignacio Lopez Moreno, et al. 2018. Transfer learning from speaker verification to multispeaker text-to-speech synthesis. *arXiv preprint arXiv:1806.04558*.

Hirokazu Kameoka, Takuhiro Kaneko, Kou Tanaka, and Nobukatsu Hojo. 2018. Stargan-vc: Non-parallel many-to-many voice conversion using star generative adversarial networks. In *2018 IEEE Spoken Language Technology Workshop (SLT)*, pages 266–273. IEEE.

Takuhiro Kaneko, Hirokazu Kameoka, Nobukatsu Hojo, Yusuke Ijima, Kaoru Hiramatsu, and Kunio Kashino. 2017a. Generative adversarial network-based postfilter for statistical parametric speech synthesis. In *2017 IEEE International Conference on Acoustics, Speech and Signal Processing (ICASSP)*, pages 4910–4914. IEEE.

Takuhiro Kaneko, Hirokazu Kameoka, Kou Tanaka, and Nobukatsu Hojo. 2020. Cyclegan-vc3: Examining and improving cyclegan-vcs for mel-spectrogram conversion. *arXiv preprint arXiv:2010.11672*.

Takuhiro Kaneko, Shinji Takaki, Hirokazu Kameoka, and Junichi Yamagishi. 2017b. Generative adversarial network-based postfilter for stft spectrograms. In *Interspeech*, pages 3389–3393.

Jaehyeon Kim, Sungwon Kim, Jungil Kong, and Sungroh Yoon. 2020. Glow-tts: A generative flow for text-to-speech via monotonic alignment search. *arXiv preprint arXiv:2005.11129*.

Zhifeng Kong, Wei Ping, Jiaji Huang, Kexin Zhao, and Bryan Catanzaro. 2020. Diffwave: A versatile diffusion model for audio synthesis. *arXiv preprint arXiv:2009.09761*.

Kaizhi Qian, Yang Zhang, Shiyu Chang, Xuesong Yang, and Mark Hasegawa-Johnson. 2019. Autovc: Zero-shot voice style transfer with only autoencoder loss. In *International Conference on Machine Learning*, pages 5210–5219. PMLR.

Yi Ren, Chenxu Hu, Xu Tan, Tao Qin, Sheng Zhao, Zhou Zhao, and Tie-Yan Liu. 2020. Fastspeech 2: Fast and high-quality end-to-end text to speech. *arXiv preprint arXiv:2006.04558*.

Jonathan Shen, Ruoming Pang, Ron J Weiss, Mike Schuster, Navdeep Jaitly, Zongheng Yang, Zhifeng Chen, Yu Zhang, Yuxuan Wang, Rj Skerrv-Ryan, et al. 2018. Natural tts synthesis by conditioning wavenet on mel spectrogram predictions. In *2018 IEEE International Conference on Acoustics, Speech and Signal Processing (ICASSP)*, pages 4779–4783. IEEE.

Yao Shi, Hui Bu, Xin Xu, Shaoji Zhang, and Ming Li. 2020. Aishell-3: A multi-speaker mandarin tts corpus and the baselines. *arXiv preprint arXiv:2010.11567*.

David Snyder, Daniel Garcia-Romero, Gregory Sell, Daniel Povey, and Sanjeev Khudanpur. 2018. X-vectors: Robust dnn embeddings for speaker recognition. In *2018 IEEE International Conference on Acoustics, Speech and Signal Processing (ICASSP)*, pages 5329–5333. IEEE.

Ashish Vaswani, Noam Shazeer, Niki Parmar, Jakob Uszkoreit, Llion Jones, Aidan N Gomez, Łukasz Kaiser, and Illia Polosukhin. 2017. Attention is all you need. In *Advances in neural information processing systems*, pages 5998–6008.

Li Wan, Quan Wang, Alan Papir, and Ignacio Lopez Moreno. 2018. Generalized end-to-end loss for speaker verification. In *2018 IEEE International Conference on Acoustics, Speech and Signal Processing (ICASSP)*, pages 4879–4883. IEEE.

Xin Wang Wang, Junichi Yamagishi Yamagishi, Yusuke Yasuda Yasuda, and Shinji Takaki Takaki. 2019. Investigation of enhanced tacotron text-to-speech synthesis systems with self-attention for pitch accent language.

The 33rd Conference on Computational Linguistics and Speech Processing (ROCLING 2021)
Taoyuan, Taiwan, October 15-16, 2021. The Association for Computational Linguistics and Chinese Language Processing

Identify Bilingual Patterns and Phrases from a Bilingual Sentence Pair

Yi-Jyun Chen
Department of Computer Science
National Tsing Hua University
yijyun@nlplab.cc

Hsin-Yun Chung
Department of Mathematics
National Chung Cheng University
maggie100573@gmail.com

Jason S. Chang
Department of Computer Science
National Tsing Hua University
jason@nlplab.cc

Abstract

This paper presents a method for automatically identifying bilingual grammar patterns and extracting bilingual phrase instances from a given English-Chinese sentence pair. In our approach, the English-Chinese sentence pair is parsed to identify English grammar patterns and Chinese counterparts. The method involves generating translations of each English grammar pattern and calculating translation probability of words from a word-aligned parallel corpora. The results allow us to extract the most probable English-Chinese phrase pairs in the sentence pair. We present a prototype system that applies the method to extract grammar patterns and phrases in parallel sentences. An evaluation on randomly selected examples from a dictionary shows that our approach has reasonably good performance. We use human judge to assess the bilingual phrases generated by our approach. The results have potential to assist language learning and machine translation research.

Keywords: Pattern Grammar, Phrase Translation, Word Alignment

1 Introduction

Verb phrases are prominent components of any sentence. If we can correctly extract English-Chinese bilingual grammar patterns and phrases in a bilingual sentence pair, it will be helpful for English and Chinese language learners and machine translation systems. These results can be used to demonstrate the synchronous structure of parallel sentences. However, Chinese sentence parsing technology is still immature, which leads to difficulties in obtaining grammar patterns and phrases in Chinese sentences.

There are still many problems with existing Chinese parsers. To extract Chinese patterns and phrases more accurately, we utilize an English sentence parser which is much more mature than Chinese parsing technology to parse English sentences and extract English patterns and phrases. We also utilize some statistical methods to estimate translation probability of word pairs using bilingual corpora. Then, we extract Chinese patterns and phrases more accurately by finding counterparts of English patterns and phrases with statistical results from bilingual corpora.

We present a system that returns bilingual verb patterns and phrases of a bilingual sentence pair. Our system identifies phrases in sentences by using the pattern table and translation probability model created in advance. The pattern table created by parsing English sentences and calculating counterparts in bilingual parallel corpus with word alignment. The translation probability model is created by the alignment probability of each English and Chinese word pair with consideration of not only the word itself but also related words.

At the runtime, our system starts with an English-Chinese bilingual sentence pair submitted by the user. The system parses the English sentence and extracts English patterns and phrases, and retrieves the counterpart of the pattern from the table created in advance to be Chinese pattern. Then, the system extracts the counterpart of words in the English phrase by the probability model created in advance. Finally, The system combines the Chinese pattern and the counterpart of words in the English phrase to form a Chinese phrase.

The system can assist language learning or be used to generate training data for machine translation research, especially research related to phrases. The rest of the article is organized as follows. We review the related work in the next section. Then we present our method for automatically identifying bilingual phrases from a bilingual sentence pair in section 3. The experiment and an evaluation based on human judgment are described in Section 4. Finally, we summarize our conclusions in Section 5.

2 Related Work

Machine Translation is a time-honored and yet active research area. Shifting from the rule-based approach toward data-intensive approach after the seminal paper by Brown et al.,1990, an increasing number of bilingual corpora have made statistical machine translation more and more feasible. In our work we address an aspect of machine translation is not a direct focus of Brown et al. (1990). We also consider on more general linguistic class of units in translation where the translation may not be litateral and may need a presentation that reflects the similarity and differences between two languages involved, and the user might be interested in multiple ways (structures) of translating a phrase (e.g., consider the phrase "harmful to the ocean" and its translation).

More recent researches concentrate on learning word translation and extracting bilingual word translation pairs from bilingual corpus, and then calculate the degree of mutual relationship between word pairs in parallel sentences, thereby deriving the precise translation (Catizone et al. (1989); Brown et al. (1990); Gale and Church (1991); Wu and Xia (1994); Fung (1995); Melamed (1995); Moore (2001)).

In our system, we focus on identifying patterns and phrases by a patterns table and a word translation model which are created using statistical methods in bilingual corpora with word alignment.

In the area of phrase alignment, Ko (2006) proposed a method for verb phrase translation. For specific verb fragments (e.g. make a report to police), automatic alignment is applied to calculate the collocation relationship across two language (e.g. when make and report appear together, report often corresponds to "報案"), then word and phrase correspondences are generated (e.g. make a report to police correspond to "向 警察 報案") ,to tally translations and counts. Chen et al. (2020) focus on the translation of noun prepositional collocations. Using statistical methods to extract translations of nouns and prepositions from bilingual parallel corpora with sentence alignment, and then adjust the translations with additional information of Chinese collocations extracted from a Chinese corpus.

3 Methodology

We attempt to identify bilingual grammar patterns and phrases in an English-Chinese sentence pair using a lexical translation model and bilingual grammar patterns. Our identification process is shown in Figure 1.

(1) Create Bilingual Grammar Patterns and Phrases Table (section 3.1) (2) Create Word Translation Probability Model (section 3.2) (3) System Runtime - Extracting Pattern Grammar and Phrases in Sentence Pair (section 3.3)

Figure 1. Identification process

3.1 Creating Bilingual Grammar Patterns and Phrases Table

In the first stage of the identification process (Step (1) in Figure 1), we extract Chinese grammar patterns for each English grammar pattern. For example, the verb "use" has a grammar pattern "use n to inf", our goal is to extract Chinese counterparts such as "使用 n 來 v" and "使用 n 去 v" for "use n to inf" .

The input to this stage is English-Chinese sentence pairs in a word-aligned bilingual parallel corpus. We parse each English sentence into a tree structure to reveal the dependency of words in the sentence and use a recursive approach to extract the grammar pattern and the phrase for each verb in the sentence. Then, we extract Chinese counterparts of the English grammar pattern in the Chinese sentence according to the word alignment, and convert them into Chinese grammar patterns according to the English word in English pattern each Chinese word corresponds to.

For example, for the sentence pair "We use computers to solve the problem. " and " 我們 使用 電腦 來 解決 問題" , we extract the English grammar pattern "use n to inf" and

English phrase "use computer to solve problem" for the verb "use". Then, we extract the Chinese counterparts "使用 電腦 來 解決 問題" and convert it into Chinese pattern "使用 n 來 v" with converting "電腦" into "n" and converting "解決 問題" into "v" according to their correspondence to English phrase and pattern.

For each English grammar pattern, we compute the frequency of Chinese patterns, and filter patterns with high frequency. Then, we sort the patterns by counts and by pattern length as shown in table 1.

English Grammar Pattern	Chinese Grammar Pattern	Count	Rank
use n to inf	使用 n 來 v	180	1
use n to inf	用 n 來 v	157	2
use n to inf	利用 n 來 v	70	3
use n to inf	用 n 去 v	41	4
use n to inf	使用 n v	287	5
use n to inf	用 n v	186	6

Table 1. Chinese grammar pattern for English pattern "use n to inf", ranked based on frequency count and pattern lengths. Note that the English are based on a pre-determined templates and the Chinese patterns are automatically derived through word alignment.

The output of this stage is a table which contains sorted Chinese patterns for each English grammar pattern.

3.2 Creating Word Translation Probability

In the second stage of the identification process (Step (2) in Figure 1), we calculate lexical translation probability for each English word and Chinese word pair.

The input to this stage is English-Chinese sentence pairs in a word-aligned bilingual parallel corpus. We calculate the counts and probability of each Chinese word aligned to each English word in the bilingual corpus. For each English-Chinese word pair in the bilingual corpus, we compute weighted translation probability of the Chinese word to the English word. We also take into consideration the tense, synonym and derivative words of English words. We set weight for these English words according to their degree of relevance to the English word in the pair. Then, we multiply the probability by their weight and sum up these weighted probabilities to generate an adjusted probability for the word pair to represent how likely they are to translate to each other.

For example, we calculate the probability of word pair (討論, discussion) with consideration of the words related to "discussion" such as "discuss" and "talk" and give them weight. Some words we consider for the pair (討論,discussion) are shown in Table 2. After multiplying the probability by their weight and summing up these weighted probabilities, we finally get a adjusted probability 0.62 to represent the probability of "討論" as a translation of "discussion".

word	probability	Weight
discussing	0.29	1
discussed	0.24	1
talk	0.03	0.5

Table 2. Word forms related the pair (討論,discussion) and weights according to morphology and synonyms

Note that because there are many errors in automatic word alignment, we only consider words with original alignment probability more than 0.01. This approach makes the adjusted probabilities of most word pairs with unrelated meanings will be zero. For example, the word pair ("他"," you") has zero probability as shown in Table 4.

Beside creating the translation probability model, for each English word, we also filter some Chinese words with high translation probability to it to be its translations. Translations of some English words are shown in table 3.

Word	Translations
use	應用、利用、採用、運用、使用、用、用途 、動用
discuss	討論、商討、探討、論述、談
mate	伴侶 、交配、隊友 、搭檔 、配偶 、夥伴、大副

Table 3. Translations of some English words

The output of this stage is a model which gives adjusted estimation of lexical translation probability of English and Chinese words in the bilingual corpus, and translations of each English word. A sample of the translation probability model is shown in table 4.

Chinese Word	English Word	Adjsuted Probabilty
玩	play	0.43

吸引	attract	0.51
產品	product	0.79
推銷	product	0.02
他	you	0

Table 4. A sample of the translation probability model

3.3 System Runtime - Extracting Pattern Grammar and Phrases in Sentence Pair

Once the bilingual grammar pattern table and weighted word translation probability model are created, our system then evaluates a given sentence pair using the procedure in Figure 2.

(1) Extract English Pattern Grammar and Phrase in English Sentence
(2) Find Suitable Counterparts for Words in English Phrase
(3) Select Chinese Grammar Pattern and Compose Chinese Phrase

Figure 2. Runtime evaluation procedure

The input to the system is an English-Chinese sentence pair such as "Peacocks use their beautiful tails to attract mates" versus "蝴蝶 用 美麗 的 尾巴 來 吸引 配偶".

In the first step (Step (1) in Figure 2), we parse the English sentence and extract the grammar pattern and phrase as described in section 3.1. For example, the pattern grammar "use n to inf" and the phrase "use tail to attract mate" will be extracted from "Peacocks use their beautiful tails to attract mates".

In the second step (Step (2) in Figure 2), for each word in the English phrase except those in the grammar pattern, we find its suitable counterpart in the Chinese sentence using the weighted word translation probability model described in Section 3.2. For each English word w in English phrase, if there are some words in Chinese sentence that have non-zero translation probability to w, we choose the one with the highest probability to be the counterpart of w.

For example, in the sentence pair "Peacocks use their beautiful tails to attract mates" versus "蝴蝶 用 美麗 的 尾巴 來 吸引 配偶", for word "tail" in phrase "use tail to attract mates", we consider the weighted translation probabilities of word pairs ("蝴蝶", "tail"), ("用", "tail"), ("美麗", "tail"), ..., ("配偶", "tail"). Because the word pair ("尾巴"," tail") has highest probability, we select "尾巴" to be the counterpart of "tail".

If there are not any Chinese words that have non-zero translation probability to w, we consider their similarity to the translations of w selected in advance by using word embedding. For each word c in the Chinese sentence, we multiply its similarity to each translation c_pre of w by the weighted translation probability of c_pre to w and sum up to be the new probability of c. Then, we choose the one with the highest new probability to be the counterpart of w.

In the final step (Step (3) in Figure 2), we consider the sorted Chinese grammar patterns of the English grammar pattern extracted in Step (1) according to the table created in advance (described in Section 3.1) and the counterparts of words in the English phrase selected in Step (2). We check each Chinese pattern in order whether it is contained in the Chinese sentence and whether the position of the counterpart of each word in English phrase is reasonable. If so, we select the grammar pattern to be the counterpart of the English grammar pattern and combine it with the counterpart of each word in English phrase to form a Chinese phrase.

For example, the Chinese pattern "用 n 來 v" is contained in sentence "蝴蝶 用 美麗 的 尾巴 來 吸引 配偶" and the most suitable counterpart of "tail", "attract" and "mate" in the phrase "use tail to attract mate" are "尾巴"," 吸引" and " 配偶" and the position of counterparts is reasonable. We combine pattern "用 n 來 v" and words "尾巴"," 吸引" and " 配偶" to form the phrase "用 尾巴 來 吸引 配偶".

For a verb in the pattern such as the "v" in the "用 n 來 v", we also consider its own bilingual pattern to find its counterparts instead of only by translation probabilities of its words. For example, in the sentence pair "she want to send her son to the school" versus " 她 想 把 兒子 送到 這所 學校", there is English pattern "want to inf" with Chinese pattern "想 v" for verb "want", and English pattern "send n1 to n2" with Chinese pattern "把 n1 送到 n2" for verb "send". By replacing the "inf" in "want to inf" by "send n1 to n2" and replacing the "v" in "想 v" by "把 n1 送到 n2", the bilingual pattern pair "want to send n1 to n2" versus "想 把 n1 送到 n2" is generated and then the bilingual phrase pair "want to send son to school" versus "想 把 兒子 送到 學校" can be extracted from the sentence pair.

The output of the system is bilingual grammar patterns and phrases extracted from the bilingual sentence pair. For example, the grammar patterns "use n to inf" versus "用 n 來 v" and the phrases "use tail to attract mates" versus "用 尾巴 來 吸引 配偶" are the output of the input sentence pair "Peacocks use their beautiful tails to attract mates" versus "蝴蝶 用 美麗 的 尾巴 來 吸引 配偶".

4 Evaluation and Discussion

The purpose of our system is to allow users to retrieve the bilingual patterns and phrases from a bilingual sentences pair. Therefore, in this section, we report the results of preliminary evaluations on the extraction of bilingual patterns and phrases. The evaluation process was conducted on a set of bilingual sentence pairs along with their patterns and phrases extracted.

4.1 Experimental setting

The bilingual parallel corpora we used are the Minutes of Legislative Council of the Hong Kong Special Administrative from the legislative council of Hong Kong with 1,640,007 bilingual sentence pairs, and the UM-corpus (Liang, 2014) from university of Macau with 1,827,014 bilingual sentence pairs. We used CKIP (Ma and Chen, 2003) which is a Chinese knowledge and information processing system developed by academic sinica to process Chinese word segmentation and used fast-align (Dyer et al., 2013) to process word alignment of bilingual parallel sentences.

We used Spacy (Honnibal and Montani, 2017) to parse English sentences and extract patterns with their counterparts to create a bilingual patterns table as we described in section 3.1. Then, we calculate and create a probability model for bilingual word pairs as we describe in section 3.2. Finally, we get the result by using our system to evaluate given sentence pairs as we describe in section 3.3.

4.2 Evaluation Metrics

The output of our method are bilingual grammar patterns and phrases of all verbs in sentence pairs. To evaluate our approach, we randomly selected 50 valid sentences (66 verb patterns) from examples in Cambridge dictionary and Macmillan dictionary. The grammar patterns and phrases in each sentence are evaluated by a linguist. Note that the verb "be" and the verb "have" are excluded from our evaluation since they often don't have a direct translation in the Chinese sentence. In some English sentences, there are not any verb grammar patterns with length greater than 1. We treat such sentence pairs as invalid and they would not be included in the 50 sentence pairs. There are totally 66 verb patterns and phrases with length greater than 1 in the 50 English sentences. We evaluated the correctness of Chinese patterns and phrases of these 66 verb patterns. Some patterns and phrases successfully identified are shown in table 5. The overall accuracy is 79% and the overall recall is 29%.

4.3 Discussion

The results of evaluation has high precision rate and low recall rate. It shows that most of the Chinese patterns and phrases identified by our method are correct, but there are many phrases that have not been successfully identified. Because of the limit of the amount of data of parallel corpora, many correct and common patterns are not successfully extracted to put into the pattern table, and then cannot be identified from the sentence pairs submitted at the runtime. It may be the main reason that causes the low recall.

English Pattern	English Phrase	Chinese Pattern	Chinese Phrase
fall on n	fell on floor	掉 在 n	掉 在 地 上
word for n	work for company	為 n 工作	為 公司 工作
agree to inf	agree to form league	同意 v	同意 結成 聯盟
provide n	provide evidence	提供 n	提供 證據
commit n	committed crime	犯 n	犯 罪

Table 5. Some patterns and phrases successfully identified

Counterparts of words in an English phrase are extracted by a probability model which is a weighted probability model adjusted from word alignment probability in the parallel corpora. That means, only words which appear and have sufficient frequency in the parallel corpora are in the model. Although we also design methods by word embedding to process words which are not in the model, they still brought a relatively high error rate.

5 Conclusion and Future Work

Many avenues exist for future research and improvement of our system. As we mentioned in section 4.3, lack of bilingual patterns in our table created in advance causes that many phrases cannot be identified. One such avenue is to design methods to expand the amount of the patterns. For example, we can consider collocations calculated in the Chinese monolingual corpus which contains a larger amount of sentences, or consider the synonyms of the words in the pattern by using word embedding or dictionaries like WordNet, to generate more bilingual patterns.

In summary, we have introduced a method for identifying patterns and phrases that allow users to submit an English-Chinese sentence pair and get bilingual patterns and phrases in the sentence pair. The method involves parsing English sentences and extracting counterparts of English patterns and phrases by using a bilingual pattern table and word translation probability model created in advance. The result of the evaluations show that our method is highly accurate.

References

Peter F Brown, John Cocke, Stephen A Della Pietra, Vincent J Della Pietra, Frederick Jelinek, John Lafferty, Robert L Mercer, and Paul S Roossin. 1990. A statistical approach to machine translation. *Computational linguistics*, 16(2):79–85.

Roberta Catizone, Graham Russell, and Susan Warwick. 1989. Deriving translation data from bilingual texts. In *Proceedings of the First International Lexical Acquisition Workshop*, pages 1–7.

Yi-Jyun Chen, Ching-Yu Helen Yang, and Jason S. Chang. 2020. Improve word alignment for extraction phrasal translations. *International Journal of Computational Linguistics Chinese Language Processing*, 25(2):37–54

Chris Dyer, Victor Chahuneau, and Noah A Smith. 2013. A simple, fast, and effective reparameterization of ibm model 2. In *Proceedings of the 2013 Conference of the North American Chapter of the Association for Computational Linguistics: Human Language Technologies*, pages 644–648

Pascale Fung. 1995. A pattern matching method for finding noun and proper noun translations from noisy parallel corpora. *arXiv preprint cmp-lg/9505016*.

William A Gale and Kenneth Church. 1991. Identifying word correspondences in parallel texts. In *Speech and Natural Language: Proceedings of a Workshop Held at Pacific Grove, California, February 19-22, 1991*.

Matthew Honnibal and Ines Montani. 2017. spacy 2: Natural language understanding with bloom embeddings, convolutional neural networks and incremental parsing. *To appear*, 7(1):411–420.

M. H. Ko. 2006. Alignment of Multi-word Expressions in Parallel Corpora. Master's thesis, National Tsing Hua University, Taiwan.

Wei-Yun Ma and Keh-Jiann Chen. 2003. Introduction to ckip chinese word segmentation system for the first international chinese word segmentation bakeoff. In *Proceedings of the second SIGHAN workshop on Chinese language processing*, pages 168–171.

I Dan Melamed. 1995. Automatic evaluation and uniform filter cascades for inducing n-best translation lexicons. *arXiv preprint cmp-lg/9505044*.

Robert C Moore. 2001. Towards a simple and accurate statistical approach to learning translation relationships among words. In *Proceedings of the ACL 2001 Workshop on Data-Driven Methods in Machine Translation*.

Liang Tian, Derek F. Wong, Lidia S. Chao, Paulo Quaresma, Francisco Oliveira, Shuo Li, Yiming Wang, Yi Lu, "UM-Corpus: A Large English-Chinese Parallel Corpus for Statistical Machine Translation". In *Proceedings of the 9th International Conference on Language Resources and Evaluation* (LREC'14), Reykjavik, Iceland, 2014.

Dekai Wu and Xuanyin Xia. 1994. Learning an english-chinese lexicon from a parallel corpus. In *Proceedings of the First Conference of the Association for Machine Translation in the Americas*

The 33rd Conference on Computational Linguistics and Speech Processing (ROCLING 2021)
Taoyuan, Taiwan, October 15-16, 2021. The Association for Computational Linguistics and Chinese Language Processing

Extracting Academic Senses: Towards An Academic Writer's Dictionary

Hsin-Yun, Chung
NLP Lab
National Tsing Hua University
maggie100573@gmail.com

Li-Kuang Chen
Institute of Information Systems and Applications
National Tsing Hua University
lkchen@nlplab.cc

Jason S. Chang
Department of Computer Science
National Tsing Hua University
jason@nlplab.cc

Abstract

We present a method for determining intended sense definitions of a given academic word in an academic keyword list. In our approach, the keyword list are converted into unigram of all possible Mandarin translations, intended or not. The method involve converting words in the keyword list into all translations using a bilingual dictionary, computing the unigram word counts of translations, and computing character counts from the word counts. At run-time, each definition (with associated translation) of the given word is scored with word and character counts, and the definition with the highest count is returned. We present a prototype system for the Academic Keyword List to generate definitions and translation for pedagogy purposes. We also experimented with clustering definition embeddings of all words and definitions, and identifying intended sense in favor of embedding in larger clusters. Preliminary evaluation shows promising performance. This endeavor is a step towards creating a full-fledged dictionary from an academic word list.

Keywords: word sense disambiguation, academic writing, academic keywords

1 Introduction

Many learners of English as a second language are writing in English for academic purposes (EAP) (e.g., papers, grant proposals, essays) every day, and many academic word lists specifically target vocabulary for EAP. For example, Academic Word List (Coxhead, 2000)[1] was developed from a small corpus (3.5 m words) of written academic English by computing the frequency, range, and uniformity of occurrence of words not in the General Service List of 2,000 words (West, 1953).

Word lists such as the AWL (Coxhead, 2000) often come without definitions (Figure 1)[2]. However, the best vocabulary learning materials for the EAP learners should contain not just words (e.g., *propose* or *argument*), but also the senses of the word (e.g., propose intended as "to offer or suggest a possible plan or action") that are relevant in an academic discourse (e.g. "We propose a method for ⋯"). Intuitively, by identifying senses that are the most similar to other words (e.g., present, introduce, and describe) in the list with an EAP prospective, we can identify the intended sense of a given word in an EAP word list. Similarity can be measured in terms of translation, definition wording, and word embeddings.

Consider the word "propose" in AKL. The best "academic" sense of this word is probably not "to ask someone to marry you" , but rather "to offer or suggest a possible plan or action." The intended academic senses are typically "used to refer to those activities that characterize academic work, organize scientific discourse and build the rhetoric of academic texts" (Paquot, 2010). These senses can be identified by computing the counts of their translations. Intuitively, by requiring the senses to have translations that are shared by many words in the academic keyword list, we can bias the sense disambiguation process towards identifying these academic senses so as to best facilitate the vocabulary building and provide the learners with deep vocabulary knowledge of the academic words. Details and examples of our method will be described in

[1]The AWL can be found at `www.wgtn.ac.nz/lals/resources/academicwordlist`

[2]The entire AKL can be found at `uclouvain.be/en/research-institutes/ilc/cecl/academic-keyword-list.html`

233 verbs

accept, account (for), achieve, acquire, act, adapt, adopt, advance, advocate, affect, aid, aim, allocate, allow, alter, analyse, appear, apply, argue, arise, assert, assess, assign, associate, assist, assume, attain, attempt, attend, attribute, avoid, base, be, become, benefit, can, cause, characterise, choose, cite, claim, clarify, classify, coincide, combine, compare, compete, comprise, concentrate, concern, conclude, conduct, confine, conform, connect, consider, consist, constitute, construct, contain, contrast, contribute, control, convert, correspond, create, damage, deal, decline, define, demonstrate, depend, derive, describe, design, destroy, determine, develop, differ, differentiate, diminish, direct, discuss, display, distinguish, divide, dominate, effect, eliminate, emerge, emphasize, employ, enable, encounter, encourage, enhance, ensure, establish, evaluate, evolve, examine, exceed, exclude, exemplify, exist, expand, experience, explain, expose, express, extend, facilitate, fail, favour, finance, focus, follow, form, formulate, function, gain, generate, govern, highlight, identify, illustrate, imply, impose, improve, include, incorporate, increase, indicate, induce, influence, initiate, integrate, interpret, introduce, investigate, involve, isolate, label, lack, lead, limit, link, locate, maintain, may, measure, neglect, note, obtain, occur, operate, outline, overcome, participate, perceive, perform, permit, pose, possess, precede, predict, present, preserve, prevent, produce, promote, propose, prove, provide, publish, pursue, quote, receive, record, reduce, refer, reflect, regard, regulate, reinforce, reject, relate, rely, remain, remove, render, replace, report, represent, reproduce, require, resolve, respond, restrict, result, retain, reveal, seek, select, separate, should, show, solve, specify, state, stimulate, strengthen, stress, study, submit, suffer, suggest, summarise, supply, support, sustain, tackle, tend, term, transform, treat, undermine, undertake, use, vary, view, write, yield

Figure 1: A sample of the AKL.
From https://uclouvain.be/en/research-institutes/ilc/cecl/academic-keyword-list.html

Section 3.

The rest of the paper is organized as follows. We review the related work in the next section. Then we present our method for automatically learning to determine intended senses of words of a keyword list for a specific genre (Section 3). As part of our evaluation, we compare the quality of the senses generated by the proposed method with a clustering based method in the literature (Section 4).

2 Related Work

Word sense disambiguation (WSD) is an important research area in Natural Language Processing. Most methods (e.g., (Navigli, 2009; Ranjan Pal and Saha, 2015)) proposed over the years use the context of an ambiguous word occurrence to determine the intended sense.

A task more closely related to our work is disambiguating words in groups (e.g. a list of synonyms in a thesaurus) without context. These groups of words do not come with a context often used in typical WSD setting. In previous work, external lexical resources were often employed to make up for the lack of context. Dagan and Itai (1994) suggested resolving lexical ambiguities of the target language using statistical data from another language. Resnik (1999) proposed to disambiguate a related group of nouns using Wordnet hypernyms (Miller, 1995). Tuan et al. (2020) employed clustering the definition-based word sense vectors to filter out unrelated senses and obtain intended senses of the given group. Our method, which we will describe in detail in the next section, addresses a similar problem of assigning senses relevant in an academic context to a given much larger list of academic keywords.

In the research area of developing word lists for EAP and ESL teaching and learning, the best known work is West (1953)'s General Service List (GSL), a list consisting of approximately 2000 words to represent the most frequently-used part of the English vocabulary. Later, Coxhead (2000) compiled the Academic Word List (AWL), which places emphasis on words more frequently used in academic texts, excluding words in the GSL. It includes words that are observed in various academic disciplines with frequencies above a given threshold, but are relatively uncommon in other kinds of texts. Paquot (2010) comes up with a list that marks a departure from AWL. With words in GSL allowed, the Academic Keyword List (AKL) is compiled from various academic writing corpora of different disciplines. AKL words are selected based on comparative analysis of an academic corpus with a fiction corpus to find words that carry more academic importance and that are shared across academic disciplines.

In contrast to the WSD and EAP work described above, we exploit translation ngrams and clusters of sense-definition-based embeddings to identify intended, EAP-relevant sense. Although being relatively simple, preliminary evaluation shows the method yields satisfactory results. The results also offer the benefit of combining the resources of an EAP word list and existing dictionaries (e.g., Cambridge learner dictionary) to generate more pedagogically useful EAP materials for as pointed out in (Paquot, 2010).

3 Finding intended senses of a word list

Using contexts from a running text to find the intended sense of words in EAP word list might not work very well, as existing WSD methods typically have low accuracy rates and typically require an annotated dataset for training. We exploit the nature of the EAP genre and word list: there are often more than one way to express the same concept. By computing sense to sense similarity based on translation and word embedding, and selecting the sense with the highest similarity based on translations, we propose a method for identifying intended senses for each word in an EAP word list. We now formally state the problem we are addressing:

Problem statement: Given a set of words W of a known application (in this case, academic use), and all senses $s_{w,i}$ of each word $w_i \in W$. Our goal is to identify the sense $s_{w,i'}$ for each word w_i such that $s_{w,i'}$ is the sense that is used to facilitate academic writing.

The steps to our solution is as follows:

propose-1 (verb)

DIFFICULTY: B2

to offer or suggest a possible plan or action for other people to consider

SYNONYMS: suggest-1, propound-1, submit-2, float-5

ANTONYMS: withdraw-1, deny-2, refuse-1

EXAMPLE SENTENCES:

- I **propose** that we wait until the budget has been announced before committing ourselves to any expenditure.
- He **proposed** dealing directly with the suppliers.

Figure 2: A example of the disambiguation result

In the final result, the correct sense of each word is shown along with its English definition, guide word, difficulty level, and example sentences (Figure 2).

As an example, consider the group of words: (propose, suggest, argue): Figure 3 shows the count of each translation. For *propose*, since the sense [“建議”, “提議”, “提出”] contains the translations ’建議’ and ’提議’, which both occurred twice, the sense is selected as the ’correct’ sense. Similarly, the sense [“提議”, “建議”] is selected for *suggest*. On the other hand, since all translations of *argue* only occur once within the group, the ’correct’ academic sense cannot be identified, and its first sense [“爭論”, “爭吵”, “爭辯”] is selected.

Algorithm 1: Algorithm for finding the most likely sense given a group of semantically similar words W, based on the number of occurrences of all translated senses

def FreqDisambiguate(W, S);

Input :

W : A set of words to disambiguate;

S : A set of translated senses for each word in W, where each sense of word w is $s_i^w \in S$, and each translated sense $s_{i,t}^w \in s_i^w$;

F : A hash table with translated sense $s_{w,i}$ as keys and their frequencies in W as values.

Output:

D: A hash table with words as keys and 1 disambiguate sense for each word as values

for each w_i **in** W
    initialize $maxSenseCnt$
    initialize $topSense$
    for each s_i^w **in** s^w
        for each $s_{i,t}^w$ **in** s_i^w
            if F$[s_{i,t}^w] > maxSenseCnt$ **then**
                $maxSenseCnt \leftarrow F[s_{i,t}^w]$
                $topSense \leftarrow s_{i,t}^w$
    D$[w_i] \leftarrow topSense$
return D

4 Experimental results

We conducted two sets of experiments: the first experiment disambiguate word senses based on the frequencies of the translated senses, as in Algorithm 1. The second experiment employs definition embedding and clustering, which requires only lexical resources from one language, as opposed to our first

```
argue [['爭論', '爭吵', '爭辯'], ['論證', '說理', '辯論'], ['顯示出', '表明']]
propose [['建議', '提議', '提出'], ['提名', '推薦（某人）擔任某職（或參加某組織）'], ['求婚'], ['計劃',
'打算']]
suggest [['提議', '建議'], ['暗示', '間接表明', '意味著'], ['使想到', '使聯想到']]

{'爭論': 1, '爭吵': 1, '爭辯': 1, '論證': 1, '說理': 1, '辯論': 1, '顯示出': 1, '表明': 1, '建議': 2
, '提議': 2, '提出': 1, '提名': 1, '推薦（某人）擔任某職（或參加某組織）': 1, '求婚': 1, '計劃': 1, '打
算': 1, '暗示': 1, '間接表明': 1, '意味著': 1, '使想到': 1, '使聯想到': 1}

argue ['爭論', '爭吵', '爭辯']
propose ['建議', '提議', '提出']
suggest ['提議', '建議']
```

Figure 3: A sample of the disambiguation process and result: The first block displays all senses of each word. The second block displays counts of each translation. The third block shows the senses chosen.

experiment where translation in another language is needed.

4.1 The Vanilla Approach: Most Frequent Translation

In our experiment, we retrieve the Mandarin translation of each word from the online Cambridge Dictionary (Cambridge University Press, 2021). The Cambridge Dictionary is an ideal external resource for this task because it is compiled by experienced lexicographers and provide rich information useful for learners, including proficiency level, English definitions, guide words, example sentences, and translations in many L1 languages.

The AKL consists of 930 potential academic words and phrases, categorized into 5 groups: nouns, verbs, adjectives, adverbs, and others. Table 1 is a summary of word distribution of the original and the translated AKL. The number of unique words and their occurrences are greater than the numbers from the original AKL because each word or phrase is often provided with more than one translation. Since words on the AKL are semantically related, translations of the same senses tend to occur multiple times, which enable us to identify the "correct" academic sense for each word by choosing the sense whose translation has the highest occurrences among all senses.

4.2 The Monolingual Approach: Clustering with Definition Embedding

While our method based on Mandarin translation is effective, it requires translations of a second language to work. The method would not function when translations are not available, or when counting the occurrences of translated token is not as simple as those in Mandarin, for instance, languages that involves extensive inflections. In this case, a pretrained sense embedding model could be a valid alternative.

Word embeddings have exploded in use since Mikolov et al. (2013). The ability to represent words in a continuous vector space enables a whole new array of applications. In recent years, sentence encoding models (or "language models") that utilize embeddings as word representations have evolved to achieve state-of-the-art results, notably seq2seq (Sutskever et al., 2014), ELMo (Peters et al., 2018), the Transformer (Vaswani et al., 2017), and most recently BERT (Devlin et al., 2018). These models typically encode the input sequences with Long Short-Term Memory (LSTM) (Hochreiter and Schmidhuber, 1997) or self-attention into hidden states, and map the hidden states to an output sequences with a decoder. Although several studies (Kågebäck and Salomonsson, 2016; Raganato et al., 2017; Ahmed et al., 2018; Wiedemann et al., 2019; Huang et al., 2020) have used these models to perform WSD, these studies all focus on WSD within context, whereas our task concerns a special case where context is not available. In addition, individual senses are implicitly incorporated in the hidden states or embeddings, which poses challenges for interpretability and downstream tasks that specifically require embeddings for individual senses. Last but not least, these language models are expensive to train, which makes them unsuitable for our task at hand.

Bosc and Vincent (2018) proposed an alternate method for encoding embeddings, where embeddings are encoded from dictionary defi-

Part of speech	AKL entries	Unique trsl. words	Total trsl. words
NOUN	355	1785	2174
VERB	233	1158	1415
ADJECTIVE	180	798	954
ADVERB	87	300	347

Table 1: This table shows the number of AKL entries and number of words after translation. Total translated words include repeated words.

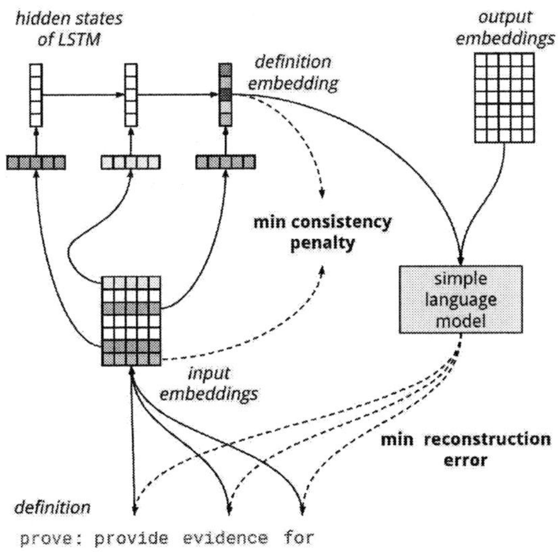

Figure 4: An overview of the CPAE model. Graph from Bosc and Vincent (2018)

nition. In Bosc and Vincent (2018), definition embeddings are encoded by passing the definition of a sense to an LSTM and a linear transformation. The authors also proposed a method called *consistency penalty*, where the objective function defined as the distance between the embedding produced by the LSTM and the embedding being fed into the LSTM is to be minimized. Fig. 4 provides an overview of the architecture of the model. In their final step, all definition embeddings of a word are concatenated into one embedding. For our purpose of extracting the correct sense from all other senses, we choose not to concatenate the definition embeddings and instead encode each definition as a separate embedding, enabling the actions for our next step. For our embeddings, definitions from Cambridge Dictionary are used as input data.

Based on the assumption that senses that are semantically related tend to be closer to each other in a vector space, we perform a clustering algorithm as in Tuan et al. (2020) on a complete graph derived from the sense embeddings of words in AKL:

1. Obtain pairwise similarity between all pairs of senses of all words. The pairwise similarity is calculated as the cosine similarity between two definition embeddings.

2. Build a complete graph with senses as nodes and their pairwise similarity as edges.

3. Perform density-based spatial clustering as in Campello et al. (2013) and obtain the largest cluster.

4. Senses within the largest cluster are selected as disambiguated senses.

5. Words whose senses are not included within the cluster are assigned the disambiguation result from the translation method.

5 Evaluation and Discussion

We randomly select 10 percent of identified senses from each category for evaluation. We have two human experts evaluate whether each sense identified is of academic use. For the baseline, the first sense listed for each word in Cambridge Dictionary is chosen as the "correct" sense. The accuracies of the translation method, the clustering method, and the baseline are summarized in Table 2.

Our method performs significantly better than the baseline, averaging at 90% accuracy, whereas the baseline has an average of 79% accuracy. The seemingly impossible 100% accuracy for adverbs is due to small group size, and the relatively lower degrees of sense ambiguity (1.9 senses per word vs. the average 2.6 senses per word).

part of speech	translation accuracy	clustering accuracy	baseline accuracy
NOUN	**91%**	**91%**	71%
VERB	**83%**	**83%**	75%
ADJECTIVE	**89%**	83%	83%
ADVERB	**100%**	**100%**	94%
AVERAGE	**90%**	87%	79%

Table 2: Accuracies of academic sense disambiguation

Interestingly, our evaluation also shows that using sense embeddings with clustering does not necessarily yield better results than the knowledge adn translation-based approach, although the embedding based approach also performs much better than the baseline. There could be several reasons for its lesser performance: One is that the sense embeddings might not have encompassed the complete semantic content for some senses, placing those senses at positions further away from the main cluster where other sense vectors are. On the other hand, the words grouped together in AKL might not necessarily be closely-enough related semantically to form a large cluster. Despite its lower accuracies, the clustering method still outperforms the baseline, and serves as an effective disambiguation method when sense translations of the target word groups are not available.

6 Conclusion and Future Work

We have introduced a method for disambiguating senses for academic usage for words in the Academic Keyword List. The method involves retrieving translations of each sense in another language and extracting English senses that correspond to the most frequently-occurring translation. We have also experimented with disambiguating senses with the clustering of sense embeddings. Both methods yields reasonable good results in disentagling academic senses from other senses. More importantly, our work marks a step towards building an academic writers' dictionary.

Many avenues exist for future research and improvement for our method. For building an academic writers' dictionary, the next step is to include all potentially-academic senses for each word on the AKL. Disambiguating AKL words within running text would largely benefit learners of EAP. Synonyms, antonyms, and example sentences of the disambiguated senses could be generated to further assist ESL learners.

Additionally, another direction of research would be to experiment on using translations in languages other than Mandarin for potentially better disambiguation results, as well as a more profound understanding of the properties of human sense-making.

Acknowledgments

The authors would like to thank the reviewers for their invaluable suggestions and feedback. Thanks also due to GLORIA Operation Center for offering a short course on Academic English Writing which provides the impetus of this research

References

Mahtab Ahmed, Muhammad Rifayat Samee, and Robert Mercer. 2018. A novel neural sequence model with multiple attentions for word sense disambiguation. In *2018 17th IEEE International Conference on Machine Learning and Applications (ICMLA)*, pages 687–694. IEEE.

Tom Bosc and Pascal Vincent. 2018. Auto-encoding dictionary definitions into consistent word embeddings. In *Proceedings of the 2018 Conference on Empirical Methods in Natural Language Processing*, pages 1522–1532, Brussels, Belgium. Association for Computational Linguistics.

2021 Cambridge University Press. 2021. Cambridge dictionary. `https://dictionary.cambridge.org`. Accessed: 2021-08-01.

Ricardo J. G. B. Campello, Davoud Moulavi, and Joerg Sander. 2013. Density-based clustering based on hierarchical density estimates. In *Advances in Knowledge Discovery and Data Mining*, pages 160–172, Berlin, Heidelberg. Springer Berlin Heidelberg.

Averil Coxhead. 2000. A new academic word list. *TESOL Quarterly*, 34(2):213–238.

Ido Dagan and Alon Itai. 1994. Word sense disambiguation using a second language monolingual corpus. *Comput. Linguist.*, 20(4):563—596.

Jacob Devlin, Ming-Wei Chang, Kenton Lee, and Kristina Toutanova. 2018. Bert: Pre-training of deep bidirectional transformers for language understanding. *arXiv preprint arXiv:1810.04805.*

Sepp Hochreiter and Jürgen Schmidhuber. 1997. Long short-term memory. *Neural Computation*, 9(8):1735–1780.

Luyao Huang, Chi Sun, Xipeng Qiu, and Xuanjing Huang. 2020. Glossbert: Bert for word sense disambiguation with gloss knowledge.

Mikael Kågebäck and Hans Salomonsson. 2016. Word sense disambiguation using a bidirectional lstm. *arXiv preprint arXiv:1606.03568.*

Tomas Mikolov, Kai Chen, Greg Corrado, and Jeffrey Dean. 2013. Efficient estimation of word representations in vector space.

George A. Miller. 1995. Wordnet: A lexical database for english. *Commun. ACM*, 38(11):39—41.

Roberto Navigli. 2009. Word sense disambiguation: A survey. *ACM Comput. Surv.*, 41(2).

Magali Paquot. 2010. *Academic vocabulary in learner writing: From extraction to analysis.* Bloomsbury Publishing.

Matthew E Peters, Mark Neumann, Mohit Iyyer, Matt Gardner, Christopher Clark, Kenton Lee, and Luke Zettlemoyer. 2018. Deep contextualized word representations. *arXiv preprint arXiv:1802.05365.*

Alessandro Raganato, Claudio Delli Bovi, and Roberto Navigli. 2017. Neural sequence learning models for word sense disambiguation. In *Proceedings of the 2017 Conference on Empirical Methods in Natural Language Processing*, pages 1156–1167.

Alok Ranjan Pal and Diganta Saha. 2015. Word sense disambiguation: A survey. *International Journal of Control Theory and Computer Modeling*, 5(3):1—16.

P. Resnik. 1999. *Disambiguating Noun Groupings with Respect to WordNet Senses*, pages 77–98. Springer Netherlands, Dordrecht.

Ilya Sutskever, Oriol Vinyals, and Quoc V. Le. 2014. Sequence to sequence learning with neural networks.

Kai-Wen Tuan, Yi-Chien Lin, Jason S Chang, Kuan-Lin Lee, and Li-Kuang Chen. 2020. Consenses: Disambiguating content word groups based on knowledge base and definition embedding. In *2020 International Conference on Technologies and Applications of Artificial Intelligence (TAAI)*, pages 260–265. IEEE.

Ashish Vaswani, Noam Shazeer, Niki Parmar, Jakob Uszkoreit, Llion Jones, Aidan N Gomez, Łukasz Kaiser, and Illia Polosukhin. 2017. Attention is all you need. In *Advances in neural information processing systems*, pages 5998–6008.

Michael West. 1953. *A General Service List of English Words.* Addison-Wesley Longman Ltd, London.

Gregor Wiedemann, Steffen Remus, Avi Chawla, and Chris Biemann. 2019. Does bert make any sense? interpretable word sense disambiguation with contextualized embeddings.

The 33rd Conference on Computational Linguistics and Speech Processing (ROCLING 2021)
Taoyuan, Taiwan, October 15-16, 2021. The Association for Computational Linguistics and Chinese Language Processing

SCUDS at ROCLING-2021 Shared Task: Using Pretrained Model for Dimensional Sentiment Analysis Based on Sample Expansion Method

Hsiao-Shih Chen
School of Big Data Management, Soochow University, Taiwan
07170235@gm.scu.edu.tw

Pin-Chiung Chen
School of Big Data Management, Soochow University, Taiwan
07170140@gm.scu.edu.tw

Shao-Cheng Huang
School of Big Data Management, Soochow University, Taiwan
07170123@gm.scu.edu.tw

Yu-Cheng Chiu
School of Big Data Management, Soochow University, Taiwan
jean199925@gmail.com

Jheng-Long Wu
Department of Data Science, Soochow University, Taiwan
jlwu@gm.scu.edu.tw

摘要

情感分析已成為現今非常熱門的研究議題，而在教育文本的情感分析仍是一大重點。根據文獻指出，產生極為相似的語句，將有效幫助機器學習的學習成效，因此可被控制的訓練樣本擴充法將成為預測模型提升效果的主要元素。本研究將提出採用詞性篩選結合 Word2Vec 模型計算相似字詞來擴充訓練樣本，以達到相似字詞替換後，仍保有較高品質的情感表達。而在預測模型方面，本研究採用 DistilBERT 預訓練模型作為基礎，再進行句子的 Valence-Arousal 情感分數學習與預測。根據實驗結果顯示，採用本研究所提出的擴充訓練樣本時，可以獲得降低 80% *MAE* 和提升 28% *PCC*。

Abstract

Sentiment analysis has become a popular research issue in recent years, especially on educational texts which is an important problem. According to literature, the similar sentence generation can help the prediction performance of machine learning. Therefore, the process of controlled expansional samples is a key component to prediction models. The paper proposed a sample expansion method which combined part-of-speech filter and similar word finder of Word2Vec. The generate samples have high quality with similar sentiment representation. The DistilBERT pretrained model is used to learn and predict Valence-Arousal scores from the expansion samples. Experimental result displays that the using the expansion samples as training data into prediction model has outperforms original training data without expansion, and obtains 80% mean square error reducing and 28% pearson correlation coefficient increasing.

關鍵字：情感分析、預訓練模型、樣本擴充法

Keywords: Sentiment analysis, Pretrained model, Sample expansion method

1 緒論

1.1 背景與動機

隨著社群媒體的快速發展，以及網路資源、行動裝置的普及，造就現今社會時時刻刻都能透過各大社群網站獲取大量資訊，包括新聞網站、影音平台與直播平台等都有提供留言或即時聊天的功能，讓世界各地的人能在偌大的網路虛擬世界進行交流。在各大論壇上，曾經發表過的言論，都會被記錄下來，這些大量的文字資訊，經常在自然語言領域，當作是模型訓練的語料庫。

情感分析是一種用來識別文本中情感資訊的重要技術。通常會針對一個文本作兩極性的分類。分類的目的在於判斷文字中表達的情緒是正向（positive）、負向（negative）或中性（neutral）。在早期情感分析領域提出研究主要是在探測商品評論與電影影評的兩極觀點（Turney, 2002）。而另一種方法是以維度的方式將情感狀態以連續數值表示在多個維度上，像是 Valence-Arousal（VA）（Russell,

1980）。Valence 代表環境帶給人類的情緒影響，當值為正向時，代表歡樂、和平與喜悅等正面情緒；值為負時，代表生氣、無趣與悲傷等負面情緒。Arousal 代表情緒的強烈、壓力程度，當值為高時，代表快樂、興奮；值為低時，代表憂鬱、無聊。本研究將採用 ROCLING 2021 Shared Task 所提供的語料庫，其中包含以句子為單位的 CVAT 2.0（Yu et al., 2016）、以單詞為單位的 CVAW 4.0（Yu et al., 2016）以及以片語為單位的 CVAP 2.0（Yu et al., 2017）。由於本研究要解決句子型態的情感狀態，即預測句子的 VA 值，則使用 CVAT 2.0 語料庫作為本研究的主要訓練資料，包含來自六個不同類別的網路評論，每個句子手動標記成二維的向量，分別代表情緒的正負面及語氣的興奮程度，共計 2,969 筆句子。而 CVAW 4.0 語料庫有 5,512 個單詞，以及 CVAP 2.0 語料庫則有 2,998 個片語。

由於以句子為單位的語料庫僅有 2,969 筆，其樣本數略顯不足。根據過去的相關訓練樣本數不足的研究，已經證實擴充訓練樣本後，能夠提供更多樣性的訓練樣本，使得機器學習模型可以從中學習更多的樣本，避免機器學習只能參考少部分樣本分布，使得機器學習模型在預測的精確度有所提升（Shorten and Khoshgoftaar, 2019）。而在自然語言處理相關研究中，深度學習（Deep Learning）的 BERT 模型（Devlin et al., 2018）已經取得相當大幅度的改善，透過預訓練的方式，從超大量語料庫中學習後，再僅透過一個額外的輸出層進行後續任務微調或特定架構修改等就能夠獲得預測效果的改善。而另一個傳統的機器學習預測模型，則是使用 TF-IDF（Term Frequecny-Inverse document Frequency）（Ramos, 2003）將文字轉換成特徵向量後，再透過全域求解的 SVM（Support Vector Machine）（Cortes and Vapnik, 1995）演算法來建立模型。為了有效預測以句子為單位的教育文本之情感分數，本研究將採取多種訓練樣本擴充法搭配機器學習及深度學習的模型進行訓練與預測。所以自動化預測句子的情感分數，相關單位可以透過分數的高低來判斷該句子可能想要表達的情緒，甚至能分析學生的學習狀況。

1.2 目的

圖 1 為本研究的實驗流程圖，為了要提高模型預測的準確度，本次任務將 CVAT 2.0 語料庫透過斷詞及詞性標注後，再找出情感單詞的近義詞和計算情感單詞與近義詞的相似度分數，並重新計算替換過後的句子 VA 值，因此透過替換方式所擴充出相似句子，可用於訓練樣本的資料量。再者，透過 DistilBERT 預訓練模型及 SVM 模型進行情感分數的訓練與預測。本研究藉由上述所提出的流程來訓練與預測教育文本（學生自我評價）的句子在維度情感分析任務中應有的分數。本研究的目的為建構一套樣本擴充法與採用強大的預測模型，可以從網路評論的訓練樣本學習到規則，進而用來預測教育文本的資料集，即學生自我評價的句子所表達的 Valence 和 Arousal 值。

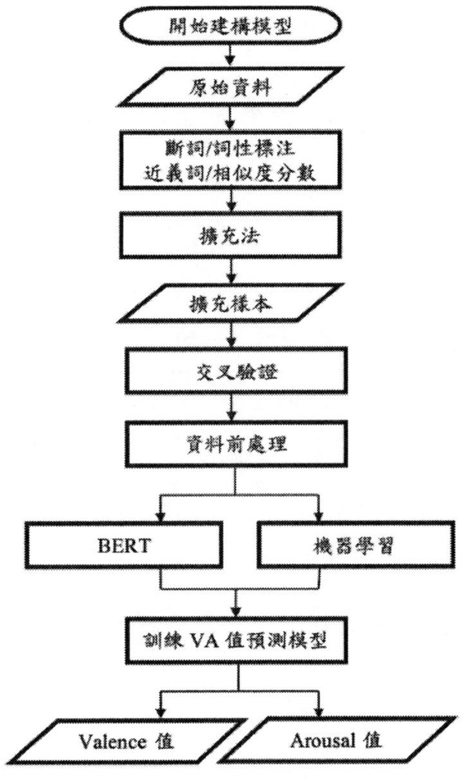

圖 1：研究實驗流程圖

2 系統方法

本研究的系統方法包括資料擴充法以及預測模型建構。資料擴充法使得模型有更多的訓練資料量可以用來學習，而再訓練機器學習與深度學習的模型獲得預測模型，並透過交叉驗證法得出表現最好的模型來做為最終預測使用。

2.1 資料擴充法

首先參考 EDA（Easy Data Augmentation techniques）模型（Wei and Zou, 2019），此為一種傳統的文本擴充方法，可以以四種方式來進行資料擴充，包含：同義詞替換、隨機插入、隨機交換與隨機刪除。接著參考 Word2Vec 模型（Mikolov et al., 2013）的字詞相似度概念，使用一個向量來表示一個詞，將文本空間中的某個 word，透過語言模型的訓練後，將該詞相關的資訊嵌入（embedding）於所屬向量空間，因此可以透過餘弦相似度（cosine-similarity）方法來計算詞與詞之間的相似程度，進而做到找尋相近詞的功用。

2.1.1 斷詞與詞性標注

多數與英文相關的語言，字詞與字詞之間都有明顯的空白做為分隔，所以很容易就能判斷出單詞。然而，中文則是一長串文字的組合，字詞與字詞間沒有明顯的符號來做區隔，因此斷詞為文字預處理不可或缺的過程。本研究使用 Python Synonyms 套件[1]，來進行斷詞與詞性標註，這樣可以針對特定的詞性作為替換的規則，斷詞與詞性標註範例如圖 2 所示。

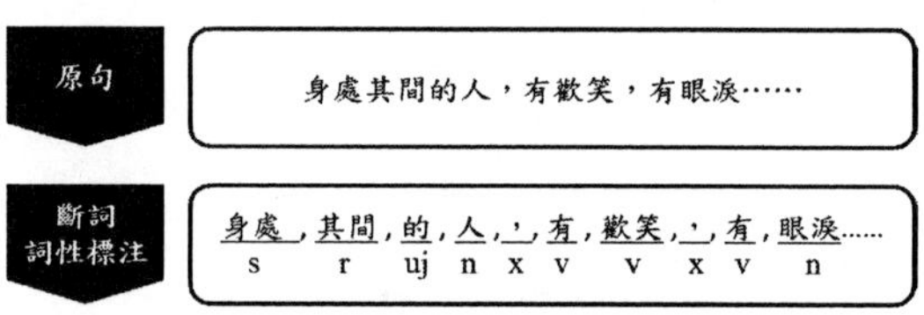

圖 2：斷詞及詞性標注

2.1.2 近義詞與餘弦相似度分數

為了達成產生相似句子的目的，本研究將採取找尋合適的近義詞，以替換句子斷詞後的單詞，此可產生一句新的擴充句子。例如單詞「心碎」可與其近義單詞計算餘弦相似度，分數愈接近 1 則代表該詞與「心碎」的語意愈相近，如「心痛」的餘弦相似度值為 0.76，其餘相似單詞的相似度如圖 3 所示。

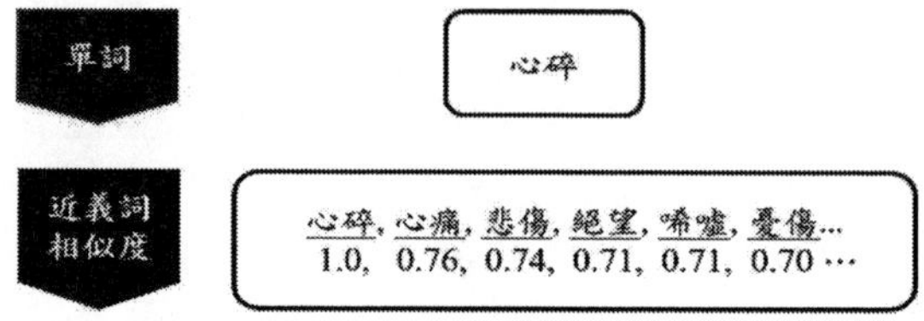

圖 3：近義詞及相似度分數

本研究預計透過四種方法來擴充原始資料，並會使用同一原始句子來做說明，此範例的原始句子如：

- 身處其間的人，有歡笑，有眼淚，有快樂，有悲傷，有甜蜜，有心碎，可是應該是不會後悔的吧。
- Valence：5.75、Arousal：5。

以下小節是擴充法說明：

2.1.3 擴充法 1

當句子斷詞後的單詞出現在 CVAW 4.0 單詞語料庫時，找尋其要被替換的單詞之 VA 值，相差正負 0.1 內，便可替換該詞，以產生新的擴充句子，其擴充句子的 VA 值將與原始句子相同。以下為擴充法 1 所產生的擴充句子（粗體表示替換過的單詞）與其對應的 VA 值：

- 身處其間的人，有**歡喜**、有眼淚，有快樂，有**傲慢**，有**強壯**，有心碎，可是應該是**犯錯乞討**的吧。
- Valence：5.75、 Arousal：5。

2.1.4 擴充法 2

基本操作同擴充法 1 相似，差別在於指定**動詞**為範圍找出可被替之同義詞，且符合餘弦相似度大於 0.7，並採取隨機替換。而情感分數方面，以原始詞與被替換詞的各別 VA 值之差乘以 5% 作為新 VA 值調整。以下為擴充法 2 所產生的擴充句子與其對應的 VA 值：

- 身處其間的人，有**歡樂**，有眼淚，有快樂，有悲傷，有甜蜜，有**憂傷**，可是應該是**無法懊悔**的吧。
- Valence：5.79、Arousal：4.99

[1] 中文近义词工具包 Synonyms. 網址：https://github.com/chatopera/Synonyms

2.1.5 擴充法 3

基本操作與擴充法 2 相似，差別在於指定**名詞與動詞**為範圍找出可被替之同義詞。以下為擴充法 3 所產生的擴充句子與其對應的 VA 值：

- 身處其間的人，有**歡樂**，有眼淚，有快樂，有悲傷，有甜蜜，有**心痛**，可是應該是**無法生氣**的吧。
- Valence：5.73、Arousal：5.1

2.1.6 擴充法 4

基本操作與擴充法 2 相似，差別在於指定**名詞**、**動詞**、**名詞＋動詞**為範圍，找出被替換詞之同義詞，一次替換一個詞至一次替換五個詞，排列所有可能。以下為擴充法 4 所產生的擴充句子與其對應的 VA 值：

- 身處其間的人，有**歡樂**，有**流淚**，有快樂，有悲傷，有甜蜜，有**憂傷**，可是應該是**不能慚愧**的吧。
- Valence：5.81、Arousal：4.86

2.2 交叉驗證

為了得到可靠且穩定的模型，本研究使用交叉驗證法來評估模型的學習效果，避免資料的分布不均所造成的學習效果不佳。本研究以 5-fold 交叉驗證將資料分成訓練集與驗證集，就是把資料切成五個子集合，其中一個子集合需被保留作為驗證，其餘四個子樣本用來訓練，重複五次，每個子集合都必須輪流作為驗證集一次。然而，先前提到的資料擴充法所產生的擴充句子，將作為訓練樣本來加強模型訓練，所以在每個 fold 中，只會在訓練樣本額外加上擴充句子進行訓練，並不會將擴充資料版本納入驗證子樣本進行驗證，以避免擴充資料影響整體模型驗證效果。

2.3 預測模型訓練

2.3.1 DistilBERT 模型與超參數設定

本研究使用 CVAT 2.0 句子語料庫作為訓練集，將輸入句字進行斷詞（Tokenizer），也就是轉換成 BERT 模型當中單個 Token 的編號，並且統一每個輸入的長度，未滿長度者以 0 補齊，最多為 512 個單詞。再者透過 Hugging Face 的套件（Wolf et al., 2020）所提供的預訓練模型 DistilBERT（distilbert-base-multilingual-cased）作為預測模型基礎。

並透過調整模型超參數以取得最佳模型，本研究分別定義 Batch Size，Learning Rate 和 Epochs 等三個超參數，總共訂定六組超參數，表 1 為 DistilBERT 所使用的超參數設定。

Experiment	Batch size	Learning rate	Epochs
EXP1	16	5e-2	50
EXP2	16	5e-3	50
EXP3	16	5e-5	50
EXP4	8	5e-2	50
EXP5	8	5e-3	50
EXP6	8	5e-5	50

表 1：DistilBERT 模型之超參數設定

2.3.2 SVM 機器學習模型與超參數設定

SVM 模型訓練則將所有輸入句子採用 CKIP-Transformers（Li et al., 2020）工具進行斷詞，接著訓練資料建立詞彙表，再計算各樣本的 TF-IDF 值。而 SVM 透過調整不同超參數以取得最佳模型，SVM 的超參數設定如表 2 所示。

Kernel	Cost	Degree	Gamma
Linear	1	-	auto
RBF	1	-	auto
	1	-	scale
	20	-	0.5
Sigmoid	1	-	auto
	1	-	scale
	10	-	0.1
Poly	1	3	auto
	1	3	scale
	10	3	0.5
	10	3	1
	10	3	2
	10	3	0.1

表 2：SVM 模型之超參數設定

2.4 評估指標介紹

根據 ROCLING 2021 Shared Task 所示，為了評估模型的表現，使用平均絕對誤差（Mean Square Error, MAE）與皮爾森相關係數

（Pearson Correlation Coefficient, PCC），如公式(1)與公式(2)所示。

- MAE：計算各次真實值與預測值誤差取絕對值後再求平均值。

$$MAE = \frac{1}{n}\sum_{i=1}^{n} | A_i - P_i | \quad (1)$$

- PCC：表示真實值與預測值是否共同產生變化的關聯程度。

$$PCC = \frac{1}{n}\sum_{i=1}^{n}(\frac{A_i - \bar{A}}{\sigma_A})(\frac{P_i - \bar{P}}{\sigma_P}) \quad (2)$$

A_i 為手動標記評分，P_i為模型預測評分，n為測試樣本數量，$\bar{A}$和$\bar{P}$分別為手動標記評分與模型預測評分的總平均，σ為標準差。

2.4.1 最佳模型挑選準則

先前提到為了避免模型訓練偏差，使用 5-fold 交叉驗證來穩定模型，而評估指標計算方法則是將得到的五次 *MAE* 與 *PCC* 之結果各自取平均值作為此超參數最終的評估指標，以挑選出最佳模型。

3 實驗結果與比較

3.1 擴充句子統計量

將 CVAT 2.0 句子語料庫（2,969 筆）做為版本一的訓練資料版本，版本二至版本五分別使用擴充法 1 至 4 來生成的訓練擴充樣本分別加上版本一，最後版本六為合併版本一至版本五的所有資料，並刪除重複生成句子（共計移除 9,977 筆）。表 3 為各版本之擴充量統計數據。

資料版本	**規則**	**總數量 (+擴充量)**
版本一	原始擴充資料集	29,69 (+0)
版本二	使用擴充法 1	5,444 (+2,475)
版本三	使用擴充法 2	7,008 (+4,039)
版本四	使用擴充法 3	6,921 (+3,952)
版本五	使用擴充法 4	31,433 (+28,464)
版本六	合併第一至第五版，並刪除重複句子	34,892 (+31,923)

表 3：訓練資料版本規則與統計量

3.2 DistilBERT 模型之預測效果

本研究使用 DistilBERT 預訓練模型作為此 VA 預測模型的起點，表 4 與表 5 為統整每個資料版本中表現最佳超參數組合，以及對應的 *MAE* 與 *PCC*，其中最佳超參數是以最低的 *MAE* 或最高的 *PCC* 篩選而得。然而進一步觀察得知無論是 Valence 還是 Arousal 表現最好的皆為資料版本六，和版本一（無擴充資料集）相比，大幅降低了 *MAE* 評估指標，Valence 從 0.6723 降至 0.1378，Arousal 則從 0.7265 降至 0.1436，兩個預測目標幾乎都降了 80%。

資料版本	**Valence**		
	Experiment	***MAE***	***PCC***
版本一	EXP3	0.672	0.757
版本二	EXP3	0.224	0.957
版本三	EXP3	0.310	0.915
版本四	EXP3	0.264	0.931
版本五	EXP3	0.296	0.917
版本六	**EXP3**	**0.138**	**0.971**

表 4：DistilBERT 之 Valence 預測結果

資料版本	**Arousal**		
	Experiment	***MAE***	***PCC***
版本一	EXP3	0.727	0.469
版本二	EXP6	0.247	0.897
版本三	EXP3	0.341	0.829
版本四	EXP3	0.292	0.867
版本五	EXP3	0.306	0.850
版本六	**EXP3**	**0.144**	**0.939**

表 5：DistilBERT 之 Arousal 預測結果

3.3 SVM 機器學習之預測效果

由 DistilBERT 預訓練模型可得知資料版本六的預測效果大幅領先，因此在 SVM 模型的訓練將直接採用資料版本六進行訓練，根據不同的超參數組合，最佳模型的超參數設置為：Kernel 採用 RBF，Gamma 設定 0.5、Cost 設定 20，其設定在預測 VA 值皆得到最好的效果，如表 6 所示。與最差的 SVM 模型比較下，最佳的 SVM 模型在 Valence 改善約 0.10 的 *MAE*，

Arousal 則是改善約 0.05 的 *MAE*。有此可知，再不同的超參數組合下，對 SVM 模型沒有產生極大差異，顯示 SVM 模型相當穩定。

Target	*MAE*	*PCC*
Valence	0.235	0.952
Arousal	0.218	0.919

表 6：SVM 之預測結果

3.4 SVM 與 DistilBERT 模型之預測結果比較

表 7 為將 SVM 和 DistilBERT 模型所訓練的最佳成果比較，可以看到 DistilBERT 模型的 *MAE* 都比 SVM 要來得低，在 Valence 的部分，兩模型的 *MAE* 相差約 9.7%；在 Arousal 的部分則相差約 7.4%，因此可以得知 DistilBERT 的表現相較於 SVM 傳統機器學習模型來的佳，且大幅改善。

Model	Valence		Arousal	
	MAE	*PCC*	*MAE*	*PCC*
DistilBERT	0.138	0.971	0.144	0.939
SVM	0.235	0.952	0.218	0.919

表 7：DistilBERT 與 SVM 模型預測結果之比較

3.5 不同 BERT 的預訓練模型之比較

由於官方提供的資料集與本研究的擴充資料版本皆為繁體中文，DistilBERT 是一種多語言的預訓練模型，為了探究預訓練模型的文本語言是否會影響 VA 的預測效果，所以本研究利用中央研究院開發繁體中文的預訓練模型 CKIPlabBERT[2]（ckiplab/bert-base-chinese）再次作為預訓練模型，並訓練本研究的擴充資料。首先採用資料版一作為基礎，比較無擴充訓練樣本的預測效果。圖 4 表示在無擴充資料版本一的比較結果，CKIPlabBERT 都比 DistilBERT 模型來得優秀，在 VA 的 *MAE* 分別差 0.152 和 0.027，而 *PCC* 則是分別差 0.1 和 0.051。

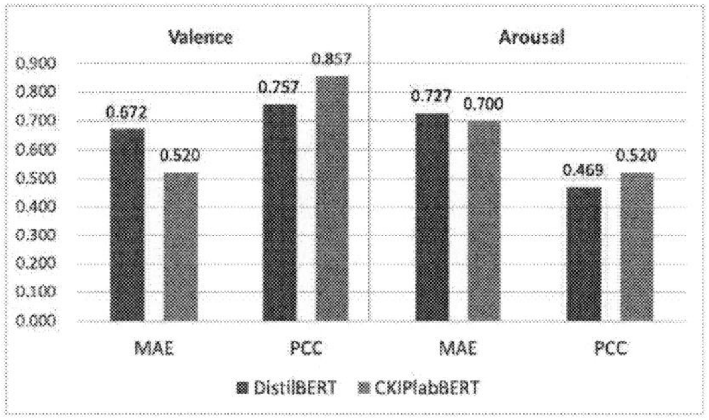

圖 4：版本一預訓練模型比較

然而，圖 5 表示有擴充資料的版本六的比較結果，反而是 DistilBERT 比 CKIPlabBERT 來的優秀，在 VA 的 *MAE* 分別差 0.016 和 0.035，而 *PCC* 則是分別差 0.004 和 0.003。但相較於無擴充資料版本一時，其差距變得非常小。

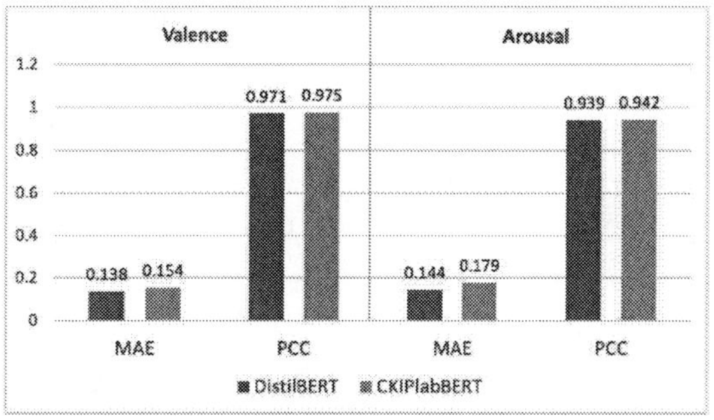

圖 5：版本六預訓練模型比較

3.6 最佳模型選擇

模型訓練完成後，以驗證集作為基準，從 SVM、DistilBERT 和 CKIPlabBERT 中挑選最佳模型作為最終繳交使用之預測模型。本研究選擇 DistilBERT 和 CKIPlabBERT 兩模型搭配先前表現最好的超參數組合 EXP3 和 EXP6，作為預測模型進行比較，並使用無擴充資料的版本一作為預測集。由表 8 與表 9 可見，在 DistilBERT 模型中，VA 值的驗證效果皆為超參數組合 EXP3 較好，而在預測集的結果，其 *MAE* 又更低，兩者相差約 9%。而在 CKIPlabBERT 模型中，Valence 的驗證集效果

[2] CKIP LAB 所開發之 CKIP Transformers 為繁體中文的 transformers 模型，網址：https://huggingface.co/CKIP_lab

為超參數組合 EXP3 較好，其在預測集的結果亦為 *MAE* 較低，兩者相差了約 6.87%；Arousal 的驗證集則是超參數組合 EXP6 較好，其在預測集的結果亦為 *MAE* 較低，兩者相差了約 8.72%。然而兩個模型在預測 VA 值的效果上，超參數組合不論是 EXP3 或 EXP6 皆是 DistilBERT 模型表現得較出色，其整體在預測集的 *MAE* 都是 CKIPlabBERT 模型的約 0.5 倍，所以根據前述的最佳模型挑選準則，最後選擇了 DistilBERT 模型搭配超參數組合 EXP3 與 EXP6 作為兩個最終模型。

Model / Experiment	驗證集		預測集	
	MAE	*PCC*	*MAE*	*PCC*
DistilBERT / EXP3	0.138	0.971	0.045	0.998
DistilBERT / EXP6	0.142	0.967	0.045	0.998
CKIPlabBERT / EXP3	0.154	0.975	0.085	0.999
CKIPlabBERT / EXP6	0.174	0.970	0.084	0.998

表 8：DistilBERT 與 CKIPlabBERT 模型在驗證集與預測集的 Valence 預測效果之比較

Model / Experiment	驗證集		預測集	
	MAE	*PCC*	*MAE*	*PCC*
DistilBERT / EXP3	0.144	0.939	0.044	0.997
DistilBERT / EXP6	0.159	0.935	0.052	0.996
CKIPlabBERT / EXP3	0.179	0.944	0.094	0.997
CKIPlabBERT / EXP6	0.171	0.938	0.084	0.997

表 9：DistilBERT 與 CKIPlabBERT 模型在驗證集與預測集的 Arousal 預測效果之比較

3.7 測試集評估結果

根據 ROCLING 2021 Shared Task 提供的測試集，所提交的兩個預測模型為 DistilBERT 搭配超參數組合 EXP3 與 EXP6，其預測結果如表 10 所示，在 Valence 的 *MAE* 最低為 0.953 和 *PCC* 最高為 0.694；在 Arousal 的 *MAE* 最低為 1.039 和 *PCC* 最高為 0.375。

Model / Experiment	Valence		Arousal	
	MAE	*PCC*	*MAE*	*PCC*
DistilBERT / EXP3	0.953	0.694	1.054	0.375
DistilBERT / EXP6	0.975	0.667	1.039	0.354

表 10：DistilBERT 模型與 EXP3 和 EXP6 超參數組合在測試集的評估結果

然而，ROCLING 2021 Shared Task 釋出測試集答案後，本研究也將 CKIPlabBERT 模型進行預測，並進行評估，其評估結果如表 11 所示，在 Valence 很明顯可以看出比 CKIP_LAB_BERT 比 DistilBERT 模型表現來得好，*MAE* 降低約 20%，PCC 增加約 17%，而 Arousal 的 *MAE*，CKIPlabBERT 降低約 5%，*PCC* 也增加約 17%。

Model / Experiment	Valence		Arousal	
	MAE	*PCC*	*MAE*	*PCC*
CKIPlab_BERT / EXP3	0.767	0.814	0.983	0.480
CKIPlabBERT / EXP6	0.857	0.766	0.982	0.443

表 11：CKIPlabBERT 模型與 EXP3 和 EXP6 超參數組合在測試集的評估結果

由於在提交測試集的預測結果時，無從得知測試集答案，就標準實驗流程而言，根據本研究中預測集所表現最好的 DistilBERT 模型作為當前的最佳模型，並提交該最佳模型在測試集的預測結果，固然在測試集的效果是 CKIPlabBERT 模型較佳，但也無法作為最終被挑選為最終預測模型。

4 結論

本研究已經提出了一種有效的訓練樣本擴充方法。根據情感字詞的特性，透過預訓練的 Word2Vec 模型找尋相似字詞，以及與情感較相關的詞性進行篩選，限縮替換範圍，將可以使替換之字詞聚焦於情感方面，避免過度發散，意味著有效的控制替換字詞的品質，也就可以產生高品質的擴充句子。除了訓練樣本擴充可帶來效果外，本研究也再次證實，相較於機器學習模型，較為新進的 DistilBERT 模型可以有效的提升 VA 的預測效果，甚至根據測試集的評估可以得知，專門為繁體中文所預訓練的 CKIPlabBERT 模型可以更進一步獲得改善。總之，未來研究仍可以朝向資料擴充法的探索，像是採用 Generative Adversarial Network 作為仿生句子的訓練，達到更具多樣性的擴充句子，並保有合適的 VA 情感分數。

參考文獻

Connor Shorten and Taghi M. Khoshgoftaar. 2019. A survey on Image Data Augmentation for Deep Learning. *Journal of Big Data, 6, Article number: 60.* https://doi.org/10.1186/s40537-019-0197-0.

Corinna Cortes and Vladimir Vapnik. 1995. Support-Vector Networks. *Machine Learning volume 20,* pages 273–297.

James A. Russell. 1980. A circumplex model of affect. *Journal of Personality and Social Psychology,* 39(6):1161. https://doi.org/10.1037/h0077714.

Jacob Devlin, Ming-Wei Chang, Kenton Lee, and Kristina Toutanova. 2018. *BERT: Pre-training of Deep Bidirectional Transformers for Language Understanding. Computation and Language.* arXiv:1810.04805. Version 2.

Juan Ramos. 2003. Using TF-IDF to Determine Word Relevance in Document Queries.

Jason Wei and Kai Zou. 2019. *EDA: Easy data augmentation techniques for boosting performance on text classification tasks. Computation and Language*, arXiv:1901.11196. Version 2.

Liang-Chih Yu, Lung-Hao Lee, Shuai Hao, Jin Wang, Yunchao He, Jun Hu, K. Robert Lai, and Xuejie Zhang. 2016. Building Chinese affective resources in valence-arousal dimensions. In *Proceedings of NAACL/HLT-16*, pages 540-545.

Liang-Chih Yu, Lung-Hao Lee, Jin Wang, and Kam-Fai Wong. 2017. IJCNLP-2017 Task 2: Dimensional Sentiment Analysis for Chinese Phrases. In *Proceedings of IJCNLP-17*, Shared Tasks, pages 9-16.

Peter Turney. 2002. Thumbs Up or Thumbs Down? Semantic Orientation Applied to Unsupervised Classification of Reviews. In *Proceedings of the 40th Annual Meeting of the Association for Computational Linguistics, Philadelphia, Pennsylvania,* pages 417-424. https://doi.org/10.3115/1073083.1073153.

Peng-Hsuan Li, Tsu-Jui Fu, and Wei-Yun Ma. 2020. Why Attention? Analyze BiLSTM Deficiency and Its Remedies in the Case of NER. In *Proceedings of AAAI 2020. Computation and Language,* arXiv:1908.11046. Version 3.

Tomas Mikolov, Kai Chen, Greg Corrado, and Jeffrey Dean. 2013. *Efficient estimation of word representations in vector space. Computation and Language*, arXiv:1301.3781. Version 3.

Thomas Wolf, Lysandre Debut, Victor Sanh, Julien Chaumond, Clement Delangue, Anthony Moi, Pierric Cistac, et al. 2020. Transformers: State-of-the-Art Natural Language Processing. In *Proceedings of the 2020 Conference on Empirical Methods in Natural Language Processing: System Demonstrations*. Association for Computational Linguistics, pages 38-45. https://aclanthology.org/2020.emnlp-demos.6.

The 33rd Conference on Computational Linguistics and Speech Processing (ROCLING 2021)
Taoyuan, Taiwan, October 15-16, 2021. The Association for Computational Linguistics and Chinese Language Processing

ntust-nlp-1 at ROCLING-2021 Shared Task: Educational Texts Dimensional Sentiment Analysis using Pretrained Language Models

王繹崴
Yi-Wei Wang
國立台灣科技大學
Nation Taiwan University of Science and Technology

張維哲
Wei-Zhe Chang
國立台灣科技大學
Nation Taiwan University of Science and Technology

方柏翰
Bo-Han Fang
國立台灣科技大學
Nation Taiwan University of Science and Technology

陳奕嘉
Yi-Chia Chen
國立台灣科技大學
Nation Taiwan University of Science and Technology

黃偉愷
Wei-Kai Huang
國立台灣科技大學
Nation Taiwan University of Science and Technology

陳冠宇
Kuan-Yu Chen
國立台灣科技大學
Nation Taiwan University of Science and Technology

摘要

本研究為 Rocling 2021 共同任務：教育文本的維度式情感分析之成果報告。為了分析中文文本的情緒效價(Valence)與喚起程度(Arousal)，本研究基於當前流行的預訓練語言模型 BERT 與近期基於全詞遮蔽(Whole Word Masking)進行預訓練的 MacBERT，觀察模型在不同設定下的預測成果，並比較 BERT 與 MacBERT 在中文文本情緒預測效能的差異。我們發現，相較於 BERT，MacBERT 可以在驗證集上獲得些許的效能提升。因此，我們將數個使用不同訓練方法所得的預測模型進行預測結果平均，作為最終的輸出。

Abstract

This technical report aims at the ROCLING 2021 Shared Task: Dimensional Sentiment Analysis for Educational Texts. In order to predict the affective states of Chinese educational texts, we present a practical framework by employing pre-trained language models, such as BERT and MacBERT. Several valuable observations and analyses can be drawn from a series of experiments. From the results, we find that MacBERT-based methods can deliver better results than BERT-based methods on the verification set. Therefore, we average the prediction results of several models obtained using different settings as the final output.

關鍵字：情感分析、預訓練語言模型、BERT、MacBERT

Keywords: Sentiment Analysis, Pre-trained Language Model, BERT, MacBERT

1 緒論 (Introduction)

情緒分析已經是自然語言處理中備受矚目的任務之一，屬於文本分類的子任務，目標在於面對不同的文本時，能夠辨識出文本所欲表達的各類情緒量值，比如：正面、負面、情緒高漲、情緒低落等(Wei et al., 2011; Malandrakis et al., 2013; Wang et al., 2016; Du and Zhang, 2016; Wu et la., 2017; Yu et al., 2020, Kim et al., 2010; Paltoglou et al, 2013; Goel et la., 2017; Zhu et al., 2019; Wang et al., 2019; 2020)。情緒辨識可以廣泛地應用在我們的生活中，比如：分析網路上的社群評論、售後產品的相關回饋、客服機器人的應答等。

此次的共同任務：教育文本的維度式情感分析，其目標在於分析出中文教育文本中的喚起程度(Arousal)以及效價程度(Valence) (Russell, 1980)，其中喚起程度的高低意味著語者是興奮或是平靜，而效價程度則是代表語者自身處於積極或是消極的態度(Patricia E. G. Bestelmeyer, 2017)。預訓練語言模型，能夠為文本萃取出含有豐富語意資訊的特徵向量，而這個特徵向量可被應用於其它下游任務中，完成各式不同的自然語言處理任務。因此在本次任務中，我們將會使用 BERT (Jac ob Devlin, 2018)與 MacBERT (Yiming Cui, 2020)作為文件的編碼器，透過編碼器產生具有語意資訊的特徵向量，接著將其輸入至下游任務的模型內，讓模型在預測喚起程度以及效價程度時，可以獲得更佳精確的結果。

2 研究背景 (Research Background)

在本章節中，我們將會介紹在自然語言處理任務中，處理文本資料時常會使用到的重要技術-詞嵌入。此外，由於本次任務為分數預測，屬於回歸任務的一種，因此在本章節中也會對回歸任務進行介紹。最後，在本章節的末段，我們將會介紹近年來在各項自然語言處理任務中大放異彩的預訓練語言模型-BERT 及其衍生模型 MacBERT。

2.1 詞嵌入 (Word Embedding)

詞嵌入的核心概念為「將一個單詞透過一個向量進行表示」。近年來較為熟悉的相關研究有 word2vec (Tomas Mikolov, 2013)、fast-text (Armand Joulin, 2016)和 Glove (Jeffrey Pennington, 2014) 。上述的這些研究都使用各自的方法將文字表達成向量，也成功地在很多自然語言處理任務上達到優秀的成果。不過這些詞嵌入的方法在「相同單詞但是不同語意」的時候，其表示向量卻是一樣的，為了解決此一問題，後續研究提出各式「動態」的詞嵌入表示法，比如：Cove (Bryan McCann, 2017)、ELMo (Matthew E. Peters, 2018)和 BERT (Jacob Devlin, 2018)。這種類型的詞嵌入方法會透過一個語言模型，將輸入文本根據其內容的語意，給予每一個詞一個基於上下文的詞嵌入表示向量(Enkhbold Bataa, 2019)。

2.2 回歸任務 (Regression)

回歸任務是讓機器根據訓練集的資料，學習如何為輸入的資料抽取特徵，並利用這些特徵資訊，轉換成正確的標記數值。本次的任務是分析輸入文本的喚起程度(Arousal)以及效價程度(Valence)，因此我們將這個任務視為一個回歸任務。

2.3 BERT

BERT 為 Bidirectional Encoder Representation from Transformer 的簡稱，為相當經典的預訓練語言模型，其架構為多層的 Bidirectional Transformer 層，而 BERT 在訓練上分為預訓練(Pre-training)與微調(fine-tuning)兩個步驟。在預訓練步驟裡，會使用大量的無標記文本來訓練 BERT 模型，而訓練方式則包括遮罩語言模型(Masked Language Model)以及下一句預測任務(Next Sentence Prediction)。在遮罩語言模型的任務中，會有一部分的字符(token)隨機的被遮罩或是替換成類似的字符，而模型必須去預測遮罩處的正確字符為何。下一句預測則是讓模型去判斷兩個連續的句子，後一句是否確實是接在前一句之後。在微調階段，模型將被訓練於解決目標任務。相較於預訓練，模型微調使用少量的標記資料，來對模型參數進行調整，使其得以符合下游任務的需求。

2.4 MacBERT

MacBERT(MLM as correlation BERT)是一個特別針對中文語言處理所設計的中文預訓練模型，跟 BERT 不同的地方在於：

- MacBERT 在填空部分使用全詞遮蔽(Whole Word Masking)，也就是在進行遮罩的時候，是以詞為遮罩單位而非單一個字符(token)為單位，避免一些連貫性很強的字符序列，就算被遮罩一部分，模型仍可輕易地預測出被遮罩的部分。

- 在遮罩方式上，追加使用 N 元遮罩(N-gram Masking)以及 Mac 遮罩(Mac-Masking)。N 元遮罩即將連續的 N 個字符一起遮罩；Mac 遮罩則是將所有被遮罩的字符都以向量上相近的字符作為替代，而非單純的$< mask >$符號，這是考慮到$< mask >$是不會出現在下游任務的。

- MacBERT 並非選擇使用預測下一句作為預訓練的任務，而是以語句順序判斷(Sentence Order Prediction)作為訓練目標。在語句順序判斷的任務中，模型必須辨識出兩句連續句子之間的先後關係。

以上三種與 BERT 不同的預訓練方式，使得 MacBERT 更能夠彌補預訓練階段與下游任務的差異性，也使得 MacBERT 在不同任務的中文資料集上都能夠得到比 BERT 還要優秀的成績。

3 方法 (Methods)

有鑑於近年來人工智慧、深度學習相關技術的蓬勃發展，尤其是 BERT 及其衍生模型在各式自然語言處理相關任務上大放異彩，刷新了各項成績。因此，在本研究中，我們將使用 BERT 及其衍生模型 MacBERT 進行後續實驗與討論，探究預訓練語言模型在中文教育文本的維度式情感分析任務上的成效。

3.1 模型架構 (Model Architectures)

圖 1 為本研究所使用之模型架構。在模型的輸入方面，我們在字符序列的最前面加上一個特別的字符$[CLS]$，在後續的分數預測時，我們則將這個特別字符的向量輸入至全連接層，分別得到輸入句子所對應之情緒效價與喚起程度的預測分數。

3.2 模型訓練 (Model Training)

由於本次任務屬於回歸任務，因此在誤差函式的設計方面，我們使用均方誤差(Mean Square Error, MSE)計算模型預測出的情緒效價分數V_i、喚起程度分數A_i，與正確答案$\widehat{V_i}$與$\widehat{A_i}$的誤差，並透過此誤差來優化模型的參數，完成模型的訓練：

$$MSE = \frac{1}{n}\sum_{i=1}^{n}(V_i - \widehat{V_i})^2 + (A_i - \widehat{A_i})^2 \quad (1)$$

在模型訓練方面，我們使用多種方法來對模型進行訓練，方法包括將多個模型參數進行平均、多個模型預測結果平均、使用模型預測的結果當作虛擬標籤，並將虛擬標籤資料與原始訓練資料結合，進行二次訓練等方法。我們將於第四章節中詳細描述各個訓練方法的實作細節，並且比較各個方法所訓練出來的模型在驗證資料及測試資料上的效能表現。

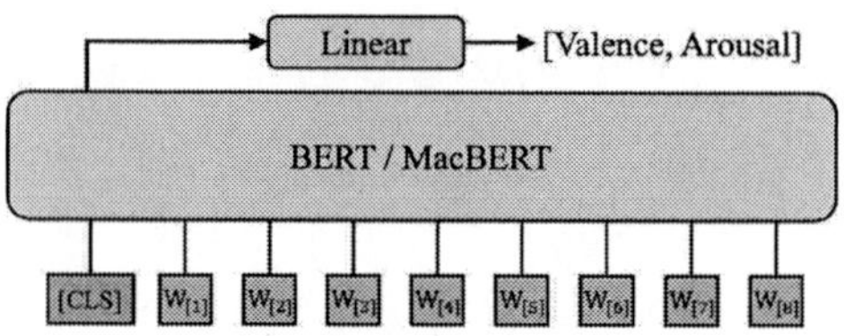

圖 1. 模型架構圖。

4 實驗 (Experiments)

在實驗的部分，我們使用了 5 種不同的設定方法，訓練出了 5 個子模型。而最終的輸出，則是這 5 個子模型的預測數值之平均。在本節中，我們將展示實作細節以及在測試集上模型集成（Ensemble）的結果。

4.1 訓練資料 (Training Data)

我們將 CVAW 4.0 的 5,512 個詞及 CVAP 2.0 的 2,998 個片語以及從 CVAT 2.0 的 2,969 個句子中抽取出 80%（2,375 筆）的句子合併作為訓練集；CVAT 2.0 剩餘的 20%（594 筆）個句子作為驗證集。經上述處理後，訓練集共有 10,885 筆文件，驗證集則有 594 筆資料。

4.2 子模型 (Sub-models)

各式子模型架構皆如表 1 所示，我們採用 BERT 或 MacBERT 作為基礎，藉由不同的訓練方法與設定，產生六個不同的子模型。

- **方法 1**：使用 BERT-base[1]作為基礎模型，採用 Adam 做為模型優化器，共迭代訓練 20 次，並使用 Noam(Ashish Vaswani, 2017)學習率調整器，再將 warmup_steps 設定為 25,000 來調整訓練時的學習率。最終，我們將訓練過程中，在驗證集上誤差最低的 5 個模型參數進行平均，作為最終的模型參數。

- **方法 2**：與方法 1 相同，只是基礎模型用 MacBERT-base[2]。

- **方法 3**：與方法 2 一樣使用 MacBERT-base 作為基礎模型，選擇 SGD 作為優化器，並迭代 5 次，而學習率固定為 1e-3。之後，我們額外加入 dianping[3]資料集做

[1] https://huggingface.co/bert-base-chinese
[2] https://huggingface.co/hfl/chinese-macbert-base
[3] https://github.com/zhangxiangxiao/glyph

	Mean Absolute Error		Pearson Correlation Coefficient	
Sub-models	Valence	Arousal	Valence	Arousal
方法 1	0.463	0.614	0.890	0.674
方法 2	0.442	0.634	0.895	0.659
方法 3	0.514	0.679	0.880	0.624
方法 4	0.487	0.649	0.885	0.664
方法 5	0.469	0.623	0.888	0.667
方法 6	0.477	0.662	0.900	0.637

表 1：驗證集結果

	Mean Absolute Error		Pearson Correlation Coefficient	
	Valence	Arousal	Valence	Arousal
方法 1	0.586	0.885	0.901	0.585
集成模型	0.684	0.906	0.912	0.607
CYUT-run1	1.695	1.177	-0.017	0.040
CYUT-run2	1.685	1.252	0.007	-0.021
NCU-NLP-run1	0.625	0.938	0.900	0.549
NCU-NLP-run2	0.611	0.989	0.904	0.582
ntust-nlp-2-run1	0.654	0.880	0.905	0.581
ntust-nlp-2-run2	0.667	0.866	0.913	0.616
SCUDS-run1	0.953	1.054	0.694	0.375
SCUDS-run2	0.975	1.039	0.667	0.354
SoochowDS-run1	2.421	1.327	0.073	0.051
SoochowDS-run2	1.073	1.125	0.584	0.228

表 2：測試集結果

偽標籤（Pseudo Labeling），迭代 5 次，學習率固定為 1e-4。

- **方法 4：**與方法 2 一樣使用 MacBERT-base 作為基礎模型，迭代 20 次後，選出在驗證集上誤差最低的 4 個模型，我們將這四個模型的輸出結果取平均，作為最終的輸出。與方法 2 不同的是，方法 4 是對輸出結果做平均，而方法 2 是對模型參數做平均。
- **方法 5：**使用 BERT-base-uncased[4]、RoBERTa-wwm-ext[5]、MacBERT-base 作為基礎模型，三種基礎模型皆使用 Adam 優化器，學習率 2e-5，各自迭代 3 次後，選出在驗證集上誤差最低的模型參數。我們將 BERT、RoBERTa 與 MacBERT 輸出的結果取平均，作為最終的輸出。
- **方法 6：**使用 MacBERT-large[6]作為基礎模型，採用 SGD 為優化器迭代 12 次，學習率固定為 1e-4。我們將訓練集透過 word 軟體分別翻譯成英文、法文、德文、日文、俄語、義大利文後再翻譯回中文，因此相較於其他方法，方法 6 的訓練資料量擴增至原本的 7 倍。

4.3 實驗結果 (Experimental Results)

表 1 為各子模型在驗證集上的實驗結果。由於共同任務最終僅能繳交兩組系統，因此我們保留方法 1，作為一組系統；此外，我們將方法 2 至方法 6 的預測結果取平均，作為一個集成系統，當成第二組輸出。表 2 為方法 1 以及集成模型在測試集上的結果。

從表 2 中的數據可以發現，集成模型的均方誤差比方法 1 還要高，我們推測原因可能來自於：

[4] https://huggingface.co/bert-base-uncased
[5] https://huggingface.co/hfl/chinese-roberta-wwm-ext
[6] https://huggingface.co/hfl/chinese-macbert-large

- 方法 2 至方法 6 所訓練出來的子模型效能表現參差不一，觀察表 1，除了方法 2 之外，其餘方法的結果皆明顯比方法 1 差，因此即便進行預測結果整合，也無法彌補模型效能上的缺陷，導致預測結果不盡理想。

- 經觀察測試資料後，我們發現測試資料中的句子與訓練資料中的句子形式上有所差異。測試資料中的句子長度普遍較短，且內容相較於訓練資料差異較大。因此我們認為另一個照成集成模型效能較差的原因是集成模型的預測結果過於 overfitting 在訓練資料上，因此在測試資料上的預測表現不是很好。

5 結論 (Conclusions)

在 Rocling 2021 共同任務：教育文本的維度式情感分析的任務中，我們的方法 1 在情緒效價與喚起程度的均方誤差分別為 0.586 與 0.885，他們的皮爾森相關係數則分別為 0.901 與 0.585。與其他隊伍相較，我們成功取得本次共同任務裡最低的情緒效價均方誤差。因而證實我們所提出的方法能在教育文本的維度式情感分析的任務上擁有較好的效能表現。

Acknowledgment

This work was supported by the Ministry of Science and Technology of Taiwan under Grant MOST 110-2636-E-011-003 (Young Scholar Fellowship Program). We thank to National Center for High-performance Computing (NCHC) for providing computational and storage resources.

References

Patricia E. G. Bestelmeyer, Sonja A. Kotz, and Pascal Belin. 2017. *Effects of emotional valence and arousal on the voice perception network https://www.ncbi.nlm.nih.gov/pmc/articles/PMC5597854/pdf/nsx059.pdf*

Yiming Cui, Wanxiang Che, Ting Liu, Bing Qin, Shijin Wang, and Guoping Hu. 2020. *Revisiting pre-trained models for chinese natural language processing*. In Findings of EMNLP. Association for Computational Linguistics.

Jacob Devlin, Ming-Wei Chang, Kenton Lee, and Kristina Toutanova. 2018. *Bert: Pre-training of deep bidirectional transformers for language understanding*. In arXiv preprint arXiv: 1810.04805v2

Tomas Mikolov, Kai Chen, Greg Corrado and Jeffrey Dean. 2013. *Efficient Estimation of Word Representations in Vector Space*. In arXiv preprint arXiv: 1301.3781v3

Armand Joulinm Edouard Grave, Piotr Bojanowski and Tomas Mikolov. 2016. *Bag of Tricks for Efficient Text Classification*. In arXiv preprint arXiv:1607.01759v3

Jeffrey Pennington, Richard Socher and Christopher D. Manning. 2014. *GloVe: Global Vectors for Word Representation*. https://aclanthology.org/D14-1162.pdf

Bryan McCann, James Bradbury, Caiming Xiong and Richard Socher. 2017. *Learned in Translation: Contextualized Word Vectors* https://papers.nips.cc/paper/2017/file/20c86a628232a67e7bd46f76fba7ce12-Paper.pdf

Matthew E. Peters†, Mark Neumann†, Mohit Iyyer†, Matt Gardner†, Christopher Clark*, Kenton Lee* and Luke Zettlemoyer†*. 2018. *Deep contextualized word representations*. In arXiv preprint arXiv:1802.05365v2

Enkhbold Bataa and Joshua Wu. 2019. *An Investigation of Transfer Learning-Based Sentiment Analysis in Japanese* https://aclanthology.org/P19-1458.pdf

Ashish Vaswani, Noam Shazeer, Niki Parmar, Jakob Uszkoreit, Llion Jones, Aidan N. Gomez, Łukasz Kaiser and Illia Polosukhin. 2017. *Attention Is All You Need*. In arXiv preprint arXiv:1706.03762v5

Rafael A. Calvo, and Sunghwan Mac Kim. 2013. Emotions in text: dimensional and categorical models. Computational Intelligence, 29(3):527-543. https://www.dhi.ac.uk/san/waysofbeing/data/health-jones-calvo-2013a.pdf

James A. Russell. 1980. A circumplex model of affect. Journal of Personality and Social Psychology, 39(6):1161.

Wen-Li Wei, Chung-Hsien Wu, and Jen-Chun Lin. 2011. A regression approach to affective rating of Chinese words from ANEW. In Proc. of ACII-11, pages 121-131.

N. Malandrakis, A. Potamianos, E. Iosif, and S. Narayanan. 2013. Distributional semantic models for affective text analysis. IEEE Transactions on Audio, Speech, and Language Processing, 21(11): 2379-2392.

Liang-Chih Yu, Lung-Hao Lee, Shuai Hao, Jin Wang, Yunchao He, Jun Hu, K. Robert Lai, and Xuejie Zhang. 2016a. Building Chinese affective resources in valence-arousal dimensions. In Proc. of NAACL/HLT-16, pages 540-545.

Steven Du and Xi Zhang. 2016. Aicyber's system for IALP 2016 shared task: Character-enhanced word vectors and Boosted Neural Networks, in Proc. of IALP-16, pages 161–163.

Chuhan Wu, Fangzhao Wu, Yongfeng Huang, Sixing Wu and Zhigang Yuan. 2017. THU NGN at IJCNLP-2017 Task 2: Dimensional sentiment analysis for Chinese phrases with deep LSTM, in Proc. of IJCNLP-17, pages 42-52.

Liang-Chih Yu, Jin Wang, K. Robert Lai and Xuejie Zhang. 2020. Pipelined neural networks for phrase-level sentiment intensity prediction, IEEE Transactions on Affective Computing, 11(3), 447-458.

Sunghwan Mac Kim, Alessandro Valitutti, and Rafael A. Calvo. 2010. Evaluation of unsupervised emotion models to textual affect recognition. In Proc. of the NAACL HLT 2010 Workshop on Computational Approaches to Analysis and Generation of Emotion in Text, pages 62-70.

Georgios Paltoglou, Mathias Theunis, Arvid Kappas, and Mike Thelwall. 2013. Predicting emotional responses to long informal text. IEEE Trans. Affective Computing, 4(1):106-115.

Pranav Goel, Devang Kulshreshtha, Prayas Jain and Kaushal Kumar Shukla. 2017. Prayas at EmoInt 2017: An Ensemble of Deep Neural Architectures for Emotion Intensity Prediction in Tweets, in Proc. of WASSA-17, pages 58–65.

Suyang Zhu, Shoushan Li and Guodong Zhou. 2019. Adversarial attention modeling for multi-dimensional emotion regression, in Proc. of ACL-19, pages 471–480.

Jin Wang, Liang-Chih Yu, K. Robert Lai and Xuejie Zhang. 2016. Community-based weighted graph model for valence-arousal prediction of affective words, IEEE/ACM Trans. Audio, Speech and Language Processing, 24(11):1957-1968.

Jin Wang, Liang-Chih Yu, K. Robert Lai and Xuejie Zhang. 2020. Tree-structured regional CNN- LSTM model for dimensional sentiment analysis, IEEE/ACM Transactions on Audio Speech and Language Processing, 28, 581–591.

The 33rd Conference on Computational Linguistics and Speech Processing (ROCLING 2021)
Taoyuan, Taiwan, October 15-16, 2021. The Association for Computational Linguistics and Chinese Language Processing

ntust-nlp-2 at ROCLING-2021 Shared Task: BERT-based semantic analyzer with word-level information

盧克函
Ke-Han Lu
國立臺灣科技大學
National Taiwan University
of Science and Technology
khlu@nlp.csie.ntust.edu.tw

陳冠宇
Kuan-Yu Chen
國立臺灣科技大學
National Taiwan University
of Science and Technology
kychen@ntust.edu.tw

摘要

本論文提出基於 BERT 架構之維度式情感辨識器，透過增加基於詞層級的資訊，我們的模型在「ROCLING 2021 共享任務：教學文本之維度式情感辨識」四項指標中拿到了三項最佳成績。通過一連串的實驗，我們比較了不同預訓練方法對於結果的影響，也證明了我們基於預訓練模型所提出的方法，顯著的改進了模型的表現，最後我們針對實驗結果，提出關於模型和資料集的深入分析與討論。

Abstract

In this paper, we proposed a BERT-based dimensional semantic analyzer, which is designed by incorporating with word-level information. Our model achieved three of the best results in four metrics on "ROCLING 2021 Shared Task: Dimensional Sentiment Analysis for Educational Texts". We conducted a series of experiments to compare the effectiveness of different pretrained methods. Besides, the results also proofed that our method can significantly improve the performances than classic methods. Based on the experiments, we also discussed the impact of model architectures and datasets.

關鍵字：情感辨識、預訓練語言模型、BERT

Keywords: Semantic analysis, Pretrained Language Model, BERT

1 緒論

情感辨識一直是自然語言處理領域中相當熱門的研究方向，可分爲分類式及維度式的情感辨識任務 (Calvo and Kim, 2013)。分類式的情感辨識爲將情緒分爲不同類別，如：快樂、悲傷、憤怒、厭惡等；維度式的情感辨識則是將情緒表示爲不同維度中的不同尺度，如：可以將一個詞 (Wei et al., 2011; Malandrakis et al., 2013; Wang et al., 2016; Du and Zhang, 2016; Wu et al., 2017; Yu et al., 2020) 或一串句子 (Kim et al., 2010; Paltoglou et al., 2013; Goel et al., 2017; Zhu et al., 2019; Wang et al., 2020) 的情緒表示於以正負性（Valence）與喚醒度（Arousal）組成的二維空間中 (Russell, 1980)，如圖1所示，其中正負性代表情緒的正面、負面程度，而喚醒度是指情緒的激動程度。

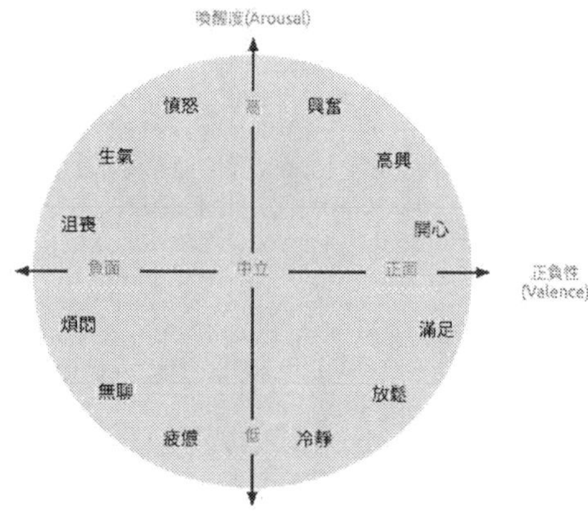

圖 1: 正負性—喚醒度空間

在教育現場，老師們常需要評估學生的學習狀況，常見的方法有出席率、考試成績、課堂發言次數等結構性的資料，而非結構性的資料，像是學生的自我評述，不僅可能紀錄著上課與課後的點點滴滴，也可能含有學生對這門課與老師的評價與回饋，豐富的情感資訊通常蘊含其中。爲了探究機器是否可以準確地自動分析這類文本，ROCLING 2021 提出了一個共享任務：教學文本之維度式情感辨識（ROCLING 2021 Shared Task: Dimensional Sentiment Analysis for Educational Texts），目標爲對學生的評語文本進行維度式的情感評分，也就是需將一段句子映射到正負性—喚醒度的空間中。

在這個共享任務裡，主辦方所提供的資料集

爲 CVAW 4.0(Yu et al., 2016)、CVAP 2.0(Yu et al., 2017) 及 CVAT 2.0(Yu et al., 2016)，分別爲單詞、片語、句子所對應的正負性與喚醒度，我們將在第2章介紹資料集的蒐集方式與特性。評估模型的方式爲預測分數與標記分數的平均絕對誤差 (Mean Absolute Error) 與皮爾森相關係數 (Pearson Correlation Coefficient)。第3章介紹我們所提出的基於預訓練 BERT(Devlin et al., 2019) 架構之維度式情感辨識器，除了句子以外，我們將詞層級的正負性與喚醒度作爲額外的訓練目標去微調最終的模型。我們使用了不同預訓練方法，包含 BERT(Devlin et al., 2019)、RoBERTa(Liu et al., 2019) 與 MacBERT(Cui et al., 2020) 以驗證我們方法的有效性。第4章展示了我們模型參數設定及實驗細節。最後，在第5章我們分析了不同預訓練方法對於此任務的影響，也證明了我們所提出的方法有效的增強了模型的表現。在測試集的表現上我們的方法可以在四項指標中獲得其中三項指標最好的成績。此外，我們更進一步地對模型及資料集做了深入的討論。

2 資料集

本研究僅使用由主辦方提供的 CVAW 4.0、CVAP 2.0 及 CVAT 2.0，上述資料集爲搜集文本後由數位標記員分別根據相同標準標記，在剔除標記差距過大的資料後整理而成，表1爲從資料中選取的範例。

CVAW 4.0: 包含 5,512 個常見與情緒有關的單詞。

CVAP 2.0: 共 2,998 個以副詞、動詞、形容詞所組成之片語，包含不同程度（如：極度、非常、略微等）、帶有懷疑（如：也許、可能、應該等）、反向（如：不、沒有、不能等）等不同排列組合的修飾。

CVAT 2.0: 共 2,969 則對於書本、旅館評論、汽車討論、電腦討論、新聞、政治評論等六類的評價內容，大部份是網路上蒐集的句子，平均長度爲 57.515，99.8% 句子中包含 CVAW 4.0 或 CVAP 2.0 所出現的單詞或片語。

3 方法

3.1 Baseline 模型

我們將維度式情感辨識任務視爲一種迴歸任務，採用基於 BERT 架構的模型，以 CLS Token 的輸出，輸入迴歸器得到預測的結果。

更明確地，我們首先將一個輸入的中文句子表示爲一連串的 Token 序列 $W = \{w_{\text{cls}}, w_1, ..., w_{|T|}, w_{\text{sep}}\}$，其中 w_{cls} 與 w_{sep} 爲兩個特殊的 Token 分別插入在句首與句尾。接著，經過嵌入層（Embedding Layer），W 可以轉換爲一連串的向量表示法（Embeddings）$E = \{e_{\text{cls}}, e_1, ..., e_{|T|}, e_{\text{sep}}\}$。然後，我們將 E 輸入數層的 Transformer 後，以對應於 w_{cls} 之輸出 h_{cls} 作爲此一輸入文本的向量表示法，藉由經過一層前饋神經網路（Feed-forward Neural Network），得到迴歸預測的數值：

$$H = \text{BERT}(E)$$
$$[y^v, y^a] = \text{FFN}(h_{\text{cls}})$$

$[y^v, y^a]$ 爲模型所預測之正負性及喚醒度。爲了達成此一目的，在模型訓練方面，我們使用均方根誤差（Mean Square Error, MSE）計算預測與答案之間的誤差，並以此作爲模型訓練的目標函數：

$$\mathcal{L}_t = \text{MSE}([y^v, y^a], [\hat{y}^v, \hat{y}^a])$$

其中，$\hat{y}^v$ 和 $\hat{y}^a$ 表示正負性及喚醒度的正確答案。

3.2 Enhanced 模型

我們注意到在訓練資料集 CVAT 2.0 中，有 99.8% 的句子含有 CVAW 4.0 及 CVAP 2.0 所出現的詞，且目標文本 (測試集) 可能存在與訓練資料分佈不同的情況，因此若將情感詞作爲額外的資訊，應可以提升預測結果的準確性。

爲了讓模型不只是學到如何爲句子評分，也同時能學到句子中出現的詞的情感分數，我們基於 Baseline 系統，額外地增加了以詞的正負性、喚醒度爲迴歸目標的增強式模型，模型架構如圖2所示。更明確地，我們首先抽取句子中最多 k 個長度小於 m 的詞或片語 $\{w_1, ..., w_k\}$，其方法如演算法1所示，這些詞或片語會以 SEP token 隔開，串接在原始的句子詞嵌入序列之後 $\hat{E} = \{e_{\text{cls}}, e_1, ..., e_{|T|}, e_{\text{sep}}, e_{w_{11}}, e_{w_{12}}, ..., e_{w_{km}}, e_{\text{sep}}\}$，其中 $e_{w_{ij}}$ 表示爲第 i 個詞的第 j 個 Token，由於每個詞經過分詞器可能表示爲多個 Token，我們將每個詞所對應到的 Transformer 輸出取平均，再經過共享參數的前饋神經網路，得到

資料集	文本	正負性	喚醒度
CVAW 4.0	開心	7.2	6.6
	愉快	7	4.8
	溫柔	6.6	4.2
	廢物	2.9	6.0
	於事無補	1.7	3.4
CVAP 2.0	極度失望	1.630	7.244
	非常失望	2.000	7.00
	略微失望	2.313	5.870
CVAT 2.0	(Book) 故事情節的發展，我心中甜蜜，酸楚，失落，幸福	5.125	4.571
	(Hotel) 服務好，前臺接待員挺熱情	6.667	4.111
	(News) 新竹縣一名 55 歲男子，曾持刀刺傷父親也曾放火燒屋，他這個月 6 日不滿父親拒喝湯，竟然把熱湯潑在父親身上，再動手痛毆父親，造成老父 2 根肋骨斷裂住院。	1.875	6.875
測試集	不知道爲什麼要趕課，一直跳投影片，都不知道重點在哪	1.75	7.08
	今天教了許多以前沒有學過的東西，所以上起課來很新鮮	6.8	5.2
	覺得課程進度有點快，內容難以消化	3.0	4.0

表 1: 各個資料集的範例資料。註：在比賽結束後才得到測試集的標記。

演算法 1

```
procedure ExtractEmotion(T)
    S ← {}
    P ← {...}            ▷ 依長度排列之片語和詞
    i ← 0
    while i < len(T) and S.size() < k do
        j ← min(m, len(T) − i))
        while j > 0 do
            s ← T[i : i + j]
            if s ∈ P then
                S ← S ∪ {s}
                i ← i + j − 1
                break
            end if
            j ← j − 1
        end while
        i ← i + 1
    end while
    return S
end procedure
```

該詞的預測結果：

$$H = \mathrm{BERT}(\hat{E})$$

$$h_{w_i} = \mathrm{Mean}([h_{w_{i1}}, ..., h_{w_{im}}])$$

$$[y^v_{w_i}, y^a_{w_i}] = \mathrm{FFN}(h_{w_i}), i \in \{1, ..., k\}$$

$$\mathcal{L} = (1-\alpha)\mathcal{L}_t + \alpha \sum_{i=1}^{k} \mathrm{MSE}([y^v_{w_i}, y^a_{w_i}], [\hat{y}^v_{w_i}, \hat{y}^a_{w_i}])$$

最終，我們以超參數 α 調節 $\mathcal{L}_t$ 與我們新加入的目標函數之訓練比重。

4 實驗設置

4.1 資料前處理

將所有資料（CVAT 2.0、CVAP 2.0 與 CVAW 4.0）使用 Microsoft Office Word 從繁體中文轉爲簡體中文，並將 CVAT 2.0 中 20% 的資料隨機切割作爲發展集，剩餘 80 % 資料作爲訓練集，訓練集共有 2,375 句，發展集則有 594 句，Enhanced 模型使用全部的 CVAP 2.0 和 CVAW 4.0 做爲額外的訓練資料，後續實驗中我們將固定此發展集，以評估不同模型之間的表現。我們也將正負性和喚醒度的標記答案從 1 至 9 分正規化爲 -4 至 4 分，以利模型訓練。

4.2 模型設定

本論文中使用 Huggingface (Wolf et al., 2020) 所提供的 Transformer 架構，以哈工大訊飛聯合實驗室所釋出的預訓練 BERT (chinese-bert-wwm-ext)、RoBERTa (chinese-RoBERTa-wwm-ext) 及 MacBERT (chinese-MacBERT-base) 初始化模型參數。

Baseline 及 Enhanced 模型同樣以學習率（Learning Rate）10^{-4} 與批次大小（Batch Size）80 訓練 7 個 Epoch，以在發展集上均方根誤差最低的模型作爲最優模型，我們注意到不同的隨機種子對訓練結果的影響很大，我們最終展示以三個不同的隨機種子訓練的模型成績之平均。

Enhanced 模型抽取句子中最多 6 個長度小於 6 的詞或片語 (即 $k = 6$ 且 $m = 6$)，輸入時

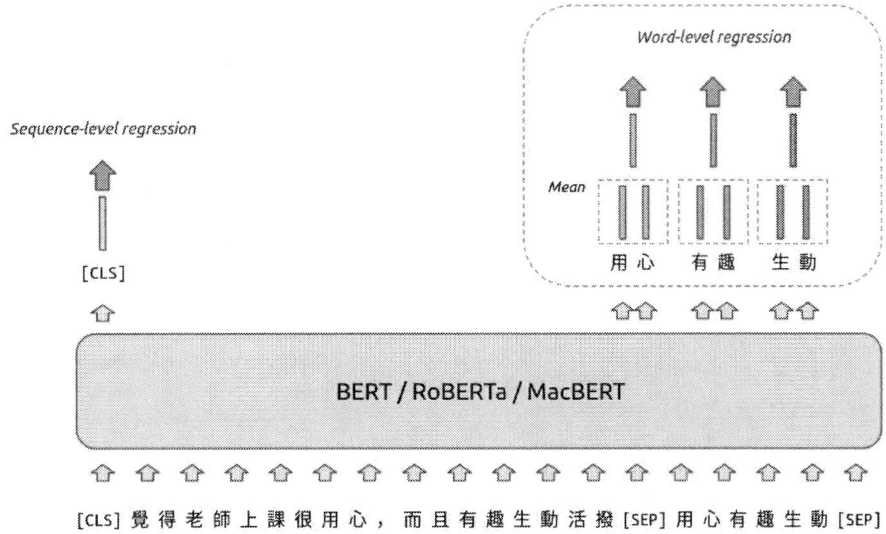

圖 2: Caption

模型	$\text{Valence}_{\text{MAE}}$	$\text{Valence}_{\text{r}}$	$\text{Arousal}_{\text{MAE}}$	$\text{Arousal}_{\text{r}}$
Baseline-BERT	0.518(0.019)	0.871(0.011)	0.694(0.010)	0.585(0.007)
Baseline-RoBERTa	0.497(0.009)	0.886(0.004)	0.691(0.001)	0.590(0.003)
Baseline-MacBERT	0.497(0.015)	0.886(0.007)	0.704(0.007)	0.577(0.009)
Enhanced-BERT	0.489(0.007)	0.890(0.003)	0.676(0.001)	0.610(0.004)
Enhanced-RoBERTa	0.485(0.003)	0.895(0.004)	**0.675(0.000)**	**0.614(0.001)**
Enhanced-MacBERT	**0.480(0.003)**	**0.898(0.001)**	0.679(0.009)	0.613(0.015)

表 2: 以三個不同的隨機種子訓練的模型在發展集上的成績平均（標準差）。

長度不足的部份以 PAD token 補足，輸出時僅計算非 PAD token 之向量平均與損失。超參數 α 設定爲 0.5，調整與傳統目標函數的比例。

4.3 集成學習

基於對實驗的觀察，我們使用兩組集成模型作爲最後測試集的預測。首先，我們用不同的隨機種子切割訓練集與發展集，並訓練了各 5 個不同的 BERT、RoBERTa、MacBERT 共 15 個模型。我們將 5 個 MacBERT 的預測結果平均作爲第一個測試結果；另外，在所訓練的 15 個模型中，剔除每筆資料最大與最小的極值後取平均，作爲第二組測試結果。

5 實驗結果與討論

表2展示 Baseline 模型及 Enhanced 模型在使用不同的預訓練參數所得到的成績，我們以平均絕對誤差（越低越好）與皮爾森相關係數（越高越好）兩個指標來評估模型的表現。

首先，在所有的結果中，Enhanced 模型皆優於 Baseline 模型，代表我們所新增的以詞輔助的迴歸目標，使用了額外的資訊，可以預期無論是正負性或喚醒度都可以帶來正向的影響。

接著我們討論不同維度之間的差異，在正負性的兩個指標中，BERT 模型在 Baseline 及 Enhanced 模型中皆略遜於另兩個模型，RoBERTa 則相同或略遜於 MacBERT。在喚醒度的部份，MacBERT 在三者之中表現最不理想，RoBERTa 有最好的成績。BERT 因爲是最早期的模型，所以我們期待基於 BERT 改進的 RoBERTa 與 MacBERT 表現應該會較優，但從實驗顯示 MacBERT 沒辦法在喚醒度和正負性有相當的表現。

從結果中可以看到正負性的成績皆優於喚醒度的成績，代表喚醒度對我們所設計的模型來說是比較困難的任務。經過人工對資料集的分析，我們認爲喚醒度在標記答案時較爲主觀，相較於正負性來說，較難客觀評估情緒的激動程度，相似的句子可能會有相當不同的標記，即使 MacBERT 可以在 Baseline 及 Enhanced 模型的正負性中取得最好的成績，在喚醒度部份則表現較差，我們猜測原因可能與預訓練

Model	$\text{Valence}_{\text{MAE}}$	$\text{Valence}_{\text{r}}$	$\text{Arousal}_{\text{MAE}}$	$\text{Arousal}_{\text{r}}$
CYUT-run1	1.695	-0.017	1.177	0.040
CYUT-run2	1.685	0.007	1.252	-0.021
NCU-NLP-run1	0.625	0.900	0.938	0.549
NCU-NLP-run2	0.611	0.904	0.989	0.582
ntust-nlp-1-run1	0.684	0.912	0.906	0.607
ntust-nlp-1-run2	**0.586**	0.901	0.885	0.585
SCUDS-run1	0.953	0.694	1.054	0.375
SCUDS-run2	0.975	0.667	1.039	0.354
SoochowDS-run1	2.421	0.073	1.327	0.051
SoochowDS-run2	1.073	0.584	1.125	0.228
Enhanced-MacBERT(X5)	0.654	0.880	0.905	0.581
Enhanced(X15)	0.667	**0.913**	**0.866**	**0.616**

表 3: 提交的測試集結果。註：Enhanced-MacBERT(X5) 與 Enhanced(X15) 分別爲 ntust-nlp-2-run1 與 ntust-nlp-2-run2

資料	正負性	喚醒度
CVAT 2.0	4.80(1.34)	4.84(1.04)
測試集	5.32(1.69)	4.51(1.32)
Ensemble-MacBERT(X5)	5.39(1.10)	4.60(0.54)
Ensemble(X15)	5.41(1.05)	4.65(0.55)

表 4: 資料集與預測結果中的所有資料的平均（標準差）。

的方式有關，MacBERT 在預訓練時將詞彙替換爲相似的詞彙以達到更好的語言模型效果，但在情感辨識任務中，由於標記的主觀性，相似的詞，例如表1中的「開心」與「愉快」，在語意上相近，但在喚醒度卻相差很大，這可能使 MacBERT 無法發揮原本的優勢，而我們所設計的 Enhanced 模型，以詞層級的資訊讓模型學會分辨不同相似詞的情緒關係，修正了 MacBERT 本身的這項缺點。最終提交結果時，我們使用集成學習的方式（請參考4.3節）產生了兩組結果，表3可以看出使用多種模型的效果最佳，但在正負性的平均絕對誤差卻相對表現較差。

經過對測試資料與其標記答案的分析，我們注意到訓練資料和測試資料之間存在明顯的差異。在 CVAT 2.0 中蒐集的內容爲書本、旅館評論、汽車討論、電腦討論、新聞、政治評論等六類內容，其中不乏較激進、狂喜、憤怒的言論；相對地，在測試資料中普遍爲學生的課堂自評，情感上相對訓練資料是比較溫和、集中的。表4顯示了以正確答案計算所得的平均值與標準差，我們將 Ensemble-MacBERT(X5) 與 Ensemble(X15) 兩個模型對於測試集的預測結果，同樣計算平均值與標準差，並列於表4中。透過上述統計，我們發現兩個模型所預測的結果中，正負性平均較 CVAT 2.0 大，反應了學生自評中較多正向句的觀察。而喚醒度標準差明顯較 CVAT 2.0 小很多，代表模型傾向給予測試資料更集中的評分，符合我們前述學生自評情緒較溫和的預期。

當我們進一步地以人工方式檢視資料，發現最終釋出的測試集標記答案與訓練資料有很大的不同，兩個資料集分開來看可以看出各個資料集的分佈類似，但兩者標記的尺度存在不小的差異。舉例來說，如表1所示，訓練資料集中「新竹縣一名 55 歲男子，曾持刀刺傷父親也曾放火燒屋，他這個月 6 日不滿父親拒喝湯，竟然把熱湯潑在父親身上，再動手痛毆父親，造成老父 2 根肋骨斷裂住院。」與測試資料集中「不知道爲什麼要趕課，一直跳投影片，都不知道重點在哪」兩者正負性和喚醒度接近，但以訓練資料的角度來看，測試資料的標記明顯較爲誇大了正負性與喚醒度。

最後，我們比較表2與表3，可以發現發展集及測試集平均絕對誤差有明顯的退步，但皮爾森相關係數卻能保持接近的成績，我們認爲原因就是因爲標記尺度不同，所以模型雖然能依訓練資料的尺度評分，但平均絕對誤差則會大幅退步，不過相關性仍能保有一定的預測水準。

6 結論

我們針對維度式的情感辨識任務「ROCLING 2021 共享任務：教學文本之維度式情感辨識」提出了基於預訓練語言模型 BERT 架構的迴歸模型，測試結果顯示我們的模型可以達到有競爭力的表現，我們也透過一連串的分析，證明我們所提出的模型設計能有比較好的表現，也注意到仍有許多可以改進的問題留待未來繼續研究。

7 Acknowledgment

This work was supported by the Ministry of Science and Technology of Taiwan under Grant MOST 110-2636-E-011-003 (Young Scholar Fellowship Program). We thank to National Center for High-performance Computing (NCHC) for providing computational and storage resources.

References

Rafael A. Calvo and Sunghwan Mac Kim. 2013. Emotions in text: dimensional and categorical models. *Computational Intelligence*, 29(3):527–543.

Yiming Cui, Wanxiang Che, Ting Liu, Bing Qin, Shijin Wang, and Guoping Hu. 2020. Revisiting pre-trained models for Chinese natural language processing. In *Findings of the Association for Computational Linguistics: EMNLP 2020*, pages 657–668, Online. Association for Computational Linguistics.

Jacob Devlin, Ming-Wei Chang, Kenton Lee, and Kristina Toutanova. 2019. BERT: Pre-training of deep bidirectional transformers for language understanding. In *Proceedings of the 2019 Conference of the North American Chapter of the Association for Computational Linguistics: Human Language Technologies, Volume 1 (Long and Short Papers)*, pages 4171–4186, Minneapolis, Minnesota. Association for Computational Linguistics.

Steven Du and Xi Zhang. 2016. Aicyber's system for ialp 2016 shared task: Character-enhanced word vectors and boosted neural networks. In *2016 International Conference on Asian Language Processing (IALP)*, pages 161–163.

Pranav Goel, Devang Kulshreshtha, Prayas Jain, and Kaushal Kumar Shukla. 2017. Prayas at EmoInt 2017: An ensemble of deep neural architectures for emotion intensity prediction in tweets. In *Proceedings of the 8th Workshop on Computational Approaches to Subjectivity, Sentiment and Social Media Analysis*, pages 58–65, Copenhagen, Denmark. Association for Computational Linguistics.

Sunghwan Mac Kim, Alessandro Valitutti, and Rafael A. Calvo. 2010. Evaluation of unsupervised emotion models to textual affect recognition. In *Proceedings of the NAACL HLT 2010 Workshop on Computational Approaches to Analysis and Generation of Emotion in Text*, pages 62–70, Los Angeles, CA. Association for Computational Linguistics.

Yinhan Liu, Myle Ott, Naman Goyal, Jingfei Du, Mandar Joshi, Danqi Chen, Omer Levy, Mike Lewis, Luke Zettlemoyer, and Veselin Stoyanov. 2019. Roberta: A robustly optimized bert pretraining approach. Cite arxiv:1907.11692.

Nikolaos Malandrakis, Alexandros Potamianos, Elias Iosif, and Shrikanth Narayanan. 2013. Distributional semantic models for affective text analysis. *IEEE Transactions on Audio, Speech, and Language Processing*, 21(11):2379–2392.

Georgios Paltoglou, Mathias Theunis, Arvid Kappas, and Mike Thelwall. 2013. Predicting emotional responses to long informal text. *IEEE Transactions on Affective Computing*, 4(1):106–115.

James A. Russell. 1980. *A circumplex model of affect*. 1161, Journal of Personality and Social Psychology, 39(6).

Jin Wang, Liang-Chih Yu, K. Robert Lai, and Xuejie Zhang. 2016. Community-based weighted graph model for valence-arousal prediction of affective words. *IEEE/ACM Transactions on Audio, Speech, and Language Processing*, 24(11):1957–1968.

Jin Wang, Liang-Chih Yu, K. Robert Lai, and Xuejie Zhang. 2020. Tree-structured regional cnn-lstm model for dimensional sentiment analysis. *IEEE/ACM Transactions on Audio, Speech, and Language Processing*, 28:581–591.

Wen-Li Wei, Chung-Hsien Wu, and Jen-Chun Lin. 2011. A regression approach to affective rating of chinese words from anew. In *Affective Computing and Intelligent Interaction*, pages 121–131, Berlin, Heidelberg. Springer Berlin Heidelberg.

Thomas Wolf, Lysandre Debut, Victor Sanh, Julien Chaumond, Clement Delangue, Anthony Moi, Pierric Cistac, Tim Rault, Rémi Louf, Morgan Funtowicz, Joe Davison, Sam Shleifer, Patrick von Platen, Clara Ma, Yacine Jernite, Julien Plu, Canwen Xu, Teven Le Scao, Sylvain Gugger, Mariama Drame, Quentin Lhoest, and Alexander M. Rush. 2020. Transformers: State-of-the-art natural language processing. In *Proceedings of the 2020 Conference on Empirical*

Methods in Natural Language Processing: System Demonstrations, pages 38–45, Online. Association for Computational Linguistics.

Chuhan Wu, Fangzhao Wu, Yongfeng Huang, Sixing Wu, and Zhigang Yuan. 2017. THU_NGN at IJCNLP-2017 task 2: Dimensional sentiment analysis for Chinese phrases with deep LSTM. In *Proceedings of the IJCNLP 2017, Shared Tasks*, pages 47–52, Taipei, Taiwan. Asian Federation of Natural Language Processing.

Liang-Chih Yu, Lung-Hao Lee, Shuai Hao, Jin Wang, Yunchao He, Jun Hu, K. Robert Lai, and Xuejie Zhang. 2016. Building Chinese affective resources in valence-arousal dimensions. In *Proceedings of the 2016 Conference of the North American Chapter of the Association for Computational Linguistics: Human Language Technologies*, pages 540–545, San Diego, California. Association for Computational Linguistics.

Liang-Chih Yu, Lung-Hao Lee, Jin Wang, and Kam-Fai Wong. 2017. IJCNLP-2017 task 2: Dimensional sentiment analysis for Chinese phrases. In *Proceedings of the IJCNLP 2017, Shared Tasks*, pages 9–16, Taipei, Taiwan. Asian Federation of Natural Language Processing.

Liang-Chih Yu, Jin Wang, K. Robert Lai, and Xuejie Zhang. 2020. Pipelined neural networks for phrase-level sentiment intensity prediction. *IEEE Transactions on Affective Computing*, 11(3):447–458.

Suyang Zhu, Shoushan Li, and Guodong Zhou. 2019. Adversarial attention modeling for multi-dimensional emotion regression. In *Proceedings of the 57th Annual Meeting of the Association for Computational Linguistics*, pages 471–480, Florence, Italy. Association for Computational Linguistics.

The 33rd Conference on Computational Linguistics and Speech Processing (ROCLING 2021)
Taoyuan, Taiwan, October 15-16, 2021. The Association for Computational Linguistics and Chinese Language Processing

CYUT at ROCLING-2021 Shared Task: Based on BERT and MacBERT

Xie-Sheng Hong
Department of CSIE
Chaoyang University of Technology
Taichung, Taiwan
kk6251433@gmail.com

Shih-Hung Wu
Department of CSIE
Chaoyang University of Technology
Taichung, Taiwan
shwu@cyut.edu.tw

Abstract

This paper present a description for the ROCLING 2021 shared task in dimensional sentiment analysis for educational texts. We submitted two runs in the final test. Both runs use the standard regression model. The Run1 uses Chinese version of BERT as the base, and in Run2 we use the early version of MacBERT that Chinese version of RoBERTa-like BERT model, RoBERTa-wwm-ext. Using powerful pre-training model of BERT for text embedding to help train the model.

Keywords:
Natural Language Processing, Dimensional Sentiment Analysis, Deep learning

1 Introduction

The ROCLING 2021 Shared Task was inherited from a task about dimensional sentiment analysis task for Chinese words at IALP2016. The task is extended to include both word- and phrase-level dimensional sentiment analysis. It explores the sentence-level dimensional sentiment analysis task on educational texts.

In view of structured information such as attendance, in-class participation have been extensively studied to predict students' learning performance. For this reason, the organizers of task wanted participants to use unstructured information such as self- evaluation comments written by students. Using dimensional sentiment analysis to identify valence-arousal ratings from texts. To analyze the affective states contained in them to help illuminate students' affective states.

In the three training sets provided, there are several sentences, phrases, or words with their corresponding real-valued or average scores for both valence and arousal dimensions. The two dimensions range from 1 (highly negative or calm) to 9 (highly positive or excited) where valence represents the degree of positive and negative sentiment, and arousal represents the degree of calm and excitement(Yu et al., 2016). For example, the questions and answers used in this shared task are shown below:

Input:

今天教了許多以前沒有學過的東西，所以上起課來很新鮮

Output:

Valence: 6.8

Arousal: 5.2

In short, the specific goal of this shared task is to input a sentence and let our proposed system predict the score on two indexes, Valence and Arousal.

Therefore, this task can be defined as a two-objective regression task. We used the Chinese versions of the BERT and RoBERTa pre-training models to construct the regression models. In the experiment, we chose different motivation functions in the two tests. We also adjusted some of the parameters in order to find a more suitable method. The rest of the paper will give the details of our method, show the experiment setting and results, also discussions on the results, In the final section, we will give conclusion and future works.

2 Method

For comparison, we fine-tune two Transformer Models, bert-base-chinese and RoBERTa-wwm-ext. The former uses the official Chinese version of BERT provided by Google(Devlin et al., 2019), while the latter uses the Chinese version of the RoBERTa-like model proposed by State Key Laboratory of Cognitive Intelligence, iFLYTEK Research (HFL)(Cui et al., 2019, 2020). We fine-tun the two models, and combine two different activation functions, ReLU and LeakyReLU, to build the regression model. In this section, we present our ideas and attempts on the models, as well as the methods and procedures used to build them.

2.1 Model-1: BERT

In Run1, our system is based on the standard Chinese version of the BERT pre-training model proposed by Google. BERT is a deep, two-way unsupervised language representation trained using only plain text corpus. Unlike word2vector(Mikolov et al.) and GloVe(Pennington et al., 2014), which do not use context.Transformers is a new simple network structure proposed by Google, which is based only on attention mechanisms and does not require recursion and convolution at all. The results of the two translator tasks presented in their study show that the model can improve considerably with this network.Also, it is easier to perform parallelization, and the training time required for the model is significantly reduced(Vaswani et al., 2017).BERT takes into account the context in which a particular word appears each time it is used in an article. Therefore, even if the same word occurs repeatedly, BERT can generate different word vectors according to different contexts(Devlin et al., 2019).

We consider that the text data used for training the model is clean and does not contain tags such as <br>, which are not useful for model training. So, we just organize the training data and convert it into a data form that can be read by the BERT model. In this part, we use Pytorch(Paszke et al., 2019) and call HuggingFace(Wolf et al., 2020) to fine-tune and build the whole model.

2.2 Model-2: Chinese-RoBERTa-wwm

As a comparison with Run1, our system is built using a RoBERT-like model called RoBERTa-wwm-ext in Run2. First, the original version of RoBERTa (Robustly optimized BERT approach)(Liu et al., 2019), which can be simply understood as an enhanced optimization of the original BERT model. It was jointly proposed by Facebook and the University of Washington. RoBERTa has the following main improvements over the original BERT. It uses a larger number of model parameters, a larger batch size, and increases the training data. In the model training process, RoBERTa adopts a dynamic mask, so that the model generates a new mask pattern for each input sequence. In this way, the model can gradually adapt to different mask patterns as the data is input. Then, considering the controversy over the validity of the NSP task used on BERT(Devlin et al., 2019; Lample and Conneau, 2019; Joshi et al., 2020), RoBERTa has also adapted the NSP task.

MacBERT is a new pre-training model proposed by the HFL after improving the models same proposed by them, such as Chinese-BERT-wwm and Chinese-RoBERTa-wwm(Cui et al., 2020, 2019). Therefore, in this paper we call the RoBERTa-wwm-ext model as the early version MacBERT. The model's full name is RoBERTa Whole Word Masking Extended data. The "wwm" here refers to the updated version released by the author of the original BERT in 2019, named Whole Word Masking. It mainly mitigates the drawbacks in original BERT's Wordpice. If the masked WordPiece token belongs to a whole word, then all the WordPiece tokens will be masked, so that it forms a complete word, not just WordPices in the training task. It is beneficial to design more powerful models(Wu et al., 2016; Cui et al., 2019).

The model we use is called RoBERTa-like because this pre-trained model is made by the original author by integrating the advantages of RoBERTa and BERT-wwm. In essence, it is not RoBERTa, but a BERT model trained according to the training method similar to RoBERTa. They used the wwm strategy for mask instead of Dynamic masking in the pre-training phase, eliminated the NSP loss, and adjusted the length of MAX Len and the number of training steps(Cui et al., 2019, 2020).

As Model-1, we also used Pytorch and called HuggingFace to fine-tune and build the whole model.

2.3 ReLU and LeakyReLU

In the current study, we used two activation functions, ReLU and LeakyReLU, to construct the regression models for our two systems. In order to make a larger difference between the two tests, we used LeakyReLU in the BERT-based model and used common ReLU in RoBERTa-like model.

ReLU (rectified linear activation function) is a widely used activation function in deep neural networks(Ramachandran et al., 2017). It can be as a piecewise linear function that modifies the negative part to zero and keeps the positive part. In other words, the value of ReLU is zero when it is smaller than zero and remains the same when it is larger(Nair and Hinton, 2010; Sun et al., 2014). It is a non-saturated excitation function, which has many advantages over saturated functions such as sigmoid and tanh.

Since ReLU can maintain the original state when the output is above zero, this property can keep the gradient invariant and can effectively mitigate the vanishing gradient and exploding gradient problems(Clevert et al., 2016; Xu et al., 2015)that easily occur in the sigmoid and tanh functions. In addition, ReLU has an important property that the result of activation by it is sparse. Although some scholars have question(Xu et al., 2015), it is generally accepted that the sparse property of ReLU can lead to excellent performance(Glorot et al., 2011; He et al., 2014). The reason is that the sparsity of ReLU can separate the features in the data, make the dense features sparse, and make the features linearly separable(Glorot et al., 2011). Therefore, ReLU can learn the features of data more flexibly and effectively.

LeakyReLU is a variant of ReLU. The biggest difference with ReLU is that LeakyReLU is given a non-zero slope in the negative part, the negative part is no longer set to zero at all times. This change solves the dying ReLU problem. It refers to the fact that when the activation value of ReLU is always negative, the gradient obtained is also always zero. As a result, the neuron can no longer learn, like it is "dead" . The adjustment solves this problem, so that it has the advantage of ReLU, but also solves some of the original shortcomings of ReLU(Xu et al., 2015; Maas, 2013).

The detailed shapes of the two models can be seen in Figure 1 (a) and Figure 1 (b).

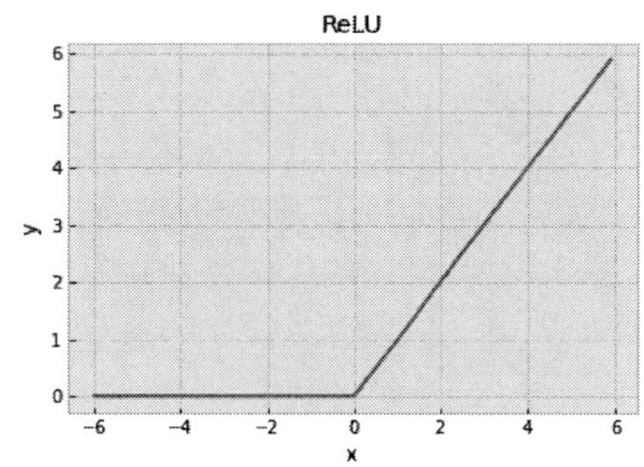

(a) ReLU Function

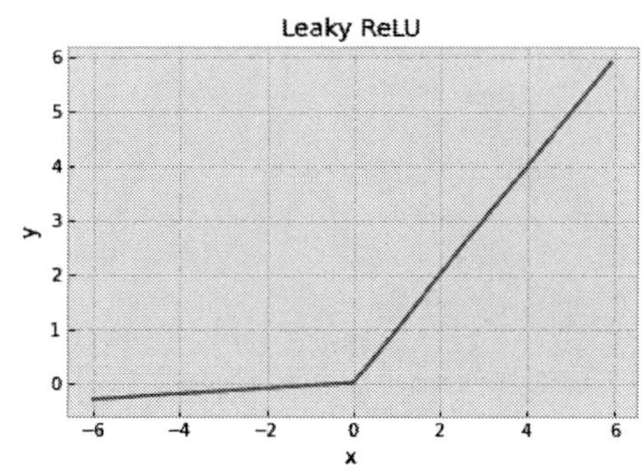

(b) LeakyReLU Function

Figure 1: ReLU and LeakyReLU Function

3 Experiments

Figure 2 shows the overall flow of our study, which can be roughly divided into the following processes. We first do a simple preprocessing of the raw data to be used for training the model, and build a dataloader to facilitate the training.Then we construct a BERT/RoBERTa-like neural network model and train it.After the training, the test data are also organized into a dataloader and given to the model for prediction.Finally, the prediction results of the model are organized into a prescribed format.

In this section, we describe in detail the various settings of our system and analyze the results and errors.

3.1 Parameters and Setting

For Run1, we use a batch size of 16 to run the training. We use AdamW(Loshchilov and

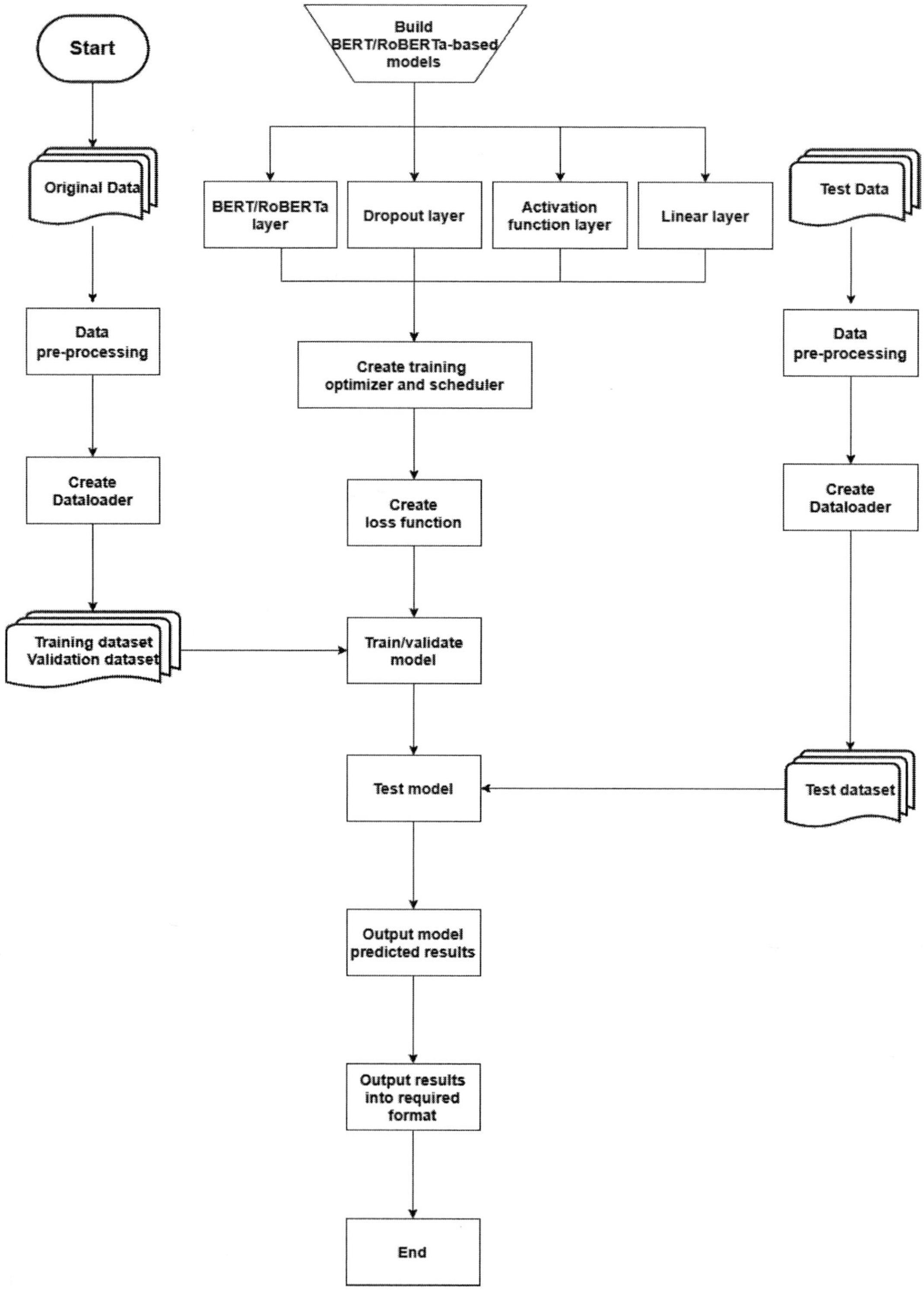

Figure 2: The flow chart of our study

Hutter, 2019) as the optimizer of the model, which is a variant of another classical optimizer, Adam(Kingma and Ba, 2017). The authors of AdamW propose simple modifications to improve the weight decay and improve its generalization performance. We set the learning rate of the optimizer to 2e-5, correct_bias to False, and keep the rest of the relevant parameters as default. Run2 is the same as Run1 except that the batch size is changed to 32. Finally, the maximum length of the training data is set to 200 for both.

For the model architecture, Run1 and Run2 are basically the same. Both of them use two linear layers, two activation layers and two dropout layers with p=0.2 for Run1, with 0.1 for Run2, to avoid overfitting.

During the model training, Run1 and Run2 are trained for 100 epochs by default. A parameter called "patience" is set as the threshold. The training is terminated early if the model does not improve its loss for three consecutive epochs. Run1 is automatically terminated at the 60th epoch, and Run2 is manually terminated at 26 epochs to avoid overfitting.

3.2 Official Run and Fixed Run Result

Table 1 show the prediction results of our system for the two targets in two Runs. Since we made a mistake when submitting the final test, the predicted answers were misaligned with the questions in our submitted results. As a result, we got unexpected predicted scores from the organizer's validation. The scores is named "Official" in tables. After fixing the program, we verified the model prediction with the same verification method as the organizer, mean absolute error and pearson correlation coefficient, and got a different result. The new results are shown in Table 1, too.

3.3 Result and Error Analysis

From Section 3.3, our system returned to a more normal value after correcting the error. Thanks to the power of BERT, our system is able to perform to a certain extent even if we do not do too much complex processing of training data or neural network models.

Briefly summarizing Tables 1, Run2 (RoBERTa-wwm-ext + ReLU) is better than Run1 (BERT + LeakyReLU) in both objectives. It seems to show that the RoBERTa-wwm-ext trained with more pretraining data is still better than the original BERT, even with the LeakyReLU assist, when the other settings are similar.

Table 3 shows the performance of our system in the two Runs after the correction in comparison with the other groups' systems. It is found that our system is able to have a similar degree of correctness as the other groups after the correction. After looking at the results for each group and ours, we were surprised to find that the systems in each group performed slightly worse on the "Arousal" index than on the "Valence" index.

Therefore, we list the prediction results and questions of "Arousal" that are partially better (loss<=0.001) and worse (loss>=3) on our Run2-system to facilitate our comparison:

Better cases:

我覺得老師講的有一點快，需要時間消化
Error = 0.00070

我認爲可以稍微補充以及多舉些例子，好讓我們比較容易理解
Error = -0.00078

能把今天的課程學好，未來應該很受用
Error = 0.00094

Worse cases:

今天收穫很多
Error = 3.197

受益良多，頗有趣
Error = 3.054

內容生動有趣
Error = 3.158

上課時老師善用舉例，讓我有更具體的思考邏輯，對於整個架構也比較了解
Error = -3.317

Looking at our prediction results with Table 1 and Table 3, we found that our system seemed to have a higher recognition rate for the more complete sentences.As you can see from the example we gave, if the student's description of the emotional state is more detailed, the more accurate our system is in predicting the answer. When the student describes the situation in a more concise manner, our system is most likely unable to make

Run	Valence MAE	Valence r	Arousal MAE	Arousal r
Run1-Official	1.695	-0.017	1.177	0.040
Run2-Official	1.685	0.007	1.252	-0.021
Run1-Fixed	0.674	0.870	0.901	0.531
Run2-Fixed	0.600	0.900	0.877	0.565

Table 1: Official and Fixed Run Result

Run	Valence MAE	Valence r	Arousal MAE	Arousal r
Run1	0.512	0.887	0.666	0.753
Run2	0.462	0.911	0.652	0.774

Table 2: Development Result

Run	Valence MAE	Valence r	Arousal MAE	Arousal r
CYUT-Run1-Fixed	0.674	0.870	0.901	0.531
CYUT-Run2-Fixed	0.600	0.900	0.877	0.565
NCU-NLP-Run1	0.625	0.900	0.938	0.549
NCU-NLP-Run2	0.611	0.904	0.989	0.582
ntust-nlp-1-Run1	0.684	0.912	0.906	0.607
ntust-nlp-1-Run2	0.586	0.901	0.885	0.585
ntust-nlp-2-Run1	0.654	0.905	0.880	0.581
ntust-nlp-2-Run2	0.667	0.913	0.866	0.616
SCUDS-Run1	0.953	0.694	1.054	0.375
SCUDS-Run2	0.975	0.667	1.039	0.354
SoochowDS-Run1	2.421	0.073	1.327	0.051
SoochowDS-Run2	1.073	0.584	1.125	0.228

Table 3: Comparison of results with other groups

a correct prediction. It is worth noting that, as we have shown, there are also some sentences where our system is unable to make a correct prediction although there is a more detailed description. For this, we have the following inference.

Table 2 shows the results of the validation of our model on the development set after the training. However, it is important to note that even in the development set with standard answers, "Arousal" still only has a Pearson correlation coefficient of about 0.7. We believe that this may be the reason for the poor performance of the predictions of "Arousal". Perhaps the information we provide to the model for learning may not be relevant enough to the answer we are trying to predict. Considering this study, we only did simple pre-processing and Tokenizer on the text data used to train the model. We did not filter the key features in the text. Hence, our model may need more narratives to predict the answer and cannot make judgments based on key features alone. This makes it difficult for our model to predict short sentences. We think this is one of the parts of our system that needs to be improved in the future, filtering out the key features beforehand to improve the feature strength. Enhance the relevance of the model in training and prediction.

4 Conclusion and Future Works

In this paper, we describe our proposed approach on ROCLING 2021 shared task in dimensional sentiment analysis for educational texts. Our system is based on the Chinese version of the BERT and RoBERTa-wwm-ext models. Although the results were not good in the official run because of a program error, after fixing the error, our system has a standard result. It is worth noting that we only used some standard methods and parameters and do not use any complex methods. But because of this, our system' s shortcomings are also obvious. As "Arousal" problem this time, the direct use of training data may not be sufficient to train the model completely. In the future, we can adjust the pre-processing part of the data, such as finding the key features in the sentences in advance, or increasing the training data. For the neural network model, we can try to add classical neural networks such as LSTM(Hochreiter and Schmidhuber, 1997) or GRU(Chung et al., 2014) for training, and improve the depth of the model in the future.

References

Junyoung Chung, Caglar Gulcehre, KyungHyun Cho, and Yoshua Bengio. 2014. Empirical evaluation of gated recurrent neural networks on sequence modeling.

Djork-Arné Clevert, Thomas Unterthiner, and Sepp Hochreiter. 2016. Fast and accurate deep network learning by exponential linear units (elus).

Yiming Cui, Wanxiang Che, Ting Liu, Bing Qin, Shijin Wang, and Guoping Hu. 2020. Revisiting pre-trained models for Chinese natural language processing. In *Proceedings of the 2020 Conference on Empirical Methods in Natural Language Processing: Findings*, pages 657–668, Online. Association for Computational Linguistics.

Yiming Cui, Wanxiang Che, Ting Liu, Bing Qin, Ziqing Yang, Shijin Wang, and Guoping Hu. 2019. Pre-training with whole word masking for chinese bert. *arXiv preprint arXiv:1906.08101*.

Jacob Devlin, Ming-Wei Chang, Kenton Lee, and Kristina Toutanova. 2019. Bert: Pre-training of deep bidirectional transformers for language understanding.

Xavier Glorot, Antoine Bordes, and Yoshua Bengio. 2011. Deep sparse rectifier neural networks. In *Proceedings of the Fourteenth International Conference on Artificial Intelligence and Statistics*, volume 15 of *Proceedings of Machine Learning Research*, pages 315–323, Fort Lauderdale, FL, USA. PMLR.

Kaiming He, Xiangyu Zhang, Shaoqing Ren, and Jian Sun. 2014. Spatial pyramid pooling in deep convolutional networks for visual recognition. *Lecture Notes in Computer Science*, page 346—361.

Sepp Hochreiter and Jürgen Schmidhuber. 1997. Long Short-Term Memory. *Neural Computation*, 9(8):1735–1780.

Mandar Joshi, Danqi Chen, Yinhan Liu, Daniel S. Weld, Luke Zettlemoyer, and Omer Levy. 2020. Spanbert: Improving pre-training by representing and predicting spans.

Diederik P. Kingma and Jimmy Ba. 2017. Adam: A method for stochastic optimization.

Guillaume Lample and Alexis Conneau. 2019. Cross-lingual language model pretraining.

Yinhan Liu, Myle Ott, Naman Goyal, Jingfei Du, Mandar Joshi, Danqi Chen, Omer Levy, Mike Lewis, Luke Zettlemoyer, and Veselin Stoyanov. 2019. Roberta: A robustly optimized bert pretraining approach.

Ilya Loshchilov and Frank Hutter. 2019. Decoupled weight decay regularization.

Andrew L. Maas. 2013. Rectifier nonlinearities improve neural network acoustic models.

Tomas Mikolov, Kai Chen, Greg Corrado, and Jeffrey Dean. Efficient Estimation of Word Representations in Vector Space.

Vinod Nair and Geoffrey E. Hinton. 2010. Rectified linear units improve restricted boltzmann machines. In *Proceedings of the 27th International Conference on International Conference on Machine Learning*, ICML'10, page 807—814, Madison, WI, USA. Omnipress.

Adam Paszke, Sam Gross, Francisco Massa, Adam Lerer, James Bradbury, Gregory Chanan, Trevor Killeen, Zeming Lin, Natalia Gimelshein, Luca Antiga, Alban Desmaison, Andreas Köpf, Edward Yang, Zach DeVito, Martin Raison, Alykhan Tejani, Sasank Chilamkurthy, Benoit Steiner, Lu Fang, Junjie Bai, and Soumith Chintala. 2019. Pytorch: An imperative style, high-performance deep learning library.

Jeffrey Pennington, Richard Socher, and Christopher Manning. 2014. GloVe: Global vectors for word representation. In *Proceedings of the 2014 Conference on Empirical Methods in Natural Language Processing (EMNLP)*, pages 1532–1543, Doha, Qatar. Association for Computational Linguistics.

Prajit Ramachandran, Barret Zoph, and Quoc V. Le. 2017. Searching for activation functions.

Yi Sun, Xiaogang Wang, and Xiaoou Tang. 2014. Deeply learned face representations are sparse, selective, and robust.

Ashish Vaswani, Noam Shazeer, Niki Parmar, Jakob Uszkoreit, Llion Jones, Aidan N. Gomez, Lukasz Kaiser, and Illia Polosukhin. 2017. Attention is all you need.

Thomas Wolf, Lysandre Debut, Victor Sanh, Julien Chaumond, Clement Delangue, Anthony Moi, Pierric Cistac, Tim Rault, Rémi Louf, Morgan Funtowicz, Joe Davison, Sam Shleifer, Patrick von Platen, Clara Ma, Yacine Jernite, Julien Plu, Canwen Xu, Teven Le Scao, Sylvain Gugger, Mariama Drame, Quentin Lhoest, and Alexander M. Rush. 2020. Huggingface's transformers: State-of-the-art natural language processing.

Yonghui Wu, Mike Schuster, Zhifeng Chen, Quoc V. Le, Mohammad Norouzi, Wolfgang Macherey, Maxim Krikun, Yuan Cao, Qin Gao, Klaus Macherey, Jeff Klingner, Apurva Shah, Melvin Johnson, Xiaobing Liu, Łukasz Kaiser, Stephan Gouws, Yoshikiyo Kato, Taku Kudo, Hideto Kazawa, Keith Stevens, George Kurian, Nishant Patil, Wei Wang, Cliff Young, Jason Smith, Jason Riesa, Alex Rudnick, Oriol Vinyals, Greg Corrado, Macduff Hughes, and Jeffrey Dean. 2016. Google's neural machine translation system: Bridging the gap between human and machine translation.

Bing Xu, Naiyan Wang, Tianqi Chen, and Mu Li. 2015. Empirical evaluation of rectified activations in convolutional network.

Liang-Chih Yu, Lung-Hao Lee, Shuai Hao, Jin Wang, Yunchao He, Jun Hu, K. Robert Lai, and Xuejie Zhang. 2016. Building Chinese affective resources in valence-arousal dimensions. In *Proceedings of the 2016 Conference of the North American Chapter of the Association for Computational Linguistics: Human Language Technologies*, pages 540–545, San Diego, California. Association for Computational Linguistics.

The 33rd Conference on Computational Linguistics and Speech Processing (ROCLING 2021)
Taoyuan, Taiwan, October 15-16, 2021. The Association for Computational Linguistics and Chinese Language Processing

SoochowDS at ROCLING-2021 Shared Task: Text Sentiment Analysis Using BERT and LSTM

Ruei-Cyuan Su, Sing-Seong Chong, Tzu-En Su and Ming-Hsiang Su
Soochow University, Taiwan
70613rex, chongzhishan123, 70614roy, huntfox.su@gmail.com

摘要

在這次的挑戰賽中，本研究提出結合BERT-based 詞向量模型和 LSTM 預測模型進行文本 Valence和 Arousal 數值預測。其中 BERT-based 詞向量為 768 維，並依序將文句中每個詞向量依序輸入LSTM 模型中進行預測。實驗結果得知我們所提出的 BERT 結合 LSTM 模型遠優於 Lasso Regression 回歸模型的結果。

Abstract

In this shared task, this paper proposes a method to combine the BERT-based word vector model and the LSTM prediction model to predict the Valence and Arousal values in the text. Among them, the BERT-based word vector is 768-dimensional, and each word vector in the sentence is sequentially fed to the LSTM model for prediction. The experimental results show that the performance of our proposed method is better than the results of the Lasso Regression model.

關鍵字：BERT、LSTM、Lasso Regression
Keywords: BERT、LSTM、Lasso Regression

1 Introduction

情緒分析是一個非常熱門的研究領域，學者們提出許多創新方法去分析和預測。公司可以根據資料(如產品留言)，進行顧客對產品的評價分析或尋找產品銷售問題，以便提高銷售量等。在文字情緒分析中，學者們採用兩大指標，別是 Valence和 Arousal，進行文本情緒分析。其中 Valence 主要是區別情感正向與負向，而 Arousal 則是判斷情感是沉靜還是喚起。這兩大指標普遍用於檢測與識別文本情感訊息。如"最近上課遇到很多問題，情緒低落"對應的 Valence 和 Arousal 分別為 1.75 和 5.64。

會議紀錄對市場走勢起著重要作用，因為它們提供了對市場走勢的鳥瞰圖。 因此，人們越來越有興趣從大型金融文本中分析和提取各個方面的情緒以進行經濟預測。然而由於缺乏大型標記數據集，Aspect-based Sentiment Analysis (ABSA) 並未廣泛用於金融數據。於是 Wang [1] 提出一個模型來訓練ABSA 的金融文件，並分析其對各種宏觀經濟指標的預測能力。Wang [1] 運用 FinBERT 技術合併文字來達到文件級別的分析。其實驗結果顯示 Federal Open Market Committee (FOMC) 的報告文件可以解釋63%市場的成長率，員工的情緒與通貨膨脹能解釋47%和 19%相對應的經濟因數。

網路的普及創造了一個振興的數位媒體。隨著新聞點擊次數驅動的貨幣化，在網路新聞競爭激烈的氛圍中，記者們調整他們的報告以適應這樣的氛圍。由此產生的消極偏見是有害的，會導致焦慮和情緒障礙。Kumar 等人 [2] 在各種數據集上訓練 4 個管線化情感分析模型(Sequential、LSTM、BERT 和 SVM 模型)。 經過組合後，行動裝置 APP 只顯示會鼓舞人心的故事供用戶閱讀。結果顯示有 1,300 名用戶對該 APP 評價為 4.9 星，85% 的用戶回饋通過使用此 APP 改善了心理健康。

由於來自不同文化和教育背景的人對網路的使用呈指數增長，具仇恨攻擊的線上言論偵測已成為當今的一個關鍵問題。區分文本消息是否屬於仇恨言論和攻擊性語言是自動檢測文本內容的關鍵挑戰。Bencheng 等人 [3] 提出一種將推文自動分類為三類的方法：仇恨、攻擊性和兩者都不是。他們利用公共推文數據集，首先進行實驗構建 BERT-based embedding 結合 Bi-Directional Long Short-Term Memory (BI-LSTM) 模型，然後他們也嘗試使用預訓練的 Glove-based embedding 結合相同的神經網絡架構。實驗考慮不同的神經網絡架構、學習率和歸一化方法，對他們所提之 BI-LSTM 模型進行超參數調整分析。在調整模型並使用最佳參數組合後，在測試數據上對其進行評估時達到了 92% 以上的準確率。在參考上述研究後，本研究提出結合 BERT-based 詞向量模型和 LSTM 模型進行訓練，以完成 Valence 和 Arousal 文本預測。

2 資料集說明

本研究第一個採用的是 CVAT 1.0 及 CVAT 2.0 中文維度情感語料庫 [4]，是一個情感語料庫。其中包含從網路中提取的 2,969 的條列句子(CVAT 2.0)及 2,009 的條列句子(CVAT 1.0)，並且分為六個不同類別：新聞文章、政治論壇、汽車論壇、酒店評論、書評和筆記本電腦評論。每個句子都用人工分類的方式標明了 Valence 和 Arousal 之維度的實值分數。這兩個維度的範圍從 1（高度消極或平靜）到 9（高度積極或興奮）。本研究第二個採用的是 CVAW 4.0 中文維度情感詞典，包含了 5,512 個單詞。每個單詞都使用人工分類的方式標明 Valence 和 Arousal 維度的實值分數。本研究第三個採用的是 CVAP 2.0 中文維度情感片語，包含 2,998 個多詞短語。每個短語由一個情感詞和一個或多個修飾詞組成，例如修飾詞的否定詞、情態詞和程度副詞。最後再使用測試資料來完成 Valence 和 Arousal 文本預測。

3 System framework

在系統架構說明中，本研究首先使用 Jiba 斷詞工具將 CVAT 1.0 及 CVAT 2.0 這兩個資料集進行斷詞處理。本研究使用了中文維度情感辭典 CVAW、中文維度型情感片語 CVAP 資料集、地名或人名等加入 Jiba 的字典裡，使斷詞更加正確。接著本研究以 word2vector, doc2vector 和 BERT 進行詞向量模型訓練。最後分別進行 Lasso Regression 和 LSTM 模型對 Valence 和 Arousal 進行訓練，並用以預測測試集得到 Valence 和 Arousal 的結果。

3.1 斷詞模型

目前中文有兩個斷詞模型可用，一個是 Jieba 斷詞工具，而另一個是中研院的 CKIP 斷詞工具。本研究分析使用 Jieba 斷詞工具，這個工具有 python 的介面，使用上非常容易，可輸入繁體字典。 因 Jiba 的本身斷詞效果有限，因此本研究加入中文維度情感辭典 CVAW、中文維度型情感片語 CVAP 資料集。實驗結果發現加入字典的地名、人名、專業名稱並無有效修正，因此本研究再整理出應修正的名稱加入字典，得到正確的斷詞結果。

3.2 詞向量模型

Word2Vector [5]是輕量級的神經網絡，其模型僅僅包括輸入層、隱藏層和輸出層，模型框架根據輸入輸出的不同，主要包括 CBOW 和 Skip-gram 模型。CBOW 的方式為知道詞w_t的上下文$w_{t-2}, w_{t-1}, w_{t+1}, w_{t+2}$的情況預測當前詞$w_t$，而 Skip-gram 則是知道了詞$w_t$的情況，對詞的上下文$w_{t-2}, w_{t-1}, w_{t+1}, w_{t+2}$進行預測。

首先介紹 Simple CBOW Mode，在我們的設置中，詞彙量大小為V隱藏層大小為N。輸入x是一層 one-hot representation vector，這意味著對於給定的輸入上下文詞$\{x_1 \dots x_V\}$，裡面共V個單元，其中只有一個為 1，所有其他單元為 0。例如$x = [0, \dots, 1, \dots, 0]$。輸入層和輸出層之間的權重可以用一個$\mathrm{V} \times \mathrm{N}$矩陣$\mathrm{W}$表示。$W_{\mathrm{V}\times\mathrm{N}} = \{w_{ki}\}$的每一行是輸入層關聯詞的$N$維向量表示$v_w$。給定一個上下文（一個詞），假設 $x_k = 1, x_{k'} = 0, k \neq k'$，得

$$h = x^T W = W_{(k,\cdot)}^T \coloneqq v_{wI}^T \quad (1)$$

這只是將W的第k行複製到 h。v_{wI}是輸入詞 wI的向量表示。從隱藏層至輸出層，權重矩陣為

$$W'_{N\times V} = \{w'_{ij}\} \quad (2)$$

這是一個$\mathrm{N} \times \mathrm{V}$的矩陣。使用這些權重，我們可以計算詞彙中每單詞的分數u_i，

$$u_j = {v'_{wj}}^T \cdot h \quad (3)$$

其中 v'_{wj}是矩陣W'的第j列。然後我們可以使用 softmax 得到詞的後驗分佈，這是一個多項式分佈。

$$p = (w_j | w_I) = y_j = \frac{\exp(u_j)}{\sum_{j'=1}^{V} \exp(u_{j'})} \quad (4)$$

其中y_i是輸出層中第j個單元的輸出。對於損失函數，在訓練目標是在給定輸入上下文詞 w_I的權重的情況下，最大化觀察實際輸出詞 w_0將其在輸出層中的相應索引表示為j^*的條件概率

$$\max p(w_0 | w_I) \quad (5)$$

$$= u_{j^*} - log \sum_{j'=1}^{V} \exp(u_{j'}) := -E$$

而$E = -logp(w_O|w_I)$為損失函數，其中j^*是輸出層中實際輸出詞的索引。

而在 Skip-gram Model 中，我們仍然使用 Simple CBOW Mode 對隱藏層輸出 h 相同的定義。在輸出層，我們不是輸出一個多項式分佈，而是輸出c個多項式分佈，

$$p(w_{c,j} = w_{O,c}|w_I) = \frac{\exp(u_{c,j})}{\sum_{j'=1}^{V} \exp(u_{j'})} \quad (6)$$

其中$w_{c,j}$是輸出層第 c 個面板上的第j個單詞；$w_{O,c}$是實際第C 個輸出上下文詞中的詞；w_I是唯一的輸入詞；$y_{c,j}$是第j個的輸出輸出層第C個面板上的單元；$u_{c,j}$是第j個單元在第c個單元上的淨輸入輸出層面板。其中因為輸出層面板共享相同的權重，因此$u_{c,j} = u_j = {v'_{wj}}^T \cdot h,\ c = 1,2, \ldots, C$，其他參數如同 Simple CBOW Mode。損失函數與 Simple CBOW Mode 沒有太大差別，

$$E = -logp(w_{O,1}, w_{O,2}, \ldots, w_{O,C}|w_I)$$
$$= -log \prod_{c=1}^{C} \frac{\exp(u_{c,j_c^*})}{\sum_{j'=1}^{V} \exp(u_{j'})} \quad (7)$$

最後詞向量模型為 BERT 模型(Bidirectional Encoder Representations from Transformer)，是 Google 以無監督的方式利用大量無標記文本的模型。訓練資料來源于 Wikipedia (2.5B 字) 加上 Book coupus (800M 字)。批量大小為 1024 序列*128 長度或 256 序列*512 長度。BERT 分為兩種 BERT-Base (12-layer, 768-Hidden, 12-head)和 BERT-Large (24-layer, 1024hidden, 16-head)。BERT 無需標記好的資料或解釋即可進行分析。Transformer 是 BERT 的核心模組，而 Attention 是 transformer 的核心部分，主要是增強語義向量，在不同的字結合中，代表識別字所帶來的意思。

3.3 Lasso Regression

線性回歸(linear regression)，為用線性函數(hypothesis) $f(x) = wx + b$ 去擬合一組數據 $D = \{(x_1, y_1), (x_2, y_2), \ldots (x_n, y_n)\}$，找到一組$(w^*, b^*)$，使損失$J = \frac{1}{n}\sum_{i=1}^{n}(f(x_i) - y_i)^2$ (mse)最小。Lasso 的全稱 Least Absolute Shrinkage and Selection Operator，又譯最小絕對值收斂和選擇算子、套索算法，其 cost function 為

$$J = \frac{1}{n}\sum_{i=1}^{n}(f(x_i) - y_i)^2 + \lambda\|w\|_1 \quad (8)$$

其中λ為乘子。目標為$min_{w,b}J$，因此也將它寫成

$$min_{w,b}\ \frac{1}{n}\sum_{i=1}^{n}(f(x_i) - y_i)^2, \quad s.t. \|w\|_1 \le t \quad (9)$$

其中 t 可理解為正規化力度。以$x \in R^2$為例，對 w 的限制空間為正方形，因此 $argmin_{w,b}\ \frac{1}{n}\sum_{i=1}^{n}(f(x_i) - y_i)^2$的解容易切在 w 某一維為 0 的點可解決過度擬和問題以及來做 feature selection。

3.4 LSTM 模型

LSTM 是為了解決 RNN 的缺點，如不能準確處理長期序列、時間的資料。LSTM 是由四個結構所組成，輸入門 (Input Gate)，儲存細胞（Memory Cell），遺忘門 (Forget Gate)，輸出門 (Output Gate)。Input gate 主要負責控制這個值輸入，Memory Cell 儲存值，下階段在使用，Output Gate 輸出 output，Forget Gate 是否保留或刪除特徵(feature)。LSTM 操作思路就是把輸入到類神經網路層處理產生出結果，過程當中，記住某些特徵，然後會跟著這些經驗來判斷或學習。其中 (10)-(15)分別為 Input Gate, Forget Gate 和 Output Gate 計算公式。

$$f_t = \sigma(W_f \cdot [X_t, h_{t-1}] + b_f) \quad (10)$$
$$i_t = \sigma(W_i \cdot [X_t, h_{t-1}] + b_i) \quad (11)$$
$$c_t = tanh(W_c \cdot [X_t, h_{t-1}] + b_c) \quad (12)$$
$$C_t = f_t \times C_{t-1} + i_t \times c_t \quad (13)$$
$$o_t = \sigma(W_o \cdot [X_t, h_{t-1}] + b_o) \quad (14)$$
$$h_t = o_t \times tanh(C_t) \quad (15)$$

4 實驗結果

4.1 皮爾遜相關係數

皮爾遜相關係數 (Pearson product-moment correlation coefficient) [6]，又稱作 PPMCC 或 PCCs，常用 r 或 Pearson's r 表示。在統計學上，用於度量兩個變數x和y之間的相關程度（線性相依），其值介於-1 與 1 之間。於自然科學領域中，該係數廣用於度量兩個變數之間的線性相依程度。本使用的r為(x_i, y_i)樣本點的標準分數的均值估算：

$$r = \frac{1}{n}\sum_{i=1}^{n}(\frac{x_i - \bar{x}}{\sigma_x})(\frac{y_i - \bar{y}}{\sigma_y}) \quad (16)$$

其中 $\frac{x_i-\bar{x}}{\sigma_x}$ 為 x_i 樣本的標準分數，$\bar{x}$為x_i樣本的平均值，σ_x為x_i樣本的標準差。

4.2 平均絕對誤差

平均絕對誤差（Mean Absolute Error, MAE），對同一物理量，進行多次測量時，其各次測量值和其絕對誤差不會相同，因此把各次測量的絕對誤差取絕對值後再求平均值，稱為平均絕對誤差，由於離差被絕對值化，不會出現正負相抵消的情況，因能更佳地反映預測值誤差的實際情形。指各個變量值平均數的離差絕對值的算術平均數。f_i為預測值，y_i為真實值，$e_i = |f_i - y_i|$為絕對誤差，

$$\text{MAE} = \frac{1}{n}\sum_{i=1}^{n}|f_i - y_i| = \frac{1}{n}\sum_{i=1}^{n}|e_i| \qquad (17)$$

從上可知， MAE 就是指你的預測值與真實值之間平均相差多大。

4.3 實驗參數設定

詞向量模型部分，使用的 Word2Vec 為 CBOW Multi-Word Context Model 的採用均值的方式。 在表示當前詞與預測詞在一個句子的最大距離設為 10，對字典做截斷的詞頻次數少於 1 的單詞會被丟棄。訓練並行數為 4。使用 negative sampling 的技巧，採用 negative sampling 設置 5 個 noise words，初始化權重則使用 python 的 hash 函數。替代次數為 5，在分配 word index 的時候會先對單詞基於頻率降序排序，每一批的傳遞單詞數量為 10000，學習速率為 0.025。特徵向量的維度為 200。

使用的 Lasso Regression 的替代次數固定為 10000，調整調整正則化的強度的值(alpha)來尋找最佳模型，再使用預測出的數值和正確數值本身算出 MAE 和皮爾遜相關係數。Alpha(A)為 Arousal Lasso regression(簡 Arousal LR)模型參數的數值，Alpha (V) 為 Valence Lasso regression (簡 Valence LR) 模型參數的數值。

而 LSTM 模型中，我們設定一層 LSTM 和一層 Neural Network，作為預測模型，其中輸入為 BERT 所輸出之詞向量串接、Loss Function 是 Mean Square Error、Optimizer 是 Adam、訓練 epochs 是 200。

4.4 實驗模型選擇

分析數值後，我們對 Arousal LR 模型以及 Valence LR 模型，每個取 Alpha=0.00001 和 Alpha=0.0001 去預測正確結果。結果發現無論在 Arousal LR 模型或 Valence LR 模型，對於 Alpha=0.00001 所預測出的結果有些超過 Arousal 和 Valence 維度限制範圍 (1~9) 過多，因此最後使用 Alpha=0.0001 的數值作為 Arousal LR 模型和 Valence LR 模型的參數，並以之預測結果。其中 Table 1 和 Table 2 為 Lasso Regression 模型實驗結果，Table 3 為不同模型實驗結果，最後我們選擇 BERT+LSTM model 作為最終架構。

Table 1: Arousal Lasso Regression Evaluation

Alpha(α)	MAE	Pearson's r
0.00001	0.5338	-0.192
0.0001	0.8099	-0.052
0.001	0.8142	-0.046
0.01	0.8205	-0.033
0.1	0.8361	-

Table 2: Valence Lasso Regression Evaluation

Alpha(α)	MAE	Pearson's r
0.00001	0.6842	0.837
0.0001	1.1199	0.241
0.001	1.1346	0.211
0.01	1.1509	0.172
0.1	1.1702	0.081

Table 3: Model Evaluation

Model	MAE	Pearson's r
Arousal Lasso Regression	1.0107	-0.046
Valence Lasso Regression	1.3176	0.211
BERT+LSTM	**0.052**	**0.998**

5 Conclusion and Future Work

在這次的挑戰賽中，我們提出結合 BERT-based 詞向量模型和 LSTM 預測模型進行文本 Valence 和 Arousal 數值預測。實驗結果得知我們所提出的模型遠優於 Lasso Regression 回歸模型的結果。在未來的研究中，我們將持續修正模型中的參數設定和字典的擴增，以期能提升整體系統的效能。

References

[1] Sarah-Yifei Wang. 2021. *Aspect-based Sentiment Analysis in Document - FOMC Meeting Minutes on Economic Projection*, arXiv:2108.04080.

[2] Saurav Kumar, Rushil Jayant, and Nihaar Charagulla. 2021. *Sentiment Analysis on the News to Improve Mental Health*, arXiv:2108.07706.

[3] Bencheng Wei, Jason Li, Ajay Gupta, Hafiza Umair, Atsu Vovor, Natalie Durzynski. 2021. *Offensive Language and Hate Speech Detection with Deep Learning and Transfer Learning*. arXiv:2108.03305.

[4] Liang-Chih Yu, Lung-Hao Lee, Shuai Hao, Jin Wang, Yunchao He, Jun Hu, K. Robert Lai, and Xuejie Zhang. 2016. Building Chinese affective resources in valence-arousal dimensions. In Proceedings of NAACL/HLT-16, pages 540-545.

[5] Rong, Xin. 2014. *word2vec parameter learning explained*, arXiv:1411.2738.

[6] Lee Rodgers, Joseph, and W. Alan Nicewander. 1988. Thirteen ways to look at the correlation coefficient. *The American Statistician*, 42(1): 59-66. https://doi.org/10.1080/00031305.1988.10475524.

The 33rd Conference on Computational Linguistics and Speech Processing (ROCLING 2021)
Taoyuan, Taiwan, October 15-16, 2021. The Association for Computational Linguistics and Chinese Language Processing

NCU-NLP at ROCLING-2021 Shared Task: Using MacBERT Transformers for Dimensional Sentiment Analysis

洪滿珍 Man-Chen Hung, 陳昭沂 Chao-Yi Chen
陳品蓉 Pin-Jung Chen, 李龍豪 Lung-Hao Lee
國立中央大學電機工程學系
Department of Electrical Engineering
National Central University
{109521068, 107501543, 107303034}@ncu.edu.tw, lhlee@ee.ncu.edu.tw

摘要

我們運用 MacBERT 模型在 CVAT 與 CVAS 資料集微調使其適用於 ROCLING 2021 的評測任務，並比較 MacBERT 與 BERT 和 RoBERTa 這兩個不同的模型，在 Valence 與 Arousal 維度上的效能差異。我們以平均絕對誤差 (MAE) 與關係係數 (r) 作為評分指標，在測試資料上能夠在 Valence 達到 MAE 與 r 分別為 0.611 與 0.904；而在 Arousal 達到 MAE 與 r 分別為 0.938 與 0.549 的效能。

Abstract

We use the MacBERT transformers and fine-tune them to ROCLING-2021 shared tasks using the CVAT and CVAS data. We compare the performance of MacBERT with the other two transformers BERT and RoBERTa in the valence and arousal dimensions, respectively. MAE and correlation coefficient (r) were used as evaluation metrics. On ROCLING-2021 test set, our used MacBERT model achieves 0.611 of MAE and 0.904 of r in the valence dimensions; and 0.938 of MAE and 0.549 of r in the arousal dimension.

關鍵字：情感運算、學習情緒、深度學習
Keywords: affective computing, learning emotions, deep learning

1 介紹

情感運算 (affective computing) 的目標是希望機器能夠讀懂人類的情感，進而做出相對應的動作，情感分析(sentiment analysis) 是自然語言處理研究中重要的研究領域，主要在於如何有效的提取文本中的情感資訊。根據情感的表達形式不同，可以區分為以下兩種方式：分類型情感分析或是維度型情感分析 (Calvo and Kim, 2013)。

傳統作法採用分類型 (categorical) 情感分析，將所有情感詞分成某幾個類別，例如：常見的正面、中立、負面三類情緒； 以及 Ekman (1992) 的六個基本情緒包含：憤怒 (anger)、高興 (happiness)、恐懼 (fear)、悲傷 (sadness)、厭惡 (disgust) 和驚喜 (surprise)，廣泛地應用各個領域 (Schouten and Frasincar, 2015; Pontiki et al., 2015)。

由於分類型情感分析無法精準的表達情緒詞中所帶有的情感，因此衍生出維度型 (dimensional) 情感分析，在多個情緒維度上，用連續性數值表示情感 (Russell, 1980)。圖 1 為常見的 Valance-Arousal 情感維度，採用二維平面表示，橫軸為 Valance 軸 (簡稱 V) 代表情感的正負面，數值範圍是 1 到 9 分，數值 1 表示最負面，數值 9 表示最正面，數值 5 則是中立沒有偏向。縱軸為 Arousal 軸 (簡稱 A) 表示情感激動程度， 1 為最平靜、9 為最激動，5 為中間值。任何字詞、片語、句子、篇章、段落都可以這個 VA 二維平面上表示，例如：「感激」這個詞在中文維度型情感字典 (CVAW) (Yu et al., 2016a) 的 VA 值分別為 6.8 和 7.2，位於 VA 平面屬於情緒正面且激動程度高的第一象限；「冷漠」一詞 (V: 4.0, A: 2.8) 則被歸到情緒負面且激動程度低的第三象限。任何情緒都可以在這個 VA 二維平面上用連續的

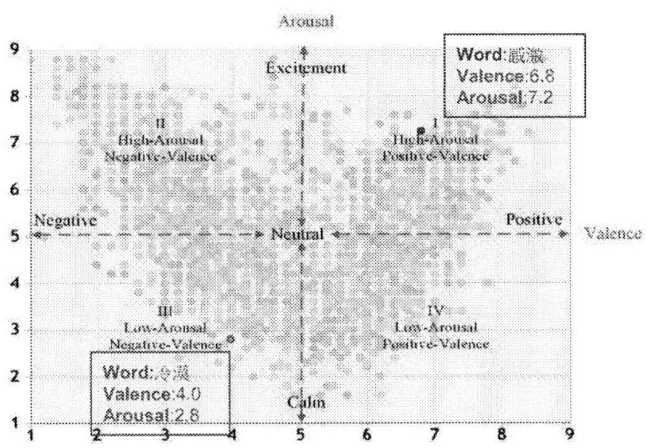

圖 1：VA 二維平面

數值表示，能更加細微的表達情感的差異，擴大應用領域。

IALP 2016 評測任務的目標是將此維度型分析應用在中文字詞 (Chinese words) (Yu et al; 2016b)；IJCNLP 2017 評測任務則是中文片語 (Chinese phrases)，近一步探討修飾語對於情感詞的情感狀態值變化 (Yu et al., 2017)。ROCLING 2021 今年的評測任務則專注於領域自調適(domain adaption)問題，目標是教育領域的學生學習心得情緒分析。在這個任務中，輸入一則學生的中文學習心得，情感分析系統需要分別對 Valence (V) 和 Arousal (A) 兩個維度，分析該輸入句蘊含的情感，各自輸出 1 到 9 的實數值，以下為編號 1 的中文心得，系統輸出值分別是 V 值 6.8 及 A 值 5.2。

- Input: 1, 今天教了許多以前沒有學過的東西，所以上起課來很新鮮。
- Output: 1, 6.8, 5.2

我們開發的 NCU-NLP 情感分析系統採用 MacBERT 作為主要的模型架構 (Cui et al., 2020)。我們用 CVAT 資料集 (Yu et al., 2016b) 以及自行建置的 CVAS 資料集，微調預訓練好的 MacBERT 模型，在測試資料上在 Valence 的 MAE 與 r 分別達到 0.611 與 0.904；在 Arousal 的 MAE 與 r 分別達到 0.938 與 0.549。

本文其他章節如下，第二章是維度型情感分析的相關研究，第三章敘述我們使用的模型架構，第四部份為實驗結果和效能比較，最後則是結論。

2 相關研究

維度型情感分析 VA 值預測模型，大致可分成三大類：辭典法 (lexicon-based)、回歸法 (regression-based)、以及神經網路法 (neural-network-based)。

辭典法將句子中出現的字詞，與情感字典進行比對，最後平均所有情感詞的 VA 值，將此平均結果當成文本的 VA 值預測結果 (Paltoglou et al., 2012)。

回歸法曾是最常被研究拿來預測 VA 值的方法，為了解決中文與英文這種跨語言的文字問題，Wei et al. (2011) 提出半自動標記中文詞語的方式，以英文為底，轉換成中文，最後才進行回歸模型的訓練，這種方式容易造成擬合度不足(underfitting)。因此，Wanget al. (2016b) 提出區域性加權回歸方式(a locally weighted method)，可以提升預測精準度。Wang et al. (2016a) 進一步提出 Community-based 加權圖模型 (weighted graph model)，能讓未見過的詞，有更相似的 Seed 字詞，對 VA 估計過程更有幫助，對英文和中文數據集都有更好的預測效能。此外，Amir et al. (2015) 同樣利用回歸法，並加上詞嵌入向量分析推特上的情緒成分。

近年來，深度學習方法廣泛用於維度型情感分析，有許多研究朝向使用詞嵌入向量和類神經網路的方式來預測 VA 情感值。在 IALP 2016 評測任務中，Du and Zhang (2016) 採用集成式單層增強神經網路 (an ensemble of several boosted one layer neural networks) 完成 VA 情感值的預測。在 IJCNLP 2017 的評測任務中，Wu et al. (2017)中提出連結緊密的長短期記憶模型 (Long Short-Term Memory, LSTM) 預測中文詞語及片語。Yu et al. (2020) 採用兩層 NN 模型的疊接，第一層決定單詞的強度，第二層決定修飾詞語的位移權重，將有助於提升片語的精確度。Zhu et al. (2019) 使用基於注意力的對抗神經網路 (Adversarial Attention Network)，著重訓練為輸入詞加權的注意力層 (attention layer)，以達到確定某些詞語為特定情感做出的貢獻。之後更提出結合 CNN 和 LSTM 模型兩種類神經網路模型，將文本一部份當作 CNN 模型的輸入，以提取特徵值，而產生樹狀區域的 CNN-LSTM 模型，實驗結果顯示比以前單純的類神經網路結構，效果更好 (Wang et al., 2020)。

學生的學習表現都會呈現在成績上，結構化的資料比如說是出席率、作業完成率及繳交率、課堂上的參與程度等等，都被老師來評斷成學生的學習狀況。學生學習心得這種非結構化的資料，因為不易結構化很容易被忽略掉，學生上課時的心得通常都富含情感詞，內容大多是對於課堂吸收程度的第一手情感資料，如果可以有效分析，將非常有助於課堂的調整，或是讓老師了解那些學生需要加強，對於教育領域很有幫助(Yu et al., 2018)。

3 NCU-NLP 模型架構

我們所使用的模型為 MacBERT (MLM as correction BERT) (Cui et al., 2020)，並對模型進行微調。MacBERT 是基於 BERT 改良的模型，該模型與 BERT 共享相同的預訓練任務，並對遮罩語言模型 (Masked Language Model, MLM) 任務進行修改：使用全詞遮罩及 n-gram 遮罩策略來選擇遮罩的詞候選，詞級別 1-gram 到 4-gram 的遮罩比例為 40%、30%、20%、10%。此外，MacBERT 不使用 [MASK] 符號來進行遮罩，因為在詞與符號的微調階段並沒有出現過 [MASK]，而改採用相似單詞進行遮罩，使用基於同義詞工具 (synonyms toolkit) 與 Word2vec (Mikolov et al., 2013)來計算相似度。若選擇一個 n-gram 來進行遮罩，則將會分別尋找相似的單詞，在找不到相似單詞時，則會降級使用隨機的單詞替換。MacBERT 使用 15% 的輸入文字來進行遮罩， 80% 替換為相似的單詞， 10% 替換為隨機單詞，剩下的 10% 為保留原本的輸入單詞。

4 實驗與評估

4.1 資料集

訓練資料來自中文維度型情感語料庫 (Chinese Valence-Arousal Text, CVAT) (Yu et al., 2016b) 及自行建置的 CVAS (Chinese Valence-Arousal Sentences)資料集。CVAT 資料集 (ver. 2.0) 內包含 2,969 個中文評論段落(Yu et al., 2016a)，CVAS 資料集包含 2582 個中文情感句子，皆已標記 VA 值。測試資料為主辦單位提供的學生中文學習心得，共有 1600 句。

4.2 實驗設定

我們比較以下三個模型的效能差異：BERT (Devlin et al., 2019)、RoBERTa (Liu et al.,2019) 與 MacBERT (Cui et al., 2020)。實驗採五折交互驗證，學習率 (learning rate) 設定為 5e-5，批次大小為 64，以及訓練次數 (epoch) 為 50 次。此外，我們比較只有 CVAT 資料集作為訓練資料，以及 CVAT 資料集加入 CVAS 資料集的效能差異。

4.3 評分指標

模型的表現程度，將情緒正負面(V 值)和激動程度(A 值)分開計算，以模型預測結果和標準答案間作比對，使用平均絕對誤差(Mean absolute error, MAE) 及皮爾森相關係數 (Pearson correlation coefficient)來衡量。

- 平均絕對誤差 (Mean absolute error, MAE)

$$\text{MAE} = \frac{1}{n}\sum_{i=1}^{n}|A_i - P_i| \quad (1)$$

- 皮爾森相關係數 (Pearson correlation coefficient)

$$\text{r} = \frac{1}{n-1}\sum_{i=1}^{n}\left(\frac{A_i - \bar{A}}{\sigma_A}\right)\left(\frac{P_i - \bar{P}}{\sigma_P}\right) \quad (2)$$

4.4 結果

只有 CVAT 資料集的交互驗證結果如表 1，MacBERT 在 Valence 的 MAE 與 r 分數都較其他兩個模型來得更好；而在 Arousal 的 MAE 比其他兩者來的好，但 r 與 RoBERTa 有些微的落差。整體而言，MacBERT 的表現比 RoBERTa 與 BERT 佳。

表 1 與表 2 為 CVAT 與 CVAS 兩個資料集的交互驗證結果，MacBERT 與 RoBERTa 的 MAE 和 r 在 Valence 與 Arousal 都只有些微的差距，但都比 BERT 還要來得好。

綜合上述結果，我們決定採用MacBERT 作為系統架構，選擇兩種不同資料組合 (CVAT, CVAT+CVAS) 微調後的模型，作為 NCU-NLP 系統在測試集的效能。

CVAT		
Valence	MAE	r
BERT	0.475	0.854
RoBERTa	0.469	0.895
MacBERT	0.457	0.897
Arousal	MAE	r
BERT	0.668	0.62
RoBERTa	0.659	0.695
MacBERT	0.652	0.639

表 1、CVAT 資料集實驗結果

CVAT+CVAS		
Valence	MAE	r
BERT	0.531	0.854
RoBERTa	0.51	0.868
MacBERT	0.513	0.865
Arousal	MAE	r
BERT	0.763	0.582
RoBERTa	0.757	0.596
MacBERT	0.754	0.592

表 2、CVAT＋CVAS 資料集實驗結果

4.5 比較

表 3 為測試結果。在 Valence 上，CVAT+CVAS 資料集微調過的 MacBERT 模型的 MAE 分數，比只有 CVAT 資料集的少了 0.014，且 r 的分數也只高了 0.004。在 Arousal 上，只有 CVAT 資料集的 MAE 分數，比 CVAT+CVAS 資料集的分數少了 0.051，但 CVAT+CVAS 資料集的 r 分數，比只有 CVAT 資料集的分數還要好 0.033。

整體來說，以相關係數 r 來看，整體上 CVAT+CVAS 資料集的分數在 Valence 與 Arousal 上都比只有 CVAT 的來得高，而 MAE 在 Valence 上 CVAT+CVAS 資料集的分數較好，Arousal 則是只有 CVAT 資料集的分數較佳。

5 結論

在本次的評測任務中，經由 CVAT 資料集微調後的 MacBERT，在 Valence 的 MAE 與 r 分別為 0.625 與 0.9；在 Arousal 的 MAE 與 r 分別為 0.938 與 0.549。而經由 CVAT+CVAS 資料集微調後的 MacBERT ，在 Valence 的 MAE 與 r 分別為 0.611 與 0.904；在 Arousal 的 MAE 與 r 分別為 0.989 與 0.582，且在 r 指標都得到較好的成績。

ROCLING-2021 Test Set		
Valence	MAE	r
MacBERT - CVAT	0.625	0.9
MacBERT - CVAT +CVAS	0.611	0.904
Arousal	MAE	r
MacBERT - CVAT	0.938	0.549
MacBERT - CVAT +CVAS	0.989	0.582

表 3、ROCLING-2021 Test Set 實驗結果

致謝

This work was partially supported by the Ministry of Science and Technology, Taiwan under the grant MOST 108-2218-E-008-017-MY3.

參考資料

Silvio Amir, Ranmon F. Astudillo, Wang Ling, Bruno Martins, Mario Silva, and Isabel Trancoso. 2015. INESC-ID: A regression model for large scale twitter sentiment lexicon induction. In *Proceedings of the 9th International Workshop on Semantic Evaluation*, pages 613-618. https://doi.org/10.18653/v1/S15-2102

Rafael A. Calvo and Sunghwan Mac Kim. 2013. Emotions in text: dimensional and categorical models. *Computational Intelligence*, 29(3):527-543. https://doi.org/10.1111/j.1467-8640.2012.00456.x

Yiming Cui, Wanxiang Che, Ting Liu, Bing Qin, Shijin Wang, Guoping Hu. 2020. Revisiting Pre-Trained Models for Chinese Natural Language Processing. *Association for Computational Linguistics,* pages 657–668.https://doi.org/10.18653/v1/2020.findings-emnlp.58.

Jacob Devlin, Ming-Wei Chang, Kenton Lee, and Kristina Toutanova. 2019. BERT: Pre-training of Deep Bidirectional Transformers for Language Understanding. In *Proceedings of the 2019 Conference of the North American Chapter of the Association for Computational Linguistics: Human Language Technologies, Volume 1 (Long and Short Papers). Human Language Technologies, pages 4171-4186.* https://doi.org/10.18653/v1/N19-1423.

Steven Du and Xi Zhang. 2016. Aicyber's system for IALP 2016 shared task: Character-enhanced word vectors and Boosted Neural Networks. In *Proceedings of 2016 International Conference on Asian Language Processing,* pages 161-163. http://doi.org/10.1109/IALP.2016.7875958

Paul Ekman. 1992. An argument for basic emotions. *Cognition and Emotion*, 6(3-4):169-200. https://doi.org/10.1080/02699939208411068

Tomas Mikolov, Ilya Sutskever, Kai Chen, Greg Corrado, and Jeffrey Dean. 2013. Distributed representations of words and phrases and their compositionality. In C. J. C. Burges, L. Bottou, M. Welling, Z. Ghahramani, and K. Q. Weinberger, editors, *Advances in Neural Information Processing Systems 26*, pages 3111–3119. https://proceedings.neurips.cc/paper/2013/file/9aa42b31882ec039965f3c4923ce901b-Paper.pdf.

Georgios Paltoglou, Mathias Theunis, Arvid Kappas, and Mike Thelwall. 2012. Predicting emotional responses to long informal text. *IEEE Transactions on Affective Computing*, 4(1):106-115. http://doi.org/2010.1109/T-AFFC.2012.26

Maria Pontiki, Dimitrios Galanis, Haris Papageorgiou, Suresh Manandhar, and Ion Androutsopoulos. 2015. SemEval-2015 task 12: Aspect based sentiment analysis. In *Proceedings of the 9th International Workshop on Semantic Evaluation*, pages 486-495. https://doi.org/10.18653/v1/S15-2082

Jame A. Russell. 1980. A circumplex model of affect. *Journal of personality and social psychology*, 39(6):1161. https://doi.org/10.1037/h0077714

Kim Schouten and Flavius Frasincar. 2015. Survey on aspect-level sentiment analysis. *IEEE Transactions on Knowledge and Data Engineering*, 28(3):813-830. https://doi.org/10.1109/TKDE.2015.2485209

Jin Wang, Liang-Chih Yu, K. Robert Lai, and Xuejie Zhang. 2016a. Community-based weighted graph model for valence-arousal prediction of affective words. *IEEE/ACM Transactions on Audio, Speech, and Language Processing*, 24(11):1957-1968. https://doi.org/10.1109/TASLP.2016.2594287

Jin Wang,Liang-Chih Yu, K. Robert Lai, and Xuejie Zhang. 2016b. Locally weighted linear regression for cross-lingual valence-arousal prediction of affective words. *Neurocomputing*, 194:271-278. https://doi.org/10.1016/j.neucom.2016.02.057

Jin Wang, Liang-Chih Yu, K. Robert Lai, and Xuejie Zhang. 2020. Tree-structured regional CNN-LSTM model for dimensional sentiment analysis. *IEEE/ACM Transactions on Audio, Speech, and Language Processing*, 28:581-591. http:/doi.org/10.1109/TASLP.2019.2959251

Wen-Li Wei, Chung-Hsien Wu, and Jen-Chun Lin. 2011. A regression approach to affective rating of Chinese words from ANEW. In *Proceedings of International Conference on Affective Computing and Intelligent Interaction*, pages 121-131. https://doi.org/10.1007/978-3-642-24571-8_13

Chuhan Wu, Fangzhao Wu, Yongfeng Huang, Sixing Wu, and Zhigang Yuan. 2017. THU_NGN at IJCNLP-2017 task 2: Dimensional sentiment analysis for Chinese phrases with deep LSTM. In *Proceedings of the 8th International Joint Conference on Natural Language Processing: Shared Tasks*, pages 47-52.

Yinhan Liu, Myle Ott, Naman Goyal, Jingfei Du, Mandar Joshi, Danqi Chen, Omer Levy, Mike Lewis, Luke Zettlemoyer, and Veselin Stoyanov. 2019. Roberta: A robustly optimized bert pretraining approach. https://arxiv.org/pdf/1907.11692.pdf

Liang-Chih Yu, Lung-Hao Lee, Shuai Hao, Jin Wang, Yunchao He, Jun Hu, K. Robert Lai, Xuejie Zhang 2016a. Building Chinese affective resources in valence-arousal dimensions. In *Proceedings of the 2016 Conference of the North American Chapter of the Association for Computational Linguistics: Human Language Technologies*, pages 540-545 https://doi.org/10.18653/v1/N16-1066

Liang-Chih Yu, Lung-Hao Lee, and Kam-Fai Wong. 2016b. Overview of the IALP 2016 shared task on dimensional sentiment analysis for Chinese words. In *International Conference on Asian Language Processing*, pages 156-160. http://doi.org/10.1109/IALP.2016.7875957

Liang-Chih Yu, Lung-Hao Lee, Jin Wang, and Kam-Fai Wong. 2017. IJCNLP-2017 Task 2: Dimensional Sentiment Analysis for Chinese Phrases. In *Proceedings of the 8th International Joint Conference on Natural Language Processing: Shared Tasks*, pages 9-16.

Liang-Chih Yu, Jin Wang, K. Robert Lai, and Xuejie Zhang. 2020. Pipelined neural networks for phrase-level sentiment intensity prediction. *IEEE Transactions on Affective Computing*, 11(3): 447-458. http://doi.org/10.1109/TAFFC.2018.2807819

Liang-Chih Yu, C.-W. Lee, H.I. Pan, C.Y. Chou, P.Y. Chao, Z.H. Chen, S.F. Tseng, C.L. Chan, and K.R. Lai. 2018. Improving early prediction of academic failure using sentiment analysis on self-evaluated comments. *Journal of Computer Assisted Learning*, 34(4):358-365. https://doi.org/10.1111/jcal.12247

Suyang Zhu, Shoushan Li, and Guodong Zhou. 2019. Adversarial attention modeling for multi-dimensional emotion regression. In *Proceedings of the 57th Annual Meeting of the Association for Computational Linguistics*, pages 417-480. http://doi.org/10.18653/v1/P19-1045

The 33rd Conference on Computational Linguistics and Speech Processing (ROCLING 2021)
Taoyuan, Taiwan, October 15-16, 2021. The Association for Computational Linguistics and Chinese Language Processing

ROCLING-2021 Shared Task: Dimensional Sentiment Analysis for Educational Texts

Liang-Chih Yu[1], Jin Wang[2], Bo Peng[3], Chu-Ren Huang[3]
[1]Department of Information Management, Yuan Ze University
[2] School of Information Science and Engineering, Yunnan University
[3]Department of Chinese and Bilingual Studies, The Hong Kong Polytechnic University
Contact: lcyu@saturn.yzu.edu.tw, wangjin@ynu.edu.cn, peng-bo.peng@polyu.edu.hk, churen.huang@polyu.edu.hk

Abstract

This paper presents the ROCLING 2021 shared task on dimensional sentiment analysis for educational texts which seeks to identify a real-value sentiment score of self-evaluation comments written by Chinese students in the both valence and arousal dimensions. Valence represents the degree of pleasant and unpleasant (or positive and negative) feelings, and arousal represents the degree of excitement and calm. Of the 7 teams registered for this shared task for two-dimensional sentiment analysis, 6 submitted results. We expected that this evaluation campaign could produce more advanced dimensional sentiment analysis techniques for the educational domain. All data sets with gold standards and scoring script are made publicly available to researchers.

1 Introduction

The goal of sentiment analysis is to automatically identify affective information within texts. There are two major models to represent affective states: categorical and dimensional approaches (Calvo and Kim, 2013). The categorical approach represents affective states as several discrete classes (e.g., positive, negative, neutral), while the dimensional approach represents affective states as continuous numerical values on multiple dimensions, such as valence-arousal (VA) space (Russell, 1980), as shown in Fig. 1. The valence represents the degree of pleasant and unpleasant (or positive and negative) feelings, and the arousal represents the degree of excitement and calm. Based on this two-dimensional representation, any affective state can be represented as a point in the VA coordinate plane by determining the degrees of valence and arousal of given words (Wei et al., 2011; Malandrakis et al., 2013; Wang et al., 2016a; Du and Zhang, 2016; Wu et la., 2017) or texts (Paltoglou et al, 2013; Goel et la., 2017; Zhu et al., 2019; Wang et al., 2019; 2020; Cheng et al, 2021; Wu et al., 2021, Xie et al., 2021). In 2016, we hosted a first dimensional sentiment analysis task for Chinese words (Yu et al., 2016b). In 2017, we extended this task to include both word- and phrase-level dimensional sentiment analysis (Yu et al., 2017). This year, we explore the sentence-level dimensional sentiment analysis task on educational texts (students' self-evaluated comments).

Structured data such as attendance, homework completion and in-class participation have been extensively studied to predict students' learning performance. Unstructured data, such as self-evaluation comments written by students, is also a useful data resource because it contains rich emotional information that can help illuminate the emotional states of students (Yu et al., 2018). Dimensional sentiment analysis is an effective technique to recognize the valence-arousal ratings from texts, indicating the degree from most negative to most positive for valence, and from most calm to most excited for arousal. This shared task provides an evaluation platform for the development and implementation of advanced techniques for dimensional sentiment analysis in the educational domain.

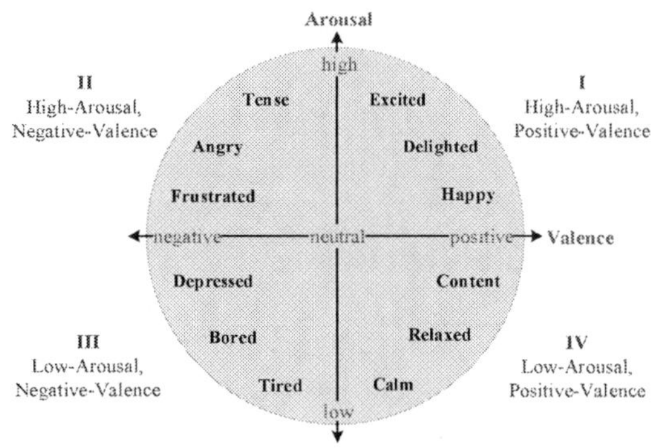

Figure 1: Two-dimensional valence-arousal space.

2 Task Description

In this task, participants are asked to provide a real-valued score from 1 to 9 for both valence and arousal dimensions for each self-evaluation comment. The input format is "sentence_id, sentence", and the output format is "sentence_id, valence_rating, arousal_rating". Below are the input/output formats of the example sentences.

Example 1:
Input: 1, 今天教了許多以前沒有學過的東西，所以上起課來很新鮮
Output: 1, 6.8, 5.2

Example 2:
Input: 2, 覺得課程進度有點快，內容難以消化
Output: 2, 3.0, 4.0

3 Datasets

Training set: There are three datasets annotated with valence-arousal ratings for training: 1) Chinese Valence-Arousal Words (CVAW)[1] (Yu et al., 2016a), which contains 5,512 single words; 2) Chinese Valence-Arousal Words (CVAP)[2] (Yu et al., 2017), which contains 2,998 multi-word phrases; 3) Chinese Valence-Arousal Words (CVAT)[3] (Yu et al., 2016a), which contains 2,969 sentences.

Test set: A total of 1,600 sentences were collected from the self-evaluated comments written by university students. Each sentence was then annotated with valence-arousal ratings by seven annotators and the average ratings were taken as ground truth. Once the rating process was finished, a corpus clean-up procedure was performed to remove outlier ratings that did not fall within the mean plus/minus 1.5 standard deviations. They were then excluded from the calculation of the average ratings for each sentence.

The policy of this shared task was implemented as is an open test. That is, in addition to the above official datasets, participating teams were allowed to use other publicly available data for system development, but such sources should be specified in the final technical report.

4 Evaluation Metrics

Prediction performance is evaluated by examining the difference between machine-predicted ratings and human-annotated ratings, in which valence and arousal are treated independently. The evaluation metrics include Mean Absolute Error (MAE) and Pearson Correction Coefficient (r), as shown in the following equations.

- **Mean absolute error (MAE)**

$$MAE = \frac{1}{n}\sum_{i=1}^{n}| A_i - P_i | \quad (1)$$

- **Pearson correlation coefficient (r)**

$$PCC = \frac{1}{n-1}\sum_{i=1}^{n}(\frac{A_i - \overline{A}}{\sigma_A})(\frac{P_i - \overline{P}}{\sigma_P}) \quad (2)$$

where A_i is the actual value, P_i is the predicted value, n is the number of test samples, $\overline{A}$ and $\overline{P}$ respectively denote the arithmetic mean of A and P, and σ is the standard deviation. The MAE measures the error rate and the PCC measures the linear correlation between the actual values and the predicted values. A lower MAE and a higher PCC indicate more accurate prediction performance.

5 Evaluation Results

5.1 Participants

Table 1 summarizes the submission statistics for 7 participating teams (CYUT, NCU-NLP, DeepNLP, NTUST-NLP-1, NTUST-NLP-2, SCUDS and SoochowDS). In the testing phase, each team was allowed to submit at most two runs. Six teams submitted two runs, yielding a total of 12 runs for comparison.

[1] http://nlp.innobic.yzu.edu.tw/resources/cvaw.html
[2] http://nlp.innobic.yzu.edu.tw/resources/cvap.html
[3] http://nlp.innobic.yzu.edu.tw/resources/cvat.html

Team	**Affiliation**	**#Run**
CYUT	Chaoyang University of Technology	2
NCU-NLP	National Central University	2
DeepNLP	Nanjing University	0
NTUST-NLP-1	National Taiwan University of Science and Technology	2
NTUST-NLP-2	National Taiwan University of Science and Technology	2
SCUDS	Soochow University	2
SoochowDS	Soochow University	2

Table 1: Submission statistics for all participating teams.

Team	**Valence MAE**	**Valence *r***	**Arousal MAE**	**Arousal *r***
Baseline	1.143	0.457	0.954	0.278
CYUT-run1	1.695	-0.017	1.177	0.040
CYUT-run2	1.685	0.007	1.252	-0.021
NCU-NLP-run1	0.625	0.900	0.938	0.549
NCU-NLP-run2	0.611	0.904	0.989	0.582
ntust-nlp-1-run1	0.684	0.912	0.906	0.607
ntust-nlp-1-run2	**0.586**	0.901	0.885	0.585
ntust-nlp-2-run1	0.654	0.905	0.880	0.581
ntust-nlp-2-run2	0.667	**0.913**	**0.866**	**0.616**
SCUDS-run1	0.953	0.694	1.054	0.375
SCUDS-run2	0.975	0.667	1.039	0.354
SoochowDS-run1	2.421	0.073	1.327	0.051
SoochowDS-run2	1.073	0.584	1.125	0.228
Late-CYUT-run1	0.674	0.870	0.901	0.531
Late-CYUT-run2	0.600	0.900	0.877	0.565

Table 2: Comparative results of valence-arousal prediction on the test set.

5.2 Baseline

We implemented a baseline using a lexicon-based method to calculate the VA ratings of texts by averaging the VA ratings of affective words match between the texts and CVAW 4.0 (Yu et al., 2016a). For the test instances that contain no affective words in the lexicon, their VA ratings will be assigned with 5.

5.3 Results

Tables 2 shows the results of valence-arousal prediction on the test set. Most of the results outperformed the baseline. The three best performing systems are summarized as follows.

- Valence MAE: NTUST-NLP-1-run2, NCU-NLP-run2 and NCU-NLP-run1
- Valence *r*: NTUST-NLP-2-run2, NTUST-NLP-1-run1 and NTUST-NLP-2-run1
- Arousal MAE: NTUST-NLP-2-run2, NTUST-NLP-2-run1 and NTUST-NLP-1-run2
- Arousal *r*: NTUST-NLP-2-run2, NTUST-NLP-1-run1 and NTUST-NLP-1-run2

There is a late submission for the CYUT team because the order of their scores in the initial submission is not consistent with that of the test set, thus yielding a negative correlation. The results of the late submission show the actual performance of their proposed method.

6 Conclusions

This study describes an overview of the ROCLING 2021 shared task on dimensional sentiment analysis for educational texts, including task design, data preparation, performance metrics and evaluation results. We hope the data sets collected and annotated for this shared task can facilitate and expedite future development in this research area. Therefore, all data sets with gold standard and scoring script are publicly available[4].

Acknowledgments

This work was supported by the Ministry of Science and Technology, Taiwan, ROC, under Grant No. MOST 110-2628-E-155-002.

References

Rafael A. Calvo and Sunghwan Mac Kim. 2013. Emotions in text: dimensional and categorical models. *Computational Intelligence*, 29(3):527-543.

Yu-Ya Cheng, Yan-Ming Chen, Wen-Chao Yeh, and Yung-Chun Chang.2021. Valence and Arousal-Infused Bi-Directional LSTM for Sentiment Analysis of Government Social Media Management. *Applied Sciences*, 11(2):880.

Steven Du and Xi Zhang. 2016. Aicyber's system for IALP 2016 shared task: Character-enhanced word vectors and Boosted Neural Networks. In *Proc. of IALP-16*.

Pranav Goel, Devang Kulshreshtha, Prayas Jain and Kaushal Kumar Shukla. 2017. Prayas at EmoInt 2017: An Ensemble of Deep Neural Architectures for Emotion Intensity Prediction in Tweets. In *Proc. WASSA-17*, page 58–65.

Nikos Malandrakis, Alexandros Potamianos, Elias Iosif, and Shrikanth Narayanan, 2011. Kernel models for affective lexicon creation. In *Proc. of INTERSPEECH-11*, pages 2977-2980.

Georgios Paltoglou, Mathias Theunis, Arvid Kappas, and Mike Thelwall. 2013. Predicting emotional responses to long informal text. *IEEE Trans. Affective Computing*, 4(1):106-115.

James A. Russell. 1980. A circumplex model of affect. *Journal of Personality and Social Psychology*, 39(6):1161.

Jin Wang, Liang-Chih Yu, K. Robert Lai and Xuejie Zhang. 2016a. Community-based weighted graph model for valence-arousal prediction of affective words, *IEEE/ACM Trans. Audio, Speech and Language Processing*, 24(11):1957-1968.

Jin Wang, Liang-Chih Yu, K. Robert Lai, and Xuejie Zhang. 2016b. Dimensional sentiment analysis using a regional CNN-LSTM model. In *Proc. of ACL-16*, pages 225-230.

Jin Wang, Liang-Chih Yu, K. Robert Lai and Xuejie Zhang. 2019. Investigating Dynamic Routing in Tree-Structured LSTM for Sentiment Analysis. In *Proc. of EMNLP/IJCNLP-19*, pages 3423-3428.

Jin Wang, Liang-Chih Yu, K. Robert Lai and Xuejie Zhang. 2020. Tree-Structured Regional CNN-LSTM Model for Dimensional Sentiment Analysis. *IEEE/ACM Trans. Audio, Speech and Language Processing*, 28:581-591.

Wen-Li Wei, Chung-Hsien Wu, and Jen-Chun Lin. 2011. A regression approach to affective rating of Chinese words from ANEW. In *Proc. of ACII-11*, pages 121-131.

Chuhan Wu, Fangzhao Wu, Yongfeng Huang, Sixing Wu and Zhigang Yuan. 2017. THU_NGN at IJCNLP-2017 Task 2: Dimensional Sentiment Analysis for Chinese Phrases with Deep LSTM. In *Proc. of IJCNLP-17, Shared Tasks*, pages 47–52.

Jheng-Long Wu, Min-Tzu Huang, Chi-Sheng Yang, and Kai-Hsuan Liu. 2021. Sentiment analysis of stock markets using a novel dimensional valence–arousal approach. *Soft Computing*, 25:4433–4450.

Housheng Xie, Wei Lin, Shuying Lin, Jin Wang, and Liang-Chih Yu. 2021. A multi-dimensional relation model for dimensional sentiment analysis. *Information Sciences*, 579:832-844.

Liang-Chih Yu et al. 2018. Improving Early Prediction of Academic Failure Using Sentiment Analysis on Self-evaluated Comments. *Journal of Computer Assisted Learning*, 34(4):358-365.

Liang-Chih Yu, Lung-Hao Lee, Shuai Hao, Jin Wang, Yunchao He, Jun Hu, K. Robert Lai, and Xuejie Zhang. 2016a. Building Chinese affective resources in valence-arousal dimensions. In *Proc. of NAACL/HLT-16*, pages 540-545.

Liang-Chih Yu, Lung-Hao Lee and Kam-Fai Wong. 2016b. Overview of the IALP 2016 shared task on dimensional sentiment analysis for Chinese words, in *Proc. of IALP-16*, pages 156-160.

Liang-Chih Yu, Lung-Hao Lee, Jin Wang and Kam-Fai Wong. 2017. IJCNLP-2017 Task 2: Dimensional Sentiment Analysis for Chinese Phrases. In *Proc. of IJCNLP-17, Shared Tasks*, pages 9-16.

Suyang Zhu, Shoushan Li and Guodong Zhou. 2019. Adversarial Attention Modeling for Multi-dimensional Emotion Regression. In *Proc. of ACL-19*, pages 471–480.

[4] https://rocling2021.github.io/

Association for Computational Linguistics
209 N. Eighth Street
Stroudsburg, Pennsylvania 18360

ISBN 978-1-7138-3924-8

CURRAN ASSOCIATES INC.
proceedings.com